SAT*

Prep Course

with Software

JEFF KOLBY

NOVA PRESS

* SAT is a registered trademark of
the College Entrance Examination
Board, which was not involved in
the production of, and does not
endorse, this book.

Additional educational titles from Nova Press:

GRE Prep Course (624 pages, includes software)

GMAT Prep Course (624 pages, includes software)

Master The LSAT (560 pages, includes an official LSAT exam)

The MCAT Physics Book (444 pages)

The MCAT Biology Book (416 pages)

Law School Basics: A Preview of Law School and Legal Reasoning (224 pages)

Vocabulary 4000: The 4000 Words Essential for an Educated Vocabulary (160 pages)

ISBN 1–889057–28–2

11659 Mayfield Ave., Suite 1
Los Angeles, CA 90049

Phone: 1-800-949-6175
E-mail: info@novapress.net
Website: www.novapress.net

ABOUT THIS BOOK

If you don't have a pencil in your hand, get one now! Don't just read this book—write on it, study it, scrutinize it! In short, for the next six weeks, this book should be a part of your life. When you have finished the book, it should be marked-up, dog-eared, tattered and torn.

Although the SAT is a difficult test, it is a *very* learnable test. This is not to say that the SAT is "beatable." There is no bag of tricks that will show you how to master it overnight. You probably have already realized this. Some books, nevertheless, offer "inside stuff" or "tricks" which they claim will enable you to beat the test. These include declaring that answer-choices B, C, or D are more likely to be correct than choices A or E. This tactic, like most of its type, does not work. It is offered to give the student the feeling that he or she is getting the scoop on the test.

The SAT cannot be "beaten." But it can be mastered—through hard work, analytical thought, and by training yourself to think like a test writer. Many of the exercises in this book are designed to prompt you to think like a test writer. For example, in the math section, you will find "Duals." These are pairs of similar problems in which only one property is different. They illustrate the process of creating SAT questions.

The SAT is not easy—nor is this book. To improve your SAT score, you must be willing to work; if you study hard and master the techniques in this book, your score will improve—significantly.

This book will introduce you to numerous analytic techniques that will help you immensely, not only on the SAT but in college as well. For this reason, studying for the SAT can be a rewarding and satisfying experience.

Although the quick-fix method is not offered in this book, about 15% of the material is dedicated to studying how the questions are constructed. Knowing how the problems are written and how the test writers think will give you useful insight into the problems and make them less mysterious. Moreover, familiarity with the SAT's structure will help reduce your anxiety. The more you know about this test, the less anxious you will be the day you take it.

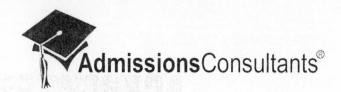

ACKNOWLEDGMENT

Behind any successful test-prep book, there is more than just the author's efforts.

I would like to thank Kathleen Pierce for her many contributions to the book and for her continued support and inspiration.

Reading passages were drawn from the following sources:

Passage page 35, from *The Two Faces of Eastern Europe,* © 1990 Adam Michnik.

Passage page 38, from *Deschooling Society,* © 1971 Harper & Row, by Ivan Illich.

Passage page 45, from *The Cult of Multiculturalism,* © 1991 Fred Siegel.

Passage page 49, from *Ways of Seeing,* © 1972 Penguin Books Limited, by John Berger.

Passage page 54, from *Placebo Cures for the Incurable*, Journal of Irreproducible Results, © 1985 Thomas G. Kyle.

Passage page 59, from *Women, Fire, and Dangerous Things,* © George Lakoff.

Passage page 63, from *Screening Immigrants and International Travelers for the Human Immunodeficiency Virus,* © 1990 New England Journal of Medicine.

Passage page 67, from *The Perry Scheme and the Teaching of Writing,* © 1986 Christopher Burnham.

Passage page 69, from *Man Bites Shark,* © 1990 Scientific American.

Passage page 71, from *Hemingway: The Writer as Artist*, © 1952 Carlos Baker.

Passage page 73, from *The Stars in Their Courses,* © 1931 James Jeans.

CONTENTS

ORIENTATION

- **WHAT DOES THE SAT MEASURE?**

- **FORMAT OF THE SAT**

- **PACING**

- **SCORING THE SAT**

- **SKIPPING AND GUESSING**

- **ORDER OF DIFFICULTY**

- **THE PSAT**

- **THE "2 OUT OF 5" RULE**

- **HOW TO USE THIS BOOK**
  Shortened Study Plan

- **QUESTIONS AND ANSWERS**

What Does the SAT Measure?

The SAT is an aptitude test. Like all aptitude tests, it must choose a medium in which to measure intellectual ability. The SAT has chosen math and English.

OK, the SAT is an aptitude test. The question is—does it measure aptitude for college? The SAT's ability to predict performance in college is only a little better than chance.

No test can measure all aspects of intelligence. Thus any admission test, no matter how well written, is inherently inadequate. Nevertheless, some form of admission testing is necessary. It would be unfair to base acceptance to college solely on grades; they can be misleading. For instance, would it be fair to admit a student with an A average earned in easy classes over a student with a B average earned in difficult classes? A school's reputation is too broad a measure to use as admission criteria: many students seek out easy classes and generous instructors, in hopes of inflating their GPA. Furthermore, a system that would monitor the academic standards of every class would be cost prohibitive and stifling. So until a better system is proposed, the admission test is here to stay.

Format of the SAT

The SAT is a three-hour and 45-minute test. Only three hours and twenty minutes of the test count toward your score—the experimental section is not scored. There are ten sections in the test.

Section	Type	Time
Reading	19 Sentence Completions 48 Reading Comprehension 67 Total Questions	70 minutes (two 25-minute sections and one 20-minute section)
Writing	49 Grammar 1 Essay 49 Total Questions + Essay	60 minutes (two 25-minute sections and one 10-minute section)
Math	44 Multiple-choice 10 Grid-ins 54 Total Questions	70 minutes (two 25-minute sections and one 20-minute section)
Experimental	Reading, Writing, or Math	25 minutes

The order of the format is not fixed: the sections can occur in any order.

The SAT is a standardized test. Each time it is offered, the test has, as close as possible, the same level of difficulty as every previous test. Maintaining this consistency is very difficult—hence the experimental section. The effectiveness of each question must be assessed before it can be used on the SAT. A problem that one person finds easy another person may find hard, and vice versa. The experimental section measures the relative difficulty of potential questions; if responses to a question do not perform to strict specifications, the question is rejected.

The experimental section, which is not scored, can be a reading section, a writing section, or a math section. You won't know which section is experimental. You will know which type of section it is, though, since there will be an extra one of that type.

Because the "bugs" have not been worked out of the experimental section, this portion of the test is often more difficult and confusing than the other parts.

This brings up an ethical issue: How many students have run into the experimental section early in the test and have been confused and discouraged by it? Crestfallen by having done poorly on, say, the first—though experimental—section, they lose confidence and perform below their ability on the rest of the test. Some testing companies are becoming more enlightened in this regard and are administering experimental sections as separate practice tests.

Knowing that the experimental section can be disproportionately difficult, if you do poorly on a particular section you can take some solace in the hope that it may have been the experimental section. In other words, do not allow one difficult section to discourage your performance on the rest of the test.

Pacing

Although time is strictly limited on the SAT, working <u>too</u> quickly can damage your score. Many problems hinge on subtle points, and most require careful reading of the setup. Because high school can put heavy reading loads on students, many will follow their academic conditioning and read questions quickly, looking only for the gist of what each is asking. Once they have found it, they mark their answer and move on, confident they have answered it correctly. Later, many are startled to discover that they missed questions because they either misread the problems or overlooked subtle points.

Practice with a Timer
The simplest way to practice pacing is to use a timer. The Silent Timer™ is a special timer made for managing time on the SAT. It tells you when you have taken too long on any question and helps you set a pace to finish your test on time. It is the perfect timing tool to help you *Master The SAT*.

www.SilentTimer.com

Use promotion code **MTSKOL** and get 5% OFF your timer online! Read more about this timer at the end of the book.

To do well in your classes, you have to attempt to solve every, or nearly every, problem on a test. Not so with the SAT. In fact, if you try to solve every problem on the test, you will probably decimate your score. For the vast majority of people, the key to performing well on the SAT is not the number of questions they answer, within reason, but the percentage they answer correctly.

Scoring the SAT

The three parts of the test are scored independently. You will receive a reading score, a writing score, and a math score. Each score ranges from 200 to 800, with a total test score of 600–2400. The average score of each section is about 500. Thus, the total average score is about 1500.

In addition to the scaled score, you will be assigned a percentile ranking, which gives the percentage of students with scores below yours. For instance, if you score in the 80th percentile, then you will have scored better than 80 out of every 100 test takers.

Skipping and Guessing

Some questions on the SAT are rather hard. Many test takers should skip these questions. We'll talk about how to identify hard questions as we come to them.

Often students become obsessed with a particular problem and waste valuable time trying to solve it. To get a top score, learn to cut your losses and move on because all questions are worth the same number of points, regardless of difficulty level. So often it is best to skip the hardest questions and concentrate on the easy and medium ones.

Though there is a small guessing penalty on the SAT, if you can eliminate even one of the answer-choices it is to your advantage to guess.

Order of Difficulty

Like most standardized tests, the SAT lists problems in ascending order of difficulty. So deciding which questions to skip is easy—skip the last ones. Note, some SAT sections have subsections. Within these subsections, the problems also ascend in order of difficulty. For example, one of the writing sections has three subsections: *error identification, improving sentences,* and *improving paragraphs.* So if the section starts with improving sentences, then Question 1 will be the easiest and Question 11 (the last of improving sentences questions) will be the hardest. Then Question 12 (the first error identification question) will be the easiest, and so on.

The PSAT

The only difference between the SAT and the PSAT is the format and the number of questions (fewer), except for Algebra II questions, which do not appear. Hence, all the techniques developed in this book apply just as well to the PSAT.

The "2 out of 5" Rule

It is significantly harder to create a good but incorrect answer-choice than it is to produce the correct answer. For this reason usually only two attractive answer-choices are offered. One correct; the other either intentionally misleading or only partially correct. The other three answer-choices are usually fluff. This makes educated guessing on the SAT immensely effective. If you can dismiss the three fluff choices, your probability of answering the question successfully will increase from 20% to 50%.

How to Use this Book

The parts of this book are independent of one another. However, to take full advantage of the system presented in the book, it is best to tackle each part in the order given.

This book contains the equivalent of a six-week course which meets two hours a day, five days a week. Ideally you have bought the book at least four weeks before your scheduled test date. However, if the test is only a week or two away, there is still a truncated study plan that will be useful.

Shortened Study Plan

Reading:

Reading Comprehension: *(The Six Questions)*
Sentence Completions

Writing:

Grammar
General Tips on Writing Your Essays
Present Your Perspective on an Issue

Math:

Substitution
Functions
Math Notes
Number Theory
Geometry
Elimination Strategies

Questions and Answers

When is the SAT given?

The test is administered seven times a year—in October, November, December, January, March, May, and June—on Saturday mornings. Special arrangements for schedule changes are available.

If I didn't mail in a registration form, may I still take the test?

On the day of the test, walk-in registration is available, but you must call ETS in advance. You will be accommodated only if space is available—it usually is.

How important is the SAT and how is it used?

It is crucial! Although colleges may consider other factors, the majority of admission decisions are based on only two criteria: your SAT score and your GPA.

How many times should I take the SAT?

Most people are better off preparing thoroughly for the test, taking it one time and getting their top score. You can take the test as often as you like, but some schools will average your scores. You should call the schools to which you are applying to find out their policy. Then plan your strategy accordingly.

Can I cancel my score?

Yes. To do so, you must notify ETS within 5 days after taking the test.

Where can I get the registration forms?

Most high schools have the forms. You can also get them directly from ETS by writing to:

Scholastic Assessment Test
Educational Testing Service
P.O. Box 6200
Princeton, NJ 08541

Or calling
609-771-7600

Or through the Internet:
www.ets.org

Part One

Reading

Format of the Reading Section

The SAT includes 3 reading sections: Two 25-minute sections and one 20-minute section. Each section consists of two types of questions: *Sentence Completions* and *Reading Comprehension*. They are designed to test your ability to reason using the written word. The sentence Completion questions are listed in ascending order of difficulty, but the reading comprehension questions are not. There is a total of 19 sentence completion questions, and a total of 48 reading comprehension questions, which are drawn from both long passages (400–850 words) and short passages (about 150 words). The long and short passages have the same type of questions.

TYPICAL FORMAT
Questions 1–8: Sentence Completions
Questions 9–24: Reading Comprehension (two short passages and one long passage)

Vocabulary

The reading section is essentially a vocabulary test. If you know the word, you will probably be able to answer the question correctly. Thus, it is crucial that you improve your vocabulary. Yet, even if you have a strong vocabulary, you will still encounter unfamiliar words on the SAT. Much of the reading portion of this book is dedicated to studying techniques that will help you discern the meaning of words you barely recognize.

Nevertheless, don't rely on just these techniques—you must study word lists. Obviously, you cannot attempt to memorize the dictionary, and you don't need to. The SAT tests a surprisingly limited number of words. Toward the end of the reading portion of this book, you will find a list of 4000 essential words. Granted, memorizing a list of words is rather dry, but it is probably the most effective way of improving your performance on the reading section.

Attempt the reading comprehension only after you have completed the sentence completions. As mentioned before, each question on the SAT is worth the same number of points, whether it is long and hard or short and easy. Sentence completion questions take only a fraction of the time that the reading comprehension questions do.

READING COMPREHENSION

- **INTRODUCTION**
  The Source for the Passages

- **READING METHODS**
  Why Speed Reading Doesn't Work
  Why Previewing the Questions Doesn't Work
  Pre-reading the Topic Sentences

- **THE SIX QUESTIONS**
  Main Idea Questions
  Description Questions
  Writing Technique Questions
  Extension Questions
  Application Questions
  Tone Questions

- **PIVOTAL WORDS**

- **THE THREE STEP METHOD**
  1. (Optional) Preview the First Sentences
  2. Note the Six Questions
  3. Circle the Pivotal Words and Annotate

- **EXTRA READING**

Introduction

On the SAT, 48 of the 67 reading questions are on reading comprehension. Hence, this section is particularly important. Each SAT passage is about 150 to 850 words long, and each is followed by two to thirteen questions. The subject matter of a passage can be almost anything, but the most common themes are politics, history, culture, and science.

Most people find the passages difficult because the subject matter is dry and unfamiliar. Obscure subject matter is chosen so that your reading comprehension will be tested, not your knowledge of a particular subject. Also the more esoteric the subject the more likely everyone taking the test will be on an even playing field. However, because the material must still be accessible to laymen, you won't find any tracts on subtle issues of philosophy or abstract mathematics. In fact, if you read books on current affairs and the Op/Ed page of the newspaper, then the style of writing used in the SAT passages will be familiar and you probably won't find the reading comprehension section particularly difficult.

The passages use a formal, compact style. They are typically taken from articles in academic journals, but they are rarely reprinted verbatim. Usually the chosen article is heavily edited until it is honed down to about 150 to 850 hundred words. The formal style of the piece is retained but much of the "fluff" is removed. The editing process condenses the article to about one-third its original length. Thus, an SAT passage contains about three times as much information for its length as does the original article. This is why the passages are similar to the writing on the Op/Ed page of a newspaper. After all, a person writing a piece for the Op/Ed page must express all his ideas in about 500 words, and he must use a formal (grammatical) style to convince people that he is well educated.

Reading Methods

Reading styles are subjective—there is no best method for approaching the passages. There are as many "systems" for reading the passages as there are test-prep books—all "authoritatively" promoting their method, while contradicting some aspect of another. A reading technique that is natural for one person can be awkward and unnatural for another person. However, I find it hard to believe that many of the methods advocated in certain books could help anyone. Be that as it may, I will throw in my own two-cents worth— though not so dogmatically.

Some books recommend speed-reading the passages. This is a mistake. Speed reading is designed for ordinary, nontechnical material. Because this material is filled with "fluff," you can skim over the nonessential parts and still get the gist—and often more—of the passage. As mentioned before, however, SAT passages are dense. Some are actual quoted articles (when the writers of the SAT find one that is sufficiently compact). Most often, however, they are based on articles that have been condensed to about one-third their original length. During this process no essential information is lost, just the "fluff" is cut. This is why speed reading will not work here—the passages contain too much information. You should, however, read somewhat faster than you normally do, but not to the point that your comprehension suffers. You will have to experiment to find your optimum pace.

Many books recommend that the questions be read before the passage. This strikes me as a cruel joke. In some of these books it seems that many of the methods, such as this one, are advocated merely to give the reader the feeling that he or she is getting the "inside stuff" on how to ace the test. But there are two big problems with this method. First, some of the questions are a paragraph long, and reading a question twice can use up precious time. Second, there are up to thirteen questions per passage, and psychologists have shown that we can hold in our minds a maximum of about three thoughts at any one time (some of us have trouble simply remembering phone numbers). After reading all thirteen questions, the student will turn to the passage with his mind clouded by half-remembered thoughts. This will at best waste his time and distract him. More likely it will turn the passage into a disjointed mass of information.

However, one technique that you may find helpful is to preview the passage by reading the first sentence of each paragraph. Generally, the topic of a paragraph is contained in the first sentence. Reading the first sentence of each paragraph will give an overview of the passage. The topic sentences act in essence as a summary of the passage. Furthermore, since each passage is only four to eight paragraphs long, previewing the topic sentences will not use up an inordinate amount of time. (I don't use this method myself, however. I prefer to see the passage as a completed whole, and to let the passage unveil its main idea to me as I become absorbed in it. I find that when I try to pre-analyze the passage it tends to become disjointed, and I lose my concentration. Nonetheless, as mentioned before, reading methods are subjective, so experiment—this may work for you.)

The Six Questions

The key to performing well on the passages is not the particular reading technique you use (so long as it's neither speed reading nor pre-reading the questions). Rather the key is to become completely familiar with the question types—there are only six—so that you can anticipate the questions that *might* be asked as you read the passage and answer those that *are* asked more quickly and efficiently. As you become familiar with the six question types, you will gain an intuitive sense for the places from which questions are likely to be drawn. This will give you the same advantage as that claimed by the "pre-reading-the-questions" technique, without the confusion and waste of time. Note, the order in which the questions are asked roughly corresponds to the order in which the main issues are presented in the passage. Early questions should correspond to information given early in the passage, and so on.

The following passage and accompanying questions illustrate the six question types. Read the passage slowly to get a good understanding of the issues.

There are two major systems of criminal procedure in the modern world—the adversarial and the inquisitorial. The former is associated with common law tradition and the latter with
5 civil law tradition. Both systems were historically preceded by the system of private vengeance in which the victim of a crime fashioned his own remedy and administered it privately, either personally or through an agent.
10 The vengeance system was a system of self-help, the essence of which was captured in the slogan "an eye for an eye, a tooth for a tooth." The modern adversarial system is only one historical step removed from the private vengeance system
15 and still retains some of its characteristic features. Thus, for example, even though the right to institute criminal action has now been extended to all members of society and even though the police department has taken over the
20 pretrial investigative functions on behalf of the prosecution, the adversarial system still leaves the defendant to conduct his own pretrial investigation. The trial is still viewed as a duel between two adversaries, refereed by a judge who, at the
25 beginning of the trial has no knowledge of the investigative background of the case. In the final analysis the adversarial system of criminal procedure symbolizes and regularizes the punitive combat.

30 By contrast, the inquisitorial system begins historically where the adversarial system stopped its development. It is two historical steps removed from the system of private vengeance. Therefore, from the standpoint of legal anthro-
35 pology, it is historically superior to the adversarial system. Under the inquisitorial system the public investigator has the duty to investigate not just on behalf of the prosecutor but also on behalf of the defendant. Additionally, the public
40 prosecutor has the duty to present to the court not only evidence that may lead to the conviction of the defendant but also evidence that may lead to his exoneration. This system mandates that both parties permit full pretrial discovery of the evi-
45 dence in their possession. Finally, in an effort to make the trial less like a duel between two adversaries, the inquisitorial system mandates that the judge take an active part in the conduct of the trial, with a role that is both directive and
50 protective.
  Fact-finding is at the heart of the inquisitorial system. This system operates on the philosophical premise that in a criminal case the crucial factor is not the legal rule but the facts of
55 the case and that the goal of the entire procedure is to experimentally recreate for the court the commission of the alleged crime.

MAIN IDEA QUESTIONS

All authors have a point they want to make in their writing. Main idea questions test your ability to identify and understand an author's intent. The main idea is usually stated in the last—occasionally the first—sentence of the first paragraph. If it's not there, it will probably be the last sentence of the entire passage. Main idea questions are usually the first questions asked.

Some common main idea questions are

☐   Which one of the following best expresses the main idea of the passage?

☐   The primary purpose of the passage is to . . .

☐   In the passage, the author's primary concern is to discuss . . .

Main idea questions are rarely difficult; after all the author wants to clearly communicate her ideas to you. If, however, after the first reading, you don't have a feel for the main idea, review the first and last sentence of each paragraph; these will give you a quick overview of the passage.

Because main idea questions are relatively easy, the SAT writers try to obscure the correct answer by surrounding it with close answer-choices ("detractors") that either overstate or understate the author's main point. Answer-choices that stress specifics tend to understate the main idea; choices that go beyond the scope of the passage tend to overstate the main idea.

> The answer to a main idea question will summarize the author's argument, yet be neither too specific nor too broad.

In most SAT passages the author's primary purpose is to persuade the reader to accept her opinion. Occasionally, it is to describe something.

Example: (Refer to passage on page 21.)

The primary purpose of the passage is to

(A)   explain why the inquisitorial system is the best system of criminal justice
(B)   explain how the adversarial and the inquisitorial systems of criminal justice both evolved from the system of private vengeance
(C)   show how the adversarial and inquisitorial systems of criminal justice can both comple-ment and hinder each other's development
(D)   show how the adversarial and inquisitorial systems of criminal justice are being combined into a new and better system
(E)   analyze two systems of criminal justice and deduce which one is better

The answer to a main idea question will summarize the passage without going beyond it. (A) violates these criteria by *overstating* the scope of the passage. The comparison in the passage is between two specific systems, not between *all* systems. (A) would be a good answer if "best" were replaced with "better." **Beware of extreme words**. (B) violates the criteria by *understating* the scope of the passage. Although the evolution of both the adversarial and the inquisitorial systems is discussed in the passage, it is done to show why one is superior to the other. As to (C) and (D), both can be quickly dismissed since neither is mentioned in the passage. Finally, the passage does two things: it presents two systems of criminal justice and shows why one is better than the other. (E) aptly summarizes this, so it is the best answer.

Following is a short passage. The types of questions for short passages are the same as those for long passages. Only the lengths of the passages differ.

Application: *(Short passage)*

As Xenophanes recognized as long ago as the sixth century before Christ, whether or not God made man in His own image, it is certain that man makes gods in his. The gods of Greek mythology first appear in the writings of Homer and Hesiod, and, from the character and actions of these picturesque and, for the most part, friendly beings, we get some idea of the men who made them and brought them to Greece.

But ritual is more fundamental than mythology, and the study of Greek ritual during recent years has shown that, beneath the belief or skepticism with which the Olympians were regarded, lay an older magic, with traditional rites for the promotion of fertility by the celebration of the annual cycle of life and death, and the propitiation of unfriendly ghosts, gods or demons. Some such survivals were doubtless widespread, and, prolonged into classical times, probably made the substance of Eleusinian and Orphic mysteries. Against this dark and dangerous background arose Olympic mythology on the one hand and early philosophy and science on the other.

In classical times the need of a creed higher than the Olympian was felt, and Aeschylus, Sophocles and Plato finally evolved from the pleasant but crude polytheism the idea of a single, supreme and righteous Zeus. But the decay of Olympus led to a revival of old and the invasion of new magic cults among the people, while some philosophers were looking to a vision of the uniformity of nature under divine and universal law.

From Sir William Cecil Dampier, *A Shorter History of Science*, ©1957, Meridian Books.

The main idea of the passage is that

(A)   Olympic mythology evolved from ancient rituals and gave rise to early philosophy.
(B)   early moves toward viewing nature as ordered by divine and universal law coincided with monotheistic impulses and the disintegration of classical mythology.
(C)   early philosophy followed from classical mythology.
(D)   the practice of science, i.e., empiricism, preceded scientific theory.

Most main idea questions are rather easy. This one is not—mainly, because the passage itself is not an easy read. Recall that to find the main idea of a passage, we check the last sentence of the first paragraph; if it's not there, we check the closing of the passage. Reviewing the last sentence of the first paragraph, we see that it hardly presents a statement, let alone the main idea. Turning to the closing line of the passage, however, we find the key to this question. The passage describes a struggle for ascendancy amongst four opposing philosophies: (magic and traditional rites) vs. (Olympic mythology) vs. (monotheism [Zeus]) vs. (early philosophy and science). The closing lines of the passage summarize this and add that Olympic mythology lost out to monotheism (Zeus), while magical cults enjoyed a revival and the germ of universal law was planted. Thus the answer is (B).

As to the other choices, (A) is false. "Olympic mythology [arose] on one hand and early philosophy and science on the other" (closing to paragraph two); thus they initially developed in parallel. (C) is also false. It makes the same type of error as (A). Finally, (D) is not mentioned in the passage.

DESCRIPTION QUESTIONS

Description questions, as with main idea questions, refer to a point made by the author. However, description questions refer to a minor point or to incidental information, not to the author's main point.

Again, these questions take various forms:

☐   According to the passage . . .

☐   In line 37, the author mentions . . . for the purpose of . . .

☐   The passage suggests that which one of the following would . . .

The answer to a description question must refer <u>directly</u> to a statement in the passage, not to something implied by it. However, the correct answer will paraphrase a statement in the passage, not give an exact quote. In fact, exact quotes ("Same language" traps) are often used to bait wrong answers.

Caution: When answering a description question, you must find the point in the passage from which the question is drawn. Don't rely on memory—too many obfuscating tactics are used with these questions.

Not only must the correct answer refer directly to a statement in the passage, it must refer to the relevant statement. The correct answer will be surrounded by wrong choices which refer directly to the passage but don't address the question. These choices can be tempting because they tend to be quite close to the actual answer.

Once you spot the sentence to which the question refers, you still must read a few sentences before and after it, to put the question in context. If a question refers to line 20, the information needed to answer it can occur anywhere from line 15 to 25. Even if you have spotted the answer in line 20, you should still read a couple more lines to make certain you have the proper perspective.

Example: (Refer to passage on page 21.)

According to the passage, the inquisitorial system differs from the adversarial system in that

(A)   it does not make the defendant solely responsible for gathering evidence for his case
(B)   it does not require the police department to work on behalf of the prosecution
(C)   it does not allow the victim the satisfaction of private vengeance
(D)   it requires the prosecution to drop a weak case
(E)   a defendant who is innocent would prefer to be tried under the inquisitorial system

This is a description question, so the information needed to answer it must be stated in the passage—though not in the same language as in the answer. The needed information is contained in lines 37–40, which state that the public prosecutor has to investigate on behalf of both society and the defendant. Thus, the defendant is not solely responsible for investigating his case. Furthermore, the paragraph's opening implies that this feature is not found in the adversarial system. This illustrates why you must determine the context of the situation before you can safely answer the question. The answer is (A).

The other choices can be easily dismissed. (B) is the second best answer. Lines 19–21 state that in the adversarial system the police assume the work of the prosecution. Then lines 30–32 state that the inquisitorial system begins where the adversarial system stopped; this implies that in both systems the police work for the prosecution. (C) uses a false claim ploy. The passage states that both systems are removed from the system of private vengeance. (D) is probably true, but it is neither stated nor directly implied by the passage. Finally, (E) uses a reference to the passage to make a true but irrelevant statement. People's attitude or preference toward a system is not a part of that system.

Application: *(Short passage)*

If dynamic visual graphics, sound effects, and automatic scorekeeping are the features that account for the popularity of video games, why are parents so worried? All of these features seem quite innocent. But another source of concern is that the games available in arcades have, almost without exception, themes of physical aggression.... There has long been the belief that violent content may teach violent behavior. And yet again our society finds a new medium in which to present that content, and yet again the demand is nearly insatiable. And there is evidence that violent video games breed violent behavior, just as violent television shows do....

The effects of video violence are less simple, however, than they at first appeared. The same group of researchers who found negative effects [from certain video games] have more recently found that two-player aggressive video games, whether cooperative or competitive, reduce the level of aggression in children's play....

It may be that the most harmful aspect of the violent video games is that they are solitary in nature. A two-person aggressive game (video boxing, in this study) seems to provide a cathartic or releasing effect for aggression, while a solitary aggressive game (such as Space Invaders) may stimulate further aggression. Perhaps the effects of television in stimulating aggression will also be found to stem partly from the fact that TV viewing typically involves little social interaction.

From Patricia Marks Greenfield, *Mind and Media: The Effects of Television, Video Games, and Computers.* © 1984 by Harvard University Press.

According to the passage, which of the following would be likely to stimulate violent behavior in a child playing a video game?

   I.   Watching the computer stage a battle between two opponents
   II.   Controlling a character in battle against a computer
   III.   Challenging another player to a battle in a non-cooperative two-person game

(A)   II only
(B)   III only
(C)   I and II only
(D)   II and III only

Item I, True: Stimulation would occur. This choice is qualitatively the same as passively watching violence on television. **Item II, True:** Stimulation would also occur. This is another example of solitary aggression (implied by the second sentence of the last paragraph). **Item III, False:** No stimulation would occur. Two-player aggressive games are "cathartic" (again the needed reference is the second sentence of the last paragraph). The answer is (C).

Often you will be asked to define a word or phrase based on its context. For this type of question, again you must look at a few lines before and after the word. Don't assume that because the word is familiar you know the definition requested. Words often have more than one meaning, and the SAT often asks for a peculiar or technical meaning of a common word. For example, as a noun *champion* means "the winner," but as a verb *champion* means "to be an advocate for someone." You must consider the word's context to get its correct meaning.

On the SAT the definition of a word will not use as simple a structure as was used above to define *champion.* One common way the SAT introduces a defining word or phrase is to place it in apposition to the word being defined.

Don't confuse "apposition" with "opposition": they have antithetical [exactly opposite] meanings. Words or phrases in apposition are placed next to each other, and the second word or phrase defines, clarifies, or gives evidence for the first word or phrase. The second word or phrase will be set off from the first by a comma, semicolon, hyphen, or parentheses. (Note: If a comma is not followed by a linking word—such as *and, for, yet*—then the following phrase is probably appositional.)

Example:

The discussions were acrimonious, frequently degenerating into name-calling contests.

After the comma in this sentence, there is no linking word (such as *and, but, because, although,* etc.). Hence the phrase following the comma is in apposition to *acrimonious*—it defines or further clarifies the word. Now acrimonious means bitter, mean-spirited talk, which would aptly describe a name-calling contest.

Application: *(Short passage)*

The technical phenomenon, embracing all the separate techniques, forms a whole.... It is useless to look for differentiations. They do exist, but only secondarily. The common features of the technical phenomenon are so sharply drawn that it is easy to discern that which is the technical phenomenon and that which is not.

... To analyze these common features is tricky, but it is simple to grasp them. Just as there are principles common to things as different as a wireless set and an internal-combustion engine, so the organization of an office and the construction of an aircraft have certain identical features. This identity is the primary mark of that thoroughgoing unity which makes the technical phenomenon a single essence despite the extreme diversity of its appearances.

As a corollary, it is impossible to analyze this or that element out of it—a truth which is today particularly misunderstood. The great tendency of all persons who study techniques is to make distinctions. They distinguish between the different elements of technique, maintaining some and discarding others. They distinguish between technique and the use to which it is put. These distinctions are completely invalid and show only that he who makes them has understood nothing of the technical phenomenon. Its parts are ontologically tied together; in it, use is inseparable from being.

From Jacques Ellul, *The Technological Society*, ©1964 by Alfred A. Knopf, Inc.

The "technical phenomenon" referred to in the opening line can best be defined as

(A)   all of the machinery in use today
(B)   the abstract idea of the machine
(C)   a way of thinking in modern society
(D)   what all machines have in common

(A): No, it is clear from the passage that the technical phenomenon is more abstract than that, since it is described in the opening paragraph as uniting all the separate "techniques" (not machines) and as comprising the "features" that such things as an office and an aircraft have in common. (B): No, the passage states that the technical phenomenon is something that includes both techniques and their use (See closing lines of the passage); it is thus broader that just the idea of machinery. **(C): Yes,** this seems to be the best answer; it is broad enough to include both techniques and their uses and abstract enough to go beyond talking only about machines. (D): No, the passage suggests that it is something that techniques have in common and techniques can include airplanes or offices.

WRITING TECHNIQUE QUESTIONS

All coherent writing has a superstructure or blueprint. When writing, we don't just randomly jot down our thoughts; we organize our ideas and present them in a logical manner. For instance, we may present evidence that builds up to a conclusion but intentionally leave the conclusion unstated, or we may present a position and then contrast it with an opposing position, or we may draw an extended analogy.

There is an endless number of writing techniques that authors use to present their ideas, so we cannot classify every method. However, some techniques are very common to the type of explanatory or opinionated writing found in SAT passages.

A.   Compare and contrast two positions.

This technique has a number of variations, but the most common and direct is to develop two ideas or systems (comparing) and then point out why one is better than the other (contrasting).

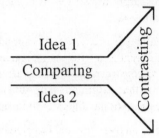

Some common tip-off phrases to this method of analysis are

- By contrast
- Similarly

Some typical questions for these types of passages are

- According to the passage, a central distinction between a woman's presence and a man's presence is:
- In which of the following ways does the author imply that birds and reptiles are similar?

Writing-technique questions are similar to main idea questions; except that they ask about how the author <u>presents</u> his ideas, not about the ideas themselves. Generally, you will be given only two writing methods to choose from, but each method will have two or more variations.

Example: (Refer to passage on page 21.)
Which one of the following best describes the organization of the passage?

(A)   Two systems of criminal justice are compared and contrasted, and one is deemed to be better than the other.
(B)   One system of criminal justice is presented as better than another. Then evidence is offered to support that claim.
(C)   Two systems of criminal justice are analyzed, and one specific example is examined in detail.
(D)   A set of examples is furnished. Then a conclusion is drawn from them.
(E)   The inner workings of the criminal justice system are illustrated by using two systems.

Clearly the author is comparing and contrasting two criminal justice systems. Indeed, the opening to paragraph two makes this explicit. The author uses a mixed form of comparison and contrast. He opens the passage by developing (comparing) both systems and then shifts to developing just the adversarial system. He opens the second paragraph by contrasting the two criminal justice systems and then further develops just the inquisitorial system. Finally, he closes by again contrasting the two systems and implying that the inquisitorial system is superior.

Only two answer-choices, (A) and (B), have any real merit. They say essentially the same thing—though in different order. Notice in the passage that the author does not indicate which system is better until the end of paragraph one, and he does not make that certain until paragraph two. This contradicts the order given by (B). Hence the answer is (A). (Note: In (A) the order is not specified and therefore is harder to attack, whereas in (B) the order is definite and therefore is easier to attack. Remember that a measured response is harder to attack and therefore is more likely to be the answer.)

B.   Show cause and effect.

In this technique, the author typically shows how a particular cause leads to a certain result or set of results. It is not uncommon for this method to introduce a sequence of causes and effects. A causes B, which causes C, which causes D, and so on. Hence B is both the effect of A and the cause of C. The variations on this rhetorical technique can be illustrated by the following schematics:

$$\text{C} \longrightarrow \text{E} \qquad \text{C} \Big\langle\!\!\!\begin{array}{c} \longrightarrow \text{E} \\ \longrightarrow \text{E} \\ \longrightarrow \text{E} \end{array} \qquad \text{C} \longrightarrow \text{C/E} \longrightarrow \text{C/E} \longrightarrow \text{E}$$

Example: *(Short passage)*

Thirdly, I worry about the private automobile. It is a dirty, noisy, wasteful, and lonely means of travel. It pollutes the air, ruins the safety and sociability of the street, and exercises upon the individual a discipline which takes away far more freedom than it gives him. It causes an enormous amount of land to be unnecessarily abstracted from nature and from plant life and to become devoid of any natural function. It explodes cities, grievously impairs the whole institution of neighborliness, fragmentizes and destroys communities. It has already spelled the end of our cities as real cultural and social communities, and has made impossible the construction of any others in their place. Together with the airplane, it has crowded out other, more civilized and more convenient means of transport, leaving older people, infirm people, poor people and children in a worse situation than they were a hundred years ago. It continues to lend a terrible element of fragility to our civilization, placing us in a situation where our life would break down completely if anything ever interfered with the oil supply.

George F. Kennan

Which of the following best describes the organization of the passage?

(A)   A problem is presented and then a possible solution is discussed.
(B)   The benefits and demerits of the automobile are compared and contrasted.
(C)   A topic is presented and a number of its effects are discussed.
(D)   A set of examples is furnished to support a conclusion.

This passage is laden with effects. Kennan introduces the cause, the automobile, in the opening sentence and from there on presents a series of effects—the automobile pollutes, enslaves, and so on. Hence the answer is (C). Note: (D) is the second-best choice; it is disqualified by two flaws. First, in this context, "examples" is not as precise as "effects." Second, the order is wrong: the conclusion, *"I worry about the private automobile"* is presented first and then the examples: it pollutes, it enslaves, etc.

C.   State a position and then give supporting evidence.

This technique is common with opinionated passages. Equally common is the reverse order. That is, the supporting evidence is presented and then the position or conclusion is stated. And sometimes the evidence will be structured to build up to a conclusion which is then left unstated. If this is done skillfully the reader will be more likely to arrive at the same conclusion as the author.

Following are some typical questions for these types of passages:

- According to the author, which of the following is required for one to become proficient with a computer?

- Which of the following does the author cite as evidence that the bald eagle is in danger of becoming extinct?

EXTENSION QUESTIONS

Extension questions are the most common. They require you to go beyond what is stated in the passage, asking you to draw an inference from the passage, to make a conclusion based on the passage, or to identify one of the author's tacit assumptions.

You may be asked to draw a conclusion based on the ideas or facts presented:

☐   It can be inferred from the passage that . . .

☐   The passage suggests that . . .

Since extension questions require you to go beyond the passage, the correct answer must say *more* than what is said in the passage. Beware of same language traps with these questions: the correct answer will often both paraphrase and extend a statement in the passage, but it will not directly quote it.

> **"Same Language" traps:** For extension questions, any answer-choice that explicitly refers to or repeats a statement in the passage will probably be wrong.

The correct answer to an extension question will not require a quantum leap in thought, but it will add significantly to the ideas presented in the passage.

Example: (Refer to passage on page 21.)

The author views the prosecution's role in the inquisitorial system as being

   (A)   an advocate for both society and the defendant
   (B)   solely responsible for starting a trial
   (C)   a protector of the legal rule
   (D)   an investigator only
   (E)   an aggressive but fair investigator

This is an extension question. So the answer will not be explicitly stated in the passage, but it will be strongly supported by it.

The author states that the prosecutor is duty bound to present any evidence that may prove the defendant innocent and that he must disclose all pretrial evidence (i.e., have no tricks up his sleeve). This is the essence of fair play. So the answer is probably (E).

However, we should check all the choices. (A) overstates the case. Although the prosecutor must disclose any evidence that might show the defendant innocent, the prosecutor is still advocating society's case against the defendant—it must merely be measured advocacy. This is the second-best answer. As for (B), although it is implied that in both systems the right to initiate a case is extended to all people through the prosecutor, it is not stated or implied that this is the only way to start a case. Finally, neither (C) nor (D) is mentioned or implied in the passage. The answer, therefore, is (E).

Application: *(Short passage)*

> Often, the central problem in any business is that money is needed to make money. The following discusses the sale of equity, which is one response to this problem.
>
> *Sale of Capital Stock*: a way to obtain capital through the sale of stock to individual investors beyond the scope of one's immediate acquaintances. Periods of high interest rates turn entrepreneurs to this equity market. This involves, of necessity, a dilution of ownership, and many owners are reluctant to take this step for that reason. Whether the owner is wise in declining to use outside equity financing depends upon the firm's long-range prospects. If there is an opportunity for substantial expansion on a continuing basis and if other sources are inadequate, the owner may decide logically to bring in other owners. Owning part of a larger business may be more profitable than owning all of a smaller business.
>
> *Small-Business Management*, 6th Ed., © 1983 by South-Western Publishing Co.

The passage implies that an owner who chooses not to sell capital stock despite the prospect of continued expansion is

   (A)   subject to increased regulation
   (B)   more conservative than is wise under the circumstances
   (C)   likely to have her ownership of the business diluted
   (D)   sacrificing security for rapid growth

(A): No. This is not mentioned in the passage. **(B): Yes.** The passage states that *"the owner may decide logically to bring in other owners";* in other words, the owner would be wise to sell stock in this situation. (C): No. By NOT selling stock, the owner retains full ownership. (D) No. Just the opposite: the owner would be sacrificing a measure of security for growth if she did sell stock.

APPLICATION QUESTIONS

Application questions differ from extension questions only in degree. Extension questions ask you to apply what you have learned from the passage to derive new information about the same subject, whereas application questions go one step further, asking you to apply what you have learned from the passage to a different or hypothetical situation.

The following are common application questions:

☐   Which one of the following is the most likely source of the passage?

☐   Which one of the following actions would be most likely to have the same effect as the author's actions?

You may be asked to complete a thought for the author:

☐   The author would most likely agree with which one of the following statements?

☐   Which one of the following sentences would the author be most likely to use to complete the last paragraph of the passage?

To answer an application question, take the author's perspective. Ask yourself: what am I arguing for? what might make my argument stronger? what might make it weaker?

Because these questions go well beyond the passage, they tend to be the most difficult. Furthermore, because application questions and extension questions require a deeper understanding of the passage, skimming (or worse yet, speed-reading) the passage is ineffective. Skimming may give you the main idea and structure of the passage, but it is unlikely to give you the subtleties of the author's attitude.

Example: (Refer to passage on page 21.)

Based on the information in the passage, it can be inferred that which one of the following would most logically begin a paragraph immediately following the passage?

(A)   Because of the inquisitorial system's thoroughness in conducting its pretrial investigation, it can be concluded that a defendant who is innocent would prefer to be tried under the inquisitorial system, whereas a defendant who is guilty would prefer to be tried under the adversarial system.

(B)   As the preceding analysis shows, the legal system is in a constant state of flux. For now the inquisitorial system is ascendant, but it will probably be soon replaced by another system.

(C)   The accusatorial system begins where the inquisitorial system ends. So it is three steps removed from the system of private vengeance, and therefore historically superior to it.

(D)   Because in the inquisitorial system the judge must take an active role in the conduct of the trial, his competency and expertise have become critical.

(E)   The criminal justice system has evolved to the point that it no longer seems to be derivative of the system of private vengeance. Modern systems of criminal justice empower all of society with the right to instigate a legal action, and the need for vengeance is satisfied through a surrogate—the public prosecutor.

The author has rather thoroughly presented his position, so the next paragraph would be a natural place for him to summarize it. The passage compares and contrasts two systems of criminal justice, implying that the inquisitorial system is superior. We expect the concluding paragraph to sum up this position. Now all legal theory aside, the system of justice under which an innocent person would choose to be judged would, as a practical matter, pretty much sum up the situation. Hence the answer is (A).

Application: *(Short passage)*

The idea of stuff expresses no more than the experience of coming to a limit at which our senses or our instruments are not fine enough to make out the pattern.

Something of the same kind happens when the scientist investigates any unit or pattern so distinct to the naked eye that it has been considered a separate entity. He finds that the more carefully he observes and describes it, the more he is *also* describing the environment in which it moves and other patterns to which it seems inseparably related. As Teilhard de Chardin has so well expressed it, the isolation of individual, atomic patterns "is merely an intellectual dodge."

...Although the ancient cultures of Asia never attained the rigorously exact physical knowledge of the modern West, they grasped in principle many things which are only now occurring to us. Hinduism and Buddhism are impossible to classify as religions, philosophies, sciences, or even mythologies, or again as amalgamations of all four, because departmentalization is foreign to them even in so basic a form as the separation of the spiritual and the material.... Buddhism ... is not a culture but a critique of culture, an enduring nonviolent revolution, or "loyal opposition," to the culture with which it is involved. This gives these ways of liberation something in common with psychotherapy beyond the interest in changing states of consciousness. For the task of the psychotherapist is to bring about a reconciliation between individual feeling and social norms without, however, sacrificing the integrity of the individual. He tries to help the individual to be himself and to go it alone in the world (of social convention) but not of the world.

From Alan W. Watts, *Psychotherapy East and West*, © 1961 by Pantheon Books, a division of Random House.

What does the passage suggest about the theme of the book from which it is excerpted?

(A) The book attempts to understand psychotherapy in the context of different and changing systems of thought.

(B) The book argues that psychotherapy unites elements of an exact science with elements of eastern philosophy.

(C) The book describes the origins of psychotherapy around the world.

(D) The book compares psychotherapy in the West and in the East.

(A): Yes, this is the most accurate inference from the passage. The passage discusses how the more carefully a scientist views and describes something the more he describes the environment in which it moves, and the passage traces similarities between psychotherapy and Eastern systems of (evolving) thought. (B): No, this is too narrow an interpretation of what the whole book would be doing. (C): No, too vague; the passage is too philosophical to be merely a history. (D): No, also too vague, meant to entrap those of you who relied on the title without thinking through the passage.

TONE QUESTIONS

Tone questions ask you to identify the writer's attitude or perspective. Is the writer's feeling toward the subject positive, negative, or neutral? Does the writer give his own opinion, or does he objectively present the opinions of others?

> Before you read the answer-choices, decide whether the writer's tone is positive, negative, or neutral. It is best to do this without referring to the passage.

However, if you did not get a feel for the writer's attitude on the first reading, check the adjectives that he chooses. Adjectives and, to a lesser extent, adverbs express our feelings toward subjects. For instance, if we agree with a person who holds strong feelings about a subject, we may describe his opinions as impassioned. On the other hand, if we disagree with him, we may describe his opinions as excitable, which has the same meaning as "impassioned" but carries a negative connotation.

Example: (Refer to passage on page 21.)

The author's attitude toward the adversarial system can best be described as

(A)   encouraged that it is far removed from the system of private vengeance
(B)   concerned that it does not allow all members of society to instigate legal action
(C)   pleased that it does not require the defendant to conduct his own pretrial investigation
(D)   hopeful that it will be replaced by the inquisitorial system
(E)   doubtful that it is the best vehicle for justice

The author does not reveal his feelings toward the adversarial system until the end of paragraph one. Clearly the clause "the adversarial system of criminal procedure symbolizes and regularizes the punitive combat" indicates that he has a negative attitude toward the system. This is confirmed in the second paragraph when he states that the inquisitorial system is historically superior to the adversarial system. So he feels that the adversarial system is deficient.

The "two-out-of-five" rule is at work here: only choices (D) and (E) have any real merit. Both are good answers. But which one is better? Intuitively, choice (E) is more likely to be the answer because it is more measured. To decide between two choices attack each: the one that survives is the answer. Now a tone question should be answered from what is directly stated in the passage—not from what it implies. Although the author has reservations toward the adversarial system, at no point does he say that he hopes the inquisitorial system will replace it, he may prefer a third system over both. This eliminates (D); the answer therefore is (E).

The remaining choices are not supported by the passage. (A), using the same language as in the passage, overstates the author's feeling. In lines 12–14, he states that the adversarial system is only *one* step removed from the private vengeance system—not *far* removed. Remember: Be wary of extreme words. (A) would be a better choice if "far" were dropped. (B) makes a false claim. In lines 16–18, the author states that the adversarial system *does* extend the right to initiate legal action to all members of society. Finally, (C) also makes a false claim. In lines 21–23, the author states that the defendant in the adversarial system is still left to conduct his own pretrial investigation.

Application: *(Short passage)*

An elm in our backyard caught the blight this summer and dropped stone dead, leafless, almost overnight. One weekend it was a normal-looking elm, maybe a little bare in spots but nothing alarming, and the next weekend it was gone, passed over, departed, taken....

The dying of a field mouse, at the jaws of an amiable household cat, is a spectacle I have beheld many times. It used to make me wince.... Nature, I thought, was an abomination.

Recently I've done some thinking about that mouse, and I wonder if his dying is necessarily all that different from the passing of our elm. The main difference, if there is one, would be in the matter of pain. I do not believe that an elm tree has pain receptors, and even so, the blight seems to me a relatively painless way to go. But the mouse dangling tail-down from the teeth of a gray cat is something else again, with pain beyond bearing, you'd think, all over his small body. There are now some plausible reasons for thinking it is not like that at all.... At the instant of being trapped and penetrated by teeth, peptide hormones are released by cells in the hypothalamus and the pituitary gland; instantly these substances, called endorphins, are attached to the surfaces of other cells responsible for pain perception; the hormones have the pharmaco-logic properties of opium; there is no pain. Thus it is that the mouse seems always to dangle so languidly from the jaws, lies there so quietly when dropped, dies of his injuries without a struggle. If a mouse could shrug, he'd shrug....

Pain is useful for avoidance, for getting away when there's time to get away, but when it is end game, and no way back, pain is likely to be turned off, and the mechanisms for this are wonderfully precise and quick. If I had to design an ecosystem in which creatures had to live off each other and in which dying was an indispensable part of living, I could not think of a better way to manage.

From Lewis Thomas, *On Natural Death,* © 1979 by Lewis Thomas.

Which one of the following would best characterize the author's attitude toward the relationship between pain and death?

(A)   Dismay at the inherent cruelty of nature
(B)   Amusement at the irony of the relationship between pain and death
(C)   Admiration for the ways in which animal life functions in the ecosystem
(D)   A desire to conduct experiments on animals in order to discover more about the relation-ship between pain and death

The author's attitude toward the relationship between pain and death evolves through three stages. First, he expresses revulsion at the relationship. This is indicated in the second paragraph by the words *"wince"* and *"abomination."* Then in the third paragraph, he adopts a more analytical attitude and questions his previous judgment. This is indicated by the clause, *"I wonder if his dying is necessarily all that different from the passing of our elm."* And in closing the paragraph, he seems resigned to the fact the relationship is not all that bad. This is indicated by the sentence, *"If a mouse could shrug, he'd shrug."* Finally, in the last paragraph, he comes to express admiration for the relationship between pain and death. This is indicated by the phrase *"wonderfully precise and quick,"* and it is made definite by the closing line, *"If I had to design an ecosystem . . . in which dying was an indispensable part of living, I could not think of a better way to manage."* Thus, the answer is (C).

The other choices are easily ruled out. Choice (A) is perhaps superficially tempting. In the second paragraph the author does express dismay at the ways of nature, but notice that his concerns are in the past tense. He is *now* more understanding, wiser of the ways of nature. As to (B), the author is subtly reverential, never ironical, toward nature. Finally, (D) is not mentioned or alluded to in the passage.

Beware of answer-choices that contain extreme emotions. Remember the passages are taken from academic journals. In the rarefied air of academic circles, strong emotions are considered inappropriate and sophomoric. The writers want to display opinions that are considered and reasonable, not spontaneous and off-the-wall. So if an author's tone is negative, it may be disapproving—not snide. Or if her tone is positive, it may be approving—not ecstatic.

Furthermore, the answers must be indisputable. If the answers were subjective, then the writers of the SAT would be deluged with letters from angry test takers, complaining that their test-scores are unfair. To avoid such a difficult position, the writers of the SAT never allow the correct answer to be either controversial or grammatically questionable.

Let's use these theories to answer the following questions.

Example:

Which one of the following most accurately characterizes the author's attitude with respect to Phillis Wheatley's literary accomplishments?

(A) enthusiastic advocacy
(B) qualified admiration
(C) dispassionate impartiality
(D) detached ambivalence
(E) perfunctory dismissal

Even without reference to the passage, this is not a difficult question to answer.

Scholars may advocate each other's work, but they are unlikely to be enthusiastic advocates. Furthermore, the context stretches the meaning of advocacy—to defend someone else's cause or plight. So (A) is unlikely to be the answer.

(B) is the measured response and therefore is probably the answer.

"Dispassionate impartiality" is a rather odd construction; additionally, it is redundant. It could never be the answer to an SAT question. This eliminates (C).

"Detached ambivalence" is not as odd as "dispassionate impartiality," but it is unusual. So (D) is unlikely to be the answer.

Remember, scholars want their audience to consider their opinions well thought out, not off-the-wall. But *perfunctory* means "hasty and superficial." So (E) could not be the answer.

Hence, even without the passage we can still find the answer, (B).

Example:

Which one of the following best describes the author's attitude toward scientific techniques?

(A) critical
(B) hostile
(C) idealistic
(D) ironic
(E) neutral

(A) is one of two measured responses offered. Now a scholar may be critical of a particular scientific technique, but only a crackpot would be critical of *all* scientific techniques—eliminate (A).

"Hostile" is far too negative. Scholars consider such emotions juvenile—eliminate (B).

"Idealistic," on the other hand, is too positive; it sounds pollyannaish—eliminate (C).

"Ironic" seems illogical in this context. It's hard to conceive of a person having an ironic attitude toward scientific techniques—eliminate (D).

(E) is the other measured response, and by elimination it is the answer.

Description, extension, and application questions make up about 80% of the reading comprehension questions, main idea questions about 10%, and tone and writing technique questions about 5% each.

Points to Remember

1. The order of the passage questions roughly corresponds to the order in which the issues are presented in the passage.

2. The six questions are
    Main Idea
    Description
    Writing Technique
    Extension
    Application
    Tone

3. The main idea of a passage is usually stated in the last, sometimes the first, sentence of the first paragraph. If it's not there, it will probably be the last sentence of the entire passage.

4. If after the first reading, you don't have a feel for the main idea, review the first and last sentence of each paragraph.

5. The answer to a description question must refer directly to a statement in the passage, not to something implied by it. However, the correct answer will paraphrase a passage statement, not quote it exactly. In fact, exact quotes are used with these questions to bait wrong answers.

6. When answering a description question, you must find the point in the passage from which the question is drawn.

7. If a description question refers to line 20, the information needed to answer it can occur anywhere from line 15 to 25.

8. Some writing techniques commonly used in the SAT passages are
    A. Compare and contrast two positions.
    B. Show cause and effect.
    C. State a position; then give supporting evidence.

9. For extension questions, any answer-choice that refers explicitly to or repeats a statement in the passage will probably be wrong.

10. Application questions differ from extension questions only in degree. Extension questions ask you to apply what you have learned from the passage to derive new information about the same subject, whereas application questions go one step further, asking you to apply what you have learned from the passage to a different or hypothetical situation.

11. To answer an application question, take the perspective of the author. Ask yourself: what am I arguing for? what might make my argument stronger? what might make it weaker?

12. Because application questions go well beyond the passage, they tend to be the most difficult.

13. For tone questions, decide whether the writer's tone is positive, negative, or neutral before you look at the answer-choices.

14. If you do not have a feel for the writer's attitude after the first reading, check the adjectives that she chooses.

15. Beware of answer-choices that contain extreme emotions. If an author's tone is negative, it may be disapproving—not snide. Or if her tone is positive, it may be approving—not ecstatic.

16. The answers must be indisputable. A correct answer will never be controversial or grammatically questionable.

17. Description, extension, and application questions make up about 80% of the reading comprehension questions, main idea questions about 10%, and tone and writing technique questions about 5% each.

Mentor Exercise

From Romania to Germany, from Tallinn to Belgrade, a major historical process—the death of communism—is taking place. The German Democratic Republic no longer exists as a separate
5   state. And the former German Democratic Republic will serve as the first measure of the price a post-Communist society has to pay for entering the normal European orbit. In Yugoslavia we will see whether the federation can survive without communism.

10   One thing seems common to all these countries: dictatorship has been defeated and freedom has won, yet the victory of freedom has not yet meant the triumph of democracy. Democracy is something more than freedom. Democracy is freedom institu-
15   tionalized, freedom submitted to the limits of the law, freedom functioning as an object of compromise between the major political forces on the scene.

We have freedom, but we still have not achieved the democratic order. That is why this freedom is so
20   fragile. In the years of democratic opposition to communism, we supposed that the easiest thing would be to introduce changes in the economy. In fact, we thought that the march from a planned economy to a market economy would take place within
25   the framework of the bureaucratic system, and that the market within the Communist state would explode the totalitarian structures. Only then would the time come to build the institutions of a civil society; and only at the end, with the completion of the
30   market economy and the civil society, would the time of great political transformations finally arrive.

The opposite happened. First came the big political change, the great shock, which either broke the monopoly and the principle of Communist Party rule
35   or simply pushed the Communists out of power. Then came the creation of civil society, whose institutions were created in great pain, and which had trouble negotiating the empty space of freedom. Only then, as the third moment of change, the final
40   task was undertaken: that of transforming the totalitarian economy into a normal economy where different forms of ownership and different economic actors will live one next to the other.

Today we are in a typical moment of transition.
45   No one can say where we are headed. The people of the democratic opposition have the feeling that we won. We taste the sweetness of our victory the same way the Communists, only yesterday our prison guards, taste the bitterness of their defeat. Yet, even
50   as we are conscious of our victory, we feel that we are, in a strange way, losing. In Bulgaria the Communists have won the parliamentary elections and will govern the country, without losing their social legitimacy. In Romania the National Salvation
55   Front, largely dominated by people from the old Communist bureaucracy, has won. In other countries democratic institutions seem shaky, and the political horizon is cloudy. The masquerade goes on: dozens of groups and parties are created, each announces
60   similar slogans, each accuses its adversaries of all possible sins, and each declares itself representative of the national interest. Personal disputes are more important than disputes over values. Arguments over values are fiercer than arguments over ideas.

1. The author originally thought that the order of events in the transformation of communist society would be represented by which one of the following?

(A)   A great political shock would break the totalitarian monopoly, leaving in its wake a civil society whose task would be to change the state-controlled market into a free economy.

(B)   The transformation of the economy would destroy totalitarianism, after which a new and different social and political structure would be born.

(C)   First the people would freely elect political representatives who would transform the economy, which would then undermine the totalitarian structure.

(D)   The change to a democratic state would necessarily undermine totalitarianism, after which a new economic order would be created.

(E)   The people's frustration would build until it spontaneously generated violent revolution, which would sentence society to years of anarchy and regression.

2.   Beginning in the second paragraph, the author describes the complicated relationship between "freedom" and "democracy." In the author's view, which one of the following statements best reflects that relationship?

(A)   A country can have freedom without having democracy.

(B)   If a country has freedom, it necessarily has democracy.

(C)   A country can have democracy without having freedom.

(D)   A country can never have democracy if it has freedom.

(E)   If a country has democracy, it cannot have freedom.

3.   From the passage, a reader could conclude that which one of the following best describes the author's attitude toward the events that have taken place in communist society?

(A)   Relieved that at last the democratic order has surfaced.

(B)   Clearly wants to return to the old order.

(C)   Disappointed with the nature of the democracy that has emerged.

(D)   Confident that a free economy will ultimately provide the basis for a true democracy.

(E)   Surprised that communism was toppled through political rather than economic means.

1. This is a description question, so you should locate the point in the passage from which it was drawn. It is the third paragraph. In lines 22–28, the author recalls his expectation that, by introducing the market system, the communist system would topple from within.

Be careful not to choose (A). It chronicles how the events actually occurred, not how they were *anticipated* to occur. (A) is baited with the words "great shock," "monopoly," and "civil society."

The answer is (B).

2. This is an extension question, so the answer must say more than what is said in the passage, without requiring a quantum leap in thought. The needed reference is *"Democracy is something more than freedom"* (lines 13–15). Since freedom can exist without democracy, freedom alone does not insure democracy.

The answer is (A).

3. This is a tone question. The key to answering this question is found in the closing comments. There the author states *"The masquerade goes on,"* referring to nascent democracies. So he has reservations about the newly emerging democracies.

Watch out for (E). Although it is supported by the passage, it is in a supporting paragraph. The ideas in a concluding paragraph take precedence over those in a supporting paragraph.

The answer is (C).

4. A cynic who has observed political systems in various countries would likely interpret the author's description of the situation at the end of the passage as

    (A) evidence that society is still in the throws of the old totalitarian structure.
    (B) a distorted description of the new political system.
    (C) a necessary political reality that is a pre-lude to "democracy."
    (D) a fair description of many democratic political systems.
    (E) evidence of the baseness of people.

4. This is an application question. These are like extension questions, but they go well beyond what is stated in the passage. In this case we are asked to interpret the author's comments from a cynic's perspective. Because application questions go well beyond the passage, they are often difficult, as is this one.

Hint: A cynic looks at reality from a negative perspective, usually with a sense of dark irony and hopelessness.

Don't make the mistake of choosing (E). Although a cynic is likely to make such a statement, it does not address the subject of the passage—political and economic systems. The passage is not about human nature, at least not directly.

The answer is (D).

5. Which one of the following does the author imply may have contributed to the difficulties involved in creating a new democratic order in eastern Europe?

    I.   The people who existed under the totalitarian structure have not had the experience of "negotiating the empty space of freedom."
    II. Mistaking the order in which political, economic, and social restructuring would occur.
    III. Excessive self-interest among the new political activists.

    (A) I only
    (B) II only
    (C) I and III only
    (D) II and III only
    (E) I, II, and III

5. This is an extension question. Statement I is true. In lines 36–38, the author implies that the institutions of the new-born, free society were created in great pain because the people lacked experience. Statement II is true. Expectations that the market mechanisms would explode totalitarianism and usher in a new society were dashed, and having to readjust one's expectations certainly makes a situation more difficult. Finally, statement III is true. It summarizes the thrust of the passage's closing lines.

The answer is (E).

6. By stating "even as we are conscious of our victory, we feel that we are, in a strange way, losing" (lines 49–51) the author means that

    (A) some of the old governments are still unwilling to grant freedom at the individual level.
    (B) some of the new governments are not strong enough to exist as a single federation.
    (C) some of the new democratic governments are electing to retain the old political parties.
    (D) no new parties have been created to fill the vacuum created by the victory of freedom.
    (E) some of the new governments are reverting to communism.

6. This is a hybrid extension and description question. Because it refers to a specific point in the passage, you must read a few sentences before and after it. The answer can be found in lines 51–64.

The answer is (C).

Exercise

Directions: This passage is followed by a group of questions to be answered based on what is <u>stated</u> or <u>implied</u> in the passage. Choose the <u>best</u> answer; the one that most accurately and completely answers the question.

In the United States the per capita costs of schooling have risen almost as fast as the cost of medical treatment. But increased treatment by both doctors and teachers has shown steadily declining
5   results. Medical expenses concentrated on those above forty-five have doubled several times over a period of forty years with a resulting 3 percent increase in the life expectancy of men. The increase in educational expenditures has produced
10   even stranger results; otherwise President Nixon could not have been moved this spring to promise that every child shall soon have the "Right to Read" before leaving school.

In the United States it would take eighty
15   billion dollars per year to provide what educators regard as equal treatment for all in grammar and high school. This is well over twice the $36 billion now being spent. Independent cost projections prepared at HEW and at the University of Florida
20   indicate that by 1974 the comparable figures will be $107 billion as against the $45 billion now projected, and these figures wholly omit the enormous costs of what is called "higher education," for which demand is growing even faster. The United
25   States, which spent nearly eighty billion dollars in 1969 for "defense," including its deployment in Vietnam, is obviously too poor to provide equal schooling. The President's committee for the study of school finance should ask not how to support or
30   how to trim such increasing costs, but how they can be avoided.

Equal obligatory schooling must be recognized as at least economically unfeasible. In Latin America the amount of public money spent on each
35   graduate student is between 350 and 1,500 times the amount spent on the median citizen (that is, the citizen who holds the middle ground between the poorest and the richest). In the United States the discrepancy is smaller, but the discrimination is
40   keener. The richest parents, some 10 percent, can afford private education for their children and help them to benefit from foundation grants. But in addition they obtain ten times the per capita amount of public funds if this is compared with the
45   per capita expenditure made on the children of the 10 percent who are poorest. The principal reasons for this are that rich children stay longer in school, that a year in a university is disproportionately more expensive than a year in high school, and that
50   most private universities depend—at least indirectly—on tax-derived finances.

Obligatory schooling inevitably polarizes a society; it also grades the nations of the world according to an international caste system.
55   Countries are rated like castes whose educational dignity is determined by the average years of schooling of its citizens, a rating which is closely related to per capita gross national product, and much more painful.

1.   Which one of the following best expresses the main idea of the passage?

(A)   The educational shortcomings of the United States, in contrast to those of Latin America, are merely the result of poor allocation of available resources.

(B)   Both education and medical care are severely underfunded.

(C)   Defense spending is sapping funds which would be better spent in education.

(D)   Obligatory schooling must be scrapped if the goal of educational equality is to be realized.

(E)   Obligatory education does not and cannot provide equal education.

2.   The author most likely would agree with which one of the following solutions to the problems presented by obligatory education?

(A)   Education should not be obligatory at all.

(B)   Education should not be obligatory for those who cannot afford it.

(C)   More money should be diverted to education for the poorest.

(D)   Countries should cooperate to establish common minimal educational standards.

(E)   Future spending should be capped.

3. According to the passage, education is like health care in all of the following ways EXCEPT:

   (A) It has reached a point of diminishing returns, increased spending no longer results in significant improvement.
   (B) It has an inappropriate "more is better" philosophy.
   (C) It is unfairly distributed between rich and poor.
   (D) The amount of money being spent on older students is increasing.
   (E) Its cost has increased nearly as fast.

4. Why does the author consider the results from increased educational expenditures to be "even stranger" than those from increased medical expenditures?

   (A) The aging of the population should have had an impact only on medical care, not on education.
   (B) The "Right to Read" should be a bare minimum, not a Presidential ideal.
   (C) Educational spending has shown even poorer results than spending on health care, despite greater increases.
   (D) Education has become even more discriminatory than health care.
   (E) It inevitably polarizes society.

5. Which one of the following most accurately characterizes the author's attitude with respect to obligatory schooling?

   (A) qualified admiration
   (B) critical
   (C) neutral
   (D) ambivalent
   (E) resentful

6. By stating "In Latin America the amount of public money spent on each graduate student is between 350 and 1,500 times the amount spent on the median citizen" and "In the United States the discrepancy is smaller" the author implies that

   (A) equal education is possible in the United States but not in Latin America.
   (B) equal education for all at the graduate level is an unrealistic ideal.
   (C) educational spending is more efficient in the United States.
   (D) higher education is more expensive than lower education both in Latin America and in the United States, but more so in Latin America.
   (E) underfunding of lower education is a world-wide problem.

Answers and Solutions to Exercise

1.   The answer to a main idea question will summarize the passage, without going beyond it.

(A) fails to meet these criteria because it makes a false claim. Lines 33–38 imply that the discrepancy in allocation of funds is greater in Latin America. Besides, Latin America is mentioned only in passing, so this is not the main idea.

(B) also makes a false claim. The author implies that increased funding for education is irrelevant, if not counterproductive. In fact, the sentence *"The President's committee for the study of school finance should ask not how to support or how to trim such increasing costs, but how they can be avoided"* implies that he thinks an increase in funding would be counterproductive.

(C) is implied by the sentence *"The United States . . . is obviously too poor to provide equal schooling,"* but the author does not fully develop this idea. Besides, he implies that the problem is not financial.

(D) is the second-best answer-choice. The answer to a main idea question should sum up the passage, not make a conjecture about it. Clearly the author has serious reservations about obligatory schooling, but at no point does he state or imply that it should be scrapped. He may believe that it can be modified, or he may be resigned to the fact that, for other reasons, it is necessary. We don't know.

Finally, (E) aptly summarizes the passage, without going beyond it. The key to seeing this is the opening to paragraph three, *"Equal obligatory schooling must be recognized as at least economically unfeasible."* In other words, regardless of any other failings, it cannot succeed economically and therefore cannot provide equal education.

2.   This is an application question. These questions tend to be rather difficult, though this one is not. To answer an application question, put yourself in the author's place. If you were arguing his case, which of the solutions would you advocate?

As to (A), although we rejected the recommendation that obligatory education be eliminated as Question 1's answer, it is the answer to Question 2. The author does not merely imply that obligatory education has some shortcomings; he suggests that it is fundamentally flawed. Again this is made clear by the opening to paragraph three, *"Equal obligatory schooling must be recognized as at least economically unfeasible."* Still, there is a possible misunderstanding here: perhaps the author believes that obligatory education is a noble but unrealistic

idea. This possibility, however, is dispelled by the closing paragraph in which he states that obligatory education polarizes society and sets up a caste system. Obviously, such a system, if this is true, should be discarded. The answer is (A).

The other choices can be easily dismissed. (B) is incorrect because nothing in the passage suggests that the author would advocate a solution that would polarize society even more. Indeed, at the end of paragraph three, he suggests that the rich already get more than their fair share.

(C) is incorrect because it contradicts the author. Paragraph two is dedicated to showing that the United States is too poor to provide equal schooling. You can't divert money you don't have.

(D) is incorrect. It reads too much into the last paragraph.

Finally, (E) is the second-best answer-choice. Although the author probably believes that future spending should be restrained or capped, this understates the thrust of his argument. However, he might offer this as a compromise to his opponents.

3.   This is a description question, so we must find the place from which it is drawn. It is the first paragraph. The sentence *"But increased treatment by both doctors and teachers has shown steadily declining results"* shows that both have reached a point of diminishing returns. This eliminates (A) and (B). Next, the passage states *"Medical expenses concentrated on those above forty-five have doubled several times"* (lines 5–6) and that the demand and costs of higher education are growing faster than the demand and costs of elementary and high school education. This eliminates (D). Next, the opening to the passage states that the costs of education *"have risen almost as fast as the cost of medical treatment."* This eliminates (E). Hence, by process of elimination, the answer is (C). We should, however, verify this. In paragraph three, the author does state that there is a "keen" discrepancy in the funding of education between rich and poor, but a survey of the passage shows that at no point does he mention that this is also the case with health care.

4.   This is an extension question. We are asked to interpret a statement by the author. The needed reference is the closing sentence to paragraph one. Remember: extension questions require you to go beyond the passage, so the answer won't be explicitly stated in the reference—we will have to interpret it.

The implication of President Nixon's promise is that despite increased educational funding many children cannot even read when they graduate from school. Hence the answer is (B).

Don't make the mistake of choosing (C). Although at first glance this is a tempting inference, it would be difficult to compare the results of education and medical care directly (how would we do so?). Regardless, the opening line to the passage states that educational costs have risen "almost as fast" as medical costs, not faster.

(A) is incorrect because the passage never mentions the aging of the population. The same is true for (D).

Many students who cannot solve this question choose (E)—don't. It uses as bait language from the passage, *"inevitably polarizes a society."* Note: The phrase "Right to Read" in (B) is not a same language trap; it is merely part of a paraphrase of the passage. The correct answer to an extension question will often both paraphrase and extend a passage statement but will not quote it directly, as in (E).

5.   Like most tone questions this one is rather easy. Although choice (A) is a measured response, the author clearly does not admire the obligatory school system. This eliminates (A); it also eliminates (C) and (D). Of the two remaining choices, (B) is the measured response, and it is the answer. Although the author strongly opposes obligatory schooling, "resentful" is too strong and too personal. A scholar would never directly express resentment or envy, even if that is his true feeling.

6.   This is another extension question. By stating that the amount of funding spent on graduate students is more than 350 times the amount spent on the average citizen, the author implies that it would be impossible to equalize the funding. Hence the answer is (B).

None of the other choices have any real merit. (A) is incorrect because the import of the passage is that the rich get better schooling and more public funds in the United States and therefore discrimination is "keener" here (lines 39–40).

(C) and (D) are incorrect because they are neither mentioned nor implied by the passage.

(E) is the second-best choice. Although this is implied by the numbers given, it has little to do with the primary purpose of the passage—to show that obligatory education is perhaps not such a good idea.

Pivotal Words

As mentioned before, each passage contains 150 to 850 words and only two to thirteen questions, so you will <u>not</u> be tested on most of the material in the passage. Your best reading strategy, therefore, is to identify the places from which questions will most likely be drawn and concentrate your attention there.

Pivotal words can help in this regard. Following are the most common pivotal words.

PIVOTAL WORDS

But	**Although**
However	**Yet**
Despite	**Nevertheless**
Nonetheless	**Except**
In contrast	**Even though**

As you may have noticed, these words indicate contrast. Pivotal words warn that the author is about to either make a U-turn or introduce a counter-premise (concession to a minor point that weakens the argument).

Example: (Counter-premise)

I submit that the strikers should accept the management's offer. Admittedly, it is less than what was demanded. But it does resolve the main grievance—inadequate health care. Furthermore, an independent study shows that a wage increase greater than 5% would leave the company unable to compete against Japan and Germany, forcing it into bankruptcy.

The conclusion, "the strikers should accept the management's offer," is stated in the first sentence. Then "Admittedly" introduces a concession (counter-premise); namely, that the offer was less than what was demanded. This weakens the speaker's case, but it addresses a potential criticism of his position before it can be made. The last two sentences of the argument present more compelling reasons to accept the offer and form the gist of the argument.

Pivotal words mark natural places for questions to be drawn. At a pivotal word, the author changes direction. The SAT writers form questions at these junctures to test whether you turned with the author or you continued to go straight. Rarely do the SAT writers let a pivotal word pass without drawing a question from its sentence.

As you read a passage, circle the pivotal words and refer to them when answering the questions.

Let's apply this theory to the passage on criminal justice. For easy reference, the passage is reprinted here in the left-hand column, with explanations in the right-hand column. The pivotal words are marked in bold.

There are two major systems of criminal procedure in the modern world—the adversarial and the inquisitorial. The former is associated with common law tradition and the latter with civil law tradition. Both systems were historically preceded by the system of private vengeance in which the victim of a crime fashioned his own remedy and administered it privately, either personally or through an agent. The vengeance system was a system of self-help, the essence of which was captured in the slogan "an eye for an eye, a tooth for a tooth." The modern adversarial system is only one historical step removed from the private vengeance system and still retains some of its characteristic features. Thus, for example, **even though** the right to institute criminal action has now been extended to all members of society and **even though** the police department has taken over the pretrial investigative functions on behalf of the prosecution, the adversarial system still leaves the defendant to conduct his own pretrial investigation. The trial is still viewed as a duel between two adversaries, refereed by a judge who, at the beginning of the trial has no knowledge of the investigative background of the case. In the final analysis the adversarial system of criminal procedure symbolizes and regularizes the punitive combat.

By contrast, the inquisitorial system begins historically where the adversarial system stopped its development. It is two historical steps removed from the system of private vengeance. Therefore, from the standpoint of legal anthropology, it is historically superior to the adversarial system. Under the inquisitorial system the public investigator has the duty to investigate not just on behalf of the prosecutor **but also** on behalf of the defendant. Additionally, the public prosecutor has the duty to present to the court not only evidence that may lead to the conviction of the defendant **but also** evidence that may lead to his exoneration. This system mandates that both parties permit full pretrial discovery of the evidence in their possession. Finally, in an effort to make the trial less like a duel between two adversaries, the inquisitorial system mandates that the judge take an active part in the conduct of the trial, with a role that is both directive and protective.

Fact-finding is at the heart of the inquisitorial system. This system operates on the philosophical premise that in a criminal case the crucial factor is not the legal rule but the facts of the case and that the goal of the entire procedure is to experimentally recreate for the court the commission of the alleged crime.

Even though—Here "even though" is introducing a concession. In the previous sentence, the author stated that the adversarial system is only one step removed from the private vengeance system. The author uses the two concessions as a hedge against potential criticism that he did not consider that the adversarial system has extended the right to institute criminal action to all members of society and that police departments now perform the pretrial investigation. But the author then states that the adversarial system still leaves the defendant to conduct his own pretrial investigation. This marks a good place from which to draw a question. Many people will misinterpret the two concessions as evidence that the adversarial system is two steps removed from the private vengeance system.

By contrast—In this case the pivotal word is not introducing a concession. Instead it indicates a change in thought: now the author is going to discuss the other criminal justice system. This is a natural place to test whether the student has made the transition and whether he will attribute the properties soon to be introduced to the inquisitorial system, not the adversarial system.

But also—In both places, "but also" indicates neither concession nor change in thought. Instead it is part of the coordinating conjunction "not only . . . but also . . . ." Rather than indicating contrast, it emphasizes the second element of the pair.

Let's see how these pivotal words can help answer the questions in the last section. The first is from the Description Section:

Example:

According to the passage, the inquisitorial system differs from the adversarial system in that

(A)   it does not make the defendant solely responsible for gathering evidence for his case
(B)   it does not require the police department to work on behalf of the prosecution
(C)   it does not allow the victim the satisfaction of private vengeance
(D)   it requires the prosecution to drop a weak case
(E)   a defendant who is innocent would prefer to be tried under the inquisitorial system

The pivotal phrase "by contrast" flags the second paragraph as the place to begin looking. The pivotal phrase "but also" introduces the answer—namely that the prosecutor must also investigate "on behalf of the defendant." The answer is (A).

The next question is from the Writing Techniques Section:

Example:

Which one of the following best describes the organization of the passage?

(A)   Two systems of criminal justice are compared and contrasted, and one is deemed to be better than the other.
(B)   One system of criminal justice is presented as better than another. Then evidence is presented to support that claim.
(C)   Two systems of criminal justice are analyzed, and one specific example is examined in detail.
(D)   A set of examples is presented. Then a conclusion is drawn from them.
(E)   The inner workings of the criminal justice system are illustrated by using two systems.

The pivotal phrase "by contrast" gives this question away. The author is comparing and contrasting two criminal justice systems, which the opening pivotal word introduces. Hence the answer is (A).

For our final example, consider the question from the Extension Section:

Example:

The author views the prosecution's role in the inquisitorial system as being

(A)   an advocate for both society and the defendant
(B)   solely responsible for starting a trial
(C)   a protector of the legal rule
(D)   an investigator only
(E)   an aggressive but fair investigator

The information needed to answer this question is introduced by the pivotal phrase, "but also." There it is stated that the prosecutor must present evidence that may exonerate the defendant; that is, he must act fairly. The answer is (E).

Points to Remember

1.   Pivotal words indicate that the author is about to make a U-turn in thought or introduce a counter-premise (concession to a minor point that weakens the argument).

2.   The following are the most common pivotal words:

But	**Although**	**Except**
However	**Yet**	**Even though**
Despite	**Nevertheless**	**In contrast**
Nonetheless		

3.   Pivotal words mark natural places for questions to be drawn. At a pivotal word, the author changes direction. The SAT writers form questions at these junctures to test whether you made the turn with the author or whether you continued to go straight. Rarely do the SAT writers pass a pivotal word without drawing a question from its sentence.

4.   As you read each passage, circle the pivotal words.

Mentor Exercise

<u>Directions:</u> This passage is followed by a group of questions to be answered based on what is <u>stated</u> or <u>implied</u> in the passage. Choose the <u>best</u> answer; the one that most accurately and completely answers the question. Hints, insights, and answers are given in the right-hand column.

The premise with which the multiculturalists begin is unexceptional: that it is important to recognize and to celebrate the wide range of cultures that exist in the United States. In what sounds like a reflection of traditional American pluralism, the multiculturalists argue that we must recognize difference, that difference is legitimate; in its kindlier versions, multiculturalism represents the discovery on the part of minority groups that they can play a part in molding the larger culture even as they are molded by it. And on the campus multiculturalism, defined more locally as the need to recognize cultural variations among students, has tried with some success to talk about how a racially and ethnically diverse student body can enrich everyone's education.

Phillip Green, a political scientist at Smith and a thoughtful proponent of multiculturalism, notes that for a significant portion of the students the politics of identity is all-consuming. Students he says "are unhappy with the thin gruel of rationalism. They require a therapeutic curriculum to overcome not straightforward racism but ignorant stereotyping."

(1) But multiculturalism's hard-liners, who seem to make up the majority of the movement, damn as racism any attempt to draw the myriad of American groups into a common American culture. For these multiculturalists, differences are absolute, irreducible, intractable—occasions not for understanding but for separation. The multiculturalist, it turns out, is not especially interested in the great American hyphen, in the syncretistic (and therefore naturally tolerant) identities that allow Americans to belong to more than a single culture, to be both particularists and universalists.

The time-honored American mixture of assimilation and traditional allegiance is denounced as a danger to racial and gender authenticity. This is an extraordinary reversal of the traditional liberal commitment to a "truth" that transcends parochialisms. In the new race/class/gender formation, universality is replaced by, among other things, feminist science Nubian numerals (as part of an Afro-centric science), and what Marilyn Frankenstein of the University of Massachusetts-Boston describes as "ethno-mathematics," in which the cultural basis of counting comes to the fore.

There are two critical pivotal words in this passage—(1) **But**, and (2) **however**.

(1) **But**. Until this point, the author did not reveal his feeling toward multiculturalism. He presented an objective, if not positive, view of the movement. However, "**But**" introduced an abrupt change in direction (a U-turn). Before he talked about the "kindlier" multiculturalism—to which he appears to be sympathetic. Now he talks about "hard-line" multiculturalism, which he implies is intolerant and divisive.

The pivotal word "**but**" doesn't just change the direction of the passage, it introduces the main idea: that multiculturalism has become an extreme and self-contradictory movement.

The multiculturalists insist on seeing all perspectives as tainted by the perceiver's particular point of view. Impartial knowledge, they argue, is not possible, because ideas are simply the expression of individual identity, or of the unspoken but inescapable assumptions that are inscribed in a culture or a language. The problem, **(2) however,** with this warmed-over Nietzscheanism is that it threatens to leave no ground for anybody to stand on. So the multiculturalists make a leap, necessary for their own intellectual survival, and proceed to argue that there are some categories, such as race and gender, that do in fact embody an unmistakable knowledge of oppression. Victims are at least epistemologically lucky. Objectivity is a mask for oppression. And so an appalled former 1960s radical complained to me that self-proclaimed witches were teaching classes on witchcraft. "They're not teaching students how to think," she said, "they're telling them what to believe."

(2) however. This is the second critical pivotal word. The author opened this paragraph by presenting the multiculturalist's view; now he will criticize their positions.

1. Which one of the following ideas would a multiculturalist NOT believe?

   (A)   That we should recognize and celebrate the differences among the many cultures in the United States.
   (B)   That we can never know the "truth" because "truth" is always shaped by one's culture.
   (C)   That "difference" is more important than "sameness."
   (D)   That a school curriculum should be constructed to compensate for institutionalized racism.
   (E)   That different cultures should work to assimilate themselves into the mainstream culture so that eventually there will be no excuse for racism.

1. The sentence introduced by the pivotal word **"But"** gives away the answer to this question.

The answer is (E).

2. According to a hard-line multiculturalist, which one of the following groups is most likely to know the "truth" about political reality?

   (A)   Educated people who have learned how to see reality from many different perspectives.
   (B)   A minority group that has suffered oppression at the hands of the majority.
   (C)   High government officials who have privileged access to secret information.
   (D)   Minorities who through their education have risen above the socioeconomic position occupied by most members of their ethnic group.
   (E)   Political scientists who have thoroughly studied the problem.

2. This is a rather hard extension question.

   Hint: A subjugated minority group has at least the "unmistakable knowledge of oppression" (last paragraph).

   Don't make the mistake of choosing (D). Upper class minorities have simply exchanged one tainted point of view for another—and probably a more tainted one since the adopted position does not allow for knowledge of "oppression."

The answer is (B).

3. The author states that in a "kindlier version" of multiculturalism, minorities discover "that they can play a part in molding the larger culture even as they are molded by it." If no new ethnic groups were incorporated into the American culture for many centuries to come, which one of the following would be the most probable outcome of this "kindlier version"?

(A) At some point in the future, there would be only one culture with no observable ethnic differences.

(B) Eventually the dominant culture would overwhelm the minority cultures, who would then lose their ethnic identities.

(C) The multiplicity of ethnic groups would remain but the characteristics of the different ethnic groups would change.

(D) The smaller ethnic groups would remain, and they would retain their ethnic heritage.

(E) The minority cultures would eventually overwhelm the dominant culture, which would then lose its identity.

4. The author speaks about the "politics of identity" that Phillip Green, a political scientist at Smith, notes is all-consuming for many of the students. Considering the subject of the passage, which one of the following best describes what the author means by "the politics of identity"?

(A) The attempt to discover individual identities through political action

(B) The political agenda that aspires to create a new pride of identity for Americans

(C) The current obsession for therapy groups that help individuals discover their inner selves

(D) The trend among minority students to discover their identities in their ethnic groups rather than in their individuality

(E) The increased political activism of minorities on college campuses

3. This application question clearly goes well beyond the passage.

If no new ethnic groups were incorporated into the American culture, then the interplay between the larger and smaller groups would continue, with both groups changing, until there would be only one common (and different from any original) group.

The answer is (A).

4. This is an extension question. You may find the classification of the these problems as "application" or "extension" to be somewhat arbitrary or even disagree with a particular classification. As mentioned before, application and extension questions differ only in degree. Question 3 is clearly an application question; by asking you to make a conjecture about the future, it goes well beyond the passage. How to classify Question 4, however, is not so clear. I classified it as an extension question because it seems to be asking merely for the author's true meaning of the phrase "the politics of identity." That is, it stays within the context of the passage.

Don't be led astray by (B); it uses the word "political" to tempt you. Although it is perhaps a good description, it is not within the context of the passage, which focuses on ethnic politics, not national identities through "roots."

The answer is (D).

5. Which one of the following best describes the attitude of the writer toward the multicultural movement?

    (A) Tolerant. It may have some faults, but it is well-meaning overall.
    (B) Critical. A formerly admirable movement has been taken over by radical intellectuals.
    (C) Disinterested. He seems to be presenting an objective report.
    (D) Enthusiastic. The author embraces the multiculturalist movement and is trying to present it in a favorable light.
    (E) Ambivalent. Like a moth to a flame he is simultaneously attracted and repulsed by the movement.

5. Like most tone questions this one is rather easy.

    To get a feel for the author's attitude, check the adjectives he chooses. The author starts by introducing the "kindlier" version of multiculturalism and describes a proponent of multiculturalism, Phillip Green, as "thoughtful." Then he introduces the "hard liners" who "damn" any attempt at cultural assimilation. He feels that the movement has changed; that it has gone bad.

    The answer is (B).

6. "Multiculturalist relativism" is the notion that there is no such thing as impartial or objective knowledge. The author seems to be grounding his criticism of this notion on

    (A) the clear evidence that science has indeed discovered "truths" that have been independent of both language and culture.
    (B) the conclusion that relativism leaves one with no clear notions of any one thing that is true.
    (C) the absurdity of claiming that knowledge of oppression is more valid than knowledge of scientific facts.
    (D) the agreement among peoples of all cultures as to certain undeniable truths— e.g., when the sky is clear, day is warmer than night.
    (E) the fact that "truth" is not finitely definable and therefore that any discussion of impartial or objective truth is moot.

6. This is an another extension question.

    Hint: The answer can be derived from the pivotal sentence containing "however" (2).

    The answer is (B).

Exercise

Directions: This passage is followed by a group of questions to be answered based on what is stated or implied in the passage. Choose the best answer; the one that most accurately and completely answers the question.

According to usage and conventions which are at last being questioned but have by no means been overcome, the social presence of a woman is different in kind from that of a man. A man's
5 presence is dependent upon the promise of power which he embodies. If the promise is large and credible his presence is striking. If it is small or incredible, he is found to have little presence. The promised power may be moral, physical,
10 temperamental, economic, social, sexual—but its object is always exterior to the man. A man's presence suggests what he is capable of doing to you or for you. His presence may be fabricated, in the sense that he pretends to be capable of what he
15 is not. But the pretense is always toward a power which he exercises on others.

By contrast, a woman's presence expresses her own attitude to herself, and defines what can and cannot be done to her. Her presence is
20 manifest in her gestures, voices, opinions, expressions, clothes, chosen surroundings, taste— indeed there is nothing she can do which does not contribute to her presence. Presence for a woman is so intrinsic to her person that men tend to think
25 of it as an almost physical emanation, a kind of heat or smell or aura.

To be born a woman has been to be born, within an allotted and confined space, into the keeping of men. The social presence of women
30 has developed as a result of their ingenuity in living under such tutelage within such a limited space. But this has been at the cost of a woman's self being split into two. A woman must continu- ally watch herself. Whilst she is walking across a
35 room or whilst she is weeping at the death of her father, she can scarcely avoid envisaging herself walking or weeping. From earliest childhood she has been taught and persuaded to survey herself continually.

40 And so she comes to consider the *surveyor* and the *surveyed* within her as the two constituent yet always distinct elements of her identity as a woman.

She has to survey everything she is and
45 everything she does because how she appears to others, and ultimately how she appears to men, is of crucial importance for what is normally thought of as the success of her life. Her own sense of being in herself is supplanted by a sense of being
50 appreciated as herself by another. Men survey women before treating them. Consequently how a woman appears to a man can determine how she will be treated. To acquire some control over this process, women must contain it and internalize it.
55 That part of a woman's self which is the surveyor treats the part which is the surveyed so as to demonstrate to others how her whole self would like to be treated. And this exemplary treatment of herself by herself constitutes her presence.
60 Every woman's presence regulates what is and is not "permissible" within her presence. Every one of her actions—whatever its direct purpose or motivation—is also read as an indication of how she would like to be treated. If a woman throws a
65 glass on the floor, this is an example of how she treats her own emotion of anger and so of how she would wish to be treated by others. If a man does the same, his action is only read as an expression of his anger. If a woman makes a good joke this
70 is an example of how she treats the joker in herself and accordingly of how she as joker-woman would like to be treated by others. Only a man can make a good joke for its own sake.

1. According to "usage and conventions," appearance is NECESSARILY a part of reality for

    (A) men
    (B) women
    (C) both men and women
    (D) neither men nor women
    (E) men always and women occasionally

2. In analyzing a woman's customary "social presence," the author hopes to

    (A) justify and reinforce it.
    (B) understand and explain it.
    (C) expose and discredit it.
    (D) demonstrate and criticize it.
    (E) sanction and promote it.

3. It can be inferred from the passage that a woman with a Ph.D. in psychology who gives a lecture to a group of students is probably MOST concerned with

    (A) whether her students learn the material.
    (B) what the males in the audience think of her.
    (C) how she comes off as a speaker in psychology.
    (D) finding a husband.
    (E) whether a man challenges her.

4. The passage portrays women as

    (A) victims
    (B) liars
    (C) actresses
    (D) politicians
    (E) ignorant

5. Which one of the following is NOT implied by the passage?

    (A) Women have split personalities.
    (B) Men are not image-conscious.
    (C) Good looks are more important to women than to men.
    (D) A man is defined by what he does, whereas a woman is defined by how she appears.
    (E) A man's presence is extrinsic, whereas a woman's is intrinsic.

6. The primary purpose of the passage is to

    (A) compare and contrast woman's presence and place in society with that of man's.
    (B) discuss a woman's presence and place in society and to contrast it with a man's presence and place.
    (C) illustrate how a woman is oppressed by society.
    (D) explain why men are better than women at telling jokes.
    (E) illustrate how both men and women are hurt by sexism.

Answers and Solutions to Exercise

This passage is filled with pivotal words, some of which are crucial to following the author's train of thought. We will discuss only the critical pivotal words. The first pivotal word, "but" (line 16), introduces a distinction between a man's presence and a woman's: a man's is external, a woman's internal. The second pivotal word, "by contrast," introduces the main idea of the passage. The author opened the passage by defining a man's presence; now she will define a woman's presence. The last pivotal word, "but" (lines 32–33), also introduces a change in thought. Now the author discusses how a woman's presence has split her identity into two parts—the *surveyor* and the *surveyed*. By closing with, *"Only a man can make a good joke for its own sake,"* the author is saying a man can concentrate on the punch line, whereas a woman must concentrate on its delivery.

1. This is a description question. The needed reference is contained in lines 22–25: *"there is nothing [a woman] can do which does not contribute to her presence. Presence for a woman is intrinsic to her person . . ."* If something is intrinsic to you, then it necessarily is part of your reality. Hence the answer is (B).

Note the question refers to "usage and conventions" discussed in the passage, not to any other way of viewing the world—such as your own!

2. Although the author opens the passage with a hint that she doesn't like the customary sex roles (*"conventions which are at last being questioned"*), the rest of the passage is explanatory and analytical. So (C) and (D) are too strong. The answer is (B).

3. This is an application question; we are asked to apply what we have learned from the passage to a hypothetical situation.

The best way to analyze this question is to compare the speaker to a joke-teller. The passage paints a portrait of a woman as most concerned with the image she presents to the world. She is not concerned with the speech or joke, *per se*, rather with how she delivers it. *"Only a man can make a good joke for its own sake."* The answer is (C).

Don't make the mistake of choosing (B). Although men have, in the main, molded her self-image, she has gone beyond that; she now measures herself in the abstract: "how will I come off to the ultimately critical audience?" and not "how will actual audience members see me?"

4. This description question is a bit tricky because the second-best choice is rather good. Women are concerned with the image they present, so they cannot be themselves—they must act their part. Hence the answer is (C).

You may have been tempted by (A). According to the passage, women are thrown into the role of an actress, "into the keeping of men." So, like victims, they are not responsible for their social position. However, nothing in the passage directly suggests that it is wrong for women to be in this position or that women attempt to refuse this role. According to the passage, therefore, women are not, strictly speaking, victims. (*Victim* means "someone not in control of something injurious happening to him or her.")

5. This is an extension question. The passage discusses the fact that a man may fabricate his image (lines 13–15). This suggests that men *are* conscious of their images, but the passage also states that image is not intrinsic to their personalities, as it is for women. The answer is (B).

6. This is a rather hard main idea question because the second-best choice, (A), is quite good.

The passage does open with a discussion of a man's presence. But in paragraph two the pivotal phrase "by contrast" introduces a woman's presence; from there the discussion of a man's presence is only in regard to how it affects a woman's. So a woman's presence is the main idea; contrasting it with a man's presence is secondary. (B) gives the proper emphasis to these two purposes.

The Three Step Method

Now we apply all the methods we have learned to another passage. First let's summarize the reading techniques we have developed and express them in a three-step attack strategy for reading SAT passages:

THE THREE STEP METHOD

1. **(Optional) Preview the first sentence of each paragraph.**

2. **Read the passage at a faster than usual pace (but not to the point that comprehension suffers). Stay alert to places from which any of the six questions might be drawn:**

    a.) **Main Idea**
    b.) **Description**
    c.) **Writing Technique**
    d.) **Extension**
    e.) **Application**
    f.) **Tone**

3. **Annotate the passage and circle any pivotal words. Then use them as reference points when answering the questions. Following are some common annotation marks (you may want to add to this list):**

    A = Author's Attitude
    C = Complex point
    ? = **Question?** I don't understand this part (you can bet that this area will be important to *at least* one question)
    SP = Significant point
    ! = **Exclamation!** Strong opinion
    W = Weak, questionable or unsupported argument or premise

Notice how the three-step process proceeds from the general to the specific. The **first step**, previewing the first sentences, gives you an overview of the passage. This will help you answer main idea questions. The **second step**, reading the passage at a slightly faster than usual pace, brings out the passage's structure (i.e., does the author compare and contrast, show cause and effect, etc.). Further, it will clue you into the author's attitude (positive, negative, objective, indifferent, etc.). Finally, the **third step**, circling pivotal words and annotating, will solidify your understanding of the passage and highlight specific details.

The three step method should be viewed as a dynamic, and not a static, process. The steps often overlap and they are not performed in strict order. Comprehending a passage is an ebb and flow process. Analyzing a passage to understand how it is constructed can be compared to dismantling an engine to understand how it was built—you may stop occasionally and reassemble parts of it to review what you just did; then proceed again to dismantle more. Likewise, when reading a passage, you may first read and annotate a paragraph (disassembling it) and then go back and skim to reassemble it. During this process, comprehension proceeds from the global to the specific. This can be represented by an inverted pyramid:

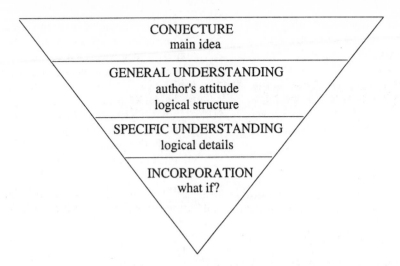

In the conjecture stage, we form a tentative main idea—one which we may have to modify or even reject as we read more deeply into the passage. In the general understanding stage, we develop a feel for the author's tone and discover the schema that she uses to present her ideas. In the specific understanding stage, we fill in the minor gaps in our understanding. Finally, in the incorporation stage, we integrate the ideas presented in the passage into our own thought process. We now understand the ideas sufficiently to defend them, apply them to other situations, or evaluate their validity in a hypothetical situation. Only with complete understanding of the passage can this be done.

Let's apply the three step method to the passage on the next page. Begin by previewing the first sentence of each paragraph:

The sentence *"That placebos can cure everything from dandruff to leprosy is well known"* implies that the passage is about placebos and that they are perhaps cure-alls.

The sentence *"Every drug tested would prove effective if special steps were not taken to neutralize the placebo effect"* gives the first bit of evidence supporting the topic sentence.

The sentence *"Most people feel that the lucky patients in a drug test get the experimental drug because the real drug provides them a chance to be cured"* might be introducing a counter-premise or pivotal point; we won't know until we read the passage.

The sentence *"Placebos regularly cure more than five percent of the patients and would cure considerably more if the doubts associated with the tests were eliminated"* provides more support for the topic sentence.

The sentence *"The actual curing power of placebos probably stems from the faith of the patient in the treatment"* explains why the topic sentence is true.

The sentence *"It may take a while to reach the ten percent level of cure because any newly established program will not have cultivated the word-of-mouth advertising needed to insure its success"* is hard to interpret. This does not help us.

The sentence *"Unfortunately, placebo treatment centers cannot operate as nonprofit businesses"* seems to be off the subject. Again, this does not help us.

In summary, although the last two sentences were not useful, we now have a good idea of what the passage is about: *how* and *why* placebos are effective. We now read the passage—looking for places from which any of the six questions might be drawn, circling the pivotal words, and annotating key points.

Passage begins on the next page.

That placebos can cure everything from dandruff to leprosy is well known. They have a long history of use by witch doctors, faith healers, and even modern physicians, all of whom refuse to 5 admit their efficacy. Modern distribution techniques can bring this most potent of medicines to the aid of everyone, not just those lucky enough to receive placebos in a medical testing program.

Every drug tested would prove effective if 10 special steps were not taken to neutralize the placebo effect. This is why drug tests give half the patients the new medication and half a harmless substitute. These tests prove the value of placebos because approximately five percent of the patients 15 taking them are cured even though the placebos are made from substances that have been carefully selected to be useless.

Most people feel that the lucky patients in a drug test get the experimental drug because the real 20 drug provides them a chance to be cured. **(1) Yet** analysis shows that patients getting the placebo may be the lucky ones because they may be cured without risking any adverse effects the new drug may have. Furthermore, the drug may well be 25 found worthless and to have severe side effects. No harmful side effects result from placebos.

Placebos regularly cure more than five percent of the patients and would cure considerably more if the doubts associated with the tests were 30 eliminated. Cures are principally due to the patient's faith, **(2) yet** the patient must have doubts knowing that he may or may not be given the new drug, which itself may or may not prove to be an effective drug. Since he knows the probability of 35 being given the true drug is about fifty percent, the placebo cure rate would be more than doubled by removing these doubts if cures are directly related to faith.

The actual curing power of placebos probably 40 stems from the faith of the patient in the treatment. This suggests that cure rates in the ten percent range could be expected if patients are given placebos under the guise of a proven cure, even when patients know their problems are incurable.

45 It may take a while to reach the ten percent level of cure because any newly established program will not have cultivated the word-of-mouth advertising needed to insure its success. One person saying "I was told that my problem was beyond 50 medical help, but they cured me," can direct countless people to the treatment with the required degree of faith. Furthermore, when only terminal illnesses are treated, those not cured tell no one of the failure.

Unfortunately, placebo treatment centers 55 cannot operate as nonprofit businesses. The nonprofit idea was ruled out upon learning that the first rule of public medicine is never to give free medicine. Public health services know that medicine not paid for by patients is often not taken 60 or not effective because the recipient feels the medicine is worth just what it cost him. **(3) Even though** the patients would not know they were taking sugar pills, the placebos cost so little that the patients would have no faith in the treatment. 65 Therefore, though it is against higher principles, treatment centers must charge high fees for placebo treatments. This sacrifice of principles, however, is a small price to pay for the greater good of the patients.

1. Which one of the following best expresses the main idea of the passage?

(A) Placebo treatment is a proven tool of modern medicine and its expanded use would benefit society's health.

(B) Because modern technology allows for distribution of drugs on a massive scale, the proven efficacy of the placebo is no longer limited to a privileged few.

(C) The curative power of the placebo is so strong that it should replace proven drugs because the patients receiving the placebo will then be cured without risking any adverse side effects.

(D) The price of placebo treatment must be kept artificially high because patients have little faith in inexpensive treatments.

(E) Semi-placebos—drugs that contain only a small amount of the usual dosage—are even more effective curatives than either the placebo or the full-strength drug.

2. Which one of the following is most analogous to the idea presented in the last paragraph?

    (A) Buying a television at a discount house
    (B) Making an additional pledge to charity
    (C) Choosing the most expensive dishwasher in a manufacturer's line
    (D) Waiting until a book comes out in paperback
    (E) Contributing one dollar to the Presidential Campaign fund on your tax return

3. According to the passage, when testing a new drug medical researchers give half of the subjects the test drug and half a placebo because

    (A) proper statistical controls should be observed.
    (B) this method reduces the risk of maiming too many subjects if the drug should prove to be harmful.
    (C) all drugs which are tested would prove to be effective otherwise.
    (D) most drugs would test positively otherwise.
    (E) the cost of dispensing drugs to all the patients is prohibitive.

4. It can be inferred from the passage that the author might

    (A) believe that the benefits of a placebo treatment program which leads patients to believe they were getting a real drug would outweigh the moral issue of lying.
    (B) support legislation outlawing the use of placebos.
    (C) open up a medical clinic that would treat patients exclusively through placebo methods.
    (D) believe that factors other than faith are responsible for the curative power of the placebo.
    (E) believe that placebo treatment centers should be tax-exempt because they are nonprofit businesses.

5. Which one of the following best describes the organization of the material presented in the passage?

    (A) A general proposition is stated; then evidence for its support is given.
    (B) Two types of drug treatment—placebo and non-placebo—are compared and contrasted.
    (C) A result is stated, its cause is explained, and an application is suggested.
    (D) A dilemma is presented and a possible solution is offered.
    (E) A series of examples is presented; then a conclusion is drawn from them.

6. Which one of the following most accurately characterizes the author's attitude toward placebo treatment?

    (A) reserved advocacy
    (B) feigned objectivity
    (C) summary dismissal
    (D) perplexed by its effectiveness
    (E) zealous promotion

The first item is a main idea question:

1.   Which one of the following best expresses the main idea of the passage?

   (A)   Placebo treatment is a proven tool of modern medicine and its expanded use would benefit society's health.
   (B)   Because modern technology allows for distribution of drugs on a massive scale, the proven efficacy of the placebo is no longer limited to a privileged few.
   (C)   The curative power of the placebo is so strong that it should replace proven drugs because the patients receiving the placebo will then be cured without risking any adverse side effects.
   (D)   The price of placebo treatment must be kept artificially high because patients have little faith in inexpensive treatments.
   (E)   Semi-placebos—drugs that contain only a small amount of the usual dosage—are even more effective curatives than either the placebo or the full-strength drug.

As we found by previewing the topic sentences, the passage is about the efficacy of placebo treatment. Careful reading shows that the passage also promotes expanded use of placebos. Hence the answer is (A).

The other choices can be quickly dismissed. (B) is the second-best choice: the author *does* mention that modern distribution techniques can bring the curative power of placebos to everyone, but he does not fully develop that idea. This answer-choice is tempting because it is contained in the topic paragraph. As to (C), it overstates the author's claim. Although in the third paragraph, the author states that those who receive the placebos may be the lucky ones, this is referring to new, unproven drugs, not to established drugs. As to (D), it, like (B), is mentioned in the passage but is not fully developed. It's tempting because it appears in the last paragraph—a natural place for the conclusion. Finally, (E) is neither mentioned nor implied by the passage.

The second item is an application question.

2.   Which one of the following is most analogous to the idea presented in the last paragraph?

   (A)   Buying a television at a discount house
   (B)   Making an additional pledge to charity
   (C)   Choosing the most expensive dishwasher in a manufacturer's line
   (D)   Waiting until a book comes out in paperback
   (E)   Contributing one dollar to the Presidential Campaign fund on your tax return

The information needed to answer this question is heralded by the pivotal phrase "Even though" (lines 61–64). The implication of that sentence is "you get what you pay for." This would motivate one to buy the most expensive item in a manufacturer's line. Hence the answer is (C).

The third item is a description question.

3.   According to the passage, when testing a new drug medical researchers give half of the subjects the test drug and half a placebo because

   (A)   proper statistical controls should be observed.
   (B)   this method reduces the risk of maiming too many subjects if the drug should prove to be harmful.
   (C)   all drugs which are tested would prove to be effective otherwise.
   (D)   most drugs would test positively otherwise.
   (E)   the cost of dispensing drugs to all the patients is prohibitive.

Since this is a description question, you must refer to the passage to answer it. The opening sentence to paragraph two contains the needed information. That sentence states "Every drug would prove effective if special steps were not taken to neutralize the placebo effect." Hence the answer is (C).

Choice (D) illustrates why you must refer directly to the passage to answer a description question: unless you have a remarkable memory, you will be unsure whether the statement was that **all** or that **most** drugs would prove effective.

The fourth item is an extension question.

4.   It can be inferred from the passage that the author might

(A)   believe that the benefits of a placebo treatment program that lead patients to believe they were getting a real drug would outweigh the moral issue of lying.
(B)   support legislation outlawing the use of placebos.
(C)   open up a medical clinic that would treat patients exclusively through placebo methods.
(D)   believe that factors other than faith are responsible for the curative power of the placebo.
(E)   believe that placebo treatment centers should be tax-exempt because they are nonprofit businesses.

The answer is (A). One of the first clues to the author's view on this issue is contained in the pivotal clause "yet the patient . . . effective drug" (lines 31–34). Later, in paragraph six, the author nearly advocates that the patient should not be told that he or she might be receiving a placebo. Finally, the closing line of the passage cinches it. There, the author implies that certain principles *can be* sacrificed for the greater good of the patients.

The fifth item is a writing technique question.

5.   Which one of the following best describes the organization of the material presented in the passage?

(A)   A general proposition is stated; then evidence for its support is given.
(B)   Two types of drug treatment—placebo and non-placebo—are compared and contrasted.
(C)   A result is stated, its cause is explained, and an application is suggested.
(D)   A dilemma is presented and a possible solution is offered.
(E)   A series of examples is presented; then a conclusion is drawn from them.

In the first paragraph the author claims that placebos can cure everything from dandruff to leprosy—this is a result. Then in paragraphs two, three, four, and five, he explains the causes of the result. Finally, he alludes to an application—the placebo treatment centers. The answer is (C).

The sixth item is a tone question.

6.   Which one of the following most accurately characterizes the author's attitude toward placebo treatment?

(A)   reserved advocacy
(B)   feigned objectivity
(C)   summary dismissal
(D)   perplexed by its effectiveness
(E)   zealous promotion

This question is a little tricky. Only choices (A) and (B) have any real merit. Although the passage has a detached, third-person style, the author nonetheless *does* present his opinions—namely that placebos work and that their use should be expanded. However, that advocacy is reserved, so the answer is (A).

The other choices can be quickly eliminated:

"Summary dismissal" is not supported by the passage. Besides, a scholar would never summarily dismiss something; he would consider it carefully—or at least give the impression that he has—before rejecting it. This eliminates (C).

Given the human ego, we are unlikely to admit that we don't understand the subject we are writing about. This eliminates (D).

"Zealous promotion" is too strong; "promotion" itself is probably too strong. This eliminates (E).

<u>Points to Remember</u>

1. <u>THE THREE STEP METHOD</u>

   1.   (Optional) Preview the first sentence of each paragraph.

   2.   Read the passage at a faster than usual pace (but not to the point that comprehension suffers), being alert to places from which any of the six questions might be drawn:

      a.)   Main Idea
      b.)   Description
      c.)   Writing Technique
      d.)   Extension
      e.)   Application
      f.)   Tone

   3.   Annotate the passage and circle any pivotal words. Then use these as reference points for answering the questions. Following are some common annotation marks (you may want to add to this list):

      A = **A**uthor's **A**ttitude
      C = **C**omplex point
      ? = **Question?** I don't understand this part (you can bet that this area will be important to *at least* one question)
      SP = **S**ignificant **p**oint
      ! = **Exclamation!** Strong opinion
      W = **W**eak, questionable or unsupported argument or premise

Mentor Exercise

> Directions: This passage is followed by a group of questions to be answered based on what is <u>stated</u> or <u>implied</u> in the passage. Choose the <u>best</u> answer; the one that most accurately and completely answers the question.

Following the Three Step Method, we preview the first sentence of each paragraph in the passage: (The body of the passage will be presented later.)

The enigmatic opening sentence *"Many readers, I suspect, will take the title of this article [Women, Fire, and Dangerous Things] as suggesting that women, fire, and dangerous things have something in common—say, that women are fiery and dangerous"* does not give us much of a clue to what the passage is about.

The sentence *"The classical view that categories are based on shared properties is not entirely wrong"* is more helpful. It tells us the passage is about categorization and that there are at least two theories about it: the classical view, which has merit, and the modern view, which is apparently superior.

The sentence *"Categorization is not a matter to be taken lightly"* merely confirms the subject of the passage.

Although only one sentence was helpful, previewing did reveal a lot about the passage's subject matter—categorization. Now we read the passage, circling pivotal words, annotating, and noting likely places from which any of the six questions might be drawn. After each paragraph, we will stop to analyze and interpret what the author has presented:

> Many readers, I suspect, will take the title of this article [*Women, Fire, and Dangerous Things*] as suggesting that women, fire, and dangerous things have something in common—say, that women are fiery and dangerous. Most feminists I've mentioned it to have loved the title for that reason, though some have hated it for the same reason. But the chain of inference—from conjunction to categorization to commonality—is the norm. The inference is based on the common idea of what it means to be in the same category: things are categorized together on the basis of what they have in common. The idea that categories are defined by common properties is not only our everyday folk theory of what a category is, it is also the principle technical theory—one that has been with us for more than two thousand years.

In this paragraph, the author introduces the subject matter of the passage—categorization. And the pivotal sentence, introduced by "but," explains the classical theory of categorization, albeit rather obtusely. Namely, like things are placed in the same category.

Now we consider the second paragraph:

> The classical view that categories are based on shared properties is not entirely wrong. We often do categorize things on that basis. But that is only a small part of the story. In recent years it has become clear that categorization is far more complex than that. A new theory of categorization, called *prototype theory*, has emerged. It shows that human categorization is based on principles that extend far beyond those envisioned in the classical theory. One of our goals is to survey the complexities of the way people really categorize. For example, the title of this book was inspired by the Australian aboriginal language Dyirbal, which has a category, *balan*, that actually includes women, fire, and dangerous things. It also includes birds that are *not* dangerous, as well as exceptional animals, such as the platypus, bandicoot, and echidna. This is not simply a matter of categorization by common properties.

In this paragraph, the second pivotal word—but—is crucial. It introduces the main idea of the passage--the prototype theory of categorization. Now everything that is introduced should be attributed to the prototype theory, <u>not</u> to the classical theory. Wrong answer-choices are likely to be baited with just the opposite.

The author states that the prototype theory goes "far beyond" the classical theory. Although he does not tell us what the prototype theory *is*, he does tell us that it *is not* merely categorization by common properties.

Now we turn to the third paragraph:

Categorization is not a matter to be taken lightly. There is nothing more basic than categorization to our thought, perception, action and speech. Every time we see something as a *kind* of thing, for example, a tree, we are categorizing. Whenever we reason about *kinds* of things—chairs, nations, illnesses, emotions, any kind of thing at all—we are employing categories. Whenever we intentionally perform any *kind* of action, say something as mundane as writing with a pencil, hammering with a hammer, or ironing clothes, we are using categories. The particular action we perform on that occasion is a *kind* of motor activity, that is, it is in a particular category of motor actions. They are never done in exactly the same way, yet despite the differences in particular movements, they are all movements of a kind, and we know how to make movements of that kind. And any time we either produce or understand any utterance of any reasonable length, we are employing dozens if not hundreds of categories: categories of speech sounds, of words, of phrases and clauses, as well as conceptual categories. Without the ability to categorize, we could not function at all, either in the physical world or in our social and intellectual lives.

Though the author does not explicitly state it, this paragraph defines the theory of prototypes. Notice the author likes to use an indirect, even cryptic, method of introducing or switching topics, which makes this a classic SAT type passage. The SAT writers have many opportunities here to test whether you are following the author's train of thought.

Now we attack the questions.

1. The author probably chose *Women, Fire, and Dangerous Things* as the title of the article because

    I. he thought that since the Dyirbal placed all three items in the same category, women, fire, and dangerous things necessarily had something in common.

    II. he was hoping to draw attention to the fact that because items have been placed in the same category doesn't mean that they necessarily have anything in common

    III. he wanted to use the Dyirbal classification system as an example of how primitive classifications are not as functional as contemporary Western classification systems.

    (A) I only
    (B) II only
    (C) III only
    (D) II and III only
    (E) I, II, and III

1. This is an extension question. The second paragraph contains the information needed to answer it. There the author states that women, fire, and dangerous things belong to a category called *balan* in an Australian aboriginal language, which is <u>not</u> simply based on common properties. This eliminates Statement I and confirms Statement II.

The answer is (B).

2. According to the author,

    I. categorizing is a fundamental activity of people.

    II. whenever a word refers to a kind of thing, it signifies a category.

    III. one has to be able to categorize in order to function in our culture.

    (A) I only
    (B) II only
    (C) I and II only
    (D) II and III only
    (E) I, II, and III

2. This is a description question, so we must find the points in the passage from which the statements were drawn. Remember, the answer to a description question will not directly quote a statement from the passage, but it will be closely related to one—often a paraphrase. The needed references for Statements I, II, and III are all contained in the closing paragraph.

The answer is (E).

3. Which one of the following facts would most weaken the significance of the author's title?

    (A) The discovery that all the birds and animals classified as *balan* in Dyirbal are female

    (B) The discovery that the male Dyirbal culture considers females to be both fiery and dangerous

    (C) The discovery that all items in the *balan* category are considered female

    (D) The discovery that neither fire nor women are considered dangerous

    (E) The discovery that other cultures have categories similar to the *balan* category

3. To weaken an argument, attack one or more of its premises. Now the implication of the title is that *women*, *fire*, and *dangerous things* <u>do not</u> have anything in common. To weaken this implication, the answer should state that all things in the *balan* category <u>have</u> something in common.

The answer is (C).

4.   If linguistic experts cannot perceive how women, fire, and dangerous things in the category *balan* have at least one thing in common, it follows that

(A)   there probably is something other than shared properties that led to all items in *balan* being placed in that category.

(B)   the anthropologists simply weren't able to perceive what the items had in common.

(C)   the anthropologists might not have been able to see what the items had in common.

(D)   the items do not have anything in common.

(E)   the Australian aboriginal culture is rather mystic.

4. This is an extension question; we are asked to draw a conclusion based on the passage.

Hint: The thrust of the passage is that commonality is not the only way to categorize things.

The answer is (A).

5.   Which one of the following sentences would best complete the last paragraph of the passage?

(A)   An understanding of how we categorize is central to any understanding of how we think and how we function, and therefore central to an understanding of what makes us human.

(B)   The prototype theory is only the latest in a series of new and improved theories of categorization; undoubtedly even better theories will replace it.

(C)   The prototype theory of categories has not only unified a major branch of linguistics, but it has applications to mathematics and physics as well.

(D)   An understanding of how the prototype theory of categorization evolved from the classical theory is essential to any understanding of how we think and how we function in society.

(E)   To fully understand how modern Australian society functions, we must study how it is influenced by aboriginal culture—most specifically how aborigines organize and classify their surroundings.

5. This is a application question; we are asked to complete a thought for the author.

Most of the third paragraph is introducing the prototype theory of categorization. But in the last sentence the author changes direction somewhat—without any notice, as is typical of his style. Now he is discussing the importance of the ability to categorize. The clause *"Without the ability to categorize, we could not function at all"* indicates that this ability is fundamental to our very being.

Be careful not to choose (D). Although it is probably true, it is too specific: in the final sentence the author is discussing categorization in general.

The answer is (A).

EXERCISE

Directions: This passage is followed by a group of questions to be answered based on what is stated or implied in the passage. Choose the best answer; the one that most accurately and completely answers the question.

Global strategies to control infectious disease have historically included the erection of barriers to international travel and immigration. Keeping people with infectious diseases outside
5 national borders has reemerged as an important public health policy in the human immunodeficiency virus (HIV) epidemic. Between 29 and 50 countries are reported to have introduced border restrictions on HIV-positive foreigners,
10 usually those planning an extended stay in the country, such as students, workers, or seamen.

Travel restrictions have been established primarily by countries in the western Pacific and Mediterranean regions, where HIV seropreva-
15 lence is relatively low. However, the country with the broadest policy of testing and excluding foreigners is the United States. From December 1, 1987, when HIV infection was first classified in the United States as a contagious disease,
20 through September 30, 1989, more than 3 million people seeking permanent residence in this country were tested for HIV antibodies. The U.S. policy has been sharply criticized by national and international organizations as being
25 contrary to public health goals and human-rights principles. Many of these organizations are boycotting international meetings in the United States that are vital for the study of prevention, education, and treatment of HIV infection.

30 The Immigration and Nationality Act requires the Public Health Service to list "dangerous contagious diseases" for which aliens can be excluded from the United States. By 1987 there were seven designated diseases—
35 five of them sexually transmitted (chancroid, gonorrhea, granuloma inguinale, lymphog-ranuloma venereum, and infectious syphilis) and two non-venereal (active tuberculosis and infectious leprosy). On June 8, 1987, in response to a
40 Congressional direction in the Helms Amendment, the Public Health Service added HIV infection to the list of dangerous contagious diseases.

A just and efficacious travel and immigra-
45 tion policy would not exclude people because of their serologic status unless they posed a danger to the community through casual transmission. U.S. regulations should list only active tuberculosis as a contagious infectious disease. We
50 support well-funded programs to protect the health of travelers infected with HIV through appropriate immunizations and prophylactic treatment and to reduce behaviors that may transmit infection.

55 We recognize that treating patients infected with HIV who immigrate to the United States will incur costs for the public sector. It is inequitable, however, to use cost as a reason to exclude people infected with HIV, for there are
60 no similar exclusionary policies for those with other costly chronic diseases, such as heart disease or cancer.

Rather than arbitrarily restrict the movement of a subgroup of infected people, we must
65 dedicate ourselves to the principles of justice, scientific cooperation, and a global response to the HIV pandemic.

1. According to the passage, countries in the western Pacific have

   (A) a very high frequency of HIV-positive immigrants and have a greater reason to be concerned over this issue than other countries.

   (B) opposed efforts on the part of Mediterranean states to establish travel restrictions on HIV-positive residents.

   (C) a low HIV seroprevalence and, in tandem with Mediterranean regions, have established travel restrictions on HIV-positive foreigners.

   (D) continued to obstruct efforts to unify policy concerning immigrant screening.

   (E) joined with the United States in sharing information about HIV-positive individuals.

2.   The authors of the passage conclude that

(A)   it is unjust to exclude people based on their serological status without the knowledge that they pose a danger to the public.

(B)   U.S. regulations should require more stringent testing to be implemented at all major border crossings.

(C)   it is the responsibility of the public sector to absorb costs incurred by treatment of immigrants infected with HIV.

(D)   the HIV pandemic is largely overstated and that, based on new epidemiological data, screening immigrants is not indicated.

(E)   only the non-venereal diseases active tuberculosis and infectious leprosy should be listed as dangerous and contagious diseases.

3.   It can be inferred from the passage that

(A)   more than 3 million HIV-positive people have sought permanent residence in the United States.

(B)   countries with a low seroprevalence of HIV have a disproportionate and unjustified concern over the spread of AIDS by immigration.

(C)   the United States is more concerned with controlling the number of HIV-positive immigrants than with avoiding criticism from outside its borders.

(D)   current law is meeting the demand for prudent handling of a potentially hazardous international issue.

(E)   actions by countries in the western Pacific and Mediterranean regions to restrict travel are ineffective.

4.   Before the Helms Amendment in 1987, seven designated diseases were listed as being cause for denying immigration. We can conclude from the passage that

(A)   the authors agree fully with this policy but disagree with adding HIV to the list.

(B)   the authors believe that sexual diseases are appropriate reasons for denying immigration but not non-venereal diseases.

(C)   the authors disagree with the amendment.

(D)   the authors believe that non-venereal diseases are justifiable reasons for exclusion, but not sexually transmitted diseases.

(E)   the authors believe that no diseases should be cause for denying immigration.

5.   In referring to the "costs" incurred by the public (line 58), the authors apparently mean

(A)   financial costs.
(B)   costs to the public health.
(C)   costs in manpower.
(D)   costs in international reputation.
(E)   costs in public confidence.

Answers and Solutions to Exercise

Previewing the first sentence of each paragraph shows that the passage is about restricting travel of HIV-positive persons and that the authors feel there should be no restrictions. There are two pivotal words: "however" (line 15), and "Rather than" (line 63), which introduces the concluding paragraph.

1.   This is a description question, so we must find the point in the passage from which the question is drawn. It is the opening sentence to paragraph two. There it is stated that countries in the western Pacific and Mediterranean regions have a low incidence of HIV infection and have introduced border restrictions. The answer, therefore, is (C).

2.   This is another description question. The answer is (A). This is directly supported by the opening sentence of paragraph four. Note that (A) is a paraphrase of that sentence.

Be careful with (C). Although this is hinted at in paragraph five, it is never directly stated that the public sector is <u>responsible</u> for these costs, only that it would in fact pick up these costs. Remember: A description question must be answered from what is directly stated in the passage, not from what it implies.

3.   This is an extension question. Lines 23–24 state *"U.S. policy has been sharply criticized by national and international organizations."* Given that this criticism has not caused the United States to change its policies, it must be more concerned with controlling the number of HIV-positive immigrants than with avoiding criticism. The answer, therefore, is (C).

Don't be tempted by (A); it's a same language trap. Every word in it is taken from the passage. However, the passage states that over 3 million people were tested for HIV antibodies (lines 20–22), <u>not</u> that they were tested "positive" for HIV antibodies.

4.   This is another extension question. In lines 48–49, the authors state that only active tuberculosis should be listed as a dangerous contagious disease. We expect that they would oppose adding HIV to the list. The answer is (C).

5.   Although governments have ostensibly restricted the immigration of HIV-positive persons out of fear that they may spread the disease, the authors apparently are referring to financial costs, not costs to public health. This is indicated by lines 57–62, where they describe heart disease and cancer as non-contagious and costly, yet still admissible. The answer, therefore, is (A).

EXTRA READING

Directions: Each passage in this group is followed by questions based on its content. After reading a passage, choose the best answer to each question. Answer all questions following a passage on the basis of what is <u>stated</u> or <u>implied</u> in that passage.

Most students arrive at [college] using "discrete, concrete, and absolute categories to understand people, knowledge, and values." These students live with a *dualistic* view, seeing "the world in polar terms
5 of we-right-good vs. other-wrong-bad." These students cannot acknowledge the existence of more than one point of view toward any issue. There is one "right" way. And because these absolutes are assumed by or imposed on the individual from exter-
10 nal authority, they cannot be personally substantiated or authenticated by experience. These students are slaves to the generalizations of their authorities. An eye for an eye! Capital punishment is apt justice for murder. The Bible says so.

15 Most students break through the dualistic stage to another equally frustrating stage—*multiplicity*. Within this stage, students see a variety of ways to deal with any given topic or problem. However, while these students accept multiple points of view,
20 they are unable to evaluate or justify them. To have an opinion is everyone's right. While students in the dualistic stage are unable to produce evidence to support what they consider to be self-evident absolutes, students in the multiplistic stage are unable to
25 connect instances into coherent generalizations. Every assertion, every point, is valid. In their democracy they are directionless. Capital punishment? What sense is there in answering one murder with another?

30 The third stage of development finds students living in a world of *relativism*. Knowledge is relative: right and wrong depend on the context. No longer recognizing the validity of each individual idea or action, relativists examine everything to find its
35 place in an overall framework. While the multiplist views the world as unconnected, almost random, the relativist seeks always to place phenomena into coherent larger patterns. Students in this stage view the world analytically. They appreciate authority for
40 its expertise, using it to defend their own generalizations. In addition, they accept or reject ostensible

authority *after systematically* evaluating its validity. In this stage, however, students resist decision making. Suffering the ambivalence of finding several
45 consistent and acceptable alternatives, they are almost overwhelmed by diversity and need means for managing it. Capital punishment is appropriate justice—in some instances.

In the final stage students manage diversity
50 through individual *commitment*. Students do not deny relativism. Rather they assert an identity by forming commitments and assuming responsibility for them. They gather personal experience into a coherent framework, abstract principles to guide their actions,
55 and use these principles to discipline and govern their thoughts and actions. The individual has chosen to join a particular community and agrees to live by its tenets. The accused has had the benefit of due process to guard his civil rights, a jury of peers has
60 found him guilty, and the state has the right to end his life. This is a principle my community and I endorse.

1. It can be inferred from the passage that the author would consider which of the following to be good examples of "dualistic thinking"?

   I. People who think "there is a right way and a wrong way to do things"
   II. Teenagers who assume they know more about "the real world" than adults do
   III. People who back our country "right or wrong" when it goes to war

   (A) I only
   (B) II only
   (C) III only
   (D) I and II only
   (E) I and III only

2. Students who are "dualistic" thinkers may not be able to support their beliefs convincingly because

    (A) most of their beliefs *cannot* be supported by arguments.

    (B) they have accepted their "truths" simply because authorities have said these things are "true."

    (C) they half-believe and half-disbelieve just about everything.

    (D) their teachers almost always think that "dualistic" thinkers are wrong.

    (E) they are enslaved by their authorities.

3. Which one of the following assertions is supported by the passage?

    (A) *Committed* thinkers are not very sure of their positions.

    (B) *Relativistic* thinkers have learned how to make sense out of the world and have chosen their own positions in it.

    (C) *Multiplicity* thinkers have difficulty understanding the relationships between different points of view.

    (D) *Dualistic* thinkers have thought out the reasons for taking their positions.

    (E) *Dualistic* thinkers fear the power of authority.

4. In paragraph two, the author states that in their "democracy" students in the *multiplicity* stage are directionless. The writer describes *multiplicity* students as being in a "democracy" because

    (A) there are so many different kinds of people in a democracy.

    (B) in an "ideal" democracy, all people are considered equal; by extension, so are their opinions.

    (C) Democrats generally do not have a good sense of direction.

    (D) although democracies may grant freedom, they are generally acknowledged to be less efficient than more authoritarian forms of government.

    (E) in a democracy the individual has ultimate authority over himself, not the state.

5. Which one of the following kinds of thinking is NOT described in the passage?

    (A) People who assume that there is no right or wrong in any issue

    (B) People who make unreasoned commitments and stick by them

    (C) People who believe that right or wrong depends on the situation

    (D) People who commit themselves to a particular point of view after having considered several alternative concepts

    (E) People who think that all behavior can be accounted for by cause and effect relationships

6. If students were asked to write essays on the different *concepts* of tragedy as exemplified by Cordelia and Antigone, and they all responded by showing how each character exemplified a traditional definition of tragedy, we could, according to the passage, hypothesize which one of the following about these students?

    (A) The students were locked into the relativist stage.

    (B) The students had not advanced beyond the dualist stage.

    (C) The students had at least achieved the multiplicity stage.

    (D) The students had reached the commitment stage.

    (E) We have no indication of which cognitive stage the students were in.

7. Which one of the following best describes the organization of the passage?

    (A) Four methods of thought are compared and contrasted.

    (B) It is shown how each of four types of thought evolved from each other.

    (C) Four methods of thought are presented, and each is shown to complement the other.

    (D) The evolution of thought from simplistic and provincial through considered and cosmopolitan is illustrated by four stages.

    (E) The evolution of thought through four stages is presented, and each stage is illustrated by how it views capital punishment.

A growing taste for shark steaks and shark-fin soup has for the first time in 400 million years put the scourge of the sea at the wrong end of the food chain. Commercial landings of this toothsome fish
5 have doubled every year since 1986, and shark populations are plunging. It is hardly a case of good riddance. Sharks do for gentler fish what lions do for the wildebeest: they check populations by feeding on the weak. Also, sharks apparently do not get
10 cancer and may therefore harbor clues to the nature of that disease.

Finally, there is the issue of motherhood. Sharks are viviparous. That is, they bear their young alive and swimming (not sealed in eggs) after gesta-
15 tion periods lasting from nine months to two years. Shark mothers generally give birth to litters of from eight to twelve pups and bear only one litter every other year.

This is why sharks have one of the lowest
20 fecundity rates in the ocean. The female cod, for example, spawns annually and lays a few million eggs at a time. If three quarters of the cod were to be fished this year, they could be back in full force in a few years. But if humans took that big of a bite out
25 of the sharks, the population would not recover for 15 years.

So, late this summer, if all goes according to plan, the shark will join the bald eagle and the buffalo on the list of managed species. The federal
30 government will cap the U.S. commercial catch at 5,800 metric tons, about half of the 1989 level, and limit sportsmen to two sharks per boat. Another provision discourages finning, the harvesting of shark fins alone, by limiting the weight of fins to 7
35 percent of that of all the carcasses.

Finning got under the skin of environmentalists, and the resulting anger helped to mobilize support for the new regulations. Finning itself is a fairly recent innovation. Shark fins contain noodle-
40 like cartilaginous tissues that Chinese chefs have traditionally used to thicken and flavor soup. Over the past few years rising demand in Hong Kong has made the fins as valuable as the rest of the fish. Long strands are prized, so unusually large fins can
45 be worth considerably more to the fisherman than the average price of about $10 a pound.

But can U.S. quotas save shark species that wander the whole Atlantic? The blue shark, for example, migrates into the waters of something like
50 23 countries. John G. Casey, a biologist with the National Marine Fisheries Service Research Center in Narragansett, R.I., admits that international coordination will eventually be necessary. But he supports U.S. quotas as a first step in mobilizing
55 other nations. Meanwhile the commercial fishermen are not waiting for the new rules to take effect.

"There's a pre-quota rush on sharks," Casey says, "and it's going on as we speak."

8. According to the passage, shark populations are at greater risk than cod populations because

(A) sharks are now being eaten more than cod.
(B) the shark reproduction rate is lower than that of the cod.
(C) sharks are quickly becoming fewer in number.
(D) sharks are now as scarce as bald eagles and buffalo.
(E) sharks are scavengers and therefore more susceptible to disease.

9. According to the passage, a decrease in shark populations

I. might cause some fish populations to go unchecked.
II. would hamper cancer research.
III. to one-quarter the current level would take over a decade to recover from.

(A) II only
(B) III only
(C) I and III only
(D) I and II only
(E) I, II, and III

10. If the species *Homo logicus* was determined to be viviparous and to have extremely low fecundity rates on land, we might expect that

   (A) *Homo logicus* could overpopulate its niche and should be controlled.
   (B) *Homo logicus* might be declared an endangered species.
   (C) *Homo logicus* would pose no danger to other species and would itself be in no danger.
   (D) *Homo logicus* would soon become extinct.
   (E) None of these events would be expected with certainty.

11. Which one of the following best describes the author's attitude toward the efforts to protect shark populations?

   (A) strong advocate
   (B) impartial observer
   (C) opposed
   (D) perplexed
   (E) resigned to their ineffectiveness

12. It can be inferred from the passage that

   I.   research efforts on cancer will be hindered if shark populations are threatened.
   II. U.S. quotas on shark fishing will have limited effectiveness in protecting certain species.
   III. some practices of Chinese chefs have angered environmentalists.

   (A) I only
   (B) II only
   (C) I and II only
   (D) II and III only
   (E) I, II, and III

13. An irony resulting from the announcement that sharks will be placed on the managed list is

   (A) we will now find out less about cancer, so in effect by saving the sharks, we are hurting ourselves.
   (B) sharks are far more dangerous to other fish than we are to them.
   (C) more chefs are now using the cartilaginous tissues found in shark fins.
   (D) more sharks are being killed now than before the announcement.
   (E) man will now protect a creature that he has been the victim of.

"A writer's job is to tell the truth," said Hemingway in 1942. No other writer of our time had so fiercely asserted, so pugnaciously defended or so consistently exemplified the writer's obligation to speak truly. His
5 standard of truth-telling remained, moreover, so high and so rigorous that he was ordinarily unwilling to admit secondary evidence, whether literary evidence or evidence picked up from other sources than his own experience. "I only know what I have seen," was a
10 statement which came often to his lips and pen. What he had personally done, or what he knew unforgettably by having gone through one version of it, was what he was interested in telling about. This is not to say that he refused to invent freely. But he always made it a
15 sacrosanct point to invent in terms of what he actually knew from having been there.

The primary intent of his writing, from first to last, was to seize and project for the reader what he often called "the way it was." This is a characteristi-
20 cally simple phrase for a concept of extraordinary complexity, and Hemingway's conception of its meaning subtly changed several times in the course of his career—always in the direction of greater complexity. At the core of the concept, however, one can invariably
25 discern the operation of three aesthetic instruments: the sense of place, the sense of fact, and the sense of scene.

The first of these, obviously a strong passion with Hemingway, is the sense of place. "Unless you have geography, background," he once told George Antheil,
30 "you have nothing." You have, that is to say, a dramatic vacuum. Few writers have been more place-conscious. Few have so carefully charted out the geographical ground work of their novels while managing to keep background so conspicuously unobtrusive.
35 Few, accordingly, have been able to record more economically and graphically the way it is when you walk through the streets of Paris in search of breakfast at a corner café . . . Or when, at around six o'clock of a Spanish dawn, you watch the bulls running from the
40 corrals at the Puerta Rochapea through the streets of Pamplona towards the bullring.

"When I woke it was the sound of the rocket exploding that announced the release of the bulls from the corrals at the edge of town.
45 Down below the narrow street was empty. All the balconies were crowded with people. Suddenly a crowd came down the street. They were all running, packed close together. They passed along and up the street toward the bull-
50 ring and behind them came more men running faster, and then some stragglers who were really running. Behind them was a little bare space, and then the bulls, galloping, tossing their heads up and down. It all went out of sight around the
55 corner. One man fell, rolled to the gutter, and lay quiet. But the bulls went right on and did not notice him. They were all running together."

This landscape is as morning-fresh as a design in India ink on clean white paper. First is the bare white
60 street, seen from above, quiet and empty. Then one sees the first packed clot of runners. Behind these are the thinner ranks of those who move faster because they are closer to the bulls. Then the almost comic stragglers, who are "really running." Brilliantly behind
65 these shines the "little bare space," a desperate margin for error. Then the clot of running bulls—closing the design, except of course for the man in the gutter making himself, like the designer's initials, as inconspicuous as possible.

14. According to the author, Hemingway's primary purpose in telling a story was

(A) to construct a well-told story that the reader would thoroughly enjoy.

(B) to construct a story that would reflect truths that were not particular to a specific historical period.

(C) to begin from reality but to allow his imagination to roam from "the way it was" to "the way it might have been."

(D) to report faithfully reality as Hemingway had experienced it.

(E) to go beyond the truth, to "create" reality.

15. From the author's comments and the example of the bulls (paragraph 4), what was the most likely reason for which Hemingway took care to include details of place?

(A) He felt that geography in some way illuminated other, more important events.

(B) He thought readers generally did not have enough imagination to visualize the scenes for themselves.

(C) He had no other recourse since he was avoiding the use of other literary sources.

(D) He thought that landscapes were more important than characters to convey "the way it was."

(E) He felt that without background information the readers would be unable to follow the story.

16. One might infer from the passage that Hemingway preferred which one of the following sources for his novels and short stories?

(A) Stories that he had heard from friends or chance acquaintances

(B) Stories that he had read about in newspapers or other secondary sources

(C) Stories that came to him in periods of meditation or in dreams

(D) Stories that he had lived rather than read about

(E) Stories adapted from myths

17. It has been suggested that part of Hemingway's genius lies in the way in which he removes himself from his stories in order to let readers experience the stories for themselves. Which of the following elements of the passage support this suggestion?

I. The comparison of "the designer's initials" to the man who fell and lay in the gutter (lines 55–56) during the running of the bulls

II. Hemingway's stated intent to project for the reader "the way it was" (line 19)

III. Hemingway's ability to invent fascinating tales from his own experience

(A) I only

(B) II only

(C) I and II only

(D) I and III only

(E) I, II, and III

18. From the passage, one can assume that which of the following statements would best describe Hemingway's attitude toward knowledge?

(A) One can learn about life only by living it fully.

(B) A wise person will read widely in order to learn about life.

(C) Knowledge is a powerful tool that should be reserved only for those who know how to use it.

(D) Experience is a poor teacher.

(E) One can never truly "know" anything.

19. The author calls "the way it was" a "characteristically simple phrase for a concept of extraordinary complexity" (lines 20–21) because

(A) the phrase reflects Hemingway's talent for obscuring ordinary events.

(B) the relationship between simplicity and complexity reflected the relationship between the style and content of Hemingway's writing.

(C) Hemingway became increasingly confused about "the way it was" throughout the course of his career.

(D) Hemingway's obsession for geographic details progressively overshadowed the dramatic element of his stories.

(E) it typifies how Hemingway understated complex issues.

Imagine that we stand on any ordinary seaside pier, and watch the waves rolling in and striking against the iron columns of the pier. Large waves pay very little attention to the columns—they divide right and left and re-unite
5   after passing each column, much as a regiment of soldiers would if a tree stood in their way; it is almost as though the columns had not been there. But the short waves and ripples find the columns of the pier a much more formidable obstacle. When the short waves impinge on
10 the columns, they are reflected back and spread as new ripples in all directions. To use the technical term, they are "scattered." The obstacle provided by the iron columns hardly affects the long waves at all, but scatters the short ripples.

15   We have been watching a working model of the way in which sunlight struggles through the earth's atmosphere. Between us on earth and outer space the atmosphere interposes innumerable obstacles in the form of molecules of air, tiny droplets of water, and small parti-
20 cles of dust. They are represented by the columns of the pier.

        The waves of the sea represent the sunlight. We know that sunlight is a blend of lights of many colors—as we can prove for ourselves by passing it through a prism,
25 or even through a jug of water, or as Nature demonstrates to us when she passes it through the raindrops of a summer shower and produces a rainbow. We also know that light consists of waves, and that the different colors of light are produced by waves of different lengths, red
30 light by long waves and blue light by short waves. The mixture of waves which constitutes sunlight has to struggle through the obstacles it meets in the atmosphere, just as the mixture of waves at the seaside has to struggle past the columns of the pier. And these obstacles treat the
35 light waves much as the columns of the pier treat the sea-waves. The long waves which constitute red light are hardly affected, but the short waves which constitute blue light are scattered in all directions.

        Thus, the different constituents of sunlight are
40 treated in different ways as they struggle through the earth's atmosphere. A wave of blue light may be scattered by a dust particle, and turned out of its course. After a time a second dust particle again turns it out of its course, and so on, until finally it enters our eyes by a path
45 as zigzag as that of a flash of lightning. Consequently, the blue waves of the sunlight enter our eyes from all directions. And that is why the sky looks blue.

20. We know from experience that if we look directly at the sun, we will see red light near the sun. This observation is supported by the passage for which one of the following reasons?

(A)   It seems reasonable to assume that red light would surround the sun because the sun is basically a large fireball.

(B)   It seems reasonable to assume that the other colors of light would either cancel each other or combine to produce red.

(C)   It seems reasonable to assume that red light would not be disturbed by the atmospheric particles and would consequently reach us by a relatively direct path from the sun to our eyes.

(D)   It is not supported by the passage. The author does not say what color of light should be near the sun, and he provides no reasons that would allow us to assume that the light would be red.

(E)   Gazing directly at the sun forces the eye to focus on the longer red waves.

21. Scientists have observed that shorter wavelength light has more energy than longer wavelength light. From this we can conclude that

(A)   red light will exert more energy when it hits the surface of the earth than will blue light.

(B)   lightning is caused by the collision of blue light with particles in the air.

(C)   red light will travel faster than blue light.

(D)   blue light has more energy than red light.

(E)   blue light has less energy than red light.

22. A scientist makes new observations and learns that water waves of shorter wavelengths spread in all directions not only because they scatter off piers but also because they interact with previously scattered short water waves. Drawing upon the analogy between water waves and light waves, we might hypothesize which of the following?

(A) Blue light waves act like ripples that other blue light waves meet and scatter from.

(B) Red light waves will be scattered by blue light waves like incoming long water waves are scattered by outgoing ripples.

(C) Red light waves can scatter blue light waves, but blue light waves cannot scatter red.

(D) The analogy between water and light waves cannot be extended to include the way in which short water waves become ripples and scatter one another.

(E) The scattering effect of blue light waves is canceled by that of red.

23. Which one of the following is a reason for assuming that sunlight is constituted of waves of many colors?

(A) The mixture of waves that make up sunlight has to struggle through a variety of obstacles in the atmosphere.

(B) When passing through water in the atmosphere, sunlight is sometimes broken down into an array of colors.

(C) Many different wavelengths of light enter our eyes from all directions.

(D) The mere fact that light waves can be scattered is a reason for assuming that sunlight is constituted of waves of different colors.

(E) When passing through dust in the atmosphere, sunlight is sometimes broken down into an array of colors.

24. From the information presented in the passage, what can we conclude about the color of the sky on a day with a large quantity of dust in the air?

(A) The sky would be even bluer

(B) The sky would be redder

(C) The sky would not change colors

(D) We do not have enough information to determine a change in color

(E) The sky would assume a violet hue

25. We all know that when there is a clear sky, the western sky appears red as the sun sets. From the information presented in the passage, this phenomenon would seem to be explained by which of the following?

I. Light meets more obstacles when passing parallel to the earth's surface than when traveling perpendicular. Consequently, even red light is diffused.

II. The blue light may not make it through the denser pathway of the evening sky, leaving only the long light waves of red.

III. The short red light waves have more energy and are the only waves that can make it through the thick atmosphere of the evening sky.

(A) I only

(B) II only

(C) I and II only

(D) II and III only

(E) I, II, and III

26. Which one of the following does the author seem to imply?

(A) Waves of light and waves of water are identical.

(B) Waves of light have the same physical shape as waves of water.

(C) Waves of light and waves of water do not have very much in common.

(D) Waves of water are only models of waves of light.

(E) There are colors of light waves just as there are colors of water waves.

Passage 1

Every year, Americans spend millions of dollars on diet programs, diet supplements, and gym memberships. These are wasted dollars when you consider that all you need for weight loss is general information about carbohydrates. Carbohydrates help the body produce insulin which helps maintain a balance of blood-sugar levels. This is important for the body to function properly; however, too many carbohydrates sends blood-sugar levels plunging because of an excess of insulin. It's at this time you reach for a "quick-fix"—often a candy bar—to replenish your energy. When you replace healthy protein snacks with sweets, proper weight loss never takes place.

To lose weight, it is imperative that you cut back on your carbohydrate intake. By making this adjustment, even a couch potato can lose weight! With a reduction in carbohydrates in your system, you will burn enough energy just sitting in a chair, that you can shed the pounds. You can't ask for an easier way to diet.

Passage 2

In America, the latest fads are diets. With the revolving door on such diets, it's no wonder that the rate of obesity continues to grow in the United States. What Americans need to do is go back to the basics: a well-rounded, healthy diet and a regular exercise regiment. A well-rounded diet includes eating the recommended daily allowance of fruits, vegetables, meats, and grains. Sweets and oils should be consumed sparingly, although not totally eliminated. Many dieters attempt to go "cold turkey" off of sweets and fatty foods, and they end up failing miserably. This failure leads to a lack of confidence and perseverance in dieting.

Rather than making a physical decision to "diet," Americans should simply eat sensibly and couple this with exercise. Exercise is one of the most important components of losing weight and being healthy. Individuals should receive 20 minutes of exercise at least three times per week. If America will only get back to the basics, the nation will be back to fit and healthy.

27. Consider two people who eat from the same low-carbohydrate menu. Which of the following would weaken the author's argument in Passage 1?

(A) Person A does not exercise. Person B does not exercise. Person A loses two more pounds than Person B.
(B) Person A does not exercise. Person B exercises regularly. Person B loses more weight than Person A.
(C) Person A exercises regularly. Person B does not exercise. Person B loses 5 more pounds than Person A.
(D) Person A exercises regularly. Person B exercises regularly. Neither loses any weight.
(E) Person A does not exercise. Person B does not exercise. Both lose the same amount of weight.

28. In Passage 2, diets are compared to fads because

(A) they come and go.
(B) they are adopted by younger generations.
(C) there is often a cost associated with them.
(D) they stay the same.
(E) they became popular within a year.

29. On what main idea do the authors of both passages agree?

(A) Americans don't diet often enough.
(B) An exercise regiment in your diet is irrelevant.
(C) Americans consume too much junk food.
(D) Americans make dieting too complicated.
(E) Too many Americans suffer from obesity.

30. On what main issue do the authors of both passages disagree?

(A) Sweets should be cut from your diet.
(B) Carbohydrates should be a part of your diet.
(C) You should eat more meats and vegetables in a healthy diet.
(D) You should eat less fat in your diet.
(E) A diet should include regular exercise.

Passage 1

We've all been through Biology class, so we're familiar with Punic squares and the likelihood that two brown-eyed parents will have brown-eyed children. And we also know that genetics has something to do with our hair color, height, and build. But what about our personality? Nature vs. nurture is an age-old controversy. It is one argument that has yet to be won, and theories abound. One thing is clear, however: there is definitely more to it than nature. A family with multiple children makes this obvious because each child has his or her own distinct personality. Rarely is there a family, even one with twins, where each child exhibits identical personality traits to that of his siblings; rather, each child develops his own personality through nurture. Anyone who has a mother, a father, or a sibling can attest to the fact that there is a lot more to it than nature.

Passage 2

Whether a person is shy or extroverted, conservative or adventurous, that person inherited these traits from his parents. Although personality is not completely dependent upon genetics, heredity lays the foundation for a person's personality traits and tendencies. After the foundation has been laid, nurture then steps in and works to develop what nature has presented. For example, through nurture a shy person can learn to become more outgoing; however, this manifestation of personality will never be completely natural for this person because extroversion is not the foundation nature built for him. Equally, a child who does not seem to have natural musical talent may, through nurture, learn to play the piano; however, he will likely have to work twice as hard to become musically fluent as another child who is an inherently talented musician. Clearly, nature and nurture both play a very important role in the development of personality, but it is nature that initially forms a personality, and it is nature that ultimately shines through no matter how much nurturing takes place.

31. Which of the following would weaken the argument presented by the author in Passage 1?

    (A) A mother and daughter who exhibit some of the same personality traits.
    (B) An adopted child who exhibits many of the same personality traits as his adopted parents.
    (C) Two brothers: one is an introvert, and one is an extrovert.
    (D) Twins separated at birth who exhibit many of the same personality traits.
    (E) A mother and daughter who have different personality traits.

32. According to Passage 2, which of the following best defines *inherently*?

    (A) Typically
    (B) Something given to you when someone dies
    (C) Innately
    (D) Extremely
    (E) Clearly

33. Which of the following would best describe the relationship between the two passages?

    (A) Both passages offer essentially the same argument.
    (B) Passage 1 gives an argument which Passage 2 completely refutes.
    (C) Passage 1 gives a generalization, while Passage 2 offers a specific example.
    (D) Passage 1 offers a generalization, while Passage 1 gives a specific example.
    (E) Passage 1 completely refutes an point of view described in Passage 2.

34. Which of the following best defines *nature vs. nurture*?

    (A) outdoor vs. indoor recreation
    (B) genetics vs. heredity
    (C) personality vs. physical appearance
    (D) introversion vs. extroversion
    (E) heredity vs. upbringing

Answers and Solutions

Answers to Questions

1.	E	10.	E	19.	B
2.	B	11.	B	20.	C
3.	C	12.	B	21.	D
4.	B	13.	D	22.	D
5.	E	14.	D	23.	B
6.	B	15.	A	24.	D
7.	E	16.	D	25.	C
8.	B	17.	C	26.	D
9.	C	18.	A		

Questions 1–7

Before we turn to the answers, three pivotal words in the first passage should be noted: "However" (line 18), "however" (line 44), and "Rather" (line 51).

1.   This is an extension question. Statement I is true. This is the essential characteristic of dualistic (right/wrong) thinkers (lines 3–8). This eliminates (B) and (C). Statement II is false. Dualistic thinkers grant authority (right thinking) to adults and adult figures. This is clear from the sentence, *"These students are slaves to the generalizations of their authorities."* This eliminates (D). Unfortunately, we have to check Statement III. It is true since Dualistic thinkers believe *their* group is right and the *other* group is wrong. (Again, see lines 3–8.) The answer, therefore, is (E).

2.   This is another extension question. Dualistic thinkers probably cannot give cogent arguments for their beliefs since they have adopted them unquestioningly from authority figures; dualistic thinkers do not know (have never thought of) the reasons for which their beliefs are right or wrong. Hence the answer is (B).

3.   This is a description question. (A) is false. After carefully thinking through their reasons, committed thinkers are reasonably sure of their position. (B) is also false. Relativistic thinkers make sense of the world, but they have not chosen their position; indeed they cannot even choose a position. (C) is true. Multiplicity thinkers see the world as randomly organized; they can't see the relationships that connect different positions. (See the first pivotal word, "however" [line 18].)

4.   This is an extension question. Multiplicity students view all opinions as equally valid. They have yet to learn how to rank opinions (truths)—all votes (thoughts) count equally. The answer is (B).
       Note, (C) is offered to humor Republicans. The test-makers sometimes run out of tempting wrong choices. Don't dwell on such humorous nonsense.

5.   This is another description question. (A): No, these are the Multiplists. (B): No, Dualists think this

way. (C): No, this describes Relativists. Don't confuse (A) and (C). Multiplists acknowledge no right or wrong; whereas Relativists acknowledge a morality, but one that is context dependent. (D): No, Committed thinkers fit this description rather nicely. Hence, by process of elimination, we have learned the answer is (E).

6.   This is an application question. Since all the students showed how the characters exemplified the *same* concept of "tragedy," they must be working from a common definition of tragedy (the traditional one). They have accepted "authority's" definition of tragedy and have shown how each character fits it. It never occurred to them that there may be other ways to view a tragedy. Hence they are all dualistic thinkers. The answer is (B).

7.   This is a writing technique question. In each paragraph the author shows how a stage of thought evolved from a previous stage—except the dualistic stage, which starts the analysis. Further, the thought process in each stage is illustrated by how it views capital punishment. Hence the answer is (E).

       Be careful not to choose (D). Although dualistic thinking certainly is simplistic and provincial, and committed thinking seems to be considered and cosmopolitan, neither of these judgments is stated nor implied by the passage.

Questions 8–13

8.   This is a description question. Paragraph 3 contains the information needed to answer it. There it is stated that the cod population can replenish itself in a few years, but the shark population would take 15 years. Hence the answer is (B).
       Don't make the mistake of choosing (C). Although it is certainly supported by the passage, it does not state how this relates to cod—they too may be decreasing in number. (C) uses the true-but-irrelevant ploy.

9.   This is a description question. Statement I is true. It is supported by the analogy drawn between lions and sharks (lines 7–9). This eliminates (A) and (B). Statement II is false. It is too strong an inference to draw from the information in lines 9–11. If sharks were on the verge of extinction, this "could hamper" research. But given that the author does not claim or imply that sharks are near extinction, "would hamper" is too strong. Besides, the author does not state that sharks are being used in research, just that they may be useful in that regard. This eliminates (D) and (E). Hence, by process of elimination, we have learned the answer is (C).

10.   This is an application question; we are asked to apply what we have learned in the passage to a hypothetical situation. A review of the passage shows that only (B) and (E) have any real merit. But sharks have survived for 400 million years with an extremely low fecundity rate. This eliminates (B). Hence the answer is (E).

11.   This is a rather easy tone question. The passage has a matter-of-fact or journalistic tone to it. So the answer is (B).

12.   This is an extension question. Statement I is incorrect. Like Statement II in Question 9, it overstates the case. Statement II is correct. We know from lines 48–50 that some species of sharks migrate into the waters of over 20 countries. U.S. quotas alone cannot "protect" these sharks, even if the quotas reduce the rate of killing in U.S. waters. Statement III is incorrect. The environmentalists are angry at the finning fishermen who are over-fishing the waters, there is nothing in the passage to suggest that this anger is also directed towards the chefs. The answer is (B).

13.   By announcing the impending classification, the federal government ironically encourages fishermen to kill as many sharks as they can before the regulations go into effect—stimulating the opposite of what was intended, i.e., the saving of sharks. The answer is (D).

Questions 14–19

14.   This is a description question. (A) is false. The enjoyment of the reader was incidental to Hemingway's primary purpose—truth-telling. (B) is false, though very tempting. The first half of this item "*to construct a story that would reflect truths*" looks very good. The second half, however, spoils it by adding the qualifier "*not particular to a specific historical period.*" Reviewing the passage reveals no indication that Hemingway is trying to create any kind of "general truth." In fact, one can argue that Hemingway's emphasis on developing a strong "sense of place" (lines 27–30), and his belief that when trying to tell the truth "I only know what I have seen" (line 9)

support the inference that Hemingway sees truth as subjective, not objective. (C) is also false. The passage gives no indication that Hemingway was interested in the way things "might have been." (D) is true. This is clearly the author's interpretation of Hemingway's purpose. Look at the first few sentences of both the first and the second paragraphs. Notice that this question item emphasizes subjective truth, or the truth "as Hemingway had experienced it."

   Strategy: In this question, you have two choices—(B) and (D)—which at first glance seem very close. Let's assume you don't understand exactly why a "close second" is wrong. When confronted with this situation, it's a good idea to take a few seconds and try to get into the *Question-Writer's* mindset. What are you missing that the Question-Writer thinks is an important point in this passage? In this case, the Question-Writer is focusing on the subtle point that Hemingway sees his perspective as "subjective," that certain things, true in some places or to some people, may not be true in other places or to other people. In other words, there is no "objective reality."

   If intuition is the only way to distinguish between the two close choices, then you should mark them in your test booklet as *close*, perhaps like this

(B)
(C) , to show that you had to choose between
(D)

them, and move on. If you have trouble with later questions on the same passage, you may want to go back, analyze the passage, and determine the real difference between the earlier "close pair." The Question-Writer may be testing the same question from a different angle, in which case time is well spent pondering the issue.

15.   This is an extension question. In lines 27–30, Hemingway effectively equates geography with background, and says that without them "you have nothing." In lines 32–34, the author refers to the "geographical groundwork" of Hemingway's novels. Both of these statements imply that details of place set the stage for other, more important events. Hence the answer is (A). Don't try to draw a distinction between "geography," "background," and "landscape." The author uses them interchangeably when referring to details of place. Such latitude with labels is often mimicked by the Question-Writers.

   Choice (D) is a close second-best. The author indicates that geography, background, and landscape are quite important to Hemingway. In fact, "first" in the opening to paragraph 3 almost indicates that details of place are the most important aspect of his writing. Looking closely, however, we see that the passage gives no indication of Hemingway's perspective on characters. So no comparison can be made.

16.   Hemingway's primary intent was to project for the reader "the way it was," as seen through his eyes. The answer is (D).

17.   This is an extension question. Statement I is true. The last line of the passage states that the designer's initials (i.e., the writer's presence) are made as inconspicuous as possible. Statement II is also true. Readers cannot see "the way it was" if they are looking through another medium (the author). Hemingway appears to say, in effect: *"I'm striving to report exactly what happened (and not my opinions about it). The readers must draw their own conclusions."* Statement III is false. In fact, a good case could be made that writing only from personal experience would tend to increase, not decrease, the presence of the writer in his writings. The answer is (C).

18.   This is an application question; we are asked to put ourselves in Hemingway's mind. From Hemingway's statement "I only know what I have seen" and from the author's assertion that Hemingway refused to honor secondary sources, we can infer that he believed one can "know" only through experience. Hence the answer is (A).

19.   This is an extension question. The answer is (B). There is a great parallel here. *Phrase* (in the passage) corresponds to *style* (in the answer-choice), and *concept* corresponds to *content*.

Questions 20–26

20.   This is an extension question. According to the passage, red light would not be significantly deflected and consequently would pass through a relatively direct route from the sun to our eyes. Hence the answer is (C).

21.   This is another extension question. Since the passage is a science selection, we should expect a lot of extension questions. (A): No, if anything, blue light would exert more energy. (B): No. We can not infer this. The collision of blue light with particles in the air is the reason for a blue sky, not for lightning. (C): No. Speed of light is not mentioned in the passage. **(D): Yes.** Blue light has a shorter wavelength, consequently it has more energy than red light.

22.   This is an application question since it introduces new information about water waves and asks us to conclude how the behavior of light waves might be similarly affected. Given this information, however, we can justify no conclusion about whether light waves imitate water waves in this new regard. The analogy might hold or it might break down. We don't yet know. (To find out we would have to do an experiment using light.) The answer is (D).

23.   (A): No. We do not know anything about a "variety" of obstacles; even if we did, we would have no reason to assume that light is constituted of different colors. **(B): Yes.** See lines 22–27. Rainbows occur because light is constituted of many colors. (C): No. This is a distortion of lines 45–47, and it sounds illogical to boot. (D): No. This gives no reason to assume that light is constituted of many colors. (E): No. Water vapor in the atmosphere causes rainbows, not dust.

24.   (A): No. Although dust is mentioned as one of the three important obstacles (lines 17–20), we simply do not have enough information to conclude how dust density would change sky color. (B): No. While this idea may fit with the common lore that a lot of dust in the air creates great, red sunsets, the passage itself gives no basis to any conclusion regarding color change. (C): No. Same reason as in (A) and (B). **(D): Yes.** There is not enough information in the passage to determine a relationship between color change and dust density. The dust may give off a certain color of its own—we can't say for certain.

25.   Statement I is true. There are obviously more particles on a horizontal than a vertical path. The glowing red sky is reasonable evidence for some diffusion. Note that Question 24 asks "what can we *conclude*" while this question asks what seems *plausible* (what "would seem to be explained"). So, while we are attempting to make very similar inferences in both questions, what we can do with the data depends, among other things, on the degree of certainty requested. Statement II is true. The path of evening light probably has a greater average density, since it spends more time passing through a zone of thicker atmosphere. It is reasonable to assume this significantly greater density, or the absolute number of particles, might present an obstacle to blue light. Statement III is false. There are two things wrong with this answer: (1) red light waves are not short, relative to blue; (2) we do not know that waves with more energy will more readily pass through obstacles. The passage, in fact, implies just the opposite. The answer is (C).

26.   (A): No. Water waves offer only a model for light waves. As a model, they are identical in some ways but not in others. (B): No. This is not implied by the passage. What they have in common is the way they act when they impinge on obstacles. (C): No. Waves of water are used as a model because they have much in common with waves of light. **(D): Yes.** See explanation for (A).

27. Choice A is incorrect. Passage 1 argues that exercise does not matter with weight loss. Neither person exercised in this choice. Therefore, it is irrelevant that Person A lost two more pounds than Person B. It does not weaken the author's supposition that exercise does not matter.

Choice C is incorrect because it would not weaken the author's argument. Rather, it would strengthen it since the person who did not exercise lost the most weight.

Choice D is incorrect. Both exercised and neither lost weight. This works to support the author, not to weaken his argument.

Choice E is incorrect. The author argues that you can lose weight just by sitting on the couch. Both Person A and Person B did just that and lost the same amount of weight. This is what the author said would happen; therefore, it does not weaken his argument.

Choice B is the correct answer. In this answer-choice, Person B exercises regularly and is the one who loses weight. This weakens the author's argument that exercise is inconsequential when it comes to weight loss.

28. Choice B is incorrect because fads are not necessarily only adopted by the younger people of a population.

Choice C is incorrect. A fad is not defined by any type of monetary cost.

Choice D is incorrect. In fact, it offers a definition that is completely opposite of what fads actually are.

Choice E is incorrect. Although fads do take awhile to spread their popularity, there is no set amount of time.

Choice A is your answer because fads, by definition, come and go. The author compares diets to fads because new diet ideas come and go.

29. Choice A is incorrect. If anything, the authors believe that Americans diet too often.

Choice B is incorrect. While the author of Passage 1 believes that exercise is irrelevant, the author of Passage 2 believes exercise is imperative to weight loss and healthy living.

Choice C is incorrect. Sweets are mentioned in each passage but neither author infers that Americans eat too much junk food. Passage 1 uses a candy bar as an example of a poor choice for a snack, and Passage 2 states that while junk food consumption should be curbed to some extent, it should not be eliminated. Therefore, neither has a real strong opinion about junk food.

Choice E is incorrect. Passage 2 mentions obesity and indicates that more and more people in the United States are suffering from obesity. However, he does not conclude that, even with the rising rate, there are "too many" who suffer from obesity. The author of

Passage 1 does not even mention obesity. Therefore, this answer-choice is not right.

Choice D is correct. Both passages discuss all of the different ways Americans attempt to diet. Both passages agree that there is a simpler way. The author of Passage 1 states that "all you need is general information." The author of Passage 2 states that what "Americans need to do is go back to the basics." Both authors attempt to offer simplicity in the complicated world of dieting.

30. Choice A is incorrect. The author of Passage 1 suggests that sweet snacks should be replaced with protein snacks. However, he does not say that sweets should be completely cut from a diet. Along the same lines, the author in Passage 2 suggests using sweets sparingly in your diet, but cautions that you must not completely cut them from your diet as going "cold-turkey" can result in failure. Neither author suggests cutting sweets completely from your diet. Therefore, they agree on this topic, and this is not your answer.

Choice B is incorrect. The author of Passage 1 clearly feels that carbohydrate intake should be reduced; however, he seems to recommend a low-carbohydrate diet, not a no-carbohydrate diet. The author of Passage 2 suggests that Americans need to eat the recommended daily allowance of grains, which would include carbohydrates. The two authors do not fully disagree on this topic, so this is not your answer.

Choice C is incorrect. The author in Passage 1 does not mention meat and vegetables; however, for the dieter who cuts back on her carbohydrate intake, it can be assumed that meats and healthier carbohydrates like vegetables would play a larger role in her diet. Passage 2 suggests that Americans eat the recommended daily allowance for meats and vegetables. This is not to say that each person should necessarily increase their intake, but the author seems to assume that many Americans are probably not eating enough since he suggests "getting back" to the basics. In both cases, the authors do not offer a strong opinion, nor do they disagree on this topic.

Choice D is incorrect as the authors do not clearly disagree on this topic. Passage 1 does not even mention fatty foods. The author of Passage 2 suggests consuming fatty foods sparingly but cautions against cutting them completely from a diet. The authors do not clearly disagree on this topic.

Choice E is the correct answer. The author of Passage 1 clearly explains that you do not need to exercise in order to lose weight. This idea is in direct opposition of the author of Passage 2 who views exercise as an integral part of losing weight and living a healthy life.

31. Choice A is incorrect. This option is rather ambiguous and therefore does not work to weaken the argument presented in Passage 1. A mother and daughter could share some of the same personality traits because of nature or nurture. The author talks more of nurture, but it is impossible to determine from this instance which played a larger role in giving the daughter *some* of the same traits as her mother.

Choice B is incorrect as it completely supports the author's view that nurture plays a very large role in personality development. If an adopted child exhibits many of the same personality traits as his adopted parents, these traits were gained through nurture. In order to weaken the author's argument, the adoptee would have to have many of the same traits as his biological parents.

Choice C is incorrect because it supports the author's argument that family members, despite the fact that they carry the same genes, often develop different personalities through nurture.

Choice E is incorrect for the same reason as Choice C.

Choice D is the correct answer. If twins were separated at birth but exhibit the same personality traits, this would indicated that nature, not nurture, played a very large role in the development of their personality. This weakens the author's argument that favors nurture.

32. Choice A is incorrect because *inherently* does not mean "like normal."

Choice B is incorrect and is confusing the word *inherently* with *inheritance*.

Choice D is incorrect because *inherently* does not mean "to an extreme."

Choice E is not correct because it does not properly define *inherently*.

Choice C is correct because the root word of *innately—innate—*refers to something that is "inborn" or naturally within a person. This is a synonym to *inherently*.

33. Choice B is incorrect. Passage 1 discusses both nature and nurture and seems to suggest that nurture plays a larger role in personality development. However, it does not refute the role of nature. Passage 2 seems to suggest that nature plays a larger role; however, it does not refute the role of nurture.

Choice C is incorrect. A generalization is typically a more vague description of a topic than is presented in Passage 1. Both passages give fairly specific examples to support their topics and perspectives.

Choice D is incorrect for the same reason as Choice C.

Choice E is incorrect for the same reason as Choice B.

Choice A is the correct answer. Both passages describe the roles of nature and nurture in the development of personality. Both passages seem to agree that personality does not develop without some input from both nature and nurture.

34. Choice A is clearly not the right answer. *Nature* has something to do with the outdoors, but *nurture* has nothing to do with indoor recreation.

Choice B is incorrect. Genetics and heredity are synonymous in this instance, and *nature* and *nurture* are not.

Choice C is not correct. Personality involves both *nature* and *nurture*. While physical appearance is generally attributed to *nature*, *nurture* can play some role in how a person cares for his physical appearance.

Choice D is incorrect. Introversion and extroversion do not define *nature* and *nurture*.

Choice is correct. When discussing the controversy of *nature* vs. *nurture*, the *nature* side is referring to the role that genes and heredity play in a person's development. *Nurture* refers to a persons upbringing.

CRITICAL REASONING

Argument Analysis

To reason analytically is to break down a thought (passage) into its constituent parts. Then discover how those parts are related to one another and thereby better understand the whole thought (passage).

This process rests on the premise that you are more familiar with (better understand) the parts than the whole thought. For an analogy, we can again use the example, in the chapter *The Three Step Method*, of dismantling an engine to better understand how it works. Once we have separated the starter, generator, radiator, pistons, etc., from the engine, it would be more enlightening if we knew how each of the parts functioned and how they related to one another. This is where premises and conclusions come in. They are the *parts* of an argument. Although the conclusion is often said to follow from the premises, we will study conclusions first, because the first step in analyzing an argument is to identify its conclusion.

Note: In common jargon, an argument means a heated debate between two people. However, as used on the SAT, a passage argument is a formal presentation of facts and opinions in order to support a position.

Conclusions

In most cases, successfully analyzing an argument hinges on determining the conclusion of the argument. The conclusion is the main idea of the argument. It is what the writer is trying to persuade the reader to believe. Most often the conclusion comes at the end of the argument. The writer organizes the facts and his opinions so that they build up to the conclusion. Sometimes, however, the conclusion will come at the beginning of an argument. Rarely does it come in the middle. And occasionally, for rhetorical effect, the conclusion is not even stated.

Example:

The police are the armed guardians of the social order. The blacks are the chief domestic victims of the American social order. <u>A conflict of interest exists, therefore, between the blacks and the police</u>— Eldridge Cleaver, *Soul on Ice*

Here the first two sentences anticipate or setup the conclusion. By changing the grammar slightly, the conclusion can be placed at the beginning of the argument and still sound natural:

<u>A conflict of interest exists between the blacks and the police</u> because the police are the armed guardians of the social order and the blacks are the chief domestic victims of the American social order.

The conclusion can also be forced into the middle:

The police are the armed guardians of the social order. So a <u>conflict of interest exists between the blacks and the police</u> because the blacks are the chief domestic victims of the American social order.

It is generally awkward, as in the pervious paragraph, to place the conclusion in the middle of the argument because then it cannot be fully anticipated by what comes before nor fully explained by what comes after. On the rare occasion when a conclusion comes in the middle of an argument, most often either the material that comes before it or the material that comes after it is not essential.

When determining the meaning of a conclusion, be careful not to read any more into it than what the author states. For example, many people will interpret the sentence

"Every Republican is not a conservative"

to mean that some republicans are not conservative.* SAT passages are typically taken from academic journals, and the writers in those journals do not use grammar (logic) that loosely. On the SAT, the above sentence would mean what it literally states—that no Republican is a conservative.

To illustrate further, consider the meaning of *some* in the sentence "Some of Mary's friends went to the party." It would be unwarranted, based on this statement, to assume that some of Mary's friends did not go to the party. Although it may seem deceiving to say that *some* of Mary's friends went to the party when in fact *all* of them did, it is nonetheless technically consistent with the meaning of *some*.

As mentioned before, the conclusion usually comes at the end of an argument, sometimes at the beginning, but rarely in the middle. Writers use certain words to indicate that the conclusion is about to be stated. Following is a list of the most common conclusion indicators:

CONCLUSION INDICATORS

hence	therefore
so	accordingly
thus	consequently
follows that	shows that
conclude that	implies
as a result	means that

These conclusion flags are very helpful, but you must use them cautiously because many of these words have other functions.

Example:

All devout Muslims abstain from alcohol. Steve is a devout Muslim. <u>Thus</u>, he abstains from alcohol.

In this example, "thus" anticipates the conclusion that necessarily follows from the first two sentences. Notice the different function of *thus* in the following sentence.

Example:

The problem is simple when the solution is <u>thus</u> stated.

In this example, *thus* means "in that manner."

Most often the conclusion of an argument is put in the form of a statement (as in all the examples we have considered so far). Sometimes, however, the conclusion is given as a command or obligation.

Example:

All things considered, you ought to vote.

Here, the author implies that you are obliged to vote.

Example:

Son, unless you go to college, you will not make a success of yourself. No Carnegie has ever been a failure. So you will go to college.

Here the conclusion is given as an imperative command.

---

* To give the sentence that meaning reword it as "Not every republican is a conservative".

The conclusion can even be put in the form of a question. This rhetorical technique is quite effective in convincing people that a certain position is correct. We are more likely to believe something if we feel that we concluded it on our own, or at least if we feel that we were not told to believe it. A conclusion put in question form can have this result.

Example:

The Nanuuts believe that they should not take from nature anything she cannot replenish during their lifetime. This assures that future generations can enjoy the same riches of nature that they have. At the current rate of destruction, the rain forests will disappear during our lifetime. Do we have an obligation to future generations to prevent this result?

Here the author trusts that the power of her argument will persuade the reader to answer the question affirmatively.

Taking this rhetorical technique one step further, the writer may build up to the conclusion but leave it unstated. This allows the reader to make up his own mind. If the build-up is done skillfully, the reader will be more likely to agree with the author and still not feel manipulated.

Example:

He who is without sin should cast the first stone. There is no one here who does not have a skeleton in his closet.

The unstated but obvious conclusion here is that none of the people has the right to cast the first stone.

When determining the conclusion's scope be careful not to read any more or less into it than the author states. SAT writers often create wrong answer-choices by slightly overstating or understating the author's claim. Certain words limit the scope of a statement. These words are called quantifiers—pay close attention to them. Following is a list of the most important quantifiers:

Quantifiers

all	**except**	**likely**
some	**most**	**many**
only	**could**	**no**
never	**always**	**everywhere**
probably	**must**	**alone**

Example: *(Short-passage)*

Whether the world is Euclidean or non-Euclidean is still an open question. However, if a star's position is predicted based on non-Euclidean geometry, then when a telescope is pointed to where the star should be it will be there. Whereas, if the star's position is predicted based on Euclidean geometry, then when a telescope is pointed to where the star should be it won't be there. This strongly indicates that the world is non-Euclidean.

Which one of the following best expresses the main idea of the passage?

(A)   The world may or may not be Euclidean.
(B)   The world is probably non-Euclidean.
(C)   The world is non-Euclidean.
(D)   The world is Euclidean.
(E)   The world is neither Euclidean nor non-Euclidean.

Choice (A) understates the main idea. Although the opening to the passage states that we don't know whether the world is non-Euclidean, the author goes on to give evidence that it is non-Euclidean. Choice (C) overstates the main idea. The author doesn't say that the world is non-Euclidean, just that evidence strongly indicates that it is. In choice (B), the word "probably" properly limits the scope of the main idea, namely, that the world is probably non-Euclidean, but we can't yet state so definitively. The answer is (B).

Warm-Up Drill I

Directions: Find, then underline, the conclusion to each of the following arguments. If an argument does not state the conclusion, complete it with the most natural conclusion. Answers and solutions begin on page 89.

1. When a man is tired of London, he is tired of life; for there is in London all that life can afford.— Samuel Johnson

2. Some psychiatrists claim that watching violent movies dissipates aggression. Does watching pornography dissipate one's libido?

3. By the age of 10 months, purebred golden retrievers display certain instinctive behaviors. Because this 11-month-old golden retriever does not display these instinctive behaviors, it is not a purebred.

4. Most people would agree that it is immoral to lie. But if a kidnaper accosts you on the street and asks which way his escaped victim went, would it be immoral to point in the opposite direction?

5. Beware, for I am fearless, and therefore, powerful.—Mary Shelley, *Frankenstein*

6. The continuous stream of violent death depicted on television has so jaded society that murder is no longer shocking. It's hardly surprising, then, that violent crime so permeates modern society.

7. Where all other circumstances are equal, wages are generally higher in new than in old trades. When a projector attempts to establish a new manufacture, he must at first entice his workmen from other employments by higher wages than they can either earn in their old trades, or than the nature of his work would otherwise require, and a considerable time must pass away before he can venture to reduce them to the common level.—Adam Smith, *The Wealth of Nations*

8. Existentialists believe that our identity is continually evolving, that we are born into this world without an identity and do not begin to develop one until the act of retrospection. So one's identity is always trailing oneself like the wake of a boat. As one goes through life, the wake becomes wider and wider defining him more and more precisely.

9. In time I began to recognize that all of these smaller complaints about rigidity, emotional suffocation, the tortured logic of the law were part of a more fundamental phenomenon in the law itself. Law is at war with ambiguity, with uncertainty. In the courtroom, the adversary system—plaintiff against defendant—guarantees that someone will always win, someone loses. No matter if justice is evenly with each side, no matter if the issues are indefinite and obscure, the rule of law will be declared.— Scott Turow, *One L*

10. Either God controls all of man's behavior or God does not control any of man's behavior. God must not control man's behavior since there is so much evil in the world.

11. The more deeply I understand the central role of caring in my own life, the more I realize it to be central to the human condition.—Milton Mayeroff, *On Caring*

Premises

Once you've found the conclusion, most often everything else in the argument will be either premises or "noise." The premises provide evidence for the conclusion; they form the foundation or infrastructure upon which the conclusion depends. To determine whether a statement is a premise, ask yourself whether it supports the conclusion. If so, it's a premise. Earlier we saw that writers use certain words to flag conclusions; likewise writers use certain words to flag premises. Following is a partial list of the most common premise indicators:

PREMISE INDICATORS

because	**for**
since	**is evidence that**
if	**in that**
as	**owing to**
suppose	**inasmuch as**
assume	**may be derived from**

Premise indicators are very helpful. As with conclusion indicators, though, you must use them cautiously because they have other functions. For example, *since* can indicate a premise, or it can merely indicate time.

Example:

Since the incumbent's views are out of step with public opinion, he probably will not be reelected.

Here "since" is used to flag the premise that the incumbent's positions are unpopular. Contrast this use of "since" with the following example.

Example:

Since the incumbent was elected to office, he has spent less and less time with his family.

In this case, "since" merely expresses a temporal relationship. The statement as a whole expresses an observation, rather than an argument.

SUPPRESSED PREMISES

Most arguments depend on one or more unstated premises. Sometimes this indicates a weakness in the argument, an oversight by the writer. More often, however, certain premises are left tacit because they are too numerous, or the writer assumes that his audience is aware of the assumptions, or he wants the audience to fill in the premise themselves and therefore be more likely to believe the conclusion.

Example:
Conclusion: I knew he did it.
Premise: Only a guilty person would accept immunity from prosecution.

The suppressed premise is that he did, in fact, accept immunity. The speaker assumes that his audience is aware of this fact or at least is willing to believe it, so to state it would be redundant and ponderous. If the unstated premise were false (that is, he did not accept immunity), the argument would not technically be a lie; but it would be very deceptive. The unscrupulous writer may use this ploy if he thinks that he can get away with it. That is, his argument has the intended effect and the false premise, though implicit, is hard to find or ambiguous. Politicians are not at all above using this tactic.

Example:

Politician: A hawk should not be elected president because this country has seen too many wars.

The argument has two tacit premises—one obvious, the other subtle. Clearly, the politician has labeled his opponent a hawk, and he hopes the audience will accept that label. Furthermore, although he does not state it explicitly, the argument rests on the assumption that a hawk is likely to start a war. He hopes the audience will fill in that premise, thereby tainting his opponent as a war monger.

A common SAT question asks you to find the suppressed premise of a passage. Finding the suppressed premise—or assumption—of an argument can be difficult. However, on the SAT you have an advantage—the suppressed premise is listed as one of the five answer-choices. To test whether an answer-choice is a suppressed premise, ask yourself whether it would make the argument more plausible If so, then it is very likely a suppressed premise.

Example: *(Short-passage)*

American attitudes tend to be rather insular, but there is much we can learn from other countries. In Japan, for example, workers set aside some time each day to exercise. And many of the corporations provide elaborate exercise facilities for their employees. Few American corporations have such exercise programs. Studies have shown that the Japanese worker is more productive and healthier than the American worker. It must be concluded that the productivity of American workers will lag behind their Japanese counterparts, until mandatory exercise programs are introduced.

The argument presented in the passage depends on the assumption that:

(A)   even if exercise programs do not increase productivity, they will improve the American worker's health.
(B)   the productivity of all workers can be increased by exercise.
(C)   exercise is an essential factor in the Japanese worker's superior productivity.
(D)   American workers can adapt to the longer Japanese workweek.

The unstated essence of the argument is that exercise is an integral part of productivity and that Japanese workers are more productive than American workers because they exercise more. The answer is (C).

Example: *(Short-passage)*

Kirkland's theory of corporate structure can be represented by a truncated pyramid. There are workers, middle management, and executive management, but no head of the corporation. Instead, all major decisions are made by committee. As a consequence, in Kirkland's structure, risky, cutting-edge technologies cannot be developed.

Implicit in the passage is the assumption that:

(A)   Cutting-edge technologies are typically developed by entrepreneurs, not by big corporations.
(B)   Only single individuals make risky decisions.
(C)   An individual is more likely to take a gamble on his own than in a group.
(D)   All heads of corporations reached their positions by taking risks.

The link that allows the conclusion to be drawn is the assumption that <u>only</u> individuals make risky decisions. The answer is (B).

Both (A) and (C) are close second-best choices. Both are supported by the passage, but each understates the scope of the suppressed premise. The argument states that in Kirkland's model of corporate structure cutting edge-technologies <u>cannot</u> be developed, not that they are less likely to be developed.

Another common passage-question asks you to either strengthen or weaken an argument. Typically, to answer such questions, you need to show that a suppressed premised is true or that it is false.

Example: *(Short-passage)*

The petrochemical industry claims that chemical waste dumps pose no threat to people living near them. If this is true, then why do they locate the plants in sparsely populated regions. By not locating the chemical dumps in densely populated areas the petrochemical industry tacitly admits that these chemicals are potentially dangerous to the people living nearby.

Which of the following, if true, would most weaken the author's argument?

(A)   Funding through the environmental Super Fund to clean up poorly run waste dumps is reserved for rural areas only.
(B)   Until chemical dumps are proven 100% safe, it would be imprudent to locate them were they could potentially do the most harm.

(C)   Locating the dumps in sparsely populated areas is less expensive and involves less government red tape.

(D)   The potential for chemicals to leach into the water table has in the past been underestimated.

The suppressed, *false* premise of the argument is that all things being equal there is no reason to prefer locating the sites in sparsely populated areas. To weaken the argument, we need to show it is <u>not</u> true that all things are equal. In other words, there are advantages other than safety in locating the sites in sparsely populated areas. Choice (C) gives two possible advantages—cost and ease. Hence (C) is the answer.

Warm-Up Drill II

Directions: For each of the following arguments, identify the suppressed premise and state whether it is a reasonable assumption for the author to make. Answers and solutions are on page 90.

1.   Sacramento is the capital of California; thus it is located northeast of San Francisco.

2.   I read it in a book, so it must be true.

3.   Any government action that intrudes on the right of privacy is unconstitutional. Therefore, requiring government employees to take a drug test is unconstitutional.

4.   After studying assiduously for three months, Sean retook the SAT and increased his score by more than four hundred points. Therefore, the Educational Testing Service canceled his score.

5.   When explorers arrived in the Americas in the 1500s A.D., they observed the natives hunting with bronze tipped arrows. Archaeological evidence shows that bronze was not smelted in the Americas until the 1200s A.D. Therefore, native Americans must have begun hunting with arrows sometime between 1200 and 1500 A.D.

6.   Fiction is truer than history, because it goes beyond the evidence.—E. M. Forster

7.   In Knox's theory of military strategy, all decisions about troop deployment must be made by a committee of generals. If, however, his model of command were in effect during World War II, then daring and successful operations—such as Patton's unilateral decision to land paratroopers behind enemy lines during the Battle of the Bulge—would not have been ordered.

8.   In recent years many talented and dedicated teachers have left the public school system for the private sector because the public school system's salary scale is not sufficient for a family to maintain a quality standard of living. To lure these dedicated teachers back to the public schools, we must immediately raise the pay scale to a level comparable to that of the private sector, and thereby save our schools.

Solutions to Warm-Up Drills

Drill I

1.   <u>When a man is tired of London, he is tired of life</u>; for there is in London all that life can afford.—Samuel Johnson

2.   The conclusion is not stated, but the arguer implies that watching violent movies does *not* dissipate aggression.

3.   By the age of 10 months, purebred golden retrievers display certain instinctive behaviors. Because this 11 month-old golden retriever does not display these instinctive behaviors, <u>it is not a purebred.</u>

4.   No conclusion is stated. But the author implies that to lie is not always immoral.

5.   Beware, for I am fearless, and therefore, <u>powerful</u>.—Mary Shelley, *Frankenstein*

6.   The implied conclusion is that violence depicted on television contributes to society's high rate of violence.

7.   Where all other circumstances are equal, <u>wages are generally higher in new than in old trades</u>. When a projector attempts to establish a new manufacture, he must at first entice his workmen from other employments by higher wages than they can either earn in their old trades, or than the nature of his work would otherwise require, and a considerable time must pass away before he can venture to reduce them to the common level.—Adam Smith, *The Wealth of Nations*

8.   Existentialists believe that our identity is continually evolving, that we are born into this world without an identity and do not begin to develop one until the act of retrospection. So <u>one's identity is always trailing oneself</u> like the wake of a boat. As one goes through life, the wake becomes wider and wider defining him more and more precisely.

9.   In time I began to recognize that all of these smaller complaints about rigidity, emotional suffocation, the tortured logic of the law were part of a more fundamental phenomenon in the law itself. <u>Law is at war with ambiguity, with uncertainty</u>. In the courtroom, the adversary system—plaintiff against defendant—guarantees that someone will always win, someone loses. No matter if justice is evenly with each side, no matter if the issues are indefinite and obscure, the rule of law will be declared.— Scott Turow, *One L*

10.   Either God controls all of man's behavior or God does not control any of man's behavior. <u>God must not control man's behavior</u> since there is so much evil in the world.

11.   The more deeply I understand the central role of caring in my own life, the more I realize <u>it to be central to the human condition</u>.—Milton Mayeroff, *On Caring*

Drill II

1.   The suppressed premise is that the capital of California is located northeast of San Francisco. This is a reasonable assumption because it is true!

2.   The suppressed premise is that only the truth is published. Clearly this is not a reasonable assumption.

3.   The suppressed premise is that being forced to take a drug test is an invasion of privacy. This is a reasonable assumption.

4.   ETS's suppressed premise is that extremely high score improvements indicate cheating. This is arguably a reasonable assumption, but it is not consistent with the tradition of assuming one innocent until proven otherwise. (By the way, this is a true story. Sean sued ETS and the courts ordered them to release his score.)

5.   The suppressed premise is that hunting with arrows did not begin until the arrows were tipped with bronze. This seems to be a questionable assumption.

6.   The suppressed premise is that what goes beyond the evidence is truer that what does not. This is a questionable assumption; arguably just the opposite is the case.

7.   The suppressed premise is that only decisions made by a single individual can be daring. This assumption has some truth to it, but it's a bit extreme.

8.   The suppressed premise is that comparable pay would be sufficient to entice the teachers to change their careers again. This is probably a reasonable assumption since the teachers were described as dedicated.

Inductive Arguments

In this chapter we will classify and study the major types of inductive arguments.

An argument is deductive if its conclusion *necessarily* follows from its premises—otherwise it is inductive. In an inductive argument, the author presents the premises as evidence or reasons for the conclusion. The validity of the conclusion depends on how compelling the premises are. Unlike deductive arguments, the conclusion of an inductive argument is never certain. The *truth* of the conclusion can range from highly likely to highly unlikely. In reasonable arguments, the conclusion is likely. In fallacious arguments, it is improbable. We will study both reasonable and fallacious arguments.

First, we will classify the three major types of inductive reasoning—generalization, analogy, and causal—and their associated fallacies. Next, we will study common fallacies.

Generalization

Generalization and analogy, which we consider in the next section, are the main tools by which we accumulate knowledge and analyze our world. Many people define *generalization* as "inductive reasoning." In colloquial speech, the phrase "to generalize" carries a negative connotation. To argue by generalization, however, is neither inherently good nor bad. The relative validity of a generalization depends on both the context of the argument and the likelihood that its conclusion is true. Polling organizations make predictions by generalizing information from a small sample of the population, which hopefully represents the general population. The soundness of their predictions (arguments) depends on how representative the sample is and on its size. Clearly, the less comprehensive a conclusion is the more likely it is to be true.

Example:

During the late seventies when Japan was rapidly expanding its share of the American auto market, GM surveyed owners of GM cars and asked them whether they would be more willing to buy a large, powerful car or a small, economical car. Seventy percent of those who responded said that they would prefer a large car. On the basis of this survey, GM decided to continue building large cars. Yet during the '80s, GM lost even more of the market to the Japanese.

Which one of the following, if it were determined to be true, would best explain this discrepancy.

(A) Only 10 percent of those who were polled replied.
(B) Ford which conducted a similar survey with similar results continued to build large cars and also lost more of their market to the Japanese.
(C) The surveyed owners who preferred big cars also preferred big homes.
(D) GM determined that it would be more profitable to make big cars.
(E) Eighty percent of the owners who wanted big cars and only 40 percent of the owners who wanted small cars replied to the survey.

The argument generalizes *from* the survey *to* the general car-buying population, so the reliability of the projection depends on how representative the sample is. At first glance, choice (A) seems rather good, because 10 percent does not seem large enough. However, political opinion polls are typically based on only .001 percent of the population. More importantly, we don't know what percentage of GM car owners received the survey. Choice (B) simply states that Ford made the same mistake that GM did. Choice (C) is irrelevant. Choice (D), rather than explaining the discrepancy, gives even more reason for GM to continue making large cars. Finally, choice (E) points out that part of the survey did not represent the entire public, so (E) is the answer.

Analogy

To argue by analogy is to claim that because two things are similar in some respects, they will be similar in others. Medical experimentation on animals is predicated on such reasoning. The argument goes like this: the metabolism of pigs, for example, is similar to that of humans, and high doses of saccharine cause cancer in pigs. Therefore, high doses of saccharine probably cause cancer in humans.

Clearly, the greater the similarity between the two things being compared the stronger the argument will be. Also the less ambitious the conclusion the stronger the argument will be. The argument above would be strengthened by changing "probably" to "may." It can be weakened by pointing out the dissimilarities between pigs and people.

The following words usually indicate that an analogy is being drawn:

ANALOGY INDICATORS

like	**likewise**
similar	**also**
too	**compared to**
as with	**just as ... so too ...**

Often, however, a writer will use an analogy without flagging it with any of the above words.

Example:

Just as the fishing line becomes too taut, so too the trials and tribulations of life in the city can become so stressful that one's mind can snap.

Which one of the following most closely parallels the reasoning used in the argument above?

(A)   Just as the bow may be drawn too taut, so too may one's life be wasted pursuing self-gratification.

(B)   Just as a gambler's fortunes change unpredictably, so too do one's career opportunities come unexpectedly.

(C)   Just as a plant can be killed by over watering it, so too can drinking too much water lead to lethargy.

(D)   Just as the engine may race too quickly, so too may life in the fast lane lead to an early death.

(E)   Just as an actor may become stressed before a performance, so too may dwelling on the negative cause depression.

The argument compares the tautness in a fishing line to the stress of city life; it then concludes that the mind can snap just as the fishing line can. So we are looking for an answer-choice that compares two things and draws a conclusion based on their similarity. Notice that we are looking for an argument that uses similar reasoning, but not necessarily similar concepts.

As to choice (A), the analogy between a taut bow and self-gratification is weak, if existent. Choice (B) offers a good analogy but no conclusion. Choice (C) offers both a good analogy and a conclusion; however, the conclusion, "leads to lethargy," understates the scope of what the analogy implies. Choice (D) offers a strong analogy and a conclusion with the same scope found in the original: "the engine blows, the person dies"; "the line snaps, the mind snaps." The answer is (D).

Causal Reasoning

Of the three types of inductive reasoning we will discuss, causal reasoning is both the weakest and the most prone to fallacy. Nevertheless, it is a useful and common method of thought.

To argue by causation is to claim that one thing causes another. A causal argument can be either weak or strong depending on the context. For example, to claim that you won the lottery because you saw a shooting star the night before is clearly fallacious. However, most people believe that smoking causes cancer because cancer often strikes those with a history of cigarette use. Although the connection between smoking and cancer is virtually certain, as with all inductive arguments it can never be 100 percent certain. Cigarette companies have claimed that there may be a genetic predisposition in some people to both develop cancer and crave nicotine. Although this claim is highly improbable, it is conceivable.

There are two common fallacies associated with causal reasoning:

1.   **Confusing <u>Correlation</u> with <u>Causation</u>.**

   To claim that A caused B merely because A occurred immediately before B is clearly questionable. It may be only coincidental that they occurred together, or something else may have caused them to occur together. For example, the fact that insomnia and lack of appetite often occur together does not mean that one necessarily causes the other. They may both be symptoms of an underlying condition.

2.   **Confusing Necessary Conditions with Sufficient Conditions.**

   A is necessary for B means "B cannot occur without A." *A is sufficient for B* means "A causes B to occur, but B can still occur without A." For example, a small tax base is sufficient to cause a budget deficit, but excessive spending can cause a deficit even with a large tax base. A common fallacy is to assume that a necessary condition is sufficient to cause a situation. For example, to win a modern war it is necessary to have modern, high-tech equipment, but it is not sufficient, as Iraq discovered in the Persian Gulf War.

Common Fallacies

Contradiction

Contradiction is the most glaring type of fallacy. It is committed when two opposing statements are simultaneously asserted. For example, saying "it is raining *and* it is not raining" is a contradiction. If all contradictions were this basic, there would not be much need to study them. Typically, however, the arguer obscures the contradiction to the point that the argument can be quite compelling. Take, for instance, the following argument:

   "We cannot know anything, because we intuitively realize that our thoughts are unreliable."

This argument has an air of reasonableness to it. But "intuitively realize" means "to know." Thus the arguer is in essence saying that we *know* that we don't know anything. This is self-contradictory.

Example:
In the game of basketball, scoring a three-point shot is a skill that only those with a soft shooting touch can develop. Wilt Chamberlain, however, was a great player, so even though he did not have a soft shooting touch he would have excelled at scoring three point shots.

Which one of the following contains a flaw that most closely parallels the flaw contained in the passage?
(A)   Eighty percent of the freshmen at Berkeley go on to get a bachelor's degree. David is a freshman at Berkeley, so he will probably complete his studies and receive a bachelor's degree.
(B)   If the police don't act immediately to quell the disturbance, it will escalate into a riot. However, since the police are understaffed, there will be a riot.
(C)   The meek shall inherit the earth. Susie received an inheritance from her grandfather, so she must be meek.
(D)   During the Vietnam War, the powerful had to serve along with the poor. However, Stevens' father was a federal judge, so Stevens was able to get a draft deferment.
(E)   All dolphins are mammals and all mammals breathe air. Therefore, all mammals that breathe air are dolphins.

The argument clearly contradicts itself. So look for an answer-choice that contradicts itself in like manner. Choice (A) is not self-contradictory. In fact, it's a fairly sound argument—eliminate it. Choice (B), on the other hand, is not a very sound argument. The police, though understaffed, may realize the seriousness of the situation and rearrange their priorities. Nevertheless, (B) does not contain a contradiction—eliminate it. Choice (C), though questionable, does not contain a contradiction—eliminate it. Choice (D), however, does contain a contradiction. It begins by stating that both the powerful and the poor had to serve in Vietnam and ends by stating that some powerful people—namely, Stevens—did not have to serve. This is a contradiction, so (D) is probably the answer. Choice (E), like the original argument, is invalid but does not contain a contradiction—eliminate it. The answer is (D).

Equivocation

Equivocation is the use of a word in more than one sense during an argument. It is often done intentionally.

Example:

Individual rights must be championed by the government. It is right for one to believe in God.
So government should promote the belief in God.

In this argument, *right* is used ambiguously. In the phrase "individual rights" it is used in the sense of a privilege, whereas in the second sentence *right* is used to mean correct or moral. The questionable conclusion is possible only if the arguer is allowed to play with the meaning of the critical word *right*.

Example:

Judy: Traditionally, Republican administrations have supported free trade. But the President must veto the North American Free Trade Act because it will drain away American jobs to Mexico and lead to wholesale exploitation of the Mexican workers by international conglomerates.

Tina: I disagree. Exploitation of workers is the essence of any economic system just like the exploitation of natural resources.

Judy and Tina will not be able to settle their argument unless they

(A)   explain their opinions in more detail
(B)   ask an expert on international trade to decide who is correct
(C)   decide whose conclusion is true but irrelevant
(D)   decide whose conclusion is based on a questionable premise
(E)   define a critical word

Clearly, Judy and Tina are working with different definitions of the word *exploitation*. Judy is using the meaning that most people attribute to exploitation—abuse. We can't tell the exact meaning Tina intends, but for her exploitation must have a positive, or at least neutral, connotation, otherwise she would be unlikely to defend it as essential. Their argument will be fruitless until they agree on a definition for *exploitation*. Hence the answer is (E).

Circular Reasoning

Circular reasoning involves assuming as a premise that which you are trying to prove. Intuitively, it may seem that no one would fall for such an argument. However, the conclusion may appear to state something additional, or the argument may be so long that the reader may forget that the conclusion was stated as a premise.

Example:

The death penalty is appropriate for traitors because it is right to execute those who betray their own country and thereby risk the lives of millions.

This argument is circular because "right" means essentially the same thing as "appropriate." In effect, the writer is saying that the death penalty is appropriate because it is appropriate.

Example:

Democracy is the best form of government yet created. Therefore, we must be vigilant in its defense; that is, we must be prepared to defend the right to freedom. Because this right is fundamental to any progressive form of government, it is clear that democracy is better than any other form of government.

Which one of the following illustrates the same flawed reasoning as found in the passage?

(A)   I never get a headache when I eat only Chinese food, nor when I drink only wine. But when I eat Chinese food and drink wine, I get a headache. So the combination of the two must be the cause of my headaches.

(B)   The two times I have gone to that restaurant something bad has happened. The first time the waiter dropped a glass and it shattered all over the table. And after the second time I went there, I got sick. So why should I go there again—something bad will just happen again.

(C)   I would much rather live a life dedicated to helping my fellow man than one dedicated to gaining material possessions and seeing my fellow man as a competitor. At the end of each day, the satisfaction of having helped people is infinitely greater than the satisfaction of having achieved something material.

(D)   I'm obsessed with volleyball; that's why I play it constantly. I train seven days a week, and I enter every tournament. Since I'm always playing it, I must be obsessed with it.

(E)   In my academic studies, I have repeatedly changed majors. I decide to major in each new subject that I'm introduced to. Just as a bee lights from one flower to the next, tasting the nectar of each, I jump from one subject to the next getting just a taste of each.

The argument in the passage is circular (and filled with non-sequiturs). It is incumbent on the writer to give evidence or support for the conclusion. In this argument, though, the writer first states that democracy is the best government, the rest is merely "noise," until he restates the conclusion.

Choice (A) is a reasonably valid causation argument—eliminate. (B) argues by generalization. Although it is of questionable validity, it is not circular because the conclusion, "it will happen again," is not stated, nor is it implicit in the premises—eliminate. (C) is not circular because the conclusion is mentioned only once—eliminate. (D) begins by stating, "I'm obsessed with volleyball." It does not, however, provide compelling evidence for that claim: training seven days a week, rather than indicating obsession, may be required for, say, members of the Olympic Volleyball Team. Furthermore, the argument repeats the conclusion at the end. So it is circular in the same manner as the original. Hence (D) is our answer.

Shifting the Burden of Proof

As mentioned before, it is incumbent upon the writer to provide evidence or support for her position. To imply that a position is true merely because no one has disproved it is to shift the burden of proof to others.

Example:

Since no one has been able to prove God's existence, there must not be a God.

There are two major weaknesses in this argument. First, the fact that God's existence has yet to be proven does not preclude any future proof of existence. Second, if there is a God, one would expect that his existence is independent of any proof by man.

Reasoning by shifting the burden of proof is not always fallacious. In fact, our legal system is predicated on this method of thought. The defendant is *assumed* innocent until proven guilty. This assumption shifts the onus of proof to the state. Science can also validly use this method of thought to better understand the world—so long as it is not used to claim "truth." Consider the following argument: "The multitude of theories about our world have failed to codify and predict its behavior as well as Einstein's theory of relativity. Therefore, our world is probably Einsteinian." This argument is strong so long as it is qualified with "probably"—otherwise it is fallacious: someone may yet create a better theory of our world.

Example:

Astronomers have created a mathematical model for determining whether life exists outside our solar system. It is based on the assumption that life as we know it can exist only on a planet such as our own, and that our sun, which has nine planets circling it, is the kind of star commonly found throughout the universe. Hence it is projected that there are billions of planets with conditions similar to our own. So astronomers have concluded that it is highly probable, if not virtually certain, that life exists outside our solar system. Yet there has never been detected so much as one planet beyond our solar system. Hence life exists only on planet Earth.

Which one of the following would most weaken the above argument?

(A)   Thousands of responsible people, people with reputations in the community to protect, have claimed to have seen UFOs. Statistically, it is virtually impossible for this many people to be mistaken or to be lying.

(B)   Recently it has been discovered that Mars has water, and its equatorial region has temperatures in the same range as that of northern Europe. So there may be life on Mars.

(C)   Only one percent of the stars in the universe are like our sun.

(D)   The technology needed to detect planets outside our solar system has not yet been developed.

(E)   Even if all the elements for life as we know it are present, the probability that life would spontaneously generate is infinitesimal.

This argument implies that since no planet has been discovered outside our solar system, none exist and therefore no life exists elsewhere in the universe. Hence the burden of proof is shifted from the arguer to the astronomers.

Although choice (A) weakens the argument, it has a flaw: the UFOs may not be life forms. Choice (B) is irrelevant. Although the argument states that the only life in the universe is on Earth, it is essentially about the possibility of life beyond our solar system. Choice (C) also weakens the argument. However, one percent of billions is still a significant number, and it is not clear whether one percent should be considered "common." Now, the underlying premise of the argument is that since no other planets have been detected, no others exist. Choice (D) attacks this premise directly by stating that no planets outside our solar system have been discovered because we don't yet have the ability to detect them. This is probably the best answer, but we must check all the choices. Choice (E) strengthens the argument by implying that even if there were other planets it would be extremely unlikely that they would contain life. The answer, therefore, is (D).

Unwarranted Assumptions

The *fallacy of unwarranted assumption* is committed when the conclusion of an argument is based on a premise (implicit or explicit) that is false or unwarranted. An assumption is unwarranted when it is false— these premises are usually suppressed or vaguely written. An assumption is also unwarranted when it is true but does not apply in the given context—these premises are usually explicit. The varieties of unwarranted assumptions are too numerous to classify, but a few examples should give you the basic idea.

Example: *(False Dichotomy)*

Either restrictions must be placed on freedom of speech or certain subversive elements in society will use it to destroy this country. Since to allow the latter to occur is unconscionable, we must restrict freedom of speech.

The conclusion above is unsound because

(A)   subversives do not in fact want to destroy the country
(B)   the author places too much importance on the freedom of speech
(C)   the author fails to consider an accommodation between the two alternatives
(D)   the meaning of "freedom of speech" has not been defined
(E)   subversives are a true threat to our way of life

The arguer offers two options: either restrict freedom of speech, or lose the country. He hopes the reader will assume that these are the only options available. This is unwarranted. He does not state how the so-called "subversive elements" would destroy the country, nor for that matter why they would want to destroy it. There may be a third option that the author did not mention; namely, that society may be able to tolerate the "subversives"; it may even be improved by the diversity of opinion they offer. The answer is (C).

Example: *(False Dichotomy)*

When workers do not find their assignments challenging, they become bored and so achieve less than their abilities would allow. On the other hand, when workers find their assignments too difficult, they give up and so again achieve less than what they are capable of achieving. It is, therefore, clear that no worker's full potential will ever be realized.

Which one of the following is an error of reasoning contained in the argument?

(A)   mistakenly equating what is actual and what is merely possible
(B)   assuming without warrant that a situation allows only two possibilities
(C)   relying on subjective rather than objective evidence
(D)   confusing the coincidence of two events with a causal relation between the two
(E)   depending on the ambiguous use of a key term

This argument commits the fallacy of false dichotomy. It assumes that workers have only two reactions to their work—either it's not challenging or it's too challenging. Clearly, there is a wide range of reactions between those two extremes. The answer is (B).

Example:
To score in the ninetieth percentile on the SAT, one must study hard. If one studies four hours a day for one month, she will score in the ninetieth percentile. Hence, if a person scored in the top ten percent on the SAT, then she must have studied at least four hours a day for one month.
Which one of the following most accurately describes the weakness in the above argument?
(A)   The argument fails to take into account that not all test-prep books recommend studying four hours a day for one month.
(B)   The argument does not consider that excessive studying can be counterproductive.
(C)   The argument does not consider that some people may be able to score in the ninetieth percentile though they studied less than four hours a day for one month.
(D)   The argument fails to distinguish between how much people should study and how much they can study.
(E)   The author fails to realize that the ninetieth percentile and the top ten percent do not mean the same thing.

You may have noticed that this argument uses the converse of the fallacy *"Confusing Necessary Conditions with Sufficient Conditions"* mentioned earlier. In other words, it assumes that something which is sufficient is also necessary. In the given argument, this is fallacious because some people may still score in the ninetieth percentile, though they studied less than four hours a day for one month. Therefore the answer is (C).

Example:
Of course Steve supports government sponsorship of the arts. He's an artist.
Which one of the following uses reasoning that is most similar to the above argument?
(A)   Of course if a person lies to me, I will never trust that person again.
(B)   Conservatives in the past have prevented ratification of any nuclear arms limitation treaties with the Soviet Union (or Russia), so they will prevent the ratification of the current treaty.
(C)   Mr. Sullivan is the police commissioner, so it stands to reason that he would support the NRA's position on gun control.
(D)   Following her conscience, Congresswoman Martinez voted against the death penalty, in spite of the fact that she knew it would doom her chances for reelection.
(E)   You're in no position to criticize me for avoiding paying my fair share of taxes. You don't even pay your employees a fair wage.

This argument is fallacious—and unfair—because it assumes that all artists support government sponsorship of the arts. Some artists, however, may have reasons for not supporting government sponsorship of the arts. For example, they may believe that government involvement stifles artistic expression. Or they may reject government involvement on purely philosophical grounds. The argument suggests a person's profession taints his opinion. Choice (C) does the same thing, so it is the answer.

True But Irrelevant

This tactic is quite simple: the arguer bases a conclusion on information that is true but not germane to the issue.

Example:
This pain relief product can be bought over the counter or in a stronger form with a prescription. But according to this pamphlet, for the prescription strength product to be effective it must be taken at the immediate onset of pain, it must be taken every four hours thereafter, and it cannot be taken with any dairy products. So it actually doesn't matter whether you use the prescription strength or the over-the-counter strength product.
Which one of the following best identifies the flaw in the above argument?
(A)   The fact that many people could not live a full life without the prescription strength product cannot be ignored.
(B)   It cannot be concluded that just because the prescription strength product has certain guidelines and restrictions on its use that it is not more effective.
(C)   It does not consider that complications may arise from the prescription strength product.
(D)   It fails to consider that other products may be more effective in relieving pain.
(E)   It is unreasonable to assume that the over-the-counter strength product does not have similar restrictions and guidelines for its use.

It is unreasonable to reject the effectiveness of a product merely because it has modest requirements for use. All medications have directions and restrictions. Hence the answer is (B). Don't make the mistake of choosing (A). Although it is a good rebuttal, it does not address the flaw in the argument. Interestingly, it too is true but irrelevant.

Appeal to Authority

To appeal to authority is to cite an expert's opinion as support for one's own opinion. This method of thought is not necessarily fallacious. Clearly, the reasonableness of the argument depends on the "expertise" of the person being cited and whether he or she is an expert in a field relevant to the argument. Appealing to a doctor's authority on a medical issue, for example, would be reasonable; but if the issue is about dermatology and the doctor is an orthopedist, then the argument would be questionable.

Example:

The legalization of drugs is advocated by no less respectable people than William F. Buckley and federal judge Edmund J. Reinholt. These people would not propose a social policy that is likely to be harmful. So there is little risk in experimenting with a one-year legalization of drugs.

In presenting her position the author does which one of the following?

(A)   Argues from the specific to the general.
(B)   Attacks the motives of her opponents.
(C)   Uses the positions of noted social commentators to support her position.
(D)   Argues in a circular manner.
(E)   Claims that her position is correct because others cannot disprove it.

The only evidence that the author gives to support her position is that respected people agree with her. She is appealing to the authority of others. Thus, the answer is (C).

Personal Attack

In a personal attack (ad hominem), a person's character is challenged instead of her opinions.

Example:

Politician: How can we trust my opponent to be true to the voters? He isn't true to his wife!

This argument is weak because it attacks the opponent's character, not his positions. Some people may consider fidelity a prerequisite for public office. History, however, shows no correlation between fidelity and great political leadership.

Example:

A reporter responded with the following to the charge that he resorted to tabloid journalism when he rummaged through and reported on the contents of garbage taken from the home of Henry Kissinger.

"Of all the printed commentary . . . only a few editorial writers thought to express the obvious point that when it comes to invasion of privacy, the man who as National Security Advisor helped to bug the home phones of his own staff members is one of our nation's leading practitioners."—Washington Monthly, October 1975

In defending his actions, the reporter does which one of the following?

(A)   Attacks the character of Henry Kissinger.
(B)   Claims Henry Kissinger caused the reporter to act as he did.
(C)   Claims that "bugging" is not an invasion of privacy.
(D)   Appeals to the authority of editorial writers.
(E)   Claims that his actions were justified because no one was able to show otherwise.

The reporter justifies his actions by claiming that Kissinger is guilty of wrong doing. So, instead of addressing the question, he attacks the character of Henry Kissinger. The answer is (A).

Sentence Completions

Sentence completions begin each reading section. This is fortunate since the sentence completions are a good warm-up for the harder reading comprehension. The sentence completions form the most straightforward part of the test, and most students do well on them.

Before You Look at The Answer-Choices, Think of a Word That "Fits" The Sentence

Example :

Crestfallen by having done poorly on the SAT, Susan began to question her abilities. Her self-confidence was _____ .

(A) appeased
(B) destroyed
(C) placated
(D) elevated
(E) sustained

If somebody is crestfallen (despairing) and has begun to question herself, then her self-confidence would be destroyed. Hence, the answer is (B).

If a Sentence Has Two Blanks, Plug in the First Word in Each Answer-Choice, Eliminating any that Don't Make sense.

After eliminating the answer-choices that don't make sense with the first word plugged in, turn to the remaining answer-choices and plug in the second word.

Example :

The plane had been redesigned so many times before it reached the assembly line that its _____ conception was no longer _____ .

(A) appropriate . . visible
(B) dilapidated . . relevant
(C) original . . recognizable
(D) initial . . understandable
(E) promised . . viable

An "appropriate conception" does not make sense in this context, eliminate (A). A "dilapidated conception" probably does not make sense in any context, eliminate (B). A "promised conception" is an odd construction, probably eliminate. Now, "original" and "initial" both work in the first blank. However, "understandable" does not make sense in the second blank. A redesign could clarify the original design, but it's hard to imagine how it would make the original design unintelligible, eliminate (D). Finally, "recognizable" *does* make sense. Since the plane was redesigned many times, is it likely to look quite different from its original design. The answer is (C).

Most often the answer-choices to sentence completion problems are not simple or common words, that is, words we use in daily speech. Nevertheless, don't hesitate to use a common word. Although an everyday word is unlikely to be the answer, it will help guide you to the answer. Further, it will help eliminate wrong answer-choices.

99

Be Alert to Transitional Words

Transitional words tell you what is coming up. They indicate that the author is now going to draw a contrast with something stated previously, or support something stated previously.

Contrast Indicators

To contrast two things is to point out how they differ. In this type of sentence completion problem, we look for a word that has the opposite meaning (an antonym) of some key word or phrase in the sentence. Following are some of the most common contrast indicators:

BUT	**YET**
DESPITE	**ALTHOUGH**
HOWEVER	**NEVERTHELESS**
WHEREAS	**IN CONTRAST**

Example :

Although the warring parties had settled a number of disputes, past experience made them _____ to express optimism that the talks would be a success.

- (A)   rash
- (B)   ambivalent
- (C)   scornful
- (D)   overjoyed
- (E)   reticent

"Although" sets up a contrast between what has occurred—success on some issues—and what can be expected to occur—success for the whole talks. Hence, the parties are reluctant to express optimism. The common word "reluctant" is not offered as an answer-choice, but a synonym—reticent—is. The answer is (E).

Support Indicators

Supporting words support or further explain what has already been said. These words often introduce synonyms for words elsewhere in the sentence. Following are some common supporting words:

AND	**ALSO**
FURTHERMORE	**LIKEWISE**
IN ADDITION	**FOR**
INDEED	**SIMILARY**

Example :

Davis is an opprobrious and _____ speaker, equally caustic toward friend or foe—a true curmudgeon.

- (A)   lofty
- (B)   vituperative
- (C)   unstinting
- (D)   retiring
- (E)   laudatory

"And" in the sentence indicates that the missing adjective is similar in meaning to "opprobrious," which is very negative. Now, *vituperative*—the only negative word—means "abusive." Hence, the answer is (B).

Example :

The belief that sanctions and tactical military strikes can turn the people of a country against a dictator is folly; indeed, as we are witnessing in the Balkans, this _____ causes the population to rally around the dictator.

(A) sometimes
(B) rarely
(C) invariably
(D) never
(E) occasionally

"Indeed" in the sentence indicates that the second clause supports and emphasizes what is stated in the first clause: that sanctions and tactical military strikes will not work. Now, something that will not work will *invariably* (always) fail. The answer is (C).

Cause and Effect Indicators

These words indicate that one thing causes another to occur. Some of the most common cause and effect indicators are

BECAUSE	**FOR**
THUS	**HENCE**
THEREFORE	**IF __ , THEN ___ .**
ACCORDINGLY	**DUE TO**

Example :

Because the Senate has the votes to override a presidential veto, the President has no choice but to _____ .

(A) object
(B) abdicate
(C) abstain
(D) capitulate
(E) compromise

Since the Senate has the votes to pass the bill or motion, the President would be wise to compromise and make the best of the situation. The answer is (E).

Apposition

This rather advanced grammatical structure is very common on the SAT. (Don't confuse "apposition" with "opposition": they have opposite meanings.)

Words or phrases in apposition are placed next to each other, and the second word or phrase defines, clarifies, or gives evidence to the first word or phrase. The second word or phrase will be set off from the first by a comma, semicolon, hyphen, or parentheses. Note: If a comma is not followed by a linking word—such as *and, for, yet*—then the following phrase is probably appositional.

Identifying an appositional structure, can greatly simplify a sentence completion problem since the appositional word, phrase, or clause will define the missing word.

Example :

His novels are _____ ; he uses a long circumlocution when a direct coupling of a simple subject and verb would be best.

(A) prolix   (B) pedestrian   (C) succinct   (D) vapid   (E) risqué

The sentence has no linking words (such as *because, although,* etc.). Hence, the phrase following the comma is in apposition to the missing word—it defines or further clarifies the missing word. Now, writing filled with circumlocutions is aptly described as prolix. The answer is (A).

Problem Set A: Answers and solutions begin on page 106.

1. Because of his success as a comedian, directors were loath to consider him for _____ roles.

    (A) supporting
    (B) leading
    (C) dramatic
    (D) comedic
    (E) musical

2. The aspiring candidate's performance in the debate all but _____ any hope he may have had of winning the election.

    (A) nullifies
    (B) encourages
    (C) guarantees
    (D) accentuates
    (E) contains

3. She is the most _____ person I have ever met, seemingly with an endless reserve of energy.

    (A) jejune
    (B) vivacious
    (C) solicitous
    (D) impudent
    (E) indolent

4. Despite all its _____, a stint in the diplomatic core is invariably an uplifting experience.

    (A) merits
    (B) compensation
    (C) effectiveness
    (D) rigors
    (E) mediocrity

5. Robert Williams' style of writing has an air of _____: just when you think the story line is predictable, he suddenly takes a different direction. Although this is often the mark of a beginner, Williams pulls it off masterfully.

    (A) ineptness
    (B) indignation
    (C) reserve
    (D) jollity
    (E) capriciousness

6. Liharev talks about being both a nihilist and an atheist during his life, yet he never does _____ faith in God.

    (A) affirm
    (B) lose
    (C) scorn
    (D) aver
    (E) supplicate

7. Existentialism can be used to rationalize evil: if one does not like the rules of society and has no conscience, he may use existentialism as a means of _____ a set of beliefs that are advantageous to him but injurious to others.

    (A) thwarting
    (B) proving
    (C) promoting
    (D) justifying
    (E) impugning

8. These categories amply point out the fundamental desire that people have to express themselves and the cleverness they display in that expression; who would have believed that the drab, mundane DMV would become the _____ such creativity?

    (A) catalyst for
    (B) inhibitor of
    (C) disabler of
    (D) referee of
    (E) censor of

9. This argues well that Erikson exercised less free will than Warner; for even though Erikson was aware that he was misdirected, he was still unable to _____ free will.

    (A) defer
    (B) facilitate
    (C) proscribe
    (D) prevent
    (E) exert

10. Man has no choice but to seek truth, he is made uncomfortable and frustrated without truth—thus, the quest for truth is part of what makes us _____ .

   (A) noble
   (B) different
   (C) human
   (D) intelligent
   (E) aggressive

11. Though most explicitly sexist words have been replaced by gender-neutral terms, sexism thrives in the _____ of many words.

   (A) indistinctness
   (B) similitude
   (C) loquacity
   (D) implications
   (E) obscurity

12. Though a small man, J. Egar Hoover appeared to be much larger behind his desk; for, having skillfully designed his office, he was _____ by the perspective.

   (A) augmented
   (B) comforted
   (C) apprehended
   (D) lessened
   (E) disconcerted

13. Man is violent and therefore any theory of conflict resolution between nations that _____ to account for this is _____ flawed.

   (A) declines . . . supposedly
   (B) refuses . . . pejoratively
   (C) fails . . . inherently
   (D) consents . . . manifestly
   (E) flinches . . . innately

14. Ironically, the foreign affairs policies of democracies are more likely to met with protests than similar policies of totalitarian regimes because a democracy is _____ protest; whereas in a totalitarian regime, no one is listening.

   (A) impassive to
   (B) indifferent to
   (C) imperiled by
   (D) sensitive to
   (E) inured to

15. Although the buildings and streets of this small beach town appear _____, the property values are quite _____ .

   (A) expensive . . steep
   (B) dilapidated . . high
   (C) artistic . . pedestrian
   (D) refurbished . . low
   (E) quaint . . reasonable

16. Though he claimed the business was _____, his irritability _____ that claim.

   (A) sound . . belied
   (B) expanding . . supported
   (C) downsizing . . vindicated
   (D) static . . contradicted
   (E) booming. . affirmed

17. The rules of engagement for United Nations troops stationed in Bosnia prohibit deadly force unless all _____ actions have be exhausted.

   (A) comparable
   (B) menacing
   (C) alternative
   (D) augmented
   (E) extraordinary

18. Despite its lofty goal—truth—many scholars maintain that law as _____ is a highly regulated street fight.

   (A) a dogma
   (B) a study
   (C) a profession
   (D) a philosophy
   (E) a lifestyle

19. The vigorous dispute over where to place a comma in the Republican platform was motivated not by any _____ change in meaning but by a desire not to show any deference to the other side.

   (A) specific
   (B) discredited
   (C) tarnished
   (D) petulant
   (E) infinite

20. The citizenry had become so _____ by the presidents _____ that the latest financial scandal did not even make the front page of the newspapers.
    - (A) fascinated . . impropriety
    - (B) disgusted . . peccadilloes
    - (C) distraught . . magnanimity
    - (D) regretful . . personification
    - (E) jaded . . indiscretions

21. In these politically correct times, it has become _____ to discuss certain subjects at all.
    - (A) safe
    - (B) eccentric
    - (C) precarious
    - (D) efficacious
    - (E) effortless

22. Although the stock market has experienced strong _____ in the past two years, there have been short periods in which the market has_____ precipitously.
    - (A) expansion . . stagnated
    - (B) growth . . fallen
    - (C) augmentation. . steadied
    - (D) extension . . stabilized
    - (E) development . . increased

23. Rather than increasing its security by developing nuclear weapons, a nascent nuclear power is viewed as a _____ by its enemies.
    - (A) benefactor
    - (B) protector
    - (C) target
    - (D) patron
    - (E) non entity

24. Her stern attitude toward the child was complemented with plenty of _____.
    - (A) love
    - (B) spite
    - (C) indifference
    - (D) malice
    - (E) ambivalence

25. The interviewer was startled to hear the otherwise gracious author make the _____ remark: "My novels are too sophisticated for the American public."
    - (A) apt
    - (B) enigmatic
    - (C) lofty
    - (D) vacuous
    - (E) insightful

26. The judge openly associated with racist organizations; nevertheless, he showed no _____ in his decisions during his career.
    - (A) favoritism
    - (B) benevolence
    - (C) openness
    - (D) prejudice
    - (E) altruism

27. The condemnatory drivel of critics directed toward Steven Spielberg's latest film attests to the fact that the pretentious critics have lost sight of the purpose of movies: _____.
    - (A) to exalt
    - (B) to correct
    - (C) to mislead
    - (D) to convert
    - (E) to entertain

28. Though in acting circles he has a reputation of being a consummate professional, at times he can be quite _____ on the stage.
    - (A) stern
    - (B) efficient
    - (C) playful
    - (D) adept
    - (E) aloof

29. Because a comprehensive _____ has yet to be done on the effects of radiation from computer monitors, we don't even know the amount of time the typical office worker spends at a computer monitor.
    - (A) theory
    - (B) strategy
    - (C) solution
    - (D) illness
    - (E) study

30. The general accused the senator of naiveté for _____ that air strikes alone could stop the aggressors.

    (A) advocating
    (B) denying
    (C) obfuscating
    (D) mishandling
    (E) disallowing

31. Hundreds of citizens showed up to _____ the planning commission's master plan for regional centers, claiming that adding 800,000 additional people to the metro area by the year 2010 would cause overcrowding and gridlock.

    (A) vote on
    (B) protest
    (C) celebrate
    (D) view
    (E) stop

32. Though _____ toward his own needs, he was always magnanimous toward others.

    (A) miserly
    (B) charitable
    (C) profligate
    (D) improvident
    (E) condemnatory

33. The intelligence community should not be _____ for not foreseeing the fall of the Soviet Union; even Hedrick Smith, author of *The Russians*, stated in 1986 that the Soviet Union is the world's most stable society.

    (A) applauded
    (B) contradicted
    (C) faulted
    (D) preempted
    (E) engendered

34. Although prices _____ during the fuel shortage, the suppliers actually saw _____ in profits.

    (A) increased . . a loss
    (B) stabilized . . a boon
    (C) shot up . . an expansion
    (D) fluctuated . . a deprivation
    (E) decreased . . a windfall

35. In the 1950s, integration was _____ to most Americans; now, however, most Americans accept it as _____ .

    (A) welcome . . normal
    (B) an anathema . . desirable
    (C) voluntary . . mandatory
    (D) common . . sporadic
    (E) an abhorrence. . unusual

36. A more admirable character would have been one who overcame his _____ impulses and became good; rather than one who merely lacked the _____ to be bad.

    (A) forbearing . . patience
    (B) ire . . drama
    (C) baser . . intensity
    (D) depraved . . goodness
    (E) evil . . sophistication

37. Although World War II ended more than half a century ago, Russia and Japan still have not signed a formal peace treaty; and both countries have been _____ to develop more _____ relations.

    (A) reticent . . amiable
    (B) inhibited . . colder
    (C) loath . . hostile
    (D) averse . . controversial
    (E) inimical . . blasé

Solutions to problems

Problem Set A:

1. If the public expects a comedian to always make them laugh, then they might not accept a comedian in a serious role. Hence, the directors would be loath (reluctant) to cast a comedian in a dramatic role. The answer is (C).

2. The phrase "all but" implies that the debate was a make-or-break event for the candidate. Suppose the candidate did well. Then his spirits would be high, and we would expect the missing word to be positive. However, a positive word in the phrase *"all but _____ any hope"* is awkward. Hence, the candidate must have done poorly in the debate and had his hopes for election nixed. So we turn to the answer-choices looking for "nixed." It's not there, but a synonym—nullifies—is. The answer is (A).

3. Since no connecting word—such as *and, for, so*, etc.—follows the comma, the phrase *"seemingly with an endless reserve of energy"* defines the missing word. Now, a person with an endless reserve of energy would be lively, which is the meaning of "vivacious." The answer is (B).

4. "Despite" sets up a contrast between the key phrase "uplifting experience" and the missing word. The implication is that in spite of the rewards, the job is harsh and trying; in other words, rigorous. The answer is (D).

5. There is no connecting word following the colon. Hence, the description, *"just when you think the story line is predictable, he suddenly takes a different direction,"* defines the missing word. Now, something that is unpredictable because it's continually changing direction is capricious. Thus, the answer is (E).

6. "Yet" draws a contrast between what one would expect an Atheist to do (renounce faith in God) and what Liharev did (maintained faith in God). In other words, he did not lose faith in God. The answer is (B).

7. To rationalize evil is to make excuses for wrong doing. Now, the words following the colon explain how existentialism can be used to excuse or justify evil. The answer is (D).

8. The phrase "who would have believed" implies that the reality is the opposite of what one would expect. Now, one would not expect the drab DMV to be a catalyst for creativity. The answer is (A).

9. The sentence implies that even when Erikson knows he is taking the wrong path in life, he still cannot stop. That is, he cannot exert free will. The answer is (E).

10. If man have no choice but to seek truth, then this is a defining characteristic of man. In other words, it is part of what makes us human. The answer is (C).

11. The sentence is saying that although a word may not be explicitly sexist it may contain sexist connotations or implications. The answer is (D).

12. The passage states that when sitting behind his desk J. Egar Hoover looked larger than he actually was. So the perspective must have increased the appearance of his size. The only word that means to increase is "augmented." The answer is (A).

13. Since man is violent, any useful theory of conflict resolution must incorporate this fact. The answer is (C).

14. The clause "whereas in a totalitarian regime, no one is listening" implies that a democracy does listen to protests. In other words, it is sensitive to protests. The answer is (D).

15. "Although" sets up a contrast between what the property values are (high) and what one would expect them to be in a dilapidated (run down) community. The answer is (B).

16. If the business was not sound, his irritability would belie (contradict) his claim that the business was sound. The answer is (A).

17. The word "exhausted" implies that all other actions (alternatives) have been tried. The answer is (C).

18. The sentence is pointing out that as a practical matter the legal profession pursues the truth through a rough and tumble path. The answer is (C).

19. The clause "a desire not to show any deference to the other side" implies that the issue was who would win not who was right. So the placement of the comma did not affect the specific meaning of the sentence. The answer is (A).

20. A financial scandal is an indiscretion; and it may not have made the front page because the public was jaded (worn out) by an excess of scandals. The answer is (E).

21. The sentence is suggesting that it is risky to discuss certain subjects regardless of what you say. The answer is (C).

22. "Although" sets up a contrast between what happened in the market over a two year period (growth) and what happened in some shorter periods during that time (no growth). The answer is (B).

23. The phrase "rather than" sets up a contrast between what a country hopes to achieve by developing nuclear weapons (increased security) and what it actually achieves (becoming a target). The answer is (C).

24. A complement is something that makes up a whole, bringing it to perfection. Of the answer-choices offered, only "love" could complement "stern" in such a manner. The answer is (A).

25. We are told that the author is gracious, yet she makes the churlish comment: "My novels are to sophisticated for the American public." Such an out of character comment is enigmatic. The answer is (B).

26. "Nevertheless" points out a contrast in how the judge felt (prejudice) and how he acted (without prejudice). The answer is (D).

27. The word "pretentious" indicates that the writer believes that the critics take themselves and movies too seriously. That is, the main purpose of a movie is merely to entertain. The answer is (E).

28. "Though" sets up a contrast between the behavior one would expect from a "consummate professional" and the behavior that the actor sometimes displays. Now from a consummate professional, one would expect a serious, work-like attitude, not playfulness. The answer is (C).

29. To determine the amount of time the typical office worker spends at a computer monitor, a study would need to be conducted. The answer is (E).

30. The general is accusing the senator of being naive (unsophisticated) for believing that air strikes alone could stop the aggressors. The answer is (A).

31. People are likely to protest a plan that they believe will cause overcrowding and gridlock. The answer is (B).

32. "Though" sets up a contrast between "magnanimous" (charitable) and "miserly." The answer is (A).

33. The sentence is implying that no one could have foreseen the collapse of the Soviet Union. The answer is (C).

34. The sentence is pointing out that in spite of the higher prices the suppliers lost money. The answer is (A).

35. The sentence is pointing out the difference between the attitudes of people in the '50s and the attitudes today. The answer is (B).

36. The writer is pointing out that one who overcomes evil is more admirable than one who is born simple but good. The answer is (E).

37. If no peace treaty has been signed after 50 years, then the countries are probably reticent (reluctant) to develop more amiable (friendly) relations. The answer is (A).

The Ubiquitous 400

The SAT tests a surprisingly limited number of words. In the following lists, you will find words that occur frequently on the SAT. Granted, memorizing a list of words is rather dry, but it is probably the most effective way to improve your performance on the reading section.

As you read through the lists, mark any words that you do not know with a check mark. Then when you read through the list again, mark any that you do not remember with two checks. Continue in this manner until you have learned the words.

The first list, The Ubiquitous 400, contains words that have appeared frequently on the SAT. Over the years, our second list, Vocabulary 4000, has been an invaluable tool for students who have both the time and the determination to wade through it. It's chock-full of words that are prime candidates for the SAT.

abash humiliate, embarrass

abdicate relinquish power or position

aberrant abnormal

abet aid, encourage (typically of crime)

abeyance postponement

aboriginal indigenous

abridge shorten

abstemious moderate

acclimate accustom oneself to a climate

accost to approach and speak to someone

acquiesce agree passively

acumen insight

adamant insistent

admonish warn gently

adulterate contaminate, corrupt

adversity hardship

aegis that which protects

aesthetic pleasing to the senses, beautiful

affable friendly

affinity fondness

aggregate total, collect

aghast horrified

alacrity swiftness

alienate estrange, antagonize

alleviate lessen, assuage

altruism benevolence, generosity

amalgamation mixture

ambiguous unclear

ambivalence conflicting emotions

amenable agreeable

amorphous shapeless

anachronistic out of historical order

analogous similar

anarchy absence of government

anathema curse

animus hate

anomalous abnormal

antipathy repulsion, hatred

antipodal exactly opposite

antiquated outdated, obsolete

apathy indifference

appease pacify

approbation approval

artless naive, simple

ascetic self-denying

assiduous hard-working

assimilate absorb

audacity boldness

auspicious favorable

austere harsh, Spartan

autonomous self-governing

avarice greed

axiom self-evident truth

banal trite

belie misrepresent

belittle disparage

bellicose warlike

benefactor patron

boisterous noisy

boor vulgar person

bourgeois middle class

bucolic rustic

buttress support

cachet prestige

cacophony dissonance, harsh noise

callow inexperienced

canon rule

capacious spacious

capitulate surrender

castigate criticize

cathartic purgative, purifying

catholic universal, worldly

caustic scathing (of speech)

censure condemn

chagrin embarrassment

charlatan quack

chary cautious

coagulate thicken

coda concluding passage

cogent well-put, convincing

collusion conspiracy

commensurate proportionate

commiserate empathize

compensatory redeeming

compliant submissive

conciliatory reconciling

condone overlook wrong doing

conducive helping

connoisseur an expert, gourmet

consensus general agreement

contentious argumentative

conundrum puzzle, enigma

convoluted twisted, complicated

covenant agreement, pact

covert secret

credence belief

credulous believing

cynical scornful of the motives of others

dauntless courageous

dearth scarcity

defamation (noun) slander

deference courteously yielding to another

deleterious harmful

delineate draw a line around, describe

demur take exception

denigrate defame

deprecate belittle

desiccate dehydrate

despot tyrant

destitute poor

desultory without direction in life

deterrent hindrance

devoid empty

devout pious

diatribe long denunciation

dichotomy a division into two parts

didactic instructional

diffident shy

digress ramble

disabuse correct a misconception

discerning observant

discord lack of harmony

discrete separate

discretion prudence

disingenuous deceptive

disparate various

disseminate distribute

dissent disagree

dissolution disintegration

dissonance discord

distend swell

divest strip, deprive

divulge disclose

dogmatic certain, unchanging in opinion

dormant asleep

eclectic from many sources

efficacy effectiveness

effigy likeness, mannequin

effloresce to bloom

effrontery insolence

elicit provoke

eloquent well-spoken

emancipate liberate

embellish exaggerate

endemic peculiar to a particular region

enervate weaken

engender generate

ennui boredom

enumerate count

esoteric known by only a few

esthetic artistic

euphemism genteel expression

euphoria elation

evanescent fleeting, very brief

exacerbate worsen

exasperate irritate

exhibitionist one who draws attention to himself

exonerate free from blame

expedite hasten

extemporize improvise

extol praise highly

facetious joking, sarcastic

facilitate make easier

fallacy false belief

fathom understand

fervor intensity

fickle always changing one's mind

filibuster long speech

fledgling just beginning, struggling

flout to show disregard for the law or rules

foment instigate

forsake abandon

fortuitous lucky

foster encourage

frugal thrifty

fulminate denounce, menace

furtive stealthy

gainsay contradict

germane relevant

glib insincere manner

gratuitous unwarranted, uncalled for

gregarious sociable

halcyon serene

hamper obstruct

harangue tirade

harry harass

hedonism excessive pursuit of pleasure in life

hegemony authority, domination

histrionic overly dramatic

homogeneous uniform

hyperbole exaggeration

hypocritical deceiving, two-faced

iconoclast one who rails against sacred institutions

idiosyncrasy peculiarity

imminent about to happen

impecunious indigent

imperative vital, pressing

imperturbable calm

impervious impenetrable

impetuous impulsive

implicit implied

impolitic unwise

impulsive to act suddenly

impunity exemption from harm

inadvertent unintentional

incendiary inflammatory

incipient beginning

incontrovertible indisputable

incorrigible unreformable

indifferent unconcerned

indigent poor

indolent lazy

indomitable invincible

ineffable inexpressible

inert inactive

inherent innate, inborn

inhibit restrain

inimical adverse, hostile

insatiable gluttonous

insidious treacherous

insipid flat, dull

insufferable unbearable

insular narrow-minded

intangible not perceptible by touch

internecine mutually destructive

intractable unmanageable

intrepid fearless

inundate flood

inure accustom, habituate, harden

invective verbal insult

inveigle lure

irascible irritable

irresolute hesitant, uncertain

itinerary route

judicious prudent

laconic brief, terse

lassitude lethargy

laudatory commendable

levity frivolity

lucid clearly understood

lurid ghastly

Machiavellian politically crafty, cunning

magnanimous generous, kindhearted

magnate a powerful, successful person

malevolence bad intent, malice

malinger shirk

malleable moldable, tractable

misanthrope hater of mankind

miscreant evildoer

mitigate lessen the severity

mundane ordinary

nadir lowest point

narcissism self-love

nascent incipient

neologism newly coined expression

nonplus confound

noxious toxic

obfuscate bewilder, muddle

obtuse stupid

obviate make unnecessary

odious despicable

officious forward, obtrusive

omnipotent all-powerful

onerous burdensome

opprobrium disgrace

oscillate waver

paean a song of praise

paradigm a model

paragon standard of excellence

parody imitation, ridicule

parsimonious stingy

paucity scarcity

pedagogical pertaining to teaching

pedantic bookish

penchant inclination

penury poverty

pernicious destructive

perpetuity eternity

perspicacious keen

pervade permeate

philanthropic charitable

phlegmatic sluggish

piety devoutness

pious devout, holy

piquant tart-tasting, spicy

pithy concise

platitude trite remark

platonic nonsexual

plethora overabundance

polemic a controversy

posthumous after death

pragmatic practical

precarious dangerous, risky

precipitate cause

precursor forerunner

preponderance predominance

presumptuous assuming

pretentious affected, inflated

pretext excuse

prevaricate lie

probity integrity

problematic uncertain

prodigal wasteful

prodigious marvelous, enormous

prodigy a person with extraordinary ability or talent

profligate licentious, prodigal

profound deep, knowledgeable

profusion overabundance

prolific fruitful, productive

propensity inclination

proportionate commensurate

propriety decorum

prosaic uninspired, flat

proscribe prohibit

protuberance bulge

pundit politically astute person

pungent sharp smell or taste

qualms misgivings

quash put down, suppress

querulous complaining

quixotic impractical, romantic

raconteur story teller

recalcitrant stubborn

recant retract

redoubtable formidable, steadfast

refractory obstinate

relegate assign to an inferior position

renege break a promise

renounce disown

reprehensible blameworthy

reproach blame

reprobate miscreant

repudiate disavow

requisite necessary

rescind revoke

resolute determined

reticent reserved

retribution reprisal

reverent respectful

rhapsody ecstasy

rhetoric elocution, grandiloquence

sanctimonious self-righteous

sanction approval

sanguinary gory, murderous

satiate satisfy fully

satire ridicule

schism rift

secular worldly, nonreligious

sedulous diligent

severance division

skeptical doubtful

solicitous considerate, concerned

solvent financially sound

sophistry specious reasoning

specious false but plausible

spurious false, counterfeit

squander waste

stolid impassive

stupefy deaden, dumfound

stymie hinder, thwart

sullen sulky, sour

supercilious arrogant

superfluous overabundant

surfeit overabundance

synthesis combination

tacit understood without being spoken

temerity boldness

tenuous thin, insubstantial

terse concise

torpid lethargic, inactive

tractable docile, manageable

transient fleeting, temporary

trenchant incisive, penetrating

truculent fierce, savage

ubiquitous omnipresent, pervasive

ulterior hidden, covert

untenable cannot be achieved

untoward perverse

urbane refined, worldly

vacillate waver

venerable revered

veracity truthfulness

verbose wordy

vernacular common speech

vex annoy

viable capable of surviving

vilify defame

virulent deadly, poisonous

vitriolic scathing

vituperative abusive

vivacious lively

volatile unstable

voluminous bulky, extensive

voracious hungry

xenophobia fear of foreigners

zealot fanatic

Vocabulary 4000

A

a cappella without accompaniment

à la carte priced separately

a priori reasoning based on general principles

aback unexpected

abacus counting device

abandon desert, forsake

abase degrade

abash humiliate, embarrass

abate lessen

abatement alleviation

abbey monastery

abbreviate shorten

abdicate relinquish power or position

abdomen belly

abduct kidnap

aberrant abnormal

abet aid, encourage (typically of crime)

abeyance postponement

abhor detest

abide submit, endure

abject wretched

abjure renounce

ablate cut away

ablution cleansing

abode home

abolish annul

abominable detestable

aboriginal indigenous

abortive unsuccessful

abound be plentiful

abreast side-by-side

abridge shorten

abroad overseas

abrogate cancel

abrupt ending suddenly

abscess infected and inflamed tissue

abscond to run away (secretly)

absolve acquit

abstain refrain

abstract theoretical, intangible

abstruse difficult to understand

abut touch, border on

abysmal deficient, sub par

abyss chasm

academy school

accede yield

accentuate emphasize

accession attainment of rank

accessory attachment

acclaim recognition, fame

acclimate accustom oneself to a climate

acclivity ascent, incline

accolade applause

accommodate adapt

accomplice one who aids a lawbreaker

accord agreement

accost to approach and speak to someone

accouter equip

accredit authorize

accrete grow larger

accrue accumulate

accumulate amass

acerbic caustic (of speech)

acme summit

acolyte assistant

acoustic pertaining to sound

acquaint familiarize

acquiesce agree passively

acquit free from blame

acrid pungent, caustic

acrimonious caustic, bitter

acrophobia fear of heights

actuate induce, start

acumen insight

acute sharp, intense

ad nauseam to a ridiculous degree

ad-lib improvise

adage proverb

adamant insistent

adapt adjust to changing conditions

adaptable pliable

addendum appendix

adduce offer as example

adept skillful

adhere stick to

adherent supporter

adieu farewell

adipose fatty

adjacent next to

adjourn discontinue

adjudicate judge

adjunct addition

administer manage

admissible allowable

admonish warn gently

ado fuss

Adonis beautiful man

adroit skillful

adulation applause

adulterate contaminate, corrupt

adumbration overshadow

advent arrival

adventitious accidental

adversary opponent

adverse unfavorable

adversity hardship

advise give counsel

advocate urge

aegis that which protects

aerial pertaining to the air

aerobics exercise

aesthetic pleasing to the senses, beautiful

affable friendly

affect influence

affectation pretense

affidavit sworn written statement

affiliate associate

affiliation connection

affinity fondness

affix fasten

affliction illness

affluent abundant, wealthy

affray brawl

affront insult

aficionado devotee, ardent follower

afoul entangled

aft rear

aftermath consequence

agape wonder

agenda plan, timetable

agent provocateur agitator

aggrandize exaggerate

aggravate worsen

aggregate total, collect

aggressor attacker

aggrieve mistreat

aggrieved unjustly injured

aghast horrified

agile nimble

agitate stir up

agnate related on the father's side

agnostic not knowing whether God exists

agrarian pertaining to farming

agronomy science of crop production

air discuss, broadcast

airs pretension

akimbo with hands on hips

akin related

al fresco outdoors

alacrity swiftness

albatross large sea bird

albino lacking pigmentation

alcove recess, niche

alfresco outdoors

alias assumed name

alibi excuse

alienate estrange, antagonize

alight land, descend

allay to reassure

allege assert without proof

allegiance loyalty

Quiz 1 (Matching)

Match each word in the first column with its definition in the second column.

1.	ABASE	A.	applause
2.	ABSTAIN	B.	caustic
3.	ACOLYTE	C.	shorten
4.	ABEYANCE	D.	applause
5.	ABRIDGE	E.	assistant
6.	ACCOLADE	F.	postponement
7.	ACRIMONIOUS	G.	refrain
8.	ADDUCE	H.	exercise
9.	ADULATION	I.	degrade
10.	AEROBICS	J.	offer as example

---

allegory fable

allegro fast

alleviate lessen, assuage

alliteration repetition of the same sound

allocate distribute

allot allocate

allude refer to indirectly

ally unite for a purpose

almanac calendar with additional information

alms charity

aloof arrogant

altercation argument

altitude height

alto low female voice

altruism benevolence, generosity

amalgamation mixture

amass collect

ambient surrounding, environment

ambiguous unclear

ambivalence conflicting emotions

ambulatory able to walk

ameliorate improve

amenable agreeable

amend correct

amenities courtesies, comforts

amenity pleasantness

amiable friendly

amid among

amiss wrong, out of place

amity friendship

amnesty pardon

amoral without morals

amorous loving, sexual

amorphous shapeless

amortize pay by installments

amphibious able to operate in water and land

amphitheater oval-shaped theater

amuck murderous frenzy

amulet charm, talisman

amuse entertain

anachronistic out of historical order

anaerobic without oxygen

anagram a word formed by rearranging the letters of another word

analgesic pain-soother

analogous similar

analogy point by point comparison

anarchist terrorist

anarchy absence of government

anathema curse

anecdote story

aneurysm bulging in a blood vessel

angst anxiety, dread

animadversion critical remark

animated exuberant

animosity dislike

animus hate

annals historical records

annex to attach

annihilate destroy

annotate to add explanatory notes

annul cancel

annular ring-shaped

anodyne pain soothing

anoint consecrate

anomalous abnormal

anonymity state of being anonymous

antagonistic hostile

antagonize harass

antechamber waiting room

antediluvian ancient, obsolete

anthology collection

anthrax disease

antic caper, prank

antipathy repulsion, hated

antipodal exactly opposite

antiquated outdated, obsolete

antiquity ancient times

antithesis direct opposite

apartheid racial segregation

apathetic unconcerned

apathy indifference

ape mimic

aperture opening

apex highest point

aphasia speechless

aphorism maxim

aplomb poise

apocalyptic ominous, doomed

apocryphal of doubtful authenticity

apoplexy stroke

apostate one who abandons one's faith

apotheosis deification

appall horrify

apparition phantom

appease pacify

appellation title

append affix

apposite apt

apprehensive anxious

apprise inform

approbation approval

apropos appropriate

apt suitable

aptitude ability

aquatic pertaining to water

arbiter judge

arbitrament final judgment

arbitrary tyrannical, capricious

arcane secret

archaic antiquated

archetype original model

archipelago group of island

archives public records

ardent passionate

ardor passion

arduous hard

argonauts gold-seekers, adventurers

argot specialized vocabulary

aria operatic song

arid dry, dull

aristocrat nobleman

armada fleet of ships

armistice truce

arraign indict

array arrangement

arrears in debt

arrogate seize without right

arroyo gully

arsenal supply

artful skillful, cunning

articulate well-spoken

artifice trick

artless naive, simple

ascend rise

ascendancy powerful state

ascertain discover

ascetic self-denying

ascribe to attribute

aseptic sterile

ashen pale

asinine stupid

askance to view with suspicion

askew crooked

aspersion slander

asphyxiate suffocate

aspirant contestant

aspiration ambition

assail attack

assassin murderer

assent agree

assert affirm

assess appraise

assiduous hard-working

assimilate absorb

assonance partial rhyme

assuage lessen (pain)

astral pertaining to stars

astringent causing contraction, severe

astute wise

asunder apart

asylum place of refuge

asymmetric uneven

atavistic exhibiting the characteristics of one's forebears

atelier workshop

atoll reef

atomize vaporize

atone make amends

atrophy the wasting away of muscle

attenuate weaken

attest testify

attire dress

attribute ascribe

attrition deterioration, reduction

atypical abnormal

au courant well informed

audacity boldness

audient listening, attentive

audition tryout

augment increase

augur predict

august noble

aura atmosphere, emanation

auspices patronage, protection

auspicious favorable

austere harsh, Spartan

authorize grant, sanction

automaton robot

autonomous self-governing

auxiliary secondary

avail assistance

avant garde vanguard

avarice greed

avatar incarnation

averse loath, reluctant

avert turn away

avian pertaining to birds

avid enthusiastic

avocation hobby

avouch attest, guarantee

avow declare

avuncular like an uncle

awry crooked

axiom self-evident truth

aye affirmative vote

azure sky blue

B

babbittry smugness

Quiz 2 (Matching)

Match each word in the first column with its definition in the second column.

1.	ANATHEMA	A.	hard
2.	ANNIHILATE	B.	curse
3.	ANOMALOUS	C.	gully
4.	APATHETIC	D.	suffocate
5.	ARCHAIC	E.	antiquated
6.	ARDUOUS	F.	destroy
7.	ARROYO	G.	abnormal
8.	ASPHYXIATE	H.	unconcerned
9.	ASTRINGENT	I.	make amends
10.	ATONE	J.	causing contraction

---

bacchanal orgy

badger pester

badinage banter

bagatelle nonentity, trifle

bailiwick area of concern or business

baleen whalebone

baleful hostile, malignant

balk hesitate

balky hesitant

ballad song

ballast counterbalance

ballistics study of projectiles

balm soothing ointment

banal trite

bandy exchange

bane poison, nuisance

barbarian savage

bard poet

baroque ornate

barrister lawyer

bask take pleasure in, sun

basso low male voice

bastion fort

bathos sentimentality

batten fasten, board up

battery physical attack

bauble trinket

beatify sanctify

beatitude state of bliss

beckon lure

becoming proper

bedlam uproar

befit to be suitable

beget produce, procreate

begrudge resent, envy

beguile deceive, seduce

behemoth monster

behest command

beholden in debt

belabor assail verbally

belated delayed, overdue

beleaguer besiege

belfry bell tower

belie misrepresent

belittle disparage

bellicose warlike

belligerent combative

bellow shout

bellwether leader, guide

bemoan lament

bemused bewildered

benchmark standard

benediction blessing

benefactor patron

benevolent kind

benign harmless

bent determined

bequeath will

bequest gift, endowment

berate scold

bereave rob

bereft deprived of

berserk crazed

beseech implore

beset harass, encircle

besiege beleaguer, surround

besmirch slander, sully

bespeak attest

bestial beast-like, brutal

bestow offer, grant

betrothed engaged

bevy group

bibliography list of sources of information

bicameral having two legislative branches

bicker quarrel

biennial occurring every two years

bilateral two-sided

bilious ill-tempered

bilk swindle

biodegradable naturally decaying

biopsy removing tissue for examination

biped two-footed animal

bistro tavern, cafe

bivouac encampment

blandish flatter, grovel

blasé bored with life

blasphemy insulting God

bleak cheerless

blight decay

bliss happiness

blithe joyous

bloated swollen

bode portend

bogus forged, false

bogy bugbear

boisterous noisy

bolt move quickly and suddenly

bombast pompous speech

bon vivant gourmet, epicure

bona fide made in good faith

bonanza a stroke of luck

boon payoff

boor vulgar person

bootless unavailing

booty loot

botch bungle

bourgeois middle class

bovine cow-like

boycott abstain in protest

bracing refreshing

brackish salty

brandish display menacingly

bravado feigned bravery

bravura technically difficult

brawn strength

brevity shortness of expression

brigand robber

brink edge

broach bring up a topic of conversation

bromide cliché

brook tolerate

browbeat to bully

brusque curt

bucolic rustic

buffet blow

buffoon fool

bulwark fortification

buncombe empty, showy talk

buoyant floatable

burgeon sprout

burlesque farce

burly husky

buttress support

C

cabal plot

cabaret night club

cache hiding place

cachet prestige

cacophony dissonance, harsh noise

cadaver corpse

cadaverous haggard

cadence rhythm

cadet a student of a military academy

cadge beg

cadre small group

cajole encourage, coax

calamity disaster

calculating scheming

caliber ability

callous insensitive

callow inexperienced

calumny slander

camaraderie fellowship

canaille rabble

canard hoax

candid frank, unrehearsed

candor frankness

canine pertaining to dogs

canon rule

cant insincere speech

cantankerous peevish

cantata musical composition

canvass survey

capacious spacious

capillary thin tube

capital most significant, pertaining to wealth

capitol legislative building

capitulate surrender

capricious fickle, impulsive

caption title

captious fond of finding fault in others

captivate engross, fascinate

carafe bottle

carbine rifle

carcinogenic causing cancer

carcinoma tumor

cardinal chief

cardiologist one who studies the heart

careen swerve

carrion decaying flesh

cartographer mapmaker

cascade waterfall

cashmere fine wool from Asia

Cassandra unheeded prophet

castigate criticize

castrate remove the testicles

casuistry specious reasoning

cataclysm catastrophe

catastrophic disastrous

categorical absolute, certain

cathartic purgative, purifying

catholic universal, worldly

caucus meeting

cause célèbre celebrated legal case

caustic scathing (of speech)

cauterize to sear

cavalier disdainful, nonchalant

caveat warning

caveat emptor buyer beware

cavil quibble

cavort frolic

cede transfer ownership

celestial heavenly

celibate abstaining from sex

cenotaph empty tomb

censorious condemning speech

censure condemn

ceramics pottery

cerebral pertaining to the brain

Quiz 3 (Matching)

Match each word in the first column with its definition in the second column.

1.	BESMIRCH	A.	unheeded prophet
2.	BICAMERAL	B.	peevish
3.	BILATERAL	C.	pertaining to dogs
4.	BOOTLESS	D.	plot
5.	BRANDISH	E.	farce
6.	BURLESQUE	F.	display menacingly
7.	CABAL	G.	unavailing
8.	CANINE	H.	two-sided
9.	CANTANKEROUS	I.	having two legislative branches
10.	CASSANDRA	J.	sully

---

cessation a stoping

chafe abrade

chagrin embarrassment

chalice goblet

champion defend

chaperon escort

charade pantomime

charlatan quack

chartreuse greenish yellow

chary cautious

chaste pure, virgin

chasten castigate

chateau castle

cheeky brass, forward

cherub cupid

cherubic sweet, innocent

chicanery trickery

chide scold

chimerical imaginary, dreamlike

choleric easily angered

chortle laugh, snort

chronic continual

chronicle a history

chronology arrangement by time

churl a boor

chutzpah gall

Cimmerian dim, unlit

cipher zero

circa about

circuitous roundabout

circumcise remove the foreskin

circumlocution roundabout expression

circumspect cautious

circumvent evade

citadel fortress

citation summons to appear in court

clamor noise

clan extended family

clandestine secret

claustrophobia fear of enclosed places

cleave split

cleft split

clemency forgiveness

clique a small group

cloister refuge

clone duplicate

clout influence

cloven split

cloy glut

cloyed jaded

co-opt preempt, usurp

coagulate thicken

coalesce combine

coda concluding passage

coddle pamper

codicil supplement to a will

coercion force

coffer strong box

cogent well-put, convincing

cogitate ponder

cognate from the same source

cognizant aware

cognomen family name

cohabit live together

cohere stick together

cohort an associate

coiffure hairdo

collaborate work together

collar seize

collateral securities for a debt

colloquial informal speech

colloquy conference

collusion conspiracy

colonnade row of columns

comatose stupor

combine unite, blend

commandeer seize for military use

commemorate observe

commend praise

commensurate proportionate

commiserate empathize

commissary food store

commission authorization to perform a task

commodious spacious

commodity product

commodore naval officer

communion fellowship

commutation exchange, substitution

commute lessen punishment

compact covenant

compassion kindness

compatible well-matched, harmonious

compatriot countryman

compelling convincing

compendium summary

compensate make up for

compensatory redeeming

competence skillfulness

compile collect

complacent self-satisfied

compliant submissive

complicity guilt by association

comport to conduct oneself

composed cool, self-possessed

compound augment

comprehensive thorough

comprise consist of

compulsive obsessive

compulsory obligatory

compunction remorse

concatenate link

concave curving inward

concede yield, grant

concerted done together

conch spiral shell

conciliatory reconciling

concise brief

conclusive convincing, ending doubt

concoct devise

concomitant accompanying, concurrent

concord accord

concordat agreement

concourse throng

concubine mistress

concur agree

concurrent simultaneous

condescend patronize, talk down to

condiment seasoning

condolence commiseration

condone overlook wrong doing, pardon

conducive helping

conduit pipe

confabulate discuss

confection candy

confederacy alliance

confer bestow

conference meeting

confidant trusted friend

confide trust another (with secrets)

confiscate seize

conflagration large fire

confluence flowing together

confound bewilder

confront challenge

confuse perplex

confute disprove

congeal solidify

congenial friendly

congenital inborn, existing from birth

congeries pile

congruence conformity

coniferous bearing cones

conjecture hypothesis

conjugal pertaining to marriage

conjure summon

connive conspire

connoisseur an expert, gourmet

consanguineous related by blood

conscientious honorable, upright

conscription draft, enlistment

consecrate make holy

consecutive one after another

consensus general agreement

considered well thought out, contemplated

consign assign

consolation comfort

console comfort

consolidate unite, strengthen

consonant harmonious

consort spouse

consortium cartel

conspicuous obvious

conspire plot

constellation arrangement of stars

consternation anxiety, bewilderment

constrained confined

construe interpret

consummate perfect

contagion infectious agent

contemplate meditate

contempt disdain

contend struggle

contented satisfied

contentious argumentative

contiguous adjacent, abutting

continence self-control

contingent conditional

contort twist

contraband illicit goods

contraction shrinkage

contractual related to a contract

contrariety opposition

contrast difference, comparison

contravene oppose

contretemps unfortunate occurrence

contrite apologetic

contrive arrange, artificial

controversial subject to dispute

controvert dispute

contumacy disobedience

contusion bruise

conundrum puzzle, enigma

convene assemble (a group)

conventional customary, standard

converge come together

conversant familiar

converse opposite

convex curving outward

convey communicate

conviction strongly held belief

Quiz 4 (Matching)

Match each word in the first column with its definition in the second column.

1.	COMMANDEER	A.	seize for military use
2.	COMMUNION	B.	apologetic
3.	COMPATRIOT	C.	perfect
4.	CONCERTED	D.	accord
5.	CONCORD	E.	done together
6.	CONFLUENCE	F.	pile
7.	CONGERIES	G.	flowing together
8.	CONSONANT	H.	harmonious
9.	CONSUMMATE	I.	countryman
10.	CONTRITE	J.	fellowship

---

convivial sociable, festive

convocation gathering

convoke convene, summon

convoluted twisted, complicated

copious abundant

coquette a flirt

cordial friendly

cordon bond, chain

cornucopia cone-shaped horn filled with fruit

corollary consequence

coronation crowning of a sovereign

corporeal of the body

corps group of people

corpulent fat

corroborate confirm

cortege procession

coruscate sparkle

cosmopolitan worldly, sophisticated

cosset coddle

coterie small group

countenance facial expression

countermand overrule

counterstrike strike back

countervail counterbalance

coup master stroke

coup de grâce final stroke, a blow of mercy

court-martial military trial

courtesan prostitute

courtier member of the king's court

covenant agreement, pact

covert secret

covet desire

cower showing fear

crass crude

crave desire

craven cowardly

credence belief

credenza buffet

credulity gullibility

credulous believing

creed belief

crescendo becoming louder

crestfallen dejected

crevice crack

cringe cower

criterion a standard used in judging

critique examination, criticism

croon sing

cruet bottle

crux gist, key

cryptic mysterious

cubism a style of painting

cudgel club

culinary pertaining to cooking

cull pick out, select

culminate climax

culpable blameworthy

culprit offender

culvert drain

cumbersome unwieldy

cumulative accumulate

cupidity greed

curb restrain, block

curmudgeon boor

curriculum course of study

curry seek favor by flattery

cursory hasty

curt abrupt, rude

curtail shorten

cyclone storm

cynical scornful of the motives of others

cynosure celebrity

czar Russian emperor

D

dab touch lightly

dais platform

dally procrastinate

dank damp

dauntless courageous

de facto actual

de jure legally

de rigueur very formal

deadpan expressionless

dearth scarcity

debacle a rout, defeat

debase degrade

debauch corrupt

debauchery indulgence

debilitate weaken

debonair sophisticated, affable

debrief interrogate

debunk refute, expose

debutante a girl debuting into society

decadence decay (e.g. moral or cultural)

decant pour

decapitate kill by beheading

decathlon athletic contest

deceive trick

deciduous shedding leaves

decimate destroy

decipher decode

decline decrease in number

decommission take a ship out of service

decorous seemly

decorum protocol

decree official order

decrepitude enfeeblement

decry castigate

deduce conclude

deduct subtract

deem judge

deface mar, disfigure

defamation (noun) slander

defame (verb) slander .

defeatist one who is resigned to defeat

defer postpone

deference courteously yielding to another

deficit shortage

defile pollute

definitive conclusive, final

deflect turn aside

deflower despoil

defraud swindle

defray pay

deft skillful

defunct extinct

degrade demean

dehydrate dry out

deign condescend

deity a god

delectable delicious

delegate authorize

delete remove

deleterious harmful

deliberate ponder

delineate draw a line around, describe

delinquent negligent, culpable

delirium mental confusion, ecstasy

delude deceive

deluge a flood

delve dig, explore (of ideas)

demagogue a politician who appeals to base instincts

demean degrade

demeanor behavior

demented deranged

demise death

demobilize disband

demography study of human populations

demoralize dishearten

demote lower in rank

demur take exception

demure sedate, reserved

denigrate defame

denizen dweller

denomination class, sect

denote signify, stand for

denouement resolution

denounce condemn

denude strip bare

depart leave

depict portray

deplete exhaust

deplore condemn

deploy arrange forces

deportment behavior

deposition testimony

depravity immorality

deprecate belittle

depredation preying on, plunder

deprive take away

deracinate uproot

derelict negligent

deride ridicule

derisive mocking

derogatory degrading

derrick crane

desecrate profane

desiccate dehydrate

designate appoint

desist stop

desolate forsaken

despicable contemptible

despise loathe

despondent depressed

despot tyrant

destitute poor

desuetude disuse

desultory without direction in life

detached emotionally removed

detain confine

détente truce

detention confinement

deter discourage, prevent

deterrent hindrance

detract lessen

detractor one who criticizes

detrimental harmful

detritus debris

devastate lay waste

deviate turn away from

devise plan

devoid empty

devotee enthusiast, follower

devout pious

diabolical devilish

dialectic pertaining to debate

diaphanous sheer, translucent

diatribe long denunciation

Quiz 5 (Matching)

Match each word in the first column with its definition in the second column.

1.	DEBUNK	A.	decode
2.	DECIPHER	B.	refute
3.	DEDUCE	C.	conclusive
4.	DEFINITIVE	D.	conclude
5.	DEFUNCT	E.	to draw a line around
6.	DELINEATE	F.	extinct
7.	DENOMINATION	G.	belittle
8.	DEPRECATE	H.	sect
9.	DESOLATE	I.	pertaining to debate
10.	DIALECTIC	J.	forsaken

dicey risky

dichotomy a division into two parts

dictate command

dictum saying

didactic instructional

diffident shy

digress ramble **dilapidated** neglected

dilate enlarge

dilatory procrastinating

dilemma a difficult choice

dilettante amateur, dabbler

diligent hard-working

diminution reduction

diocese district

dire dreadful

dirigible airship, blimp

disabuse correct

disaffect alienate

disarray disorder

disavow deny

disband disperse

disburse pay out

discernible visible

discerning observant

disclaim renounce

disconcert confuse

disconsolate inconsolable

discord lack of harmony

discourse conversation

discreet prudent

discrepancy difference

discrete separate

discretion prudence

discriminating able to see differences

discursive rambling

disdain contempt

disengage release, detach

disfigure mar, ruin

disgruntle disappointed

dishevel muss

disinclination unwillingness

disingenuous deceptive

disinter unearth

disinterested impartial

disjointed disconnected, incoherent

dismal gloomy

dismantle take apart

dismay dread

disparage belittle

disparate various

disparity difference

dispassionate impartial

dispatch send

dispel cause to banish

disperse scatter

dispirit discourage

disposition attitude

dispossess take away possessions

disputatious fond of arguing

dispute debate

disquietude anxiety

disquisition elaborate treatise

disrepute disgrace

dissemble pretend

disseminate distribute

dissent disagree

dissertation lecture

dissidence disagreement

dissipate scatter

dissolute profligate, immoral

dissolution disintegration

dissonance discord

dissuade deter

distend swell

distortion misinterpret, lie

distract divert

distrait preoccupied, absent-minded

distraught distressed

distrust suspect

dither move without purpose

diurnal daily

diva prima donna

diverge branch off

diverse varying

diversion pastime

diversity variety

divest strip, deprive

dividend distributed profits

divine foretell

divisive causing conflict

divulge disclose

docile domesticated, trained

dock curtail

doctrinaire dogmatic

document verify

dodder tremble

dogged persistent

doggerel poor verse

dogmatic certain, unchanging in opinion

dolce sweetly

doldrums dullness

doleful sorrowful

dolorous gloomy

domicile home

dominion authority

don assume, put on

donor contributor

dormant asleep

dossier file

dotage senility

doting attending

double-entendre having two meanings one of which is sexually suggestive

doughty resolute, unafraid

dour sullen

dowager widow

doyen dean of a group

draconian harsh

dregs residue, riffraff

drivel inane speech

droll amusing

drone speak in a monotonic voice

dubious doubtful

ductile stretchable

dudgeon resentment, indignant humor

duenna governess

duet twosome

dulcet melodious

dupe one who is easily trick, victim

duplicity deceit, treachery

duress coercion

dynamic energetic

E

ebb recede

ebullient exuberant

eccentric odd, weird

ecclesiastical churchly

echelon degree

éclat brilliance

eclectic from many sources

ectoderm top layer of skin

ecumenical universal

edict order

edifice building

edify instruct

editorialize express an opinion

educe draw forth, evoke

efface obliterate

effeminate unmanly

effervescence exuberance

effete worn out

efficacious effective

efficacy effectiveness

effigy likeness, mannequin

effloresce to bloom

effrontery insolence

effulgent brilliant

effusion pouring forth

egocentric self-centered

egregious grossly wrong

egress exit

ejaculate exclaim

eke to supplement with great effort, strain

elaboration detailed explanation

elate raise spirits

electorate voters

eleemosynary pertaining to charity

elegant refined, exquisite

elegiac sad

elephantine large

elicit provoke

elide omit

elite upper-class

ellipsis omission of words

eloquent well-spoken

elucidate make clear

elude evade

elusive evasive

emaciated underfed, gaunt

emancipate liberate

emasculate castrate, dispirit

embargo restriction

embellish exaggerate

embezzlement theft

emblazon imprint, brand

embody personify

embrace accept

embrangle embroil

embroil involve

embryonic rudimentary

emend correct

emergent appearing

emeritus retired, but retaining title

eminent distinguished, famous

emissary messenger

emote to display exaggerated emotion

empathy compassion, sympathy

employ use

empower enable, grant

emulate imitate

enact decree, ordain

enamored charmed, captivated

enate related on the mother's side

encapsulate condense

enchant charm

enclave area enclosed within another region

encomium praise

encompass contain, encircle

encore additional performance

encroach trespass

encumber burden

encyclopedic comprehensive

endear enamor

endeavor attempt, strive

endemic peculiar to a particular region

endocrinologist one who studies glands of internal secretion

endoderm within the skin

endorse approve

endowment property, gift

endure suffer

enervate weaken

enfranchise liberate

engaging enchanting, charming

engender generate

engrave carve into a material

engross captivate

engulf overwhelm

enhance improve

enigmatic puzzling

enjoin urge, order

enlighten inform

enlist join

enmity hostility, hatred

ennoble exalt

ennui boredom

enormity large, tragic

ensemble musical group

enshroud cover

ensnare trap

ensue follow immediately

entail involve, necessitate

enterprise undertaking

enthrall mesmerize

entice lure

entomology the study of insects

entourage assemblage

entreat plead

entrench fortify

entrepreneur businessman

enumerate count

enviable desirable

envision imagine

envoy messenger

eon long period of time

ephemeral short-lived

epic majestic

epicure gourmet

epidemic spreading rapidly

epidemiology study of the spread of disease

epigram saying

episode incident

epistemology the branch of philosophy dealing with knowledge

Quiz 6 (Matching)

Match each word in the first column with its definition in the second column.

1.	DORMANT	A.	exuberant
2.	DOUGHTY	B.	puzzling
3.	DUET	C.	comprehensive
4.	EBULLIENT	D.	asleep
5.	EFFEMINATE	E.	omission of words
6.	ELLIPSIS	F.	unmanly
7.	EMANCIPATE	G.	charm
8.	ENCHANT	H.	liberate
9.	ENCYCLOPEDIC	I.	twosome
10.	ENIGMATIC	J.	resolute

---

epithet name, appellation

epoch era

epoxy glue

equable even-tempered

equanimity composure

equine pertaining to horses

equitable fair

equivocate make intentionally ambiguous

era period of time

eradicate abolish

ergo therefore

erode wear away

err mistake, misjudge

errant wandering

erratic constantly changing

erroneous mistaken

ersatz artificial

erudite learned

erupt burst forth

escalate intensify

escapade adventure

escarpment a steep slope

eschew avoid

esoteric known by only a few

esplanade boardwalk

espouse advocate

esteem respect

esthetic artistic

estimable meritorious

estrange alienate

eternal endless

ethereal light, airy

ethical conforming to accepted standards of behavior

ethos beliefs of a group

etiquette manners

etymology study of words

euphemism genteel expression

euphoria elation

euthanasia mercy-killing

evade avoid

evanescent fleeting, very brief

evangelical proselytizing

evasive elusive

eventful momentous

eventual ultimate, coming

eventuate bring about

evidential pertaining to evidence

evince attest, demonstrate

eviscerate disembowel

evoke draw forth

evolution gradual change

ewe female sheep

ex officio by virtue of position

exacerbate worsen

exact use authority to force payment

exacting demanding, difficult

exalt glorify

exasperate irritate

excerpt selection, extract

excision removal

exclaim shout

exclude shut out

exclusive prohibitive

excommunicate expel

excruciate torture

execrable abominable

execute put into effect

exegesis interpretation

exemplary outstanding

exempt excuse

exhaustive thorough

exhibitionist one who draws attention to himself

exhort strongly urge

exhume uncover

exigency urgency

exiguous scanty

exile banish

exodus departure, migration

exonerate free from blame

exorbitant expensive

exorcise expel

expanse extent of land

expansive sweeping

expedient advantageous

expedite hasten

expel drive out

expertise knowledge, ability

expiate atone

expletive oath

expliate atone

explicate explain

explicit definite, clear

exploit utilize, milk

expose divulge

expostulate protest

expound explain

expropriate dispossess

expunge erase

exquisite beautifully made

extant existing

extemporize improvise

extent scope

extenuate mitigate

extirpate seek out and destroy

extol praise highly

extort extract, force

extract to pull out, exact

extradite deport, deliver

extraneous not essential

extrapolate infer

extremity farthest point

extricate disentangle

extroverted outgoing

extrude force out

exuberant joyous

exude emit

exult rejoice

F

fabrication a lie

facade mask

facet aspect

facetious joking, sarcastic

facile easy

facilitate make easier

facility skill

facsimile duplicate

faction clique, sect

factious causing disagreement

factitious artificial

factotum handyman

fallacious false

fallacy false belief

fallow unproductive, unplowed

falsetto high male voice

falter waver

fanaticism excessive zeal

fane temple

fanfare publicity

farcical absurd

farrago mixture

fascism totalitarianism

fastidious meticulous

fatal resulting in death

fathom understand

fatuity foolishness

fatuous inane, stupid

fauna animals

faux pas false step, mistake

fealty loyalty

feasible likely to succeed

feat deed

febrile feverish, delirious

feckless incompetent

fecund fertile

feign pretend

felicity happiness

felonious criminal

femme fatale a woman who leads men to their destruction

fend ward off

feral untamed, wild

ferment turmoil

ferret rummage through

fertile fruitful

fervor intensity

fester decay

festive joyous

festoon decorate

fete to honor

fetid stinking

fetters shackles

fey eccentric, whimsical

fiasco debacle

fiat decree

fickle always changing one's mind

fictitious invented, imaginary

fidelity loyalty

figment falsehood, fantasy

filch steal

filial son

filibuster long speech

fillip stimulus

finale conclusion

finesse skill

firebrand agitator

firmament sky

fiscal monetary

fitful irregular

fjord inlet

flabbergasted amazed, bumdfounded

flagellate whip

flagrant outrageous

flail whip

fledgling just beginning, struggling

flippant pert

florid ruddy

flout to show disregard for the law or rules

fluctuate waver, vary

foible weakness, minor fault

foil defeat

foist palm off a fake

foment instigate

font source, fountainhead, set of type

forage search for food

foray raid

forbear abstain

force majeure superior force

Quiz 7 (Matching)

Match each word in the first column with its definition in the second column.

1.	EXHORT	A.	free from blame
2.	EXONERATE	B.	strongly urge
3.	EXPOSTULATE	C.	agitator
4.	EXTRADITE	D.	untamed
5.	EXULT	E.	debacle
6.	FACTITIOUS	F.	inane
7.	FATUOUS	G.	artificial
8.	FERAL	H.	deport
9.	FIASCO	I.	rejoice
10.	FIREBRAND	J.	protest

---

foreclose exclude

forensic pertaining to debate

foresight ability to predict the future

forestall thwart

forgo relinquish

forsake abandon

forswear deny

forthright frank

forthwith immediately

fortify strengthen

fortitude patience, courage

fortuitous lucky

foster encourage

founder sink

fracas noisy fight

fragile easily broken

fragmented broken into fragments

fraternity brotherhood

fraught filled

frenetic harried, neurotic

fret worry

fritter squander

frivolity playfulness

frolic romp, play

frond bending tree

frugal thrifty

fruitful productive

fruition realization, completion

fruitless unprofitable, barren

fulminate denounce, menace

fulsome excessive, insincere

fuming angry

furlough leave of absence

furor commotion

furtive stealthy

fusillade bombardment

futile hopeless

G

gaffe embarrassing mistake

gainful profitable

gainsay contradict

galvanize excite to action

gambit plot

gamut range

gargantuan large

garner gather

garnish decorate

garrote stranglehold

garrulous talkative

gauche awkward

genealogy ancestry

generic general

genesis beginning

genetics study of heredity

genre kind, category

genteel elegant

genuflect kneel in reverence

genuine authentic

geriatrics pertaining to old age

germane relevant

ghastly horrible

gibe heckle

gingivitis inflammation of the gums

gist essence

glabrous without hair

glaucoma disorder of the eye

glean gather

glib insincere manner

glower stare angrily

glut surplus, excess

glutton one who eats too much

gnarl deform

gnome dwarf-like being

goad encourage

googol a very large number

gorge stuff, satiate

gorgon ugly person

gormandize eat voraciously

gory bloody

gossamer thin and flimsy

Gothic medieval

gouge overcharge

gracious kindness

gradient incline, rising by degrees

gradual by degrees

grandiose impressive, large

granular grainy

grapple struggle

gratis free

gratitude thankfulness

gratuitous unwarranted, uncalled for

gratuity tip

gravamen the essential part of an accusation

gravity seriousness

gregarious sociable

grievous tragic, heinous

grimace expression of disgust

grisly gruesome

grovel crawl, obey

grudging reluctant

guffaw laughter

guile deceit

gullible easily deceived

gusto great enjoyment

guttural throaty

gyrate whirl

H

habitat natural environment

habituate accustom

hackneyed trite

haggard gaunt

halcyon serene

hale healthy

hallucination delusion

hamper obstruct

hapless unlucky

harangue tirade

harass torment

harbinger forerunner

harbor give shelter, conceal

hardy healthy

harlequin clown

harp complain incessantly

harridan hag

harrowing distressing

harry harass

haughty arrogant

haven refuge

havoc destruction

hearsay gossip

hedonism the pursuit of pleasure in life

heed follow advice

heedless careless

hegemony authority, domination

hegira a journey to a more pleasant place

heinous vile

heliocentric having the sun as a center

helix a spiral

helots slaves

herald harbinger

herbivorous feeding on plants

Herculean powerful, large

hermetic airtight, sealed

hermit one who lives in solitude

herpetologist one who studies reptiles

heterodox departing form established doctrines

heuristic teaching device or method

hew cut

heyday glory days

hiatus interruption

hibernal wintry

hidalgo nobleman

hidebound prejudiced

hideous horrible

hie to hasten

highbrow intellectual

hirsute bearded

histrionic overly dramatic

holograph written entirely by hand

homage respect

homely plain

homily sermon

homogeneous uniform

homonym words that are identical in spelling and pronunciation

hone sharpen

horde group

hortatory inspiring good deeds

hospice shelter

hovel shanty, cabin

hoyden tomboy

hubris arrogance

hue color

humane compassionate

humanities languages and literature

humility humbleness

hummock knoll, mound

humus soil

husbandry management

hybrid crossbreed

hydrophobia fear of water

hygienic sanitary

hymeneal pertaining to marriage

hymn religious song

hyperactive overactive

hyperbole exaggeration

hypertension elevated blood pressure

hypocritical deceiving, two-faced

hypoglycemic low blood sugar

hypothermia low body temperature

I

ibidem in the same place

ichthyology study of fish

iconoclast one who rails against sacred institutions

idiosyncrasy peculiarity

idyllic natural, picturesque

ignoble dishonorable

ilk class, clan

illicit unlawful

illimitable limitless

illusory fleeting

illustrious famous

imbibe drink

imbue infuse

immaculate spotlessly clean

immaterial irrelevant

immense huge

Quiz 8 (Matching)

Match each word in the first column with its definition in the second column.

1.	GRANDIOSE	A.	drink
2.	GRIEVOUS	B.	pertaining to marriage
3.	HALCYON	C.	arrogance
4.	HARLEQUIN	D.	prejudiced
5.	HEDONISM	E.	teaching device or method
6.	HEURISTIC	F.	the pursuit of pleasure in life
7.	HIDEBOUND	G.	clown
8.	HUBRIS	H.	serene
9.	HYMENEAL	I.	heinous
10.	IMBIBE	J.	impressive

immerse bathe

imminent about to happen

immobile still

immolate sacrifice

immunity exemption from prosecution

immure build a wall around

immutable unchangeable

impair injure

impale pierce

impartial not biased

impasse deadlock

impassioned fiery, emotional

impassive calm

impeach accuse, charge

impeccable faultless

impecunious indigent

impede hinder

impediment obstacle

impel urge, force

impending approaching

imperative vital, pressing

imperceptible slight, intangible

imperialism colonialism

imperil endanger

imperious domineering

impertinent insolent

imperturbable calm

impervious impenetrable

impetuous impulsive

impetus stimulus, spark

impinge encroach, touch

implant instill

implausible unlikely

implement carry out, execute

implicate incriminate

implicit implied

implore entreat

implosion bursting inward

impolitic unwise

imponderable difficult to estimate

import meaning, significance

importune urgent request

imposing intimidating

imposition intrusion

impotent powerless

impound seize

imprecation curse, inculcate

impregnable invincible

impresario promoter

impressionable susceptible, easily influenced

impressionism a style of painting

imprimatur sanction

impromptu spontaneous

improvise invent

impudence insolence

impugn criticize

impulse inclination

impulsive to act suddenly

impunity exemption from harm

impute charge

in toto in full, entirely

inadvertent unintentional

inadvisable not recommended

inalienable that which cannot be taken away

inane vacuous, stupid

inanimate inorganic, lifeless

inaudible cannot be heard

inaugurate induct

inborn innate

incalculable immeasurable

incandescent brilliant

incantation chant

incapacitate disable

incarcerate imprison

incarnate embody, personify

incendiary inflammatory

incense enrage

incentive stimulus

incessant unceasing

incest sex among family members

inchoate just begun

incidental insignificant, minor

incinerate burn

incipient beginning

incision cut

incisive keen, penetrating

incite foment, provoke

incivility disdain

inclement harsh

inclusive comprehensive

incognito disguised

incommunicado unable to communicate with others

incomparable peerless

incompatibility inability to live in harmony

inconceivable unthinkable

incongruous out of place, absurd

inconsiderate thoughtless

inconspicuous not noticeable

incontrovertible indisputable

incorporate combine

incorrigible unreformable

incredulous skeptical

increment step, increase

incriminate accuse

incubus nightmare

inculcate instill, indoctrinate

inculpate accuse

incumbent obligatory

incursion raid

indecent offensive

indecorous unseemly

indelible permanent

indemnity insurance

indict charge

indifferent unconcerned

indigenous native

indigent poor

indignant resentment of injustice

indiscreet lacking sound judgment, rash

indiscriminate random

indispensable vital, essential

indistinct blurry, without clear features

indolent lazy

indomitable invincible

indubitable unquestionable

induce persuade

indulge succumb to desire

indurate harden

industrious hard-working

inebriate intoxicate

ineffable inexpressible

ineffectual futile

ineluctable inescapable

inept unfit

inert inactive

inestimable priceless

inevitable unavoidable, predestined

inexorable relentless

infallible unerring

infamous notorious

infamy shame

infantry foot soldiers

infatuate immature love

infer conclude

infernal hellish

infidel nonbeliever

infidelity disloyalty

infiltrate trespass

infinitesimal very small

infirmary clinic

infirmity ailment

inflammatory incendiary

influx inflow

infraction violation

infringe encroach

infuriate enrage

infuse inspire, instill

ingenious clever

ingrate ungrateful person

ingratiate pleasing, flattering, endearing

ingress entering

inherent innate, inborn

inhibit restrain

inimical adverse, hostile

inimitable peerless

iniquitous unjust, wicked

iniquity sin

initiate begin

initiation induction ceremony

injunction command

inkling hint

innate inborn

innervate invigorate

innocuous harmless

innovative new, useful idea

innuendo insinuation

inopportune untimely

inordinate excessive

inquest investigation

inquisition interrogation

inquisitive curious

insatiable gluttonous

inscribe engrave

inscrutable cannot be fully understood

insensate without feeling

insidious treacherous

insignia emblems

insinuate allude

insipid flat, dull

insolent insulting

insolvent bankrupt

insouciant nonchalant

installment portion

instant at once

instigate incite

insubordinate disobedient

insufferable unbearable

insular narrow-minded

insuperable insurmountable

insurgent rebellious

insurrection uprising

intangible not perceptible by touch

integral essential

integrate make whole

integration unification

integument a covering

intelligentsia the intellectual elite of society

intensive extreme

inter bury

Quiz 9 (Matching)

Match each word in the first column with its definition in the second column.

1.	INCONGRUOUS	A.	harden
2.	INCONSPICUOUS	B.	relentless
3.	INDECOROUS	C.	hostile
4.	INDIGNANT	D.	cannot be fully understood
5.	INDURATE	E.	out of place, absurd
6.	INEXORABLE	F.	not noticeable
7.	INIMICAL	G.	unseemly
8.	INSCRUTABLE	H.	resentment of injustice
9.	INSOUCIANT	I.	nonchalant
10.	INSUPERABLE	J.	insurmountable

---

intercede plead on behalf of another

intercept prevent

interdict prohibit

interject interrupt **interloper** intruder

interlude intermission

interminable unending

internecine mutually destructive

interpolate insert

interpose insert

interregnum interval between two successive reigns

interrogate question

intersperse scatter

interstate between states

intervene interfere, mediate

intestate leaving no will

intimate allude to

intractable unmanageable

intransigent unyielding

intrepid fearless

intricate complex

intrigue plot, mystery

intrinsic inherent

introspection self-analysis

inundate flood

inure accustom, habituate, harden

invalidate disprove

invective verbal insult

inveigh to rail against

inveigle lure

inventive cleaver, resourceful

inverse directly opposite

inveterate habitual, chronic

invidious incurring ill-will

invincible cannot be defeated

inviolate sacred

invocation calling on God

irascible irritable

irate angry

ironic oddly contrary to what is expected

irrational illogical

irrelevant unrelated, immaterial

irreparable cannot be repaired

irresolute hesitant, uncertain

irrevocable cannot be rescinded

isosceles having two equal sides

itinerant wandering

itinerary route

J

jabberwocky nonsense

jaded spent, bored with one's situation

jargon specialized vocabulary

jaundiced biased, embittered

jeer mock

jejune barren

jest joke

jilt reject

jingoistic nationalistic, warmongering

jocular humorous

jostle push, brush against

journeyman reliable worker

joust combat between knights on horses

jubilant in high spirits

judicious prudent

juggernaut unstoppable force

jugular throat

juncture pivotal point in time

junoesque stately beauty

junta small ruling group

jurisdiction domain

jurisprudence law

justify excuse, mitigate

juvenescent making young

juxtapose to place side by side

K

kaleidoscope series of changing events

keen of sharp mind

ken purview, range of comprehension

kindle arouse, inspire

kindred similar

kinetic pertaining to motion

kismet fate

kite bad check

kitsch trashy art

kleptomania impulse to steal

knave con man

knead massage

knell sound of a bell

Koran holy book of Islam

kowtow behave obsequiously

kudos acclaim

L

labyrinth maze

lacerate tear, cut

lachrymose tearful

lackey servant

laconic brief, terse

lactic derived from milk

lacuna a missing part, gap

laggard loafer

lagniappe bonus

laity laymen

lambent softly radiant

lament mourn

lamina layer

lampoon satirize

languish weaken

lanyard short rope

larceny theft

largess generous donation

lascivious lustful

lassitude lethargy

latent potential

laudatory commendable

laurels fame

lave wash

lavish extravagant

lax loose, careless

laxity carelessness

layman nonprofessional

lectern reading desk

leery cautious

legacy bequest

legerdemain trickery

legible readable

legislate make laws

legitimate lawful

lenient forgiving

lethargic drowsy, sluggish

levee embankment, dam

leviathan a monster

levity frivolity

liable responsible

liaison relationship, affair

libertarian one who believes in complete freedom

libertine roué, rake

libidinous lustful

licentious lewd, immoral

lien financial claim

lieutenant one who acts in place of another

ligature bond

ligneous woodlike

Lilliputian very small

limerick poem

limn portray, describe

limpid transparent, clearly understood

linchpin something that is indispensable

lineage ancestry

linguistics study of language

liquidate eliminate

lissome agile, supple

listless lacking spirit or interest

litany list

lithe supple

litigate contest

litotes two negative statements that cancel to make a positive statement

liturgy ceremony

livid enraged

loath reluctant

loathe abhor

lofty high

logistics means of supplying troops

logo symbol

logy sluggish

loquacious talkative

lothario rake, womanizer

lout goon

lucid clearly understood

lucrative profitable

lucre money, profit

ludicrous absurd

lugubrious sad

luminous bright

lupine wolf-like

lure entice

lurid ghastly

luster gloss

luxuriant lush

lynch hang without trial

M

macabre gruesome

Machiavellian politically crafty, cunning

machination plot

macrobiosis longevity

macroscopic visibly large

maelstrom whirlpool

magisterial arbitrary, dictatorial

magnanimous generous, kindhearted

magnate a powerful, successful person

magnitude size

magnum opus masterpiece

maim injure

maladjusted disturbed

maladroit clumsy

malady illness

malaise uneasiness, weariness

malapropism comical misuse of a word

malcontent one who is forever dissatisfied

malediction curse

malefactor evildoer

malevolence bad intent, malice

malfeasance wrong doing

malice spite

malign defame

malignant virulent, pernicious

Quiz 10 (Matching)

Match each word in the first column with its definition in the second column.

1.	LACHRYMOSE	A.	trickery
2.	LAGGARD	B.	roué
3.	LASCIVIOUS	C.	very small
4.	LEGERDEMAIN	D.	tearful
5.	LIBERTINE	E.	loafer
6.	LILLIPUTIAN	F.	lustful
7.	LOQUACIOUS	G.	talkative
8.	MACHIAVELLIAN	H.	comical misuse of a word
9.	MAGISTERIAL	I.	arbitrary, dictatorial
10.	MALAPROPISM	J.	politically crafty, cunning

malinger shirk

malleable moldable, tractable

malodorous fetid

mammoth huge

manacle shackle

mandate command

mandatory obligatory

mandrill baboon

mania madness

manifest obvious, evident

manifesto proclamation

manifold multiple, diverse

manslaughter killing someone without malice

manumit set free

manuscript unpublished book

mar damage

marauder plunderer

marginal insignificant

marionette puppet

maroon abandon

marshal array, mobilize

martial warlike

martinet disciplinarian

martyr sacrifice, symbol

masochist one who enjoys pain

masticate chew

mastiff large dog

mastodon extinct elephant

maternal motherly

maternity motherhood

matriarch matron

matriculate enroll

matrix array

matutinal early

maudlin weepy, sentimental

maul rough up

mausoleum tomb

maverick a rebel

mawkish sickeningly sentimental

mayhem mutilation

mea culpa my fault

meager scanty

meander roam, ramble

median middle

mediocre average

medley mixture

megalith ancient stone monument

melancholy reflective, gloomy

melee riot

mellifluous sweet sounding

melodious melodic

memento souvenir

memoir autobiography

memorabilia things worth remembering

memorandum note

menagerie zoo

mendacity untruth

mendicant beggar

menial humble, degrading

mentor teacher

mercantile commercial

mercenary calculating, venal

mercurial changeable, volatile

metamorphosis a change in form

mete distribute

meteoric swift

meteorology science of weather

methodical systematic, careful

meticulous extremely careful, precise

metier occupation

metonymy the substitution of a phrase for the name itself

mettle courage, capacity for bravery

miasma toxin

mien appearance, bearing

migrate travel

milieu environment

militant combative

militate work against

milk extract

millennium thousand-year period

minatory threatening

mince chop, moderate

minion subordinate

minstrel troubadour

minuscule small

minute very small

minutiae trivia

mirage illusion

mire marsh

mirth jollity

misanthrope hater of mankind

misappropriation use dishonestly

misbegotten illegitimate

miscarry abort

miscegenation intermarriage between races

miscellany mixture of items

misconstrue misinterpret

miscreant evildoer

misgiving doubt

misnomer wrongly named

misogyny hatred of women

misshapen deformed

missive letter

mitigate lessen the severity

mnemonics that which aids the memory

mobilize assemble for action

mobocracy rule by mob

modicum pittance

modish chic

module unit

mogul powerful person

molest bother

mollify appease

molten melted

momentous of great importance

monocle eyeglass

monolithic large and uniform

monologue long speech

monstrosity distorted, abnormal form

moot disputable

moral ethical

morale spirit, confidence

morass swamp, difficult situation

moratorium postponement

mordant biting, sarcastic

mores moral standards

moribund near death

morose sullen

morphine painkilling drug

morsel bite, piece

mortify humiliate

mosque temple

mote speck

motif theme

motive reason

motley diverse

mottled spotted

motto slogan, saying

mountebank charlatan

mousy drab, colorless

muckraker reformer

muffle stifle, quiet

mulct defraud

multifarious diverse, many-sided

multitude throng

mundane ordinary

munificent generous

murmur mutter, mumble

muse ponder

muster to gather one's forces

mutability able to change

mute silent

mutilate maim

mutiny rebellion

mutter murmur, grumble

muzzle restrain

myopic narrow-minded

myriad innumerable

myrmidons loyal followers

mystique mystery, aura

mythical fictitious

N

nadir lowest point

narcissism self-love

narrate tell, recount

nascent incipient

natal related to birth

nativity the process of birth

naturalize grant citizenship

ne'er-do-well loafer, idler

nebulous indistinct

necromancy sorcery

nefarious evil

negate cancel

negligible insignificant

nemesis implacable foe

neologism newly coined expression

neonatal newborn

neophyte beginner

nepotism favoritism

nervy brash

nether under

nettle irritate

neurotic disturbed

neutralize offset, nullify

nexus link

nicety euphemism

niche nook

niggardly stingy

nimble spry

nirvana bliss

noctambulism sleepwalking

nocturnal pertaining to night

nocturne serenade

noisome harmful

nomad wanderer

nomenclature terminology

nominal slight, in name only

nominate propose

nominee candidate

nonchalant casual

noncommittal neutral, circumspect

nondescript lacking distinctive features

nonentity person of no significance

nonesuch paragon, one in a thousand

nonpareil unequaled, peerless

Quiz 11 (Matching)

Match each word in the first column with its definition in the second column.

1.	MISCELLANY	A.	peerless
2.	MISSIVE	B.	to gather one's forces
3.	MOOT	C.	newly coined expression
4.	MOUNTEBANK	D.	self-love
5.	MULTIFARIOUS	E.	loyal followers
6.	MUSTER	F.	letter
7.	MYRMIDONS	G.	diverse
8.	NARCISSISM	H.	charlatan
9.	NEOLOGISM	I.	disputable
10.	NONPAREIL	J.	mixture of items

nonpartisan neutral, uncommitted

nonplus confound

notable remarkable, noteworthy

noted famous

notorious wicked, widely known

nouveau riche newly rich

nova bright star

novel new, unique

novice beginner

noxious toxic

nuance shade, subtlety

nub crux

nubile marriageable

nugatory useless, worthless

nuisance annoyance

nullify void

nullity nothingness

numismatics coin collecting

nurture nourish, foster

nymph goddess

O

oaf awkward person

obdurate unyielding

obeisance homage, deference

obelisk tall column, monument

obese fat

obfuscate bewilder, muddle

obituary eulogy

objective (adj.) unbiased

objective (noun) goal

objectivity impartiality

oblation offering, sacrifice

obligatory required

oblige compel

obliging accommodating, considerate

oblique indirect

obliquity perversity

obliterate destroy

oblong elliptical, oval

obloquy slander

obscure vague, unclear

obsequious fawning, servile

obsequy funeral ceremony

observant watchful

obsolete outdated

obstinate stubborn

obstreperous noisy, unruly

obtain gain possession

obtrusive forward, meddlesome

obtuse stupid

obviate make unnecessary

Occident the West

occlude block

occult mystical

octogenarian person in her eighties

ocular optic, visual

ode poem

odious despicable

odoriferous pleasant odor

odyssey journey

offal inedible parts of a butchered animal

offertory church collection

officiate supervise

officious forward, obtrusive

offset counterbalance

ogle flirt

ogre monster, demon

oleaginous oily

oligarchy aristocracy

olio medley

ominous threatening

omnibus collection, compilation

omnipotent all-powerful

omniscient all-knowing

onerous burdensome

onslaught attack

ontology the study of the nature of existence

onus burden

opaque nontransparent

operative working

operetta musical comedy

opiate narcotic

opine think

opportune well-timed

oppress persecute

oppressive burdensome

opprobrious abusive, scornful

opprobrium disgrace

oppugn assail

opt decide, choose

optimum best condition

optional elective

opulence wealth

opus literary work or musical composition

oracle prophet

oration speech

orator speaker

orb sphere

orchestrate organize

ordain appoint

orderly neat

ordinance law

ordnance artillery

orient align

orison prayer

ornate lavishly decorated

ornithology study of birds

orthodox conventional

oscillate waver

ossify harden

ostensible apparent, seeming

ostentatious pretentious

ostracize ban

otherworldly spiritual

otiose idle

ouster ejection

outmoded out-of-date

outré eccentric

outset beginning

ovation applause

overrule disallow

overture advance, proposal

overweening arrogant, forward

overwhelm overpower

overwrought overworked, high-strung

ovum egg, cell

P

pachyderm elephant

pacifist one who opposes all violence

pacify appease

pact agreement

paean a song of praise

pagan heathen, ungodly

page attendant

pageant exhibition, show

pains labor

painstaking taking great care

palatial grand, splendid

palaver babble, nonsense

Paleolithic stone age

paleontologist one who studies fossils

pall to become dull or weary

palliate assuage

pallid pale, sallow

palpable touchable

palpitate beat, throb

palsy paralysis

paltry scarce

pan criticize

panacea cure-all

panache flamboyance

pandemic universal

pandemonium din, commotion

pander cater to people's baser instincts

panegyric praise

pang pain

panoply full suit of armor

panorama vista

pant gasp, puff

pantomime mime

pantry storeroom

papyrus paper

parable allegory

paradigm a model

paragon standard of excellence

parameter limit

paramount chief, foremost

paramour lover

paranoid obsessively suspicious, demented

paranormal supernatural

parapet rampart, defense

paraphernalia equipment

paraphrase restatement

parcel package

parchment paper

pare peel

parenthetical in parentheses

pariah outcast

parish fold, church

parity equality

parlance local speech

parlay increase

parley conference

parochial provincial

parody imitation, ridicule

parole release

paroxysm outburst, convulsion

parrot mimic

parry avert, ward off

parsimonious stingy

parson clergyman

partake share, receive

partial incomplete

partiality bias

parting farewell, severance

partisan supporter

partition division

parvenu newcomer, social climber

pasquinade satire

passé outmoded

passim here and there

pastel pale

pasteurize disinfect

pastoral rustic

patent obvious

paternal fatherly

pathetic pitiful

pathogen agent causing disease

Quiz 12 (Matching)

Match each word in the first column with its definition in the second column.

1.	ORDNANCE	A.	a model
2.	ORTHODOX	B.	local speech
3.	OUTMODED	C.	convulsion
4.	PALAVER	D.	stingy
5.	PANEGYRIC	E.	agent causing disease
6.	PARADIGM	F.	artillery
7.	PARLANCE	G.	conventional
8.	PAROXYSM	H.	out-of-date
9.	PARSIMONIOUS	I.	babble
10.	PATHOGEN	J.	praise

---

pathogenic causing disease

pathos emotion

patrician aristocrat

patrimony inheritance

patronize condescend

patronymic a name formed form the name of a father

patter walk lightly

paucity scarcity

paunch stomach

pauper poor person

pavilion tent

pawn (noun) tool, stooge

pawn (verb) pledge

pax peace

peaked wan, pale, haggard

peal reverberation, outburst

peccadillo a minor fault

peculate embezzle

peculiar unusual

peculiarity characteristic

pedagogical pertaining to teaching

pedagogue dull, formal teacher

pedant pedagogue

pedantic bookish

peddle sell

pedestrian common

pedigree genealogy

peerage aristocracy

peevish cranky

pejorative insulting

pell-mell in a confused manner

pellucid transparent

pen write

penance atonement

penchant inclination

pend depend, hang

pending not decided

penitent repentant

pensive sad

penurious stingy

penury poverty

peon common worker

per se in itself

perceptive discerning

percolate ooze, permeate

perdition damnation

peregrination wandering

peremptory dictatorial

perennial enduring, lasting

perfectionist purist, precisionist

perfidious treacherous (of a person)

perforate puncture

perforce by necessity

perfunctory careless

perigee point nearest to the earth

perilous dangerous

peripatetic walking about

periphery outer boundary

perish die

perishable decomposable

perjury lying

permeate spread throughout

permutation reordering

pernicious destructive

peroration conclusion

perpendicular at right angles

perpetrate commit

perpetual continuous

perpetuate cause to continue

perpetuity eternity

perplex puzzle, bewilder

perquisite reward, bonus

persecute harass

persevere persist, endure

persona social facade

personable charming

personage official, dignitary

personify embody, exemplify

personnel employees

perspicacious keen

perspicacity discernment, keenness

persuasive convincing

pert flippant, bold

pertain to relate

pertinacious persevering

pertinent relevant

perturbation agitation

peruse read carefully

pervade permeate

pessimist cynic

pestilence disease

petite small

petition request

petrify calcify, shock

petrology study of rocks

pettifogger unscrupulous lawyer

petty trivial

petulant irritable, peevish

phantasm apparition

phenomena unusual natural events

philanthropic charitable

philanthropist altruist

philatelist stamp collector

philippic invective

Philistine barbarian

philosophical contemplative

phlegmatic sluggish

phobia fear

phoenix rebirth

physic laxative, cathartic

physique frame, musculature

picaresque roguish, adventurous

picayune trifling

piecemeal one at a time

pied mottled, brindled

piety devoutness

pilfer steal

pillage plunder

pillory punish by ridicule

pine languish

pinnacle highest point

pious devout, holy

piquant tart-tasting, spicy

pique sting, arouse interest

piscine pertaining to fish

piteous sorrowful, pathetic

pithy concise

pitiable miserable, wretched

pittance alms, driblet

pittance trifle

pivotal crucial

pixilated eccentric, possessed

placard poster

placate appease

placid serene

plagiarize pirate, counterfeit

plaintive expressing sorrow

platitude trite remark

platonic nonsexual

plaudit acclaim

pleasantry banter, persiflage

plebeian common, vulgar

plebiscite referendum

plenary full

plentiful abundant

pleonasm redundancy, verbosity

plethora overabundance

pliable flexible

pliant supple, flexible

plight sad situation

plucky courageous

plumb measure

plummet fall

plutocrat wealthy person

plutonium radioactive material

poach steal

podgy fat

podium stand, rostrum

pogrom massacre, mass murder

poignant pungent, sharp

polemic a controversy

polity methods of government

poltroon dastard

polychromatic many-colored

polygamist one who has many wives

ponder muse, reflect

ponderous heavy, bulky

pontiff bishop

pontificate to speak at length

pootroon coward

porcine pig-like

porous permeable, spongy

porridge stew

portend signify, augur

portent omen

portly large

portmanteau suitcase

posit stipulate

posterior rear, subsequent

posterity future generations

posthaste hastily

posthumous after death

postulate supposition, premise

potent powerful

potentate sovereign, king

potion brew

potpourri medley

potter aimlessly busy

pragmatic practical

prate babble

prattle chatter

preamble introduction

precarious dangerous, risky

precedent an act that serves as an example

precept principle, law

precinct neighborhood

precipice cliff

precipitate cause

precipitous steep

précis summary

precise accurate, detailed

preclude prevent

precocious advanced

preconception prejudgment, prejudice

precursor forerunner

predacious plundering

predecessor one who proceeds

predestine foreordain

predicament quandary

predicate base

predilection inclination

predisposed inclined

preeminent supreme

preempt commandeer

preen groom

prefabricated ready-built

prefect magistrate

preference choice

preferment promotion

prelate primate, bishop

preliminary introductory

prelude introduction

premeditate plan in advance

premonition warning

prenatal before birth

preponderance predominance

prepossessing appealing, charming

preposterous ridiculous

prerequisite requirement

prerogative right, privilege

presage omen

prescribe urge

presentable acceptable, well-mannered

preside direct, chair

pressing urgent

prestidigitator magicians

prestige reputation, renown

presume deduce

presumptuous assuming

presuppose assume

pretense affectation, excuse

pretentious affected, inflated

preternatural abnormal, supernatural

pretext excuse

prevail triumph

prevailing common, current

prevalent widespread

prevaricate lie

prick puncture

priggish pedantic, affected

prim formal, prudish

primal first, beginning

primate head, master

primogeniture first-born child

primp groom

princely regal, generous

prismatic many-colored, sparkling

pristine pure, unspoiled

privation hardship

privy aware of private matters

probe examine

probity integrity

problematic uncertain

proboscis snout

procedure method

Quiz 13 (Matching)

Match each word in the first column with its definition in the second column.

1.	PHOENIX	A.	cliff
2.	PILLORY	B.	inclination
3.	PITTANCE	C.	warning
4.	PLAUDIT	D.	acclaim
5.	PLETHORA	E.	overabundance
6.	POGROM	F.	after death
7.	POSTHUMOUS	G.	massacre
8.	PRECIPICE	H.	rebirth
9.	PREDILECTION	I.	punish by ridicule
10.	PREMONITION	J.	trifle

---

proceeds profit

proclaim announce

proclivity inclination

procreate beget

proctor supervise

procure acquire

procurer pander

prod urge

prodigal wasteful

prodigious marvelous, enormous

prodigy a person with extraordinary ability or talent

profane blasphemous

profess affirm

proffer bring forward

proficient skillful

profiteer extortionist

profligate licentious, prodigal

profound deep, knowledgeable

profusion overabundance

progenitor ancestor

progeny children

prognosis forecast

prognosticate foretell

progressive advancing, liberal

proletariat working class

proliferate increase rapidly

prolific fruitful, productive

prolix long-winded

prologue introduction

prolong lengthen in time

promenade stroll, parade

promethean inspirational

promiscuous sexually indiscreet

promontory headland, cape

prompt induce

prompter reminder

promulgate publish, disseminate

prone inclined, predisposed

propaganda publicity

propellant rocket fuel

propensity inclination

prophet prognosticator

prophylactic preventive

propinquity nearness

propitiate satisfy

propitious auspicious, favorable

proponent supporter, advocate

proportionate commensurate

proposition offer, proposal

propound propose

proprietor manager, owner

propriety decorum

prosaic uninspired, flat

proscenium platform, rostrum

proscribe prohibit

proselytize recruit, convert

prosody study of poetic structure

prospective expected, imminent

prospectus brochure

prostrate supine

protagonist main character in a story

protean changing readily

protégé ward, pupil

protocol code of diplomatic etiquette

proton particle

protract prolong

protuberance bulge

provender food

proverb maxim

proverbial well-known

providence foresight, divine protection

provident having foresight, thrifty

providential fortunate

province bailiwick, district

provincial intolerant, insular

provisional temporary

proviso stipulation

provisory conditional

provocation incitement

provocative titillating

provoke incite

prowess strength, expertise

proximity nearness

proxy substitute, agent

prude puritan

prudence discretion

prudent cautious

prudish puritanical

prurient lewd

pseudo false

pseudonym alias

psychic pertaining the psyche or mind

psychopath madman

psychotic demented

puberty adolescence

puckish impish, mischievous

puerile childish

pugilism boxing

pugnacious combative

puissant strong

pulchritude beauty

pulp paste, mush

pulpit platform, priesthood

pulsate throb

pulverize crush

pun wordplay

punctilious meticulous

pundit learned or politically astute person

pungent sharp smell or taste

punitive punishing

puny weak, small

purblind obtuse, stupid

purgative cathartic, cleansing

purgatory limbo, netherworld

purge cleanse, remove

puritanical prim

purlieus environs, surroundings

purloin steal

purport claim to be

purported rumored

purposeful determined

pursuant following, according

purvey deliver

purview range, understanding

pusillanimous cowardly

putative reputed

putrefy decay

putsch a sudden attempt to overthrow a government

pygmy dwarf

pyrotechnics fireworks

pyrrhic a battle won with unacceptable losses

Q

quack charlatan

quadrennial occurring every four years

quadrille square dance

quadruped four foot animal

quaff drink

quagmire difficult situation

quail shrink, cower

quaint old-fashioned

qualified limited

qualms misgivings

quandary dilemma

quantum quantity, particle

quarantine detention, confinement

quarry prey, game

quarter residence

quash put down, suppress

quasi seeming, almost

quaver tremble

quay wharf

queasy squeamish

queer odd

quell suppress, allay

quench extinguish, slake

querulous complaining

questionnaire interrogation

queue line

quibble bicker

quicken revive, hasten

quiddity essence

quiescent still, motionless

quietus a cessation of activity

quill feather, pen

quip joke

quirk eccentricity

quiver tremble

quixotic impractical, romantic

quizzical odd

quorum majority

quota a share or proportion

quotidian daily

R

rabble crowd

rabid mad, furious

racketeer gangster

raconteur story teller

radical revolutionary

raffish rowdy

rail rant, harangue

raiment clothing

rake womanizer

rally assemble

rambunctious boisterous

ramification consequence

rampage run amuck

rampant unbridled, raging

ramrod rod

rancid rotten

rancor resentment

randy vulgar

rankle cause bitterness, resentment

rant rage, scold

rapacious grasping, avaricious

rapidity speed

rapier sword

rapine plunder

rapport affinity, empathy

rapprochement reconciliation

rapture bliss

rash hasty, brash

rasp scrape

ratify approve

ration allowance, portion

rationale justification

Quiz 14 (Matching)

Match each word in the first column with its definition in the second column.

1.	PROTEAN	A.	bulge
2.	PROTUBERANCE	B.	changing readily
3.	PROVISIONAL	C.	steal
4.	PUNDIT	D.	majority
5.	PURLOIN	E.	temporary
6.	PURPORT	F.	a cessation of activity
7.	QUAVER	G.	line
8.	QUEUE	H.	tremble
9.	QUIETUS	I.	claim to be
10.	QUORUM	J.	politically astute person

---

ravage plunder

ravish captivate, charm

raze destroy

realm kingdom, domain

realpolitik cynical interpretation of politics

reap harvest

rebuff reject

rebuke criticize

rebus picture puzzle

rebuttal reply, counterargument

recalcitrant stubborn

recant retract

recapitulate restate, summarize

recede move back

receptacle container

receptive open to ideas

recidivism habitual criminal activity

recipient one who receives

reciprocal mutual, return in kind

recital performance

recitation recital, lesson

reclusive solitary

recoil flinch, retreat

recollect remember

recompense repay

reconcile adjust, balance

recondite mystical, profound

reconnaissance surveillance

reconnoiter to survey

recount recite

recoup recover

recourse appeal, resort

recreant cowardly

recrimination countercharge, retaliation

recruit draftee

rectify correct

recumbent reclining

recuperation recovery

recur repeat, revert

redeem buy back, justify

redeemer savior

redemption salvation

redolent fragrant

redoubt fort

redoubtable formidable, steadfast

redress restitution

redundant repetitious

reek smell

reel stagger

referendum vote

refined purified, cultured

reflux ebb

refraction bending, deflection

refractory obstinate

refrain abstain

refurbish remodel

refute disprove

regal royal

regale entertain

regalia emblems

regime a government

regiment infantry unit

regrettable lamentable

regurgitate vomit

rehash repeat

reign rule, influence

rein curb

reincarnation rebirth

reiterate repeat

rejoice celebrate

rejoinder answer, retort

rejuvenate make young again

relapse recurrence (of illness)

relegate assign to an inferior position

relent soften, yield

relentless unstoppable

relic antique

relinquish release

relish savor

remedial corrective

remiss negligent

remit forgive, send payment

remnant residue, fragment

remonstrance protest

remorse guilt

remuneration compensation

renaissance rebirth

renascent reborn

rend to tear apart

render deliver, provide

rendezvous a meeting

rendition version, interpretation

renege break a promise

renounce disown

renown fame

rent tear, rupture

reparation amends, atonement

repartee witty conversation

repatriate to send back to the native land

repellent causing aversion

repent atone for

repercussion consequence

repertoire stock of works

repine fret

replenish refill

replete complete

replica copy

replicate duplicate

repose rest

reprehensible blameworthy

repress suppress

reprieve temporary suspension

reprimand rebuke

reprisal retaliation

reprise repetition

reproach blame

reprobate miscreant

reprove rebuke

repudiate disavow

repugnant distasteful

repulse repel

repulsive repugnant

repute esteem

reputed supposed

requiem rest, a mass for the dead

requisite necessary

requisition order

requite to return in kind

rescind revoke

reserve self-control

reside dwell

residue remaining part

resigned accepting of a situation

resilience ability to recover from an illness

resolute determined

resolution determination

resolve determination

resonant reverberating

resort recourse

resound echo

resourceful inventive, skillful

respectively in order

respire breathe

respite rest

resplendent shining, splendid

restitution reparation, amends

restive nervous, uneasy

resurgence revival

resurrection rebirth

resuscitate revive

retain keep

retainer advance fee

retaliate revenge

retch vomit

reticent reserved

retiring modest, unassuming

retort quick reply

retrench cut back, economize

retribution reprisal

retrieve reclaim

retrograde regress

retrospective reminiscent

revamp recast

reveille bugle call

revel frolic, take joy in

revelry merrymaking

revenue income

revere honor

reverent respectful

reverie daydream

revert return

revile denounce, defame

revision new version

revive renew

revoke repeal

revulsion aversion

rhapsody ecstasy

rhetoric elocution, grandiloquence

rheumatism inflammation

ribald coarse, vulgar

rickety shaky, ramshackle

ricochet carom, rebound

rife widespread, abundant

riffraff dregs of society

rifle search through and steal

rift a split, an opening

righteous upright, moral

rigor harshness

rime crust

riposte counterthrust

risible laughable

risqué off-color, racy

rivet engross

robust vigorous

rogue scoundrel

roister bluster

romp frolic

roseate rosy, optimistic

roster list of people

rostrum podium

roué libertine

rouse awaken

rout vanquish

rubicund ruddy

ruck the common herd

rudiment beginning

rue regret

ruffian brutal person

ruminate ponder

rummage hunt

Quiz 15 (Matching)

Match each word in the first column with its definition in the second column.

1.	REGIME	A.	vulgar
2.	REJOINDER	B.	quick reply
3.	REMUNERATION	C.	uneasy
4.	RENDEZVOUS	D.	necessary
5.	RENT	E.	miscreant
6.	REPROBATE	F.	rupture
7.	REQUISITE	G.	a meeting
8.	RESTIVE	H.	compensation
9.	RETRIBUTION	I.	retort
10.	RIBALD	J.	a government

---

runel stream

ruse trick

rustic rural

S

Sabbath day of rest

sabbatical vacation

saber sword

sabotage treason, destruction

saccharine sugary, overly sweet tone

sacerdotal priestly

sack pillage

sacrament rite

sacred cow idol, taboo

sacrilege blasphemy

sacrosanct sacred

saddle encumber

sadist one who takes pleasure in hurting others

safari expedition

saga story

sagacious wise

sage wise person

salacious licentious

salient prominent

saline salty

sallow sickly complected

sally sortie, attack

salutary good, wholesome

salutation salute, greeting

salvation redemption

salve medicinal ointment

salvo volley, gunfire

sanctify consecrate

sanctimonious self-righteous

sanction approval

sanctuary refuge

sang-froid coolness under fire

sanguinary gory, murderous

sanguine cheerful

sans without

sapid interesting

sapient wise

sarcophagus stone coffin

sardonic scornful

sartorial pertaining to clothes

satanic pertaining to the Devil

satchel bag

sate satisfy fully

satiate satisfy fully

satire ridicule

saturate soak

saturnine gloomy

satyr demigod, goat-man

saunter stroll

savanna grassland

savant scholar

savoir-faire tact, polish

savor enjoy

savory appetizing

savvy perceptive

scabrous difficult

scant inadequate, meager

scapegoat one who takes blame for others

scarify criticize

scathe injure, denounce

scepter a rod, staff

scheme plot

schism rift

scintilla speck

scintillate sparkle

scion offspring

scoff jeer

scone biscuit

scorn disdain, reject

scoundrel unprincipled person

scour clean

scourge affliction

scruples misgivings

scrupulous principled, fastidious

scrutinize examine closely

scurf dandruff

scurrilous abusive, insulting

scurry move quickly

scuttle to sink (a ship)

scythe long, curved blade

sear burn

sebaceous like fat

secede withdraw

secluded remote, isolated

seclusion solitude

sectarian denominational

secular worldly, nonreligious

secure make safe

sedation state of calm

sedentary stationary, inactive

sedition treason

seduce lure

sedulous diligent

seedy rundown, ramshackle

seemly proper, attractive

seethe fume, resent

seismic pertaining to earthquakes

seismology study of earthquakes

self-effacing modest

semantics study of word meanings

semblance likeness

seminal fundamental

semper fidelis always loyal

senescence old age

senescent aging

seniority privilege due to length of service

sensational outstanding

sensible wise

sensory relating to the senses

sensualist epicure

sensuous appealing to the senses

sententious concise

sentient conscious

sentinel watchman

sepulcher tomb

sequacious dependent

sequel continuation, epilogue

sequester segregate

seraphic angelic

serendipity making fortunate discoveries

serene peaceful

serpentine winding

serried saw-toothed

serum vaccine

servile slavish

servitude forced labor

sessile permanently attached

session meeting

settee seat, sofa

sever cut in two

severance division

shallot onion

sham pretense

shambles disorder

shard fragment

sheen luster

sheepish shy

shibboleth password

shirk evade (work)

sliver fragment

shoal reef

shoring supporting

shortcomings deficiencies

shrew virago

shrewd clever

shrill high-pitched

shun avoid

shunt turn aside

shyster unethical lawyer

sibilant a hissing sound

sibling brother or sister

sickle semicircular blade

sidereal pertaining to the stars

sidle move sideways

siege blockade

sierra mountain range

sieve strainer

signatory signer

signet a seal

silhouette outline

silo storage tower

simian monkey

simile figure of speech

simper smile, smirk

simulacrum likeness

sinecure position with little responsibility

sinewy fibrous, stringy

singe burn just the surface of something

singly one by one

singular unique

sinister evil

sinistral left-handed

siphon extract

sire forefather, to beget

siren temptress

site location

skeptical doubtful

skinflint miser

skirmish a small battle

skittish excitable

skulk sneak about

skullduggery trickery

slake quench

slander defame

slate list of candidate

slaver drivel, fawn

slay kill

sleight dexterity

slew an abundance

slither slide

slogan motto

sloth laziness

slovenly sloppy

smattering superficial knowledge

smelt refine metal

smirk smug look

smite strike, afflict

smock apron

snare trap

snide sarcastic

snippet morsel

snivel whine

snub ignore

snuff extinguish

sobriety composed

Quiz 16 (Matching)

Match each word in the first column with its definition in the second column.

1.	SCRUPLES	A.	figure of speech
2.	SCYTHE	B.	proper, attractive
3.	SEEMLY	C.	long, curved blade
4.	SENTENTIOUS	D.	left-handed
5.	SERENDIPITY	E.	pertaining to the stars
6.	SHIBBOLETH	F.	signer
7.	SIDEREAL	G.	making fortunate discoveries
8.	SIGNATORY	H.	password
9.	SIMILE	I.	misgivings
10.	SINISTRAL	J.	concise

---

sobriquet nickname

socialite one who is prominent in society

sociology study of society

sodality companionship

sodden soaked

sojourn trip

solace consolation

solder fuse, weld

solecism ungrammatical construction

solemn serious, somber

solemnity seriousness

solicit request

solicitous considerate, concerned

soliloquy monologue

solstice furthest point

soluble dissolvable

solvent financially sound

somatic pertaining to the body

somber gloomy

somnambulist sleepwalker

somnolent sleepy

sonnet poem

sonorous resonant, majestic

sop morsel, compensation

sophistry specious reasoning

soporific sleep inducing

soprano high female voice

sordid foul, ignoble

sorority sisterhood

soubrette actress, ingenue

souse a drunk

sovereign monarch

spar fight

spasmodic intermittent

spate sudden outpouring

spawn produce

specimen sample

specious false but plausible

spectacle public display

spectral ghostly

spectrum range

speculate conjecture

speleologist one who studies caves

spew eject

spindle shaft

spindly tall and thin

spinster old maid

spire pinnacle

spirited lively

spirituous alcohol, intoxicating

spite malice, grudge

spittle spit

splay spread apart

spleen resentment, wrath

splenetic peevish

splurge indulge

spontaneous extemporaneous

sporadic occurring irregularly

sportive playful

spry nimble

spume foam

spurious false, counterfeit

spurn reject

squalid filthy

squall rain storm

squander waste

squelch crush, stifle

stagnant stale, motionless

staid demure, sedate

stalwart pillar, strong

stamina vigor, endurance

stanch loyal

stanchion prop

stanza division of a poem

stark desolate

startle surprise

stately impressive, noble

static inactive, immobile

statue regulation

staunch loyal

stave ward off

steadfast loyal

stealth secrecy, covertness

steeped soaked

stenography shorthand

stentorian loud

sterling high quality

stern strict

stevedore longshoreman

stifle suppress

stigma mark of disgrace

stiletto dagger

stilted formal, stiff

stimulate excite

stint limit, assignment

stipend payment

stipulate specify, arrange

stodgy stuffy, pompous

stoic indifferent to pain or pleasure

stoke prod, fuel

stole long scarf

stolid impassive

stout stocky

strait distress

stratagem trick

stratify form into layers

stratum layer

striate to stripe

stricture censure

strife conflict

striking impressive, attractive

stringent severe, strict

strive endeavor

studious diligent

stultify inhibit, enfeeble

stunted arrested development

stupefy deaden, dumfound

stupendous astounding

stupor lethargy

stylize formalize

stymie hinder, thwart

suave smooth

sub rosa in secret

subcutaneous beneath the skin

subdue conquer

subjugate suppress

sublet subcontract

sublimate to redirect forbidden impulses (usually sexual) into socially accepted activities

sublime lofty, excellent

sublunary earthly

submit yield

subordinate lower in rank

subsequent succeeding, following

subservient servile, submissive

subside diminish

subsidiary subordinate

subsidize financial assistance

substantiate verify

substantive substantial

subterfuge cunning, ruse

subterranean underground

subvert undermine

succor help, comfort

succulent juicy, delicious

succumb yield, submit

suffice adequate

suffrage vote

suffuse pervade, permeate

suggestive thought-provoking, risqué

sullen sulky, sour

sully stain

sultry sweltering

summon call for, arraign

sumptuous opulent, luscious

sunder split

sundry various

superb excellent

supercilious arrogant

supererogatory wanton, superfluous

superfluous overabundant

superimpose cover, place on top of

superintend supervise

superlative superior

supernumerary subordinate

supersede supplant

supervene ensue, follow

supervise oversee

supine lying on the back

supplant replace

supplication prayer

suppress subdue

surfeit overabundance

surly rude, crass

surmise to guess

surmount overcome

surname family name

surpass exceed, excel

surreal dreamlike

surreptitious secretive

surrogate substitute

surveillance close watch

susceptible vulnerable

suspend stop temporarily

sustenance food

susurrant whispering

suture surgical stitch

svelte slender

swank fashionable

swarthy dark (as in complexion)

swatch strip of fabric

sweltering hot

swivel a pivot

sybarite pleasure-seeker

sycophant flatterer, flunky

syllabicate divide into syllables

syllabus schedule

sylph a slim, graceful girl

sylvan rustic

symbiotic cooperative, working in close association

symmetry harmony, congruence

symposium panel (discussion)

symptomatic indicative

synagogue temple

syndicate cartel

syndrome set of symptoms

synod council

synopsis brief summary

synthesis combination

Quiz 17 (Matching)

Match each word in the first column with its definition in the second column.

1.	STAVE	A.	distress
2.	STEVEDORE	B.	diligent
3.	STRAIT	C.	ward off
4.	STUDIOUS	D.	longshoreman
5.	SUBJUGATE	E.	various
6.	SUBTERFUGE	F.	overabundant
7.	SUNDRY	G.	suppress
8.	SUPERFLUOUS	H.	cunning
9.	SUPINE	I.	dreamlike
10.	SURREAL	J.	lying on the back

---

systole heart contraction

T

tabernacle temple

table postpone

tableau scene, backdrop

taboo prohibition

tabulate arrange

tacit understood without being spoken

taciturn untalkative

tactful sensitive

tactics strategy

tactile tangible

taint pollute

talion punishment

tally count

talon claw

tandem two or more things together

tang strong taste

tangential peripheral

tangible touchable

tantalize tease

tantamount equivalent

taper candle

tariff tax on imported or exported goods

tarn small lake

tarnish taint

tarry linger

taurine bull-like

taut tight

tautological repetitious

tawdry gaudy

technology body of knowledge

tedious boring, tiring

teem swarm, abound

temerity boldness

temperate moderate

tempest storm

tempestuous agitated

tempo speed

temporal pertaining to time

tempt entice

tenable defensible, valid

tenacious persistent

tendentious biased

tenement decaying apartment building

tenet doctrine

tensile stretchable

tentative provisional

tenuous thin, insubstantial

tenure status given after a period of time

tepid lukewarm

terminal final

terminology nomenclature

ternary triple

terpsichorean related to dance

terrain the feature of land

terrapin turtle

terrestrial earthly

terse concise

testament covenant

testy petulant

tether tie down

theatrics histrionics

theologian one who studies religion

thesaurus book of synonyms

thesis proposition, topic

thespian actor

thews muscles

thorny difficult

thrall slave

threadbare tattered

thrive prosper

throes anguish

throng crowd

throttle choke

thwart to foil

tiara crown

tidings news, information

tiff fight

timbre tonal quality, resonance

timorous fearful, timid

tincture trace, vestige, tint

tinsel tawdriness

tirade scolding speech

titan accomplished person

titanic huge

titer laugh nervously

tithe donate one-tenth

titian auburn

titillate arouse

titular in name only, figurehead

toady fawner, sycophant

tocsin alarm bell, signal

toil drudgery

tome large book

tonal pertaining to sound

topography science of map making

```
┌─────────────────────────────────────────────────────────────────┐
│                    Quiz 18  (Matching)                            │
│                                                                   │
│  Match each word in the first column with its definition in the   │
│  second column.                                                   │
│                                                                   │
│   1.  SWATCH              A.  to foil                             │
│   2.  SYNOD               B.  anguish                            │
│   3.  TACIT               C.  concise                            │
│   4.  TALON               D.  provisional                       │
│   5.  TAURINE             E.  agitated                          │
│   6.  TEMPESTUOUS         F.  bull-like                         │
│   7.  TENTATIVE           G.  claw                             │
│   8.  TERSE               H.  understood without being spoken  │
│   9.  THROES              I.  council                          │
│  10.  THWART              J.  strip of fabric                  │
└─────────────────────────────────────────────────────────────────┘
```

torment harass

torpid lethargic, inactive

torrid scorching, passionate

torsion twisting

torus doughnut shaped object

totter stagger

touchstone standard

tousled disheveled

tout praise, brag

toxicologist one who studies poisons

tractable docile, manageable

traduce slander

tranquilize calm, anesthetize

transcribe write a copy

transfigure transform, exalt

transfix impale

transfuse insert, infuse

transgression trespass, offense

transient fleeting, temporary

transitory fleeting

translucent clear, lucid

transpire happen

transpose interchange

trauma injury

travail work, drudgery

traverse cross

travesty caricature, farce

treatise book, dissertation

trek journey

trenchant incisive, penetrating

trepidation fear

triad group of three

tribunal court

tributary river

trite commonplace, insincere

troglodyte cave dweller

trollop harlot

troublous disturbed

trounce thrash

troupe group of actors

truckle yield

truculent fierce, savage

trudge march, slog

truism self-evident truth

truncate shorten

truncheon club

tryst meeting, rendezvous

tumbler drinking glass

tumefy swell

tumult commotion

turbid muddy, clouded

turgid swollen

turpitude depravity

tussle fight

tussock cluster of glass

tutelage guardianship

twain two

twinge pain

tyrannical dictatorial

tyranny oppression

tyro beginner

U

ubiquitous omnipresent, pervasive

ulterior hidden, covert

ultimatum demand

ululate howl, wail

umbrage resentment

unabashed shameless, brazen

unabated ceaseless

unaffected natural, sincere

unanimity agreement

unassuming modest

unavailing useless, futile

unawares suddenly, unexpectedly

unbecoming unfitting

unbridled unrestrained

uncanny mysterious, inexplicable

unconscionable unscrupulous

uncouth uncultured, crude

unctuous insincere

undermine weaken

underpin support

underscore emphasize

understudy a stand-in

underworld criminal world

underwrite agree to finance, guarantee

undue unjust, excessive

undulate surge, fluctuate

unduly excessive

unequivocal unambiguous, categorical

unexceptionable beyond criticism

unfailing steadfast, unfaltering

unfathomable puzzling, incomprehensible

unflagging untiring, unrelenting

unflappable not easily upset

unfrock discharge

unfurl open up, spread out

Quiz 19 (Matching)

Match each word in the first column with its definition in the second column.

1.	TIDINGS	A.	incisive
2.	TITER	B.	omnipresent
3.	TITULAR	C.	lethargic
4.	TORPID	D.	figurehead
5.	TRADUCE	E.	unrestrained
6.	TRENCHANT	F.	news
7.	UBIQUITOUS	G.	laugh nervously
8.	ULULATE	H.	ceaseless
9.	UNABATED	I.	wail
10.	UNBRIDLED	J.	slander

ungainly awkward

uniformity sameness

unilateral action taken by only one party

unimpeachable exemplary

unison together

unkempt disheveled

unmitigated complete, harsh

unmoved firm, steadfast

unprecedented without previous occurrence

unremitting relentless

unsavory distasteful, offensive

unscathed unhurt

unseat displace

unseemly unbecoming, improper

unstinting generous

unsullied spotless

unsung neglected

untenable cannot be achieved

untoward perverse

unwarranted unjustified

unwieldy awkward

unwitting unintentional

upshot result

urbane refined, worldly

ursine bear-like

usurp seize, to appropriate

usury overcharge

utilitarian pragmatic

utopia paradise

utter complete

uxorious a doting husband

V

vacillate waver

vacuous inane

vagary whim

vain unsuccessful

vainglorious conceited

valediction farewell speech

valiant brave

validate affirm

valor bravery

vanguard leading position

vanquish conquer

vapid vacuous, insipid

variance discrepancy

vassal subject

vaunt brag

vehement adamant

venal mercenary, for the sake of money

vendetta grudge, feud

veneer false front, facade

venerable revered

venial excusable

venom poison, spite

venture risk, speculate

venturesome bold, risky

venue location

veracity truthfulness

veranda porch

verbatim word for word

verbose wordy

verdant green, lush

verdict decision

vernacular common speech

vertigo dizziness

vestige trace

veto reject

vex annoy

viable capable of surviving

viaduct waterway

viand food

vicious evil

vicissitude changing fortunes

victuals food

vie compete

vigil watch, sentry duty

vigilant on guard

vignette scene

vigor vitality

vilify defame

vindicate free from blame

vindictive revengeful

virile manly

virtuoso highly skilled artist

virulent deadly, poisonous

visage facial expression

viscid thick, gummy

visitation a formal visit

vital necessary

vitiate spoil, ruin

vitreous glassy

vitriolic scathing

vituperative abusive

vivacious lively

vivid lifelike, clear

vocation occupation

Quiz 20 (Matching)

Match each word in the first column with its definition in the second column.

1.	UNCOUTH	A.	disheveled
2.	UNDULY	B.	capable of surviving
3.	UNFLAGGING	C.	awkward
4.	UNKEMPT	D.	uncultured
5.	UNSTINTING	E.	truthfulness
6.	UNTENABLE	F.	whim
7.	UNWIELDY	G.	unrelenting
8.	VAGARY	H.	cannot be achieved
9.	VERACITY	I.	generous
10.	VIABLE	J.	excessive

vociferous adamant, clamoring

vogue fashion, chic

volant agile

volatile unstable

volition free will

voluble talkative

voluminous bulky, extensive

voracious hungry

votary fan, aficionado

vouchsafe confer, bestow

vulgarity obscenity

vulnerable susceptible

vulpine fox-like

W

wager bet

waggish playful

waive forego

wallow indulge

wan pale

wane dissipate, wither

want need, poverty

wanton lewd, abandoned

warrant justification

wary guarded

wastrel spendthrift

waylay ambush

wean remove from nursing, break a habit

weir dam

welter confusion, hodgepodge

wheedle coax

whet stimulate

whiffle vacillate

whimsical capricious

wield control

willful deliberate

wily shrewd

wince cringe

windfall bonus, boon

winnow separate

winsome charming

wistful yearning

wither shrivel

wizened shriveled

woe anguish

wont custom

woo court, seek favor

wraith ghost

wrath anger, fury

wreak inflict

wrest snatch

wretched miserable

writ summons

writhe contort

wry twisted

zealot fanatic

zenith summit

zephyr gentle breeze

X

xenophillic attraction to strangers

xenophobia fear of foreigners

xylophone musical percussion instrument

Y

yarn story

yearn desire strongly

yen desire

yore long ago

young Turks reformers

Z

zeal earnestness, passion

Answers to Quizzes

Quiz 1	Quiz 2	Quiz 3	Quiz 4	Quiz 5	Quiz 6	Quiz 7	Quiz 8	Quiz 9	Quiz 10
1. I	1. B	1. J	1. A	1. B	1. D	1. B	1. J	1. E	1. D
2. G	2. F	2. I	2. J	2. A	2. J	2. A	2. I	2. F	2. E
3. E	3. G	3. H	3. I	3. D	3. I	3. J	3. H	3. G	3. F
4. F	4. H	4. G	4. E	4. C	4. A	4. H	4. G	4. H	4. A
5. C	5. E	5. F	5. D	5. F	5. F	5. I	5. F	5. A	5. B
6. D	6. A	6. E	6. G	6. E	6. E	6. G	6. E	6. B	6. C
7. B	7. C	7. D	7. F	7. H	7. H	7. F	7. D	7. C	7. G
8. J	8. D	8. C	8. H	8. G	8. G	8. D	8. C	8. D	8. J
9. A	9. J	9. B	9. C	9. J	9. C	9. E	9. B	9. I	9. I
10. H	10. I	10. A	10. B	10. I	10. B	10. C	10. A	10. J	10. H

Quiz 11	Quiz 12	Quiz 13	Quiz 14	Quiz 15	Quiz 16	Quiz 17	Quiz 18	Quiz 19	Quiz 20
1. J	1. F	1. H	1. B	1. J	1. I	1. C	1. J	1. F	1. D
2. F	2. G	2. I	2. A	2. I	2. C	2. D	2. I	2. G	2. J
3. I	3. H	3. J	3. E	3. H	3. B	3. A	3. H	3. D	3. G
4. H	4. I	4. D	4. J	4. G	4. J	4. B	4. G	4. C	4. A
5. G	5. J	5. E	5. C	5. F	5. G	5. G	5. F	5. J	5. H
6. B	6. A	6. G	6. I	6. E	6. H	6. H	6. E	6. A	6. B
7. E	7. B	7. F	7. H	7. D	7. E	7. E	7. D	7. B	7. C
8. D	8. C	8. A	8. G	8. C	8. F	8. F	8. C	8. I	8. F
9. C	9. D	9. B	9. F	9. B	9. A	9. J	9. B	9. H	9. E
10. A	10. E	10. C	10. D	10. A	10. D	10. I	10. A	10. E	10. B

Etymology

Etymology is the study of the development of words and their forms. Many of the words in the English language have fascinating histories; familiarity with these stories and the development of the words can help you remember the meanings of the words and help you decipher the meanings of others words.

A Biography of English

It is helpful to learn some of the history of English—a language less than 2000 years old that has made its way to almost every corner of the world, making it the one true global language. Knowing something about the history of the language as well as its present qualities should not only intrigue you, but also give you more facility to acquire new vocabulary and use it well in your college writing.

It has been said that English came to Britain "on the edge of a sword." In 449 AD, Britain, at the time settled by the Celts, became the target of several invasions because other groups of people wanted its fertile land. The first group of people to invade, the Anglo-Saxons, drove the Celtic-Britons westward, settled into the fertile land, and began farming their new property. The Anglo-Saxons were an agricultural people; everyday words like *sheep*, *shepherd*, *ox*, *earth*, *dog*, *wood*, *field*, and *work* come from the Anglo-Saxon Old English. Moreover, it is nearly impossible to write a modern English sentence without using Anglo-Saxon words like *the*, *is*, *you*, *here*, and *there*.

The Vikings built on the Anglo-Saxon vocabulary with their merciless invasions. During the time of the Viking invasions, Anglo-Saxon writing reflected a bitter, negative tone. Themes like transience of life, heroism, and keeping dignity in the face of defeat permeated their writings about themes such as the cruel sea, ruined cities, war, and exile. One notable example of Old English writing is the heroic epic poem *Beowulf*. Lines 20-25 of the Prologue in Old English read:

> Swa sceal geong guma gode gewyrcean,
> fromum feohgiftum on fæder bearme,
> pæt hine on ylde eft gewunigen
> wilgesipas, ponne wig cume,
> leode gelæsten; lofdædum sceal
> in mægpa gehwære man gepeon.

These lines are translated as follows:

> So becomes it a youth to quit him well
> with his father's friends, by fee and gift,
> that to aid him, aged, in after days,
> come warriors willing, should war draw nigh,
> liegemen loyal; by lauded deeds
> shall an earl have honor in every clan.

Most likely, you found it impossible to interpret even one word of the poem as it was originally written; Old English was certainly very different from English as we know it today.

It would take yet another invasion to add just a bit of present-day "normalcy" to the language. This invasion came in 1066 and became known as the Norman Conquest. It transformed the English language, marking a turning point in the language's history from Old English to Middle English. When the Normans invaded Britain from present-day Normandy, France, and William the conqueror took the throne, English began its transformation into the melting pot of all languages.

When the Normans arrived in Britain, they found a people governed by what they considered to be inferior moral and cultural standards. Consequently, French was the language of the aristocrats, the well-bred—the language of the civilized. However, English survived for a number of reasons. First and foremost, it was too established to disappear. In addition, there was intermarriage between the French-speaking Normans and the English-speaking Anglos, and, in instances where an Anglo woman married a Norman, the children were more likely to speak their mother's language, thus carrying the language to the next generation.

Other events had an effect on the strength of English as well. The Hundred Years War caused French to lose its prestige while it bolstered nationalism for English. During the war, the Black Plague took so many lives that labor was scarce, forcing the rise of the English working man. The disease had the same effect in churches and monasteries.

Through the survival of English came many changes to its vocabulary and to its written form. The biggest change was the addition of many borrowed words, especially from French and Latin. Although English borrowed many words from French, French had little impact on the grammatical structure of the language, though there were notable changes to its form. For example, pronunciations and spelling changed as regional dialects formed. In addition, word order began to change. Through all the changes, English began to take on more of the look that we recognize today although there were still marked differences. Following is an excerpt from the Prologue of Chaucer's *Canterbury Tales*. Try deciphering the left column without consulting the translation in the right column.

Here bygynneth the Book of the tales of Caunterbury	**Here begins the Book of the Tales of Canterbury**
Whan that aprill with his shoures soote	When April with his showers sweet with fruit
The droghte of march hath perced to the roote,	The drought of March has pierced unto the root
And bathed every veyne in swich licour	And bathed each vein with liquor that has power
Of which vertu engendred is the flour;	To generate therein and sire the flower;
Whan zephirus eek with his sweete breeth	When Zephyr also has, with his sweet breath,
Inspired hath in every holt and heeth	Quickened again, in every holt and heath,
Tendre croppes, and the yonge sonne	The tender shoots and buds, and the young sun
Hath in the ram his halve cours yronne,	Into the Ram one half his course has run,
And smale foweles maken melodye,	And many little birds make melody
That slepen al the nyght with open ye	That sleep through all the night with open eye
(so priketh hem nature in hir corages);	(So Nature pricks them on to ramp and rage);
Thanne longen folk to goon on pilgrimages,	Then do folk long to go on pilgrimage,
And palmeres for to seken straunge strondes,	And palmers to go seeking out strange strands,
To ferne halwes, kowthe in sondry londes;	To distant shrines well known in sundry lands.
And specially from every shires ende	And specially from every shire's end
Of engelond to caunterbury they wende,	Of England they to Canterbury wend,
The hooly blisful martir for to seke,	The holy blessed martyr there to seek
That hem hath holpen whan that they were seeke.	Who helped them when they lay so ill and weak

Undoubtedly, you found *Canterbury Tales* easier to decipher than *Beowulf*, even in its original form. Clearer still is the following well-known excerpt from William Shakespeare's *Romeo and Juliet*:

> O Romeo, Romeo, wherefore art thou Romeo?
> Deny thy father and refuse thy name!
> Or, if thou wilt not, be but sworn my love,
> And I'll no longer be a Capulet. *(2.2.33-36)*

William Shakespeare along with King James marked the change from Middle English to Modern English although their writing reflected a use of word order that still sounds awkward in our present-day English. For example, the King James version of the Bible uses such phrases as *follow thou me, speak ye unto me, cake unleavened, things eternal, they knew him not*. Although these authors' writings may seem antiquated to us today, they both have left a lasting impression. Many present-day phrases came from Shakespeare: *good riddance, lie low, the long and the short of it, a fool's paradise, sleep a wink, green-eyed jealousy*, and *love at first sight*. King James contributed many of today's idioms: *the root of the matter, wolf in sheep's clothing, lambs to the slaughter, an eye for an eye*, and *straight and narrow*.

In comparison, English as Shakespeare and King James knew it and English as we know it is quite different. Truly, English is a changing language. And, although it seems to have already had a very full life, there is no reason to assume that it will not continue to pass through new and different stages in its life.

The Birth of a Word

Just as the English language was born and has lived a life of change, so too a word has a life. From its birth, a word can undergo changes or remain static throughout its life; it may seem immortal, or it may die. Words have ancestors; they have relatives. Words also have "friends" (*synonyms*) and "enemies" (*antonyms*). Studying the life of words is fascinating and gives you an upper hand at understanding and using words and deciphering unfamiliar words you may find on the GRE or in your graduate work.

A word's ancestor is called a *cognate*. Cognates are ancient words that bare a close resemblance to modern words. For example, in ancient Indo-European Sanskrit the word *father* is "pitar;" in Latin, "pater;" in French, "père;" in Spanish "padre." In Sanskrit, *mother* is "matar;" in Latin, "mater;" in French, "mère;" in Spanish, "madre." Sir William Jones, a British judge, was the first to point out the close relationship between languages despite the passage of time. His theory, a theory shared by many today, was that the languages of 1/3 of the human race have a common source in this Indo-European language.

This common source found in cognates should not be confused with borrowed words. Borrowing is one way that words are given birth in the English language. English has borrowed more words than any other language, especially from French and Latin—a direct result from the Norman Conquest. Borrowed words sometimes keep their original form. For example, the French word *laissez-faire* is commonly used in English and refers to the "policy of non-interference, especially as pertaining to government." In other instances, however, words change form to fit the accepted rules and pronunciation that govern the English language. For example, the word *adroit* means "right, justice." The word is from the French *à*, which means "to" and *droit* (pronounced *dwa*), which means "right." Through their transition to English, the words changed spelling to become one word, the English version lost the accent mark, and the pronunciation changed. Following are some examples of other borrowed words:

ABERRATION

Present meaning: departure from what is normal

Derived from: Latin *aberrare*, to wander away from

Details of origin: Originally a psychological term describing a person who mentally deviates from the norm.

ABOMINATE

Present meaning: loathe

Derived from: Latin *abominor*, "I pray that the event predicted by the omen may be averted"

Details of origin: A superstitious word the Romans uttered to ward off evil spirits when anyone said something unlucky.

ALOOF

Present meaning: distant (as pertaining to emotion)

Derived from: Dutch *te loef*, to windward; also used as a sailor's term *a loof*, to the luff or windward direction

Details of origin: Present meaning suggests that the use of the term to mean "keeping a ship's head to the wind and away from the shore" developed into our meaning of "distance."

EBULLIENT

Present meaning: high-spirited; exuberant

Derived from: Latin *ebullire*, to boil over

Details of origin: Much as a pot boils over, one who is ebullient "boils over" with enthusiasm.

EXPUNGE

Present meaning: erase; remove

Derived from: Latin *expungere*, to prick through or mark off

Details of origin: In ancient Rome, when a soldier would retire, a series of dots and points were placed under his name on service lists.

GREGARIOUS

Present meaning: sociable

Derived from: Latin *gregarius* and *grex*, flock or herd

Details of origin: From the idea that animals stayed in flocks or herds because they were sociable came our present-day meaning.

LETHARGY

Present meaning: drowsiness; sluggishness

Derived from: Greek *lethargia* or *lethe*, forgetfulness

Details of origin: Because of the Greeks belief in afterlife, legend had it that the dead crossed the river Lethe, which took them through Hades. Anyone who drank from the river would forget his past. This idea of forgetfulness lead to our meaning of sluggishness.

While some words are borrowed directly from another language, others are adopted from interesting people and events in history. For example, you have probably at one time or another made a *Freudian slip*, an unintentional comment based on some subconscious feeling. And did you know that a *bootlegger* was originally someone who smuggled illegal alcoholic liquor in the tops of his boots? Here are some other words with fascinating histories:

AMALGAM

Present meaning: mixture, combination

Derived from: Latin *amalgama*, alloy of mercury; Greek *malagma*, softening substance

Details of origin: Evolved to present meaning in 1775.

BOWDLERIZE

Present meaning: to remove offensive words from a book

Derived from: Scottish physician Dr. Thomas Bowdler

Details of origin: Dr. Bowdler published an edition of Shakespeare's works, omitting certain words which he deemed offensive.

CHAUVINISM

Present meaning: exaggerated patriotism

Derived from: one of Napoleon's soldiers, Nicolas Chauvin

Details of origin: After retiring from the army, Chauvin spoke so highly of himself and his feats while in battle that he became a joke and thus the term was coined.

CYNOSURE

Present meaning: center of attention or admiration

Derived from: Greek mythology *Cynosura*, dog's tail

Details of origin: The Greek god Zeus honored a nymph by placing her as a constellation in the sky. One star in the constellation in particular stood out. To many, the constellation looked like a dog's tail because of the one bright star.

DESULTORY

Present meaning: lacking in consistency; disconnected

Derived from: Romans *desultor*, a leaper

Details of origin: Often Roman soldiers would go into battle with two horses so that when one horse tired, the soldier could leap to the second horse striding alongside. This person became known as a *desultor*, or leaper. The term evolved since this leaper only stayed on one horse for a short amount of time before becoming disconnected and jumping to the other horse.

FIASCO

Present meaning: humiliating failure or breakdown

Derived from: Italian *fiasco*, flask or bottle

Details of origin: Venetian glassblowers set aside fine glass with flaws to use in making ordinary bottles. The term resulted from the fact that something fine should be turned into something ordinary.

GAMUT

Present meaning: whole series or range of something

Derived from: medieval musician Guido of Arezzo

Details of origin: Arezzo was the first to use the lines of the musical staff, and he assigned the Greek letter "gamma" for the lowest tone. This note was called "gamma ut" and thus "gamut" evolved into our present meaning.

INTRANSIGENT

Present meaning: uncompromising

Derived from: Spanish *intransigente*, not compromising

Details of origin: In 1873, Amadeus was forced to give up the throne of Spain. After this occurred, a group of people attempted to form a political party of their own. This group was known as *los intransigentes* because they would not conform to the policies of any other groups.

JOVIAL

Present meaning: merry

Derived from: Latin *Jovialis*, of Jupiter; *Jovius*, Jupiter

Details of origin: Astrologers believed that those born under the sign of Jupiter were characterized by a merry disposition.

MESMERIZE

Present meaning: fascinate; spellbind

Derived from: Austrian doctor Friedrich Anton Mesmer

Details of origin: Doctor Mesmer was the first to successfully use hypnotism. Although the term is still used today to relate to the technique of hypnotism, its meaning has broadened to encompass a general idea of fascination.

OSTRACIZE

Present meaning: to exclude from a society as by general consent

Derived from: Greek *ostrakon*, tile, shell

Details of origin: In ancient Greece, if a man was considered dangerous to society, judges would cast their votes regarding banishment by writing their names on a tile and dropping them in an urn.

QUARANTINE

Present meaning: isolation to prevent contagion

Derived from: Latin *quadraginta*, forty and *quattuor*, four; *quarantina*, space of forty days

Details of origin: This word has a rich history, originally referring to the period of time that a widow in the 1500's could live in her dead husband's house. It was also used to reference the period of 40 days during which Christ fasted in the wilderness. In the 1600's, the Venetians kept ships at bay for 40 days if their voyage originated in a disease-stricken country. Since then, the term has broadened to encompass any period of isolation.

QUISLING

Present meaning: traitor

Derived from: Norweigan army officer Vidkun Quisling

Details of origin: Although the term loosely refers to a traitor, more specifically it describes a traitor who betrays his country to serve a dictatorial government. Officer Quisling was one such traitor who betrayed Norway to join arms with the Nazis in World War II.

SYCOPHANT

Present meaning: self-seeking flatterer

Derived from: Greek *sykon*, fig; *phantes*, one who shows

Details of origin: Originally, a sycophant referred to an informer. Etymologists speculate that the term "fig-shower" was used in this context because ancient Greeks, or sycophants, would act as informers against merchants who were unlawfully exporting figs.

The process by which a word comes into being is called *neologism* or *coinage*. A new word is coined when it is used by a large number of people for a significant amount of time. Though not a very specific and measurable process, it is clearer when we look at three main reasons people begin using new words. First, new words are created when two words are combined into one. For example, the word *breakfast* evolved from the two words *break* and *fast*. Breakfast "breaks" the "fast" your body undergoes during the night. Other words like *roommate*, *housewife*, *stay-at-home*, and *doorbell* were coined by the same process of combining multiple words to form one.

The opposite process also forms new words. For example, the word *ref* is short for *referee*; *gym* is short for *gymnasium*; and *exam* is short for *examination*. It is easy to imagine how shortened words become coined—as a society, we are always looking for shortcuts, and clipping words is a convenient shortcut.

New words are also coined to avoid confusion, most often between languages. For example, have you ever wondered exactly where the tennis term *love* came from? It seems a strange term to use for scoring. Tennis is originally a French game, and since a zero is egg-shaped, the French referred to it as *l'œuf*. This term was confused in translation and only the pronunciation was adopted; English-speakers heard "love" and it stuck. Another example of confusion is the word *maudlin*, which means "tearfully sentimental." The word evolved from the British English pronunciation of "Mary Magdalene." During the Middle Ages, one of the popular plays depicted the life of the Bible's Mary Magdalene. Because the character was usually tearful in every scene and, because the British pronunciation was "Maudlin," the term picked up this meaning.

The Life of a Word

Whatever the birth story, some words live exciting lives of change while others retain their original meaning. Words can undergo changes by being clipped as mentioned above or by being combined with other words to form completely new ones. Some words become more powerful. For example, the words *filth* and *foul* were originally used to mean plain old "dirt." Originally, you might wipe down your kitchen counter at the end of the day because it was *filthy* or *foul*. Today *filthy* and *foul* have taken on a more powerful meaning so that you probably only associate *filth* and *foul* with the nearest garbage dump. Another example of a word that has gained force is *disaster*. At one time, the word simply referred to "an unlucky event." Today, we hear the word used in reference to "disaster areas" resulting from earthquakes, floods, and tornadoes. There is much more power associated with the word now.

Words can also lose power. Take the word *mortify*, for example. It originally meant "to make dead." Now it can simply refer to a moment of humiliation: He was *mortified* when he realized that his zipper was down during his important speech. Other words have powerful meanings, even as depicted in the dictionary, but in everyday speech they are used rather casually. For example, the word *atrocious* by definition refers to something that is "extremely savage or wicked." But you've probably heard the word in reference to someone's taste in style: Did you see that *atrocious* purple and green striped dress she was wearing?

Words gain power and they lose power. Words can also gain or lose a bad reputation. The word *lewd* has gained a negative connotation over the years from its original reference to all laymen. From there it evolved to present-day where it now encompasses things that are "indecent or obscene." On the other hand, *marshal* once referred to a person who took care of horses. Over the years, the position gained more respect and now not only refers to the person who controls parades, but also refers to someone in a high-ranking position such as a sheriff.

In both the example of *lewd* and the example of *marshal*, not only did the meanings change from positive to negative and vice versa, but they also changed in scope. *Lewd* became more narrow in its meaning, *marshal* more broad. *Butcher* is another example of a word that has broadened in scope. A butcher was originally a man who killed goats. Nowadays, you can expect to find a vast array of meats in a butcher shop. By contrast, the original meaning of *disease* was "ill at ease." The word has narrowed its scope over the years so that now it refers to specific ailments and maladies.

What a boring language we would speak if words did not change in so many different ways! And how mundane our speech would be if it were not colored with such flourishes as slang and colloquialisms. The word *slang* was coined by combining the word *slinging* with the word *language*. Specific to certain countries, even just to particular regions of a country, slang refers to very informal language. Slang should therefore not be used in your graduate classes. Slang generally stays with the time and examples include such words as *yuppie, valleygirl,* and *phat.* Slang can also include standard words that portray alternate, often ironic, meanings; for example, the word *bad* when used as slang can describe something that is actually good. Think of slang as language you would use only when you are *chillin'* (slang for "spending time with") with your closest friends

Colloquialisms are also informal although they are more widely accepted. Still, you should not use colloquial speech in your graduate work. You could use colloquial language with those with whom you are close but perhaps not quite as familiar as your best buddies—your parents, for example. Instead of *chillin'* with your family, you might *hang out* with them. Or you might tell a co-worker to *give you a holler* if he wants to get together for lunch. Clearly, knowing your audience is important when choosing the language you will use. Since your work on the GRE and in graduate school is for a formal audience, formal language should be favored; avoid slang and colloquialisms.

You should also avoid overusing *euphemisms,* or "delicate" language. In our world of political correctness, there is a natural tendency to substitute "nice" words for real words. For example, you might describe a "domestic engineer" who is "with child." Translation? A pregnant housewife. The best writing conveys a real point clearly and therefore euphemisms should be used sparingly.

While slang, colloquialism, and euphemism, though informal, are ways to bring the personality of a writer or speaker out in the open, a more subtle way to express such character is through connotative writing. In comparison to denotative language, connotative words possess undertones of emotion. Denotation is factual. Take the word *gentleman,* for example. *Gentleman* is a connotative word that contains much more meaning than does the denotative word *man.* To picture a man is just to picture a male human. But to picture a gentleman is to imagine a well-dressed man who brings flowers, opens doors, and pulls out chairs for his lady. And of course a lady is not just a woman but a sophisticated female who is elegant and courteous, who quietly laughs at the right time and crosses her legs when she sits down. A lady is *lovely* (connotative), not just *pretty* (denotative).

How Words Die

Although certain words are seemingly immortal like *and, the,* and *is,* others do meet their death. When a word meets its death, it becomes *obsolete.* The King James version of the Bible as well as any one of Shakespeare's plays contains a vast sum of words that, today, are obsolete. Slang words and colloquialisms are also quick to become obsolete. This is because slang and colloquialisms generally come into existence through trends. Speaking trends fade in and fade out just as quickly as the latest fashion trends.

Some words do not fade away, but their meaning does. A well-known example of such a phenomenon is the word *gay,* which at one time meant "happy." Today the word is used in reference to homosexuality. And did you know that *nice* originally referred to something that was "silly" or "foolish"? Other meanings of words are surely on their way out as technology advances. For example, very few people actually "dial" a number into their phone because there are few rotary phones still in use. Along the same lines, singers no longer put out "albums" because we now have compact discs rather than records. It is probably just a matter of time until these meanings die.

When you study the life of a word, it is easy to see that English is truly a unique language. Studying its history, its life, and its patterns is both fascinating and helpful in learning to communicate effectively. Excelling in your use of the English language in graduate school will contribute greatly to your success. Success in graduate school will lead to success in your career which is your ultimate goal. Knowing this should make you all the more diligent in your study of English and the words that make up the one true global language.

Word Analysis

In addition to the study of word origin, etymology also involves word analysis, which is the process of separating a word into its parts and then using the meanings of those parts to deduce the meaning of the original word. Take, for example, the word INTERMINABLE. It is made up of three parts: a prefix IN (not), a root TERMIN (stop), and a suffix ABLE (can do). Therefore, by word analysis, INTERMINABLE means "not able to stop." This is not the literal meaning of INTERMINABLE (endless), but it is close enough to find an antonym. For another example, consider the word RETROSPECT. It is made up of the prefix RETRO (back) and the root SPECT (to look). Hence, RETROSPECT means "to look back (in time), to contemplate."

Word analysis is very effective in decoding the meaning of words. However, you must be careful in its application since words do not always have the same meaning as the sum of the meanings of their parts. In fact, on occasion words can have the opposite meaning of their parts. For example, by word analysis the word AWFUL should mean "full of awe," or awe-inspiring. But over the years it has come to mean just the opposite—terrible. In spite of the shortcomings, word analysis gives the correct meaning of a word (or at least a hint of it) far more often than not and therefore is a useful tool.

Examples:

INDEFATIGABLE

Analysis: IN (not);   DE (thoroughly);   FATIG (fatigue);   ABLE (can do)
Meaning: cannot be fatigued, tireless

CIRCUMSPECT

Analysis: CIRCUM (around);   SPECT (to look)
Meaning: to look around, that is, to be cautious

ANTIPATHY

Analysis: ANTI (against);   PATH (to feel);   Y (noun suffix)
Meaning: to feel strongly against something, to hate

OMNISCIENT

Analysis: OMNI (all);   SCI (to know);   ENT (noun suffix)
Meaning: all-knowing

Following are some of the most useful prefixes, roots, and suffixes—memorize them.

PREFIXES

1. **ab**	from		aberration
2. **ad**—also **ac, af, ag, al, an, ap, ar, as, at**	to		adequate
3. **ambi**	both		ambidextrous
4. **an**—also **a**	without		anarchy
5. **anti**	against		antipathetic
6. **ante**	before		antecedent
7. **be**	throughout		belie
8. **bi**	two		bilateral
9. **cata**	down		catacomb
10. **circum**	around		circumscribe
11. **com**—also **con, col, cor, cog, co**	together		confluence
12. **contra**	against		contravene
13. **de**	down (negative)		debase
14. **deca**	ten		decathlon
15. **decem**	ten		decimal
16. **di**	two		digraph
17. **dia**	through, between		dialectic
18. **dis**	apart (negative)		disparity
19. **du**	two		duplicate
20. **dys**	abnormal, impaired		dysphoria
21. **epi**	upon		epicenter
22. **equi**	equal		equitable
23. **ex**	out		extricate
24. **extra**	beyond		extraterrestrial
25. **fore**	in front of		foreword
26. **hemi**	half		hemisphere
27. **hyper**	excessive		hyperbole
28. **hypo**	too little		hypothermia
29. **in**—also **ig, il, im, ir**	not		inefficient
30. **in**—also **il, im, ir**	in, very		invite, inflammable
31. **inter**	between		interloper
32. **intro**—also **intra**	inside		introspective
33. **kilo**	one thousand		kilogram
34. **meta**	changing		metaphysics
35. **micro**	small		microcosm
36. **mili**—also **milli**	one thousand		millipede
37. **mis**	bad, hate		misanthrope
38. **mono**	one		monopoly
39. **multi**	many		multifarious

40. **neo**	new	neophyte
41. **nil**—also **nihil**	nothing	nihilism
42. **non**	not	nonentity
43. **ob**—also **oc, of, op**	against	obstinate
44. **pan**	all	panegyric
45. **para**	beside	paranormal
46. **per**	throughout	permeate
47. **peri**	around	periscope
48. **poly**	many	polyglot
49. **post**	after	posterity
50. **pre**	before	predecessor
51. **prim**	first	primitive
52. **pro**	forward	procession
53. **quad**	four	quadruple
54. **re**	again	reiterate
55. **retro**	backward	retrograde
56. **semi**	half	semiliterate
57. **sub**—also **suc, suf, sug, sup, sus**	under	succumb
58. **super**—also **supra**	above	superannuated
59. **syn**—also **sym, syl**	together	synthesis
60. **trans**	across	transgression
61. **un**	not	unkempt
62. **uni**	one	unique

ROOTS

Root	Meaning	Example
1. **ac**	bitter, sharp	acrid
2. **agog**	leader	demagogue
3. **agri**—also **agrari**	field	agriculture
4. **ali**	other	alienate
5. **alt**	high	altostratus
6. **alter**	other	alternative
7. **am**	love	amiable
8. **anim**	soul	animadversion
9. **anthrop**	man, people	anthropology
10. **arch**	ruler	monarch
11. **aud**	hear	auditory
12. **auto**	self	autocracy
13. **belli**	war	bellicose
14. **ben**	good	benevolence
15. **biblio**	book	bibliophile

16.	**bio**	life	biosphere
17.	**cap**	take	caprice
18.	**capit**	head	capitulate
19.	**carn**	flesh	incarnate
20.	**ced**	go	accede
21.	**celer**	swift	accelerate
22.	**cent**	one hundred	centurion
23.	**chron**	time	chronology
24.	**cide**	cut, kill	fratricide
25.	**cit**	to call	recite
26.	**civ**	citizen	civility
27.	**cord**	heart	cordial
28.	**corp**	body	corporeal
29.	**cosm**	universe	cosmopolitan
30.	**crat**	power	plutocrat
31.	**cred**	belief	incredulous
32.	**cur**	to care	curable
33.	**deb**	debt	debit
34.	**dem**	people	demagogue
35.	**dic**	to say	Dictaphone
36.	**doc**	to teach	doctorate
37.	**dynam**	power	dynamism
38.	**ego**	I	egocentric
39.	**err**	to wander	errant
40.	**eu**	good	euphemism
41.	**fac**—also **fic, fec, fect**	to make	affectation
42.	**fall**	false	infallible
43.	**fer**	to carry	fertile
44.	**fid**	faith	confidence
45.	**fin**	end	finish
46.	**fort**	strong	fortitude
47.	**gen**	race, group	genocide
48.	**geo**	earth	geology
49.	**germ**	vital part	germane
50.	**gest**	carry	gesticulate
51.	**gnosi**	know	prognosis
52.	**grad**—also **gress**	step	transgress
53.	**graph**	writing	calligraphy
54.	**grav**	heavy	gravitate
55.	**greg**	crowd	egregious
56.	**habit**	to have, live	habituate
57.	**hema**—also **hemo**	blood	hemorrhage
58.	**hetero**	different	heterogeneous

59.	**homo**	same	homogenized
60.	**hum**	earth, man	humble
61.	**jac**—also **jec**	throw	interjection
62.	**jud**	judge	judicious
63.	**junct**—also **join**	combine	disjunctive
64.	**jus**—also **jur**	law, to swear	adjure
65.	**leg**	law	legislator
66.	**liber**	free	libertine
67.	**lic**	permit	illicit
68.	**loc**	place	locomotion
69.	**log**	word	logic
70.	**loqu**	speak	soliloquy
71.	**macro**	large	macrobiotics
72.	**magn**	large	magnanimous
73.	**mal**	bad	malevolent
74.	**manu**	by hand	manuscript
75.	**matr**	mother	matriarch
76.	**medi**	middle	medieval
77.	**meter**	measure	perimeter
78.	**mit**—also **miss**	send	missive
79.	**morph**	form, structure	anthropomorphic
80.	**mut**	change	immutable
81.	**nat**—also **nasc**	born	nascent
82.	**neg**	deny	renegade
83.	**nomen**	name	nominal
84.	**nov**	new	innovative
85.	**omni**	all	omniscient
86.	**oper**—also **opus**	work	operative
87.	**pac**—also **plais**	please	complaisant
88.	**pater**—also **patr**	father	expatriate
89.	**path**	disease, feeling	pathos
90.	**ped**—also **pod**	foot	pedestal
91.	**pel**—also **puls**	push	impulsive
92.	**pen**	hang	appendix
93.	**phil**	love	philanthropic
94.	**pict**	paint	depict
95.	**poli**	city	metropolis
96.	**port**	carry	deportment
97.	**pos**—also **pon**	to place	posit
98.	**pot**	power	potentate
99.	**put**	think	computer
100.	**rect**—also **reg**	straight	rectitude
101.	**ridi**—also **risi**	laughter	derision

102.	**rog**	beg	interrogate
103.	**rupt**	break	interruption
104.	**sanct**	holy	sanctimonious
105.	**sangui**	blood	sanguinary
106.	**sat**	enough	satiate
107.	**sci**	know	conscience
108.	**scrib**—also **script**	to write	circumscribe
109.	**sequ**—also **secu**	follow	sequence
110.	**simil**—also **simul**	resembling	simile
111.	**solv**—also **solut**	loosen	absolve
112.	**soph**	wisdom	unsophisticated
113.	**spec**	look	circumspect
114.	**spir**	breathe	aspire
115.	**strict**—also **string**	bind	astringent
116.	**stru**	build	construe
117.	**tact**—also **tang, tig**	touch	intangible
118.	**techni**	skill	technique
119.	**tempor**	time	temporal
120.	**ten**	hold	tenacious
121.	**term**	end	interminable
122.	**terr**	earth	extraterrestrial
123.	**test**	to witness	testimony
124.	**the**	god	theocracy
125.	**therm**	heat	thermodynamics
126.	**tom**	cut	epitome
127.	**tort**—also **tors**	twist	distortion
128.	**tract**	draw, pull	abstract
129.	**trib**	bestow	attribute
130.	**trud**—also **trus**	push	protrude
131.	**tuit**—also **tut**	teach	intuitive
132.	**ultima**	last	penultimate
133.	**ultra**	beyond	ultraviolet
134.	**urb**	city	urbane
135.	**vac**	empty	vacuous
136.	**val**	strength, valor	valediction
137.	**ven**	come	adventure
138.	**ver**	true	veracity
139.	**verb**	word	verbose
140.	**vest**	clothe	travesty
141.	**vic**	change	vicissitude
142.	**vit**—also **viv**	alive	vivacious
143.	**voc**	voice	vociferous
144.	**vol**	wish	volition

Suffixes determine the part of speech a word belongs to. They are not as useful for determining a word's meaning as are roots and prefixes. Nevertheless, there are a few that are helpful.

SUFFIXES

Suffix	Meaning	Example
1. **able**—also **ible**	capable of	legible
2. **acy**	state of	celibacy
3. **ant**	full of	luxuriant
4. **ate**	to make	consecrate
5. **er, or**	one who	censor
6. **fic**	making	traffic
7. **ism**	belief	monotheism
8. **ist**	one who	fascist
9. **ize**	to make	victimize
10. **oid**	like	steroid
11. **ology**	study of	biology
12. **ose**	full of	verbose
13. **ous**	full of	fatuous
14. **tude**	state of	rectitude
15. **ure**	state of, act	primogeniture

Problem Set A:

Analyze and define the following words. Solutions begin on page 209.

Example: **RETROGRADE**
Analysis: retro (backward); grade (step)
Meaning: to step backward, to regress

1.   **CIRCUMNAVIGATE**   Analysis:
                            Meaning:

2.   **MISANTHROPE**   Analysis:
                            Meaning:

3.   **ANARCHY**   Analysis:
                            Meaning:

4.   **AUTOBIOGRAPHY**   Analysis:
                            Meaning:

5.   **INCREDULOUS**   Analysis:
                            Meaning:

6.   **EGOCENTRIC**   Analysis:
                            Meaning:

7.   **INFALLIBLE**   Analysis:
                            Meaning:

8.   **AMORAL**   Analysis:
                            Meaning:

9.   **INFIDEL**   Analysis:
                            Meaning:

10. **NONENTITY**   Analysis:
                            Meaning:

11. **CORPULENT**   Analysis:
                            Meaning:

12. **IRREPARABLE**   Analysis:
                            Meaning:

13. **INTROSPECTIVE**   Analysis:
                            Meaning:

14. **IMMORTALITY**   Analysis:
                            Meaning:

15. **BENEFACTOR**   Analysis:
                            Meaning:

16. **DEGRADATION**   Analysis:
                            Meaning:

17. **DISPASSIONATE**   Analysis:
                            Meaning:

18. **APATHETIC**   Analysis:
                            Meaning:

Problem Set B:

The meanings of all the capitalized words in this exercise can be deduced by word analysis. Solutions begin on page 210.

Directions: For the following problems, choose the word most opposite in meaning to the capitalized word.

1. ABERRANT:

(A) catholic
(B) euphoric
(C) customary
(D) lax
(E) putrid

2. ADJUDICATE:

(A) abhor
(B) command
(C) vitiate
(D) revoke
(E) ignore

3. ADJUNCT:

(A) franchise
(B) accessory
(C) disjunction
(D) kismet
(E) pygmy

4. AGNOSTIC:

(A) unfaithful
(B) arcane
(C) heathen
(D) evangelical
(E) mundane

5. MALEDICTION:

(A) blessing
(B) termination
(C) shibboleth
(D) sliver
(E) simian

6. CONSANGUINITY:

(A) estrangement
(B) asylum
(C) resolve
(D) fraternity
(E) pantomime

7. ASTRINGENT:

(A) harsh
(B) lax
(C) engaging
(D) incredulous
(E) pusillanimous

8. GRATUITOUS:

(A) anomalous
(B) xenophillic
(C) whimsical
(D) restrained
(E) tactful

9. OMNIPOTENT:

(A) unabated
(B) feeble
(C) tractable
(D) sententious
(E) sedulous

10. MULTIFARIOUS:

(A) eclectic
(B) ardent
(C) manifold
(D) dismal
(E) singular

11. COUNTERMAND:

(A) compete
(B) accommodate
(C) ratify
(D) sunder
(E) preside

12. IMMUTABLE:

(A) fortuitous
(B) uniform
(C) candid
(D) volatile
(E) unvarying

13. INSCRIBE:

(A) appropriate
(B) supplant
(C) erase
(D) exchange
(E) invalidate

14. INTREPID:

(A) tremulous
(B) viable
(C) gallant
(D) jocular
(E) invidious

15. PREVARICATE:

(A) abate
(B) impede
(C) prove
(D) ululate
(E) tether

16. RECTILINEAR:

(A) circuitous
(B) tawdry
(C) overweening
(D) inimical
(E) brackish

17. PHILANTHROPIC:

(A) queasy
(B) unassuming
(C) ungainly
(D) callous
(E) openhanded

18. SANCTIMONIOUS:

(A) sententious
(B) ingenuous
(C) sinister
(D) ineffabe
(E) antiquated

Problem Set C:

Solutions begin on page 211.

1. TRANSLUCENT:

(A) opaque
(B) vitreous
(C) loquacious
(D) diaphanous
(E) judgmental

2. VERITABLE:

(A) comely
(B) innocent
(C) phenomenal
(D) truthful
(E) spurious

3. ALLY:

(A) authorize
(B) split
(C) assimilate
(D) simplify
(E) comfort

4. INSULAR:

(A) parochial
(B) restricted
(C) barbarous
(D) orthodox
(E) worldly

5. AUGMENT:

(A) encode
(B) debate
(C) conceive
(D) obviate
(E) bloat

6. PEDESTRIAN:

(A) antagonistic
(B) communal
(C) stellar
(D) hackneyed
(E) empowered

7. ASPERSION:

(A) exaltation
(B) calumny
(C) impasse
(D) indecision
(E) fantasy

8. SAP:

(A) menace
(B) quicken
(C) vex
(D) hesitate
(E) cleanse

9. IMPEDE:

(A) extenuate
(B) affix
(C) deter
(D) foster
(E) proscribe

10. TYRO:

(A) master
(B) neophyte
(C) sloth
(D) pragmatist
(E) tyrant

11. VENERABLE:

(A) distinguished
(B) soporific
(C) attenuated
(D) famous
(E) contemptible

12. GRIEVOUS:

(A) accidental
(B) iniquitous
(C) trivial
(D) corrupt
(E) uniform

13. SOLACE:

(A) adopt
(B) dishearten
(C) omit
(D) relieve
(E) feign

14. PITHY:

(A) vapid
(B) inattentive
(C) pungent
(D) jocose
(E) sickening

15. CAPITULATE:

(A) bellow
(B) botch
(C) relinquish
(D) persevere
(E) rouse

16. CONVIVIAL:

(A) antagonistic
(B) cogent
(C) gracious
(D) unsung
(E) cordial

17. PROPENSITY:

(A) approbation
(B) aversion
(C) ascendancy
(D) circumscription
(E) hiatus

18. EMBED:

(A) lionize
(B) bulge
(C) interject
(D) defraud
(E) extricate

Problem Set D:

Solutions begin on page 211.

1. REPINE:

(A) exact
(B) delight
(C) taint
(D) descend
(E) affront

2. ODIUM

(A) approbation
(B) repudiation
(C) essence
(D) circumspection
(E) disdain

3. REFRACTORY:

(A) impetuous
(B) sagacious
(C) dire
(D) futile
(E) impressionable

4. MINATORY:

(A) flighty
(B) inspiring
(C) chaste
(D) hallowed
(E) global

5. ONEROUS:

(A) antagonistic
(B) facile
(C) resourceful
(D) obliging
(E) momentary

6. DISAVOW:

(A) defile
(B) counterpoise
(C) appropriate
(D) assuage
(E) exculpate

7. QUELL:

(A) incense
(B) wallow
(C) assimilate
(D) vacillate
(E) repudiate

8. TORRID:

(A) disproportionate
(B) dispassionate
(C) inventive
(D) peevish
(E) deferential

9. PHLEGMATIC:

(A) consummate
(B) abounding
(C) animated
(D) cavalier
(E) industrious

10. SEMINAL:

(A) distinctive
(B) perturbed
(C) stifling
(D) contented
(E) categorical

11. NULLIFY:

(A) repose
(B) assuage
(C) assemble
(D) neutralize
(E) superintend

12. ESCHEW:

(A) purge
(B) prevaricate
(C) pursue
(D) indict
(E) flaunt

13. APPRISE:

(A) concede
(B) campaign
(C) succor
(D) induce
(E) enshroud

14. INTREPID:

(A) craven
(B) averse
(C) impudent
(D) contracting
(E) beguiling

15. GARROTE:

(A) calumniate
(B) emancipate
(C) jettison
(D) infuriate
(E) abide

16. SODDEN:

(A) quaint
(B) indomitable
(C) proud
(D) desiccated
(E) unadulterated

17. PITILESS:

(A) enchanting
(B) astute
(C) benevolent
(D) indurate
(E) fanatic

18. MANUMIT:

(A) indenture
(B) reconvene
(C) stymie
(D) foster
(E) waffle

Problem Set E:

Solutions begin on page 212.

1. VITREOUS:

(A) obscure
(B) pellucid
(C) effusive
(D) limpid
(E) lascivious

2. DEFINITIVE:

(A) patrician
(B) culpable
(C) singular
(D) earnest
(E) wanting

3. CONFEDERATE:

(A) enjoin
(B) hew
(C) accustom
(D) bolster
(E) thwart

4. PAROCHIAL:

(A) idiomatic
(B) restrained
(C) gracious
(D) devout
(E) cosmopolitan

5. AGGRANDIZE:

(A) encroach
(B) acquiesce
(C) depict
(D) encumber
(E) enhance

6. FATUOUS:

(A) auspicious
(B) scarce
(C) sagacious
(D) trite
(E) sanctioned

7. OBLOQUY:

(A) apotheosis
(B) infamy
(C) contingency
(D) reliance
(E) disposition

8. SUBVERT:

(A) overshadow
(B) expedite
(C) hector
(D) falter
(E) purge

9. MUCKRAKE:

(A) disoblige
(B) annex
(C) abstain
(D) secrete
(E) ostracize

10. FORSAKE:

(A) recuperate
(B) attenuate
(C) abet
(D) nullify
(E) acquiesce

11. EMINENT:

(A) conspicuous
(B) analgesic
(C) widespread
(D) customary
(E) woeful

12. FLAGITIOUS:

(A) cardinal
(B) mercenary
(C) meritorious
(D) praetorian
(E) askew

13. CONDOLE:

(A) embrace
(B) incommode
(C) attend
(D) abate
(E) contrive

14. EPIGRAMMATIC:

(A) insipid
(B) indiscriminate
(C) poignant
(D) droll
(E) invidious

15. BESTIR:

(A) revile
(B) botch
(C) saunter
(D) affront
(E) inculpate

16. CONGENIAL:

(A) cantankerous
(B) sterling
(C) clement
(D) feral
(E) courteous

17. PENCHANT:

(A) usurpation
(B) loathing
(C) dominion
(D) axiom
(E) adjournment

18. FLIGHTY:

(A) arbitrary
(B) steadfast
(C) fleeting
(D) distraught
(E) repellent

Answers and Solutions to Problems

Set B	Set C	Set D	Set E
1. C	1. A	1. B	1. A
2. E	2. E	2. A	2. E
3. C	3. B	3. E	3. B
4. D	4. E	4. B	4. E
5. A	5. D	5. B	5. D
6. A	6. C	6. C	6. C
7. B	7. A	7. A	7. A
8. D	8. B	8. B	8. B
9. B	9. D	9. C	9. D
10. E	10. A	10. C	10. C
11. C	11. E	11. C	11. E
12. D	12. C	12. C	12. C
13. C	13. B	13. E	13. B
14. A	14. A	14. A	14. A
15. C	15. D	15. B	15. C
16. A	16. A	16. D	16. A
17. D	17. B	17. C	17. B
18. B	18. E	18. A	18. B

Problem Set A:

1. CIRCUM (around); NAV (to sail); ATE (verb suffix)

Meaning: To sail around the world.

2. MIS (bad, hate); ANTHROP (man)

Meaning: One who hates all mankind.

3. AN (without); ARCH (ruler); Y (noun suffix)

Meaning: Without rule, chaos.

4. AUTO (self); BIO (life); GRAPH (to write); Y (noun suffix)

Meaning: One's written life story.

5. IN (not); CRED (belief); OUS (adjective suffix)

Meaning: Doubtful, unbelieving.

6. EGO (self); CENTR (center); IC (adjective suffix)

Meaning: Self-centered.

7. IN (not); FALL (false); IBLE (adjective suffix)

Meaning: Certain, cannot fail.

8. A (without); MORAL (ethical)

Meaning: Without morals.

Note: AMORAL does not mean immoral; rather it means neither right nor wrong. Consider the following example: Little Susie, who does not realize that it is wrong to hit other people, hits little Bobby. She has committed an AMORAL act. However, if her mother explains to Susie that it is wrong to hit other people and she understands it but still hits Bobby, then she has committed an *immoral* act.

9. IN (not); FID (belief)

Meaning: One who does not believe (of religion).

10. NON (not); ENTITY (thing)

Meaning: A person of no significance.

11. CORP (body); LENT (adjective suffix)

Meaning: Obese.

12. IR (not); REPAR (to repair); ABLE (can do)

Meaning: Something that cannot be repaired; a wrong so egregious it cannot be righted.

13. INTRO (within); SPECT (to look); IVE (adjective suffix)

Meaning: To look inward, to analyze oneself.

14. IM (not); MORTAL (subject to death); ITY (noun ending)

Meaning: Cannot die, will live forever.

15. BENE (good); FACT (to do); OR (noun suffix [one who])

Meaning: One who does a good deed, a patron.

16. DE (down—negative); GRADE (step); TION (noun suffix)

Meaning: The act of lowering someone socially or humiliating them.

17. DIS (away—negative); PASS (to feel)

Meaning: Devoid of personal feeling, impartial.

18. A (without); PATH (to feel); IC (adjective ending)

Meaning: Without feeling; to be uninterested. (The apathetic voters.)

19. Analysis: A (not); NOM (rule); Y (noun ending)

Meaning: Not following the rule, aberration.

20. Analysis: IM (not); PERTURB (upset); ABLE (can do)

Meaning: Cannot be upset, cool, collected.

Problem Set B:

1. The root "err" means "to wander," and the prefix "ab" means "away from." Hence, to wander away from. In this case, to wander away from the normal. The opposite is CUSTOMARY (common). The answer is (C).

2. The root "jud" means "to judge." The opposite of to judge is to IGNORE. The answer is (E).

3. The root "junct" means "combine." The opposite of to combine is DISJUNCTION (cleave, separate). The answer is (C).

4. The root "gnosi" means "knowledge," and the prefix "a" means "without." Hence, AGNOSTIC means "without knowledge." In this case, without knowledge that God exists. The opposite is EVANGELICAL (devout, crusading). The answer is (D).

5. The root "mal" means "bad," and the root "dic" means "to speak." Hence, MALEDICTION means to speak badly of someone (to curse). The opposite is a BLESSING. The answer is (A).

6. The prefix "con" means "together," and the root "sangui" means "blood." Hence, CONSANGUINITY means "related by blood," and by extension it means close relation or affinity. The opposite is ESTRANGEMENT. The answer is (A).

7. The root "string" means "binding, strict." Hence, ASTRINGENT means "harsh, binding.". The opposite is LAX (loose). The answer is (B).

8. The root "grat" means "free" or "freely given." By extension, GRATUITOUS means "uncalled for, unwarranted." The opposite is RESTRAINED. The answer is (D).

9. "Omni" means "all," and "pot" means "power." So, OMNIPOTENT means "all-powerful." The opposite is FEEBLE. The answer is (B).

10. The prefix "multi" means "many." The opposite of "many" is "few" or "SINGULAR." The answer is (E). MULTIFARIOUS means "many-sided, numerous."

11. The prefix "counter" means "against," and the root "mand" means "order." Hence, COUNTERMAND means "overrule" The opposite is "RATIFY." The answer is (C).

12. The prefix "im" means "not," and the root "mut" means "change." Hence, IMMUTABLE means "unchanging" The opposite is "VOLATILE (changing rapidly, explosive)." The answer is (D).

13. The prefix "in" means "in," and the root "scrib" means "to write." Hence, INSCRIBE means "to write" or "engrave." The opposite is "ERASE." The answer is (C).

14. The prefix "in" means "not," and the root "trep" means "fear." Hence, INTREPID means "fearless." The opposite is "TREMULOUS." The answer is (A).

15. The root "ver" means "true." The only word related to truth is PROVE. The answer is (C). PREVARICATE means to "lie."

16. The root "rect" means "in," and the root "lin" means "line." Hence, RECTILINEAR means "in a straight line." The opposite is CIRCUITOUS (roundabout, winding). The answer is (A).

17. The root "phil" means "love," and the root "anthrop" means "man, people." Hence, PHILANTHROPIC means "lover of mankind." By extension, it means "humane, charitable." The opposite is CALLOUS (cold-hearted). The answer is (D).

18. The root "sanct" means "holy," and SANCTIMONIOUS means "feigning righteousness, hypocritical." The opposite is INGENUOUS (naive, artless). The answer is (B).

Problem Set C:

1. TRANSLUCENT means "clear, obvious." The opposite is OPAQUE—unclear, dark, impenetrable. The answer is (A).

2. VERITABLE means "unquestionable, true." The opposite is SPURIOUS—false, deceptive. The answer is (E).

3. ALLY means "to unite or connect in a personal relationship." The opposite is SPLIT—to divide. The answer is (B).

4. INSULAR means "isolated, narrow-minded." The opposite is WORLDLY—sophisticated, cosmopolitan. The answer is (E).

5. AUGMENT means "to add to." The opposite is OBVIATE—preclude, prevent. The answer is (D).

6. PEDESTRIAN means "common, uninspired." The opposite is STELLAR—outstanding. The answer is (C).

7. ASPERSION means "defamation." The opposite is EXALTATION—glorification. The answer is (A).

8. SAP means "to deplete , to debilitate." The opposite is QUICKEN—animate, revitalize. The answer is (B).

9. IMPEDE means "to hinder." The opposite is FOSTER—to encourge, to raise. The answer is (D).

10. TYRO means "a beginner." The opposite is MASTER—an expert. The answer is (A).

11. VENERABLE means "worthy of reverence or respect." The opposite is COMTEMTIBLE—despictible. The answer is (E).

12. GRIEVOUS means "atrocious, serious, grave." The opposite is TRIVIAL. The answer is (C).

13. SOLACE means "to comfort, to console." The opposite is DISHEARTEN—to discourage. The answer is (B).

14. PITHY means "concise, well-put." The opposite is VAPID—insipid, prosaic. The answer is (A).

15. CAPITULATE means "to give up, to surrender." The opposite is PERSEVERE. The answer is (D).

16. CONVIVIAL means "sociable, congenial." The opposite is ANTAGONISTIC. The answer is (A).

17. PROPENSITY means "inclination, penchant." The opposite is AVERSION—dislike. The answer is (B).

18. EMBED means "to implant." The opposite is EXTRICATE—to remove. The answer is (E).

Problem Set D:

1. REPINE means "to sulk, to fret." The opposite is DELIGHT. The answer is (B).

2. ODIUM means "abhorrence, discredit." The opposite is APPROBATION—approval. The answer is (A).

3. REFRACTORY means "obstinate." The opposite is IMPRESSIONABLE. The answer is (E).

4. MINATORY means "menacing." The opposite is INSPIRING. The answer is (B).

5. ONEROUS means "difficult, burdensome." The opposite is FACILE—easy, effortless. The answer is (B).

6. DISAVOW means "to reject" The opposite is APPROPRIATE—to adopt, to seize. The answer is (C).

7. QUELL means "to subdue, to allay." The opposite is INCENSE—inflame. The answer is (A).

8. TORRID means "passionate, burning." The opposite is DISPASSIONATE. The answer is (B).

9. PHLEGMATIC means "listless." The opposite is ANIMATED—spirited. The answer is (C).

10. SEMINAL means "creative, far-reaching." The opposite is STIFLING—confining The answer is (C).

11. NULLIFY means "to void." The opposite is ASSEMBLE—bring together, manufacture. The answer is (C).

12. ESCHEW means "to avoid." The opposite is PURSUE. The answer is (C).

13. APPRISE means "to inform." The opposite is ENSHROUD—conceal. The answer is (E).

14. INTREPID means "fearless." The opposite is CRAVEN—cowardly. The answer is (A).

15. GARROTE means "to strangle" The opposite is EMANCIPATE—to liberate. The answer is (B).

16. SODDEN means "wet." The opposite is DESICCATED—dry. The answer is (D).

17. PITILESS means "fierce" The opposite is BENEVOLENT—kind, generous. The answer is (C).

18. MANUMIT means "to liberate." The opposite is INDENTURE—to enslave. The answer is (A).

Problem Set E:

1. VITREOUS means "clear." The opposite is OBSCURE—dark. The answer is (A).

2. DEFINITIVE means "conclusive, thorough." The opposite is WANTING—incomplete, lacking. The answer is (E).

3. CONFEDERATE means "to unite or connect in a close relationship." The opposite is HEW—to split. The answer is (B).

4. PAROCHIAL means "provincial." The opposite is COSMOPOLITAN—sophisticated. The answer is (E).

5. AGGRANDIZE means "to enlarge, (especially of stature)." The opposite is ENCUMBER—to hinder. The answer is (D).

6. FATUOUS means "inane, stupid." The opposite is SAGACIOUS—wise. The answer is (C).

7. OBLOQUY means "defamation." The opposite is APOTHEOSIS—deification. The answer is (A).

8. SUBVERT means "undermine." The opposite is EXPEDITE—hasten. The answer is (B).

9. MUCKRAKE means "to expose (typically political corruption)." The opposite is SECRETE—to conceal. The answer is (D).

10. FORSAKE means to abandon. The opposite is ABET, aid. The answer is (C).

11. EMINENT means "distinguished, respected." The opposite is WOEFUL—pitiful, deplorable. The answer is (E).

12. FLAGITIOUS means "criminal, vicious." The opposite is MERITORIOUS, praiseworthy. The answer is (C).

13. CONDOLE means "to comfort, to console." The opposite is INCOMMODE—to inconvenience, to disturb. The answer is (B).

14. EPIGRAMMATIC means "clever, witty." The opposite is INSIPID—dull, prosaic. The answer is (A).

15. BESTIR means "to energize, to rouse." The opposite is SAUNTER, to stroll. The answer is (C).

16. CONGENIAL means "sociable, friendly." The opposite is CANTANKEROUS, ill-tempered. The answer is (A).

17. PENCHANT means "inclination." The opposite is LOATHING, aversion, dislike. The answer is (B).

18. FLIGHTY means "characterized by capricious or unstable behavior. " The opposite is STEADFAST. The answer is (B).

Vocabulary Drills

Many students write off questions which contain words they don't recognize. This is a mistake. This chapter will introduce numerous techniques that will decode unfamiliar words and prod your memory of words you only half-remember. With these techniques you will often be able to squeeze out enough meaning from an unfamiliar word to answer a question correctly.

TECHNIQUES FOR LEARNING NEW VOCABULARY

Put The Definition In Your Own Words

The first technique for learning new words is to put the definition in your own words. It is best to try to condense the definition to only one or two words; this will make it easier to remember. You will find simple one or two word definitions provided for you in the list of 4000 essential words in this book. You may be even more likely to remember these, however, if you put the definitions in your own words. For example, take the word

Heinous

The definition of *heinous* is "abominable, vile." However, you may find it much easier to remember by the word

Horrible

Often the dictionary definition of a word can be simplified by condensing the definition into one word. Take, for example, the word

Expiate

The dictionary definition is "to put an end to; to extinguish guilt, to make amends for." This definition may be summed up by one word

Atone

Putting definitions in your own words makes them more familiar and therefore easier to remember.

Write Down The Words

Many people are visual learners and do not fully benefit from a mere review of words and their definitions as they appear in a dictionary or in the list in this book. For these learners, writing the words and their definitions may well make a dramatic difference in retaining the words and their meanings. For many, it may take several times of writing the word down along with its definition to make it all "sink in." If you think this method is best for you, get a notebook to write your words in.

Use Flashcards

If you decide to write down the new words you are learning, you might also consider accomplishing two jobs at once by creating your own set of flashcards. Cut heavyweight paper into a size that you feel is manageable. Then, when you are practicing your words by writing them down, simply write the words on one side of a flashcard and write the definition on the other side. You will then have a wonderful tool with which to learn words on your own or to use with a partner in quizzing each other.

Create A Word Picture

Creating mental word pictures is another visual technique that you can apply to many words. You may remember in grade school learning the difference between the word *principal* and the word *principle*. Your teacher probably told you that *principal* refers to "the leader of an educational institution" and the word ends with "pal." Your school principal wants to be your "pal," so this is easy to remember (after all, you always wanted to be best friends with your principal, right?). Your teacher gave you a mental word picture.

Let's take another word: *sovereign. Sovereign* means "monarch." The word itself contains the word *reign*. What do you think of when you think of *reign*? You probably think of a king—or a monarch. So, picture a king when you are trying to recall the meaning of *sovereign*, and it should be easy to remember.

How about *pestilence. Pestilence* means "disease." The word *pest* is in the word. Pests are common in a garden, and, unfortunately, they often cause diseases among the plants in a garden. So when you see this word, picture a garden and then picture all of the pests that bring diseases to your garden. Then you will remember the meaning of *pestilence*.

If you have created flashcards, it may help to draw a small reminder on the flashcard of your mental word picture to further ingrain the word in your memory. For example, for *sovereign*, you might draw a small crown; for *pestilence*, you could pencil in a pesty bug.

Creating mental word pictures helps you retain the meanings of new words and clarifies your thinking when you get to the test.

Set Goals

Whatever technique works best for you, it is necessary to set goals if you plan to learn the "Ubiquitous 400" as well as the top 4000 words that are listed in this study guide. To do so, first look ahead to your intended test date. Next, determine how many days you have before this test date. Finally, divide the list so you have a preset goal each day of how many words you will learn. This makes the task much less formidable because you will be able to measure your accomplishments each day rather than trying to attack in one sitting what seems to be an insurmountable task.

WHEN YOU DON'T KNOW THE WORD

As we mentioned, you can't possibly memorize the whole dictionary, and, while you can learn the words in a list of words that occur most frequently on the SAT, there will inevitably still be some that you do not know. Don't be discouraged. Again, there are some very effective techniques that can be applied when a word does not look familiar to you.

Put The Word In Context

In our daily speech, we combine words into phrases and sentences; rarely do we use a word by itself. This can cause words that we have little trouble understanding in sentences to suddenly appear unfamiliar when we view them in isolation. For example, take the word

Whet

Most people don't recognize it in isolation. Yet most people understand it in the following phrase:

To whet your appetite

Whet means to "stimulate."

If you don't recognize the meaning of a word, think of a phrase in which you have heard it used.

For another example, take the word

Hallow

In isolation, it may seem unfamiliar to you. However, you probably understand its use in the phrase

The hallowed halls of academia

Hallow means "to make sacred, to honor."

Problem Set A:

For the following exercise, think of a common phrase in which the capitalized word is used. Answers and solutions begin on page 223.

Directions: For the following problems, choose the word most opposite in meaning to the capitalized word.

---

1. GRATUITOUS: (A) voluntary   (B) arduous   (C) solicitous   (D) righteous   (E) befitting

2. FALLOW: (A) fatuous   (B) productive   (C) bountiful   (D) pertinacious   (E) opprobrious

3. METTLE: (A) ad hoc   (B) perdition   (C) woe   (D) trepidation   (E) apathy

4. SAVANT: (A) dolt   (B) sage   (C) attaché   (D) apropos comment   (E) state of confusion

5. RIFE: (A) multitudinous   (B) blemished   (C) sturdy   (D) counterfeit   (E) sparse

6. ABRIDGE: (A) distend   (B) assail   (C) unfetter   (D) enfeeble   (E) prove

7. PRODIGAL: (A) bountiful   (B) dependent   (C) provident   (D) superfluous   (E) profligate

8. REQUIEM: (A) humility   (B) prerequisite   (C) resolution   (D) reign   (E) hiatus

9. METE: (A) indict   (B) convoke   (C) hamper   (D) disseminate   (E) deviate

10. SEVERANCE: (A) continuation   (B) dichotomy   (C) astringency   (D) disclosure   (E) remonstrance

Change The Word Into A More Common Form

Most words are built from other words. Although you may not know a given word, you may spot the root word from which it is derived and thereby deduce the meaning of the original word.

Example 1:   PERTURBATION: (A) impotence   (B) obstruction   (C) prediction   (D) equanimity   (E) chivalry

You may not know how to pronounce PERTURBATION let alone know what it means. However, changing its ending yields the more common form of the word "perturbed," which means "upset, agitated." The opposite of upset is calm, which is exactly what EQUANIMITY means. The answer is (D).

Example 2:   TEMPESTUOUS: (A) prodigal   (B) reticent   (C) serene   (D) phenomenal   (E) accountable

TEMPESTUOUS is a hard word. However, if we drop the ending "stuous" and add the letter "r" we get the common word "temper." The opposite of having a temper is being calm or SERENE. The answer is (C).

Problem Set B:

For each of the following problems change the capitalized word into a more common form of the word and then choose a word most opposite in meaning to the capitalized word. Solutions begin on page 223.

1. HYPOCRITICAL: (A) forthright   (B) judicious   (C) circumspect   (D) puritanical   (E) unorthodox

2. VOLUMINOUS: (A) obscure   (B) cantankerous   (C) unsubstantial   (D) tenacious   (E) opprobrious

3. FANATICISM: (A) delusion   (B) fascism   (C) remorse   (D) cynicism   (E) indifference

4. INTERMINABLE: (A) finite   (B) jejune   (C) tranquil   (D) incessant   (E) imprudent   (D) incessant   (E) imprudent

5. ORNATE: (A) Spartan   (B) blemished   (C) sturdy   (D) counterfeit   (E) temporary

6. MUTABILITY: (A) simplicity   (B) apprehension   (C) frailty   (D) maverick   (E) tenacity

7. VIRULENT: (A) benign   (B) intrepid   (C) malignant   (D) hyperbolic   (E) tentative

8. ABSTEMIOUS: (A) timely   (B) immoderate   (C) bellicose   (D) servile   (E) irreligious

9. VERBOSE: (A) subliminal   (B) myopic   (C) pithy   (D) dauntless   (E) ubiquitous

10. SUFFRAGE: (A) absence of charity   (B) absence of franchise   (C) absence of pain
             (D) absence of success   (E) absence of malice

11. UPSHOT: (A) consequence   (B) descent   (C) annihilation   (D) termination   (E) inception

12. WHET: (A) obscure   (B) blunt   (C) harden   (D) imbibe   (E) enervate

13. PRODIGY: (A) vacuous comment   (B) hegemony   (C) plane   (D) common occurrence
             (E) capitulation

14. AMBULATORY: (A) immutable   (B) obdurate   (C) hospitalized   (D) pedantic   (E) stationary

15. PLATITUDE: (A) sincere comment   (B) enigmatic comment   (C) hostile comment
             (D) disingenuous comment   (E) original comment

Test Words For Positive And Negative Connotations

Testing words for positive and negative connotations is a very effective technique. Surprisingly, you can often solve a problem knowing only that a given word has a negative connotation.

Example 1:   REPUDIATE: (A) denounce   (B) deceive   (C) embrace
                                 (D) fib   (E) generalize

You may not know what REPUDIATE means, but you probably sense that it has a negative connotation. Since we are looking for a word whose meaning is opposite of REPUDIATE, we eliminate any answer-choices that are also negative. Now, "denounce," "deceive," and "fib" are all, to varying degrees, negative. So eliminate them. "Generalize" has a neutral connotation: it can be positive, negative, or neither. So eliminate it as well. Hence, by process of elimination, the answer is (C), EMBRACE.

Example 2:   NOXIOUS: (A) diffuse   (B) latent   (C) beneficial
                               (D) unique   (E) unjust

NOXIOUS has a negative connotation (strongly so). Therefore, we are looking for a word with a positive connotation. Now "diffuse" means "spread out, widely scattered." Hence, it is neutral in meaning, neither positive nor negative. Thus, we eliminate it. "Latent" and "unique" are also neutral in meaning— eliminate. "Unjust" has a negative connotation—eliminate. The only word remaining, BENEFICIAL, has a strongly positive connotation and is the answer.

• **Any SAT Word That Starts With "De," "Dis," or "Anti" Will Almost Certainly Be Negative.**

Examples: Degradation, Discrepancy, Discriminating, Debase, Antipathy

• **Any SAT Word That Includes The Notion of Going up Will Almost Certainly Be Positive, and any SAT Word That Includes The Notion of Going Down Will Almost Certainly Be Negative.**

Examples (positive): Elevate, Ascendancy, Lofty

Examples (negative): Decline, Subjugate, Suborn (to encourage false witness)

Problem Set C:

Solve the following problems by checking the capitalized word for positive and negative connotation and then choose a word most opposite in meaning to the capitalized word. Solutions begin on page 224.

1. DERISION: (A) urgency   (B) admonishment   (C) uniqueness   (D) diversity   (E) acclaim

2. ANTIPATHY: (A) fondness   (B) disagreement   (C) boorishness   (D) provocation
        (E) opprobrium

3. CAJOLE: (A) implore   (B) glance at   (C) belittle   (D) ennoble   (E) engender

4. CENSURE: (A) prevaricate   (B) titillate   (C) aggrandize   (D) obscure   (E) sanction

5. ADULATION: (A) immutability   (B) reluctance   (C) reflection   (D) defamation
        (E) indifference

6. NOISOME: (A) salubrious   (B) affable   (C) multifarious   (D) provident   (E) officious

7. CONSECRATE: (A) curb   (B) destroy   (C) curse   (D) inveigh   (E) exculpate

8. ILLUSTRIOUS: (A) bellicose   (B) ignoble   (C) theoretical   (D) esoteric   (E) immaculate

9. DEIGN: (A) inveigh   (B) gainsay   (C) speculate   (D) reject   (E) laud

10. SUBTERFUGE: (A) bewilderment   (B) artlessness   (C) deceit   (D) felicitation   (E) jeopardy

Be Alert To Secondary (Often Rare) Meanings Of Words

SAT writers often use common words but with their uncommon meanings.

Example 1: CHAMPION: (A) relinquish   (B) contest   (C) oppress   (D) modify   (E) withhold

The common meaning of CHAMPION is "winner." It's opposite would be "loser." But CHAMPION also means to support or fight for someone else. (Think of the phrase "to champion a cause.") Hence, the answer is (C), OPPRESS.

Example 2: AIR: (A) release   (B) differ   (C) expose   (D) betray   (E) enshroud

AIR is commonly used as a noun—indicating that which we breathe. A secondary meaning for AIR is to discuss publicly. The opposite is to ENSHROUD, to hide, to conceal. Hence, the answer is (E).

Problem Set D:

In solving the following problems, check the capitalized word for secondary meanings and then choose the word most opposite in meaning to the capitalized word. Solutions begin on page 225.

1. CURB: (A) bridle   (B) encourage   (C) reproach   (D) ameliorate   (E) perjure

2. DOCUMENT: (A) copy   (B) implement   (C) gainsay   (D) blanch   (E) rant

3. FLUID: (A) radiant   (B) smooth   (C) solid   (D) balky   (E) craggy

4. BOLT: (A) linger   (B) refrain from   (C) subdue   (D) strip   (E) transgress

5. TABLE: (A) palliate   (B) acclimate   (C) garner   (D) propound   (E) expedite

6. HARBOR: (A) provide shelter   (B) banish   (C) acquiesce   (D) extol   (E) capitulate

7. FLOWER: (A) burgeon   (B) exact   (C) blight   (D) refute   (E) stabilize

8. STEEP: (A) desiccate   (B) intensify   (C) pontificate   (D) whet   (E) hamper

Use Your Past Knowledge / Education

Since you are studying for the SAT, you have probably completed, or almost completed, your highschool studies. Therefore, you have a wealth of knowledge from which to draw when it comes to examining the words that will appear on the test. In your classes, you studied history and probably one or more foreign languages. You may have even taken a Latin class. Because the English language has "borrowed" many words from other languages, especially Latin and French, these classes give you valuable clues to the meanings of many of the words you may come across.

Example 1: NARCISSISTIC: (A) egocentric (B) complacent
(C) pretentious (D) unostentatious (E) unassertive

You may remember Narcissus from one of your literature and Greek mythology classes. One version of the story of Narcissus relates a man who falls in love with his own reflection in a pool. Because of his requited love, he dies. As a man in love with his own reflection, he portrays self-love to the ultimate degree. A man like this is pretentious. *Unostentatious* is the opposite of *pretentious.* Hence, the answer is (D), UNOSTENTATIOUS.

Example 2: VERDANT: (A) naïve (B) seasoned (C) ignorant (D) amateur (E) innocent

Recall from your Spanish class that *verde* means "green" and from your French class that *vert* means "green" as well. These words may remind you of the word *verdant*, which also means "green" and can refer to being "green" in experience or judgment. Therefore, in this example, (B), SEASONED, is the answer because it means "experienced."

Problem Set E:

Use your past knowledge and education to solve the following problems. Solutions begin on page 226.

1. BLARNEY: (A) eloquence (B) loquacity (C) volubleness (D) taciturnity (E) efficacy
2. BRAVADO: (A) valor (B) brevity (C) audacity (D) cowardice (E) chauvinism
3. BLASÉ: (A) satiated (B) humdrum (C) provoked (D) jovial (E) robust
4. SABOTAGE: (A) subvert (B) advocate (C) extricate (D) undermine (E) emancipate
5. GRATIS: (A) unsatisfactory (B) gratuitous (C) baneful (D) commensurable (E) extravagant
6. PROTÉGÉ: (A) prodigy (B) pedagogue (C) liegeman (D) prodigal (E) imbecile
7. PEJORATIVE: (A) depreciatory (B) candid (C) ameliorative (D) disparaging (E) veracious
8. AMOROUS: (A) abhorrent (B) congenial (C) unadorned (D) magnanimous (E) menacing
9. ACQUIESCE: (A) concede (B) bestow (C) accede (D) mete (E) dissent
10. INCOGNITO: (A) recondite (B) palpable (C) inconspicuous (D) occultation (E) disguise

Points to Remember

Techniques To Learn New Words
- Put the definition in your own words
- Write down the words
- Use flashcards
- Create a word picture
- Set goals

When You Don't Know The Word
- Put the word in context
- Change the word into a more common form
- Test words for positive and negative connotation
- Be alert to secondary (often rare) meanings of words
- Use your past education/knowledge

Tips
- If the word starts with "De," "Dis," or "Anti," the word most likely has a negative connotation.
- If the word contains the notion of going up, it will most likely have a positive connotation.
- If the word contains the notion of going down, it will most likely have a negative connotation.

EXTRA VOCABULARY DRILLS

Problem Set F: Solutions begin on page 226.

1. DISCORD:

(A) agreement
(B) supposition
(C) strife
(D) scrutiny
(E) antithesis

2. KEEN:

(A) concentrated
(B) languid
(C) rash
(D) caustic
(E) voracious

3. IRRELEVANT:

(A) moot
(B) onerous
(C) impertinent
(D) germane
(E) true

4. FACILITATE:

(A) appease
(B) expedite
(C) extol
(D) foil
(E) precipitate

5. FEND:

(A) absorb
(B) disperse
(C) intensify
(D) reflect
(E) halt

6. PORTLY:

(A) ill
(B) thin
(C) dull
(D) rotund
(E) insipid

7. DEPLETE:

(A) tax
(B) annotate
(C) replenish
(D) lecture
(E) vanquish

8. INCESSANT:

(A) intermittent
(B) continual
(C) increasing
(D) enclosing
(E) expanding

9. PERJURE:

(A) absolve
(B) forswear
(C) impeach
(D) authenticate
(E) mortify

10. PLETHORA:

(A) dishonor
(B) paucity
(C) glut
(D) resolve
(E) deluge

11. ASSIMILATE:

(A) strive
(B) adapt
(C) synchronize
(D) estrange
(E) officiate

12. INADVERTENT:

(A) accidental
(B) disingenuous
(C) forthright
(D) inconsiderate
(E) calculated

13. ABSCOND:

(A) pilfer
(B) replace
(C) glean
(D) substitute
(E) surrender

14. FOMENT:

(A) exhort
(B) dissuade
(C) cower
(D) abet
(E) fixate

15. EXTENUATE:

(A) alleviate
(B) preclude
(C) worsen
(D) subdue
(E) justify

16. NONPAREIL:

(A) consummate
(B) juvenile
(C) dutiful
(D) ordinary
(E) choice

17. FITFUL:

(A) discretionary
(B) steady
(C) volatile
(D) tumultuous
(E) elegant

18. INVETERATE:

(A) sybaritic
(B) luxuriant
(C) vulnerable
(D) articulate
(E) variable

Problem Set G: Solutions begin on page 227.

1. CONDITIONAL:

(A) erratic
(B) crystalline
(C) unrestricted
(D) dependent
(E) calculating

2. INCENTIVE:

(A) comeliness
(B) naiveté
(C) purpose
(D) impediment
(E) motive

3. PENURY:

(A) affluence
(B) sacrifice
(C) assimilation
(D) harmony
(E) insolvency

4. ASPERSION:

(A) infamy
(B) restriction
(C) resoluteness
(D) tradition
(E) obeisance

5. MALEDICTION:

(A) supremacy
(B) argument
(C) diatribe
(D) encomium
(E) languor

6. EXHAUSTIVE:

(A) antipathetic
(B) concentrated
(C) stentorian
(D) stale
(E) incomplete

7. DESICCATE:

(A) fume
(B) invest
(C) saturate
(D) resent
(E) digress

8. HYPERBOLE:

(A) intimidation
(B) understatement
(C) unemphasized
(D) vacillation
(E) disagreement

9. OSTENTATIOUS:

(A) humble
(B) gaudy
(C) unfettered
(D) grievous
(E) shrewd

10. EXEMPLARY:

(A) vainglorious
(B) ardent
(C) indolent
(D) mediocre
(E) autocratic

11. RESERVE:

(A) meek
(B) softness
(C) prodigality
(D) celebrity
(E) retention

12. RESPLENDENT:

(A) planned
(B) depraved
(C) dark
(D) impure
(E) bizarre

13. NEFARIOUS:

(A) virtuous
(B) chilling
(C) base
(D) rigorous
(E) formidable

14. PROPRIETY:

(A) saga
(B) vehemence
(C) bastion
(D) humor
(E) misconduct

15. BUSTLE:

(A) attack
(B) bungle
(C) linger
(D) repulse
(E) alleviate

16. DEMISE:

(A) commencement
(B) futility
(C) pall
(D) enhancement
(E) influence

17. EXIGENT:

(A) pompous
(B) introspective
(C) stately
(D) solemn
(E) unimportant

18. PIQUE:

(A) mortify
(B) distend
(C) interpolate
(D) gratify
(E) truncate

Problem Set H: Solutions begin on page 227.

1. IMPAIR:

(A) disoblige
(B) underwrite
(C) envenom
(D) picket
(E) circumvent

2. ARBITRATE:

(A) satiate
(B) countermand
(C) pervert
(D) recant
(E) disregard

3. UNTOWARD:

(A) propitious
(B) improvident
(C) ominous
(D) narcissistic
(E) headlong

4. ATHEISTIC:

(A) adulterous
(B) privy
(C) amoral
(D) pious
(E) tellurian

5. ABJURE:

(A) blaspheme
(B) champion
(C) gesticulate
(D) mitigate
(E) absolve

6. AFFINITY:

(A) alienation
(B) haven
(C) aspiration
(D) camaraderie
(E) accretion

7. AUSTERE:

(A) cacophonous
(B) indulgent
(C) amusing
(D) skeptical
(E) craven

8. UNWARRANTED:

(A) aberrant
(B) impertinent
(C) facetious
(D) befitting
(E) attentive

9. INDEFINITE:

(A) unabridged
(B) transitory
(C) ductile
(D) oratorical
(E) fraught

10. SUNDRY:

(A) distinctive
(B) phlegmatic
(C) multitudinous
(D) disconsolate
(E) nonexistent

11. ANNUL:

(A) toil
(B) aggravate
(C) perpetuate
(D) retract
(E) govern

12. INVARIABLE:

(A) calculated
(B) askew
(C) insidious
(D) fickle
(E) uniform

13. AVER:

(A) oppugn
(B) vex
(C) efface
(D) admonish
(E) incapacitate

14. VALOROUS:

(A) palatable
(B) prostrate
(C) chivalrous
(D) acerbic
(E) timorous

15. EQUIVOCATE:

(A) enhance
(B) disencumber
(C) assay
(D) umbrage
(E) expire

16. PIED:

(A) uniform
(B) unwieldy
(C) insolent
(D) contrary
(E) tainted

17. MUNIFICENT:

(A) ambrosial
(B) ingenious
(C) genteel
(D) indurate
(E) immoderate

18. BANAL:

(A) pithy
(B) vapid
(C) foreboding
(D) conspicuous
(E) vacuous

Problem Set I:

Solutions begin on page 228.

1.   VITIATE:

(A)   incense
(B)   emend
(C)   fester
(D)   buffet
(E)   ensnare

2.   PRESIDE:

(A)   assuage
(B)   rescind
(C)   ravage
(D)   reconvene
(E)   defer

3.   INIMICAL:

(A)   auspicious
(B)   anomalous
(C)   apocalyptic
(D)   nugatory
(E)   impetuous

4.   AGNOSTIC:

(A)   perfidious
(B)   insidious
(C)   incorrigible
(D)   devout
(E)   ebullient

5.   DISAVOW:

(A)   befoul
(B)   advocate
(C)   beckon
(D)   stimulate
(E)   pardon

6.   KINSHIP:

(A)   dissension
(B)   hermitage
(C)   solicitation
(D)   communion
(E)   accrual

7.   RIGOROUS:

(A)   scabrous
(B)   lax
(C)   ponderous
(D)   precarious
(E)   timorous

8.   WANTON:

(A)   devious
(B)   impudent
(C)   lugubrious
(D)   demure
(E)   rapt

9.   CALLOUS:

(A)   unmitigated
(B)   clement
(C)   impressionable
(D)   sententious
(E)   sedulous

10.   JEJUNE:

(A)   conventional
(B)   indolent
(C)   stint
(D)   forlorn
(E)   piquant

11.   UNAVAILING:

(A)   tranquil
(B)   affecting
(C)   efficacious
(D)   detestable
(E)   disadvantageous

12.   IMMUTABLE:

(A)   obligatory
(B)   amiss
(C)   ingenuous
(D)   protean
(E)   homogeneous

13.   SURETY:

(A)   speculation
(B)   torment
(C)   chutzpah
(D)   countenance
(E)   prodigality

14.   INTREPID:

(A)   cloying
(B)   dissipated
(C)   gallant
(D)   stanch
(E)   craven

15.   MENDACIOUS:

(A)   misconstrued
(B)   primary
(C)   maidenly
(D)   amicable
(E)   exquisite

16.   MANIFOLD:

(A)   invariable
(B)   maladroit
(C)   unassuming
(D)   inimical
(E)   vile

17.   UNSTINTING:

(A)   enchanting
(B)   astute
(C)   affected
(D)   inured
(E)   improvident

18.   PROSAIC:

(A)   inapt
(B)   insipid
(C)   prophetic
(D)   discerning
(E)   impotent

Answers and Solutions

Set A	Set B	Set C	Set D	Set E	Set F	Set G	Set H	Set I
1. E	1. A	1. E	1. B	1. D	1. A	1. C	1. B	1. B
2. B	2. C	2. A	2. C	2. A	2. B	2. D	2. E	2. E
3. D	3. E	3. C	3. D	3. C	3. D	3. A	3. A	3. A
4. A	4. A	4. E	4. A	4. B	4. D	4. E	4. D	4. D
5. E	5. A	5. D	5. E	5. E	5. A	5. D	5. B	5. B
6. A	6. E	6. A	6. B	6. B	6. B	6. E	6. A	6. A
7. C	7. A	7. C	7. C	7. C	7. C	7. C	7. B	7. B
8. D	8. B	8. B	8. A	8. A	8. A	8. B	8. D	8. D
9. B	9. C	9. E		9. E	9. D	9. A	9. B	9. B
10. A	10. B	10. B		10. B	10. B	10. D	10. E	10. E
	11. E				11. D	11. C	11. C	11. C
	12. B				12. E	12. C	12. D	12. D
	13. D				13. E	13. A	13. A	13. A
	14. E				14. B	14. E	14. E	14. E
	15. E				15. C	15. C	15. C	15. C
					16. D	16. A	16. A	16. A
					17. B	17. E	17. D	17. D
					18. E	18. D	18. D	18. D

Problem Set A:

1.   You may not recognize GRATUITOUS in isolation, but you probably understand it in the phrase: "Gratuitous sex and violence." GRATU-ITOUS means "freely given, uncalled for." The opposite is BEFITTING. The answer is (E).

2.   Think of the phrase: "Fallow youth." FALLOW means idle. The opposite is PRO-DUCTIVE. The answer is (B).

3.   Think of the phrase: "To test your mettle." (The large waves tested the surfer's mettle.) METTLE means "character, courage." The opposite is TREPIDATION, which means fear. The answer is (D).

4.   Think of the description: "Idiot-savant." An idiot-savant is a person who exhibits the characteristics of both a mentally retarded person and a mental gifted person.   SAVANT means "reflective thinker." The opposite is a DOLT. The answer is (A).

5.   You may have heard RIFE used in the following manner: "The city is rife with crime." RIFE means "widespread, permeated." The opposite is SPARSE. The answer is (E).

6.   Think of the description: "Unabridged dictionary." An unabridged dictionary is the unabbreviated version of a dictionary. Hence, ABRIDGE means "to shorten." The opposite is DISTEND: to swell or protrude. The answer is (A).

7.   Think of the description: "Prodigal son." The prodigal son is the wasteful, spoiled son—a playboy.   Hence, PRODIGAL means "immoderate." The opposite is PROVIDENT—frugal, careful. The answer is (C).

8.   Think of the phrase: "Requiem for a heavyweight." REQUIEM means "a rest from an arduous task." The opposite is REIGN, the time spent in power or at the top. The answer is (D).

9.   Think of the phrase: "to mete out justice." METE means "to dispense, to distribute." The opposite is to gather, which is the meaning of CONVOKE. The answer is (B).

10.   Think of the description: "severance pay," which is the income you continue to receive after you have stopped working for a company. SEVERANCE means "the act of breaking off (or severing) a relationship." The opposite is to continue the relationship. The answer is (A).

Problem Set B:

1.   HYPOCRITICAL contains the base word HYPOCRITE, one who deceives. The opposite is one who is honest and candid. The answer is (A), FORTHRIGHT.

2.   Embedded in the word VOLUMINOUS is the word VOLUME. So we are looking for a word that is related to size. The only answer-choice related to size is UNSUBSTANTIAL. The answer is (C). (VOLUMINOUS means "large.")

3. FANATICISM contains FANATIC which in turn contains FAN. Now, at a sporting event, fans often become overenthusiastic, which is precisely the meaning of FANATIC. Thus, we are looking for a word that means unenthusiastic. That is the meaning of INDIFFERENCE. The answer is (E).

4. INTERMINABLE comes from the base word TERMINATE—to stop. Now, the prefix *in* means "not," so INTERMINABLE means "not able to stop." The only word that contains the notion of stopping or limitedness is FINITE. Hence, the answer is (A).

5. Changing the ending of ORNATE to "ment" yields the more familiar word ORNAMENT—a decoration. The opposite is undecorated. Now, the best answer-choice is SPARTAN, which means "plain or austere." The answer is (A).

6. Changing the ending of MUTABILITY from "ability" to "ate" yields the more common word MUTATE—to change. So we're looking for a word that means "unchanging." TENACITY means "steadfastness in one's opinions." In other words, not changing one's opinion easily. The answer is (E).

7. Dropping "lent" from VIRULENT and adding "s" yields the common word VIRUS. A VIRUS is harmful, so we want a word that means harmless, which is precisely the meaning of BENIGN. The answer is (A).

8. ABSTEMIOUS comes from ABSTAIN— to refrain from doing. The opposite is to do too much. Now, IMMODERATE means "excessive, indulgent." Hence, the answer is (B).

9. VERBOSE contains the word VERB, which means "word." VERBOSE means "too many words, wordy." Now, PITHY means "well put, concise." Hence, the answer is (C).
10. SUFFRAGE is a hard word. It means "the right to vote." And FRANCHISE is a synonym for "vote." Hence, the answer is (B), ABSENCE OF FRANCHISE.

11. UPSHOT is a result. Whereas, an inception is the beginning of something, it does not follow anything. The answer is (E).

12. WHET means "to stimulate." Think of the saying "To whet your appetite." The opposite of stimulating a desire or emotion is dulling or blunting it. The answer is (B).

13. Most people associate a PRODIGY with a mentally gifted child, and the opposite would be stupid. So choice (A), VACUOUS COMMENT is tempting. However, a PRODIGY is a person with extraordinary ability or talent, but not necessarily intelligence. By extension, PRODIGY means anything extraordinary. The opposite is a COMMON OCCURRENCE. The answer is (D).

14. Now, AMBULATORY means "walking, moving about." The opposite is STATIONARY. The answer is (E).

15. One of the first associations that comes to mind with PLATITUDE is a cliché or trite comment. So the opposite might be SINCERE COMMENT. However, a PLATITUDE is insincere because not much thought goes into creating it. Hence, it is unoriginal. The opposite is original. The answer is (E), ORIGINAL COMMENT.

Problem Set C:

1. Since DERISION starts with DE, it should be negative. So we are looking for a positive word. "Urgency" and "admonishment" are both somewhat negative—eliminate. "Uniqueness" and "diversity" are both neutral—eliminate. Hence, by process of elimination, the answer is (E), "acclaim." DERISION means "scorn."

2. Since ANTIPATHY starts with ANTI, it is negative. "Disagreement" "boorishness," "provocation," and "opprobrium" are all negative to varying degrees. Hence, the answer is (A), "fondness." ANTIPATHY means "hatred."

3. CAJOLE has a positive connotation. "Implore," "ennoble," and "engender" are all neutral to positive, and they are all similar to CAJOLE—eliminate. "Glance at" is neutral— eliminate. Thus, by process of elimination, the answer is (C), "belittle." CAJOLE means "to encourage."

4. CENSURE is a hard word. Nonetheless, you may sense that it has a negative connotation. (It comes from the same root as does "censor.") Hence, we want a positive word. "Sanction" is the only positive word offered, and it is the answer. CENSURE means "to deplore." The answer is (E).

5. ADULATION has a positive connotation. "Immutability," "reluctance," "reflection," and "indifference" are all neutral in connotation—

eliminate. Thus, by process of elimination, the answer is (D), "defamation." ADULATION means "praise, applause."

6. NOISOME is a very negative word, so we are looking for a very positive word. Now, "multifarious" is neutral: it means "diverse, many-sided." "Provident" is a positive synonym for "miserly." "Officious" is negative: it means "acting like an official, sticking your nose into other people's business." Finally, both "salubrious" and "affable" are positive, but "salubrious" (healthful) is more positive. So (A) is the answer. NOISOME means "noxious."

7. CONSECRATE (to make holy) has a positive connotation. The only negative word is "curse." The answer is (C). Note: "Destroy" is neutral, not negative: you can destroy something that is good or bad.

8. ILLUSTRIOUS has a positive connotation. Now, "bellicose" and "ignoble" are equally negative. At this point you have to guess. The answer is (B), "ignoble," which means dishonorable. ILLUSTRIOUS means "honored, renowned."

9. Since DEIGN starts with DE, it should be negative. So we are looking for a positive word. "Inveigh" is negative; it means to rail against. Eliminate (A). "Gainsay" is also negative; it means "to contradict, to impugn." Eliminate (B). "Speculate" is neutral as is "reject," rejecting something may be wise or unwise depending on the circumstance—eliminate (C) and (D). Hence, by process of elimination, the answer is (E). DEIGN means "to condescend, to disdain." And LAUD means "to praise, to extol."

10. The prefix "sub" gives SUBTERFUGE the sense of going down. So we expect SUBTERFUGE to have a negative connotation. Hence, we are looking for a positive word. Now, "bewilderment" is somewhat negative—eliminate. "Artlessness" (sincere, ingenuous) is positive; it may be the answer. "Deceit" is negative—eliminate. "Felicitation" (an expression of good wishes, congratulation) is also positive; it too may be the answer. "Jeopardy" is negative—eliminate. Now, SUBTERFUGE means "deceit, conspiracy." The opposite is artlessness. The answer is (B).

Problem Set D:

1. As a verb, CURB means "to restrain or stop." The opposite of stopping an activity is encouraging it. Hence, the answer is (B).

2. As a noun, DOCUMENT means "a legal or official paper." But as a verb, DOCUMENT means "to attest to, or to supply evidence." The opposite is to contradict, which is the meaning of "gainsay." The answer is (C).

3. As an adjective, FLUID means "moving in a continuous, smooth manner." The opposite would be moving in a hesitating manner, which is the meaning of "balky." (Think of a "balk" in the game of baseball.) The answer is (D).

4. As a verb BOLT means "to move quickly." (The sprinters bolted out of the starting blocks.) The opposite is to linger. The answer is (A).

5. As a verb, TABLE means "to postpone." You may have heard it used in government: "Congress tabled the bill." The opposite is to expedite. The answer is (E). Choice (D), "propound," is second-best. However, "expedite" is more precisely opposite because it includes the notion of speeding up the consideration of a proposal.

6. As a verb HARBOR mean means "to conceal" (to harbor a criminal). The opposite is to send away, which is the meaning of banish. The answer is (B).

7. As a verb, FLOWER means "to flourish," and the opposite is blight. The answer is (C).

8. As an adjective, STEEP means "precipitous." But as a verb, STEEP means "to saturate." Think of the phrase, "Steeped in tradition." In other words, filled with tradition. The opposite is to dry up, which is the meaning of desiccate. The answer is (A).

Problem Set E:

1.   Legend has it that if you kiss a magical stone in Blarney, Ireland, you will be given the gift of flattering speech, or eloquence. The opposite of BLARNEY, then, is TACITURNITY, which means silence or reticence. The answer is (D).

2.   BRAVADO comes from Old Spanish *bravada* or French *bravade*. Someone who shows bravado shows a pretense of bravery. The opposite of a pretense of bravery is true bravery, which is the meaning of VALOR. The answer is (A).

3.   BLASÉ is a French word, which means to sicken. The meaning of the word is to become world-weary or apathetic to pleasure or excitement. PROVOKED means to arouse or provide stimulation. The answer is (C).

4.   SABOTAGE, a French word, means treason or destruction. To ADVOCATE means to support. The answer is (B).

5.   GRATIS comes from Latin, and you may also recognize it from the French word *gratuit*. It means free of charge. EXTRAVAGANT is the opposite of gratis. The answer is (E).

6.   PROTÉGÉ comes from the French word *protéger*, which means to protect. A protégé is protected by a mentor, which is the opposite of protégé. One type of mentor is a teacher or PEDAGOGUE. The answer is (B).

7.   PEJORATIVE comes from the French word *péjoratif*, which means to worsen. The opposite is ameliorative. The answer is (C).

8.   You've heard the saying "Love in any language." The meaning of AMOROUS clearly relates to love. Recall from your undergraduate classes that love in French is *amour*, in Spanish *amor*, and in Italian *amore*. The opposite of love is hate. ABHORRENT means characteristic of loathing. The answer is (A).

9.   ACQUIESCE comes from the French word *acquiescer*, which means to consent or agree passively. The opposite of acquiesce is DISSENT. The answer is (E).

10. INCOGNITO is Italian and means unknown or disguised. The word has its roots in the Latin word *cognoscere*, which means to get to know. Add the prefix *in-*, which means "not." You may also remember the Spanish word *conocer* or the French word *connaître*, both of which mean "to know." The opposite of incognito is PALPABLE. The answer is (B).

Problem Set F:

1.   DISCORD means dissension, conflict. The opposite is AGREEMENT. The answer is (A).

2.   KEEN means alert, of sharp mind. The opposite is weary, which is the meaning of LANGUID. The answer is (B).

3.   GERMANE means relevant, appropriate. The answer is (D).

4.   FACILITATE means to make things easier to complete. And FOIL means to prevent the completion of something. The answer is (D).

5.   FEND means to deflect or repel. The opposite is to ABSORB. The answer is (A).

6.   PORTLY means heavy, ample. The opposite is THIN. The answer is (B).

7.   DEPLETE means to use up, to exhaust. The opposite is to REPLENISH. The answer is (C).

8.   INCESSANT means without end, perpetual. The opposite is INTERMITTENT. The answer is (A).

9.   To PERJURE is to lie under oath. And AUTHENTICATE means to verify, to show to be true. The answer is (D).

10. PLETHORA means overabundance. PAUCITY means scarcity. The answer is (B).

11. ASSIMILATE means to absorb, especially a smaller group of people into a larger group. And ESTRANGE means to alienate or separate. The answer is (D).

12. INADVERTENT means unintentional, without forethought. And CALCULATED means premeditated, with forethought. The answer is (E).

13. ABSCOND means to flee to avoid arrest. The opposite is to SURRENDER. The answer is (E).

14. FOMENT means to encourage, to call to action. The opposite is to DISSUADE, to discourage. The answer is (B).

15. EXTENUATE means to lessen the seriousness of an offense by offering excuses. Think of the phrase "extenuating circumstances." The opposite is to WORSEN. The answer is (C).

16. NONPAREIL means without equal, excellent. The opposite is ORDINARY. The answer is (D).

17. FITFUL means erratic, characterized by bursts of activity. The opposite is STEADY. The answer is (B).

18. INVETERATE means deeply-rooted, habitual. The opposite is VARIABLE. The answer is (E).

Problem Set G:

1. CONDITIONAL means dependent, contingent. The opposite is UNRESTRICTED. The answer is (C).

2. INCENTIVE means impetus, intention. The opposite is IMPEDIMENT—hindrance. The answer is (D).

3. PENURY means poverty. The opposite is AFFLUENCE—wealth. The answer is (A).

4. ASPERSION means defamation. The opposite is OBEISANCE—an expression of respect, a bow. The answer is (E).

5. MALEDICTION means denunciation. The opposite is ENCOMIUM—commemoration. The answer is (D).

6. EXHAUSTIVE means thorough, complete. The opposite is INCOMPLETE. The answer is (E).

7. DESICCATE means to dehydrate, to dry up. The opposite is to SATURATE. The answer is (C).

8. HYPERBOLE means exaggeration. The opposite is UNDERSTATEMENT. The answer is (B).

9. OSTENTATIOUS means showing off ones wealth. The opposite is HUMBLE. The answer is (A).

10. EXEMPLARY means superlative, well-done. The opposite is MEDIOCRE. The answer is (D).

11. RESERVE means self-restraint. The opposite is PRODIGALITY—extravagance, wastefulness. The answer is (C).

12. RESPLENDENT means brilliant, bright. The opposite is DARK. The answer is (C).

13. NEFARIOUS means evil. The opposite is VIRTUOUS. The answer is (A).

14. PROPRIETY means decency, appropriateness. The opposite is MISCONDUCT. The answer is (E).

15. BUSTLE means to hasten. The opposite is to LINGER. The answer is (C).

16. DEMISE means the death or end of something. The opposite is COMMENCEMENT—the beginning of something. The answer is (A).

17. EXIGENT means urgent, serious. The opposite is to UNIMPORTANT. The answer is (E).

18. PIQUE means to stimulate, to irritate. The opposite is to GRATIFY—to please. The answer is (D).

Problem Set H:

1. IMPAIR means to worsen, to damage. The opposite is UNDERWRITE, to support. The answer is (B).

2. ARBITRATE means to moderate or referee. The opposite is DISREGARD. The answer is (E).

3. UNTOWARD means unfavorable, improper. The opposite is PROPITIOUS, favorable, auspicious. The answer is (A).

4. ATHEISTIC means unbelieving, irreligious. The opposite is PIOUS, devout. The answer is (D).

5. ABJURE means to renounce. The opposite is CHAMPION, to support, to defend. The answer is (B).

6. AFFINITY means fondness, kinship. The opposite is ALIENATION. The answer is (A).

7. AUSTERE means harsh, Spartan. The opposite is INDULGENT. The answer is (B).

8. UNWARRANTED means uncalled-for. The opposite is BEFITTING, appropriate. The answer is (D).

9. INDEFINITE means endless. The opposite is TRANSITORY, fleeting. The answer is (B).

10. SUNDRY means some, various. The opposite is NONEXISTENT. The answer is (E).

11. ANNUL means to cancel. The opposite is PERPETUATE, continue. The answer is (C).

12. INVARIABLE means unchanging. The opposite is FICKLE, erratic, capricious. The answer is (D).

13. AVER means to assert. The opposite is OPPUGN, to question, to contradict. The answer is (A).

14. VALOROUS means brave. The opposite is TIMOROUS, trembling, timid. The answer is (E).

15. EQUIVOCATE means to lie. The opposite is to ASSAY, to determine, to asses. The answer is (C).

16. PIED means splotched, patchy in color. The opposite is UNIFORM. The answer is (A).

17. MUNIFICENT means charitable. The opposite is INDURATE, obstinate, callous. The answer is (D).

18. BANAL means commonplace, unoriginal. The opposite is CONSPICUOUS. The answer is (D).

Problem Set I:

1. VITIATE means to ruin, to corrupt. The opposite is EMEND, to correct. The answer is (B).

2. PRESIDE means to moderate, to oversee. The opposite is DEFER, to comply with the opinion or wishes of another. The answer is (E).

3. INIMICAL means injurious, hostile. The opposite is AUSPICIOUS, advantageous, beneficial. The answer is (A).

4. AGNOSTIC means unbelieving, irreligious. The opposite is DEVOUT, religious. The answer is (D).

5. DISAVOW means to renounce. The opposite is ADVOCATE, to support, to defend. The answer is (B).

6. KINSHIP means fondness, relationship. The opposite is DISSENSION, discord. The answer is (A).

7. RIGOROUS means harsh, exact. The opposite is LAX. The answer is (B).

8. WANTON means unrestrained, lewd. The opposite is DEMURE, modest, prim. The answer is (D).

9. CALLOUS means cruel. The opposite is CLEMENT, merciful. The answer is (B).

10. JEJUNE means dull, boring. The opposite is PIQUANT, stimulating, savory. The answer is (E).

11. UNAVAILING means useless. The opposite is EFFICACIOUS, capable of producing the desired effect. The answer is (C).

12. IMMUTABLE means unchanging. The opposite is PROTEAN, variable. The answer is (D).

13. SURETY means assurance, collateral. The opposite is SPECULATION. The answer is (A).

14. INTREPID means brave. The opposite is CRAVEN, cowardly. The answer is (E).

15. MENDACIOUS means lying. The opposite is MAIDENLY, virtuous, honest. The answer is (C).

16. MANIFOLD means many, diverse. The opposite is INVARIABLE, uniform. The answer is (A).

17. UNSTINTING means charitable. The opposite is INURED, hardened. The answer is (D).

18. PROSAIC means dull, pointless. The opposite is DISCERNING. The answer is (D).

Part Two
WRITING

WRITING

- **INTRODUCTION**
  Format of the Writing Section
  Scoring the Writing Section

- **GRAMMAR**
  Error Identification
  Improving Sentences
  Improving Paragraphs
  Pronoun Errors
  Subject-Verb Agreement
  Misplaced and Redundant Modifiers
  Faulty Parallelism
  Faulty Verb Tense
  Idiom

- **THE ESSAY**

  - **Punctuation**
    Commas
    Semicolons
    Colons
    Dashes
    Apostrophes
    Sentence Fragments
    Run-On Sentences

  - **General Tips on Writing Your Essays**
    Structure
    Style

  - **Present Your Perspective on an Issue**
    Patterns of Development
    Writing Your Issue Essay
    Sample Issues & Essays
    Practice
    More Sample Issue Essays

Format of the Writing Section

The writing section is 60 minutes long. Thirty-five minutes is devoted to two grammar sections, and 25 minutes is devoted to an essay.

Typical Format		
Essay	1 prompt	25 minutes
Grammar	35 questions	25 minutes
Grammar	14 questions	10 minutes

The essay and the multiple-choice grammar sections are presented back-to-back. If you finish the essay early, you may move on to the grammar sections.

Scoring the Writing Section

The scoring for the writing section is fairly complex. You will receive two subscores: one for the multiple-choice grammar sections, and one for the essay. The essay counts for only 30% of your writing score. The combined score for the grammar sections ranges from 20 and 80, and the essay score ranges from 2 to 12 (Two people will read your essay, each will assign a score from 1 to 6, and the two scores will be combined). But if you write on a subject that is not assigned or your handwriting is illegible, you will receive an essay score of 0. The two separate scores are weighted and the total score is then converted into the usual 200 to 800 score range, just like the reading and math parts of the test.

Grammar

The field of grammar is huge and complex—tomes have been written on the subject. This complexity should be no surprise since grammar deals with the process of communication.

SAT grammar tests only a small part of standard written English. Grammar can be divided into two parts: Mechanics and Usage.

Mechanics concerns punctuation, capitalization, etc. It is not tested on the SAT to the same extent as usage. So don't spend too much time worrying whether the comma is in the right place or whether a particular word should be capitalized. (For a thorough discussion of punctuation, see the Essay chapter.)

Usage concerns how we choose our words and how we express our thoughts. In other words, are the connections between the words in a sentence logically sound, and are they expressed in a way that conforms to standard idiom? This is the part of grammar that is most important on the SAT. Six major categories of usage are tested:

- **Pronoun Errors**
- **Subject-Verb Agreement**
- **Misplaced and Redundant Modifiers**
- **Faulty Parallelism**
- **Faulty Verb Tense**
- **Faulty Idiom**

To do well on this portion of the test, you need to know certain basic components of English grammar and usage. The more familiar you are with the parts of speech (nouns, verbs, pronouns, adjectives, adverbs, and so forth) and how they function in a sentence, the easier the test will be for you. Let's take a look at the types of grammar questions you will encounter on the test, and then we will brush up on some of the rules that dictate proper grammar and usage in the English language.

The Three Types of Grammar Questions

ERROR IDENTIFICATION

In these questions, you will see a sentence with four underlined parts—labeled A, B, C, and D—where a grammatical error may occur. If there is no error, then the answer is E. Following is some important information about these questions:

- If a there is an error, it is underlined and lettered.

- Each sentence contains either only one error or no error.

- About 1 in 5 error identification questions are correct as written.

Example:

The tactical <u>brilliance on</u> the battlefield of Tommy Franks and Richard
　　　　　　　A

Myers <u>as a general</u> can be attributed to the <u>rigorous training</u> they
　　　　B　　　　　　　　　　　　　　　　　C

<u>received</u> in military history. No error
　　D　　　　　　　　　　　　　E

To answer error identification problems, first read the sentence at a natural pace, listening for anything that impinges on your grammatical ear. If you don't hear a mistake, break the sentence into parts and then analyze each part. Assuming we did not hear the error in the example, let's break it up:

1) The tactical <u>brilliance on</u> the battlefield of

Be alert to idiomatic errors in the use of prepositions. Here, "brilliance on" seems OK. But let's try some other prepositions to see whether they might sound better. "Brilliance at" is awkward, as is "brilliance from." So, let's go to the next part of the sentence:

2) Tommy Franks and Richard Myers <u>as a general</u>

Notice that the compound subject "Tommy Franks and Richard Myers" is plural, but the phrase "as a general" is singular. This is our error, and the answer is B.

IMPROVING SENTENCES

In error identification questions, you just have to spot the error. With improving sentences questions, you have to not only spot the error but also choose the best correction. Also, the errors tend to involve larger structures in a sentence, such as the coordination between clauses. This tends to make the questions harder. The error, if any, will appear in the underlined part, which can encompass part or all of the sentence. Following is some important information about these questions:

* Choice A always repeats the underlined part of the sentence. If there is no error, choose A.

* If you cannot spot an error, the answer-choices often can direct you where to look.

* About 1 in 5 improving sentences questions are correct as written.

Example:

A bite from the tsetse fly invariably paralyzes <u>its victims unless an antidote is administered</u> within two hours.

(A) <u>its victims unless an antidote is administered</u>
(B) <u>its victims unless an antidote can be administered</u>
(C) <u>its victims unless an antidote was administered</u>
(D) <u>its victims unless an antidote is administered to the victims</u>
(E) <u>its victims unless they receive an antidote</u>

Choice (A) is incorrect since it is unclear whether the victim or the fly should receive the antidote.

Choice (B) is incorrect since *is* is more direct than *can be*.

Choice (C) is incorrect. A statement of fact should be expressed in the present tense, not the past tense.

Choice (D) is wordy. A pronoun should be used for the phrase *the victims*.

Choice (E) is the answer since *they* correctly identifies who should receive the antidote.

IMPROVING PARAGRAPHS

In these questions, you will be given a short, first draft of an essay. The sentences of the essay will be numbered, and you will be asked to improve the sentences and the paragraphs. Some of the questions will be just like improving sentences questions, but others will require you to understand the context of the essay and to improve it by strengthening what is said in the passage. This tends to make these questions harder than error identification and improving sentences questions. You should read the questions before quickly reading the essay, because although the content questions will require you to understand the essay, most of the questions can be answered without referring to the essay. Following are the three basic types of improving paragraph questions:

REVISING SENTENCES

These questions are like the improving sentences questions. The sentence that you will be asked to revise will be reprinted in the question, and you may, but probably will not need to, refer to the essay to answer it.

COMBINING SENTENCES

As the name implies, these questions require you to combine two sentences. The sentences that you need to combine will be reprinted in the question, and you may, but probably will not need to, refer to the essay to answer it. Usually, you will be able to tell without referring to the essay whether the sentences complement each other in which case they should be joined with a word like *and*; or whether the sentences oppose each other in which case they should be joined with a word like *but*. However, the best answer will often use a complete rewrite instead of just a conjunction such as *and* or *but*.

CONTENT QUESTIONS

These questions require you to understand what the essay is trying to say. You may be asked to strengthen the argument in the essay: Which of the following sentences would be best to add at the end of the essay? Or you may be asked the purpose of a sentence: Sentence 3 is best described as . . . . Or you may be asked where to insert a new paragraph: Where is the most logical place to begin a new paragraph?

Example:

(1) Stonehenge, one of the many magnificent wonders of the ancient world, has long been shrouded in mystery. (2) Its creation and purpose have generated numerous theories down the years. (3) One thing is for certain: it took many hours of manpower to develop this amazing site.

(4) Hundreds of men would have had to have helped with the construction because there were three phases of it. (5) In Phase 1, a circular ditch and bank were dug out of the ground, probably with the use of crude tools made from animal bones. (6) Phase 2 involved transporting approximately 80 stones, each weighing about 4 tons, from 240 miles away. (7) These stones were to be arranged in a circle, and, although such construction began, it was never finished. (8) Many speculate that a majority of the 4 ton stones that were hauled in were eventually removed and replaced by the larger stones used in Phase 3. (9) Approximately 30 stones were used in Phase 3, each weighing at least 25 tons and each originating 20 miles away from the Stonehenge site. (10) These stones were arranged in an outer circle and then capped with additional stones.

(11) How workers hoisted such heavy stones to their upright positions without modern-day cranes is one of the mysteries surrounding Stonehenge. (12) Without its enigma, however, it would not be the tourist attraction it is today.

1.   What is the best version of sentence 4 (reproduced below)?

    Hundreds of men would have had to have helped with the construction because there were three phases of it.

    (A)   Hundreds of men would have had to have helped with the construction because there were three phases of it.
    (B)   Hundreds of men must have helped with the construction because there were three phases of it.
    (C)   Hundreds of men must have helped with the construction because there were three phases of construction.
    (D)   Because there were three phases of construction, hundreds of men must have helped.
    (E)   Hundreds of men must have helped with the three phases of construction.

Choice (A) requires that you make no changes to the sentence; however, there are clearly some problems with the sentence as it is. First, "would have had to have helped" is rather wordy and not very direct. Second, the "it" in the sentence is not clearly defined. Therefore, Choice (A) is incorrect.

Choice (B) is incorrect as well. Although the wordiness of the sentence has been corrected with more direct phrasing, the "it" still has not been defined. In addition, the sentence implies that since there were many men working on the project, it ended up being three phases. This takes away from the author's intended message that it took hundreds of men in order to complete the project because the project entailed three phases.

Choice (C) seems to have corrected some problems; however, although we have now defined "it", the sentence sounds a bit redundant. It also presents the same problem as Choice (B) since it sounds like the construction occurred because of the men.

Choice (D) switches the order of the sentence around a bit and is the correct answer. The sentence is a cause-effect sentence: because there were multiple phases of construction, many men must have been needed. This answer-choice correctly defines this cause and effect relationship.

Choice (E) clearly shows a sentence that does not at all depict the cause and effect relationship.

2. Which sentence would function best as a concluding sentence after sentence 12 (reproduced below)?

    Without its enigma, however, it would not be the tourist attraction it is today.

    (A) The purpose of Stonehenge is still an enigma too, although most believe that it was used as a sacred burial ground for prominent people.
    (B) Thousands visit the site in Southern England each year, and work is in progress to better preserve Stonehenge so generations can enjoy the wonder.
    (C) Tourists can stay in one of the many hotels that have been built within kilometers of Stonehenge.
    (D) Many other tourist attractions are nearby as well.
    (E) The sheer magnitude of the attraction is amazing.

Choice (A) is incorrect because it raises a new topic about Stonehenge. Therefore, it does not function well as a concluding sentence, nor does it continue the topic of tourists as introduced in sentence 12.

Choice (B) is the right answer because it continues the discussion about tourists. Moreover, it functions well as a concluding sentence because it gives a brief picture of Stonehenge's future.

Choice (C) continues the topic of tourists; however, it veers too far off of the topic of Stonehenge. The purpose of the paragraphs is to give information on Stonehenge, not to cater to tourists.

Choice (D) again veers too far off topic by bringing up other tourist attractions in the area.

Choice (E) is incorrect because, while it offers a tidbit of information that might be good for a tourist to know, it veers off subject and does not provide an effective conclusion.

3. Which transitional word or phrase would best work to improve the flow between sentences 7 and 8 (reproduced below)?

    These stones were to be arranged in a circle, and, although such construction began, it was never finished. Many speculate that a majority of the 4 ton stones that were hauled in were eventually removed and replaced by the larger stones used in Phase 3.

    (A) However, many speculate...
    (B) Nevertheless, many speculate...
    (C) Consequently, many speculate...
    (D) Therefore, many speculate...
    (E) In fact, many speculate...

Choice (A) and Choice (B) are incorrect because the transitional words "however" and "nevertheless" show contrast. There is no contrast between the two sentences; rather, the second sentence explains more about the first.

Choice (C) and Choice (D) are incorrect because the transitional words "consequently" and "therefore" are transitional words that signal a result of some kind. In this instance, the second sentence is not a result of something occurring in the first, so these words do not work here.

Choice (D) is correct because the transitional phrase "in fact" is a phrase that shows agreement. In this case, the second sentence more clearly defines the first; therefore, "in fact" works.

Pronoun Errors

A pronoun is a word that stands for a noun, known as the antecedent of the pronoun. The key point for the use of pronouns is this:

- Pronouns must agree with their antecedents in both number (singular or plural) and person (1st, 2nd, or 3rd).

    Example:

    Steve has yet to receive his degree.

Here, the pronoun *his* refers to the noun *Steve*.

Following is a list of the most common pronouns:

PRONOUNS

Singular	Plural	Both Singular and Plural
I, me	we, us	any
she, her	they	none
he, him	them	all
it	these	most
anyone	those	more
either	some	who
each	that	which
many a	both	what
nothing	ourselves	you
one	any	
another	many	
everything	few	
mine	several	
his, hers	others	
this		
that		

Reference

- A pronoun should be plural when it refers to two nouns joined by *and*.

    Example:

    Jane and Katarina believe *they* passed the final exam.

The plural pronoun *they* refers to the compound subject *Jane and Katarina*.

- A pronoun should be singular when it refers to two nouns joined by *or* or *nor*.

    Example:

    Incorrect:

    Neither Jane *nor* Katarina believes *they* passed the final.

    Correct:

    Neither Jane *nor* Katarina believes *she* passed the final.

- A pronoun should refer to one and only one noun or compound noun.

This is probably the most common pronoun error. If a pronoun follows two nouns, it is often unclear which of the nouns the pronoun refers to.

Faulty Usage

The breakup of the Soviet Union has left *nuclear weapons* in the hands of unstable, nascent *countries*. It is imperative to world security that *they* be destroyed.

Although one is unlikely to take the sentence to mean that the countries must be destroyed, that interpretation is possible from the structure of the sentence. It is easily corrected:

The breakup of the Soviet Union has left *nuclear weapons* in the hands of unstable, nascent *countries*. It is imperative to world security that **these weapons** be destroyed.

Faulty Usage

In Somalia, *they* have become jaded by the constant warfare.

This construction is faulty because *they* does not have an antecedent. The sentence can be corrected by replacing *they* with *people*:

In Somalia, *people* have become jaded by the constant warfare.

Better:

The people of Somalia have become jaded by the constant warfare.

- In addition to agreeing with its antecedent in number, a pronoun must agree with its antecedent in person.

Faulty Usage

One enters this world with no responsibilities. Then comes school, then work, then marriage and family. No wonder, *you* look longingly to retirement.

In this sentence, the subject has changed from *one* (third person) to *you* (second person). To correct the sentence either replace *one* with *you* or vice versa:

You enter this world with no responsibilities. Then comes school, then work, then marriage and family. No wonder, *you* look longingly to retirement.

One enters this world with no responsibilities. Then comes school, then work, then marriage and family. No wonder, *one* looks longingly to retirement.

Using *I* and *me* with compound subjects and direct or indirect objects

- Use *I* in the subject of the sentence

  Incorrect: Sarah and me went to Las Vegas for vacation.

  Incorrect: Me and Sarah went to Las Vegas for vacation.

  Correct: Sarah and I went to Las Vegas for vacation.

- Use *me* in the indirect object of the sentence

  Incorrect: He gave the gift to Michael and I.

  Correct: He gave the gift to Michael and me.

Here's a trick: If you have a difficult time determining if the *I* or *me* is the subject or indirect object, try reading the sentence without the other portion of the compound phrase. Use the word that sounds correct.

Example:

Mark brought flowers to the party for Allie and I.

Read it like this:

Mark brought flowers to the party for I.

Does it make sense that way? No.

Correct: Mark brought flowers to the party for Allie and me.

Example:

Me and Tina ran down the beach.

First of all, always put the other person first! Read it like this:

Me ran down the beach.

Does it make sense that way? No.

Correct: Tina and I ran down the beach.

Warm-Up Drill I

Answers and solutions begin on page 273.

1. Had the President's Administration not lost the vote on the budget reduction package, his first year in office would have been rated an A.

    (A) Had the President's Administration not lost the vote on the budget reduction package, his first year in office would have been rated an A.
    (B) If the Administration had not lost the vote on the budget reduction package, his first year in office would have been rated an A.
    (C) Had the President's Administration not lost the vote on the budget reduction package, it would have been rated an A.
    (D) Had the President's Administration not lost the vote on its budget reduction package, his first year in office would have been rated an A.
    (E) If the President had not lost the vote on the budget reduction package, the Administration's first year in office would have been rated an A.

2. The President asked the Secretary of Defense and I whether we
                                    A
   would be willing to remain in our positions for at least
         B   C
   the first year of his second term. No error
                          D   E

3. The new law requires a manufacturer to immediately notify their customers whenever the government is contemplating a forced recall of any of the manufacturer's products.

    (A) to immediately notify their customers whenever the government is contemplating a forced recall of any of the manufacturer's products.
    (B) to immediately notify customers whenever the government is contemplating a forced recall of their products.
    (C) to immediately, and without delay, notify its customers whenever the government is contemplating a forced recall of any of the manufacture's products.
    (D) to immediately notify whenever the government is contemplating a forced recall of any of the manufacturer's products that the customers may have bought.
    (E) to immediately notify its customers whenever the government is contemplating a forced recall of any of the manufacturer's products.

4. Nearly all pundits agree that in spite of his surprisingly strong
       A   B
   and close campaign Republicans are unlikely
                                C
   to renominate him in four years. No error
                 D   E

5. World War II taught the United States the folly of punishing a vanquished aggressor; so <u>after the war, they enacted the Marshall Plan to rebuild Germany.</u>

    (A) after the war, they enacted the Marshall Plan to rebuild Germany.
    (B) after the war, the Marshall Plan was enacted to rebuild Germany.
    (C) after the war, the Marshall Plan was enacted by the United States to rebuild Germany.
    (D) after the war, the United States enacted the Marshall Plan to rebuild Germany.
    (E) after the war, the United States enacted the Marshall Plan in order to rebuild Germany.

6. In the 1950's, integration was an anathema <u>to most Americans; now, however, most Americans accept it as desirable.</u>

    (A) to most Americans; now, however, most Americans accept it as desirable.
    (B) to most Americans, now, however, most Americans accept it.
    (C) to most Americans; now, however, most Americans are desirable of it.
    (D) to most Americans; now, however, most Americans accepted it as desirable.
    (E) to most Americans. Now, however, most Americans will accept it as desirable.

7. Geologists in California have discovered a fault near the famous San Andreas Fault, <u>one that they believe to be a trigger for</u> major quakes on the San Andreas.

    (A) one that they believe to be a trigger for
    (B) one they believe to be a trigger for
    (C) one that they believe triggers
    (D) that they believe to be a trigger for
    (E) one they believe acts as a trigger for

Subject-Verb Agreement

Within a sentence there are certain requirements for the relationship between the subject and the verb.

- The subject and verb must agree both in number and person.

    Example:

    We have surpassed our sales goal of one million dollars.

Here, the first person plural verb *have* agrees with its first person plural subject *we*.

Note that, ironically, third person <u>singular</u> verbs often end in *s* or *es*:

> He *seems* to be fair.

- Intervening phrases and clauses have no effect on subject-verb agreement.

    Example:

    Only one of the President's nominees was confirmed.

Here, the singular verb *was* agrees with its singular subject *one*. The intervening prepositional phrase *of the President's nominees* has no effect on the number or person of the verb.

Collective nouns followed by intervening phrases are particularly easy to miss.

    Example:

    The *content* of the boxes *is* what she wants.

    The *meaning* of her sentences *is* not clear.

    A *group* of lions *is* called a "pride."

Be careful when a simple subject is followed by a phrase beginning with *as well as, along with, together with, in addition to,* or a similar expression. Be sure to make the verb agree with the simple subject, not with a noun in the intervening phrase.

    Example:

    Our *Senator,* along with most congressmen, *opposes* the bill.

Here, the singular verb *opposes* agrees with its singular subject *Senator*. The intervening phrase *along with most congressmen* has no effect on the number or person of the verb.

- When the subject and verb are reversed, they still must agree in both number and person.

    Example:

    Attached are copies of the contract.

Here, the plural verb *are attached* agrees with its plural subject *copies*. The sentence could be rewritten as

> *Copies* of the contract *are attached.*

Although it may seem obvious that when reversing the normal order of the subject and the verb their agreement must be preserved, this *obvious* error is easy to miss.

Example (wrong):

Attached to the email *is* the graphic file and the agreement.

This ungrammatical sentence sounds natural perhaps because its error is committed so often. The compound subject of the sentence is *the graphic file and the agreement*, which must take a plural verb:

Attached to the email *are* the graphic file and the agreement.

With the natural order of the subject first and then the verb in this sentence, one would be unlikely to mistakenly choose a singular verb:

The graphic file and the agreement *are attached* to the email.

Be careful when an inverted subject verb order is introduced by construction such as *there is*, *there are*, *here is*, *here are*. In these constructions, the actual subject follows the verb.

Example:

There *is* much *disagreement* between the parties.

The word *there* introduces the singular verb *is*, which agrees with the singular subject of the sentence *disagreement*.

In these constructions, it is tempting to mistakenly use a singular verb before the plural subject.

Example (wrong):

There *is a wallet and a key* on the dresser.

The compound (plural) subject of this sentence is *a wallet and a key*. It requires a plural verb:

There *are a wallet and a key* on the dresser.

This error occurs often in daily speech because the verb has to be chosen before we fully form the subject in our minds. Since the first part of the compound subject *a wallet* is singular, we naturally introduce it with the singular verb *is*.

Warm-Up Drill II

Answers and solutions begin on page 274.

1. <u>The rising cost</u> of government bureaucracy have made it all but impossible to reign in the budget deficit.

    (A) The rising cost
    (B) Since the rising costs
    (C) Because of the rising costs
    (D) The rising costs
    (E) Rising cost

2. <u>At the foundation</u> of the anti-insurgency program, strongly endorsed
    A
    by the tribal leaders, <u>is</u> plans to offer economic redevelopment
    B
    to the <u>general population</u> if <u>they oppose</u> the insurgents. No error
                 C   D   E

3. In a co-publication agreement, ownership of both the material and <u>its means of distribution are equally shared by the parties.</u>

    (A) its means of distribution are equally shared by the parties.
    (B) its means of distribution are shared equally by each of the parties.
    (C) its means of distribution is equally shared by the parties.
    (D) their means of distribution is equally shared by the parties.
    (E) the means of distribution are equally shared by the parties.

4. <u>Being adept</u> at the Machiavellian side of politics
    A
    <u>are</u> necessary for a senator <u>to succeed</u>
    B   C
    or even <u>to finish</u> his term. No error
                  D   E

5. The rise in negative attitudes toward foreigners <u>indicate that the country is becoming less tolerant, and therefore that</u> the opportunities are ripe for extremist groups to exploit the illegal immigration problem.

    (A) indicate that the country is becoming less tolerant, and therefore that
    (B) indicates that the country is becoming less tolerant, and therefore
    (C) indicates that the country is becoming less tolerant, and therefore that
    (D) indicates that the country is being less tolerant, and therefore
    (E) indicates that the country is becoming less tolerant of and therefore that

6. <u>The harvest of grapes in the local valleys decreased in 1990 for the third straight year but were</u> still at a robust level.

    (A) The harvest of grapes in the local valleys decreased in 1990 for the third straight year but were
    (B) The harvest of grapes in the local valleys began to decrease in 1990 for the third straight year but were
    (C) In 1990, the harvest of grapes in the local valleys decreased for the third straight year but were
    (D) The harvest of grapes in the local valleys decreased for the third straight year in 1990 but was
    (E) The harvest of grapes in the local valleys began decreasing in 1990 for the third straight year but was

7. <u>Each of the book's protagonists—Mark Streit, Mary Eby, and Dr. Thomas—has</u> a powerful, dynamic personality.

    (A) Each of the book's protagonists—Mark Streit, Mary Eby, and Dr. Thomas—has
    (B) Each of the book's protagonists—Mark Streit, Mary Eby, and Dr. Thomas—have
    (C) All the book's protagonists—Mark Streit, Mary Eby, and Dr. Thomas—has
    (D) Mark Streit, Mary Eby, and Dr. Thomas—the book's protagonists—each has
    (E) Each of the book's protagonists—Mark Streit, Mary Eby, and Dr. Thomas—could have had

8. <u>More important than winning is developing the ability to work with others and developing leadership skills.</u>

    (A) More important than winning is developing the ability to work with others and developing leadership skills.
    (B) More important than winning are the ability to work with others and leadership skills.
    (C) Developing the ability to work with others and developing leadership skills is more important than winning.
    (D) More important than winning are developing the ability to work with others and developing leadership skills.
    (E) More important than winning has been the development of the ability to work with others and the development leadership skills.

9. <u>There is a number of solutions</u> to the problem of global warming that have not been considered by this committee.

    (A) There is a number of solutions
    (B) There are a number of solutions
    (C) There was a number of solutions
    (D) There were a number of solutions
    (E) There have been a number of solutions

10. Although the <u>candidates accused</u> each other of encouraging voter fraud,
                              A

    <u>most polls show</u> that a majority of voters <u>believe</u>
             B   C

    the election <u>was fair</u>. No error
                     D   E

Misplaced Modifiers

A modifier is a phrase or a clause that describes something. A misplaced modifier, therefore, is one that describes the wrong item in a sentence, often creating an illogical statement.

- As a general rule, a modifier should be placed as close as possible to what it modifies.

   Example:
   Following are some useful tips for protecting your person and property from the FBI.

As written, the sentence implies that the FBI is a threat to your person and property. To correct the sentence put the modifier *from the FBI* next to the word it modifies, *tips*:

   Following are some useful tips from the FBI for protecting your person and property.

   Example:
   I saw the senators debating while watching television.

As written, the sentence implies that the senators were debating and watching television at the same time. To improve the sentence, put the modifier *while watching television* next to the word it modifies, *I*:

   While watching television, I saw the senators debating.

The sentence can be made even clearer and more direct without the modifier:

   I saw the senators debating on television.

- When a phrase begins a sentence, make sure that it modifies the subject of the sentence.

   Example:
   Coming around the corner, a few moments passed before I could recognize my old home.

As worded, the sentence implies that the moments were coming around the corner. The sentence can be corrected as follows:

   As I came around the corner, a few moments passed before I could recognize my old home.

or

   Coming around the corner, I paused a few moments before I could recognize my old home.

   Example:
   When at summer camp, my family moved.

As worded, the sentence implies that the family was at summer camp. The sentence can be corrected as follows:

   When I was at summer camp, my family moved.

- When a prepositional phrase begins a sentence, make sure that it modifies the *true* subject of the phrase.

This error is easy to miss.

Example:

As the top programmer, I feel that only Steve can handle this project.

Who is the top programmer in this sentence, I or Steve? Since only Steve can handle the project, it's likely that he is the top programmer. The sentence can be corrected as follows:

As the top programmer, only Steve can handle this project.

or

I feel that as the top programmer only Steve can handle this project.

- When a verbal phrase ends a sentence, make sure that it cannot modify more than one idea in the main clause.

This error can be rather subtle.

Example:

Oddly, the senator known to be a strong closer performed poorly in the final two debates, causing a drop in his poll numbers.

There are two conflicting ideas expressed in the main clause of this sentence: the senator is a strong closer and he did poorly in the final debates. As written, it is not clear which one caused the drop in his poll numbers (though logically the drop was caused by his poor performance). The sentence can be made clearer as follows:

Though known to be a strong closer, the senator's poor performance in the final two debates caused his poll numbers to drop.

or

The senator's poor performance in the final two debates caused his poll numbers to drop. Oddly, he is known to be a strong closer.

REDUNDANT MODIFIERS

Be careful not to modify a word with a word that means the same thing.

Example:

The old heirlooms are priceless.

By definition, heirlooms (valuables handed down from generation to generation) are old. The sentence can be corrected by dropping the word "old":

The heirlooms are priceless.

Warm-Up Drill III
Answers and solutions begin on page 276.

1. By focusing on poverty, <u>the other causes of crime—such as the breakup of the nuclear family, changing morals, the loss of community, etc.—have been overlooked by sociologists.</u>

   (A) the other causes of crime—such as the breakup of the nuclear family, changing morals, the loss of community, etc.—have been overlooked by sociologists.
   (B) the other causes of crime have been overlooked by sociologists—such as the breakup of the nuclear family, changing morals, the loss of community, etc.
   (C) there are other causes of crime that have been overlooked by sociologists—such as the breakup of the nuclear family, changing morals, the loss of community, etc.
   (D) crimes—such as the breakup of the nuclear family, changing morals, the loss of community, etc.—have been overlooked by sociologists.
   (E) sociologists have overlooked the other causes of crime—such as the breakup of the nuclear family, changing morals, the loss of community, etc.

2. <u>Using the Hubble telescope, previously unknown galaxies are now being charted.</u>

   (A) Using the Hubble telescope, previously unknown galaxies are now being charted.
   (B) Previously unknown galaxies are now being charted, using the Hubble telescope.
   (C) Using the Hubble telescope, previously unknown galaxies are now being charted by astronomers.
   (D) Using the Hubble telescope, astronomers are now charting previously unknown galaxies.
   (E) With the aid of the Hubble telescope, previously unknown galaxies are now being charted.

3. The bitter cold the Midwest is experiencing is potentially life threatening to <u>stranded motorists unless well-insulated</u> with protective clothing.

   (A) stranded motorists unless well-insulated
   (B) stranded motorists unless being insulated
   (C) stranded motorists unless they are well-insulated
   (D) stranded motorists unless there is insulation
   (E) the stranded motorist unless insulated

4. <u>Traveling across and shooting the vast expanse of the Southwest, in 1945 Ansel Adams began his photographic</u> career.

   (A) Traveling across and shooting the vast expanse of the Southwest, in 1945 Ansel Adams began his photographic career.
   (B) Traveling across and shooting the vast expanse of the Southwest, Ansel Adams began his photographic career in 1945.
   (C) Having traveled across and shooting the vast expanse of the Southwest, in 1945 Ansel Adams began his photographic career.
   (D) Ansel Adams, in 1945 began his photographic career, traveling across and shooting the vast expanse of the Southwest.
   (E) In 1945, Ansel Adams began his photographic career, traveling across and shooting the vast expanse of the Southwest.

5.   The Harmony virus will destroy <u>a computer system unless inoculated</u> by an anti-harmony program.

    (A)   a computer system unless inoculated
    (B)   a computer system unless the system is inoculated
    (C)   a computer system unless it is inoculated
    (D)   a computer system unless inoculation occurred
    (E)   a system unless it's being inoculated

6.   <u>As head of the division, we believe</u> you should make the decision whether to retake the rebel stronghold.

    (A)   As head of the division, we believe
    (B)   Seeing as you are the head of the division, we believe
    (C)   Being the head of the division, we believe
    (D)   As head of the division, we are inclined to believe
    (E)   We believe that as head of the division

7.   <u>It is well established that the death of a parent during childhood can cause insecurity in adults.</u>

    (A)   It is well established that the death of a parent during childhood can cause insecurity in adults.
    (B)   It is well established that the death of a parent when a child can cause insecurity in adults.
    (C)   It is well established that the death of a parent occurring when a child can cause insecurity in adults.
    (D)   It is well established that people who during childhood experience the death of a parent can be insecure as adults.
    (E)   That people who during childhood experience the death of a parent can be insecure as adults is well established.

8.   <u>Based on the yarns of storytellers, linguistic archeologists are compiling a written history of Valhalla and are realizing</u> that much of what was considered myth is in fact true.

    (A)   Based on the yarns of storytellers, linguistic archeologists are compiling a written history of Valhalla and are realizing
    (B)   Basing on the yarns of storytellers, linguistic archeologists are compiling a written history of Valhalla and are realizing
    (C)   Using the yarns of storytellers, linguistic archeologists are compiling a written history of Valhalla and are realizing
    (D)   Based on the yarns of storytellers, linguistic archeologists are compiling a written history of Valhalla and are coming to the realization
    (E)   Deriving it from the yarns of storytellers, linguistic archeologists are compiling a written history of Valhalla and are realizing

Faulty Parallelism

Faulty parallelism occurs when parts of a sentence that serve similar functions are not written with similar structures. For example, the verbs in a sentence should have the same tense if the subject performs the actions simultaneously.

*   For a sentence to be parallel, similar elements must be expressed in similar form.

*   When two adjectives modify the same noun, they should have similar forms.

    Example:

    The topology course was both *rigorous* and *a challenge*.

Since both *rigorous* and *a challenge* are modifying *course*, they should have the same form:

    The topology course was both *rigorous* and *challenging*.

*   When a series of adjectives modify the same noun, they should have similar forms.

    Example:

    The interim Prime Minister is *strong*, *compassionate*, and *wants* to defeat the insurgency with a minimum of civilian casualties.

The adjectives *strong* and *compassionate* begin a series of adjectives modifying the Prime Minister. Hence, the verb clause *wants to defeat* . . . is out of balance. The sentence can be corrected by turning the verb clause into an adjective clause:

    The interim Prime Minister is *strong*, *compassionate*, and *determined* to defeat the insurgency with a minimum of civilian casualties.

Notice that the clause *determined to defeat* . . . has much more structure and information than the single word modifiers *strong* and *compassionate*. Often, this imbalance in complexity can make a sentence stilted and the lesser adjectives will need to be subordinated:

    The interim Prime Minister, who is *strong* and *compassionate*, *wants* to defeat the insurgency with a minimum of civilian casualties.

However, the first rewrite is natural and more powerful. We will discuss these structures in detail later.

*   When a series of clauses is listed, the verbs in each clause must have the same form.

    Example:

    During his trip to Europe, the President will *discuss* ways to stimulate trade, *offer* economic aid, and *trying* to forge a new coalition with moderate forces in Russia.

In this example, the first two verbs, *discuss* and *offer*, are active. But the third verb in the series, *trying*, is passive. The form of the verb should be active:

During his trip to Europe, the President will *discuss* ways to stimulate trade, *offer* economic aid, and *try* to forge a new coalition with moderate forces in Russia.

- When a series of clauses with different verbs is listed, make sure the verb in each clause is included.

Although this may seem obvious, this error of omission can be surprisingly subtle to detect.

Example:
Your battlefield debriefing should *include enemy troop strength* and *why you believe the objective is necessary.*

Notice that the second clause is missing its verb. This forces the reader to assume that the writer just elected not to repeat the verb *include*. However, using the verb *include* in the second clause would be at best imprecise. The second clause would be more balanced and clearer with the verb *explain*:

Your battlefield debriefing should *include enemy troop strength* and *explain why you believe the objective is necessary.*

- When the first half of a sentence has a certain structure, the second half should preserve that structure.

Example:
To acknowledge that one is an alcoholic is *taking* the first and hardest step to recovery.

The first half of the above sentence has an infinitive structure, *to acknowledge*, so the second half must have a similar structure:

To acknowledge that one is an alcoholic is *to take* the first and hardest step to recovery.

- To correct an unparallel structure, first try giving the similar terms the same structure. For instance, change an adjective and a noun to two adjectives. However, this can make the sentence awkward. In these cases, you may need to subordinate one term to another.

Example:
He *ranks* as one of the top volleyball players in the country and is often *solicited* by clothing companies for his endorsement.

The first clause in this sentence uses the active verb *ranks*, and the second clause uses the passive verb *solicited*. The sentence can be made parallel by making the first clause passive:

He is *ranked* as one of the top volleyball players in the country and is often *solicited* by clothing companies for his endorsement.

However, this sentence is plodding. Let's try making both clauses active:

He ranks as one of the top volleyball players in the country, and clothing companies often solicit him for his endorsement.

This sentence is both plodding and awkward. Instead of forcing a parallel structure here, let's just subordinate the first clause to the second clause:

As one of the top volleyball players in the country, he is often solicited by clothing companies for his endorsement.

- Make sure the elements of correlative conjunctions are balanced.

Following are some common correlative conjunctions:

both . . . and . . .
either . . . or . . .
neither . . . nor . . .
not only . . . but also . . .
whether . . . or . . .

Example:

Agreeing to modest cuts in health benefits is a tacit admission by the union leadership *both* of its decreased influence *and* the increased influence of workers.

Here, the prepositional phrase *of its decreased influence* and the adjective phrase *increased influence of workers* are not balanced. This can be corrected by placing the preposition *of* before the conjunction *both*:

Agreeing to modest cuts in health benefits is a tacit admission by the union leadership of *both* its decreased influence *and* the increased influence of workers.

Example:

In criticizing the team, the coach was *not only* referring to the poor shooting *but also* to the numerous turnovers.

Here, the phrase *referring to the poor shooting* and the phrase *to the numerous turnovers* are not balanced. This can be corrected by moving the word *referring* before the word *not*:

In criticizing the team, the coach was referring *not only* to the poor shooting *but also* to the numerous turnovers.

Warm-Up Drill IV
Answers and solutions begin on page 278.

1. Common knowledge tells us that sensible exercise and <u>eating properly will result</u> in better health.

    (A) eating properly will result
    (B) proper diet resulted
    (C) dieting will result
    (D) proper diet results
    (E) eating properly results

2. The startup company found it <u>much easier</u> to underbid on a job
                                                 A

    <u>than completing</u> the job on time, <u>which caused</u> financial problems
          B   C

    when their clients <u>withheld payment</u>. No error
                          D   E

3. This century began with <u>war brewing in Europe, the industrial revolution well-established, and a nascent communication age.</u>

    (A) war brewing in Europe, the industrial revolution well-established, and a nascent communication age.
    (B) war brewing in Europe, the industrial revolution surging, and a nascent communication age.
    (C) war in Europe, the industrial revolution well-established, and a nascent communication age.
    (D) war brewing in Europe, the industrial revolution well-established, and the communication age beginning.
    (E) war brewing in Europe, the industrial revolution well-established, and saw the birth of the communication age.

4. It is often better <u>to try repairing an old car than to junk it.</u>

    (A) to try repairing an old car than to junk it.
    (B) to repair an old car than to have it junked.
    (C) to try repairing an old car than to junking it.
    (D) to try and repair an old car than to junk it.
    (E) to try to repair an old car than to junk it.

5. <u>Jurassic Park, written by Michael Crichton, and which was first printed in 1988,</u> is a novel about a theme park of the future in which dinosaurs roam free.

    (A) Jurassic Park, written by Michael Crichton, and which was first printed in 1988,
    (B) Jurassic Park, written by Michael Crichton and first printed in 1988,
    (C) Jurassic Park, which was written by Michael Crichton, and which was first printed in 1988,
    (D) Written by Michael Crichton and first printed in 1988, Jurassic Park
    (E) Jurassic Park, which was written by Michael Crichton and first printed in 1988,

The following passage is a first draft of an essay. Some parts of the passage need to be rewritten.

(1) Nestled in the foothills of the Smoky Mountains, *Getaway Lodge* offers its guests hospitality, comfort, and living in luxury. (2) Guests are greeted at the door and ushered to their rooms where they are welcomed with a large gift basket filled with scrumptious snacks and bath oils. (3) Every room has magnificent, breathtaking views of the surrounding mountains. (4) The mountains offer a myriad of activities for travelers including hiking and rock climbing. (5) If outdoor recreation is not appealing, guests can lounge by the free-form pool or soak in the hot tub.

(6) After a full day's activities, dinner is served in a romantic dining room adjacent to a waterfall. (7) By the glow of candlelight, diners will enjoy savory entrees and decadent desserts. (8) After dinner, guests may enjoy a stroll through the garden or sitting by the fireplace. (9) With so many pleasurable activities, guests can easily pass a memorable week at the *Getaway Lodge*.

6. What is the best way to deal with sentence 1 (reproduced below)?

    Nestled in the foothills of the Smoky Mountains, Getaway Lodge offers its guests hospitality, comfort, and living in luxury.

    (A) Leave it as it is.
    (B) Change "its" to "their".
    (C) Change "hospitality" to "hospitable living".
    (D) Change "comfort" to "comfortable living".
    (E) Change "living in luxury" to "luxurious living".

7. Which of the following is the best revision of sentence 4 to better link it to sentence 3?

    (A) Every room also has magnificent, breathtaking views of the surrounding mountains.
    (B) Moreover, every room has magnificent, breathtaking views of the surrounding mountains.
    (C) Guests are also treated to magnificent, breathtaking views of the surrounding mountains.
    (D) In addition, guests are also shown magnificent, breathtaking views of the surrounding mountains.
    (E) Also, guests may view magnificent, breathtaking views of the surrounding mountains.

8. In context, what does the word *myriad* mean in sentence 4 (reproduced below)?

    The mountains offer a myriad of activities for travelers including hiking and rock climbing.

    (A) Enjoyable
    (B) Many
    (C) Some
    (D) Few
    (E) Difficult

9. What is the best way to deal with sentence 8 (reproduced below)?

    After dinner, guests may enjoy a stroll through the garden or sitting by the fireplace.

    (A) Leave it as it is.
    (B) Change "enjoy" to "take".
    (C) Change "a stroll" to "strolling".
    (D) Change "sitting" to "taking a seat".
    (E) Place "after dinner" at the end of the sentence.

10. If the waterfall is part of the pool, where is the pool in relationship to the restaurant?

   (A) Across from
   (B) Catty-corner to
   (C) On the other side of the lodge
   (D) Next to
   (E) Down the walkway from

11. Where would you expect to find this passage?

   (A) In a travel brochure.
   (B) As part of a restaurant review.
   (C) In an outdoor recreation magazine.
   (D) On a postcard from a guest.
   (E) On a flyer.

Faulty Verb Tense

A verb is usually defined as

a word that expresses action or state of being

Oddly, this definition is simultaneously both obscure and too precise: "state of being" is vague, and words other than verbs can carry the weight of action in a sentence. However, any attempt to better define the concept of the verb will lead us into far more detail than we have room to discuss. Let's just use the above definition to reinforce our intuitive understanding of the meaning and function of a verb in a sentence.

A verb has four principal parts:

1. **Present Tense**
   a. Used to express present tense.

   He studies hard.

   b. Used to express general truths.

   During a recession, people are cautious about taking on more debt.

   c. Used with *will* or *shall* to express future time.

   He will take the SAT next year.

2. **Past Tense**
   a. Used to express past tense.

   He took the SAT last year.

3. **Past Participle**
   a. Used to form the *present perfect tense*, which indicates that an action was started in the past and its effects are continuing in the present. It is formed using *have* or *has* and the past participle of the verb.

   He has prepared thoroughly for the SAT.

   b. Used to form the *past perfect tense*, which indicates that an action was completed before another past action. It is formed using *had* and the past participle of the verb.

   He had prepared thoroughly before taking the SAT.

   c. Used to form the *future perfect tense*, which indicates that an action will be completed before another future action. It is formed using *will have* or *shall have* and the past participle of the verb.

   He will have prepared thoroughly before taking the SAT.

4. **Present Participle (-*ing* form of the verb)**

    a. Used to form the *present progressive tense*, which indicates that an action is ongoing. It is formed using *is*, *am*, or *are* and the present participle of the verb.

He is preparing thoroughly for the SAT.

    b. Used to form the *past progressive tense*, which indicates that an action was in progress in the past. It is formed using *was* or *were* and the present participle of the verb.

He was preparing for the SAT.

    c. Used to form the *future progressive tense*, which indicates that an action will be in progress in the future. It is formed using *will be* or *shall be* and the present participle of the verb.

He will be preparing thoroughly for the SAT.

PASSIVE VOICE

- The passive voice removes the subject from the sentence. It is formed with the verb *to be* and the past participle of the main verb.

Passive:

The bill was resubmitted by the Senator.

Active:

The Senator has resubmitted the bill.

Unless you want to de-emphasize the doer of an action, you should favor the active voice. Passive sentences are usually considered loose. Notice in the above example that the sentence with the active verb is more lively, more powerful.

- Be alert to passive constructions that point to the wrong doer of an action.

Example:

The head of the insurgency *was reported killed* in the first day of action by the press.

The passive structure seems to imply that the press killed the head of the insurgency. In the construction *killed in the first day of action by the press* drop the intervening phrase *in the first day* and you get *killed by the press*. The sentence is better expressed at least partially in the active voice:

The press *reported* that the head of the insurgency *was killed* in the first day of action.

Here, the subject *press* uses the active verb *reported*, and presumably the army is alluded to by the passive verb *was killed*.

Warm-Up Drill V
Answers and solutions begin on page 281.

1. In the past few years and to this day, many teachers of math and science <u>had chosen to return to the private sector.</u>

    (A) had chosen to return to the private sector.
    (B) having chosen to return to the private sector.
    (C) chose to return to the private sector.
    (D) have chosen to return to the private sector.
    (E) have chosen returning to the private sector.

2. KFBCs <u>talented weatherman</u>, Steve Emerson,
                          A
   <u>has been</u> a reporter, a <u>news writer</u>, and
      B   C
   <u>a producer</u> of many news shows. No error
         D   E

3. <u>Most of the homes that were destroyed in last summer's brush fires were</u> built with wood-shake roofs.

    (A) Most of the homes that were destroyed in last summer's brush fires were
    (B) Last summer, brush fires destroyed most of the homes that were
    (C) Most of the homes that were destroyed in last summer's brush fires had been
    (D) Most of the homes that the brush fires destroyed last summer's have been
    (E) Most of the homes destroyed in last summer's brush fires were being

4. Although World War II ended nearly a half century ago, Russia and Japan still have <u>not signed a formal peace treaty; and both countries have been</u> reticent to develop closer relations.

    (A) have not signed a formal peace treaty; and both countries have been
    (B) did not signed a formal peace treaty; and both countries have been
    (C) have not signed a formal peace treaty; and both countries being
    (D) have not signed a formal peace treaty; and both countries are
    (E) are not signing a formal peace treaty; and both countries have been

5. Although <u>Jim worked</u> hard on the project,
                  A
   the <u>loss of</u> the potentially <u>lucrative Cuban</u> market
            B   C
   <u>caused him</u> to lose interest. No error
         D   E

6. The Democrats have accused the Republicans of resorting to dirty tricks by planting a mole on the Democrat's planning committee and then <u>used the information obtained to sabotage</u> the Democrat's campaign.

    (A) used the information obtained to sabotage
    (B) used the information they had obtained to sabotage
    (C) of using the information they had obtained to sabotage
    (D) using the information obtained to sabotage
    (E) to have used the information obtained to sabotage

Idiom

Idioms are figures of speech that convey messages which are peculiar to a language. If taken literally, the message would not have the same meaning as the speaker intended.

Accept/Except

Accept means to receive something that is offered or agree to something. *Except* means leave out or exclude something.

> The European powers would have *accepted* Iran's offer if it had included on-site and unrestricted inspections.

> All the world's industrial powers signed the treaty to reduce global warming *except* the United States.

Account for

When explaining something, the correct idiom is *account for*.

> We had to *account for* all the missing money.

When receiving blame or credit, the correct idiom is *account to*:

> You will have to *account to* the state for your crimes.

Adapted to/for/from

Adapted to means "naturally suited for." *Adapted for* means "created to be suited for." *Adapted from* means "changed to be suited for." Consider these examples:

> The polar bear is *adapted to* the subzero temperatures.

> For any "New Order" to be successful, it must be *adapted for* the continually changing world power structure.

> Lucas' latest release is *adapted from* the 1950 B-movie "Attack of the Amazons."

Affect/Effect

Affect, usually a verb, means to influence something or the act upon something. *Effect*, usually a noun, means the result.

> The anti-venom had the desired *effect*, and the boy fully recovered.

Here, *effect* is a noun meaning *result*.

> The negotiators were not *affected* by the large, violent street protests.

Here, *affected* is a verb meaning to *influence*.

All ready vs. Already

> *All ready* means "everything is ready."

> *Already* means "earlier."

Alot vs. A lot

Alot is nonstandard; *a lot* is the correct form.

Among/Between

Between should be used when referring to two things, and *among* should be used when referring to more than two things. For example,

> The young lady must choose *between* two suitors.

> The fault is spread evenly *among* the three defendants.

As/Like

A frequent mistake is to use *like* when *as* is needed. If you are connecting a clause to its subject, use *as*. If you merely need a preposition to introduce a noun, use *like*.

> It appears *as* though the peace plan has failed.
> (*As* is introducing the clause "the peace plan has failed.")

> It looks *like* rain.
> (*Like* is introducing the noun "rain.")

As to

This construction is usually imprecise or vacuous. In almost all cases, you should replace it with a more precise preposition or delete it.

(Poor)	The prosecuting attorney left little doubt *as to* the defendant's motive for the murder.
(Better)	The prosecuting attorney left little doubt *about* the defendant's motive for the murder.
(Poor)	The question *as to whether* it's better to let the bill die in committee or be voted down on the floor of the house is purely political.
(Better)	The question *whether* it's better to let the bill die in committee or be voted down on the floor of the house is purely political.

Being that vs. Since

Being that is nonstandard and should be replaced by *since*.

(Faulty)	*Being that* darkness was fast approaching, we had to abandon the search.
(Better)	*Since* darkness was fast approaching, we had to abandon the search.

Beside/Besides

Adding an *s* to *beside* completely changes its meaning: *Beside* means "next to." *Besides* means "in addition."

> We sat *beside* (next to) the host.

> *Besides* (in addition), money was not even an issue in the contract negotiations.

Center on vs. Center around

Center around is colloquial. It should not be used in formal writing.

> *(Faulty)*   The dispute *centers around* the effects of undocumented workers.
>
> *(Correct)*   The dispute *centers on* the effects of undocumented workers.

Conform to (not *with*)

> Stewart's writing does not *conform to* standard literary conventions.

Consensus of opinion

Consensus of opinion is redundant: *consensus* means "general agreement."

Correspond to/with

Correspond to means "in agreement with."

> The penalty does not *correspond to* the severity of the crime.

Correspond with means "to exchange letters."

> He *corresponded with* many of the top European leaders of his time.

Double negatives

> *(Faulty)*   *Scarcely nothing* was learned during the seminar.
>
> *(Better)*   *Scarcely anything* was learned during the seminar.

Doubt that vs. Doubt whether

Doubt whether is nonstandard.

> *(Faulty)*   I *doubt whether* his new business will succeed.
>
> *(Correct)*   I *doubt that* his new business will succeed.

Farther/Further

Use *farther* when referring to distance, and use *further* when referring to degree.

> They went no *further* (degree) than necking.
>
> He threw the discs *farther* (distance) than the top seated competitor.

Fewer/Less

Use *fewer* when referring to a number of items. Use *less* when referring to a continuous quantity.

> In the past, we had *fewer* options.
>
> The impact was *less* than what was expected.

Identical with (not *to*)

This bid is *identical with* the one submitted by you.

In contrast to (not *of*)

In *contrast to* the conservative attitudes of her time, Mae West was quite provocative.

Independent of (not *from*)

The judiciary is *independent of* the other branches of government.

It's/Its

It's is a contraction of *it is*. *Its* is the possessive form of *it*. To check whether the apostrophe is needed, merely read the sentence replacing *its* or *it's* with *it is*. If the sentence reads well, then the apostrophe is needed; otherwise it's not.

It's [it is] too early to determine *its* [possession] cause.

Likely vs. Liable

Likely simply means something will probably occur. *Liable* means vulnerability to legal responsibility or to something unpleasant.

If we don't pay the bill on time, we are *liable* to damage our credit with the company; and if we don't pay it at all, we are *liable* to be sued.

A common mistake is use *liable* to mean *likely*:

(Faulty)   The top-rated team is *liable* to win the tournament.

(Correct)   The top-rated team is *likely* to win the tournament.

Not only . . . but also

In this construction, *but* cannot be replaced with *and*.

(Faulty)   Peterson is *not only* the top salesman in the department *and also* the most proficient.

(Correct)   Peterson is *not only* the top salesman in the department *but also* the most proficient.

On account of vs. Because

Because is always better than the circumlocution *on account of*.

(Poor)   *On account of* his poor behavior, he was expelled.

(Better)   *Because* he behaved poorly, he was expelled.

One another/Each other

Each other should be used when referring to two things, and *one another* should be used when referring to more than two things.

> The members of the basketball team (more than two) congratulated *one another* on their victory.

> The business partners (two) congratulated *each other* on their successful first year.

Plus vs. And

Do not use *plus* as a conjunction meaning *and*.

> *(Faulty)*   His contributions to this community are considerable, *plus* his character is beyond reproach.

> *(Correct)*   His contributions to this community are considerable, *and* his character is beyond reproach.

Note: *Plus* can be used to mean *and* as long as it is not being used as a conjunction.

> *(Acceptable)*   His generous financial contribution *plus* his donated time has made this project a success.

In this sentence, *plus* is being used as a preposition. Note, the verb *has* is singular because an intervening prepositional phrase (*plus* his donated time) does not affect subject verb agreement.

Regard vs. Regards

Unless you are giving best wishes to someone, you should use *regard*.

> *(Faulty)*   In *regards* to your letter, we would be interested in distributing your product.

> *(Correct)*   In *regard* to your letter, we would be interested in distributing your product.

Regardless vs. Irregardless

Regardless means "not withstanding." Hence, the "ir" in *irregardless* is redundant. *Regardless* is the correct form.

Retroactive to (not *from*)

The correct idiom is *retroactive to*:

> The tax increase is *retroactive to* February.

Speak to/with

To *speak to* someone is to tell them something.

> We *spoke to* Jennings about the alleged embezzlement.

To *speak with* someone is to discuss something with them.

> Steve *spoke with* his friend Dave for hours yesterday.

The reason is because

This structure is redundant. Equally common and doubly redundant is the structure *the reason why is because*.

(Poor)   The *reason why* I could not attend the party *is because* I had to work.

(Better)   I could not attend the party *because* I had to work.

Whether vs. As to whether

The circumlocution *as to whether* should be replaced by *whether*.

(Poor)   The United Nations has not decided *as to whether* to authorize a trade embargo.

(Better)   The United Nations has not decided *whether* to authorize a trade embargo.

Whether vs. If

Whether introduces a choice; *if* introduces a condition. A common mistake is to use *if* to present a choice.

(Faulty)   He inquired *if* we had decided to keep the gift.

(Correct)   He inquired *whether* we had decided to keep the gift.

Warm-Up Drill VI
Answers and solutions begin on page 282.

1. Regarding legalization of drugs, I am not concerned so much by its potential impact on middle class America <u>but instead</u> by its potential impact on the inner city.

   (A) but instead
   (B) so much as
   (C) rather
   (D) but rather
   (E) as

2. Listening <u>at</u> the couple recite <u>their</u> kidnapping ordeal
          A   B

   the <u>bank of reporters</u> could barely restrain
            B

   <u>themselves</u> from interrupting. No error
      D   E

3. Unless you maintain at least a 2.0 GPA, <u>you will not graduate medical school.</u>

   (A) you will not graduate medical school.
   (B) you will not be graduated from medical school.
   (C) you will not be graduating medical school.
   (D) you will not graduate from medical school.
   (E) you will graduate medical school.

4. <u>The studio's retrospective art exhibit refers back to</u> a simpler time in American history.

   (A) The studio's retrospective art exhibit refers back to
   (B) The studio's retrospective art exhibit harkens back to
   (C) The studio's retrospective art exhibit refers to
   (D) The studio's retrospective art exhibit refers from
   (E) The studio's retrospective art exhibit looks back to

5. <u>Due to the chemical spill, the commute into the city will be delayed by as much as 2 hours.</u>

   (A) Due to the chemical spill, the commute into the city will be delayed by as much as 2 hours.
   (B) The reason that the commute into the city will be delayed by as much as 2 hours is because of the chemical spill.
   (C) Due to the chemical spill, the commute into the city had been delayed by as much as 2 hours.
   (D) Because of the chemical spill, the commute into the city will be delayed by as much as 2 hours.
   (E) The chemical spill will be delaying the commute into the city by as much as 2 hours.

The following passage is a first draft of an essay. Some parts of the passage need to be rewritten.

(1) A best-selling book offers "Seven Ways to Become a Better Person." (2) A radio ad promises you will feel great in 30 days or less just by taking some pills. (3) "If you buy our exercise equipment," a TV ad guarantees, "you'll have the body you've always wanted." (4) In today's society, we are continually bombarded with the latest techniques of how to better ourselves, a focus which some feel is unhealthy. (5) Additionally, a focus on self-improvement is very important in helping people grow in character.

(6) Self-improvement helps build character. (7) Building character involves taking a person's strengths and building on them. (8) Such strengths as unselfishness can be developed into a lifelong habit of generosity, a positive spirit into an unfailing compassion for others. (9) Everyone has strength in character and the ability to build on these strengths through self-improvement.

(10) Weaknesses are not flaws, but rather negative traits that, through self-improvement, can be developed into more positive traits. (11) For example, impatience can be turned into determination to accomplish goals. (12) Strong will turns into perseverance. (13) If a person can just find a way to capitalize on a weakness, it can be turned into a strength. (14) Self-improvement is the best way to do this.

6. What is the best word or phrase to use in place of the word *additionally* in sentence 5 (reproduced below)?

   Additionally, a focus on self-improvement is very important in helping people grow in character.

   (A) Moreover
   (B) On the contrary
   (C) Along those lines
   (D) Consequently
   (E) Accordingly

7. Which of the following sentences works best to insert before sentence 10 to link it to sentence 9?

   (A) In addition to strengths, everyone also has weaknesses.
   (B) Character is what develops through much self-improvement.
   (C) Self-improvement also helps improve character flaws.
   (D) The next step to building character is to take a look at a person's negative traits.
   (E) Everyone also has the ability to recognize their weaknesses.

8. What is the best way to deal with sentence 12 (reproduced below)?

   Strong will turns into perseverance.

   (A) Leave it as it is.
   (B) Add "is" before "turns" and change "turns" to "turned".
   (C) Add "shall" before "turns" and change "turns" to "turn".
   (D) Change "turns into" to "becomes".
   (E) Add "can be" before "turns" and change "turns" to "turned".

9. Which of the following best defines the word *capitalize* as it is used in sentence 13 (reproduced below)?

   If a person can just find a way to capitalize on a weakness, it can be turned into a strength.

   (A) expose
   (B) use to one's advantage
   (C) obscure from one's view
   (D) modify
   (E) transpose

10. Which of the following could logically follow this passage?

    (A) A discussion about what defines character.
    (B) A book review on a book titled, "Seven Ways to Become a Better Person."
    (C) Steps to get rid of weaknesses.
    (D) A guide to improving character through strengths and weaknesses.
    (E) A list of self-improvement books and TV shows.

11. What is the main idea of this passage?

    (A) That one's weaknesses can become one's strengths.
    (B) Society's role in self-improvement.
    (C) The validity of helping oneself improve one's character.
    (D) Steps to improving one's character.
    (E) How to turn one's flaws into strengths.

Points to Remember

1.   A pronoun should be plural when it refers to two nouns joined by *and*.

2.   A pronoun should be singular when it refers to two nouns joined by *or* or *nor*.

3.   A pronoun should refer to one and only one noun or compound noun.

4.   A pronoun must agree with its antecedent in both number and person.

5.   The subject and verb must agree both in number and person.

6.   Intervening phrases and clauses have no effect on subject-verb agreement.

7.   When the subject and verb are reversed, they still must agree in both number and person.

8.   As a general rule, a modifier should be placed as close as possible to what it modifies.

9.   When a phrase begins a sentence, make sure that it modifies the subject of the sentence.

10.   For a sentence to be parallel, similar elements must be expressed in similar form.

11.   When two adjectives modify the same noun, they should have similar forms.

12.   When a series of clauses is listed, the verbs must be in the same form.

13.   When the first half of a sentence has a certain structure, the second half should preserve that structure.

14.   An adverb modifies a verb, an adjective, or another adverb.

15.   A verb has four principal parts:

    I.   Present Tense

       a.   Used to express present tense.

       b.   Used to express general truths.

       c.   Used with *will* or *shall* to express future time.

    II.   Past Tense

       a.   Used to express past tense.

    III.   Past Participle

       a.   Used to form the *present perfect tense*, which indicates that an action was started in the past and its effects are continuing in the present. It is formed using *have* or *has* and the past participle of the verb.

       b.   Used to form the *past perfect tense*, which indicates that an action was completed before another past action. It is formed using *had* and the past participle of the verb.

       c.   Used to form the *future perfect tense*, which indicates that an action will be completed before another future action. It is formed using *will have* or *shall have* and the past participle of the verb.

    IV.   Present Participle (*-ing* form of the verb)

       a.   Used to form the *present progressive tense*, which indicates that an action is ongoing. It is formed using *is*, *am*, or *are* and the present participle of the verb.

       b.   Used to form the *past progressive tense*, which indicates that an action was in progress in the past. It is formed using *was* or *were* and the present participle of the verb.

       c.   Used to form the *future progressive tense*, which indicates that an action will be in progress in the future. It is formed using *will be* or *shall be* and the present participle of the verb.

16.   Unless you want to de-emphasize the doer of an action, you should favor the active voice.

17.   Attack strategy for identifying misplaced modifiers:

   I.   Find the subject and the verb.

   II.   Isolate the subject and the verb by deleting intervening phrases.

   III.   Follow the rule of proximity: Modifiers should describe the closest units.

   IV.   Check the punctuation. Any punctuation should create coherence and not confusion.

Solutions to Warm-Up Drill I

1.   Choice (A) is incorrect because *his* appears to refer to *the President*, but the subject of the subordinate clause is *the President's Administration*, not *the President*.

    Choice (B) changes the structure of the sentence, but retains the same flawed reference.

    In choice (C), *it* can refer to either *the President's Administration* or *the budget reduction package*. Thus, the reference is ambiguous.

    Choice (D) adds another pronoun, *its*, but still retains the same flawed reference.
    Choice (E) corrects the flawed reference by removing all pronouns. The answer is (E).

2.   Both the *Secretary of Defense* and the pronoun *I* are objects of the verb *asked*. Hence, they must be in the objective case. The correct form is the *Secretary of Defense* and *me*. The answer is (A).

3.   Choice (A) is incorrect because the plural pronoun *their* cannot have the singular noun *a manufacturer* as its antecedent.

    Although choice (B) corrects the given false reference, it introduces another one. *Their* can now refer to either *customers* or *government*, neither of which would make sense in this context.

    Choice (C) also corrects the false reference, but it introduces a redundancy: *immediately* means "without delay."

    Choice (D) corrects the false reference, but its structure is very awkward. The direct object of a verb should be as close to the verb as possible. In this case, the verb *notify* is separated from its direct object *customers* by the clause "*that the government is contemplating a forced recall of any of the manufacturer's products that.*"

    Choice (E) is correct because the singular pronoun *its* has the singular noun *a manufacturer* as its antecedent. The answer is (E).

4.   The sentence is correct as written. The answer is (E). In (A), the phrase *nearly all* does not violate any rules of grammar. (B) uses the correct possessive pronoun *his*. (C) uses the correct plural verb *are*. (D) uses the correct object pronoun *him*. This problem is hard because of the long, complex clause introduced by *that*. This entire clause is the object of the verb *agree*.

5.   Choice (A) is incorrect. Since *United States* is denoting the collective country, it is singular and therefore cannot be correctly referred to by the plural pronoun *they*.

    Choice (B) is not technically incorrect, but it lacks precision since it does not state who enacted the Marshall Plan. Further, it uses a passive construction: "*was enacted.*"

    Choice (C) states who enacted the Marshall Plan, but it retains the passive construction "*was enacted.*"

    Choice (E) is second-best. The phrase "*in order*" is unnecessary.

    Choice (D) corrects the false reference by replacing *they* with *the United States*. Further, it uses the active verb *enacted* instead of the passive verb *was enacted*. The answer is (D).

6.   The sentence is not incorrect as written. Hence, the answer is choice (A).

    Choice (B) creates a run-on sentence by replacing the semicolon with a comma. Without a connecting word—*and, or, but*, etc.—two independent clauses must be joined by a semicolon or written as two separate sentences. Also, deleting "*as desirable*" changes the meaning of the sentence.

    Choice (C) uses a very awkward construction: *are desirable of it*.

    Choice (D) contains an error in tense. The sentence progresses from the past to the present, so the verb in the second clause should be *accept*, not *accepted*.

Choice (E) writes the two clauses as separate sentences, which is allowable, but it also changes the tense of the second clause to the future: *will accept.*

7.   Choice (A) is incorrect since the relative pronoun *that* is redundant: the pronoun *one*, which refers to the newly discovered fault, is sufficient.

Although choice (C) reads more smoothly, it still contains the double pronouns.

Choice (D) is incorrect. Generally, relative pronouns such as *that* refer to whole ideas in previous clauses or sentences. Since the second sentence is about the fault and not its discovery, the pronoun *that* is appropriate.

Choice (E) is very tempting. It actually reads better than choice (A), but it contains a subtle flaw. *One* is the direct object of the verb *believes* and therefore cannot be the subject of the verb *acts*. Since *they* clearly is not the subject, the verb *acts* is without a subject.

Choice (B) has both the correct pronoun and the correct verb form. The answer is (B).

Solutions to Warm-Up Drill II

1.   Choice (A) is incorrect because the plural verb *have* does not agree with its singular subject *the rising cost.*

Both (B) and (C) are incorrect because they turn the sentence into a fragment.

Choice (E) is incorrect because *rising cost* is still singular.

Choice (D) is the correct answer since now the plural verb *have* agrees with its plural subject *the rising costs.*

2.   Although *plans* comes after the verb *is*, *plans* is the subject and therefore its verb should be the plural *are*. The answer is (B). The sentence has inverted the natural order: *Plans to offer . . . are* at the foundation . . . .

3.   Choice (A) is incorrect. Recall that intervening phrases have no effect on subject-verb agreement. In this sentence, the subject *ownership* is singular, but the verb *are* is plural. Dropping the intervening phrase clearly shows that the sentence is ungrammatical:

In a co-publication, agreement ownership are equally shared by the parties.

Choice (B) is incorrect. Neither adding *each of* nor interchanging *shared* and *equally* addresses the issue of subject-verb agreement.

Choice (D) contains a faulty pronoun reference. The antecedent of the plural pronoun *their* would be the singular noun *material.*

Choice (E) is incorrect since it still contains the plural verb *are*. The answer is choice (C).

4.   The singular concept *being adept* is the subject of the sentence and therefore requires the singular verb *is*. The answer is (B).

5.   Choice (A) has two flaws. First, the subject of the sentence *the rise* is singular, and therefore the verb *indicate* should not be plural. Second, the comma indicates that the sentence is made up of two independent clauses, but the relative pronoun *that* immediately following *therefore* forms a subordinate clause.

Choice (C) corrects the number of the verb, but retains the subordinating relative pronoun *that.*

Choice (D) corrects the number of the verb and eliminates the subordinating relative pronoun *that.* However, the verb *being* is less descriptive than the verb *becoming*: As negative attitudes toward foreigners increase, the country becomes correspondingly less tolerant. *Being* does not capture this notion of change.

Choice (E) corrects the verb's number, and by dropping the comma, makes the subordination allowable. However, it introduces the preposition *of* which does not have an object: less tolerant of what?

Choice (B) both corrects the verb's number and removes the subordinating relative pronoun *that*. The answer is (B).

6. Choice (A) is incorrect since the singular subject *the harvest* requires a singular verb, not the plural verb *were*.

Choice (B) is illogical since it states that the harvest began to decrease in 1990 and then it states that it was the third straight year of decrease.

In choice (C) the plural verb *were* still does not agree with its singular subject *the harvest*.

Choice (E) contains the same flaw as choice (B).

Choice (D) has the singular verb *was* agreeing with its singular subject *the harvest*. Further, it places the phrase *in 1990* more naturally. The answer is (D).

7. The sentence is grammatical as written. The answer is (A).

When *each*, *every*, or *many a* precedes two or more subjects linked by *and*, they separate the subjects and the verb is singular. Hence, in choice (B) the plural verb *have* is incorrect.

Choice (C) is incorrect since the singular verb *has* does not agree with the plural subject *all*.

When *each* follows a plural subject it does not separate the subjects and the verb remains plural. Hence, in choice (D) the singular verb *has* is incorrect.

Choice (E) also changes the meaning of the original sentence, which states that the protagonist <u>do</u> have powerful, dynamic personalities.

8. The answer is (D).
Choice (A) is incorrect since the compound subject *developing the ability to work with others and developing leadership skills* requires a plural verb, not the singular verb *is*.
Choice (B) uses the correct plural verb *are*, but deleting the word *developing* makes the meaning of the sentence less clear.
Choice (C) uses a the natural order of subject then verb, but it is incorrect since the compound subject *developing the ability to work with others and developing leadership skills* requires a plural verb, not the singular verb *is*.
Choice (D) has the plural verb *are* agreeing with its compound subject *developing the ability to work with others and developing leadership skills*. The answer is (D).
Choice (E) is incorrect since the compound subject *the development of the ability to work with others and the development leadership skills* requires a plural verb, not the singular verb *has*.

9. The answer is (B).
Choice (A) is incorrect since the plural subject *a number* requires a plural verb, not the singular verb *is*.
Choice (B) is the answer because it correctly uses the plural verb *are* with the plural subject *a number*.
Choice (C) is incorrect since the plural subject *a number* requires a plural verb, not the singular verb *was*. Further, the shift in verb tense from *was* to *have not been* is awkward.
Choice (D) is incorrect because the shift in verb tense from *were* to *have not been* is awkward.
Choice (E) is incorrect because it is awkward and changes the meaning of the sentence.

10. The term *a majority* is singular. Hence, its verb should be the singular *believes*. The answer is (C).

Solutions to Warm-Up Drill III

1. Choice (A) is incorrect since it implies that *the other causes of crime* are doing the focusing.

    Choice (B) has the same flaw.

    Choice (C) is incorrect. The phrase *by focusing on poverty* must modify the subject of the sentence, but *there* cannot be the subject since the construction *there are* is used to introduce a subject.

    Choice (D) implies that *crimes* are focusing on poverty.

    Choice (E) puts the subject of the sentence *sociologists* immediately next to its modifying phrase *by focusing on poverty*. The answer is (E).

2. Choice (A) is incorrect because the phrase *using the Hubble telescope* does not have a noun to modify.

    Choice (B) is incorrect because the phrase *using the Hubble telescope* still does not have a noun to modify.

    Choice (C) offers a noun, *astronomers*, but it is too far from the phrase *using the Hubble telescope*.

    In choice (E), the phrase *with the aid of the Hubble telescope* does not have a noun to modify.

    Choice (D) offers a noun, *astronomers*, and places it immediately after the modifying phrase *using the Hubble telescope*. The answer is (D).

3. Choice (A) is incorrect. As worded, the sentence implies that the cold should be well-insulated.

    Choice (B) is awkward; besides, it still implies that the cold should be well-insulated.

    Choice (D) does not indicate what should be insulated.

    Choice (E), like choices (A) and (B), implies that the cold should be well-insulated.

    Choice (C) is the answer since it correctly implies that the stranded motorists should be well-insulated with protective clothing.

4. Choice (A) has two flaws. First, the introductory phrase is too long. Second, the subject Ansel Adams should immediately follow the introductory phrase since it was Ansel Adams—not the year 1945—who was traveling and shooting the Southwest.

    Choice (B) is incorrect because the phrase *"traveling across... Southwest"* is too far from its subject Ansel Adams. As written, the sentence seems to imply that the photographic career was traveling across and shooting the Southwest.

    Choice (C) is inconsistent in verb tense. Further, it implies that Adams began his photographic career after he traveled across the Southwest.

    Choice (D) is awkward.

    The best answer is choice (E).

5. Choice (A) is incorrect because it implies that the Harmony virus should be inoculated when it's the computer system that needs to be protected.
    Choice (B) is the answer since it correctly implies that the computer system should be inoculated, not the virus.
    Choice (C) sounds better, but it is not clear what the pronoun "it" is referring to, the virus or the computer. Hence, it is not clear whether it's the virus or the computer that needs to be inoculated.
    Choice (D) is awkward, and it implies that the Harmony virus should be inoculated when it's the computer system that needs to be protected.
    Choice (E) is awkward, and it implies that the Harmony virus should be inoculated when it's the computer system that needs to be protected.

6.   Choice (A) is incorrect because it implies that *we* are the head of the division instead of the actual head of the division *you*.

Although Choice (B) makes clear who is the head of the division (*you* not *we*), the structure "Seeing as you . . ." is too lose and informal.

Choice (C) makes the same mistake as the original sentence: It implies that *we* are the head of the division instead of the actual head of the division *you*.

Choice (D) is incorrect because it merely adds unnecessary words "are inclined to" which does not correct the flaw in the original sentence: It still implies that *we* are the head of the division instead of the actual head of the division *you*.

Choice (E) is the answer because the clause "that as head of the division" correctly modifies the head of the division *you*.

7.   Choice (A) is incorrect because the phrase "during childhood" modifies "parent" illogically implying that the parent died during childhood.

Choice (B) is incorrect because the phrase "when a child" modifies "parent" illogically implying that the parent died during childhood.

Choice (C) is incorrect because the phrase "occurring when a child" modifies "parent" illogically implying that the parent died during childhood.

Choice (D) is the answer. Now, the phrase "during childhood" correctly modifies "people."

Choice (E) is very awkward. The long clause "That people who . . . as adults" is the subject of the sentence. Although perhaps not ungrammatical, Choice (E) is very hard to read.

8.   Choice (A) is incorrect because the phrase "Based on the yarns of storytellers" modifies "linguistic archeologists" illogically implying that the archeologists are based on the yarns of storytellers.

Choice (B) is incorrect because the phrase "Basing on the yarns of storytellers" modifies "linguistic archeologists" illogically implying that the archeologists are based on the yarns of storytellers. Further, the phrase "Basing on the yarns of storytellers" is very awkward.

Choice (C) is the answer. The clause "Using the yarns of storytellers" correctly modifies "linguistic archeologists," showing how they are using the yarns. The clause can also be placed after the subject it modifies: Linguistic archeologists using the yarns of storytellers . . . . Notice that the same transposition in the original sentence will make the illogical modification of the subject, linguistic archeologists, even more pronounced: Linguistic archeologists based on the yarns of storytellers . . . . Here, "based on the yarns of storytellers" modifies "Linguistic archeologists" illogically implying that the archeologists are based on the yarns of storytellers.

Choice (D) is incorrect because the phrase "coming to the realization" is wordy. Further, the phrase "Based on the yarns of storytellers" modifies "linguistic archeologists" illogically implying that the archeologists are based on the yarns of storytellers.

Choice (E) is incorrect because it is awkward and vague: what is "it" referring to?

Solutions to Warm-Up Drill IV

1.   Choice (A) is incorrect since *eating properly* (verb-adverb) is not parallel to *sensible exercise* (adjective-noun).

   Choice (B) offers two parallel nouns, *exercise* and *diet*. However, a general truth should be expressed in the present tense, not in the past tense.

   Choice (C) is not parallel since it pairs the noun *exercise* with the gerund (a verb acting as a noun) *dieting*.

   Choice (E) makes the same mistake as choice (A).

   Choice (D) offers two parallel nouns—*exercise* and *diet*—and two parallel verbs—*tells* and *results*. The answer is (D).

2.   The startup company found it <u>much easier</u> to underbid on a job
                              A

   <u>than completing</u> the job on time, <u>which caused</u> financial problems
        B   C
   when their clients <u>withheld payment</u>. No error
                            D   E

To be balanced with the infinitive *to underbid*, the expression *than completing* should also be an infinitive: *to complete*. The answer is (B).

3.   Choice (A) is incorrect. Although the first two phrases, *war brewing in Europe* and *the industrial revolution well-established*, have different structures, the thoughts are parallel. However, the third phrase, *and a nascent communication age*, is not parallel to the first two.

   Choice (B) does not make the third phrase parallel to the first two.

   Choice (C) changes the meaning of the sentence: the new formulation states that war already existed in Europe while the original sentence states that war was only developing.

   Choice (E) is not parallel since the first two phrases in the series are noun phrases, but *saw the birth of the communication age* is a verb phrase. When a word introduces a series, each element of the series must agree with the introductory word. You can test the correctness of a phrase in a series by dropping the other phrases and checking whether the remaining phrase agrees with the introductory word. In this series, each phrase must be the object of the preposition *with*:

>   This century began *with* <u>war brewing in Europe</u>

>   This century began *with* <u>the industrial revolution well-established</u>

>   This century began *with* <u>saw the birth of the communication age</u>

In this form, it is clear the verb *saw* cannot be the object of the preposition *with*.

   Choice (D) offers three phrases in parallel form. The answer is (D).

4.   Choice (A) is incorrect since the verb *repairing* is not parallel to the verb *junk*.

   In choice (B), the construction *have it junked* is awkward. Further, it changes the original construction from active to passive.

   Choice (C) offers a parallel construction (*repairing/junking*), but it is awkward.

   Choice (D) also offers a parallel construction (*repair/junk*), but the construction *try and* is not idiomatic.

   Choice (E) offers a parallel construction (*repair/junk*), and the correct idiom—*try to*. The answer is (E).

5.   Choice (A) is incorrect since the verb *written* is not parallel to the construction *which was … printed*.

Choice (B) is the correct answer since the sentence is concise and the verb *written* is parallel to the verb *printed*.

Choice (C) does offer a parallel structure (*which was written/which was printed*); however, choice (B) is more concise.

Choice (D) rambles. The introduction *Written by … 1988* is too long.

Choice (E) also offers a parallel structure (*which was written/[which was] printed*); however, choice (B) again is more concise. Note that *which was* need not be repeated for the sentence to be parallel.

6.   Choice A is incorrect. We cannot leave the sentence as it is because the elements of the sentence need to be parallel in structure.

Choice B is incorrect. The subject of the sentence is *Getaway Lodge*. The correct pronoun to substitute for the lodge is "its," not "their."

Choice C is incorrect because it makes an unnecessary change. "Hospitality" functions better than "hospitable living," so we want to leave this alone.

Choice D is incorrect for the same reason as Choice C. "Comfort" is much more effective here than "comfortable living," so let's leave it alone.

Choice E is the correct answer. As it is, "living in luxury" is not parallel to "hospitality" and "comfort." We need to change it to "luxurious living."

7.   Choice A is incorrect. The passage thus far has focused on the guests rather than the subject of the room. So, even though the gift baskets are in the room as are the magnificent views, we want to hear a sentence that focuses on the guest.

Choice B is incorrect for the same reason as Choice A.

Choice D is incorrect because it implies that guests were simply "shown" their gift baskets. The passage more clearly implies that the gift baskets are *given* to the guests.

Choice E is not correct. It is a poorly constructed sentence, and it does not provide an effective transition from the subject of gift baskets to mountain views.

Choice C is correct. Just as guests were *treated* to gift baskets, the mountain views serve as a treat as well. It works well to tie the sentences together in topic. Additionally, the guests are the focus in this sentence just as in sentence 3.

8.   Choice A is incorrect. "Enjoyable" does not properly define *myriad*. In addition, the end of the sentence says, *including…* This listing of activities implies that it is just a partial list of the many available.

Choice C is incorrect. Generally, a passage that is trying to convince its readers they can be entertained would not want to limit their description to include just "some" activities.

Choice D is incorrect for much the same reason as Choice C although it goes to an even greater extreme in saying that there are only a few activity options. Moreover, the definition "few" is the opposite of the actual definition of *myriad*.

Choice E is incorrect. Again, a passage about the wonders of a tourist attraction cannot attract tourists if all of their activities are difficult.

Choice B is correct because it accurately defines *myriad*.

9.   Choice A is incorrect. All element of the sentence need to be parallel. They are not parallel, so we cannot leave it as it is.

Choice B is incorrect. Not only does the solution not address the problem of parallel structure in the sentence, but it takes away some of the interest of the sentence by replacing the word "enjoy" with "take."

Choice D is incorrect. It changes the wording of a part of the sentence that is not parallel, but the rewrite does not change the structure of the sentence.

Choice E is incorrect because the solution does not correct the problem of balancing the parallelism of the sentence. Moreover, changing the order of the sentence takes away much of the interest of the sentence.

Choice C is the correct answer. In this sentence, we needed to make *stroll through the garden* and *sitting by the fireplace* parallel. We could have corrected this by addressing *stroll* or *sitting*. This answer-choice offers a solution by changing *stroll* to *strolling*.

10.   Choice A is incorrect. In the passage, we discover that the restaurant is adjacent to a waterfall. If the waterfall is part of the pool, we know that the restaurant must also be adjacent to the pool. Now we just have to define *adjacent*. Choice A does not accurately define *adjacent*.

Choice B does not accurately define *adjacent*.

Choices C and E are not correct for the same reason as Choices A and B.

Choice D is the correct answer because *adjacent* means "next to."

11.   Choice B is not correct because the focus of the passage is not on just the restaurant but on the lodge as a whole. A restaurant review would include mostly information on the restaurant and would exclude the additional details given in the passage.

Choice C is incorrect for the same reason as Choice B. The main focus of the passage is not on the recreational activities available to guests. An article in an outdoor recreation magazine would focus more on the details of these activities and less on the additional information offered in the passage.

Choice D is incorrect because a postcard from a guest would be much more informal and personal than the passage as it is written.

Choice E is incorrect because flyers generally include much less formal, less detailed information.

Choice A is the correct answer. A travel brochure hopes to convince tourists to visit certain sites. This passage focuses on the beauty and enjoyment a guest can indulge in at the lodge. It is a perfect passage for a travel brochure.

Solutions to Warm-Up Drill V

1.   Choice (A) is incorrect because it uses the past perfect *had chosen*, which describes an event that has been completed before another event. But the sentence implies that teachers have and are continuing to return to the private sector. Hence, the present perfect tense should be used.

   Choice (B) is incorrect because it uses the present progressive tense *having chosen*, which describes an ongoing event. Although this is the case, it does not capture the fact that the event began in the past.

   Choice (C) is incorrect because it uses the simple past *chose*, which describes a past event. But again, the sentence implies that the teachers are continuing to opt for the private sector.

   Choice (D) is the correct answer because it uses the present perfect *have chosen* to describe an event that occurred in the past and is continuing into the present.

   Choice (E) is incorrect because it leaves the thought in the sentence uncompleted.

2.   The sentence is grammatical as written. The answer is (A). The sentence correctly uses the present perfect tense to make three statements that about Steve Emerson:

> 1)   He has been a reporter
> 2)   He has been a news writer
> 3)   He has been a producer

3.   Choice (A) is incorrect because the simple past *were* does not express the fact that the homes had been built before the fire destroyed them.

   Choice (B) merely rearranges the wording while retaining the simple past *were*.

   Choice (C) is the correct answer because it uses the past perfect *had been* to indicate that the homes were completely built before they were destroyed by the fires.

   Choice (D) is incorrect because it uses the present perfect *have been*, which implies that the homes were destroyed before being built.

   Choice (E) is incorrect. Although dropping the phrase *that were* makes the sentence more concise, the past progressive *were being* implies that the homes were destroyed while being built.

4.   The sentence is grammatical as written. The present perfect verb *have ... signed* correctly indicates that they have not signed a peace treaty and are not on the verge of signing one. Further, the present perfect verb *have been* correctly indicates that in the past both countries have been reluctant to develop closer relations and are still reluctant. The answer is (A).

   In choice (B), the simple past *did* does not capture the fact that they did not sign a peace treaty immediately after the war and still have not signed one.

   Choice (C) is very awkward, and the present progressive *being* does not capture the fact that the countries have been reluctant to thaw relations since after the war up through the present.

   In choice (D), the present tense *are* leaves open the possibility that in the past the countries may have desired closer relations but now no longer do.

   In choice (E), the present progressive tense *are ... signing*, as in choice (D), leaves open the possibility that in the past the countries may have desired closer relations but now no longer do.

5.   The sentence implies that Jim's hard work ended before another event in the past—loss of the Cuba market. Hence, Jim's hard work should be expressed in past perfect tense: Although Jim *had* worked hard . . . . The answer is (A).

6.   Choice (A) is incorrect because the simple past *obtained* does not express the fact that the information was gotten before another past action—the sabotage.

Choice (B) is incorrect because *used* is not parallel to *of resorting*.

Choice (C) is correct because the phrase *of using* is parallel to the phrase *of resorting*. Further, the past perfect *had obtained* correctly expresses that a past action—the spying—was completed before another past action—the sabotage.

Choice (D) is incorrect because *using* is not parallel to *of resorting* and the past perfect is not used.

Choice (E) is incorrect because *to have used* is not parallel to *of resorting* and the past perfect is not used.

Solutions to Warm-Up Drill VI

1.   The correct structure for this type of sentence is *not so much by* _____ *as by* _____. The answer is (E).

2.   The correct idiom is *listening to*, not *listening at*. The answer is (A).

3.   Choice (A) is incorrect. In this context, *graduate* requires the word *from*: "you will not *graduate from* medical school."

The use of the passive voice in choices (B) and (C) weakens the sentence.

Choice (D) is the answer since it uses the correct idiom *graduate from*.

Choice (E) changes the meaning of the sentence and does not correct the faulty idiom.

4.   Choice (A) is incorrect. *Retrospective* means looking back on the past. Hence, in the phrase *refers back*, the word *back* is redundant.

Choice (B) is incorrect because *harkens back* is also redundant.

Choice (C) is correct. Dropping the word *back* eliminates the redundancy.

Choice (D) is incorrect because the preposition *from* is non-idiomatic.

Choice (E) is incorrect because *looks back* is also redundant.

5.   Choice (A) is incorrect. Although many educated writers and speakers begin sentences with *due to*, it is almost always incorrect.

Choice (B) is incorrect: it is both redundant and awkward.

Choice (C) is incorrect. The past perfect *had been delayed* implies the delay no longer exists. Hence, the meaning of the sentence has been changed.

Choice (D) is correct. In general, *due to* should not be used as a substitute for *because of, owing to, by reason of*, etc.

Choice (E) is incorrect. The future progressive *will be delaying* is unnecessary and ponderous. Had choice (E) used the simple future *will delay*, it would have been better that choice (D) because then it would be more direct and active.

6.   Choice A is incorrect. Sentence 4 ends with "a focus that some feel is unhealthy." Sentence 5 says that "a focus on self-improvement is very important in helping people grow in character." The content of sentence 5 is in contrast to the content of sentence 4, so we need a transition that shows contrast. "Moreover" is a transitional word used to show agreement.

Choice C is incorrect for the same reason as Choice A.

Choice D is incorrect because *consequently* is a transitional word that precedes a result in a cause-effect relationship.

Choice E is incorrect for the same reason as Choice A and C.

Choice B is correct because *on the contrary* shows the contrast between what is said in sentence 4 and what is said in sentence 5.

7.   Choice B is incorrect. The choice refers to character which is mentioned in sentence 9. However, the linking sentence must serve as a topic sentence for the paragraph. The paragraph's topic is weaknesses, so this sentence does not serve well as a topic sentence.

Choice C is incorrect. It mentions self-improvement which ties it to sentence 9; however it brings up flaws. Flaws are not the main topic of the proceeding paragraph.

Choice D is not correct because, while there is a reference to character as there is in sentence 9, the sentence veers away from the purpose of the passage. The passage has not to this point offered any steps to building character. It has suggested components to building good character, but it has not given specific instructions. Moreover, the suggestion to examine negative traits is not in line with the overall positive tone of the passage.

Choice E is incorrect. It ties in well with sentence 9 with the words that "everyone also has the ability…" However, the topic of the next paragraph does not revolve around *the ability to recognize* weaknesses, but rather it assumes a person is already aware of his weaknesses.

Choice A is the correct answer. The new sentence refers back to sentence 9 by using the transitional phrase "in addition." Moreover, in sentence 9, it is established that everyone has strengths. The new transitional sentence not only refers to this, but also introduces the topic of the new paragraph: weaknesses.

8.   Choice A is incorrect. We need to make sure that sentence 12 is parallel in structure to sentence 11 which says that "impatience can be turned…" As it is now, sentence 12 is not parallel to sentence 11, so we cannot leave it as it is.

Choice B is incorrect because the resulting new sentence would be *Strong will is turned into perseverance.* Again, this is not parallel to sentence 11, so this is not our solution.

Choice C is not correct either. Let's look at the proposed new construction of the sentence: *Strong will shall turn into perseverance.* This again is not parallel to sentence 11.

Choice D is incorrect. *Strong will becomes perseverance* is not parallel in structure.

Choice E is the correct answer. Let's check the new sentence: *Strong will can be turned into perseverance.* This is parallel to *…impatience can be turned into determination…*

9.   Choice A is incorrect. If you look at the word in context, you can see that exposing a weakness does not necessarily turn it into a strength.

Choice C is incorrect. If you are blind to a weakness, you most likely will not be able to turn it into a strength.

Choice D is incorrect. While you may be able to turn a weakness into a strength by modifying, or changing it, *modify* does not accurately define *capitalize*.

Choice E is not correct. To transpose means to switch places with. It clearly does not function well in this sentence.

Choice B is your answer. If you use your weaknesses to your advantage, they can become strengths. Moreover, to *capitalize* is defined as "using to one's advantage."

10. Choice A is not correct. The purpose of the passage is to show how self-improvement can help you strengthen your character. The passage is written with the assumption that you are already cognizant of the definition of character.

Choice B is incorrect. A book review would not have a clearly defined place after this passage, especially since this particular book was simply mentioned in a series. If the book title was given more prominence in the passage, it might serve to reason that a review could follow, but that is not the case.

Choice C is incorrect. Weaknesses were not the main point of the passage, so a focus on weaknesses would not be logical.

Choice E is incorrect. The purpose of the passage is not to persuade you to delve into self-help books and other media.

Choice D is the correct answer. It is clearly stated that self-improvement is needed to build character. In addition, the author briefly explains that strengths and weaknesses can work to build character. This passage serves well as an introduction to a self-help guide to building character through strengths and weaknesses, so this would logically follow.

11. Choice A is incorrect because the passage discusses more than just weaknesses.

Choice B is not correct because the passage includes little discussion on society's role in self-improvement except to briefly mention that some in society feel such a focus is unhealthy.

Choice D is incorrect. The passage does not offer specific steps to improving character. It offers some insight but no actual instructions.

Choice E is incorrect for the same reason as Choice A.

Choice C is the correct answer. The first paragraph of the passage works to begin persuading the reader that it is a valid decision to help yourself improve your character. The passage goes on to support the validity by examining how self-introspection can aid in building character.

The Essay

How to Get a "Top-Half" Score

Writing essays for standardized exams can raise anxieties in people who are poised when answering other kinds of test questions. Perhaps this is because critical and creative skills are being tested and evaluated in a more subjective manner than they are within the objective multiple-choice format. Performance anxiety can lead to a host of problems, from having a difficult time understanding exactly what is being asked to having debilitating uncertainties about how to begin an answer.

The best way to reduce such anxieties, and therefore increase your chance of obtaining a top-half score, is through *rehearsal*, which encompasses four activities that need to take place before taking the SAT:

1) understanding the writing tasks
2) knowing what the evaluators expect to find in top-half essays
3) anticipating an organizational scheme for the essay
4) practicing by writing an essay in response to at least one practice question in this book

Having completed these four steps, you will be in an excellent position to approach the Essay with confidence and competency.

As we have mentioned, the mechanics of your essay will not play as large a role in your score as usage and topic development; however, using proper mechanics will go a long way in making a positive impression on your scorer. Following is a good review of some of the basic rules that govern punctuation. Keeping these rules fresh in your mind will help you write a clear, coherent essay.

Punctuation

Although you can receive a high score on the essay even if your it contains some grammatical errors, the official guidelines indicate that grammar is given some weight in the scoring. Knowing the rules that govern punctuation will reduce your error rate dramatically. Moreover, knowledge of grammar and punctuation will be invaluable in your college writing, where mistakes can be costly. In this section, we will discuss the most commonly used punctuation marks: commas, semicolons, colons, dashes, apostrophes, and quotation marks. We will also discuss the use of punctuation to correct run-on sentences and sentence fragments.

Commas

Use a comma:
➢ (Rule 1) in series and lists.
➢ (Rule 2) after an introductory phrase.
➢ (Rule 3) to set off nonrestrictive clauses.
➢ (Rule 4) to set off interjections and transitional phrases.
➢ (Rule 5) with a coordinating conjunction to separate two independent clauses.

➢ **Rule 1** – Use a comma to separate each item in a series or list of three or more words, phrases, or clauses. Also, use commas with descriptive words where two or more adjectives modify the same noun.

> **Example:**
>
> I made the beds, swept the floors, vacuumed the carpet, and scrubbed the bathtub to get ready for our guests. Then I went shopping to stock the refrigerator with drinks, vegetables, and fruit. I hope I'm ready to welcome them into our home and to have a great visit.

In this example, the four underlined clauses in the opening series are separated by commas, and the three underlined words in the list are separated by commas. Notice that the concluding sentence does not contain any commas. In this sentence, the clause *to welcome them into our home* and the clause *to have a great visit* are part of a series of only two elements and are simply separated by the conjunction *and*. Note that a series of words or phrases is marked by a relationship between the elements, whereas a list is simply a notation of two or more words that may or may not be related. For instance, in the example above, the first sentence contains a series of clauses. Each clause is related because they are all actions that the person took. The second sentence contains a list of items such as you would take to the grocery store.

Commas are also used with descriptive words. Use a comma in a series of two or more adjectives that modify the same noun.

> **Example:**
>
> The long, narrow, winding road lead to a beautiful, serene lake.

In this example, *long*, *narrow*, and *winding* are adjectives that all modify the noun *road*. Thus, they are separated by commas. Likewise, *beautiful* and *serene* modify *lake* and are separated by commas. Note that no comma follows the last adjective in the series; also be careful in determining the function of the last word of the series. You must make sure that all the adjectives equally modify the noun. For example,

Before you watch TV, I want you to clean the <u>dirty, grimy kitchen sink</u>.

In this example, *kitchen sink* acts as a single noun because without *kitchen*, *sink* is not adequately identified. Therefore, *grimy* is the last adjective before the noun in the series and no comma should be placed after it.

✓ Check your work

Look through your work for any series of words, phrases or clauses. If there are two or more of these elements, place a comma after all but the last one.

Example (without punctuation):

He thought taking a road trip would <u>help him feel rejuvenated</u> <u>allow him to work through his feelings</u> and <u>provide some much needed solitude in which to get his studying done</u>.

Here the three clauses are underlined. Once you have identified these clauses, you should place commas after each clause except the last one:

He thought taking a road trip would help him feel rejuvenated, allow him to work through his feelings, and provide some much needed solitude in which to get his studying done.

This example contains a list of adjectives:

She looked longingly through the window at the lovely elegant pearl necklace.

First, identify the list of words: *lovely*, *elegant*, and *pearl* modify *necklace*. Now confirm that each adjective equally modifies the noun *necklace*. To do this, insert the word *and* in between each adjective:

She looked longingly through the window at the lovely *and* elegant *and* pearl necklace.

Clearly, the sentence does not make sense with the *and* between *elegant* and *pearl*. Therefore, you should place the commas appropriately:

She looked longingly through the window at the lovely, elegant pearl necklace.

➤ **Rule 2** – Use a comma to set off an introductory word, phrase, or clause from the independent clause that follows. Introductory elements that require a comma are prepositional phrases, subordinating clauses, transitional words or phrases, and verbal phrases.

A *prepositional phrase* begins with a preposition and includes any modifiers or objects. Prepositional phrases usually signal a relationship, particularly a relationship of time or location.

Examples:

<u>In the movie *Titanic*</u>, Leonardo di Caprio's character Jack dies.

<u>Since the accident last year</u>, she has been afraid to drive on the highway.

Both introductory clauses in these examples begin with prepositions. The clauses indicate a relationship of location (<u>*In* the movie...</u>) and time (<u>*Since* the accident...</u>) between the introductory phrases and the independent clauses that follow. Therefore, they must be set off by commas.

A *subordinating clause* begins with a *subordinator*, which is a word that indicates a relationship—usually a relationship of time or location—between the clause it begins and the independent clause that follows. This relationship makes a subordinating clause similar to a prepositional phrase. However, unlike a prepositional phrase, a subordinating clause can also be referred to as a dependent clause because it has both a subject and a verb. It is a dependent clause, not an independent clause, because it cannot stand alone as a sentence.

Example:

When I was in high school, we didn't have all the modern technological conveniences that provide such great research tools today.

Here the phrase *When I was in high school* begins with the subordinator *When*, which signals a time relationship between the subordinating clause and the independent clause that follows. Although this clause has a subject (*I*) and a verb (*was*), it cannot stand alone as a sentence and requires the independent clause to complete the thought. Here is another example:

Before I had a chance to answer, he snatched the paper out of my hands and threw it in the fire.

Here again an introductory subordinating clause requires the independent clause to complete the sentence. In both examples, a comma is required to set off the subordinating clause from the independent clause.

Transitional words and phrases add coherence to your writing. They help connect one sentence to the next. A comprehensive list of transitional words and phrases appears later in this chapter, but here are some of the most commonly used transitions: *finally, furthermore, moreover,* and *next* indicate sequence; *again, likewise,* and *similarly* indicate comparison; *although, but, however, by contrast,* and *on the other hand* indicate contrast; *for example, in fact,* and *specifically* indicate examples; *accordingly, as a result, consequently,* and *therefore* indicate cause and effect.

Example:

Dear Students,

Due to illness, I will not be in class today. Your substitute, Miss Green will be teaching your literature class. Specifically, you will be reading Act 1 of *Romeo and Juliet*. There has been a lot of extraneous talking in class lately. Consequently, you must read the play on your own; you will not be allowed to read with your reading buddy. Although I would like to continue with reading buddies, that will not be possible until you show me that you can follow the rules. Today would be a good day to follow those rules! Furthermore, since Miss Green is with you today, I hope that you will take this opportunity to be on your very best behavior. I do not want to get any negative reports.

Have a great day,
Mrs. Smith

In this example, transitional words and phrases are used to make the text flow more smoothly. A comma is required after each transitional word or phrase.

Verbal phrases contain verb elements but function as nouns, adjectives or adverbs rather than verbs. There are two kinds of verbal phrases that can act as introductory phrases and therefore must be set off by commas: participial phrases and infinitive phrases.

Participial phrases are made up of a present participle (the *–ing* form of a verb) or a past participle (the *–ed* form of a verb) as well as any modifiers or objects. Participial phrases act as adjectives because they describe, or modify, the subject in the independent clause.

Examples:

Standing alone by the door, Ricky watched the rest of the boys dance with their dates.

Angered by the kids' cutting remarks, Naomi stormed out of the room and then burst into tears.

The first example contains a participial phrase that contains the present participle *Standing*. The introductory phrase *Standing alone by the door* describes Ricky. In the second example, the past participle *Angered* makes up the participial phrase, and the full introductory phrase describes Naomi.

Infinitive phrases are made up of an infinitive as well as any modifiers or objects.

> **Examples:**
>
> To win a gold medal, you must work very hard.
>
> To earn a high score on the SAT, you must study this guide thoroughly.

To win is the infinitive in the first sentence, and *To earn* is the infinitive in the second sentence. Both infinitives serve as part of the introductory phrase, which must be set off by commas.

✔ Check your work

To find introductory phrases that should be set off with a comma, first look for the subject and verb of the independent clause. Then note any words that precede the subject and verb. Other than articles and adjectives, any words or phrases that come before the subject and verb make up the introductory phrase. You can then confirm this by identifying the introductory phrase.

> **Example:**
>
> The strongest qualities of a teacher are patience and understanding.

Here *qualities* is the subject (don't be thrown off by *of a teacher*) and *are* is the verb. *The* and *strongest* precede the subject in this sentence. *The* is an article and *strongest* is an adjective, so there is no need for a comma here. Now look at this example:

> Knowing that the strongest qualities of a teacher are patience and understanding, Beth highlighted these qualities on her résumé.

Here *Beth* is the subject and *highlighted* is the verb. The phrase *Knowing that the strongest qualities of a teacher are patience and understanding* is a participial phrase and therefore should be set off with a comma.

Many writers do not place a comma after a short introductory clause.

> **Example:**
>
> This morning I stopped at the bagel shop for coffee.

Here a comma is acceptable after *This morning*; however, it is not necessary. You can use your ear to make a decision in cases like these. Often commas may be placed where there would be a pause if the sentence is spoken. When in doubt, however, use a comma.

> ➤ **Rule 3** – Use a comma to set off nonrestrictive clauses and phrases, clauses and phrases that are not essential in identifying the words they modify. Adjectival clauses and appositives (words that rename a noun) are most often nonrestrictive.

Adjectival clauses are phrases that begin with *who, whom, whose, which, that, when, where,* or *why.* In many cases, an adjectival clause is nonrestrictive such as in the following example:

> The heart, which pumps the body's blood, is necessary to sustain life.

In this sentence, the adjectival clause *which pumps the body's blood* is set off by commas because it is not essential to the sentence. The sentence would have the same meaning without the clause. By contrast, the adjectival clause in the next sentence is restrictive because it is necessary to convey the meaning of the sentence:

> The police who are investigating the murders in Maryland are using geographic profiling to aid in their search for the perpetrator.

The adjectival clause *who are investigating the murders in Maryland* is necessary to provide the reader with full details about the police and the murderer for whom they are searching. Without this phrase, the reader would not know that the police are in Maryland and that they are investigating a murderer.

Appositives act as nouns or noun substitutes by modifying the noun that precedes the appositive. Just as with adjectival clauses, nonrestrictive appositives are set off by commas, whereas restrictive appositives are not.

Nonrestrictive examples:

My high school English teacher, <u>Mr. Roper</u>, taught me how to use commas properly.
She drove her new car, <u>a Honda Accord</u>, to the senior center to pick up her grandmother.
The book club will be meeting this Wednesday to discuss the latest book, <u>Grisham's Rainmaker</u>.

In these examples, the underlined phrases are nonrestrictive appositives, which rename the noun preceding them. These phrases add interesting description to the sentences, but they are not necessary to make the sentences complete and understandable. On the other hand, some appositives are essential to capture the full meaning of the sentence. Such restrictive appositives should not be set off with commas as shown in the following examples:

My son <u>Michael</u> is two years old, and my other son <u>Jacob</u> is five months old.
Meet me at 6:00 at the new restaurant <u>*Vinny's Vittles*</u> that just opened on Main Street.
My friend <u>Tammy</u> met me at the beach yesterday.

The appositives in these examples are necessary in specifying the subjects. This information is necessary so the reader has a clear understanding of the subject involved in the text.

✓ Check your work

Review each sentence in your writing. Identify the adjectival phrases and appositives and the nouns they modify. For each adjectival phrase or appositive, ask yourself if the phrase provides important identifying information about the noun, or if it just provides "extra" information. If you are still unsure, read the sentence without the adjectival phrase or appositive. Does the sentence still have its full meaning? If so, set the phrase off with commas. If not, omit the commas.

➤   **Rule 4** – Use a comma to set off interjections and transitional phrases.

An *interjection* is usually one or two words that interrupt the flow of a sentence and give extra information about the content of the sentence. Although an interjection provides added detail that enhances the reader's knowledge, generally the information provided by an interjection could be omitted with little or no effect on the meaning of the sentence. Therefore, most interjections should be set off by commas as in the following examples:

I could probably take, <u>say</u>, five people in my van for the carpool.
She was, <u>oddly enough</u>, the only one who entered the contest.
I was thinking, <u>by the way</u>, that we could stop by the store on the way home.

A *transitional phrase* directs the flow of an essay. Often, transitional phrases are helpful in leading to a conclusion and therefore should not be set off with commas such as in these two examples:

His strategy was to impress the boss and <u>thus</u> receive the promotion.
I was tired and <u>therefore</u> did not want to go to the party.

In these examples, the transitional words serve to fully define the meaning of the sentences. There are instances, however, where a transitional word could be omitted without affecting the meaning of the sentence.

Examples:

I was not confident, <u>however</u>, that he knew the answer.
The message when on to say, <u>furthermore</u>, that he would not be coming home for dinner.

The transitional words in these examples enhance the text by emphasizing the direction in which the meaning of the sentence is moving. However, the meaning of the sentences would be the same without the transitional words.

✔ <u>Check your work</u>

To double-check your use of commas with interjections, identify any word or words that interrupt your sentence and have little or no effect to the meaning of the sentence. Set these words off with commas. Next, check for transitional words, keeping in mind the list of common transitional phrases we discussed earlier. Once you have identified the transitional words, ask yourself if the words are necessary to convey the meaning of the sentence. If they are necessary, don't set them off with commas; if they aren't, use commas.

➢ **Rule 5** – Use a comma and a coordinating conjunction to join two independent clauses.

An *independent clause* is a group of words that contain both a subject and a verb and can stand alone as a sentence.

Example:

I drove my car to work. (*I* is the subject, and *drove* is the verb.)

A *coordinating conjunction* is a word that serves as a link between a word or group of words. These conjunctions are easy to remember by using the acronym BOYFANS:

> **B**ut
> **O**r
> **Y**et
> **F**or
> **A**nd
> **N**or
> **S**o

Short, choppy sentences can make your writing tedious to read. To provide some interest and variety to your writing, you will want to join some of the sentences in your essays. To do so, you will need to use a comma and a coordinating conjunction. Let's look at some examples:

Too choppy:

I took a long lunch. I went back to work. I got behind on my work. I had to stay late.

Better:

I took a long lunch, <u>and</u> I went back to work. I got behind on my work, <u>so</u> I had to stay late.

Too choppy:

My guests were arriving in an hour. I wanted to throw a memorable New Year's Eve party. I made the punch and hors d'oeuvres ahead of time. I found that I still had a lot to get done to get ready. I decided to put the ice in the punch. Then I discovered that my icemaker was broken. I didn't have time to go to the store. I wasn't prepared to serve anything else either. I hurried to the pantry to view my options. All I had were some tea bags. I decided to throw a New Year's Eve tea party instead.

Better:

My guests were arriving in an hour, <u>and</u> I wanted to throw a memorable New Year's Eve party. I made the punch and hors d'oeuvres ahead of time, <u>yet</u> I found that I still had a lot to get done to get ready. I decided to put the ice in the punch, <u>but</u> then I discovered that my icemaker was broken. I didn't have time to go to the store, <u>nor</u> was I prepared to serve anything else. I hurried to the pantry to view my options. All I had were some tea bags, <u>so</u> I decided to throw a New Year's Eve tea party instead.

In both examples, combining sentences with commas and conjunctions make them more interesting and easier to read. We will learn more ways to create interest in your writing when we discuss writing style later on. For now, let's make sure we can apply Rule 5 correctly.

✔ <u>Check your work</u>

To properly combine two independent clauses with a comma and a conjunction, you must check to make sure that the clauses joined by the comma and conjunction are indeed independent clauses. To do this, first find all the conjunctions. Then look at the clauses on either side of each conjunction. Does each clause have a subject and a verb? Can each clause stand alone as sentences? If so, the conjunction is properly placed and a comma should precede the conjunction.

Incorrect:

We went to the mall last night, and bought some new dresses for work.

Correct:

We went to the mall last night and bought some new dresses for work.

Correct:

We went to the mall last night, and Terri bought some new dresses for work.

In the first example, *and* is the conjunction. *We went to the mall last night* is an independent clause (*we* is the subject, *went* is the verb). However, *bought some new dresses for work* is not an independent clause because there is no subject. Therefore, the sentence can be corrected by simply omitting the comma as seen in the second example. Or, if there is a possible subject for the sentence, it can be added and the comma can stay as seen in the third example. Here is another example where the same guidelines apply:

Incorrect:

He committed the crime, but didn't think the judge's ruling was fair.

Correct:

He committed the crime but didn't think the judge's ruling was fair.

Correct:

He committed the crime, but he didn't think the judge's ruling was fair.

Using a semicolon is another way to correctly join two independent clauses, and we will discuss it next.

Semicolons

Use a semicolon
➤   (Rule 1) to join two independent clauses.
➤   (Rule 2) to join more than two independent clauses.
➤   (Rule 3) to separate items in a series.

➤   **Rule 1** – Use a semicolon to join two independent clauses that are closely related. You may also use a
       semicolon in coordination with a transitional word and in place of a comma and a conjunction.

Sometimes a period seems like too strong of a mark to use to separate two closely related sentences, but a comma does not emphasize both sentences adequately. In cases like this, you can use a semicolon to join two independent clauses. Using a semicolon to join two independent clauses gives you as the writer a subtle way of showing a relationship between two clauses. You might use a semicolon, for example, if your second sentence restates your first. Or perhaps your second sentence more clearly defines your first sentence by giving an example or by presenting a contrast. Finally, you may want to link two clauses with a semicolon if they have a cause and effect relationship.

Example:

Loyalty is the foundation upon which relationships are built; without loyalty, friendships
and marriages crumble.

In this example, the second sentence restates the first sentence. A semicolon is appropriate here and functions to convey the close relationship between the two sentences.

Example:

The puppy scooted blindly across the floor; his eyes hadn't opened yet leaving him totally dependent on his mother.

The second sentence in this example more clearly defines why the puppy is moving around blindly. The semicolon ties the explanation of the first clause to the description in the second clause. A semicolon is also functional in this last example:

Of course it's pouring down rain on the day of the picnic; it was sunny the day we were inside roller-skating!

The semicolon here emphasizes the irony that is portrayed in this sentence by connecting the two contrasting sentences.

Contrasting clauses may also be joined by using a semicolon along with a transitional word.

Example:

These days there is a cure for every ailment; however, the side effects of many medications are worse than the condition for which the medication is prescribed.

Here two independent clauses are joined with a semicolon and the transitional word *however*. The second clause shows that medicines don't always produce positive effects in contrast with the first clause, which indicates that almost every ailment can be cured. The transitional word *however* further defines this contrasting relationship. A transitional word may also serve to emphasize a cause-effect relationship such as in this example:

The drought has greatly affected many farmers; therefore, the price of produce is expected to rise.

You may choose to use semicolons to portray a close relationship between two clauses as seen in the examples above. In other cases, you may recognize that using a variety of punctuation marks adds interest to your writing. Based on this recognition, the choice to join two clauses with a semicolon and a transitional word may be a stylistic choice rather than a grammatical one. Likewise, adding variety to your writing may be the purpose when it comes to replacing a comma and conjunction with a semicolon.

Example:

The slippery rock presented the climbers with a challenge, <u>so</u> they watched their footing very closely.

Becomes:
The slippery rock presented the climbers with a challenge; they watched their footing very closely.

In the first example, the two independent clauses are joined with a comma and a conjunction, and in the second sentence, a semicolon replaces the comma and the conjunction. While both sentences are correct and function equally well, you may choose to use the semicolon this way to add variety. Sometimes, however, it is necessary to replace the comma with a semicolon in order to provide clarity. In these cases, you may or may not omit the conjunction. For example,

From such a great distance, the man could not make out the faces of the evil, crafty conspirators, but, if he moved any closer, he would be taking an unnecessary, careless risk of being seen.

Because this sentence contains so much punctuation, it is a bit tedious to read and can be confusing. To remedy this, a semicolon can be used to join the two clauses. In this case, the conjunction *but* is important in enhancing the cause and effect relationship in the sentence and therefore it should remain:

From such a great distance, the man could not make out the faces of the evil, crafty conspirators; but, if he moved any closer, he would be taking an unnecessary, careless risk of being seen.

The semicolon in the example above provides much needed clarity to the sentence by separating the two independent clauses.

✓ Check your work

To use a semicolon to join two independent clauses, analyze the two clauses carefully to make sure there is a close relationship between the two before placing the semicolon. Be careful not to misuse semicolons, especially when you use them with a transitional word or in place of a comma and conjunction. For example:

Incorrect:

I was forced; therefore, to take the detour around the construction site.

Correct:

I was forced, therefore, to take the detour around the construction site.

In this example, *therefore* is a transitional word and should be set off with commas. Furthermore, the clause *I was forced* is an independent clause and *to take the detour around the construction site* is not, so the clauses cannot be set apart by a semicolon.

Take the same caution when replacing a comma and conjunction with a semicolon. Remember that, to join two clauses with a comma and a conjunction, both clauses must be independent. That is, each clause must be able to stand alone as a separate sentence. For example,

Incorrect:

He completed the yard work, and then enjoyed a lemonade break with his mom.

Incorrect:

He completed the yard work; and then enjoyed a lemonade break with his mom.

Correct:

He completed the yard work and then enjoyed a lemonade break with his mom.

The subject in this sentence is *He* and the compound verb is *completed* and *enjoyed*. There is no subject in the second part of the sentence, so it is incorrect to use a comma and conjunction in the sentence. Likewise, a semicolon cannot be used.

➢   **Rule 2** – Use a semicolon to join more than two independent clauses.

In Rule 1, we discussed using a semicolon to join two independent clauses. Semicolons can also be used to join multiple independent clauses in more complex sentences:

Example:

After graduation, students have a lot to look forward to; hopes and dreams stretch before them like a promising road that leads to whatever destination their aspirations can achieve. Students will now enter a new phase of their lives where they can move on to college; they can gain independence through learning to live on their own; their sense of responsibility can begin to shine through as they encounter new experiences.

This example could be written as a few separate sentences; however, since the independent clauses are all closely related, it is acceptable to link them with semicolons. Joining multiple independent clauses is often a stylistic choice and an effective one because it makes an impact by more closely connecting the sentences. When not serving just a stylistic choice, joining more than two independent clauses with a semicolon adds clarity such as in the following example:

Confusing:

The Thompsons spent two exciting weeks on safari in Africa and returned with wild tales of their trip. They saw all the sights anyone who goes on safari dreams of: They saw zebras, rhinoceroses, and giraffes grazing on the savanna, they witnessed a lion chasing after an antelope, a herd of elephants stomped across the road in front of their truck, and some curious, chattering monkeys came up to their truck and took food out of their hands.

Better:

The Thompsons spent two exciting weeks on safari in Africa and returned with wild tales of their trip. They saw all the sights anyone who goes on safari dreams of: They saw zebras, rhinoceroses, and giraffes grazing on the savanna; they witnessed a lion chasing after an antelope; a herd of elephants stomped across the road in front of their truck; and some curious, chattering monkeys came up to their truck and took food out of their hands.

In the first example, the writer uses commas to separate the series of clauses. However, because the clauses themselves contain lists of words separated by commas, the sentence is confusing; the semicolons in the second example provide clarity by dividing the clauses.

✓ Check your work

To join multiple independent clauses with a semicolon, make sure the clauses you are joining are related. Also consider using a semicolon instead of a comma to join clauses. To do this, check for commas within the clauses. Too many commas cause confusion and can be eliminated by using semicolons instead. Be careful, however, not to use semicolons too often because overuse can make a writer sound pedantic. When used conservatively, semicolons can add a great deal of impact. To avoid overusing semicolons, reread your text and make sure your use of semicolons is sporadic; semicolons should never appear as often as commas or periods.

Too many semicolons:

My next interviewee came in and sat across from me; she tried to put on a confident face; she maintained eye contact throughout the interview; I could tell she was nervous, though; she played anxiously with her ring; she shifted positions every few seconds; her voice quivered a bit.

Better:

My next interviewee came in and sat across from me. She tried to put on a confident face by maintaining eye contact throughout the interview. I could tell she was nervous, though; she played anxiously with her ring, shifted positions every few seconds and her voice quivered a bit.

Semicolons are used in place of periods and almost all of the commas in the first example. In the rewrite of the example, all but one semicolon is replaced with a period. The remaining semicolon is placed after *I could tell she was nervous, though*. The clause that follows gives a description that further defines the assumption that the interviewee was nervous.

➤   **Rule 3** – Use a semicolon to separate items in a series when the items themselves contain commas.

Just as you should use semicolons to join independent clauses when the clauses contain commas, you should also use semicolons to separate words and phrases in a series when those words and phrases contain commas. For example,

> **Confusing:**
>
> I boarded a flight in Los Angeles, California, had a two-hour layover in Detroit, Michigan, and finally landed in London, England.

> **Better:**
>
> I boarded a flight in Los Angeles, California; had a two-hour layover in Detroit, Michigan; and finally landed in London, England.

This sentence contains a series of clauses, which must be separated. However, each clause contains the name of a city and a state, which also must be separated. Using only commas in this example causes confusion because it is difficult to tell which commas separate clauses and which ones separate the elements within each clause. Separating the clauses with semicolons clarifies the meaning. Here is another example:

> All students must bring a notebook, pen, and a copy of *To Kill a Mockingbird* to English class; a ruler, calculator, and graph paper to Math class; and a glass, a box of baking soda, and a bottle of vinegar to Science class.

Here again, too many commas creates confusion, so in order to simplify the sentence and make it more clear, the clauses in the series are separated by semicolons.

✔ Check your work

Check each of the independent clauses you have joined with commas. Do any of the independent clauses contain commas? If so, joining the independent clauses with a semicolon instead of a comma will probably make the sentence clearer.

> **Confusing:**
>
> My pottery class is on Mondays, Wednesdays, and Fridays, and I baby sit my nephew, niece, and neighbor's son on Tuesdays and Thursdays.

> **Better:**
>
> My pottery class is on Mondays, Wednesdays, and Fridays; and I baby sit my nephew, niece and neighbor's son on Tuesdays and Thursdays.

Again, be careful not to overuse semicolons. If, after you review your writing, you feel you have used semicolons too often, consider using other methods to join phrases. For example, you might use a period to divide clauses into separate sentences. Remember that semicolons can make a big impact but only when used conservatively and correctly.

Colons

Use a colon:
➤   (Rule 1) to introduce an explanation or example.
➤   (Rule 2) to introduce a series, list, or quotation.

➤   **Rule 1** – Use a colon to relate two independent clauses when introducing an explanation or example.

When a comma does not place adequate emphasis on the relationship between two independent clauses, you can use a semicolon. When a semicolon does not provide adequate emphasis, you can use a colon. A colon joins two independent clauses to emphasize the relationship between the two clauses and is often used to introduce an explanation or an example.

Example:

When I picture my dream house, it is set in beautiful scenery: the beach or mountains, for example, would provide an ideal setting for a home.

In this sentence, the colon serves to introduce two examples of a dream home. The colon in this example strengthens the relationship between the idea of a beach or mountain home and the subject of dream homes in the first clause. A colon can also introduce an explanation such as in the following example:

Dave and Stephanie's oral report lacked the usual enthusiasm: this could be because they were up all night working on the presentation.

The second clause in this example explains the first clause and therefore may be introduced with a colon.

✓ Check your work

Just as with semicolons, the choice to use colons can be a stylistic one. If you do choose to use a colon to introduce an explanation or example, make sure that both the preceding clause and the clause that follows are independent clauses.

Capitalize the clause that follows a colon if it is a formal statement or if the content that is introduced contains more than one sentence.

Example (formal statement):

Our club bylaws shall set forth the following: Rules for meetings, code of conduct, and membership procedures.

Example (more than one clause):

When thinking of a future career, there are many choices: Becoming a lawyer would be a good financial decision. On the other hand, teaching may provide more personal satisfaction.

➢   **Rule 2** – Use a colon after an independent clause to introduce a series, list, or quotation.

Use a colon to introduce a series or list such as in the following examples:

We need to get several things done before our trip: pay the bills, water the plants, and take the dog to the kennel.

Before we can take off, you must do the following: fasten your seat belt, turn off your cell phone, and return your tray table to its upright position.

The names of the people who made the volleyball team are as follows: Ruth, Mary Lynn, Amy, Sarah, Alicia, and Elizabeth.

Note that when the word *following* or *follows* is used to introduce a list or series you must use a colon. You should also use a colon to introduce a quotation.

Example:

As people seek to build relationships and, in so doing, break down the walls of racism, they should remember Martin Luther King, Jr.'s famous words: "I have a dream that [we] will one day live in a nation where [we] will not be judged by the color of [our] skin but by the content of [our] character."

✓ Check your work

Use a colon to introduce a series or list. Always use a colon if the clause that introduces the list or series contains the term *follows* or *following*.

Example:

The following improvements need to be made to your house before you try to sell it: new carpet should be installed, the outside trim should be painted, and the fixtures in the downstairs bathroom should be replaced.

Do not use a colon if the list or series is introduced by phrases such as *especially*, *such as*, *namely*, *for instance*, *for example*, or *that is* unless the series is made up of one or more independent clauses.

Incorrect (colon introducing a series of phrases):

Some of my life goals, for example: to ski in the Alps, bungee jump from Victoria Falls, and visit the Great Wall of China.

Correct (colon introducing a series of independent clauses):

I have set some goals that I wish to achieve before I get too old to do so. For example: I want to ski in the Alps, bungee jump from Victoria Falls, and visit the Great Wall of China.

Note that a comma would work in this sentence as well. The colon following *For example* places more emphasis on the text that follows.

Do not use a colon to introduce a series that is the object of the verb in the sentence. For example,

Incorrect:

After the maitre d' seated us, I ordered: French onion soup, a Caesar salad, and filet mignon.

Correct:

After the maitre d' seated us, I ordered French onion soup, a Caesar salad, and filet mignon.

You may use a colon to introduce a quotation and, in this instance, you must capitalize the first word of the quotation.

Example:

The principles of this country are founded on the *Declaration of Independence* and its famous words: "We hold these truths to be self-evident, that all men are created equal, that they are endowed by their Creator with certain unalienable Rights, that among these are Life, Liberty and the pursuit of Happiness."

Dashes

Use dashes
➤   (Rule 1) to interrupt a sentence.
➤   (Rule 2) to emphasize parenthetical or explanatory information.

➤   **Rule 1** – Use a dash to interrupt the normal word order of a sentence.

Example:

If you are interested in martial arts—and who wouldn't be interested in such a disciplined art?—there are many centers for instruction.

The dashes in this example allow you to break into the sentence in an informal way. Here is another example:

I was unable—unwilling, really—to head up the new committee at the office.

✓ Check your work

Although commas may be used to set off phrases that interrupt a sentence, dashes add emphasis to the clause that is set off. In addition, dashes set an informal tone in your writing. Because of their informality, dashes should be used sparingly, if ever, in graduate writing. When you do choose to use dashes, you may include question marks and exclamation points in the clauses that are set off by dashes (as in the first example above).

➢ **Rule 2** – Use dashes to set off parenthetical or explanatory information.

Example:

The editor of the *Banner Herald* often employs hyperbole—deliberate exaggeration or overstatement to show special emphasis or create humor—to express his political views.

Here dashes set apart the definition of *hyperbole*. Though not necessary to the meaning of the sentence, the definition adds useful information. Again, dashes are an informal way of setting off information; a comma would serve the same purpose here.

✓ Check your work

Review each sentence in your writing and identify any information that is parenthetical or that explains a topic in the sentence. You may set this information off with dashes. Remember, though, that dashes should seldom be used in formal writing. In formal writing, you should use commas to set off these elements from the rest of the sentence.

Apostrophes

Use an apostrophe
➢ (Rule 1) in contractions.
➢ (Rule 2) to show possession.

➢ **Rule 1** – Use an apostrophe in a contraction, a word that is a shortened combination of two words.

Contractions are used in informal writing and serve to shorten two words by leaving out some letters and joining the two words with an apostrophe. Following is a chart that lists some common contractions and the words that form them:

Words that combine to form a contraction	Contractions
it is	it's
I am	I'm
he will	he'll
they are	they're
you are	you're
we will	we'll
could not	couldn't
would not	wouldn't
cannot	can't
does not	doesn't
do not	don't
will not	won't
let us	let's
I would	I'd
they would	they'd
was not	wasn't
I will	I'll
should not	shouldn't
we had	we'd
they will	they'll

✓ <u>Check your work</u>

The use of contractions is quite simple: if you wish to shorten two words into one and it is appropriate to do so using an apostrophe, you simply replace the words with the correct contraction. There are, however, some common mistakes people make when using contractions. There are a few contractions that sound like possessive words, and these are often confused. For example, the contraction *they're* sounds like the possessive *their*, but the two words have very different meanings.

Example (they're):
I don't know where they think *they're* going, but *they're* going to end up at a dead end.

Example (their):
When I saw them heading toward the dead end, I assumed they did not know *their* way.

Example (they're and their):
They're going to run into a dead end because they don't know *their* way.

Remember that *they're* is short for *they are*. *Their* is the third person plural possessive. The next pair of words to watch out for is the contraction *you're* and the possessive *your*.

Example (you're):
You're not going to succeed in school if you don't study hard.

Example (your):
Your success in school is dependent upon hard work.

Example (you're and your):
You're not going to succeed in school if you don't try *your* best in all that you do.

You're is short for *you are*, and *your* is the second person singular possessive. The final pair of words that can be confusing are *it's* and *its*.

Example (it's):
It's seemingly impossible for a cat to travel that far to get home.

Example (its):
A cat will travel a long way to find *its* home and the family it loves.

Example (it's and its):
It's amazing the distance a cat will travel to find *its* way back home.

Be careful when you use *it's* or *its*; remember that *it's* is the contraction for *it is* and *its* is the third person singular possessive.

To check for proper use of a contraction, especially those that can be tricky, substitute the words that have been replaced by the contraction. If the full-length word makes sense, the contraction is correct. If not, you need to check your spelling. Once again, though, keep in mind that contractions are more appropriate for use in informal writing.

➤ **Rule 2** – Use an apostrophe to show possession.

To show the possessive form of singular nouns, add an apostrophe and an *–s*

Examples:
Teddy cleaned the *dog's* house before he and his family went on vacation.
The teacher used *Julia's* homework as an example because it was exceptional.
She didn't feel comfortable borrowing *Harris's* car.

To show the possessive form of plural nouns, add an –*s* and an apostrophe:

Examples:

Coach Hannigan distributed the *girls'* uniforms at soccer practice.

Some plural nouns, however, do not end in –*s*. In these instances, add an apostrophe and an –*s*.

Examples:

The *women's* meeting will be held in the gymnasium on Thursday night.
All of the *children's* bikes were parked in the driveway.
Competition between *men's* sports teams is fierce.

✓ Check your work
Check for the correct use of apostrophes with possessives by first identifying the nouns that show possession. Then identify whether the noun is singular or plural. If the noun is singular, add an apostrophe and an –*s*. If the noun is plural, add an –*s* and an apostrophe. Finally, take note of any irregular plural nouns that do not end in –*s*. Add an apostrophe and an –*s* to irregular nouns.

Quotation Marks

Use quotation marks to set off quotations and dialogue.

Example (quotation):

In his famous inaugural address, President John F. Kennedy implored, "My fellow Americans, ask not what your country can do for you: Ask what you can do for your country."

Example (dialog):

"Where are you going tonight?" asked Greg.
"Beth and I are going to the library to get some research done," Susan replied. "Then we're heading to the mall to do some shopping."

When using quotation marks
➢ (Rule 1) commas and periods go inside the quotation marks.
➢ (Rule 2) semicolons and colons go outside the quotation marks.
➢ (Rule 3) question marks and exclamation points go outside the quotation marks.

➢ **Rule 1** – Commas and periods should be placed inside quotation marks.

Example:

"I don't understand what you're trying to say," Glen said. "You need to speak up."

Don't use a comma and quotation marks for indirect quotes.

Example (direct quote):

He said, "I don't have time to take the car for an oil change today."

Example (indirect quote):

He said that he didn't have time to take the car for an oil change today.

✓ Check your work
Place commas and periods inside quotation marks. To determine if a quote is a direct or indirect quote, ask yourself if the quote comes directly from the speaker and if the quote contains the exact words of the speaker. If so, place quotation marks around the quote. If not, there should be no comma or quotation marks.

> ➢ **Rule 2** – Place semicolons and colons outside quotation marks.

   Example (semicolon):

   My mom always used to say, "A stitch in time saves nine"; I always remember that quote when I am tempted to procrastinate.

   Example (colon):

   Patrick Henry made a strong statement when he said, "Give me liberty or give me death": he felt that it would be better to die than to live in a country without freedom.

✓ Check your work

When you use quotation marks with a semicolon or colon, first determine whether you are using the semicolon or colon correctly. Then make sure you place the semicolon or colon outside the quotation marks.

> ➢ **Rule 3** – Place question marks and exclamation points outside quotation marks unless they are a part of the quotation.

   Examples (question mark):

   Did you hear Professor Johnston say, "You must read the first 500 pages for a quiz on Monday"?

   Stunned, she implored, "Why didn't you tell me you were leaving for good?"

In the first example, the quotation is a statement that does not require a question mark; however, the overall sentence that contains the quotation is a question. Therefore, the question mark goes outside the quotation marks. In the second example, though, the quotation is a question, so the question mark goes inside the quotation marks.

   Examples (exclamation point):

   I can't believe she finally said, "I love you"!

   The woman ran after the thief yelling, "Hey, come back with my purse!"

Overall, the first sentence is an exclamatory sentence, but the phrase *I love you* is not; therefore, the exclamation point goes outside the quotation marks. *Hey, come back with my purse* in the second sentence, however, is an exclamation, so the exclamation point goes inside the quotation marks.

✓ Check your work

Examine all quotations in your writing. If the quotation itself is a question or exclamation, place the appropriate punctuation mark inside the quotation marks. If, however, the overall sentence is a question or exclamation but the actual quote is not, the punctuation should be placed outside the quotation marks.

Sentence Fragments

A *sentence fragment* is a clause that is punctuated like an independent clause, but it lacks a grammatical element required to make it a complete sentence. As we discussed before, an independent clause must have a subject and a verb. Without both a subject and a verb, a clause is a sentence fragment because it cannot function alone.

   Example (independent clause):

   I ran down the road.

   Examples (sentence fragments):

   Ran down the road.

   Running down the road.

The independent clause above has both a subject (*I*) and a verb (*ran*). The first example of a sentence fragment, however, has only a verb (*ran*). The last example contains the participle *Running*, which needs a helping verb like *was* as well as a subject like *He*: He was running down the road.

To correct sentence fragments in your writing
➢   (Step 1) identify them.
➢   (Step 2) revise them.

➢   **Step 1** – Identify sentence fragments in your writing.

To find sentence fragments in your writing, first analyze each sentence. In your analysis, mark the subject and verb by underlining the subject once and the verb twice. Following are some examples:

> On our way to the store tomorrow, we need to stop at the bank.
> Sprinting toward the finish line, Dan took a deep breath and pressed on.
> Providing equal opportunity to all citizens is of utmost importance.

The first two examples begin with introductory phrases, which can be confusing so take care in identifying these types of clauses and isolating them from the independent clause. The third example contains a gerund, *providing*, which acts as a noun. Now let's analyze each sentence of a paragraph. First, we will underline each subject and each verb. Then we will flag each sentence that is a fragment with a star.

> Dan always has busy days at Meadowcreek High School. *In the morning, double-checks his homework while he's on the bus. *Upon entering the school. Dan gets his books from his locker. For the rest of the day Dan keeps busy. *Doing schoolwork and participating in class discussions. Usually Dan does not bring his own lunch, but his mom gives him money to buy school lunch. Dan's afternoon progresses in much the same way as his morning. *When he gets home. He does his homework. *Because he is so tired after doing homework. He goes to bed at 10:00.

Clearly, many of the sentences in this paragraph need to be revised. Before we can complete the revisions, though, we need to analyze what the problem is in each of the identified sentence fragments. Let's look at each sentence:

> Dan always has busy days at Meadowcreek High School. (This sentence is fine.)

> * In the morning, double-checks his homework while he's on the bus. (The introductory phrase here can make the sentence tricky because you may be tempted to identify *morning* as the subject. Although *double-checks* is the verb, the subject is missing.)

> *Upon entering the school. (This introductory phrase has been set off by itself.)

> Dan gets his books from his locker. (This sentence is fine.)

> For the rest of the day, Dan keeps busy. (This sentence is fine, but again there is an introductory phrase, which can be deceiving.)

> *. *Doing schoolwork and participating in class discussions. (This clause should act as the object of the sentence and therefore is missing both the subject and the verb.)

> Usually Dan does not bring his own lunch, but his mom gives him money to buy school lunch. (Two independent clauses are correctly joined here with a comma and a conjunction. In a sentence like this, identifying the subject and verb can be confusing. In the second clause, for example, it would be easy to mistake *his* as the subject when *his* is actually an adjective modifying the subject *mom*.)

Dan's afternoon progresses in much the same way as his morning. (This sentence is fine, but again, *Dan's* could be confused as the subject when *afternoon* is actually the subject.)

*When he gets home. (The subject here is *he*, and the verb is *gets*. However, the subordinator *when* makes the sentence a dependent clause and it therefore cannot stand alone as a sentence.)

He does his homework. (This sentence is fine.)

* Because he is so tired after doing homework. (The subject here is *he*, and the verb is *is*. However, the subordinator *because* makes the sentence a dependent clause and it therefore cannot stand alone as a sentence.)

He goes to bed at 10:00. (This sentence is fine.)

➢   **Step 2** – After you have identified the sentences that are fragments, you must revise them. There are two ways to revise sentence fragments:

- Combine sentences to make them complete.

Example:

(Fragments) Because I was at my soccer game. I didn't make it to dinner.

(Revised) Because I was at my soccer game, I didn't make it to dinner.

- Add the necessary elements to the fragment to make it complete.

Example:

(Fragments) From the beginning. Wanted to practice law in a small town.

(Revised) From the beginning, he wanted to practice law in a small town.

Now, let's revise our example from Step 1:

Dan always has busy days at Meadowcreek High School. In the morning, he double-checks his homework while he's on the bus. Upon entering the school, Dan gets his books from his locker. For the rest of the day, Dan keeps busy doing schoolwork and participating in class discussions. Usually Dan does not bring his own lunch, but his mom gives him money to buy school lunch. Dan's afternoon progresses in much the same way as his morning. *When he gets home, he does his homework. Because he is so tired after doing homework, he goes to bed at 10:00.

*In the morning, double-checks his homework while he's on the bus. (We corrected this sentence by adding the subject *he* after the introductory phrase.)

*Upon entering the school. (We corrected this sentence by replacing the period after *school* with a comma and thereby making it an introductory phrase and combining it with the next sentence.)

*Doing schoolwork and participating in class discussions. (We corrected this fragment by simply combining it with the complete clause that preceded it.)

*When he gets home. (We corrected this sentence by replacing the period after *home* with a comma and thereby making it an introductory phrase and combining it with the next sentence.)

*Because he is so tired after doing homework. (We corrected this sentence by replacing the period after *homework* with a comma and thereby making it an introductory phrase and combining it with the next sentence.)

Once you have made your revisions, make sure you reread your writing. Identify the subject and verb in each sentence once again to make sure your revisions corrected the fragments.

Run-On Sentences

A *run-on sentence* contains one or more independent clauses but does not have all the proper words and marks of punctuation that are required to join independent clauses.

Example:

David went on a field trip to an aquarium with his classmates and they saw a large variety of fish.

In this example, two independent clauses are joined with a coordinating conjunction, but there is no comma. This type of run-on sentence is called a *fused* sentence. A fused sentence can also lack both a comma and a conjunction such as in the following example:

The debate over alien existence will probably continue for years some are sure they have seen aliens.

This next sentence contains a comma but no coordinating conjunction:

Many people believe in the powers of a psychic, sometimes even detectives depend on psychics to help solve crimes.

Because this sentence contains a comma but no coordinating conjunction, it is called a *comma splice*.

To correct run-on sentences in your writing
➢ (Step 1) identify them.
➢ (Step 2) revise them.

➢ **Step 1** – Identify run-on sentences in your writing.

To find run-on sentences in your writing, first analyze each sentence. In your analysis, mark the subject and verb by underlining the subject once and the verb twice. Following are some examples:

Osteoporosis is very common among women but drinking milk and taking calcium supplements can help prevent it.

This example is a fused sentence because it contains two independent clauses linked by a coordinating conjunction but no comma.

History provides us with interesting stories, it also helps us in the future because we can learn from mistakes made in history.

This example is a comma splice because it contains two independent clauses linked by a comma but no coordinating conjunction. These examples contain only two independent clauses that are not combined correctly. Many writers also link multiple clauses incorrectly. If you are prone to this error, it is important that you take the time to go through each sentence and identify the subjects and verbs. From there, you can revise your sentences accurately.

➢ **Step 2** – Revise your run-on sentences by using one of five methods:

• Separate the clauses in to complete sentences.

Example:

(Run-on) Working together as a team is more productive than working individually, a team can get more accomplished than one person.

(Revised) Working together as a team is more productive than working individually. A team can get more accomplished than one person.

- Link the clauses with a semicolon.

Example:

(Run-on) Writing is great therapy letting off steam through the written word is a good way to work through frustration.

(Revised) Writing is great therapy; letting off steam through the written word is a good way to work through frustration.

- Link the clauses with a comma and a coordinating conjunction.

Example:

(Run-on) I went to Florida last week to go to Disney World with a friend but it rained the whole time that I was there.

(Revised) I went to Florida last week to go to Disney World with a friend, but it rained the whole time that I was there.

- Rewrite the clauses to form just one independent clause.

Example:

(Run-on) This summer has been a very hot one, it has been humid also.

(Revised) This summer has been a very hot and humid one.

- Rewrite the clauses to form one independent clause with an introductory dependent clause.

Example:

(Run-on) We re-painted our house, the old paint was peeling and fading.

(Revised) Because the old paint was peeling and fading, we re-painted our house.

Make sure you review your work after making revisions to ensure that all run-on sentences have indeed been corrected. In addition, try to use all five methods of revision in your writing; don't correct each run-on with the same method. Using different forms of revision will result in varying sentence patterns, which will enhance your writing style. We will discuss writing style shortly as well as strengthening the structure of your essay. First, however, let's make sure you know how to apply the rules of punctuation we just covered.

Warm-Up Drill I

Directions: Read each sentence and then make necessary punctuation and spelling corrections. Pay special attention to sentence fragments and run-on sentences and re-write them so that they are grammatically correct. Answers and solutions begin on the next page.

1.   Dana is a foster mother. Takes care of newborns. When babies are put up for adoption a social worker places the baby in Dana's house where the baby stays until the adoption is completed usually the baby stays no longer than six weeks unless there is no adoptee lined up yet.

2.   Buying a new car is a big decision their are many factors to consider dependability for example is a key factor in choosing the car to suit your needs.

3.   The energetic boisterous boy climbed the jungle gym hung from the monkey bars jumped down and then ran to the merry-go-round.

4.   What do you think he meant when he said, "Your going to have to figure that one out on you're own"

5.   A cool sparkling stream meandered through the peaceful forest and some deer stopped to take a drink and glanced up for a moment to look at me they disappeared into the trees.

6.   Some people claim even boast that they've never read an entire book. This is there loss because reading leads to knowledge knowledge leads to power power enables people to influence those around them.

7.   That Halloween night can't have been spookier if it had come out of a story a horror story. Patches of fog enveloped the trees in some places and the trees cast dark eerie shadows in others. Because of the full moon.

8.   The mens' group did charity work this weekend they completed the following projects they helped rebuild a church that had been damaged in a tornado they completed some of the landscaping on the church grounds and they began repairs to the pastors home nearby the church.

9.   Many people suffer from "diet fatigue" they try diet after diet only to meet failure with each one. What they should be focusing on instead is nutritional eating and fitness nutritional eating consists of eating well-balanced servings of meats vegetables fruits and grains drinking lots of water and indulging in junk food sparingly. Proper fitness can come in the form of aerobic exercise walking sports or weight training making just a few adjustments in daily eating and exercise habits can make all the difference in a persons physical and emotional well-being.

10.   The beautiful grand stain-glassed windows added a majestic feeling to the old cathedral.

Solutions to Warm-Up Drill I

1.   Dana is a foster <u>mother who takes</u> care of newborns. When babies are put up for <u>adoption,</u> a social worker places the baby in Dana's house where the baby stays until the adoption is <u>completed. Usually</u> the baby stays no longer than six weeks unless there is no adoptee lined up yet.

    Takes care of newborns is a fragment; it was corrected by joining it to the first clause *Dana is a foster mother. When babies are put up for adoption* is an introductory dependent clause and should be followed by a comma. The last clause is a run-on sentence, and it was corrected by placing a period after *completed*.

2.   Buying a new car is a big <u>decision. There</u> are many factors to <u>consider: dependability, for example,</u> is a key factor in choosing the car to suit your needs.

    The first clause is a run-on sentence and should be divided into two sentences; thus, a period was placed between *decision* and *There*. Moreover, *their* was replaced with the correct word *there*. Once you have divided the sentence into two separate clauses, notice that *dependability* is an example. Therefore, a colon should follow *consider*. In addition, *for example* should be set off by commas because it is an interjection.

3.   The <u>energetic, boisterous</u> boy climbed the jungle <u>gym, hung</u> from the monkey <u>bars, jumped</u> <u>down, and</u> then ran to the merry-go-round.

    Energetic and *boisterous* are adjectives that modify *boy*. Because there are two adjectives modifying the same noun, they should be separated by a comma. In addition, a set of four phrases follows—*climbed the jungle gym, hung from the monkey bars, jumped down,* and *then ran to the merry-go-round*—and should also be separated by commas.

4.   What do you think he meant when he said, "<u>You're</u> going to have to figure that one out on <u>your</u> <u>own</u>"?

    Your and *you're* are misspelled. The contraction *you're* should be the first word in the quotation, and the possessive *your* should precede *own*. The question mark in the sentence should be placed outside the quotation marks because the quotation itself is not a question; however, the complete sentence is a question.

5.   A <u>cool, sparkling</u> stream meandered through the peaceful <u>forest. Some</u> deer stopped to take a drink. <u>Before they disappeared into the trees, they glanced up for a moment to look at me.</u>

    First, a comma should separate the series of adjectives *cool* and *sparkling*. Second, this clause is a run-on sentence and was corrected by dividing it into two independent clauses by placing a period between *forest* and *Some*. Finally, a third clause was created by converting the sentence fragment into an introductory clause.

6.   Some people <u>claim, even boast, that</u> <u>they have</u> never read an entire book. This is <u>their</u> loss because reading leads to <u>knowledge; knowledge</u> leads to <u>power; power</u> enables people to influence those around them.

    Even boast is an interjection and should be set apart by commas. You should use commas instead of dashes because the topic of the sentences is formal. The contraction *they've* should be changed to *they have* to maintain the formality. The next sentence should contain the possessive *their*. Finally, the last clause is a run-on sentence. Because the clauses are closely related, they should be separated by semicolons.

7.   That Halloween night <u>couldn't</u> have been spookier if it had come out of a <u>story—a</u> horror story. Patches of fog enveloped the trees in some <u>places. Because of the full moon, the trees cast dark, eerie shadows in others.</u>

Can't is the wrong contraction here. You can test it by plugging in the full-length words—*That Halloween night cannot have been spookier. A horror story* at the end of the sentence provides further explanation of *story* and thus can be set apart with a dash. A dash was used instead of a comma because of the informal topic. A comma should separate the adjectives *dark* and *eerie*. Finally, *Because of the full moon* is a sentence fragment and was converted into an introductory phrase for the last independent clause.

8.   The <u>men's</u> group did charity work this <u>weekend. They</u> completed the following <u>projects: they</u> helped rebuild a church that had been damaged in a <u>tornado, they</u> completed some of the landscaping on the church <u>grounds, and</u> they began repairs to the <u>pastor's</u> home nearby the church.

Because the word *men* is a plural noun that does not end in *–s*, its possessive should be spelled with an apostrophe and then an *–s*. Also, the first clause is a run-on, so there should be a period between *weekend* and *They*. Next, there should be a colon after *projects* in order to introduce the series of clauses that follow. The word *following* is your clue to use a colon in this instance. Each clause in the series should be separated by a comma. Finally, *pastor's* is possessive and should contain an apostrophe.

9.   Many people suffer from "diet <u>fatigue"; </u> they try diet after diet only to meet failure with each one. What they should be focusing on instead is nutritional eating and <u>fitness. Nutritional</u> eating consists of eating well-balanced servings of <u>meats, vegetables, fruits, and</u> <u>grains; drinking</u> lots of <u>water; and</u> indulging in junk food sparingly. Proper fitness can come in the form of aerobic <u>exercise, walking,</u> <u>sports, or</u> weight <u>training. Making</u> just a few adjustments in daily eating and exercise habits can make all the difference in a <u>person's</u> physical and emotional well-being.

The first clause is a run-on and should be divided into two separate sentences; since they're closely related, you may use a semicolon. The semicolon should be placed outside the quotation marks around *diet fatigue*. A period should follow *fitness* in order to separate the next run-on sentence into separate sentences. In the third sentence, you are presented with a series of clauses; one of the clauses contains a list of words that require commas to separate them. Because so many commas can be confusing, the series of clauses should be separated by semicolons. The series of words in the sentence that follows should be separated by commas as well. A final sentence should be set off starting at *Making*. Finally, the possessive of *person's* must contain an apostrophe.

10.   The <u>beautiful, grand</u> stain-glassed windows added a majestic feeling to the old cathedral.

A comma should separate *beautiful* and *grand*. Notice that there is no comma after *grand*. You can double-check this by placing *and* between each adjective: *The beautiful <u>and</u> grand <u>and</u> stain-glassed window*. The *and* between *grand* and *stain-glassed* does not make sense; therefore, there should be no comma preceding *stain-glassed*.

General Tips on Writing Your Essay

Structure

Now that you know when to use a semicolon instead of a comma, how do you get started writing your essay? Learning the rules that govern written English is one thing; putting your knowledge to use is another. We will discuss some specific tips that pertain to the type of essay you will be required to write, but for now, we will look at some general techniques to make your essay the best it can be. We begin by looking at the proper structure for your introduction and for your conclusion.

Introduction
Your introduction should serve two structural purposes: It should restate your topic so that the reader need not review the given question, and it should offer a clear thesis so the reader knows what your purpose is. Simply defined, a thesis states the main idea of your essay.

Your introduction should, in effect, restate the given topic. In other words, your reader should be able to ascertain the issue or argument without reading the given topic. Suppose the SAT gives you this topic and assignment:

> Prompt:
> *The new writing section was recently added to the SAT with the idea that such a section would encourage more teaching of writing. In turn, students would be more mature writers by graduation time.*

> Assignment:
> Do you think that the added writing section will indeed improve writing skills? Plan and write an essay which depicts your point of view on this subject. Provide support on your position by pulling examples from your own experiences.

Your initial reaction to this assignment may be to begin your essay with a direct response such as *I agree with this assumption...* However, this introductory sentence does not provide adequate information because it does not specify *which* assumption and therefore it would leave the reader confused. Following is the beginning of an introduction that does give adequate information to the reader:

> Does the new SAT really help improve the writing skills of high school graduates? The impetus behind the development of the new writing section is to prompt more in-depth teaching of writing. Added writing curriculum should turn out more mature writers. This is a valid assumption because...

Not only should you restate the topic, but you should also do so in a way that will spark interest. It may seem like a tall order to restate your topic, create a thesis, AND make it captivating, but if you don't grab your reader's attention in the introduction, it doesn't matter how interesting the body of your essay is because he won't feel compelled to read on. Think of your introduction as the worm on a fishhook, just dangling there enticing the fish to bite. There are several techniques you can employ to get your reader to "bite" and, thus, read on.

- Begin your introduction with a question. Naturally, when a question is posed to your reader, he or she will want to keep reading to find out the answer.
- Begin your introduction with a quote. Because you will not have time to research your topic for the SAT test, this may not be as feasible as, say, on a term paper for a college class; however, if you can remember a specific quote pertinent to your topic, use it.
- Begin with an anecdote. An anecdote is entertaining and will thus draw in the reader.
- Begin with an illustration or a hypothetical example based on the topic you are going to discuss.
- Begin with a true-to-life example.
- Begin with vivid description of something pertaining to your topic.

It is particularly important that, in the context of the SAT, you make a concerted effort to create a captivating introduction. Keep in mind that the scorers of your essays are the scorers of everyone else's essays. They read hundreds of responses to the same issues and arguments. You must make your essay stand out. What better way to make it stand out than to make it exceptional from the beginning?

Conclusion

The conclusion of your essay is just as important as the introduction because it wraps up your thoughts and evidence and should leave your reader satisfied that a convincing discussion has just taken place. Your conclusion should include a restatement of your thesis and then end with a more general statement, perhaps a warning or a call for action. Tip: If time is running out and you get stuck trying to formulate a conclusion, try beginning with "In conclusion" or "In summary." Then continue by restating your thesis.

Style

We have examined the rules that govern the English language, and we have learned some techniques on structure. But how does a writer make a piece of writing his own? And how does a writer add interest to his essays? The way a writer uses words and phrases to add personality to his writing is called *style*. A writer is to style as a figure skater is to skating. A writer can learn all the rules that make his writing correct, just as a figure skater can learn how to accomplish her jumps and footwork. But just learning the rules of grammar is not enough to create a well-written essay; learning just the rules of skating is not enough to earn a gold medal. The writer must bring his own methods and personality to his writing just as a skater must invest her own personality and flair to her performance.

Many elements combine to form a writer's style, and, even though many of these elements can be identified, each is unique to a writer. Moreover, a good writer does not allow any elements of his style to stagnate. Rather, he continues to practice writing in order to steadily improve and develop his style. We will touch briefly on how you can develop your writing style, but first let's look at some specific elements of style.

Transitions

Transitional phrases are an important element of style because they create coherence. They guide the reader from point A to point B. On the SAT, the reader will read through your essay quickly, scoring according to his first impression of what you wrote. If your essay is choppy and does not flow well, the reader will not gain a good first impression. Therefore, it is imperative that your essay exhibits solid cohesiveness. Look at the lists below for some examples of transitional words and phrases that will help you write a smooth, coherent essay.

> **Agreement:** also, plus, in addition, further, furthermore, moreover, additionally, to add to that, next, in accordance with, accordingly, in agreement, finally, for instance, for example, in exemplification, exemplifying that, in fact, factually speaking, in terms of, and so forth, in coordination with, along those lines, collectively speaking, generally speaking, indeed, undoubtedly, obviously, to be sure, equally

> **Contrast:** however, in contrast, on the contrary, on the other hand, from a different angle, nonetheless, nevertheless, but, yet, a catch to this is, sadly enough, as a hindrance, oddly enough, instead, in direct opposition, still, rather

Result: as a result, as a consequence, consequently, thus, therefore, hence, thereby, resulting in, ultimately, in the end, finally, in the overall analysis, in hindsight, in retrospect, retrospectively, vicariously, the long term effect, as a short term result, significantly, as a major effect, effectively, heretofore, hereafter, thereafter, in short, generally, over all, concluding

Transitional words and phrases are helpful not only in linking your ideas between sentences, but also in providing cohesiveness from paragraph to paragraph. Each paragraph of your essay should include a topic sentence, which can also act as a transitional sentence. This transitional sentence should link your paragraphs by relating to some element in the preceding paragraph. Take a look at the following example:

> The size of your house will probably be a factor in how you decide to decorate. If you have a large house, you may opt for a grand, sophisticated look. Over-sized furniture and ornate fixtures will complement solid-colored walls accented with artwork. On the other hand, a cozy look suits a smaller home. This look can be achieved by choosing less formal furniture, simple accents and warm colors. Equally, patterned wall-coverings add a lovely touch to a small home.
>
> <u>Regardless of the size of your house, your financial situation will also likely play a large role in the style of décor you choose.</u> Limited funds may force you to make some of your own decorations, like curtains and knick knacks. However, unlimited funds may offer the option of hiring an interior decorator to do all the work for you.

The first sentence of the second paragraph is not only the topic sentence of the paragraph (it lets the reader know what the paragraph will be about), but also the transitional sentence that links the two paragraphs. Notice that the phrase "Regardless of the size of your house" refers to the topic of the first paragraph, thereby tying together the topics of both paragraphs. In addition, the word "also" in this sentence indicates that a second factor of decorating is being introduced.

Other more subtle transitions occur in the first paragraph. For example, "over-sized furniture" in the third sentence refers to the "large house" in the preceding sentence. This provides a transition without using a transitional word. Notice further that "large" is part of the subordinate clause in the second sentence but "over-sized" is part of the main subject in the third sentence, thus providing transition while also giving the reader some variety in sentence pattern. (We will discuss varying your sentences later on.)

More obvious are the transitional words we discussed previously. In the first paragraph, for example, the phrase "On the other hand" depicts the contrast between a large and a small house while "equally" continues the thoughts pertaining to a cozy home. In the second paragraph, "However" is used to show contrast in a pattern much like in the first paragraph.

Using transitions, both subtle and obvious, in your sentences and between paragraphs is essential in creating cohesiveness in your essay. Without this clarity, your essay will likely be choppy and difficult for the scorer to read and understand. A word of caution, however, before we move on: Since time is limited on the writing assessment sections, you must be concise and to the point. Be careful not to overuse transitional words and phrases because overuse can make you sound pedantic rather than intelligent.

Varying Your Sentences

No matter how well your essay flows, the reader will easily get bored if your essay consists only of sentences that contain the same words and follow the same structure. Consider this paragraph:

> Dogs are smarter than cats. They are often used to help handicapped people. Dogs help blind people. Dogs also help epileptic people. Dogs can sense when an epileptic person is about to have a seizure. Dogs are also used in rescue work. They help rescue skiers. They also help in catastrophic events. They rescue people after earthquakes.

There are several things wrong with this paragraph:

- Almost every sentence is the same length.
- The structure in each sentence is almost identical: Subject + Verb + Direct Object.
- The same words are used over and over: "dogs," "they," "also," "help," "rescue."
- No description is used to further illustrate the writer's points.

To add more interest to your writing, you need to vary your sentence length and structure. Try different beginnings for your sentences. Employ a variety of words and use these words to paint a vivid picture of your subject. Let's apply these tips to the paragraph above:

> Dogs are more intelligent than your average feline. A cat cannot, for example, guide a blind person across busy streets and along crowded sidewalks. Amazingly enough, a dog is also a perfect companion for a person with epilepsy because a dog seems to be able to sense when a seizure is coming on. While dogs help keep the handicapped away from danger, they also aid in rescuing people who have fallen victim to dangerous situations, like skiers trapped in an avalanche. Moreover, when catastrophic events, like earthquakes, leave victims pinned beneath debris and rubble, a canine team often comes to the rescue.

A good way to vary your sentences is to begin them in different ways. For example, you could begin your sentence with the subject and predicate and then build on them using various words and phrases. This type of sentence is called a *cumulative sentence.* By contrast, in a *periodic sentence,* you use words and phrases to build up to the subject and the predicate at the end of the sentence. Here are some examples:

Cumulative sentence:

The energetic children played hard, chasing each other in all directions, occasionally falling and then scrambling to their feet, giggling at each other's antics and never stopping for even a moment to catch their breath.

Periodic sentence:

With flour in her hair, dough in between her fingers and sauce all over her face, she attempted to make a gourmet pizza.

Both types of sentences not only add variety, but also bring rhythm and cadence to writing. This rhythm creates interest and is pleasant to the reader. Additionally, descriptive words paint a clear picture for the reader.

Figurative Language

Another excellent way to paint vivid pictures for your reader is to use figures of speech. Figures of speech—like similes, metaphors, analogies, personification, hyperbole, irony, and allusion—when used correctly, add extra flair to your writing. They add to your style of writing an element that takes your writing from ordinary to extraordinary.

Similes show a marked comparison between two things by using the phrases "like," "as," or "as if."

Example:

The cat stood poised and still as a statue, waiting for the opportune moment to pounce.

Here the cat is described "as a statue" because it is standing so still.

Metaphors show absolute comparison by omitting "like," "as," or "as if."

Example:

She is Mother Theresa when it comes to her generosity and compassion.

Here the comparison is absolute because the writer states that this person *is* Mother Theresa; the writer does not say that this person is just *like* Mother Theresa.

Analogies compare the similar features of two dissimilar things. Analogies often bring clarity to writing by showing a reader another way of seeing something. Analogies are not limited to a sentence; sometimes an analogy streams its way through an entire piece of writing.

Example:

Office cooperation is like a soccer game. Each employee has a position on the playing field, and each position dictates an employee's function. Working together, the office completes passes by communicating well within each department. Shots on goal are taken when employees meet with prospective clients to pitch ideas. And the whole office triumphs when a goal is scored and a prospect becomes a client.

Here one element, an office working together, is compared to another, a soccer team playing a game. Although an office and a soccer team are two very unrelated things, the writer sees similarities in some aspects between the two and uses these similarities to show more clearly how an office works together.

Personification gives human characteristics to animals, inanimate objects and ideas in order to make them more real and understandable.

Example:

The rusty car groaned, coughed, then gave one last sputter and died.

The car in this sentence comes to life even as it "dies" because of the human characteristics it is given.

Hyperbole uses deliberate exaggeration or overstatement to show special emphasis or create humor.

Example:

Fat-free foods have become so popular that soon all vendors will want to give it a shot. Before you know it, Kentucky Fried Chicken will have fat-free fried chicken. Big Macs will contain 0 grams of fat. And the amount of fat in a Pizza Hut cheese pizza? You guessed it—none!

In order to show how far out of hand peoples' obsession with fat-free foods has become, this description purposefully exaggerates a world where the most unlikely things are fat-free.

Irony uses language that makes a suggestion that directly contrasts with the literal word or idea. It can offer humor to writing, or a bitter tone when it is used in sarcasm.

Example:

Scientists have worked hard to develop ways to decrease infant mortality rates and increase longevity. As a result, more people are living longer and scientists will soon have to develop methods with which to control overpopulation.

This sentence uses irony by predicting that, because scientists have now discovered ways to increase a person's life span, they will soon have to deal with another problem—overpopulation. This is because, with everyone living longer, there will soon be too many people for the earth to support.

Allusion makes indirect reference to known cultural works, people or events. The familiarity allusions bring to writing helps the writer make connections with the reader.

Example:

I have so much to do today, I feel like David must have felt as he approached Goliath.

Most people are familiar with the Bible story of David and Goliath. David is a small shepherd who slays the giant, Goliath, with a slingshot and one stone after the army's best soldiers fail. Even through his feat, however, David must have felt a bit intimidated when facing Goliath, a feeling this writer intimates when thinking about everything that needs to be done.

Figures of speech to avoid

Clichés are overused phrases that prevent your writing from being fresh and original, so don't use clichés like "Cute as a button" or "Busy as a bee."

Mixed metaphors are comparisons that are not consistent; they only cause confusion. For example, "The infant was like a baby bird, opening his cavernous well for food." Here the simile that an infant is like a baby bird holds true, but the following words that equate the baby's mouth to a cavernous well are not consistent.

Tone

The words you choose will greatly affect the tone of your essay. Likewise, the tone you wish to achieve will depend on your audience. In this case, you know your audience will consist of men and women who will be quickly reading your essay and then assigning a score based on their impression and how well you handled the topic. Knowing this, you will want to use a professional, formal tone, the kind you will probably use in most of your college work. Using a formal tone means that you will want to keep some distance between you, the writer, and your audience, the scorer. Be courteous and polite but avoid being chummy or intimate in any way. Furthermore, you should avoid all colloquialisms and slang.

Diction

While tone defines the overall language you use, diction deals with the specific kinds of words and phrases you choose for your essay. Since you have already determined your audience and thus ascertained that you need to portray a formal tone in your essay, you must be consistent with your diction, or word choice. Diction may be classified as technical (*homo sapien* rather than *human*), formal (*Please inform me when you are ready to depart.*), informal or colloquial (*Give me a buzz when you're ready to go.*), or slang (*She's a real couch potato and watches the tube from early morning 'til the cows come home.*) Knowing that your audience dictates a formal tone, you must also be consistent in maintaining formal diction. Look at the following example of inconsistent diction:

> Violence in schools has become an epidemic problem. School shootings occur regularly, and fights erupt daily in the nation's classrooms. Even with the addition of metal detectors at school entrances, violence will never be eradicated because the jocks are always ganging up on the geeks. If only we could just all get along.

This example begins with a formal tone and formal diction; however, it takes a quick turn when the writer uses slang words like "jocks" and "geeks." The paragraph is concluded informally with "If only we could just all get along."

As you write your essay, and later when you proofread it, you will want to make sure that you preserve the formality your audience requires.

Person

It is important to maintain consistency in person. For example, if you begin your essay in second person (*you*) do not shift to third person (*he, she, it, one,* or *they*). Let's look at a couple of examples illustrating a shift in person:

Example:

<u>One</u> can get excellent grades in school if <u>you</u> study hard.

The switch from "one" to "you" is confusing and awkward.

Example:

Off the coast of Puerto Rico, on the island of Vieques, is an old French mansion turned hotel. Here one can enjoy spacious guest rooms and a cozy library. One can lounge around the pool and indulge in the honorary pool bar. Because the hotel is not far from the ocean, you can also take a leisurely walk down to the white sandy beach where one can spend a lazy day basking in the sun.

The switch from *one* to *you* is confusing in this paragraph and detracts from the imagery. Decide from the beginning of your essay what person you wish to employ and make a conscious effort to stick to it.

Developing Your Style

Your goal as a writer is to create interest and coherence through your unique writing style. Using figures of speech and maintaining consistent use of tone, diction and person are effective ways to create interest. Using transitions creates coherence. Also remember that part of creating coherence is being concise. Use only the details that are necessary to support your topic and avoid tedious description. This is not to say that you should avoid vivid imagery, but that you should take care to ensure that your information adds to your writing rather than detracts from your writing.

In taking all of these elements of style into account, the most important aspect to remember about developing your style is that it only comes through practice. Practice your writing and proofread, proofread, proofread. If you do all of these things, you will be well on your way to becoming an effective, skillful writer. Are you ready to start practicing? Let's move on to more specifics about the essay you will be asked to write. Before we do so, however, let's practice what we've learned so far.

Warm-Up Drill II

Directions: Read each paragraph in the following essay and rewrite it, making necessary changes in order to enhance the effectiveness of the essay. Pay close attention to all of the elements you learned about writing style. Answers and solutions begin on the next page.

Prompt:
It is more beneficial to complete independent study than to attend college.

Assignment:
Do you think that a student can benefit more from completing independent study than from attending college? Plan and develop an essay in which you provide detailed and persuasive support for your opinion.

1. This opinion is not valid and is clearly not based on any evidence that would prove its validity. One can't gain more knowledge by completing independent study instead of attending college. It is necessary to look at some evidence to prove this.

2. Some people think that there are too many distractions at college because there are so many other students who take up class time. Interaction with other students can provide valuable insight into topics you study in college. Other people's backgrounds and experience add differences in perspectives and, in some cases, valuable expertise. Professors add expertise as well since they are the experts in the areas they are teaching. When a student studies on his own, he is dependent only on what he knows. He is also dependent on what he can read about. He is also dependent on his own background and experiences. This is very limiting to the value he can obtain from his education.

3. Some people think that students can learn more discipline by studying independently at home instead of going to college. College students learn a lot of discipline. They are held accountable by their college professors. They are held accountable by fellow students too. They depend upon them to contribute to the class. Students who study on their own are only accountable to themselves. Many times, studies get set aside when life gets too busy. Studies get the boot when a student encounters a subject they're not too excited about.

4. Studying at home independently is not as beneficial as attending college because the degree you get, if you get a degree at all, will not carry as much weight with potential employers as will a college degree from an accredited college or university. Employers place more weight on someone whose expertise they can depend on. Employers feel they can depend more on the expertise of someone who has been trained at a college or university.

5. People should go to college. You can't depend on your own motivation to finish your studies at home. A student gains a lot more from the interaction they receive between other students and professors in college. Students who get a degree from a college may have a better chance of getting a good job after college.

Solutions to Warm-Up Drill II

1. The opening sentence in this paragraph does not make an effective introduction. It does not restate the topic but rather makes a direct address to the topic question. A good introduction should not require the reader to read the topic. The second sentence of the paragraph gives a concise thesis statement but should be elaborated on a bit. Also, the contraction *can't* does not fit with the formal tone of the essay. The last sentence serves as a transition to the next paragraph, but it does not show much sophistication or subtlety.

    Better:

    Should a student give up a college education in order to complete an independent study at home? Although the financial savings of independent study may be substantial, one can gain more benefits by obtaining a college or university education. Studying at a college or university can give a student a broader education, can help him learn discipline through accountability, and can pay off in the long run.

    This introduction begins with a question, which is more effective than directly addressing the question/topic. The thesis statement concisely lists three reasons a formal education is better than independent study; this sentence gives the reader a clear idea of what the essay will be about.

2. The first sentence serves as a topic sentence for the paragraph; however, it should be reworded to act as a better transitional sentence, one that would tie in with the last sentence of the preceding paragraph. The second sentence would function better with a transitional phrase like *On the contrary* to introduce it. Also in this sentence, the use of second person *you* is inconsistent with the rest of the essay. The fourth sentence uses the same two words *add* and *expertise* that were used in the preceding sentence. These should be changed to add some variety. The next three sentences are repetitive and should be combined.

    Better:

    Some people think that distractions at college from other students who take up class time results in a narrow education. On the contrary, interaction with other students can provide valuable insight into the topics one studies in college. Other people's backgrounds and experience add different perspectives and, in some cases, valuable expertise. Professors offer much value as well since they are the experts in the areas they are teaching. When a student studies on his own, he is dependent only on what he knows or can read about and on his own background and experiences. This severely limits the value he can obtain from his education.

    The first sentence works as a transition because it uses the word *narrow*, which contrasts with the word *broader* from the thesis statement in the preceding paragraph.

3. The first sentence works well as a topic sentence, but it uses the same wording as the topic sentence for the preceding paragraph. In the fifth sentence, the use of *they* and *them* is confusing because it is unclear whether the pronoun reference is to the student or fellow students. The remaining sentences are all the same length and therefore choppy. The last sentence strays from the formal tone of the essay. In addition, the word *they* does not agree in person with *a student*.

    Better:

    One valuable lesson students can learn at college is discipline. College students learn a lot of discipline because they are held accountable by their professors. Moreover, they are often held accountable by fellow students who depend upon them to contribute to the class. Students who study on their own are accountable only to themselves. Many times, studies get set aside when life gets too busy or when a student encounters a subject for which he is not enthusiastic.

    The word *valuable* ties in well with the word *value* in the last sentence of the preceding paragraph. Thus, this sentence serves not only as a topic sentence but also as a transitional sentence.

4. Again, the first sentence provides a good topic sentence but not a good transition from the preceding paragraph. The second sentence unnecessarily repeats the word *weight* from the first sentence. In the third sentence, the text shifts to second person *you*. The last sentence repeats the word *depend* from the preceding sentence.

Better:

Studying at a college or university may not make every topic seem scintillating; however, when a student is held accountable, he is more driven. As he is driven to succeed, he will eventually earn a degree. Studying at home independently is not as beneficial as attending college because the degree a student gets, if he gets a degree at all, will not carry as much weight with potential employers as will a degree from an accredited college or university. Employers place more confidence in someone whose expertise they can rely on. Employers feel they can depend more on the expertise of someone who has been trained at a college or university.

The topic sentence in this paragraph provides transition because it refers to the preceding paragraph by relating *scintillating* courses to being *enthusiastic* about subjects.

5. The first sentence does not act as a thorough topic sentence, nor does it provide a good transition. The second sentence uses *you* and *your*, which is an inconsistent use of person. In addition, the contraction *can't* takes away from the formal tone of the essay. Overall, this last paragraph is not effective; it has short, choppy sentences and does not adequately conclude the subject by restating the topic and giving final remarks.

Better:

Whether one is trained at a university or opts to stay home to study independently, an education is extremely important; however, it is clear that a student can benefit more from a formal education than from independent study. Students should not depend on their own motivation to finish their studies, nor should they miss out on the opportunity to benefit from the interaction they will receive from other students and professors in college. Despite any financial savings a student may earn by studying independently, the rewards of a college education will pay off in the long run.

The transition here works well because the first sentence uses the word *trained*, which is used in the sentence before it. This final paragraph functions effectively as a conclusion because it restates the topic. It also brings the writing full circle by once again mentioning the monetary aspect of education, which, as you recall, was mentioned in the introductory paragraph.

Present Your Perspective on an Issue

The Essay section of the SAT asks you to present your perspective on a given issue. In addition, you are required to provide solid evidence to support your position. You will be given an essay prompt, along with an assignment, and you have 25 minutes to plan and write your essay. Following is the grading scale for the essay.

SCORE

6 OUTSTANDING

A 6 essay presents a cogent, well-articulated discussion of the issue and demonstrates mastery of the elements of effective writing.

> A typical paper in this category
>
> —explores ideas and develops a position on the issue with insightful reasons and/or persuasive examples
> —sustains a well-focused, well-organized discussion of the subject
> —expresses ideas with language that is clear and precise
> —varies sentence structure and vocabulary appropriate to the subject
> —demonstrates superior facility with the conventions (grammar, usage, and mechanics) of standard written English but may have minor flaws

---

5 EFFECTIVE

A 5 essay presents a well-developed discussion of the issue and demonstrates a strong control of the elements of effective writing.

> A typical paper in this category
>
> —develops a position on the issue with well-chosen reasons and/or examples
> —is focused and generally well organized
> —uses language fluently, with varied sentence structure and appropriate vocabulary
> —demonstrates facility with the conventions of standard written English but may have minor flaws

---

4 COMPETENT

A 4 essay presents a competent discussion of the issue and demonstrates adequate control of the elements of writing.

> A typical paper in this category
>
> —develops a position on the issue with relevant reasons and/or examples
> —is adequately organized
> —expresses ideas clearly
> —demonstrates adequate control of language, including diction and syntax, but may lack sentence variety
> —demonstrates adequate control of the conventions of standard written English but may have some flaws

---

3   INADEQUATE

A 3 essay presents some competence in its discussion of the issue and in its control of the elements of writing but is clearly flawed.

A typical paper in this category exhibits <u>one or more</u> of the following characteristics:

—is vague or limited in developing a position on the issue
—is poorly focused and/or poorly organized
—is weak in the use of relevant reasons and/or examples
—has problems expressing ideas clearly
—has problems in fluency, with poorly formed sentences or inappropriate vocabulary
—has occasional major errors or frequent minor errors in grammar, usage, and mechanics

2   SERIOUSLY LIMITED

A 2 essay presents a weak discussion of the issue and demonstrates little control of the elements of writing.

A typical paper in this category exhibits <u>one or more</u> of the following characteristics:

—is unclear or seriously limited in presenting and developing a position on the issue
—is unfocused and/or disorganized
—provides few, if any, relevant reasons or examples
—has serious and frequent problems in the use of language and sentence structure
—contains frequent errors in grammar, usage, or mechanics that interfere with meaning

1   FUNDAMENTALLY LACKING

A 1 essay is seriously deficient in basic writing skills.

A typical paper in this category exhibits <u>one or more</u> of the following characteristics:

—provides little evidence of the ability to organize or develop a coherent response on the issue
—has severe and persistent errors in language and sentence structure
—contains a pervasive pattern of errors in grammar, usage, and mechanics that interfere with
  meaning

0   Any paper that is blank, totally illegible, or obviously not written on the assigned topic receives a score of zero.

Using the scoring criteria for the essay, make sure that your writing demonstrates that you can:

• develop a position (which is different from merely stating a position)
• organize to present a focused discussion
• use standard written English and appropriate vocabulary
• express ideas in clear and precise language

If you are a typical high school student, you are likely thinking that the above rubric is all well and good, but your biggest concern has yet to be addressed. You probably wish your Language Arts teacher was around to ask the all important question: *How long does it have to be?* A good rule of thumb to follow for this essay as well as for future college writing—especially when writing entrance or placement essays—is the "five-paragraph essay." In a five-paragraph essay, your first paragraph introduces your topic, three body paragraphs support your topic, and the last paragraph acts as your concluding paragraph.

Writing five paragraphs on one topic may seem a daunting task; however, there are tricks to developing your topic and organizing your thoughts into paragraphs. Let's discuss some of those tricks as they pertain to the persuasive essay at hand.

Patterns of Development

Just as there is no universal answer to every question, there are many ways to write a persuasive essay. There are specific strategies that you can use to more effectively respond to different types of issue topics. These strategies, or methods, are called patterns of development. The type of pattern you choose to employ in writing your essay is dependent upon the question or prompt to which you are responding. Usually, an essay question will contain certain clues, which enable you to determine which pattern of development to use. After choosing a method to use, you will find it much easier to develop a clear, concise thesis, which, in turn, will affect the way you organize your essay.

There are three main patterns of development. Let's examine them now so we have a better understanding of how to apply them. For each, we will discuss clues in an issue question that prompts the use of a particular pattern of development, we will look at an example of such a question, and we will determine what your assignment as a writer will be in applying this method.

Comparison – Contrast

An essay prompt that commands the use of the Comparison – Contrast pattern of development:

- will use words that suggest similarity or difference.
- will seek to persuade the reader that one item is superior to another.

Example:

"American cars are better than foreign cars."

The author uses the word *than* to compare the two cars, and he seeks to persuade the reader that an American car is a wiser choice than a foreign one.

Your assignment: By employing the Comparison – Contrast pattern of development, you will portray similarities and differences between two items to prove which one is superior, either in agreement or disagreement with the author's opinion.

Cause – Effect

An essay prompt that requires the use of the Cause – Effect method of response:

- may include an "If...then" statement.
- may lack an effect.

Example (if...then):

"If college and university faculty spent time outside the academic world working in professions relevant to the courses they teach, then the overall quality of higher education would greatly increase."

The author argues that if a certain action is taken, a desirable effect is achieved.

Your assignment: In your essay, you must prove that a particular cause results in a particular effect, either in agreement or disagreement with the author.

Example (lack of effect):

"More restrictions should be set on teenage drivers."

In this "call for action" statement, the author offers no effects that will result if the action is taken, but surely it is implied that, if the author feels the action should be taken, he assumes something positive will result.

Your assignment: In your responsive essay, it would be your responsibility to support your position in agreement with this statement or against it, thus proving or disproving the implied effect.

Definition

An essay prompt that dictates the use of the Definition pattern of development:

- will attempt to show that, by definition, a particular idea or concept is of great value.
- may portray a very limited definition of an idea or concept.

Example (great value):

"Patriotism breaks down the walls of division."

The author believes that a concept can do a great thing.

Your assignment: Define the idea or concept and show that, because of its attributes and qualities, it has value or it lacks value.

Example (limited definition):

"A person's generosity can be determined by examining what he or she has given to charity."

In this example, the author seeks to provide a very limited definition of a particular concept.

Your assignment: Support the author's definition with evidence, or show that the definition is much broader.

Planning & Writing

Now that you are familiar with the different methods you can employ to write your essay, let's get down to the nitty gritty of organizing your thoughts by using these patterns of development. Remember, you are aiming for a 6 essay, one that presents clear, concise evidence to support your view. Writing a 6 essay doesn't have to be a difficult task. All you have to do is follow seven simple steps, some of which will ask you to plug information into formulas. Note that some steps may include specific formulas for each pattern of development. Also note that you need not enter complete, descriptive sentences into the formulas; simple notes and phrases will suffice.

➢ Step 1 – Understanding the Issue

In order to properly present your perspective on an issue, you must first understand the issue you are being asked to discuss. Understanding the issue allows you to fully develop your position, presenting your evidence in a way that is most effective and appropriate for the topic. There are two steps that will help you understand the issue.

First, take a couple of minutes to read the given question carefully. Second, ask yourself the following questions:

- What does the statement mean?
- What is the issue at hand?
- What is implied by the statement?
- What is the writer's stand on the issue?
- What, if any, evidence does the writer use to support his position?
- What, specifically, is my assignment?

➢ Step 2 – Choosing Your Pattern of Development

Keeping in mind our discussion of the three patterns of development, look for the necessary criteria in your question. If you think the question requires more than one method, choose the one you think works the best. On a timed writing assignment, your essay will be fairly short and therefore you cannot adequately utilize two methods.

➢ Step 3 – Developing Your Thesis

The next, and perhaps the most important, step is to develop your thesis. Your thesis states the purpose of your essay. Without a thesis statement, your reader does not know what you are setting out to prove. And without a thesis statement, it would be very difficult to organize your essay with clarity and coherence. Don't be intimidated by the task of formulating what is to be the crux of your essay. It can be quite simple. Just use the formulas below:

THESIS FOR COMPARISON – CONTRAST ESSAY *(formula 1-1)*:

I believe that Item A, _____, is better than Item B, _____, because
1) _____, 2) _____, 3) _____.

THESIS FOR CAUSE – EFFECT ESSAY *(formula 1-2)*:

If _____, then _____, because
1) _____, 2) _____, 3) _____.

THESIS FOR DEFINITION ESSAY *(formula 1-3)*:

By definition, _____ possess(es) these qualities: 1) _____,
2) _____, 3) _____ which have a positive effect because
A) _____, B) _____, C) _____.

➢   Step 4 – Understanding Counter Arguments

Have you ever been in an argument and found that you're just not getting very far very fast? This could be because you are failing to see things from the other person's point of view. Being able to see the "flip side of the coin" can go a long way in proving your point and disarming your opponent's objections. By showing that you are aware, though perhaps not understanding, of the opposing side you are adding credibility to your argument because it is clear that you have viewed the issue from all angles. To write an effective position essay, you must present your knowledge of a counter argument. In other words, you must show that you have considered the other side of the argument. Organize your counter argument this way:

COMPARISON – CONTRAST COUNTER CLAIM *(formula 2-1)*:

Others may think Item B is better than Item A because 1) _____,
2) _____, 3) _____.
(Note that these three points should contrast directly with the three points of your thesis. (see *formula 1-1*))

CAUSE – EFFECT COUNTER CLAIM *(formula 2-2)*:

Some may feel that _____ would cause _____ based on _____.
(Note that this point should contrast directly with point #1 of your thesis. (see *formula 1-2*))

DEFINITION *(formula 2-3)*:

By definition some may feel that _____ exhibits or is defined by _____ which could be positive / negative.
(Note that this point should contrast directly with point #1 of your thesis. (see *formula 1-3*))

➢   Step 5 – Organizing Your Thoughts

Now let's organize all of our information so that writing the essay will be quick and simple. Following are formulas specific to each pattern of development. These formulas will prompt you to plug in your thesis and counter argument points. (Note that the following formulas require you to plug in the three numbered items from your thesis in succession. Although it is not necessary that you discuss them in this order, we will label it that way for simplicity.) In addition, there are spaces in the formula for you to insert 1 or 2 pieces of supporting evidence. Don't be intimidated by these formulas. They are meant to be a skeleton for organizing your essay. If you practice by writing essays using the sample prompts in this book, you'll get accustomed to using the outlines, and they will seem much less imposing.

COMPARISON – CONTRAST ESSAY FORMULA *(formula 3-1)*:
I.   Introduction – Paragraph 1
   A.   Restate your topic
   B.   Thesis statement *(formula 1-1)*
II.   Support – Paragraph 2
   A.   Counter Claim point #1 *(formula 2-1)*
   B.   Thesis point #1 *(formula 1-1)*
      1.   Support for thesis point #1
      2.   Support for thesis point #1

III. Support – Paragraph 3
    A. Counter Claim point #2 *(formula 2-1)*
    B. Thesis point #2 *(formula 1-1)*
        1. Support for thesis point #2
        2. Support for thesis point #2
IV. Support – Paragraph 4
    A. Counter Claim point #3 *(formula 2-1)*
    B. Thesis point #3 *(formula 1-1)*
        1. Support for thesis point #3
        2. Support for thesis point #3
V. Conclusion – Paragraph 5
    A. Restate thesis
    B. Issue a warning or a call for action

CAUSE - EFFECT ESSAY FORMULA *(formula 3-2)*:
I. Introduction – Paragraph 1
    A. Restate your topic
    B. Thesis statement *(formula 1-2)*
II. Support – Paragraph 2
    A. Counter Claim *(formula 2-2)*
    B. Thesis point #1 *(formula 1-2)*
        1. Support for thesis point #1
        2. Support for thesis point #1
III. Support – Paragraph 3 – Thesis point #2 *(formula 1-2)*
    A. Support for thesis point #2
    B. Support for thesis point #2
IV. Support – Paragraph 4 – Thesis point #3 *(formula 1-2)*
    A. Support for thesis point #3
    B. Support for thesis point #3
V. Conclusion – Paragraph 5
    A. Restate thesis
    B. Issue a warning or a call for action

DEFINITION ESSAY FORMULA *(formula 3-3)*:
I. Introduction – Paragraph 1
    A. Restate your topic
    B. Thesis statement *(formula 1-3)*
II. Support – Paragraph 2
    A. Counter Claim *(formula 2-3)*
    B. Thesis point #1 *(formula 1-3)*
        1. Support by using thesis point A *(formula 1-3)*
        2. Support by using thesis point A *(formula 1-3)*
III. Support – Paragraph 3 – Thesis point #2 *(formula 1-3)*
    A. Support by using point B *(formula 1-3)*
    B. Support by using point B *(formula 1-3)*
IV. Support – Paragraph 4 – Thesis point #3 *(formula 1-3)*
    A. Support by using point C *(formula 1-3)*
    B. Support by using point C *(formula 1-3)*
V. Conclusion – Paragraph 5
    A. Restate thesis
    B. Issue a warning or a call for action

➢ Step 6 – Writing Your Essay

Now that you have organized your thoughts and support, it is time to write! The best strategy under the pressure of a time restraint is to just begin writing—as quickly as you can while still being careful. (You should allow yourself about 20 of the 25 minutes for writing.) Organization should not be difficult with the help of your formulas. In following your formula, don't forget to add transitional words, phrases and sentences to help give your essay coherence. As you write, remember the mechanical rules you learned at the beginning of this chapter and keep in mind the techniques we discussed in the section *General Tips on Writing Your Essays*. The key to successful timed writings is to reserve a bit of time at the end so that you can go back and proofread and add finishing touches that will make your essay flow well and that will present your ideas clearly.

> ➢ Step 7 – Revising Your Essay

Because you have written quickly, you must spend some time, about 5-8 minutes, at the end of the section reviewing your essay, making necessary changes to enhance the clarity, coherence and grammatical accuracy of your writing. You must look for misspellings and mechanical errors while at the same time keeping in mind the following questions:

- Is my introduction captivating?
- Is my thesis statement concise?
- Do my body paragraphs clearly support my thesis?
- Have I used logical transitions that help the text flow smoothly between sentences and between paragraphs?
- Have I maintained a formal tone and diction throughout my essay?
- Have I maintained consistent use of person (i.e., first, second, third)?
- Is there a word, or are there words, which I have employed too often throughout the essay?
- Do my sentences vary in length and structure?

As you ask yourself these questions, make the necessary changes. If you still have time left after you have completed the initial revision, go back and read your essay again. A writer makes many, many revisions to his manuscript before it is ready to be published, so you can never proofread too many times!

Sample Issues & Essays

Now let's apply the 7 steps to three examples.

Example 1: Comparison – Contrast Essay

Prompt:
A new custom home is a much better purchase than an older, run-down home.

Assignment:
Is it more wise to purchase an older, run-down home than a new custom home? Based on your own experiences in your family, plan and write an essay in which you develop your opinion on the better choice between new and old homes. Provide effective support for your opinion.

> ➢ Step 1 – Understanding the Issue

- What does the statement mean? *If you are in the market to buy a house, a new home would be a better value.*
- What is the issue at hand? *What kind of home is the best to buy?*
- What is implied by the statement? *That one who purchases an old home is not making a wise choice. Also implied is that an older home is run-down.*
- What is the writer's stand on the issue? *He believes a new home is superior to an old one.*
- What, if any, evidence does the writer use to support his position? *Old houses are run-down, new homes can be custom built.*
- What, specifically, is my assignment? *To give my opinion about which home I think would make a wiser choice—a new home or an old home. To give support to persuasively develop my opinion.*

> ➢ Step 2 – Choosing My Pattern of Development

This prompt requires me to employ the Comparison – Contrast pattern of development because the statement uses the word "than," a contrasting word. Moreover, the author is trying to convince me that it is better to buy a new home than an old one.

> ➤ Step 3 – Developing My Thesis

THESIS FOR COMPARISON – CONTRAST ESSAY *(formula 1-1)*:

> I believe that Item A, <u>an old home</u>, is better than Item B, <u>a new home</u>, because
> 1) <u>an old home exemplifies old-style motifs that are unique in today's market</u>, 2) <u>foundations are stronger in older homes</u>, 3) <u>can remodel an old home in any way</u>.

> ➤ Step 4 – Understanding Counter Argument

COMPARISON – CONTRAST COUNTER CLAIM *(formula 2-1)*:

Others may think Item B is better than Item A because 1) <u>you can "keep up with the Joneses" with your modern décor</u>, 2) <u>new homes may be built quickly for easy occupancy</u>, 3) <u>new homes can be custom-built</u>. (Note that these three points should contrast directly with the three points of your thesis. (see *formula 1-1*))

> ➤ Step 5 – Organizing My Thoughts

COMPARISON – CONTRAST ESSAY FORMULA *(formula 3-1)*:

I.   Introduction – Paragraph 1
  A. Some people feel that the purchase of a new home is a smarter investment choice than the purchase of an older home.
  B. For anyone who puts stock in the aged and unique, the traditional home may be the choice of a lifetime with its old-fashioned motifs, its strong foundations, and its versatility to become the house its owner designs.
II. Support – Paragraph 2
  A. keeping up with the Joneses – modern décor
  B. bring back old-time motifs
    1. More choices – can choose from different time periods
    2. More unique versus "cookie cutter" homes of today
III. Support – Paragraph 3
  A. Homes can be built quicker
  B. As a result, foundations not as strong in new homes
    1. Mass production of homes – builder doesn't establish good foundation
    2. Older homes in better condition over long period of time because built more solidly
IV. Support – Paragraph 4
  A. Custom-built
  B. Can remodel any way owner wants
    1. No allowance restrictions placed on owner by builder
V.   Conclusion – Paragraph 5
  A. Modern homes just don't offer the old-fashioned charm an older well-built, unique home can offer.
  B. When it comes to such an important decision as purchasing a home, the choice is clear: an older home has much more to offer and will last for many years to come.

> ➤ Step 6 – Writing My Essay

Modern-day housing developments are springing up everywhere, dotting hills and filling in every open space available. Characterized by "cookie cutter" homes, houses all cut from the same mold, the look of these communities lacks distinctiveness. For anyone who puts stock in the aged and unique rather than the new and ordinary, the traditional house may be the choice of a lifetime with its old-fashioned motifs, its strong foundations, and its versatility to become the home of its owner's design.

  Many homeowners do not feel the need to be the designer behind their home. Rather, they strive to "keep up with the Joneses" by filling their houses with the same modern décor that fills the homes of their neighbors. On the flip side, when seeking to invest in a traditional home, the buyer has a plethora of options because older homes offer so much uniqueness. This uniqueness can be seen in the motifs of style, which are almost non-existent in today's market of prefabricated homes but are powerful reminders of days gone by in older structures. These are the structures that offer a homeowner an admirable individuality.

  Clearly, modern-day homes, which lack individuality, are built more quickly than homes of the past, a fact that seems to fit today's hurried society. But what does a homeowner have to show for this efficiency years down the road? There is much value added to a home constructed by a builder who takes time and pays attention to detail instead of putting up as many homes as possible in the shortest amount of time possible. For example, in the past when builders did take extra time and care, the foundations and overall structures were, and still are, much stronger. This is because many builders today, eager to make a quick buck, do not give homes ample time to "settle" on their foundation before continuing with the construction. Overall, older houses are in better condition, even over the course of time, because they were more solidly built.

Many prospective buyers today overlook the quality of a home's structure and are compelled to purchase by the alluring idea of "custom building" their house. These homebuyers enjoy the process of choosing paint colors, fixtures and floor coverings. Consider an older home, however. Here the possibilities are endless, and traditional buyers may even negotiate remodeling into the price of the house. What is more, there are no spending restrictions which contemporary builders often impose on their buyers.

Spending restrictions represent just one of many ways that freedom is limited when purchasing a new home instead of an older home. Whether one prefers an elegant, plantation-style mansion or a peaceful, rustic country getaway, the distinctive older home has much more to offer than the commonplace modern home set in communities of houses that all look the same. Simply put, it comes down to whether the prospective buyer is willing to trade quality and originality for expediency.

➢ Step 7 – Revising My Essay

When critiquing other essays, you often learn a lot about the strengths and weaknesses in your own writing. So here's an assignment: Let's take our revision questions; your job is to complete the task required for each question.

- Is the introduction captivating? Why or why not? Do you recognize a certain method the author employed to make the introduction interesting?

- Is the thesis statement concise? Does it clearly show the purpose of the essay?

- Do the body paragraphs clearly support each point made in the thesis? If not, where does the essay lack necessary support?

- Are there logical transitions that make the text flow smoothly between sentences and between paragraphs? Underline each word, phrase or sentence that acts as a transition.

- Is the tone and diction consistent throughout the essay? If not, point out the places where consistency breaks down.

- Is the use of person consistent? If not, point out the places where consistency is not maintained.

- Is there a word, or are there words, which have been used too often in the essay? List these words. Also list the words that have been used to provide variety in the essay.

- Do the sentences vary in length and structure?

Example 2: Cause – Effect Essay

Prompt:
Students should not be required to take courses outside their field of study.

Assignment:
Do you think that college students should be required to take a well-rounded selection of courses even if they do not pertain to their major? Plan and write a well-developed essay in which you discuss your opinion on this topic. Support your opinion with persuasive details.

➢ Step 1 – Understanding the Issue

- What does the statement mean? *Colleges should not make students take courses, like General Education courses, if they do not pertain to their area of study.*
- What is the issue at hand? *Whether or not students benefit from taking college courses that don't pertain to their major.*
- What is implied by the statement? *That a student will be adequately prepared for the "real world" without taking a wide range of classes.*
- What is the writer's stand on the issue? *That students should not be required to take these classes.*
- What, if any, evidence does the writer use to support his position? *The writer does not give any evidence to support his view.*
- What, specifically, is my assignment? *To show my perspective on whether college students should have to take classes that do not have anything to do with their major. I need to give support that will persuade the reader that the college student will benefit based on my opinion.*

➢ Step 2 – Choosing My Pattern of Development

This prompt is a "call for action" statement, and, although no effect is discussed, the writer implies that his recommended course of action would result in a positive effect.

➢ Step 3 – Developing My Thesis

THESIS FOR CAUSE-EFFECT ESSAY *(formula 1-2)*:

If students are not required to take courses outside their field of study, then they will not be prepared, because 1) they will be ill-prepared if they fail to get a job in their field, 2) they will be lacking in important skills – communication or thinking/reasoning skills, 3) they will be close-minded and ignorant to things happening in the world around them.

➢ Step 4 – Understanding Counter Argument

CAUSE – EFFECT COUNTER CLAIM *(formula 2-2)*:

Some may feel that requiring students to take courses only in their field of study would cause students to be more knowledgeable in their field because they would have more thoroughly studied this area. (Note that this point should contrast directly with point #1 of your thesis. (see *formula 1-2*))

➢ Step 5 – Organizing My Thoughts

CAUSE - EFFECT ESSAY FORMULA *(formula 3-2)*:

I.   Introduction – Paragraph 1
   A.   Some feel students should not be required to take courses outside their field of study.
   B.   If students are not required to take courses outside their field of study, they will be ill-prepared should they fail to get a job in their field, they will lack important skills, and they will be close-minded and ignorant to things happening in the world around them.
II. Support – Paragraph 2
   A.   Some may feel that requiring students to take courses only in their field of study would cause students to be more knowledgeable in their field because they would have more thoroughly studied this area.
   B.   Many people are unable to get a job in their field after they graduate.
      1.   Without some knowledge of other fields, these highly trained people will be stuck working menial jobs.

III. They will be lacking in important skills.
    A. Students studying the sciences will lack communication skills.
    B. Students studying the arts will lack critical thinking and reasoning skills.
IV. They will be close-minded and ignorant of things happening in the world around them.
    A. Lack of familiarity with certain fields promotes disinterest in these topics as they pertain to current events (politics, scientific research).
    B. This disinterest promotes apathy in participating in or supporting causes that result from these current events.
V. Conclusion – Paragraph 5
    A. Students must take a well-rounded schedule of classes in order to be prepared for work outside their field and so they will have adequate skills to use toward a common interest in society.
    C. Students should welcome an opportunity to learn about all areas of study.

➢   Step 6 – Writing My Essay

Colleges and universities require students, regardless of their majors, to complete General Education courses, basic courses that cover general subject areas. These classes include basic literature and writing courses, basic science and math courses, and basic arts classes like music and drama. Some feel students should not be required to take these General Education classes. However, if students are not required to take courses outside their major, they will be ill-prepared should they fail to get a job in their field, they will lack important skills, and they will be close-minded and ignorant of things happening in the world around them.

Many opponents of General Education classes are themselves unaware of the advantages of a well-rounded education. They focus only on the theory that students will be more fully prepared to enter their field as a result of more extensive study in their area. What they fail to see, however, is that many graduates are not able to find jobs in their field of expertise. So, without a broad range of knowledge, these highly trained graduates would be stuck in menial jobs.

Even if graduates do get jobs within their field, such a wide range of skills are required in the workplace in order to be successful that, without a diverse educational background, a graduate will not be fully competent in any job. For example, when a graduate begins looking for a job, she will discover that excellent communication skills are invaluable in the workplace, both in dealing with customers and with colleagues. Without some base of communication knowledge, such as a student would receive in a basic English class, the candidate will be overlooked for someone who does show strength in communication. Moreover, most jobs require strong problem-solving skills, skills that develop from learning how to think and reason critically. These skills are reinforced in math and science classes.

Lack of familiarity in certain educational arenas, like math and science, results in a provincial attitude. This lack of familiarity leads to disinterest in the areas where a student has not gained knowledge. Likewise, this disinterest leads to apathy in participating or supporting any causes that are linked to these fields of study. For example, a student who has not studied science will be indifferent to scientific ideas, ideas which could become theories and could help all of mankind. A student who does not study politics and government will likely be apathetic toward participating in important political events such as elections.

It is important that a country's citizens take part in supporting causes and concepts that generate a common interest in society. Without a well-rounded schedule of classes in college, however, the citizen base will soon be filled with people who are unprepared and indifferent to anything that does not directly pertain to their area of interest. Instead of complaining about an opportunity to gain a broad range of knowledge, students should consider it a privilege and an asset.

➢   Step 7 – Revising My Essay

Read over the essay above and then answer the following questions.

- Is the introduction captivating? Why or why not? Do you recognize a certain method the author employed to make the introduction interesting?

- Is the thesis statement concise? Does it clearly show the purpose of the essay?

- Do the body paragraphs clearly support each point made in the thesis? If not, where does the essay lack necessary support?

- Are there logical transitions that make the text flow smoothly between sentences and between paragraphs? Underline each word, phrase or sentence that acts as a transition.

- Is the tone and diction consistent throughout the essay? If not, point out the places where consistency breaks down.

- Is the use of person consistent? If not, point out the places where consistency is not maintained.

- Is there a word, or are there words, which have been used too often in the essay? List these words. Also list the words that have been used to provide variety in the essay.

- Do the sentences vary in length and structure?

Example 3: Definition Essay

Prompt:
The positive effects of competition in a society far outweigh the negative effects.

Assignment:
Do you think that competition has a positive or negative effect on a community? Write an essay in which you develop your opinion. Support your perspective by drawing from personal experience and knowledge you have gained in your life. Make sure your support is specific and persuasive.

➢ Step 1 – Understanding the Issue

- What does the statement mean? *Competition affects society in a good way, not a bad way.*
- What is the issue at hand? *Whether or not competition is good for society.*
- What is implied by the statement? *That a society benefits from competition amongst its members.*
- What is the writer's stand on the issue? *That competition is good and provides benefits.*
- What, if any, evidence does the writer use to support his position? *The writer does not give any evidence to support his view.*
- What, specifically, is my assignment? *To persuasively discuss with the reader my perspective on the effects of competition in society. I can use personal experience to make my points clear.*

➢ Step 2 – Choosing My Pattern of Development

Although the comparison between a society driven by competition and one where competition plays little or no role seems to hint that the Comparison-Contrast method should be used, the Definition pattern of development is a better fit because it is necessary to look at the qualities of *competition* that make it a positive influence rather than a negative one.

➢ Step 3 – Developing My Thesis

THESIS FOR DEFINITION ESSAY *(formula 1-3)*:

By definition, <u>competition</u> possesses these qualities: 1) <u>gives everyone the same chance at the beginning</u>, 2) <u>drives people to succeed</u>, 3) <u>provides a way to recognize people who advance</u> which have a positive effect because A) <u>no one can use the excuse that they didn't have the same opportunities; everyone has a chance to succeed</u>, B) <u>people want to be the best, and gives everyone their "place" in life</u>, C) <u>gives self-worth to those who are recognized for their accomplishments</u>.

➢ Step 4 – Understanding Counter Argument

DEFINITION *(formula 2-3)*:

By definition, some may feel that <u>competition helps only a few/pushing only a few to the top, leaving others feeling left out or insignificant</u> which could be positive or **negative**.
(Note that this point should contrast directly with point #1 of your thesis. (see *formula 1-3*))

➢ Step 5 – Organizing My Thoughts

DEFINITION ESSAY FORMULA *(formula 3-3)*:

I. Introduction – Paragraph 1
    A. Competition benefits a society.
    B. Everyone is given a chance to succeed in a society where competition drives people to be the best and recognizes the accomplishments of the many who advance.
II. Support – Paragraph 2
    A. Some feel that competition helps only a few, leaving others feeling left out or insignificant. There is a push to eliminate salutatorian/valedictorian recognition speeches at graduation.
    B. Competition gives everyone the same chance at the beginning.
       1. Just like a marathon – everyone begins at the same starting line.
       2. No one has an excuse – it is up to each individual to decide how to run the race. Some want to work harder than others and therefore deserve recognition.
III. Competition drives people to be their best
    A. Everyone's "best" is different.
    B. Gives everyone their place in life – if no competition, we'd have a world full of custodians, no CEO's or vice versa.
IV. With competition comes the chance to recognize winners.
    A. Gives self-worth to those recognized, causing them to set even greater goals.
    B. Encourages those who were not recognized to try harder so that they too may be recognized.
V. Conclusion – Paragraph 5
    A. Competition is vital to a growing and thriving society.
    B. How will you run the race? Will you strive to be the best?

➢ Step 6 – Writing My Essay

On your mark! All the runners are at the starting line. *Get set!* The runners are poised, in position. *Go!* The runners take off. The spirit of competition is the driving force behind these runners' desire to win. And, as an integral part of a society, competition brings many benefits. Everyone is given a chance to succeed in a society where competition drives people to be their best, and competition recognizes the accomplishments of those who advance.

Some feel that, although competition recognizes winners, there are so few winners that many are left feeling insignificant and alienated. This attitude has, for example, lead to a movement to eliminate salutatorian and valedictorian recognition and speeches at graduation ceremonies. Those in the movement claim that acknowledging salutatorian and valedictorian students for their scholastic achievements causes other students to feel slighted. This is a misguided assumption. Government gives everyone equal opportunity to attend school and to excel. Some students work harder than others and deserve special honors at graduation. Just like in a race, everyone begins at the same starting line and therefore has the same chance to succeed. Each person makes his own decision about how he will run the race. No one has an excuse, then, for not trying his best to succeed.

Competition drives people to achieve a goal. For most, this goal represents a person's best. Since everyone's concept of "best" is different, achievement differs for each person. Therefore, when an individual reaches his goal, this gives him a certain status. This status is different for each person, depending on the goal that was attained. This is extremely important because if competition did not place people at different positions in life, the resulting equality would be stultifying to society. For example, the work force would consist of only custodians and no CEO's or vice versa.

CEO's get to where they are only through competition. As an employee works hard and competes within a company, he is rewarded for his accomplishments with promotions. Not only does competition award people through tangible benefits like promotions, but competition also gives long-lasting psychological awards such as a feeling of self-worth or pride. This recognition encourages people who succeed to raise their personal goals even higher. Recognition also drives those who were not recognized to do better so that they too may be rewarded.

Because competition results in rewards, both tangible and emotional, it is essential for a growing and thriving society. Everyone begins at the same starting line and is given the same chance to succeed. When the starting gun fires, it is up to each runner to decide how he will run the race. This decision will ultimately determine who will become the winners. Driven by competition, these winners, along with the losers, comprise a successful society.

> ➤ Step 7 – Revising My Essay

Read over the essay above and then answer the following questions:

- Is the introduction captivating? Why or why not? Do you recognize a certain method the author employed to make the introduction interesting?

- Is the thesis statement concise? Does it clearly show the purpose of the essay?

- Do the body paragraphs clearly support each point made in the thesis? If not, where does the essay lack necessary support?

- Are there logical transitions that make the text flow smoothly between sentences and between paragraphs? Underline each word, phrase or sentence that acts as a transition.

- Is the tone and diction consistent throughout the essay? If not, point out the places where consistency breaks down.

- Is the use of person consistent? If not, point out the places where consistency is not maintained.

- Is there a word, or are there words, which have been used too often in the essay? List these words. Also list the words that have been used to provide variety in the essay.

- Do the sentences vary in length and structure?

Practice

Now it's your turn to practice some Issue essays. Consider the five prompts and assignments below and write your responsive essays, making sure you follow the 7 steps we discussed.

Prompt:
Museums should have the liberty to exhibit whatever displays they want without the interference of government censorship.

Assignment:
Do you think the government should impose censorship on controversial museum displays, or should museums be permitted to display whatever they choose? Plan and write an essay in which you discuss your perspective on this type of censorship. Support your opinion with clear and persuasive evidence.

Prompt:
When people work in teams, they are more productive than when they work individually.

Assignment:
Do you think that people work more effectively in teams or by themselves? Explain your opinion in a well-developed essay. Support your perspective by drawing from personal experience and knowledge you have gained.

Prompt:
If everyone would closely examine their past, they would realize that only a few individuals have played a role in shaping their behavior and their way of thinking.

Assignment:
Do you think your behavior and way of thinking was shaped by merely a few people, or were you impacted by many others? Thinking about your own personal experiences, plan and write an essay in which you discuss your perspective on the shaping of behavior.

Prompt:
Success is easily obtained but difficult to maintain.

Assignment:
In your opinion, is it easy or difficult to obtain success? Along the same lines, do you think that, once obtained, success is easy or difficult to maintain? Plan and write an essay in which you develop your opinion about success. Support your perspective by providing concise evidence.

Prompt:
Society is governed by two types of laws, just and unjust. People must obey just laws but are at liberty to defy those laws which they determine are frivolous or unjust.

Assignment:
Do you agree that some laws are just while others are unjust? Moreover, if you do agree with this statement, do you feel that people need only obey those laws which they deem just? Discuss your opinion about the justice of laws. Provide concrete and persuasive support for your opinion.

More Sample Issue Essays

Prompt:
There is little need for books today because one can learn just as much or more from television.

Assignment:
Do you think that television is a good replacement for books? Plan and write an essay in which you discuss your opinion on the relevance of books in today's world. Make sure you support your opinion by drawing on your experiences and knowledge.

When I was little, I would line up my stuffed animals and "read" to them. Although I was not old enough to know the letters formed words and the words formed sentences, I knew there was a story to tell, and I knew there was an audience who would be interested in hearing the story. Now I watch my two-year-old daughter do the same thing. In this media age, books often take a back seat to television, which is unfortunate because books offer so much more. Books are a better tool with which to build imagination. Moreover, readers can gain much more knowledge from the wide variety of books that are available.

Satellite dishes and improved cable offer hundreds of channels, a variety that some TV viewers argue is sufficient to replace reading. However, libraries and bookstores offer thousands, not hundreds, of titles from which to choose. Among these choices, a reader can find books on any theme he chooses, from topics of today to stories of every era in the past. Television, unfortunately, is controlled mostly by popular trends. Aside from a handful of specialty channels like *The History Channel*, there is little on TV about historical events. Furthermore, TV viewers' choices are limited since the television broadcasting companies choose what they will offer on each channel.

A limited choice of TV channels results in limited knowledge. The written word offers much more detail than television. Most TV shows are limited to two hours or less, and because of this time restriction, fewer details can be included in shows like movies and documentaries. For example, a TV documentary on orangutans would most likely be a one hour program which would offer some basic knowledge about orangutans, their habitat and their way of life. A book about orangutans, on the other hand, would educate the reader far beyond the basic knowledge he would gain from watching a television program.

In addition to offering more information on a greater number of subjects, the added description included in books helps readers improve vocabulary. In books, readers see unfamiliar words in context, enabling them to decipher the meaning. For TV viewers, unfamiliar words in conversation usually go unnoticed. In fact, many people watch TV simply to "veg," or, in other words, to sit and do nothing but be vaguely aware of the images flickering across the screen. Watching television requires little of the concentration that is required for reading books; consequently the viewer overlooks many details.

Because watching TV does not require active participation, the imagination suffers. Television programs take the viewer quickly from one scene to the next, prohibiting the viewer from taking notice of the details of the setting. Books inspire imagination, allowing the reader to picture for herself the setting and characters of the story. A book's character may be described as tall, dark complected, and wearing a bright purple robe; it is up to the reader to imagine exactly what the character looks like. Is the character Italian or perhaps Native American? Is the bright purple robe rather gaudy looking, or does it give the character an air of sophistication? Television makes those decisions for the viewer by placing in the program a specific actor in garb chosen by costume designers, thus leaving little room for imagination.

Imagination is the key to forward thinking, thinking that brings a person success in what he does. Without imagination, problems go unsolved and new and inventive ideas never make it to the drawing board. Imagination produces creativity, which inspires dreamers. I hope my daughter will continue to be a dreamer, allowing her imagination to blossom. And when the letters, then words, then sentences take form for her, she will have the added benefit of gaining boundless knowledge from books.

Prompt:
Many of today's technological conveniences were developed to save time. Ironically, these developments have created an even more hurried, fast-paced society, where people actually have less leisure time.

Assignment:
Do you think modern technological advances have resulted in a less relaxed society? Develop an essay in which you give your perspective on the effects of modern conveniences on today's society. Pull from your own experiences to persuasively support your opinion.

Ah, the good ol' days! When people sat on their front porch talking and watching the world go by instead of finishing up last-minute work on their laptops. When letters took a week to spread the latest news instead of a few seconds through e-mail. In a world of pagers, faxes, cell phones, and computers, a very hurried society is characterized by impatient workaholics whose nerves are on edge and whose lives are unknowingly empty.

Many of today's conveniences were developed to meet growing impatience with the speed it took to spread information. Through the development of such things as faxes, cell phones and e-mail, however, a new impatience was born. This new impatience is characterized by frustration with the sophistication and complexity of modern technology. Office workers grit their teeth in frustration when an e-mail takes too long to download. In annoyance, they may shut down their computer assuming there is something wrong with the machine. This wastes even more time while restarting the computer and finally retrieving the culprit e-mail. Overnight delivery services emerged to meet this all-consuming impatience as well. Oftentimes, however, even this speedy service is not expedient enough. Some find it necessary to rush a package to the airport so that it may arrive at its destination just a few hours earlier.

This annoyance with our more efficient world has thrown society into a frenzy where even the most technologically advanced equipment is unsatisfactorily slow. The resulting annoyance and impatience can turn into rage in the office and on the highway, with stressed out employees who "go postal," losing all rationale and even causing injury to colleagues. Preventable injuries occur on highways as road rage consumes drivers who are eager to get to their next destination.

In a world where people are eager to pass information ever more quickly and get to their next destination ever more quickly, this has truly become a society of workaholics. Because the transfer of information is so much more efficient with modern technologies, workers find they can accomplish much more in a given day. Driven by this fact, they work more hours. There is always time to make that last call or send a quick e-mail at the end of the day. And portable conveniences like laptops and palm pilots make it possible for people to work essentially anywhere; work is no longer confined to the office and is often completed at home.

Perhaps the most detrimental aspect of our more hurried society lies at home. Because many people spend more time working, and because work is transportable, many spouses discover that their partners spend more time with their computers and cell phones than with their family. Additionally, other conveniences like microwave meals encourage quick meals on-the-go. Rushed families rarely spend quality time together around the dinner table. Rather, they all go their separate ways to eat in front of the TV, at the computer, or at a desk reviewing reports.

At home, in the office and on the streets, a fast-paced society continues to become more hurried as technology continues to match a perpetually growing impatience. Is all of this annoyance, frustration, and rage worth the added convenience that technology has brought to our society? It hardly seems so. In fact, in looking back at the good 'ol days, it seems that in a world with far less vexation and anger, there was more happiness.

Prompt:
Character is created in a crisis.

Assignment:
Do you think character is created in a crisis or merely manifested? Plan and write an essay in which you define your opinion. Make sure you provide clear support for your answer.

In 1992, Hurricane Andrew slammed into Florida causing millions of dollars of damage. Many residents lost everything, including their homes. Those houses that had the strongest foundations withstood the storm most favorably. Additionally, the homes that had been adequately prepared to face the storm fared better than those whose windows were not boarded. Character is like a house. If your character has a strong foundation and displays traits of preparedness, you can weather a storm well. In this light, it is clear that character is not born from crisis, but rather, it merely emerges during difficult times.

It is not adversity but the small moments of life that create character. Poor decisions, regardless of how insignificant, break down your character. Anytime you are inconsistent in following your principles, no matter how small the compromise, cracks in your foundation undoubtedly weaken your character. On the positive side, though, you can learn a lot from your mistakes. In fact, lessons learned from failures are indispensable in building character. To discern the lesson to be learned, however, takes conscious effort. If you are unwilling to put effort into developing character, you will continue to repeat your mistakes, and your life will stagnate.

Part of building character and thus avoiding stagnation is building on your strengths. Taking what is good and making it exceptional is what character building is all about. Continued improvement in life makes you stronger. This too takes a conscious effort in using strengths to positively affect others around you. Channeling the positive to help others results in personal growth, which in turn builds character.

Only when you are willing to learn from your mistakes and make a conscious effort to grow can you face a crisis successfully. It is during this adversity that character comes to light. If you have learned from past failures, you will have the strength to face a crisis head on. You will have adequate problem-solving skills to overcome obstacles set before you. If you have made the conscious effort to build on your positive traits, you will have the means with which to get through the crisis positively with the will to move ahead.

The will and ability to move forward from crisis is the defining moment of your character. As you move forward, though, you should never stop working to improve, because the stronger your foundation is, the better it will weather any type of storm. What kind of storm can the foundation of your character withstand?

Prompt:
People should pursue careers that provide financial security even if they do not enjoy the work.

Assignment:
Should people make financial gain their main criteria for a career choice, or should personal satisfaction play a large role as well? Develop an essay in which you discuss your perspective about choosing a career. Make sure you support your answer with strong evidence.

"I want to be a fireman when I grow up!" A simple dream from a young child in response to the question every youngster faces at one point or another: What do you want to be when you grow up? The innocence of a child, however, protects him from the world of finances, something everyone is forced to face later on in life. And when that realization hits, what path is best for a person to take: the path that leads to a career with large financial promises, or the one that leads to a career that provides more personal satisfaction? Because contentment has so many rewards, it is better for a person to choose the job that will provide happiness even if it does not pay as well as other jobs.

Some people find it necessary to get the best paying job to make financial ends meet. Often someone in financial dire straits will stick with a good paying job just long enough to get ahead and then, because they are unhappy at the job, they quit to find work elsewhere. This has several negative effects. First, the transition to a new job is difficult, and it can be made worse for a new employee if they are followed by negativity. Company officers are reluctant to invest training time and money in employees only to have them leave after a short time and therefore may not be willing to provide favorable references. Second, workers who leave jobs after short periods of time are not with a company long enough to advance within the company. These workers may find that they would have done just as well to begin in a job that they like even if it did not pay as well, because by the time they start all over, they could have already been promoted. The increase in salary that comes with most promotions could equal the wages they were earning at the job they did not enjoy.

The potential for promotion should be a major consideration when deciding between the high paying job and the job that provides satisfaction. Employees in positions they do not enjoy often work with a poor attitude. This promotes laziness and apathy. Managers quickly pick up on this and likely pass up these types of employees for promotions. On the other hand, workers who enjoy their job greet each workday with enthusiasm, fresh creativity and perseverance. Bosses commend this type of work ethic and reward such employees with promotions.

Careers that offer promotions and, most importantly, job satisfaction stimulate self-respect and pride. These characteristics are priceless and have an enormously positive impact on a person and their job performance. The employee who has pride in what he does takes ownership. He is empowered to take charge of the position he holds and give it 110 percent. This attitude has a domino effect and soon colleagues begin to take more pride in their work as well. Managers notice this natural leadership and reward it with promotions.

Taking pride in a job leads to success, not just monetarily, but also personally. Personal success and satisfaction far outweigh monetary gain. So if the little boy still wants to be a fireman when he grows up, he should be a fireman, even if it means he will live in a modest home instead of a mansion. He will never regret the happiness and contentment he will feel by following his dream instead of following the green.

Prompt:
Public figures should expect their private lives to be scrutinized.

Assignment:
Do you think public figures like actors and politicians should expect their personal lives to be exposed? Why do you think there is so much interest in the private lives of the rich and famous? Discuss your opinion on this subject. Support your answer. You may provide some support by using examples from current or past events.

Television shows, newspapers, books, magazines and tabloids delve into the lives of singers, actors, athletes and politicians on a daily basis. Should these public figures expect to lose some of their privacy? Whether they want to or not, people who are in positions that will sometimes place them in the spotlight open themselves to scrutiny from their audience, because people have a natural curiosity and interest in those who have achieved fame.

Although public figures should expect some scrutiny in their lives, there is a point where it can become dangerous. For example, it was reported in 1997 that the driver of Princess Diana's car was driving recklessly to get away from aggressive Paparazzi. As a result, the car spun out of control killing Diana. Other similar stories report stalkers and "Peeping Toms" who take too much liberty in examining the private lives of stars, athletes and politicians. While these are extreme cases of obsession, public figures must realize that there is a natural human desire to more intimately know the familiar faces on TV or on the sports field. This is especially true of actors and actresses. Television and movie viewers get to know their favorite characters on screen and therefore have a desire to "get to know" the actors behind these characters.

Not only do people want to get to know those whom they look up to, but they also strive to be like their favorite stars. Ads on TV encourage viewers to "Be like Mike [Michael Jordan]." On Halloween, teenage girls can emulate their favorite pop singer by obtaining a Britney Spears costume. Although many people admittedly would not choose a life of glamour and fame, there is something alluring about the lifestyle, and therefore admirers of people in the limelight are driven to discover personal facts about those whom they admire. Knowing these intimate details makes a famous person seem more down-to-earth and thus allows the ordinary person to feel like they have something in common with the rich and famous.

The media makes a concerted effort to give viewers a chance to become acquainted with public figures. They splash familiar stars' faces on the cover of magazines. Channels like *E!* and *VH1* feature behind the scenes stories about singers and actors, their highs and lows and how they became famous. Tabloids are a huge business supported by readers who hungrily devour the latest gossip about their favorite star. Even the news capitalizes on human interest stories that feature public figures. For example, although long and drawn-out, OJ Simpson's murder trial dominated the news, yet no one seemed to complain.

The news often highlights human interest stories that uncover the blunders of politicians. Former President Clinton's escapades with Monica Lewinsky, for example, made headlines for months. Many public figures, especially politicians, anticipate the scrutinizing eye under which they will find themselves and proactively confess to past mistakes. This takes some of the media pressure off them. Sadly, others find themselves on the front cover of every magazine and newspaper and in every headline when marital infidelity or an encounter with drugs is exposed.

Politicians are of deep interest to the public because they are the nation's leaders. Since people must place some trust in political figures to run the country effectively, politicians should expect their private lives to be examined. Not only should they expect ordinary citizens to dig into their lives, but they should also anticipate other political figures to look closely at their lives. Political campaigns, unfortunately, often focus on tearing apart the opponent. To do this, a politician must find a way to attack his opponent, which requires investigating the personal life of the candidate. This comes with the territory. If a would-be politician cannot stomach having some negative aspect of his life exposed, he should not enter the world of politics.

Although many people work hard to achieve the fame of a popular singer, actor, athlete, or politician, some become bitterly disenchanted with the lifestyle when they realize they may lose much of their privacy. This should certainly be a matter of consideration before pursuing any career that places a person in the spotlight. It is, after all, natural that admirers will be interested in the details of the life of public figures. Public figures should consider this admiration flattery rather than an intrusion on their privacy.

Prompt:
It is necessary for a leader to compromise his principles if compromising them is favorable to a greater number of people.

Assignment:
In order to be in step with the majority, do you think a leader must sometimes compromise his principles? Discuss your perspective on leadership, pulling from your personal experience and knowledge for support.

This nation has seen many outstanding leaders, like George Washington and Abraham Lincoln. Have you ever wondered what separates great leaders from ineffective leaders? Contrary to popular belief, great leaders are not born. Rather, if you want to be an effective leader, you must realize that it takes a lot of work and perseverance. Furthermore, of all the character traits that can be cultivated to make a good leader, the ability to stick to your principles is the most important; to be a great leader, you should never compromise your principles, no matter how high the price.

As a leader, you may sometimes pay a price by losing favor with the majority because of a decision you have made. At these times, it may be tempting for you to give in to the demands of your followers. However, remember that, regardless of the capacity in which you lead, you are in a position of leadership because there are people who thought your ideas were good, and therefore they made a conscious decision to follow you. Knowing this, you should be encouraged to stick to your decisions since, in the end, even if your followers still disagree with your decision, they will respect you for standing firm on your principles. If you possess honor in your word, your followers will entrust you with more responsibility knowing that, since you did not compromise your beliefs in one decision, you are not likely to go back on your word in other situations.

As followers take note that you refuse to give in by compromising your principles, they will come to the realization that they made an excellent choice in a leader, and they will gain a deeper respect for you as their leader. As people gain new respect for you, they will be more willing to follow you in all of your decisions, even if they do not fully agree with all of them. This type of respect is important for your leadership because it creates an atmosphere conducive to cooperation and teamwork. In this cooperative environment, your followers will be willing to step up and take on some of the responsibility if they believe in you and what you stand for.

With you as their guide, your team's confidence will grow. As their confidence grows, your self-confidence will flourish. A confident leader is much more effective than one who is unsure of himself. If you do not portray confidence in what you do, others will not feel confident in your decisions either. Moreover, if you lack confidence in your ability as a leader, you will likely at some point give in to others' wishes over your own principles. Your followers will perceive you as weak and will recede from your leadership. If you believe in yourself, however, you will benefit from lifelong supporters who respect your confidence and the consistency of your principles.

Unwillingness to compromise principles breeds the stalwart leader within you. Becoming an effective leader requires this confidence in the actions that you take and the decisions that you make. The respect you will earn by standing firm in what you believe will take your leadership farther than you ever thought possible.

Prompt:
Parents must be involved in their children's education in order to make them successful.

Assignment:
How integral is parental involvement in a child's education? Plan and write an essay in which you discuss the effects of a parent's involvement in his or her child's education. Make sure you provide ample support for your opinion.

Sally is a Sophomore in high school. Although she is a bright girl and has the potential to excel in school, she lacks the ability to apply herself and therefore is not doing well. As a result, she does not enjoy school and often cuts classes to hang out at the mall with friends who share her same ethic. Sally enjoys athletics and earned a spot on the Girls' Softball team. She competed in six matches, but when progress reports were issued, she was forced to leave the team because her grades were not up to par. Sally's father is a lawyer and often works so late, the family rarely sees him. Sally's mother works in an office, but after work, she enjoys going out with her colleagues. Often, Sally is on her own when she gets home and must prepare dinner for herself and her 12-year-old sister. Sally's parents have missed countless parent-teacher conferences and have yet to meet most of her teachers. They are aware of only one instance of Sally's truancy; usually she gets home in time to erase the school's message from the answering machine. When her parents heard about her "first" unexcused absence from school, they did nothing but tell her not to do it again.

Tommy is also a Sophomore. He is intelligent and works hard to obtain near-perfect grades. He enjoys school and enthusiastically participates in all of his classes. Tommy is the goalie on the Boys' Soccer team and can be depended upon to maintain his important position on the team. Tommy's parents are divorced, and Tommy and his twin 10-year-old brothers live with their mother. She works in an office and gets home promptly by 5:30. Although she must rely on Tommy to watch the twins after school, she always prepares dinner when she gets home. After dinner, Tommy and his brothers must finish their homework before they are permitted to do anything else. Tommy's mom checks everyone's homework when they are done and helps them with work they do not understand. Although Tommy's father lives an hour away, he often meets Tommy's mother for parent-teacher conferences, and he consistently makes it to Tommy's games. Tommy has never considered skipping school because he knows the consequences at home would be great.

Two students, two very different results at school and two opposite attitudes about life. The difference? Parental involvement. Although teachers can equip a student with the tools he needs to succeed in life, it is up to parents to instill in their children the motivation and determination to use these tools to be successful. To do this, parents must be willing to be involved in every aspect of their children's lives, particularly in their education. It is unfair for parents to expect teachers and school administrators to take sole responsibility for the complete education and training that prepares a student for his adult life.

Some parents feel inadequate to help their children in school because they are unfamiliar with their children's school subjects, or because they did not do well in school themselves. No matter how little academic knowledge parents have, however, they can play an integral part in her child's education. For example, there are many opportunities to volunteer in schools. Parents can become a part of the school's Parent-Teacher Association or Parent-Teacher-Student Organization. Parents can help with sports' teams or at the very least, make an effort to support the athletes by coming to the games. If parents' jobs hinder them from attending school functions, they can play an important role at home by keeping their children accountable in school matters like homework. They can help their children with things the children do not understand or get a tutor if they do not understand it either.

Although parents cannot always help a child scholastically, they can teach their children lifelong lessons in motivation and determination. If a man wants to learn how to fish, he can obtain a net and a boat and learn how to cast the net. But he is not a fisherman simply because he has the right tools and knowledge. Someone must instill in him the motivation and determination to sit on a boat day after day performing the tedious task of casting a net that does not always produce a big catch. In the same way, a teacher can give their students the book knowledge they need to be experts in various fields; however, it is the parents who must empower their children to use the knowledge to be successful. This requires parents to teach their children the value of education and thus inspire motivation; parents must teach their children never to give up and thus inspire determination.

Only motivated learners have the determination to gain the knowledge and responsibility that will enable them to succeed in life. It is the responsibility of parents to instill in their children these qualities. One of the most effective ways parents can teach their children the importance of such qualities is by modeling them in their own lives. Parents should make an effort to model responsibility through motivation and determination in their own lives. Such examples provide the best lessons a student will ever learn.

Part Three
MATH

MATH

- **INTRODUCTION**
- **SUBSTITUTION**
- **DEFINED FUNCTIONS**
- **FUNCTIONS**
- **MATH NOTES**
- **NUMBER THEORY**
- **GEOMETRY**
- **COORDINATE GEOMETRY**
- **ELIMINATION STRATEGIES**
- **INEQUALITIES**
- **FRACTIONS & DECIMALS**
- **EQUATIONS**
- **AVERAGES**
- **RATIO & PROPORTION**
- **EXPONENTS & ROOTS**
- **FACTORING**
- **ALGEBRAIC EXPRESSIONS**
- **PERCENTS**
- **GRAPHS**
- **WORD PROBLEMS**
- **SEQUENCES & SERIES**
- **COUNTING**
- **PROBABILITY & STATISTICS**
- **MISCELLANEOUS PROBLEMS**
- **GRID-INS**
- **SUMMARY OF MATH PROPERTIES**
- **DIAGNOSTIC/REVIEW MATH TEST**

Format of the Math Sections

The Math sections include two types of questions: *Multiple-choice* and *Grid-ins*. They are designed to test your ability to solve problems, not to test your mathematical knowledge. The questions in each sub-section are listed in ascending order of difficulty. So, if a section begins with 8 multiple-choice questions followed by 10 grid-ins, then Question 1 will be the easiest multiple-choice question and Question 8 will be the hardest. Then Question 9 will be the easiest grid-in question and Question 18 will be the hardest. There will be two 25-minute math sections and one 20-minute section. The sections can appear anywhere in the test.

Level of Difficulty

The mathematical skills tested on the SAT are basic: only first year algebra, geometry (no proofs), and a few basic concepts from second year algebra. However, this does not mean that the math section is easy. The medium of basic mathematics is chosen so that everyone taking the test will be on a fairly even playing field. This way students who are concentrating in math and science don't have an undue advantage over students who are concentrating in English and humanities. Although the questions require only basic mathematics and **all** have **simple** solutions, it can require considerable ingenuity to find the simple solution. If you have taken a course in calculus or another advanced math course, don't assume that you will find the math section easy. Other than increasing your mathematical maturity, little you learned in calculus will help on the SAT.

As mentioned above, every SAT math problem has a simple solution, but finding that simple solution may not be easy. The intent of the math section is to test how skilled you are at finding the simple solutions. The premise is that if you spend a lot of time working out long solutions you will not finish as much of the test as students who spot the short, simple solutions. So if you find yourself performing long calculations or applying advanced mathematics—stop. You're heading in the wrong direction.

Tackle the math problems in the order given, and don't worry if you fail to reach the last few questions. It's better to work accurately than quickly.

You may bring a calculator to the test, but all questions can be answered without using a calculator. Be careful not to overuse the calculator; it can slow you down.

To insure that you perform at your expected level on the actual SAT, you need to develop a level of mathematical skill that is greater than what is tested on the SAT. Hence, about 10% of the math problems in this book are harder than actual SAT math problems.

Directions and Reference Material

Be sure you understand the directions below so that you do not need to read or interpret them during the test.

Directions

Solve each problem and decide which one of the choices given is best. Fill in the corresponding circle on your answer sheet. You can use any available space for scratchwork.

Notes

1. All numbers used are real numbers.
2. Figures are drawn as accurately as possible EXCEPT when it is stated that the figure is not drawn to scale. All figures lie in a plane unless otherwise indicated.
3. Unless otherwise stated, the domain of a function f should be assumed to be the set of all real numbers x for which $f(x)$ is real number.

Note 1 indicates that complex numbers, $i = \sqrt{-1}$, do not appear on the test.

Note 2 indicates that figures are drawn accurately. Hence, you can check your work and in some cases even solve a problem by "eyeballing" the figure. We'll discuss this technique in detail later. If a drawing is labeled "Figure not drawn to scale," then the drawing is not accurate. In this case, an angle that appears to be 90° may not be or an object that appears congruent to another object may not be. The statement "All figures lie in a plane unless otherwise indicated" indicates that two-dimensional figures do not represent three-dimensional objects. That is, the drawing of a circle is not representing a sphere, and the drawing of a square is not representing a cube.

Note 3 indicates that both the domain and range of a function consist of real numbers, not complex numbers. It also indicates that function is defined only on its domain. This allows us to avoid stating the domain each time a function is presented. For example, in the function $f(x) = \dfrac{1}{x-4}$, we do not need to state that the 4 is not part of the domain since $f(4) = \dfrac{1}{4-4} = \dfrac{1}{0}$ is undefined. The expression $\dfrac{1}{0}$ is not a real number; it does not even exist.

Reference Information

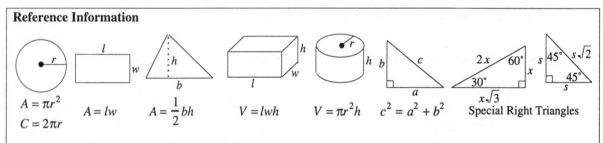

$A = \pi r^2$
$C = 2\pi r$

$A = lw$

$A = \dfrac{1}{2}bh$

$V = lwh$

$V = \pi r^2 h$

$c^2 = a^2 + b^2$

Special Right Triangles

The number of degrees of arc in a circle is 360.
The sum of the measures in degrees of the angles of a triangle is 180.

Although this reference material can be handy, be sure you know it well so that you do not waste time looking it up during the test.

Substitution

Substitution is a very useful technique for solving SAT math problems. It often reduces hard problems to routine ones. In the substitution method, we choose numbers that have the properties given in the problem and plug them into the answer-choices. A few examples will illustrate.

Example 1:   If n is an odd integer, which one of the following is an even integer?

(A) n^3

(B) $\dfrac{n}{4}$

(C) $2n + 3$

(D) $n(n + 3)$

(E) $\sqrt{n}$

We are told that n is an odd integer. So choose an odd integer for n, say, 1 and substitute it into each answer-choice. Now, n^3 becomes $1^3 = 1$, which is not an even integer. So eliminate (A). Next, $\dfrac{n}{4} = \dfrac{1}{4}$ is not an even integer—eliminate (B). Next, $2n + 3 = 2 \cdot 1 + 3 = 5$ is not an even integer—eliminate (C). Next, $n(n + 3) = 1(1 + 3) = 4$ is even and hence the answer is possibly (D). Finally, $\sqrt{n} = \sqrt{1} = 1$, which is not even—eliminate (E). The answer is (D).

• When using the substitution method, be sure to check every answer-choice because the number you choose may work for more than one answer-choice. If this does occur, then choose another number and plug it in, and so on, until you have eliminated all but the answer. This may sound like a lot of computing, but the calculations can usually be done in a few seconds.

Example 2:   If n is an integer, which of the following CANNOT be an even integer?

(A) $2n + 2$
(B) $n - 5$
(C) $2n$
(D) $2n + 3$
(E) $5n + 2$

Choose n to be 1. Then $2n + 2 = 2(1) + 2 = 4$, which is even. So eliminate (A). Next, $n - 5 = 1 - 5 = -4$. Eliminate (B). Next, $2n = 2(1) = 2$. Eliminate (C). Next, $2n + 3 = 2(1) + 3 = 5$ is not even—it *may* be our answer. However, $5n + 2 = 5(1) + 2 = 7$ is not even as well. So we choose another number, say, 2. Then $5n + 2 = 5(2) + 2 = 12$ is even, which eliminates (E). Thus, choice (D), $2n + 3$, is the answer.

Example 3:   If $\dfrac{x}{y}$ is a fraction greater than 1, then which of the following must be less than 1?

(A) $\dfrac{3y}{x}$ (B) $\dfrac{x}{3y}$ (C) $\sqrt{\dfrac{x}{y}}$ (D) $\dfrac{y}{x}$ (E) y

We must choose x and y so that $\dfrac{x}{y} > 1$. So choose $x = 3$ and $y = 2$. Now, $\dfrac{3y}{x} = \dfrac{3 \cdot 2}{3} = 2$ is greater than 1, so eliminate (A). Next, $\dfrac{x}{3y} = \dfrac{3}{3 \cdot 2} = \dfrac{1}{2}$, which is less than 1—it may be our answer. Next, $\sqrt{\dfrac{x}{y}} = \sqrt{\dfrac{3}{2}} > 1$; eliminate (C). Now, $\dfrac{y}{x} = \dfrac{2}{3} < 1$. So it too may be our answer. Next, $y = 2 > 1$; eliminate (E). Hence, we must decide between answer-choices (B) and (D). Let $x = 6$ and $y = 2$. Then $\dfrac{x}{3y} = \dfrac{6}{3 \cdot 2} = 1$, which eliminates (B). Therefore, the answer is (D).

Problem Set A:

Solve the following problems by using substitution. Solutions begin on page 521.

1. If n is an odd integer, which of the following must be an even integer?

    (A) $\dfrac{n}{2}$
    (B) $4n + 3$
    (C) $2n$
    (D) n^4
    (E) $\sqrt{n}$

2. If x and y are perfect squares, then which of the following is <u>not</u> necessarily a perfect square?

    (A) x^2
    (B) xy
    (C) $4x$
    (D) $x + y$
    (E) x^5

3. If y is an even integer and x is an odd integer, which of the following expressions could be an even integer?

    (A) $3x + \dfrac{y}{2}$
    (B) $\dfrac{x + y}{2}$
    (C) $x + y$
    (D) $\dfrac{x}{4} - \dfrac{y}{2}$
    (E) $x^2 + y^2$

4. If $0 < k < 1$, then which of the following must be less than k?

    (A) $\dfrac{3}{2}k$
    (B) $\dfrac{1}{k}$
    (C) $|k|$
    (D) $\sqrt{k}$
    (E) k^2

5. Suppose you begin reading a book on page h and end on page k. If you read each page completely and the pages are numbered and read consecutively, then how many pages have you read?

    (A) $h + k$
    (B) $h - k$
    (C) $k - h + 2$
    (D) $k - h - 1$
    (E) $k - h + 1$

6. If m is an even integer, then which of the following is the sum of the next two even integers greater than $4m + 1$?

    (A) $8m + 2$
    (B) $8m + 4$
    (C) $8m + 6$
    (D) $8m + 8$
    (E) $8m + 10$

7. If x^2 is even, which of the following must be true?

    I. x is odd.
    II. x is even.
    III. x^3 is odd.

    (A) I only
    (B) II only
    (C) III only
    (D) I and II only
    (E) II and III only

8. Suppose x is divisible by 8 but not by 3. Then which of the following CANNOT be an integer?

    (A) $\dfrac{x}{2}$

    (B) $\dfrac{x}{4}$

    (C) $\dfrac{x}{6}$

    (D) $\dfrac{x}{8}$

    (E) x

9. If p and q are positive integers, how many integers are larger than pq and smaller than $p(q + 2)$?

    (A) 3
    (B) $p + 2$
    (C) $p - 2$
    (D) $2p - 1$
    (E) $2p + 1$

10. If x and y are prime numbers, then which one of the following cannot equal $x - y$?

    (A) 1
    (B) 2
    (C) 13
    (D) 14
    (E) 20

11. If x is an integer, then which of the following is the product of the next two integers greater than $2(x + 1)$?

    (A) $4x^2 + 14x + 12$
    (B) $4x^2 + 12$
    (C) $x^2 + 14x + 12$
    (D) $x^2 + x + 12$
    (E) $4x^2 + 14x$

12. If the integer x is divisible by 3 but not by 2, then which one of the following expressions is NEVER an integer?

    (A) $\dfrac{x+1}{2}$

    (B) $\dfrac{x}{7}$

    (C) $\dfrac{x^2}{3}$

    (D) $\dfrac{x^3}{3}$

    (E) $\dfrac{x}{24}$

13. If both x and y are positive even integers, then which of the following expressions must also be even?

    I. y^{x-1}

    II. $y - 1$

    III. $\dfrac{x}{2}$

    (A) I only
    (B) II only
    (C) III only
    (D) I and III only
    (E) I, II, and III

14. Which one of the following is a solution to the equation $x^4 - 2x^2 = -1$?

    (A) 0
    (B) 1
    (C) 2
    (D) 3
    (E) 4

15. If $x \neq \dfrac{3}{4}$, which one of the following will equal -2 when multiplied by $\dfrac{3 - 4x}{5}$?

    (A) $\dfrac{5 - 4x}{4}$

    (B) $\dfrac{10}{3 - 4x}$

    (C) $\dfrac{10}{4x - 3}$

    (D) $\dfrac{3 - 4x}{5}$

    (E) $\dfrac{4x - 3}{10}$

Substitution (Plugging In): Sometimes instead of making up numbers to substitute into the problem, we can use the actual answer-choices. This is called "Plugging In." It is a very effective technique, but not as common as Substitution.

Example 1:   The digits of a three-digit number add up to 18. If the ten's digit is twice the hundred's digit and the hundred's digit is 1/3 the unit's digit, what is the number?

        (A)   246
        (B)   369
        (C)   531
        (D)   855
        (E)   893

First, check to see which of the answer-choices has a sum of digits equal to 18. For choice (A), $2 + 4 + 6 \neq$ 18. Eliminate. For choice (B), $3 + 6 + 9 = 18$. This may be the answer. For choice (C), $5 + 3 + 1 \neq 18$. Eliminate. For choice (D), $8 + 5 + 5 = 18$. This too may be the answer. For choice (E), $8 + 9 + 3 \neq 18$. Eliminate. Now, in choice (D), the ten's digit is <u>not</u> twice the hundred's digit, $5 \neq 2 \cdot 8$. Eliminate. Hence, by process of elimination, the answer is (B). Note that we did not need the fact that the hundred's digit is 1/3 the unit's digit.

Problem Set B:

Use the method of Plugging In to solve the following problems. Solutions begin on page 523.

1.   The ten's digit of a two-digit number is twice the unit's digit. Reversing the digits yields a new number that is 27 less than the original number. Which one of the following is the original number?

        (A)   12
        (B)   21
        (C)   43
        (D)   63
        (E)   83

2.   If $\dfrac{N+N}{N^2} = 1$, then $N =$

        (A) $\dfrac{1}{6}$

        (B) $\dfrac{1}{3}$

        (C)   1
        (D)   2
        (E)   3

3.   Suppose half the people on a bus exit at each stop and no additional passengers board the bus. If on the third stop the next to last person exits the bus, then how many people were on the bus?

        (A)   20
        (B)   16
        (C)   8
        (D)   6
        (E)   4

4.   The sum of the digits of a two-digit number is 12, and the ten's digit is one-third the unit's digit. What is the number?

        (A)   93
        (B)   54
        (C)   48
        (D)   39
        (E)   31

5.   If $\dfrac{x^6 - 5x^3 - 16}{8} = 1$, then x could be

        (A)   1
        (B)   2
        (C)   3
        (D)   5
        (E)   8

6.   Which one of the following is a solution to the equation $x^4 - 2x^2 = -1$?

        (A)   0
        (B)   1
        (C)   2
        (D)   3
        (E)   4

Defined Functions

Defined functions are very common on the SAT, and at first most students struggle with them. Yet once you get used to them, defined functions can be some of the easiest problems on the test. In this type of problem, you will be given a symbol and a property that defines the symbol. Some examples will illustrate.

Example 1: Define $x \nabla y$ by the equation $x \nabla y = xy - y$. Then $2 \nabla 3 =$

(A) 1 (B) 3 (C) 12 (D) 15 (E) 18

From the above definition, we know that $x \nabla y = xy - y$. So all we have to do is replace x with 2 and y with 3 in the definition: $2 \nabla 3 = 2 \cdot 3 - 3 = 3$. Hence, the answer is (B).

Example 2: If $a \Delta b$ is defined to be a^2, then what is the value of $\dfrac{z \Delta 2}{z \Delta 3}$?

(A) 2/3 (B) 1 (C) 3/2 (D) 2 (E) 3

Most students who are unfamiliar with defined functions are unable to solve this problem. Yet it is actually quite easy. By the definition above, Δ merely squares the first term. So $z \Delta 2 = z^2$, and $z \Delta 3 = z^2$. Forming the fraction yields $\dfrac{z \Delta 2}{z \Delta 3} = \dfrac{z^2}{z^2} = 1$. Hence, the answer is (B).

Example 3: If x is a positive integer, define: $\boxed{x} = \sqrt{x}$, if x is even;

$\boxed{x} = 4x$, if x is odd.

If k is a positive integer, which of the following equals $\boxed{2k-1}$?

(A) $\sqrt{2k-1}$
(B) $k-1$
(C) $8k-4$
(D) $\sqrt{8k-4}$
(E) $8k-1$

First, we must determine whether $2k - 1$ is odd or even. (It cannot be both—why?) To this end, let $k = 1$. Then $2k - 1 = 2 \cdot 1 - 1 = 1$, which is an odd number. Therefore, we use the bottom-half of the definition given above. That is, $\boxed{2k-1} = 4(2k - 1) = 8k - 4$. The answer is (C).

You may be wondering how defined functions differ from the functions, $f(x)$, you studied in Intermediate Algebra and more advanced math courses. They *don't* differ. They are the same old concept you dealt with in your math classes. The function in Example 3 could just as easily be written $f(x) = \sqrt{x}$ and $f(x) = 4x$. The purpose of defined functions is to see how well you can adapt to unusual structures. Once you realize that defined functions are evaluated and manipulated just as regular functions, they become much less daunting.

Example 4: Define $x*$ by the equation $x* = \pi - x$. Then $((-\pi)*)* =$

(A) -2π (B) -1 (C) $-\pi$ (D) 2π (E) 4π

Working from the inner parentheses out, we get

$$((-\pi)*)* = (\pi - (-\pi))* = (\pi + \pi)* = (2\pi)* = \pi - 2\pi = -\pi.$$

Hence, the answer is (C).

Method II: We can rewrite this problem using ordinary function notation. Replacing the odd symbol $x*$ with $f(x)$ gives $f(x) = \pi - x$. Now, the expression $((-\pi)*)*$ becomes the ordinary composite function $f(f(-\pi)) = f(\pi - (-\pi)) = f(\pi + \pi) = f(2\pi) = \pi - 2\pi = -\pi$.

Example 5: If x is an integer, define: $\boxed{x} = 5$, if x is odd;

$\boxed{x} = 10$, if x is even.

If u and v are integers, and both $3u$ and $7 - v$ are odd, then $\boxed{u} - \boxed{v} =$

(A) -5
(B) 0
(C) 5
(D) 10
(E) 15

Since $3u$ is odd, u is odd. (Proof: Suppose u were even, then $3u$ would be even as well. But we are given that $3u$ is odd. Hence, u must be odd.) Since $7 - v$ is odd, v must be even. (Proof: Suppose v were odd, then $7 - v$ would be even [the difference of two odd numbers is an even number]. But we are given that $7 - v$ is odd. Hence, v must be even.)

Since u is odd, the top part of the definition gives $\boxed{u} = 5$. Since v is even, the bottom part of the definition gives $\boxed{v} = 10$. Hence, $\boxed{u} - \boxed{v} = 5 - 10 = -5$. The answer is (A).

Example 6: For all real numbers a and b, where $a \cdot b \neq 0$, let $a \Diamond b = a^b$. Then which of the following must be true?

I. $a \Diamond b = b \Diamond a$

II. $(-a) \Diamond (-a) = \dfrac{(-1)^{-a}}{a^a}$

III. $(a \Diamond b) \Diamond c = a \Diamond (b \Diamond c)$

(A) I only
(B) II only
(C) III only
(D) I and II only
(E) II and III only

Statement I is false. For instance, $1 \Diamond 2 = 1^2 = 1$, but $2 \Diamond 1 = 2^1 = 2$. This eliminates (A) and (D). Statement II is true: $(-a) \Diamond (-a) = (-a)^{-a} = (-1 \cdot a)^{-a} = (-1)^{-a}(a)^{-a} = \dfrac{(-1)^{-a}}{a^a}$. This eliminates (C). Unfortunately, we have to check Statement III. It is false: $(2 \Diamond 2) \Diamond 3 = 2^2 \Diamond 3 = 4 \Diamond 3 = 4^3 = 64$ and $2 \Diamond (2 \Diamond 3) = 2 \Diamond 2^3 = 2 \Diamond 8 = 2^8 = 256$. This eliminates (E), and the answer is (B). Note: The expression $a \cdot b \neq 0$ insures that neither a nor b equals 0: if $a \cdot b = 0$, then either $a = 0$ or $b = 0$, or both. This prevents division by zero from occurring in the problem, otherwise if $a = 0$ and $b = -1$, then $0 \Diamond (-1) = 0^{-1} = \dfrac{1}{0}$.

Example 7: The operation @ is defined for all non-zero x and y by the equation $x @ y = x^y$. Then the expression $(x @ y) @ z$ is equal to

(A) x^{y^z}
(B) xyz
(C) $(xy)^z$
(D) $x^y z$
(E) $\left(x^y\right)^z$

$(x @ y) @ z = \left(x^y\right) @ z = \left(x^y\right)^z$. Hence, the answer is (E). Note, though it might appear that choices (A) and (E) are equivalent, they are not. $\left(x^y\right)^z = x^{yz}$, which is not equal to x^{y^z}.

Example 8: For all real numbers x and y, let $x \# y = (xy)^2 - x + y^2$. What is the value of y that makes $x \# y$ equal to $-x$ for all values of x ?

(A) 0   (B) 2   (C) 5   (D) 7   (E) 10

Setting $x \# y$ equal to $-x$ yields $(xy)^2 - x + y^2 = -x$

Canceling $-x$ from both sides of the equation yields $(xy)^2 + y^2 = 0$

Expanding the first term yields $x^2 y^2 + y^2 = 0$

Factoring out y^2 yields $y^2\left(x^2 + 1\right) = 0$

Setting each factor equal to zero yields $y^2 = 0$ or $x^2 + 1 = 0$

Now, $x^2 + 1$ is greater than or equal to 1 (why?). Hence, $y^2 = 0$

Taking the square root of both sides of this equation yields $y = 0$
Hence, the answer is (A).

Example 9: If $\boxed{x}$ denotes the area of a square with sides of length x, then which of the following is equal to $\boxed{9} \div \boxed{3}$?

(A) $\boxed{\sqrt{3}}$
(B) $\boxed{3}$
(C) $\boxed{\sqrt{27}}$
(D) $\boxed{27}$
(E) $\boxed{81}$

The area of a square with sides of length x is x^2. This formula yields $\boxed{9} \div \boxed{3} = 9^2 \div 3^2 = 81 \div 9 = 9$. Now, $\boxed{3} = 3^2 = 9$. Hence, the answer is (B).

Problem Set C: Solutions begin on page 523.

1. For all $p \neq 2$ define p^* by the equation $p^* = \dfrac{p+5}{p-2}$. If $p = 3$, then $p^* =$

    (A)   8/5
    (B)   8/3
    (C)   4
    (D)   5
    (E)   8

2. Let $\boxed{x}$ be defined by the equation $\boxed{x} = \dfrac{x^2}{2}$. Then which of the following equals 2?

    (A) $\boxed{2}$
    (B) $\boxed{4}$
    (C) $\boxed{6}$
    (D) $\boxed{8}$
    (E) $\boxed{10}$

3. For all a and b, define $a \# b$ to be $-\sqrt{(a+b)^2}$. Then $2 \# 3 =$

    (A) -10
    (B) -5
    (C) -3
    (D) -1
    (E) 0

4. If $\bigodot{d}$ denotes the area of a circle with diameter d, then which of the following is equal to $\bigodot{4} \cdot \bigodot{6}$?

    (A) $\bigodot{10}$

    (B) $\bigodot{12}$

    (C) $\bigodot{24}$

    (D) $\pi \cdot \bigodot{12}$

    (E) $\pi \cdot \bigodot{24}$

5. For all real numbers x, y, and z, let $\overleftrightarrow{x, y, z} = (x-y)z$. For what values of a does $\overleftrightarrow{0, 1, a} = \overleftrightarrow{1, a, 0}$?

    (A) -3 (B) -1 (C) 0 (D) 3 (E) 4

6. Let $\boxed{x} = x^2 - 2$. If $\boxed{2} - \boxed{x} = x^2$, then $x =$

    (A) $\sqrt{2}$
    (B) $\sqrt{3}$
    (C)   2
    (D)   4
    (E)   8

7. For all real numbers a and b, where $a \cdot b \neq 0$, let $a \lozenge b = ab - \dfrac{a}{b}$. Then which of the following must be true?

    I. $a \lozenge b = b \lozenge a$
    II. $a \lozenge a = (a+1)(a-1)$
    III. $(a \lozenge b) \lozenge c = a \lozenge (b \lozenge c)$

    (A)   I only
    (B)   II only
    (C)   III only
    (D)   I and II only
    (E)   I, II, and III

8. The operation $*$ is defined for all non-zero x and y by the equation $x * y = \dfrac{x}{y}$. Then the expression $(x * y) * z$ is equal to

    (A) $\dfrac{z}{xy}$

    (B) $\dfrac{y}{xz}$

    (C) xyz

    (D) $\dfrac{xz}{y}$

    (E) $\dfrac{x}{yz}$

9. Let $x \ominus y = x\sqrt{y} - y - 2x$. For what value of x does $x \ominus y = -y$ for all values of y?

    (A) 0
    (B) $\dfrac{2}{\sqrt{3}}$
    (C) $\sqrt{3}$
    (D) 2
    (E) 4

10. For all positive numbers n, $n^* = \dfrac{\sqrt{n}}{2}$.

What is the value of $\left(64^*\right)^*$?

(A) 1
(B) 2
(C) $\dfrac{\sqrt{32}}{2}$
(D) 4
(E) 16

11. If $\boxed{x} = (x+2)x$, for all x, what is the value of $\boxed{x+2} - \boxed{x-2}$?

(A) -2
(B) $x+4$
(C) 0
(D) x^2
(E) $8(x+1)$

12. For all numbers N, let $\overset{\infty}{N}$ denote the least integer greater than or equal to N. What is the value of $\overset{\infty}{-2.1}$?

(A) -4
(B) -3
(C) -2
(D) -1
(E) 0

13. Let $x \Diamond y = \sqrt{xy}$ for all positive x and y. Then $(2 \Diamond 8) - (3 \Diamond 3) =$

(A) -4
(B) 1
(C) 2
(D) 9
(E) 13

14. ϕ is a function such that $1 \phi a = 1$ and $a \phi b = b \phi a$ for all a and b. Which of the following must be true?

    I. $a \phi 1 = 1$
    II. $(1 \phi b) \phi c = 1 \phi (b \phi c)$
    III. $\dfrac{1 \phi a}{b \phi 1} = 1$

(A) I only
(B) II only
(C) III only
(D) I and II only
(E) I, II, and III

15. The symbol Θ denotes one of the operations: addition, subtraction, multiplication, or division. Further, $1 \Theta 1 = 1$ and $0 \Theta 0 = 0$. What is the value of $\pi \Theta \sqrt{2}$?

(A) $\dfrac{\pi \cdot \sqrt{2}}{3}$
(B) $\dfrac{\pi \cdot \sqrt{2}}{2}$
(C) $\pi \cdot \sqrt{2}$
(D) $2\pi \cdot \sqrt{2}$
(E) $3\pi \cdot \sqrt{2}$

Questions 16–17: Define the symbol # by the following equations:

$$x \# y = (x - y)^2, \text{ if } x > y.$$
$$x \# y = x + \frac{y}{4}, \text{ if } x \le y.$$

16. $4 \# 12 =$

(A) 4
(B) 7
(C) 8
(D) 13
(E) 64

17. If $x \# y = -1$, which of the following could be true?

    I. $x = y$
    II. $x > y$
    III. $x < y$

(A) I only
(B) II only
(C) III only
(D) I and III only
(E) I, II, and III

Questions 18–19: Define the symbol * by the following equation: $x^* = 2 - x$, for all non-negative x.

18. $(a + b^*)^* =$

(A) $b - a$
(B) $a - b - 4$
(C) $b - a + 4$
(D) $a + b - 2$
(E) $a - b$

19. If $(2 - x)^* = (x - 2)^*$, then $x =$

(A) 0
(B) 1
(C) 2
(D) 4
(E) 6

Functions

DEFINITION

A function is a special relationship (correspondence) between two sets such that for each element x in its domain there is assigned one and <u>only one</u> element y in its range.

Notice that the correspondence has two parts:

1) For each x there is assigned *one y*. (This is the ordinary part of the definition.)

2) For each x there is assigned *only one y*. (This is the special part of the definition.)

The second part of the definition of a function creates the uniqueness of the assignment: There cannot be assigned two values of y to one x. In mathematics, uniqueness is very important. We know that $2 + 2 = 4$, but it would be confusing if $2 + 2$ could also equal something else, say 5. In this case, we could never be sure that the answer to a question was the *right* answer.

The correspondence between x and y is usually expressed with the function notation: $y = f(x)$, where y is called the dependent variable and x is called the independent variable. In other words, the value of y depends on the value of x plugged into the function. For example, the square root function can be written as $y = f(x) = \sqrt{x}$. To calculate the correspondence for $x = 4$, we get $y = f(4) = \sqrt{4} = 2$. That is, the square root function assigns the unique y value of 2 to the x value of 4. Most expressions can be turned into functions. For example, the expression $2^x - \dfrac{1}{x}$ becomes the function

$$f(x) = 2^x - \frac{1}{x}$$

DOMAIN AND RANGE

We usually identify a function with its correspondence, as in the example above. However, a function consists of three parts: a domain, a range, and correspondence between them.

- The *domain* of a function is the set of x values for which the function is defined.

For example, the function $f(x) = \dfrac{1}{x-1}$ is defined for all values of $x \neq 1$, which causes division by zero. There is an infinite variety of functions with restricted domains, but only two types of restricted domains appear on the SAT: division by zero and even roots of negative numbers. For example, the function $f(x) = \sqrt{x-2}$ is defined only if $x - 2 \geq 0$, or $x \geq 2$. The two types of restrictions can be combined. For example, $f(x) = \dfrac{1}{\sqrt{x-2}}$. Here, $x - 2 \geq 0$ since it's under the square root symbol. Further $x - 2 \neq 0$, or $x \neq 2$, because that would cause division by zero. Hence, the domain is all $x > 2$.

- The *range* of a function is the set of y values that are assigned to the x values in the domain.

For example, the range of the function $y = f(x) = x^2$ is $y \geq 0$ since a square is never negative. The range of the function $y = f(x) = x^2 + 1$ is $y \geq 1$ since $x^2 + 1 \geq 1$. You can always calculate the range of a function algebraically, but is usually better to graph the function and read off its range from the y values of the graph.

GRAPHS

The graph of a function is the set of ordered pairs $(x, f(x))$, where x is in the domain of f and $y = f(x)$.

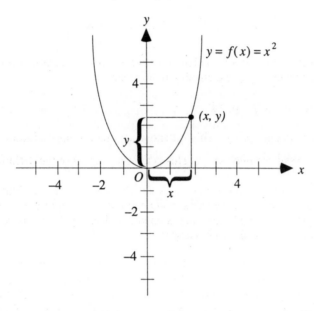

For this function, the domain is all x and the range is all $y \geq 0$ (since the graph touches the x-axis at the origin and is above the x-axis elsewhere).

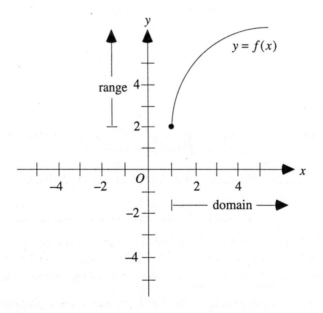

For this function, the domain is all $x \geq 1$ and the range is all $y \geq 2$.

TRANSLATIONS OF GRAPHS

Many graphs can be obtained by shifting a base graph around by adding positive or negative numbers to various places in the function. Take for example, the absolute value function $y = |x|$. Its graph is

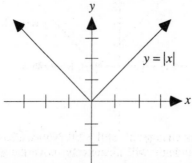

(Notice that sometimes an arrow is added to a graph to indicate the graph continues indefinitely and sometimes nothing is used. To indicate that a graph stops, a dot is added to the terminal point of the graph. Also, notice that the domain of the absolute value function is all x because you can take the absolute value of any number. The range is $y \geq 0$ because the graph touches the x-axis at the origin, is above the x-axis elsewhere, and increases indefinitely.)

To shift this base graph up one unit, we add 1 outside the absolute value symbol, $y = |x| + 1$:

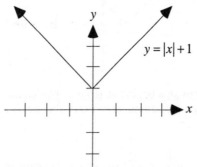

(Notice that the range is now $y \geq 1$.)

To shift the base graph down one unit, we subtract 1 outside the absolute value symbol, $y = |x| - 1$:

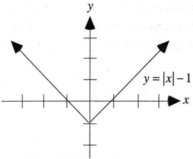

(Notice that the range is now $y \geq -1$.)

To shift the base graph to the right one unit, we subtract 1 inside the absolute value symbol, $y = |x - 1|$:

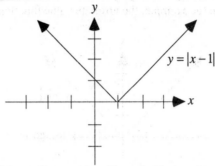

(Notice that the range did not change; it's still $y \geq 0$. Notice also that subtracting 1 moved the graph to right. Many students will mistakenly move the graph to the left because that's where the negative numbers are.)

To shift the base graph to the left one unit, we add 1 inside the absolute value symbol, $y = |x + 1|$:

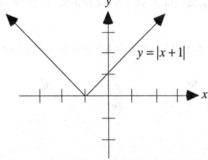

(Notice that the range did not change; it's still $y \geq 0$. Notice also that adding 1 moved the graph to left. Many students will mistakenly move the graph to the right because that's where the positive numbers are.)

The pattern of the translations above holds for all functions. So to move a function $y = f(x)$ up c units, add the positive constant c to the exterior of the function: $y = f(x) + c$. To move a function $y = f(x)$ to the right c units, subtract the constant c in interior of the function: $y = f(x - c)$. To summarize, we have

To shift up c units:	$y = f(x) + c$
To shift down c units:	$y = f(x) - c$
To shift to the right c units:	$y = f(x - c)$
To shift to the left c units:	$y = f(x + c)$

REFLECTIONS OF GRAPHS

Many graphs can be obtained by reflecting a base graph by multiplying various places in the function by negative numbers. Take for example, the square root function $y = \sqrt{x}$. Its graph is

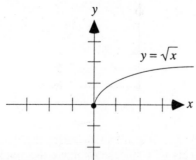

(Notice that the domain of the square root function is all $x \geq 0$ because you cannot take the square root of a negative number. The range is $y \geq 0$ because the graph touches the x-axis at the origin, is above the x-axis elsewhere, and increases indefinitely.)

To reflect this base graph about the x-axis, multiply the exterior of the square root symbol by negative one, $y = -\sqrt{x}$:

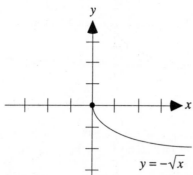

(Notice that the range is now $y \leq 0$ and the domain has not changed.)

To reflect the base graph about the y-axis, multiply the interior of the square root symbol by negative one, $y = \sqrt{-x}$:

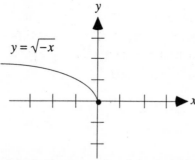

(Notice that the domain is now $x \leq 0$ and the range has not changed.)

The pattern of the reflections above holds for all functions. So to reflect a function $y = f(x)$ about the x-axis, multiply the exterior of the function by negative one: $y = -f(x)$. To reflect a function $y = f(x)$ about the y-axis, multiply the exterior of the function by negative one: $y = f(-x)$. To summarize, we have

To reflect about the x-axis: $y = -f(x)$

To reflect about the y-axis: $y = f(-x)$

Reflections and translations can be combined. Let's reflect the base graph of the square root function $y = \sqrt{x}$ about the x-axis, the y-axis and then shift it to the right 2 units and finally up 1 unit:

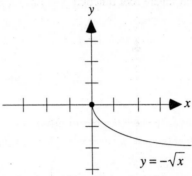

(Notice that the domain is still $x \geq 0$ and the range is now $y \leq 0$.)

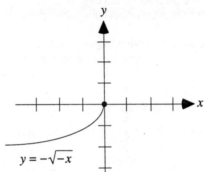

(Notice that the domain is now $x \leq 0$ and the range is still $y \leq 0$.)

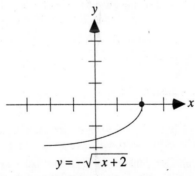

(Notice that the domain is now $x \leq 2$ and the range is still $y \leq 0$.)

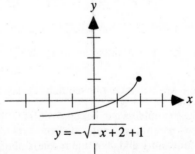

(Notice that the domain is still $x \leq 2$ and the range is now $y \leq 1$.)

EVALUATION AND COMPOSITION OF FUNCTIONS

EVALUATION

We have been using the function notation $f(x)$ intuitively; we also need to study what it actually means. You can think of the letter f in the function notation $f(x)$ as the name of the function. Instead of using the equation $y = x^3 - 1$ to describe the function, we can write $f(x) = x^3 - 1$. Here, f is the name of the function and $f(x)$ is the value of the function at x. So $f(2) = 2^3 - 1 = 8 - 1 = 7$ is the value of the function at 2. As you can see, this notation affords a convenient way of prompting the evaluation of a function for a particular value of x.

Any letter can be used as the independent variable in a function. So the above function could be written $f(p) = p^3 - 1$. This indicates that the independent variable in a function is just a "placeholder." The function could be written without a variable as follows:

$$f(\ ) = (\ )^3 - 1$$

In this form, the function can be viewed as an input/output operation. If 2 is put into the function $f(2)$, then $2^3 - 1$ is returned.

In addition to plugging numbers into functions, we can plug expressions into functions. Plugging $y + 1$ into the function $f(x) = x^2 - x$ yields

$$f(y+1) = (y+1)^2 - (y+1)$$

You can also plug other expressions in terms of x into a function. Plugging $2x$ into the function $f(x) = x^2 - x$ yields

$$f(2x) = (2x)^2 - 2x$$

This evaluation can be troubling to students because the variable x in the function is being replaced by the same variable. But the x in function is just a placeholder. If the placeholder were removed from the function, the substitution would appear more natural. In $f(\ ) = (\ )^2 - (\ )$, we plug $2x$ into the left side $f(2x)$ and it returns the right side $(2x)^2 - 2x$.

COMPOSITION

We have plugged numbers into functions and expressions into functions; now let's plug in other functions. Since a function is identified with its expression, we have actually already done this. In the example above with $f(x) = x^2 - x$ and $2x$, let's call $2x$ by the name $g(x)$. In other words, $g(x) = 2x$. Then the composition of f with g (that is plugging g into f) is

$$f(g(2x)) = f(2x) = (2x)^2 - 2x$$

You probably won't see the notation $f(g(x))$ on the test. But you probably will see one or more problems that ask you perform the substitution. For another example, let $f(x) = \dfrac{1}{x+1}$ and let $g(x) = x^2$. Then $f(g(x)) = \dfrac{1}{x^2 + 1}$ and $g(f(x)) = \left(\dfrac{1}{x+1}\right)^2$. Once you see that the composition of functions merely substitutes one function into another, these problems can become routine. Notice that the composition operation $f(g(x))$ is performed from the inner parentheses out, not from left to right. In the operation $f(g(2))$, the number 2 is first plugged into the function g and then that result is plugged in the function f.

A function can also be composed with itself. That is, substituted into itself. Let $f(x) = \sqrt{x} - 2$. Then $f(f(x)) = \sqrt{\sqrt{x} - 2} - 2$.

Example: The graph of $y = f(x)$ is shown to the right. If $f(-1) = v$, then which one of the following could be the value of $f(v)$?

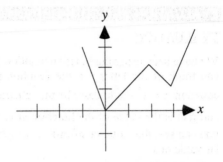

(A)   0
(B)   1
(C)   2
(D)   2.5
(E)   3

Since we are being asked to evaluate $f(v)$ and we are told that $v = f(-1)$, we are just being asked to compose f(x) with itself. That is, we need to calculate $f(f(-1))$. From the graph, $f(-1) = 3$. So $f(f(-1)) = f(3)$. Again, from the graph, $f(3) = 1$. So $f(f(-1)) = f(3) = 1$. The answer is (B).

QUADRATIC FUNCTIONS

Quadratic functions (parabolas) have the following form:

$$y = f(x) = ax^2 + bx + c$$

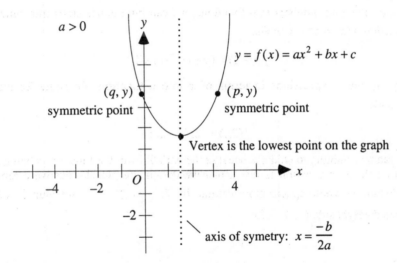

The lowest or highest point on a quadratic graph is called the vertex. The x-coordinate of the vertex occurs at $x = \dfrac{-b}{2a}$. This vertical line also forms the axis of symmetry of the graph, which means that if the graph were folded along its axis, the left and right sides of the graph would coincide.

In graphs of the form $y = f(x) = ax^2 + bx + c$ if $a > 0$, then the graph opens up.

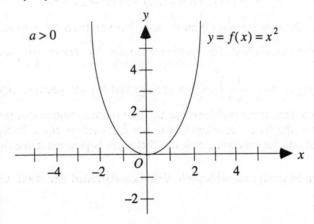

If $a < 0$, then the graph opens down.

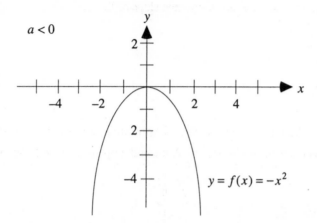

By completing the square, the form $y = ax^2 + bx + c$ can be written as $y = a(x - h)^2 + k$. You are not expected to know this form on the test. But it is a convenient form since the vertex occurs at the point (h, k) and the axis of symmetry is the line $x = h$.

We have been analyzing quadratic functions that are vertically symmetric. Though not as common, quadratic functions can also be horizontally symmetric. They have the following form:

$$x = g(y) = ay^2 + by + c$$

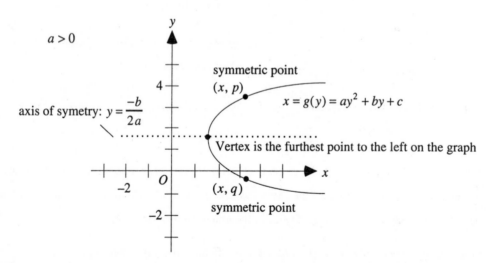

The furthest point to the left on this graph is called the vertex. The y-coordinate of the vertex occurs at $y = \dfrac{-b}{2a}$. This horizontal line also forms the axis of symmetry of the graph, which means that if the graph were folded along its axis, the top and bottom parts of the graph would coincide.

In graphs of the form $x = ay^2 + by + c$ if $a > 0$, then the graph opens to the right and if $a < 0$ then the graph opens to the left.

Example: The graph of $x = -y^2 + 2$ and the graph of the line k intersect at $(0, p)$ and $(1, q)$. Which one of the following is the smallest possible slope of line k ?

(A) $-\sqrt{2} - 1$
(B) $-\sqrt{2} + 1$
(C) $\sqrt{2} - 1$
(D) $\sqrt{2} + 1$
(E) $\sqrt{2} + 2$

Let's make a rough sketch of the graphs. Expressing $x = -y^2 + 2$ in standard form, yields $x = -1y^2 + 0 \cdot y + 2$. Since $a = -1$, $b = 0$, and $c = 2$, the graph opens to the left and its vertex is at $(2, 0)$.

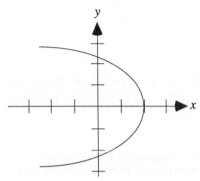

Since p and q can be positive or negative, there are four possible positions for line k (the y-coordinates in the graphs below can be calculated by plugging $x = 0$ and $x = 1$ into the function $x = -y^2 + 2$):

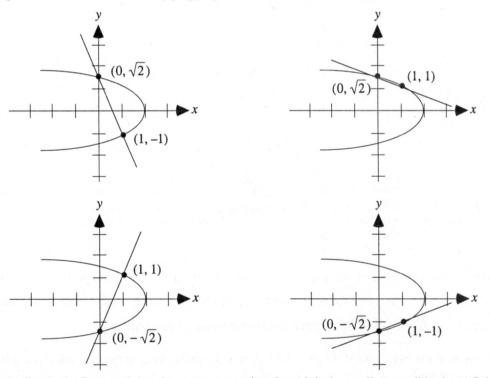

Since the line in the first graph has the steepest negative slope, it is the smallest possible slope. Calculating the slope yields

$$m = \frac{\sqrt{2} - (-1)}{0 - 1} = \frac{\sqrt{2} + 1}{-1} = -\left(\sqrt{2} + 1\right) = -\sqrt{2} - 1$$

The answer is (A).

QUALITATIVE BEHAVIOR OF GRAPHS AND FUNCTIONS

In this rather vague category, you will be asked how a function and its graph are related. You may be asked to identify the zeros of a function based on its graph. The zeros, or roots, of a function are the x-coordinates of where it crosses the x-axis. Or you may be given two graphs and asked for what x values are their functions equal. The functions will be equal where they intersect.

Example: The graphs of $y = f(x)$ and $y = 1$ are shown to the right. For how many x values does $f(x)$ equal 1?

(A)   0
(B)   1
(C)   2
(D)   3
(E)   4

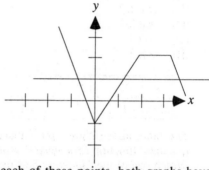

The figure shows that the graphs intersect at three points. At each of these points, both graphs have a height, or y-coordinate, of 1. The points are approximately $(-.8, 1)$, $(1.2, 1)$, and $(4, 1)$. Hence, $f(x) = 1$ for three x values. The answer is (D).

FUNCTIONS AS MODELS OF REAL-LIFE SITUATIONS

Functions can be used to predict the outcomes of certain physical events or real-life situations. For example, a function can predict the maximum height a projectile will reach when fired with an initial velocity, or the number of movie tickets that will be sold at a given price.

Example: The graph to the right shows the number of music CDs sold at various prices. At what price should the CDs be marked to sell the maximum number of CDs?

(A)   0
(B)   5
(C)   10
(D)   15
(E)   20

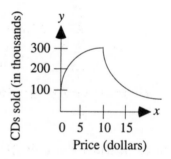

As you read the graph from left to right, it shows that sales initially increase rapidly and then slow to a maximum of about 300,000. From there, sales drop precipitously and then slowly approach zero as the price continues to increase. From the graph, sales of 300,000 units on the y-axis correspond to a price of about \$10 on the x-axis. The answer is (C).

Problem Set D: Solutions begin on page 526.

$$g(x) = (2x - 3)^{1/4} + 1$$

1.   In the function above, for what values of x is $g(x)$ a real number?

 (A) $x \geq 0$
 (B) $x \geq 1/2$
 (C) $x \geq 3/2$
 (D) $x \geq 2$
 (E) $x \geq 3$

x	–1	0	1	2
$f(x)$	1	3	1	–5

2.   The table above shows the values of the quadratic function f for several values of x. Which one of the following best represents f?

 (A) $f(x) = -2x^2$

 (B) $f(x) = x^2 + 3$

 (C) $f(x) = -x^2 + 3$

 (D) $f(x) = -2x^2 - 3$

 (E) $f(x) = -2x^2 + 3$

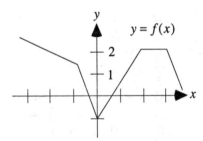

3.   In the function above, if $f(k) = 2$, then which one of the following could be a value of k?

 (A)   –1
 (B)   0
 (C)   0.5
 (D)   2.5
 (E)   4

4.   Let the function h be defined by $h(x) = \sqrt{x} + 2$. If $3h(v) = 18$, then which one of the following is the value of $h\left(\dfrac{v}{4}\right)$?

 (A)   –4
 (B)   –1
 (C)   0
 (D)   2
 (E)   4

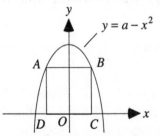

5.   The graph above shows a parabola that is symmetric about the x-axis. Which one of the following could be the equation of the graph?

 (A) $x = -(y+1)^2$

 (B) $x = -y^2$

 (C) $x = -y^2 + 1$

 (D) $x = y^2 - 1$

 (E) $x = (y+1)^2$

6.   A pottery store owner determines that the revenue for sales of a particular item can be modeled by the function $r(x) = 50\sqrt{x} - 40$, where x is the number of the items sold. How many of the items must be sold to generate \$110 in revenue?

 (A) 5   (B) 6   (C) 7   (D) 8   (E) 9

7.   At time $t = 0$, a projectile was fired upward from an initial height of 10 feet. Its height after t seconds is given by the function $h(t) = p - 10(q - t)^2$, where p and q are positive constants. If the projectile reached a maximum height of 100 feet when $t = 3$, then what was the height, in feet, of the projectile when $t = 4$?

 (A) 62   (B) 70   (C) 85   (D) 89   (E) 90

8.   The figure above shows the graph of $y = a - x^2$ for some constant a. If the square $ABCD$ intersects the graph at points A and B and the area of the square is 16, what is the value of a?

 (A) 2   (B) 4   (C) 6   (D) 8   (E) 10

Math Notes

1. **To compare two fractions, cross-multiply. The larger product will be on the same side as the larger fraction.**

   Example: Given $\dfrac{5}{6}$ vs. $\dfrac{6}{7}$. Cross-multiplying gives $5\cdot7$ vs. $6\cdot6$, or 35 vs. 36. Now 36 is larger than 35, so $\dfrac{6}{7}$ is larger than $\dfrac{5}{6}$.

2. **Taking the square root of a fraction between 0 and 1 makes it larger.**

   Example: $\sqrt{\dfrac{1}{4}} = \dfrac{1}{2}$ and $\dfrac{1}{2}$ is greater than $\dfrac{1}{4}$.

   Caution: This is not true for fractions greater than 1. For example, $\sqrt{\dfrac{9}{4}} = \dfrac{3}{2}$. But $\dfrac{3}{2} < \dfrac{9}{4}$.

3. **Squaring a fraction between 0 and 1 makes it smaller.**

   Example: $\left(\dfrac{1}{2}\right)^2 = \dfrac{1}{4}$ and $\dfrac{1}{4}$ is less than $\dfrac{1}{2}$.

4. $ax^2 \neq (ax)^2$. **In fact,** $a^2x^2 = (ax)^2$.

   Example: $3\cdot2^2 = 3\cdot4 = 12$. But $(3\cdot2)^2 = 6^2 = 36$. This mistake is often seen in the following form: $-x^2 = (-x)^2$. To see more clearly why this is wrong, write $-x^2 = (-1)x^2$, which is negative. But $(-x)^2 = (-x)(-x) = x^2$, which is positive.

   Example: $-5^2 = (-1)5^2 = (-1)25 = -25$. But $(-5)^2 = (-5)(-5) = 5\cdot5 = 25$.

5. $\dfrac{1/a}{b} \neq \dfrac{1}{a/b}$. **In fact,** $\dfrac{1/a}{b} = \dfrac{1}{ab}$ **and** $\dfrac{1}{a/b} = \dfrac{b}{a}$.

   Example: $\dfrac{1/2}{3} = \dfrac{1}{2}\cdot\dfrac{1}{3} = \dfrac{1}{6}$. But $\dfrac{1}{2/3} = 1\cdot\dfrac{3}{2} = \dfrac{3}{2}$.

6. $-(a + b) \neq -a + b$. **In fact,** $-(a + b) = -a - b$.
   Example: $-(2 + 3) = -5$. But $-2 + 3 = 1$.
   Example: $-(2 + x) = -2 - x$.

7. **Memorize the following factoring formulas—they occur frequently on the SAT.**
   A. $a^2 - b^2 = (a - b)(a + b)$
   B. $x^2 \pm 2xy + y^2 = (x \pm y)^2$
   C. $a(b + c) = ab + ac$

Problem Set E: Use the properties and techniques on the previous page to solve the following problems. Solutions begin on page 529.

1. If $x \neq 0$, then which one of the following must be true?

   (A) $2x^2 = (2x)^2$ (B) $2x^2 < (2x)^2$ (C) $2x^2 \leq (2x)^2$ (D) $2x^2 > (2x)^2$ (E) $2x^2 \geq (2x)^2$

2. Which one of the following fractions is greatest?

   (A) $\dfrac{15}{16}$ (B) $\dfrac{7}{9}$ (C) $\dfrac{13}{15}$ (D) $\dfrac{8}{9}$ (E) $\dfrac{10}{11}$

3. $1 + \dfrac{1}{1 - \dfrac{1}{2}} =$

   (A) 3   (B) 5   (C) 7   (D) 9   (E) 11

4. If the ratio of $\dfrac{1}{5}$ to $\dfrac{1}{4}$ is equal to the ratio of $\dfrac{1}{4}$ to x, then what is the value of x ?

   (A) 5/16   (B) 4/11   (C) 1   (D) 4   (E) 5

5. Which one of the following numbers is smallest?

   (A) $\left(\dfrac{7}{8}\right)^2$ (B) $\sqrt{\dfrac{7}{8}}$ (C) $\sqrt{\dfrac{8}{7}}$ (D) $\left(\dfrac{8}{7}\right)^2$ (E) $\dfrac{8}{7}$

6. Let $a \# b$ be denoted by the expression $a \# b = -b^4$. Then $x \# (-y) =$

   (A) $-y^2$ (B) y^4 (C) $-y^4$ (D) y^2 (E) $|y|$

7. $\dfrac{1}{1 - (.2)^2} =$

   (A) 25/24   (B) 25/23   (C) 24/15   (D) 23/11   (E) 21/9

8. If $0 < x < 1$, which of the following expressions is greatest?

   (A) $\dfrac{1}{\sqrt{x}}$ (B) $\sqrt{x}$ (C) $\dfrac{1}{\pi}x$ (D) x^3 (E) x^4

9. Which of the following are true?

   I. $\dfrac{\sqrt{\dfrac{5}{6}}}{\left(\dfrac{5}{6}\right)^2} > 1$ II. $\dfrac{\sqrt{\dfrac{5}{6}}}{\left(\dfrac{6}{5}\right)^2} > 1$ III. $\sqrt{\dfrac{\sqrt{\dfrac{5}{6}}}{\sqrt{\dfrac{5}{6}}}} > 1$

   (A) I only   (B) II only   (C) I and II only   (D) I and III only   (E) I, II, and III

10. If $x > y > 0$, which of the following are true?

   I. $\dfrac{x+2}{y+2} > \dfrac{x}{y}$ II. $\dfrac{x+2}{y+2} = \dfrac{x}{y}$ III. $\dfrac{x+2}{y+2} > 1$

   (A) I only   (B) II only   (C) III only   (D) I and III only   (E) II and III only

8. **Know these rules for radicals:**

A. $\sqrt{x}\sqrt{y} = \sqrt{xy}$

B. $\sqrt{\dfrac{x}{y}} = \dfrac{\sqrt{x}}{\sqrt{y}}$

9. **Pythagorean Theorem (For right triangles only):**

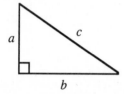

$$c^2 = a^2 + b^2$$

Example: What is the area of the triangle to the right?

    (A)   6
    (B)   7.5
    (C)   8
    (D)   11
    (E)   15

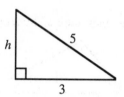

Since the triangle is a right triangle, the Pythagorean Theorem applies: $h^2 + 3^2 = 5^2$, where h is the height of the triangle. Solving for h yields $h = 4$. Hence, the area of the triangle is $\dfrac{1}{2}(base)(height) = \dfrac{1}{2}(3)(4) = 6$. The answer is (A).

10. **When parallel lines are cut by a transversal, three important angle relationships are formed:**

Alternate interior angles are equal.

Corresponding angles are equal.

Interior angles on the same side of the transversal are supplementary.

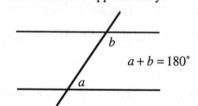

$$a + b = 180°$$

11. **In a triangle, an exterior angle is equal to the sum of its remote interior angles and therefore greater than either of them.**

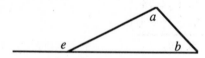

$$e = a + b \text{ and } e > a \text{ and } e > b$$

12. **A central angle has by definition the same measure as its intercepted arc.**

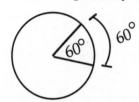

13. **An inscribed angle has one-half the measure of its intercepted arc.**

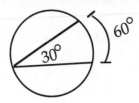

14. **There are 180° in a straight angle.**

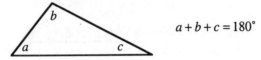

$x + y = 180°$

15. **The angle sum of a triangle is 180°.**

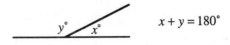

$a + b + c = 180°$

Example: In the triangle to the right, what is the degree measure of angle *c* ?

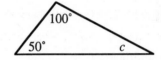

    (A)   17
    (B)   20
    (C)   30
    (D)   40
    (E)   45

Since a triangle has 180°, we get $100 + 50 + c = 180$. Solving for *c* yields $c = 30$. Hence, the answer is (C).

17. **To find the percentage increase, find the absolute increase and divide by the original amount.**

Example: If a shirt selling for \$18 is marked up to \$20, then the absolute increase is $20 - 18 = 2$.

Thus, the percentage increase is $\dfrac{increase}{original\ amount} = \dfrac{2}{18} = \dfrac{1}{9} \approx 11\%$.

18. **Systems of simultaneous equations can most often be solved by merely adding or subtracting the equations.**

Example: If $4x + y = 14$ and $3x + 2y = 13$, then $x - y =$

Solution: Merely subtract the second equation from the first:

$$
\begin{array}{r}
4x + y = 14 \\
(-)\quad 3x + 2y = 13 \\
\hline
x - y = 1
\end{array}
$$

19. **When counting elements that are in overlapping sets, the total number will equal the number in one group plus the number in the other group minus the number common to both groups. Venn diagrams are very helpful with these problems.**

   Example: If in a certain school 20 students are taking math and 10 are taking history and 7 are taking both, how many students are taking either math or history?

   Solution:

   History   Math

   10 (7) 20

   Both History and Math

   By the principle stated above, we add 10 and 20 and then subtract 7 from the result. Thus, there are $(10 + 20) - 7 = 23$ students.

20. **The number of integers between two integers <u>inclusive</u> is one more than their difference.**

   For example: The number of integers between 49 and 101 inclusive is $(101 - 49) + 1 = 53$. To see this more clearly, choose smaller numbers, say, 9 and 11. The difference between 9 and 11 is 2. But there are three numbers between them inclusive—9, 10, and 11—one more than their difference.

21. **Rounding Off:** The convention used for rounding numbers is *"if the following digit is less than five, then the preceding digit is not changed. But if the following digit is greater than or equal to five, then the preceding digit is increased by one."*

   Example: 65,439 —> 65,000 (following digit is 4)
   5.5671 —> 5.5700 (dropping the unnecessary zeros gives 5.57)

22. **Writing a number as a product of a power of 10 and a number $1 \le n < 10$ is called scientific notation. This notation has the following form: $n \times 10^c$, where $1 \le n < 10$ and c is an integer.**

   Example: $326,000,000 = 3.26 \times 10^8$
   Notice that the exponent is the number of significant places that the decimal is moved[*], not the number zeros. Students often use 6 as the exponent in the above example because there are 6 zeros.

   Example: $0.00007 = 7 \times 10^{-5}$
   Notice that for a small number the exponent is negative and for a large number the exponent is positive.

---

[*] Although no decimal is shown in the number 326,000,000, you can place a decimal at the end of the number and add as many trailing zeros as you like without changing the value of the number: 326,000,000 = 326,000,000.00 . . . .

Number Theory

This broad category is a popular source for SAT questions. At first, students often struggle with these problems since they have forgotten many of the basic properties of arithmetic. So before we begin solving these problems, let's review some of these basic properties.

- *"The remainder is r when p is divided by q"* means $p = qz + r$; the integer z is called the quotient. For instance, *"The remainder is 1 when 7 is divided by 3"* means $7 = 3 \cdot 2 + 1$.

Example 1: When the integer n is divided by 2, the quotient is u and the remainder is 1. When the integer n is divided by 5, the quotient is v and the remainder is 3. Which one of the following must be true?

    (A) $2u + 5v = 4$
    (B) $2u - 5v = 2$
    (C) $4u + 5v = 2$
    (D) $4u - 5v = 2$
    (E) $3u - 5v = 2$

Translating *"When the integer n is divided by 2, the quotient is u and the remainder is 1"* into an equation gives

$$n = 2u + 1$$

Translating *"When the integer n is divided by 5, the quotient is v and the remainder is 3"* into an equation gives

$$n = 5v + 3$$

Since both expressions equal n, we can set them equal to each other:

$$2u + 1 = 5v + 3$$

Rearranging and then combining like terms yields

$$2u - 5v = 2$$

The answer is (B).

- A number n is even if the remainder is zero when n is divided by 2: $n = 2z + 0$, or $n = 2z$.

- A number n is odd if the remainder is one when n is divided by 2: $n = 2z + 1$.

- The following properties for odd and even numbers are very useful—you should memorize them:

$$even \times even = even$$
$$odd \times odd = odd$$
$$even \times odd = even$$

$$even + even = even$$
$$odd + odd = even$$
$$even + odd = odd$$

Example 2: Suppose p is even and q is odd. Then which of the following CANNOT be an integer?

I. $\dfrac{p+q}{p}$

II. $\dfrac{pq}{3}$

III. $\dfrac{q}{p^2}$

(A) I only   (B) II only   (C) III only   (D) I and II only   (E) I and III only

For a fractional expression to be an integer, the denominator must divide evenly into the numerator. Now, Statement I cannot be an integer. Since q is odd and p is even, $p + q$ is odd. Further, since $p + q$ is odd, it cannot be divided evenly by the even number p. Hence, $\dfrac{p+q}{p}$ cannot be an integer. Next, Statement II can be an integer. For example, if $p = 2$ and $q = 3$, then $\dfrac{pq}{3} = \dfrac{2 \cdot 3}{3} = 2$. Finally, Statement III cannot be an integer. $p^2 = p \cdot p$ is even since it is the product of two even numbers. Further, since q is odd, it cannot be divided evenly by the even integer p^2. The answer is (E).

- Consecutive integers are written as $x, x + 1, x + 2, \ldots$

- Consecutive even or odd integers are written as $x + 2, x + 4, \ldots$

- The integer zero is neither positive nor negative, but it is even: $0 = 2 \cdot 0$.

- A *prime number* is an integer that is divisible only by itself and 1.
  The prime numbers are 2, 3, 5, 7, 11, 13, 17, 19, 23, 29, 31, 37, 41, . . .

- A number is divisible by 3 if the sum of its digits is divisible by 3.
  For example, 135 is divisible by 3 because the sum of its digits $(1 + 3 + 5 = 9)$ is divisible by 3.

- The absolute value of a number, $|\ |$, is always positive. In other words, the absolute value symbol eliminates negative signs.
  For example, $|-7| = 7$ and $|-\pi| = \pi$. Caution, the absolute value symbol acts only on what is inside the symbol, $|\ |$. For example, $-|-(7 - \pi)| = -(7 - \pi)$. Here, only the negative sign inside the absolute value symbol but outside the parentheses is eliminated.

Example 3: If a, b, and c are consecutive integers and $a < b < c$, which of the following must be true?

    I. $b - c = 1$

    II. $\dfrac{abc}{3}$ is an integer.

    III. $a + b + c$ is even.

    (A)   I only
    (B)   II only
    (C)   III only
    (D)   I and II only
    (E)   II and III only

Let x, $x + 1$, $x + 2$ stand for the consecutive integers a, b, and c, in that order. Plugging this into Statement I yields

$$b - c = (x + 1) - (x + 2) = -1$$

Hence, Statement I is false.

As to Statement II, since a, b, and c are three consecutive integers, one of them must be divisible by 3. Hence, $\dfrac{abc}{3}$ is an integer, and Statement II is true.

As to Statement III, suppose a is even, b is odd, and c is even. Then $a + b$ is odd since

$$even + odd = odd$$

Hence,

$$a + b + c = (a + b) + c = (odd) + even = odd$$

Thus, Statement III is not necessarily true. The answer is (B).

Example 4: If both x and y are prime numbers, which of the following CANNOT be the difference of x and y?

    (A) 1   (B) 3   (C) 9   (D) 15   (E) 23

Both 3 and 2 are prime, and $3 - 2 = 1$. This eliminates (A). Next, both 5 and 2 are prime, and $5 - 2 = 3$. This eliminates (B). Next, both 11 and 2 are prime, and $11 - 2 = 9$. This eliminates (C). Next, both 17 and 2 are prime, and $17 - 2 = 15$. This eliminates (D). Hence, by process of elimination, the answer is (E).

Example 5: If $-x = -\left|-(-2 + 5)\right|$, then $x =$

    (A) –7   (B) –3   (C) 3   (D) 7   (E) 9

Working from the innermost parentheses out, we get

$$-x = -\left|-(-2 + 5)\right|$$
$$-x = -\left|-(+3)\right|$$
$$-x = -\left|-3\right|$$
$$-x = -(+3)$$
$$-x = -3$$
$$x = 3$$

The answer is (C).

Problem Set F:

Solutions begin on page 530.

1. If the remainder is 1 when m is divided by 2 and the remainder is 3 when n is divided by 4, which of the following must be true?

    (A) m is even.
    (B) n is even.
    (C) $m + n$ is even.
    (D) mn is even.
    (E) $\dfrac{m}{n}$ is even.

2. If x and y are both prime and greater than 2, then which of the following CANNOT be a divisor of xy?

    (A) 2   (B) 3   (C) 11   (D) 15   (E) 17

3. If 2 is the greatest number that will divide evenly into both x and y, what is the greatest number that will divide evenly into both $5x$ and $5y$?

    (A) 2   (B) 4   (C) 6   (D) 8   (E) 10

4. If the average of the consecutive even integers a, b, and c is less than $\dfrac{1}{3}a$, which of the following best describes the value of a?

    (A) a is prime.   (B) a is odd.   (C) a is zero.   (D) a is positive.   (E) a is negative.

5. If $\dfrac{x+5}{y}$ is a prime integer, which of the following must be true?

    I. $y = 5x$
    II. y is a prime integer.
    III. $\dfrac{x+5}{y}$ is odd.

    (A) None
    (B) I only
    (C) II only
    (D) I and II only
    (E) II and III only

6. If x is both the cube and the square of an integer and x is between 2 and 200, what is the value of x?
    (A) 8   (B) 16   (C) 64   (D) 125   (E) 169

7. In the two-digit number x, both the sum and the difference of its digits is 4. What is the value of x?
    (A) 13   (B) 31   (C) 40   (D) 48   (E) 59

8. If p divided by 9 leaves a remainder of 1, which of the following must be true?
    I. p is even.
    II. p is odd.
    III. $p = 3 \cdot z + 1$ for some integer z.

    (A) I only
    (B) II only
    (C) III only
    (D) I and II only
    (E) I and III only

9. p and q are integers. If p is divided by 2, the remainder is 1; and if q is divided by 6, the remainder is 1. Which of the following must be true.

    I. $pq + 1$ is even.

    II. $\dfrac{pq}{2}$ is an integer.

    III. pq is a multiple of 12.

    (A) I only   (B) II only   (C) III only   (D) I and II only   (E) I and III only

10. The smallest prime number greater than 53 is

    (A) 54   (B) 55   (C) 57   (D) 59   (E) 67

11. Which one of the following numbers is the greatest positive integer x such that 3^x is a factor of 27^5?

    (A) 5   (B) 8   (C) 10   (D) 15   (E) 19

12. If x, y, and z are consecutive integers in that order, which of the following must be true?

    I. xy is even.
    II. $x - z$ is even.
    III. x^z is even.

    (A)   I only
    (B)   II only
    (C)   III only
    (D)   I and II only
    (E)   I and III only

13. If $-x - 2 = -\left|-(6 - 2)\right|$, then $x =$

    (A) –5   (B) –2   (C) 0   (D) 2   (E) 5

14. If the sum of two prime numbers x and y is odd, then the product of x and y must be divisible by

    (A)   2
    (B)   3
    (C)   4
    (D)   5
    (E)   8

15. If $\dfrac{x + y}{x - y} = 3$ and x and y are integers, then which one of the following must be true?

    (A) x is divisible by 4
    (B) y is an odd number
    (C) y is an even integer
    (D) x is an even number
    (E) x is an irreducible fraction

16. A two-digit even number is such that reversing its digits creates an odd number greater than the original number. Which one of the following cannot be the first digit of the original number?

    (A)   1
    (B)   3
    (C)   5
    (D)   7
    (E)   9

17. Let a, b, and c be three integers, and let a be a perfect square. If $a/b = b/c$, then which one of the following statements must be true?

    (A) c must be an even number
    (B) c must be an odd number
    (C) c must be a perfect square
    (D) c must not be a perfect square
    (E) c must be a prime number

18. If n > 2, then the sum, S, of the integers from 1 through n can be calculated by the following formula: $S = n(n + 1)/2$. Which one of the following statements about S must be true?

    (A) S is always odd.
    (B) S is always even.
    (C) S must be a prime number.
    (D) S must not be a prime number.
    (E) S must be a perfect square.

19. If n is an odd number greater than 5 and a multiple of 5, then what is the remainder when n is divided by 10?

    (A)   1
    (B)   3
    (C)   5
    (D)   7
    (E)   9

20. Which one of the following could be the difference between two numbers both of which are divisible by 2, 3 and 4?

    (A)   71
    (B)   72
    (C)   73
    (D)   74
    (E)   75

21. A number, when divided by 12, gives a remainder of 7. If the same number is divided by 6, then the remainder must be
    (A)   1
    (B)   2
    (C)   3
    (D)   4
    (E)   5

22. Let x be a two-digit number. If the sum of the digits of x is 9, then the sum of the digits of the number $(x + 10)$ is

    (A)   1
    (B)   8
    (C)   10
    (D)   either 8 or 10
    (E)   either 1 or 10

23. $\dfrac{39693}{3} =$

    (A)   33231
    (B)   13231
    (C)   12331
    (D)   23123
    (E)   12321

24. The number of positive integers less than 1000 that are divisible by 3 is

    (A) 332
    (B) 333
    (C) 334
    (D) 335
    (E) 336

25. If n^3 is an odd integer, which one of the following expressions is an even integer?

    (A) $2n^2 + 1$
    (B) n^4
    (C) $n^2 + 1$
    (D) $n(n + 2)$
    (E) n

26. If the product of two integers is odd, then the sum of those two integers must be

    (A) odd
    (B) even
    (C) prime
    (D) divisible by the difference of the two numbers
    (E) a perfect square

27. An odd number added to itself an odd number of times yields

    (A) an odd number
    (B) an even number
    (C) a prime number
    (D) a positive number
    (E) a perfect square

28. If the sum of three consecutive integers is odd, then the first and the last integers must be

    (A) odd, even
    (B) odd, odd
    (C) even, odd
    (D) even, even
    (E) none of the above

29. If l, m, and n are positive integers such that $l < m < n$ and $n < 4$, then $m =$

    (A) 0
    (B) 1
    (C) 2
    (D) 3
    (E) 4

30. If two non-zero positive integers p and q are such that $p = 4q$ and $p < 8$, then $q =$

    (A) 1
    (B) 2
    (C) 3
    (D) 4
    (E) 5

31. If n is an integer, then which one of the following expressions must be even?

(A) $n^2 + 1$
(B) $n(n + 2)$
(C) $n(n + 1)$
(D) $n(n + 4)$
(E) $(n + 1)(n + 3)$

32. If p and q are different prime numbers and $pq/2$ is also a prime number, then $p + q$ is

(A) an odd number
(B) an even number
(C) a prime number
(D) a negative number
(E) not a prime number

33. The sum of three consecutive positive integers must be divisible by which of the following?

(A) 2
(B) 3
(C) 4
(D) 5
(E) 6

Geometry

About one-fourth of the math problems on the SAT involve geometry. (There are no proofs.) Fortunately, the figures on the SAT are usually drawn to scale. Hence, you can check your work and in some cases even solve a problem by "eyeballing" the drawing. We'll discuss this technique in detail later.

Following is a discussion of the basic properties of geometry. You probably know many of these properties. Memorize any that you do not know.

Lines & Angles

When two straight lines meet at a point, they form an angle. The point is called the vertex of the angle, and the lines are called the sides of the angle.

The angle to the right can be identified in three ways:

1. $\angle x$
2. $\angle B$
3. $\angle ABC$ or $\angle CBA$

When two straight lines meet at a point, they form four angles. The angles opposite each other are called vertical angles, and they are congruent (equal). In the figure to the right, $a = b$, and $c = d$.

$a = b$ and $c = d$

Angles are measured in degrees, °. By definition, a circle has 360°. So an angle can be measured by its fractional part of a circle. For example, an angle that is $\dfrac{1}{360}$ of the arc of a circle is 1°. And an angle that is $\dfrac{1}{4}$ of the arc of a circle is $\dfrac{1}{4} \times 360 = 90°$.

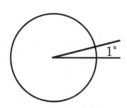

1/360 of an arc
of a circle

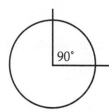

1/4 of an arc
of a circle

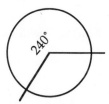

2/3 of an arc
of a circle

There are four major types of angle measures:

An **acute angle** has measure less than 90°:

A **right angle** has measure 90°:

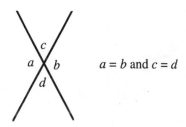

381

An **obtuse angle** has measure greater than 90°:

A **straight angle** has measure 180°:

$x + y = 180°$

Example: In the figure to the right, if the quotient of a
and b is $\dfrac{7}{2}$, then $b =$

(A) 30   (B) 35   (C) 40   (D) 46   (E) 50

Since a and b form a straight angle, $a + b = 180$. Now, translating "the quotient of a and b is $\dfrac{7}{2}$" into an

equation gives $\dfrac{a}{b} = \dfrac{7}{2}$. Solving for a yields $a = \dfrac{7}{2}b$. Plugging this into the equation $a + b = 180$ yields

$$\frac{7}{2}b + b = 180$$
$$7b + 2b = 360$$
$$9b = 360$$
$$b = 40$$

The answer is (C).

Example: In the figure to the right, what is the measure
of angle y ?

(A) 80
(B) 84
(C) 85
(D) 87
(E) 90

Since $4x$ and $2y - 40$ represent vertical angles, $4x = 2y - 40$. Since $3x$ and y form a straight angle, $3x + y = 180$. This yields the following system:

$$4x = 2y - 40$$
$$3x + y = 180$$

Solving this system for y yields $y = 84$. Hence, the answer is (B).

Two angles are supplementary if their angle sum is 180°:

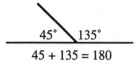

$45 + 135 = 180$

Two angles are complementary if their angle sum is 90°:

$30 + 60 = 90$

Perpendicular lines meet at right angles:

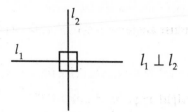

$l_1 \perp l_2$

Two lines in the same plane are parallel if they never intersect. Parallel lines have the same slope.

When parallel lines are cut by a transversal, three important angle relationships exist:

Alternate interior angles are equal.

Corresponding angles are equal.

Interior angles on the same side of the transversal are supplementary.

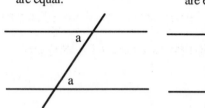

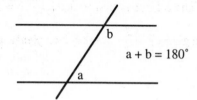

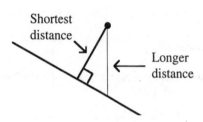

$a + b = 180°$

The shortest distance from a point to a line is along a new line that passed through the point and is perpendicular to the original line.

Shortest distance

Longer distance

Triangles

A triangle containing a right angle is called a *right triangle*. The right angle is denoted by a small square:

A triangle with two equal sides is called *isosceles*. The angles opposite the equal sides are called the base angles, and they are congruent (equal). A triangle with all three sides equal is called *equilateral*, and each angle is 60°. A triangle with no equal sides (and therefore no equal angles) is called *scalene*:

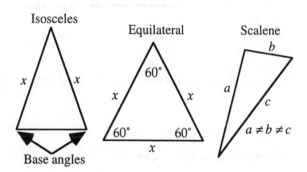

Isosceles

Equilateral

Scalene

$a \neq b \neq c$

Base angles

The altitude to the base of an isosceles or equilateral triangle bisects the base and bisects the vertex angle:

Isosceles:

Equilateral:

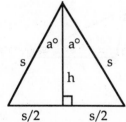

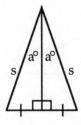

$h = \dfrac{s\sqrt{3}}{2}$

The angle sum of a triangle is 180°:

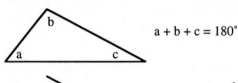

$$a + b + c = 180°$$

Example: In the figure to the right, $w =$

(A) 30   (B) 32   (C) 40   (D) 52   (E) 60

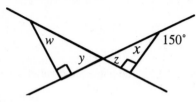

$x + 150 = 180$	since x and 150 form a straight angle
$x = 30$	solving for x
$z + x + 90 = 180$	since the angle sum of a triangle is 180°
$z + 30 + 90 = 180$	replacing x with 30
$z = 60$	solving for z
$z = y = 60$	since y and z are vertical angles
$w + y + 90 = 180$	since the angle sum of a triangle is 180°
$w + 60 + 90 = 180$	replacing y with 60
$w = 30$	solving for w

The answer is (A).

The area of a triangle is $\frac{1}{2}bh$, where b is the base and h is the height. Sometimes the base must be extended in order to draw the altitude, as in the third drawing directly below:

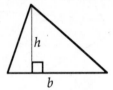 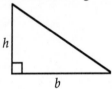 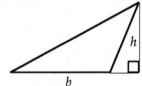

$$A = \frac{1}{2}bh$$

In a triangle, the longer side is opposite the larger angle, and vice versa:

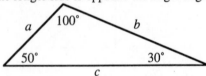

50° is larger than 30°, so side b is longer than side a.

Pythagorean Theorem (right triangles only): The square of the hypotenuse is equal to the sum of the squares of the legs.

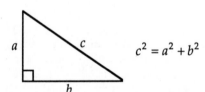

$$c^2 = a^2 + b^2$$

Pythagorean triples: The numbers 3, 4, and 5 can always represent the sides of a right triangle and they appear very often: $5^2 = 3^2 + 4^2$. Another, but less common, Pythagorean Triple is 5, 12, 13: $13^2 = 5^2 + 12^2$.

Two triangles are similar (same shape and usually different sizes) if their corresponding angles are equal. If two triangles are similar, their corresponding sides are proportional:

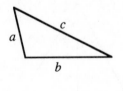 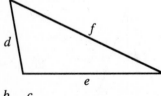

$$\frac{a}{d} = \frac{b}{e} = \frac{c}{f}$$

If two angles of a triangle are congruent to two angles of another triangle, the triangles are similar.

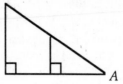

In the figure to the right, the large and small triangles are similar because both contain a right angle and they share $\angle A$.

Two triangles are congruent (identical) if they have the same size and shape.

In a triangle, an exterior angle is equal to the sum of its remote interior angles and is therefore greater than either of them:

$e = a + b$ and $e > a$ and $e > b$

In a triangle, the sum of the lengths of any two sides is greater than the length of the remaining side:

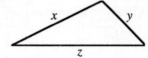

$x + y > z$
$y + z > x$
$x + z > y$

Example: In the figure to the right, what is the value of x ?

(A)   30
(B)   32
(C)   35
(D)   40
(E)   47

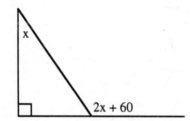

Since $2x + 60$ is an exterior angle, it is equal to the sum of the remote interior angles. That is, $2x + 60 = x + 90$. Solving for x gives $x = 30$. The answer is (A).

In a 30°–60°–90° triangle, the sides have the following relationships:

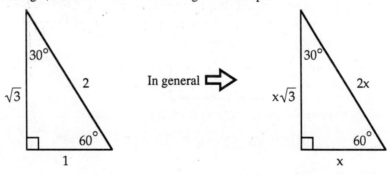

In general

In a 45°–45°–90° triangle, the sides have the following relationships:

Quadrilaterals

A *quadrilateral* is a four-sided closed figure, where each side is a straight line.

The angle sum of a quadrilateral is 360°. You can view a quadrilateral as being composed of two 180-degree triangles:

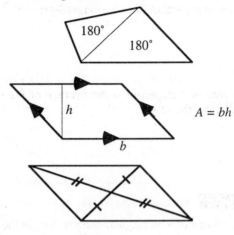

A *parallelogram* is a quadrilateral in which the opposite sides are both parallel and congruent. Its area is *base × height*:

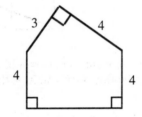

$A = bh$

The diagonals of a parallelogram bisect each other:

A parallelogram with four right angles is a *rectangle*. If *w* is the width and *l* is the length of a rectangle, then its area is $A = l \cdot w$ and its perimeter is $P = 2w + 2l$..

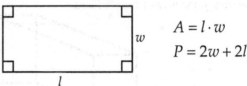

$A = l \cdot w$

$P = 2w + 2l$

Example: In the figure to the right, what is the perimeter of the pentagon?
(A)   12
(B)   13
(C)   17
(D)   20
(E)   25

Add the following line to the figure:

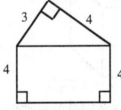

Since the legs of the right triangle formed are of lengths 3 and 4, the triangle must be a 3-4-5 right triangle. Hence, the added line has length 5. Since the bottom figure is a rectangle, the length of the base of the figure is also 5. Hence, the perimeter of the pentagon is $3 + 4 + 4 + 5 + 4 = 20$. The answer is (D).

If the opposite sides of a rectangle are equal, it is a square and its area is $A = s^2$ and its perimeter is $P = 4s$, where *s* is the length of a side:

$A = s^2$

$P = 4s$

The diagonals of a square bisect each other and are perpendicular to each other:

A quadrilateral with only one pair of parallel sides is a *trapezoid*. The parallel sides are called *bases*, and the non-parallel sides are called *legs*:

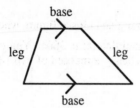

The area of a trapezoid is the average of the two bases times the height:

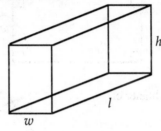

$$A = \left(\frac{b_1+b_2}{2}\right)h$$

Volume

The volume of a rectangular solid (a box) is the product of the length, width, and height. The surface area is the sum of the area of the six faces:

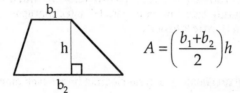

$$V = l \cdot w \cdot h$$
$$S = 2wl + 2hl + 2wh$$

If the length, width, and height of a rectangular solid (a box) are the same, it is a cube. Its volume is the cube of one of its sides, and its surface area is the sum of the areas of the six faces:

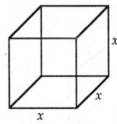

$$V = x^3$$
$$S = 6x^2$$

Example: The volume of the cube to the right is x and its surface area is x. What is the length of an edge of the cube?

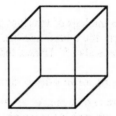

    (A)   6
    (B)   10
    (C)   18
    (D)   36
    (E)   48

Let e be the length of an edge of the cube. Recall that the volume of a cube is e^3 and its surface area is $6e^2$. Since we are given that both the volume and the surface area are x, these expressions are equal:

$$e^3 = 6e^2$$
$$e^3 - 6e^2 = 0$$
$$e^2(e-6) = 0$$
$$e^2 = 0 \text{ or } e - 6 = 0$$
$$e = 0 \text{ or } e = 6$$

We reject $e = 0$ since in that case no cube would exist. Hence, $e = 6$ and the answer is (A).

The volume of a cylinder is $V = \pi r^2 h$, and the lateral surface (excluding the top and bottom) is $S = 2\pi rh$, where r is the radius and h is the height:

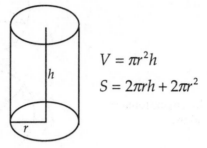

$$V = \pi r^2 h$$
$$S = 2\pi rh + 2\pi r^2$$

Circles

A circle is a set of points in a plane equidistant from a fixed point (the center of the circle). The perimeter of a circle is called the *circumference*.

A line segment from a circle to its center is a *radius*.

A line segment with both end points on a circle is a *chord*.

A chord passing though the center of a circle is a *diameter*.

A diameter can be viewed as two radii, and hence a diameter's length is twice that of a radius.

A line passing through two points on a circle is a *secant*.

A piece of the circumference is an *arc*.

The area bounded by the circumference and an angle with vertex at the center of the circle is a *sector*.

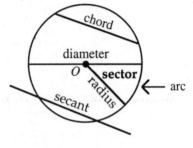

A tangent line to a circle intersects the circle at only one point. The radius of the circle is perpendicular to the tangent line at the point of tangency:

Two tangents to a circle from a common exterior point of the circle are congruent:

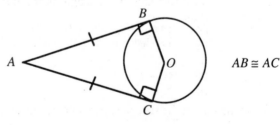

$AB \cong AC$

An angle inscribed in a semicircle is a right angle:

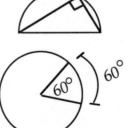

A central angle has by definition the same measure as its intercepted arc:

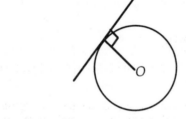

An inscribed angle has one-half the measure of its intercepted arc:

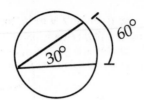

The area of a circle is πr^2, and its circumference (perimeter) is $2\pi r$, where r is the radius:

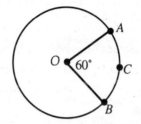

$$A = \pi r^2$$
$$C = 2\pi r$$

On the SAT, $\pi \approx 3$ is a sufficient approximation for π. You don't need $\pi \approx 3.14$.

Example: In the figure to the right, the circle has center O and its radius is 2. What is the length of arc ACB ?

(A) $\dfrac{\pi}{3}$ (B) $\dfrac{2\pi}{3}$ (C) π (D) $\dfrac{4\pi}{3}$ (E) $\dfrac{7\pi}{3}$

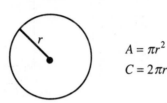

The circumference of the circle is $2\pi r = 2\pi(2) = 4\pi$. A central angle has by definition the same degree measure as its intercepted arc. Hence, arc ACB is also 60°. Now, the circumference of the circle has 360°. So arc ACB is $\dfrac{1}{6}$ (= 60/360) of the circle's circumference. Hence, arc $ACB = \dfrac{1}{6}(4\pi) = \dfrac{2}{3}\pi$. The answer is (B).

Shaded Regions

To find the area of the shaded region of a figure, subtract the area of the unshaded region from the area of the entire figure.

Example: What is the area of the shaded region formed by the circle and the rectangle in the figure to the right?
(A) $15 - 2\pi$
(B) $15 - \pi$
(C) 14
(D) $16 - \pi$
(E) 15π

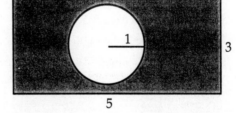

To find the area of the shaded region subtract the area of the circle from the area of the rectangle:

area of rectangle	–	area of circle
$3 \cdot 5$	–	$\pi \cdot 1^2$
15	–	π

The answer is (B).

Example: In the figure to the right, the radius of the larger circle is three times that of the smaller circle. If the circles are concentric, what is the ratio of the shaded region's area to the area of the smaller circle?

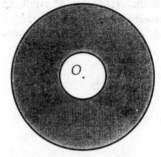

(A) 10:1
(B) 9:1
(C) 8:1
(D) 3:1
(E) 5:2

Since we are not given the radii of the circles, we can choose any two positive numbers such that one is three times the other. Let the outer radius be 3 and the inner radius be 1. Then the area of the outer circle is $\pi 3^2 = 9\pi$, and the area of the inner circle is $\pi 1^2 = \pi$. So the area of the shaded region is $9\pi - \pi = 8\pi$. Hence, the ratio of the area of the shaded region to the area of the smaller circle is $\dfrac{8\pi}{\pi} = \dfrac{8}{1}$. Therefore, the answer is (C).

"Birds-Eye" View

Most geometry problems on the SAT require straightforward calculations. However, some problems measure your insight into the basic rules of geometry. For this type of problem, you should step back and take a "birds-eye" view of the problem. The following example will illustrate.

Example: In the figure to the right, O is both the center of the circle with radius 2 and a vertex of the square OPRS. What is the length of diagonal PS?

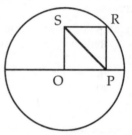

(A) 1/2 (B) $\dfrac{\sqrt{2}}{2}$ (C) 4 (D) 2 (E) $2\sqrt{5}$

The diagonals of a square are equal. Hence, line segment OR (not shown) is equal to SP. Now, OR is a radius of the circle and therefore OR = 2. Hence, SP = 2 as well, and the answer is (D).

Problem Set G:

Solutions begin on page 535.

1.   In the figure to the right, what is the value of y ?

(A) $\sqrt{23}$
(B) $\sqrt{27}$
(C) $\sqrt{29}$
(D) $\sqrt{33}$
(E) $\sqrt{35}$

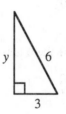

2.   In the figure to the right, circle P has diameter 2 and circle Q has diameter 1. What is the area of the shaded region?

circle P

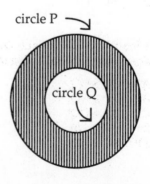

(A) $\dfrac{3}{4}\pi$
(B) 3π
(C) $\dfrac{7}{2}\pi$
(D) 5π
(E) 6π

3. In the figure to the right, QRST is a square. If the shaded region is bounded by arcs of circles with centers at Q, R, S, and T, then the area of the shaded region is

   (A) 9
   (B) 36
   (C) $36 - 9\pi$
   (D) $36 - \pi$
   (E) $9 - 3\pi$

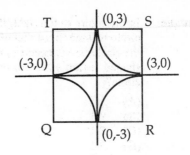

4. In the figure to the right, QRST is a square. If the area of each circle is 2π, then the area of square QRST is

   (A) $\sqrt{2}$
   (B) 4
   (C) $\sqrt{2}\pi$
   (D) $4\sqrt{2}$
   (E) 32

5. In the figure to the right, if O is the center of the circle, then $y =$

   (A) 75
   (B) 76
   (C) 77
   (D) 78
   (E) 79

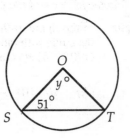

6. In the figure to the right, the value of $a + b$ is

   (A) 118
   (B) 119
   (C) 120
   (D) 121
   (E) 122

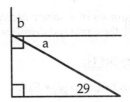

7. If $l_1 \| l_2$ in the figure to the right, what is the value of x?

   (A) 30
   (B) 45
   (C) 60
   (D) 72
   (E) 90

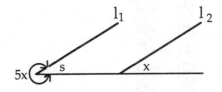

8. In the figure to the right, O is the center of the circle. Which one of the following must be true?

   (A) PQ > OQ
   (B) OP ≥ OQ
   (C) PQ = OQ
   (D) OQ < OP
   (E) PQ ≤ OP

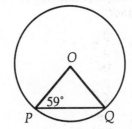

9. In the figure to the right, x is both the radius of the larger circle and the diameter of the smaller circle. The area of the shaded region is

    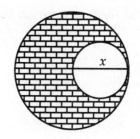

    (A) $\dfrac{3}{4}\pi x^2$

    (B) $\dfrac{\pi}{3}$

    (C) $\dfrac{4}{3}\pi x^2$

    (D) $\dfrac{3}{5}\pi x^2$

    (E) πx^2

10. In the figure to the right, the circle with center O is inscribed in the square PQRS. The combined area of the shaded regions is

    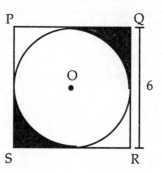

    (A) $36 - 9\pi$

    (B) $36 - \dfrac{9}{2}\pi$

    (C) $\dfrac{36 - 9\pi}{2}$

    (D) $18 - 9\pi$

    (E) $9 - \dfrac{9}{4}\pi$

11. In the figure to the right, the length of QS is

    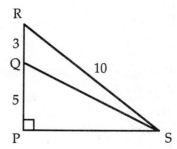

    (A) $\sqrt{51}$

    (B) $\sqrt{61}$

    (C) $\sqrt{69}$

    (D) $\sqrt{77}$

    (E) $\sqrt{89}$

12. In the figure to the right, which one of the following must be true about y ?

    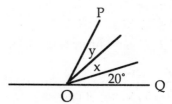

    (A) $y > 37$
    (B) $y < 35$
    (C) $y > 40$
    (D) $y > 42$
    (E) $y > 45$

    $\angle POQ = 70°$ and $x > 15$

13. In the figure to the right, if $l \| k$, then what is the value of y ?

    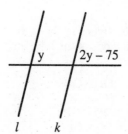

    (A)   20
    (B)   45
    (C)   55
    (D)   75
    (E)   110

14. In the figure to the right, both triangles are right triangles. The area of the shaded region is

    (A)   1/2
    (B)   2/3
    (C)   7/8
    (D)   3/2
    (E)   5/2

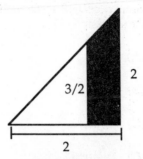

15. In the figure to the right, the radius of the larger circle is twice that of the smaller circle. If the circles are concentric, what is the ratio of the shaded region's area to the area of the smaller circle?

    (A)   10:1
    (B)   9:1
    (C)   3:1
    (D)   2:1
    (E)   1:1

16. In the figure to the right, ΔPST is an isosceles right triangle, and $PS = 2$. What is the area of the shaded region URST?

    (A)   4
    (B)   2
    (C)   5/4
    (D)   5/6
    (E)   1/2

17. In the figure to the right, the area of ΔPQR is 40. What is the area of ΔQRS?

    (A)   10
    (B)   15
    (C)   20
    (D)   25
    (E)   45

18. In the figure to the right, PQRS is a square and M and N are midpoints of their respective sides. What is the area of quadrilateral PMRN?

    (A)   8
    (B)   10
    (C)   12
    (D)   14
    (E)   16

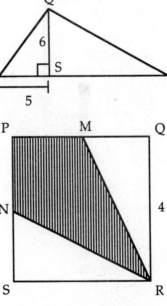

19. In the figure to the right, O is the center of the circle. If the area of the circle is 9π, then the perimeter of the sector *PRQO* is

(A) $\dfrac{\pi}{2} - 6$

(B) $\dfrac{\pi}{2} + 6$

(C) $\dfrac{3}{4}\pi + 6$

(D) $\dfrac{\pi}{2} + 18$

(E) $\dfrac{3}{4}\pi + 18$

20. Let *A* denote the area of a circular region. Which of the following denotes the circumference of that circular region?

(A) $\sqrt{\dfrac{A}{\pi}}$

(B) $2\dfrac{A}{\sqrt{\pi}}$

(C) $2\pi\sqrt{A}$

(D) $2\sqrt{\dfrac{A}{\pi}}$

(E) $2\pi\sqrt{\dfrac{A}{\pi}}$

21. Ship X and ship Y are 5 miles apart and are on a collision course. Ship X is sailing directly north, and ship Y is sailing directly east. If the point of impact is 1 mile closer to the current position of ship X than to the current position of ship Y, how many miles away from the point of impact is ship Y at this time?

(A) 1
(B) 2
(C) 3
(D) 4
(E) 5

22. The figure to the right represents a square with sides of length 4 surmounted by a circle with center *O*. What is the outer perimeter of the figure?

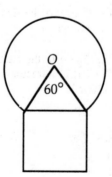

(A) $\dfrac{5}{6}\pi + 12$

(B) $\pi + 12$

(C) $\dfrac{49}{9}\pi + 12$

(D) $\dfrac{20}{3}\pi + 12$

(E) $9\pi + 12$

23. In $\triangle ABC$ to the right, $AB = AC$ and $x = 30$.
    What is the value of y?
    (A)   30
    (B)   40
    (C)   50
    (D)   65
    (E)   75

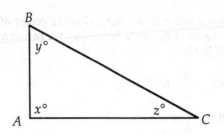

Note, figure not drawn to scale.

24. In the figure to the right, $c^2 = 6^2 + 8^2$. What is the
    area of the triangle?

    (A)   12
    (B)   18
    (C)   24
    (D)   30
    (E)   36

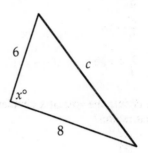

25. If the total surface area of cube S is 22, what is the volume of S?

    (A) $\dfrac{1}{3}\sqrt{\dfrac{11}{3}}$

    (B) $\dfrac{\sqrt{11}}{3}$

    (C) $\dfrac{11}{3}$

    (D) $\dfrac{11}{3}\sqrt{\dfrac{11}{3}}$

    (E) $\dfrac{121}{9}$

26. In the figure to the right, what is the area of the
    triangle?

    (A)   5
    (B)   9
    (C)   10
    (D)   15
    (E)   It cannot be determined from the informa-
          tion given

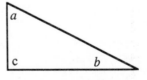

$a = x$, $b = 2x$, and $c = 3x$.

27. In the figure to the right, $\triangle ABC$ is inscribed in the circle
    and AB is a diameter of the circle. What is the radius of
    the circle?

    (A)   3/2
    (B)   2
    (C)   5/2
    (D)   5
    (E)   6

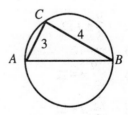

Duals

28. In the figure to the right, the circle is inscribed in the square. If the area of the square is 16 square feet, what is the area of the shaded region?

    (A) $16 - 16\pi$
    (B) $16 - 4.4\pi$
    (C) $16 - 4\pi$
    (D) 2π
    (E) 4π

29. In the figure to the right, the circle is inscribed in the square. If the area of the circle is 1.21π square feet, what is the area of the shaded region?

    (A) $14 - 14.4\pi$
    (B) $4.84 - 1.21\pi$
    (C) $8 - 3\pi$
    (D) 1.21π
    (E) $\dfrac{11}{2}\pi$

Duals

30. In $\triangle PQR$ to the right, $x = 60$. What is the value of y?

    (A)   60
    (B)   55
    (C)   50
    (D)   45
    (E)   40

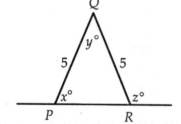

31. In $\triangle PQR$ to the right, $y + z = 150$. What is the value of y?

    (A)   60
    (B)   55
    (C)   50
    (D)   45
    (E)   40

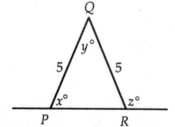

32. In the figure to the right, what is the area of the triangle?

    (A)   5
    (B)   9
    (C)   10
    (D)   15
    (E)   It cannot be determined from the information given

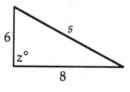

33. If point P in the figure to the right makes one complete revolution around the triangle which has height 4, what is the length of the path traveled by P?

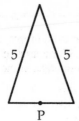

    (A) $\sqrt{150}$
    (B)   14
    (C) $\sqrt{200}$
    (D)   15
    (E)   16

34. The opposite sides of quadrilateral Q are parallel and one of the four angles of Q is 90 degrees. If θ is an angle of quadrilateral Q, which one of the following must be true?

    (A) $\theta = 80°$
    (B) $\theta = 88°$
    (C) $\theta = 90°$
    (D) $\theta = 91°$
    (E)   It cannot be determined from the information given

35. In the figure to the right, the coordinates of A are $(\sqrt{3},3)$. If $\triangle ABO$ is equilateral, what is the area of $\triangle ABO$?

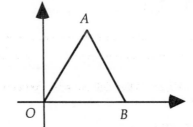

    (A) $\dfrac{1}{2}\sqrt{3}$

    (B) $\dfrac{3}{2}\sqrt{3}$

    (C) $3\sqrt{3}$

    (D) $6\sqrt{3}$

    (E) $9\sqrt{3}$

36. In the figure to the right, E is the midpoint of AD. What is the length of EB?

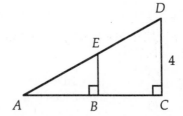

    (A)   1
    (B)   2
    (C)   11/5
    (D)   5/2
    (E)   3

37. If the sides x of the rectangle to the right are increased by 3 units, the resulting figure is a square with area 20. What was the original area?

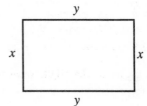

    (A) $20 - 3\sqrt{20}$
    (B) $20 - 2\sqrt{20}$
    (C) $20 - \sqrt{20}$
    (D) $20 - \sqrt{2}$
    (E)   19

Duals

38. In the figure to the right, h denotes the height and b the base of the triangle. If $2b + h = 6$, what is the area of the triangle?

    (A)   1
    (B)   2
    (C)   3
    (D)   4
    (E)   Not enough information

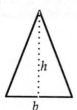

39. In the figure to the right, h denotes the height and b the base of the triangle. If $(bh)^2 = 16$, what is the area of the triangle?

    (A)   1
    (B)   2
    (C)   3
    (D)   4
    (E)   Not enough information

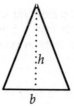

Duals

40. If the ratio of an edge of cube S and the greatest distance between two points on the cube is $1 : \sqrt{3}$, then the volume of cube S must be

    (A)   greater than 8
    (B)   less than 8
    (C)   equal to 8
    (D)   greater than or equal to 8
    (E)   Not enough information to decide

41. If the length of a diagonal across a face of cube S is 2, then the volume of cube S must be

    (A)   greater than 8
    (B)   less than 8
    (C)   equal to 8
    (D)   greater than or equal to 8
    (E)   Not enough information to decide

42. In the parallelogram to the right, $\angle BAD + \angle BCD = 140$. What is the measure of $\angle ABC$?

    (A)   100
    (B)   110
    (C)   120
    (D)   125
    (E)   142

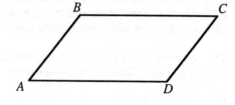

43. An equilateral triangle is inscribed in a circle, as shown to the right. If the radius of the circle is 2, what is the area of the triangle?

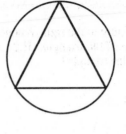

(A) $\dfrac{\sqrt{2}}{2}$

(B) $\sqrt{2}$

(C) $\sqrt{3}$

(D) $3\sqrt{3}$

(E) $10\sqrt{3}$

44. The triangle to the right has side *DC* of the square as its base. If *DM* = 5 and *M* is the midpoint of side *AB*, what is the area of the shaded region?

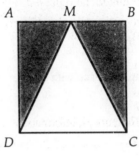

(A) $\dfrac{5}{2}$

(B) $\sqrt{10}$

(C) $\sqrt{15}$

(D) 4

(E) 10

45. A square with sides of length 3 is intersected by a line at *S* and *T*. What is the maximum possible distance between *S* and *T*?

(A) $\sqrt{6}$ (B) $2\sqrt{3}$ (C) $3\sqrt{2}$ (D) $2\sqrt{5}$ (E) 9

46. In the triangle to the right, what is the value of $\dfrac{x+y+z}{15}$?

(A) 9

(B) 10

(C) 11

(D) 12

(E) 13

47. If a square has an area of a^2 and a right-angled isosceles triangle also has area is a^2, then which one of the following must be true?

(A) The perimeter of the square is greater than the perimeter of the triangle.
(B) The perimeter of the square is less than the perimeter of the triangle.
(C) The perimeter of the square is equal to the perimeter of the triangle.
(D) The perimeter of the square is greater than or equal to the perimeter of the triangle.
(E) It cannot be determined which perimeter is greater from the information given

48. The perimeter of a square is equal to the perimeter of a rectangle whose length and width are 6*m* and 4*m*, respectively. The side of the square is

(A) 3*m*
(B) 4*m*
(C) 5*m*
(D) 6*m*
(E) 7*m*

49. If the circumference of a circle is $4m$, then the ratio of circumference of the circle to the diameter of the circle is

(A) π
(B) 4
(C) 2π
(D) 4π
(E) 16

50. In Triangle ABC, $\angle A$ is 10 degrees greater than $\angle B$, and $\angle B$ is 10 degrees greater than $\angle C$. The value of Angle B is

(A) 30
(B) 40
(C) 50
(D) 60
(E) 70

51. Two squares each with sides of length s are joined to form a rectangle. The area of the rectangle is

(A) s^2
(B) $2s^2$
(C) $4s^2$
(D) $8s^2$
(E) $16s^2$

52. A person travels 16 miles due north and then 12 miles due east. How far is the person from his initial location?

(A) 4 miles
(B) 8 miles
(C) 14 miles
(D) 20 miles
(E) 28 miles

53. The area of Triangle PQR is 6. If $PR = 4$, then the length of the hypotenuse QR is

(A) 1
(B) 2
(C) 3
(D) 4
(E) 5

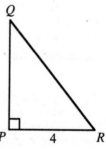

54. In the figure, the equation of line AB is $y = -\dfrac{5}{3}x + 10$.

The area of the shaded portion is

(A) 12
(B) 30
(C) 100/3
(D) 60
(E) 100

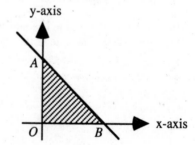

55. In the figure to the right, which one of the following must be true about the angle θ ?

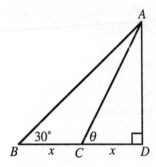

(A) $\theta = 60°$
(B) $\theta < 60°$
(C) $\theta > 60°$
(D) $\theta > 70°$
(E) It cannot be determined from the information given

56. In the figure, if $x = 54°$ and $y = 72°$, then $z =$

(A) 54°
(B) 56°
(C) 72°
(D) 76°
(E) 98°

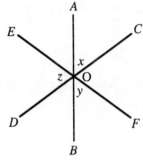

O is the point of intersection of the three lines in the figure.

57. If one of the sides of the rectangle shown in the figure has a length of 3, then the area of the rectangle is

(A) 9
(B) 13.5
(C) 18
(D) 27
(E) 54

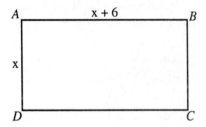

58. The value of $x + y + z =$

(A) 120°
(B) 160°
(C) 180°
(D) 270°
(E) 360°

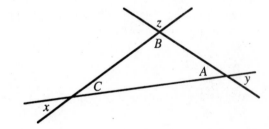

59. In the figure, what is the area of Triangle ABC ?

(A) 25
(B) 50
(C) $100/\sqrt{2}$
(D) 100
(E) $100\sqrt{2}$

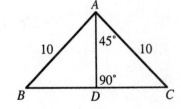

60. In the triangle to the right, $y/x = 3$. Which one of the following must be true?

(A) $4x > z$
(B) $4x < z$
(C) $4x \leq z$
(D) $4x = z$
(E) It cannot be determined from the information given

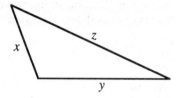

61. In the figure to the right, which one of the following statements about the circumference C of the circle and the perimeter P of Square $PQRS$ must be true?

(A) $C > P$
(B) $C < P$
(C) $C \leq P$
(D) $C = P$
(E) It cannot be determined from the information given

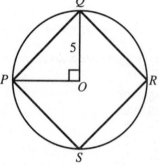

O is the center of the circle, and the radius of the circle is 5.

62. In the figure, what is the value of x?

(A) 20°
(B) 30°
(C) 40°
(D) 50°
(E) 60°

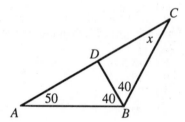

63. The area of the Triangle ABC shown in the figure is 30. The area of Triangle ADC is

(A) 5
(B) 10
(C) 15
(D) 20
(E) 25

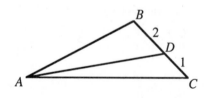

64. In the figure, what is the value of y ?

(A) 7.5
(B) 15
(C) 30
(D) 40
(E) 45

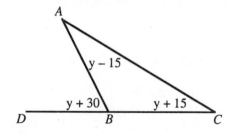

65. A circle is depicted in the rectangular coordinate system as shown. The value of x is

(A) 4
(B) 6
(C) 8
(D) 10
(E) 12

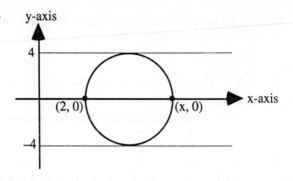

66. In the figure, the ratio of x to y is 2. What is the value of y?

(A) 108
(B) 90
(C) 68
(D) 45
(E) 36

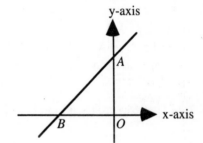

67. In the figure, the equation of line AB is $y = x + 2$. The difference of the x- and y-coordinates of any point on the line is equal to:

(A) −4
(B) −2
(C) 0
(D) 2
(E) 4

When Drawing a Geometric Figure or Checking a Given One, Be Sure to Include Drawings of Extreme Cases as Well as Ordinary Ones.

Example 1: In the figure to the right, what is the value of angle *x* ?

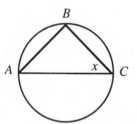

(A) $x > 45°$
(B) $x < 45°$
(C) $x = 45°$
(D) $x \geq 45°$
(E) It cannot be determined from the information given

AC is a chord.
B is a point on the circle.

Although in the drawing AC looks to be a diameter, that cannot be assumed. All we know is that AC is a chord. Hence, numerous cases are possible, three of which are illustrated below:

Case I

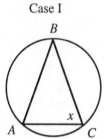

Case II

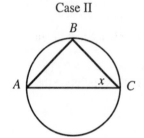

Case III

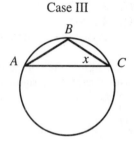

In Case I, *x* is greater than 45°; in Case II, *x* equals 45°; in Case III, *x* is less than 45°. Hence, the answer is (E).

Example 2: Three rays emanate from a common point and form three angles with measures *p*, *q*, *r*. Which one of the following is the measure of angle *q* + *r* ?

(A) $q + r > 180°$
(B) $q + r < 180°$
(C) $q + r = 180°$
(D) $q + r \leq 180°$
(E) It cannot be determined from the information given

It is natural to make the drawing symmetric as follows:

In this case, $p = q = r = 120°$, so $q + r = 240°$. However, there are other drawings possible. For example:

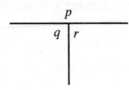

In this case, $q + r = 180°$ and therefore it cannot be determined from the information given. The answer is (E).

Problem Set H:

Solutions begin on page 565.

1. In triangle ABC, $AB = 5$ and $AC = 3$. Which one of the following is the measure of the length of side BC ?

    (A) $BC < 7$
    (B) $BC = 7$
    (C) $BC > 7$
    (D) $BC \leq 7$
    (E) It cannot be determined from the information given

2. In the figure to the right, what is the area of $\triangle ABC$?

    (A) 6
    (B) 7
    (C) 8
    (D) 9
    (E) It cannot be determined from the information given

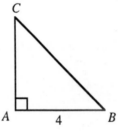

3. In the figure to the right, which one of the following is the measure of angle θ ?

    (A) $\theta < 45°$
    (B) $\theta > 45°$
    (C) $\theta = 45°$
    (D) $\theta \leq 45°$
    (E) It cannot be determined from the information given

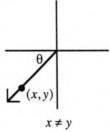

4. In isosceles triangle ABC, $CA = CB = 4$. Which one of the following is the area of triangle ABC ?

    (A) 7
    (B) 8
    (C) 9
    (D) 10
    (E) It cannot be determined from the information given

Eye-Balling

Surprisingly, on the SAT you can often solve geometry problems by merely "eye-balling" the given drawing. Even on problems whose answers you can't get directly by looking, you often can eliminate a couple of the answer-choices.

• Unless stated otherwise, all figures are drawn exactly to scale. Hence, if an angle looks like it's about 90°, it is; if one figure looks like it's about twice as large as another figure, it is.

All the problems in this section were solved before. Now, we will solve them by eye-balling the drawings.

Example 1:   In the figure to the right, if $l \| k$, then what is the value of y ?

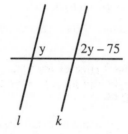

(A)   20
(B)   45
(C)   55
(D)   75
(E)   110

By eye-balling the drawing, we can see that y is less than 90°. It appears to be somewhere between 65° and 85°. But 75° is the only answer-choice in that range. Hence, the answer is (D).

Example 2:   In the figure to the right, the area of the shaded region is

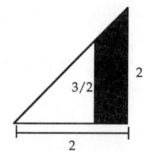

(A)   1/2
(B)   2/3
(C)   7/8
(D)   3/2
(E)   5/2

The area of the larger triangle is $A = \dfrac{1}{2} bh = \dfrac{1}{2} \cdot 2 \cdot 2 = 2$. Now, by eye-balling the drawing, the area of the shaded region looks to be about half that of the larger triangle. Therefore, the answer should be about $\dfrac{1}{2} \cdot 2 = 1$. The closest answer-choice to 1 is $\dfrac{7}{8}$. The answer is (C).

Note: On the SAT, answer-choices are listed in order of size: usually from smallest to largest (unless the question asks for the smallest or largest). Hence, in the previous example, $\dfrac{2}{3}$ is smaller than $\dfrac{7}{8}$ because it comes before $\dfrac{7}{8}$.

Problem Set I:

Solutions begin on page 567.

1. In the figure to the right, the radius of the larger circle is twice that of the smaller circle. If the circles are concentric, what is the ratio of the shaded region's area to the area of the smaller circle?

    (A) 10:1
    (B) 9:1
    (C) 3:1
    (D) 2:1
    (E) 1:1

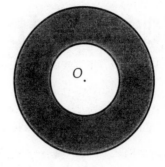

2. In the figure to the right, $\triangle PST$ is an isosceles right triangle, and $PS = 2$. What is the area of the shaded region URST?

    (A) 4
    (B) 2
    (C) 5/4
    (D) 5/6
    (E) 1/2

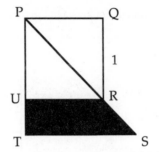

3. In the figure to the right, the area of $\triangle PQR$ is 40. What is the area of $\triangle QRS$?

    (A) 10
    (B) 15
    (C) 20
    (D) 25
    (E) 45

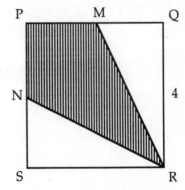

4. In the figure to the right, PQRS is a square and M and N are midpoints of their respective sides. What is the area of quadrilateral PMRN?

    (A) 8
    (B) 10
    (C) 12
    (D) 14
    (E) 16

Coordinate Geometry

On a number line, the numbers increase in size to the right and decrease to the left:

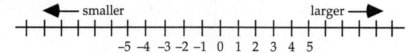

If we draw a line through the point 0 perpendicular to the number line, we will form a grid:

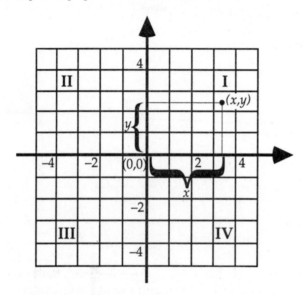

The thick horizontal line in the above diagram is called the x-axis, and the thick vertical line is called the y-axis. The point at which the axes meet, $(0, 0)$, is called the origin. On the x-axis, positive numbers are to the right of the origin and increase in size to the right; further, negative numbers are to the left of the origin and decrease in size to the left. On the y-axis, positive numbers are above the origin and ascend in size; further, negative numbers are below the origin and descend in size. As shown in the diagram, the point represented by the ordered pair (x, y) is reached by moving x units along the x-axis from the origin and then moving y units vertically. In the ordered pair (x, y), x is called the *abscissa* and y is called the *ordinate*; collectively they are called coordinates. The x and y axes divide the plane into four quadrants, numbered I, II, III, and IV counterclockwise. Note, if $x \neq y$, then (x, y) and (y, x) represent different points on the coordinate system. The points $(2, 3)$, $(-3, 1)$, $(-4, -4)$, and $(4, -2)$ are plotted in the following coordinate system:

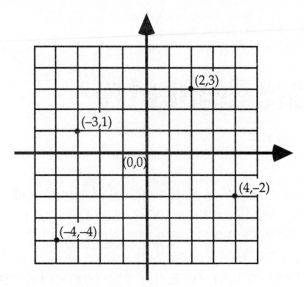

Example: In the figure to the right, polygon *ABCO* is a
square. If the coordinates of *B* are (*h*,4),
what is the value of *h* ?

(A)   4
(B) $4\sqrt{2}$
(C) $-4\sqrt{2}$
(D) -4
(E)   not enough information

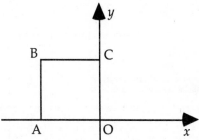

Since the *y*-coordinate of point *B* is 4, line segment *CO* has length 4. Since figure *ABCO* is a square, line
segment *AO* also has length 4. Since point *B* is in the second quadrant, the *x*-coordinate of *B* is –4. The
answer is (D). Be careful not to choose 4. *h* is the *x*-coordinate of point *B*, not the length of the square's
side.

Distance Formula:

The distance formula is derived by using the Pythagorean theorem. Notice in the figure below that the
distance between the points (*x*,*y*) and (*a*,*b*) is the hypotenuse of a right triangle. The difference *y*–*b* is the
measure of the height of the triangle, and the difference *x*–*a* is the length of base of the triangle. Applying
the Pythagorean theorem yields

$$d^2 = (x - a)^2 + (y - b)^2$$

Taking the square root of both sides this equation yields

$$d = \sqrt{(x-a)^2 + (y-b)^2}$$

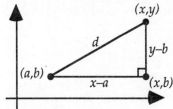

Example: In the figure to the right, the circle is centered at the origin and passes through point *P*. Which of the following points does it also pass through?

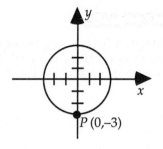

(A)   (3,3)
(B) $\left(-2\sqrt{2},-1\right)$
(C)   (2,6)
(D) $\left(-\sqrt{3},\sqrt{3}\right)$
(E)   (−3,4)

Since the circle is centered at the origin and passes through the point (0,−3), the radius of the circle is 3. Now, if any other point is on the circle, the distance from that point to the center of the circle (the radius) must also be 3.   Look at choice (B).   Using the distance formula to calculate the distance between $\left(-2\sqrt{2},-1\right)$ and (0,0) (the origin) yields

$$d = \sqrt{\left(-2\sqrt{2}-0\right)^2 + \left(-1-0\right)^2} = \sqrt{\left(-2\sqrt{2}\right)^2 + \left(-1\right)^2} = \sqrt{8+1} = \sqrt{9} = 3$$

Hence, $\left(-2\sqrt{2},-1\right)$ is on the circle, and the answer is (B).

Midpoint Formula:

The midpoint M between points (*x*,*y*) and (*a*,*b*) is given by

$$M = \left(\frac{x+a}{2}, \frac{y+b}{2}\right)$$

In other words, to find the midpoint, simply average the corresponding coordinates of the two points.

Example: In the figure to the right, polygon *PQRO* is a square and *T* is the midpoint of side *QR*. What are the coordinates of *T* ?

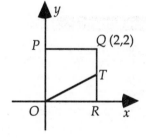

(A)   (1,1)
(B)   (1,2)
(C)   (1.5,1.5)
(D)   (2,1)
(E)   (2,3)

Since point *R* is on the *x*-axis, its *y*-coordinate is 0. Further, since *PQRO* is a square and the *x*-coordinate of *Q* is 2, the *x*-coordinate of *R* is also 2. Since *T* is the midpoint of side *QR*, the midpoint formula yields

$$T = \left(\frac{2+2}{2}, \frac{2+0}{2}\right) = \left(\frac{4}{2}, \frac{2}{2}\right) = (2,1)$$

The answer is (D).

Slope Formula:

The slope of a line measures the inclination of the line. By definition, it is the ratio of the vertical change to the horizontal change (see figure below). The vertical change is called the *rise*, and the horizontal change is called the *run*. Thus, the slope is the *rise over the run*.

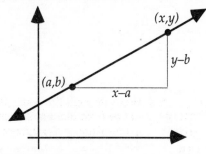

Forming the *rise over the run* in the above figure yields

$$m = \frac{y - b}{x - a}$$

Example: In the figure to the right, what is the slope of line passing through the two points?

(A) $\dfrac{1}{4}$ (B) 1   (C) $\dfrac{1}{2}$ (D) $\dfrac{3}{2}$ (E) 2

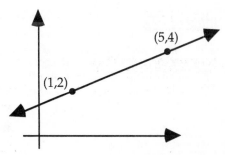

The slope formula yields $m = \dfrac{4-2}{5-1} = \dfrac{2}{4} = \dfrac{1}{2}$. The answer is (C).

Slope-Intercept Form:

Multiplying both sides of the equation $m = \dfrac{y - b}{x - a}$ by $x\text{–}a$ yields

$$y - b = m(x - a)$$

Now, if the line passes through the y-axis at $(0,b)$, then the equation becomes

$$y - b = m(x - 0)$$

or

$$y - b = mx$$

or

$$y = mx + b$$

This is called the slope-intercept form of the equation of a line, where m is the slope and b is the y-intercept. This form is convenient because it displays the two most important bits of information about a line: its slope and its y-intercept.

Example: In the figure to the right, the equation of the

line is $y = \dfrac{9}{10}x + k$. Which one of the follow-

ing must be true about line segments AO and BO ?

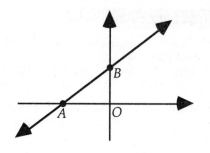

(A) $AO > BO$
(B) $AO < BO$
(C) $AO \le BO$
(D) $AO = BO$
(E) $AO = BO/2$

Since $y = \dfrac{9}{10}x + k$ is in slope-intercept form, we know the slope of the line is $\dfrac{9}{10}$. Now, the ratio of BO to

AO is the slope of the line (rise over run). Hence, $\dfrac{BO}{AO} = \dfrac{9}{10}$. Multiplying both sides of this equation by

AO yields $BO = \dfrac{9}{10}AO$. In other words, BO is $\dfrac{9}{10}$ the length of AO. Hence, AO is longer. The answer is
(A).

Intercepts:

The x-intercept is the point where the line crosses the x-axis. It is found by setting $y = 0$ and solving the resulting equation. The y-intercept is the point where the line crosses the y-axis. It is found by setting $x = 0$ and solving the resulting equation.

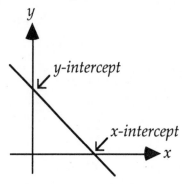

Example: Graph the equation $x - 2y = 4$.

Solution: To find the x-intercept, set $y = 0$. This yields $x - 2 \cdot 0 = 4$, or $x = 4$. So the x-intercept is (4,0). To find the y-intercept, set $x = 0$. This yields $0 - 2y = 4$, or $y = -2$. So the y-intercept is (0,–2). Plotting these two points and connecting them with a straight line yields

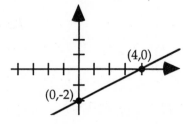

Areas and Perimeters:

Often, you will be given a geometric figure drawn on a coordinate system and will be asked to find its area or perimeter. In these problems, use the properties of the coordinate system to deduce the dimensions of the figure and then calculate the area or perimeter. For complicated figures, you may need to divide the figure into simpler forms, such as squares and triangles. A couple examples will illustrate:

Example: What is the area of the quadrilateral in the coordinate system to the right?

(A) 2
(B) 4
(C) 6
(D) 8
(E) 11

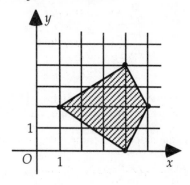

If the quadrilateral is divided horizontally through the line $y = 2$, two congruent triangles are formed. As the figure to the right shows, the top triangle has height 2 and base 4. Hence, its area is

$$A = \frac{1}{2} bh = \frac{1}{2} \cdot 4 \cdot 2 = 4$$

The area of the bottom triangle is the same, so the area of the quadrilateral is $4 + 4 = 8$. The answer is (D).

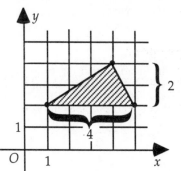

Example: What is the perimeter of Triangle ABC in the figure to the right?

(A) $5 + \sqrt{5} + \sqrt{34}$
(B) $10 + \sqrt{34}$
(C) $5 + \sqrt{5} + \sqrt{28}$
(D) $2\sqrt{5} + \sqrt{34}$
(E) $\sqrt{5} + \sqrt{28}$

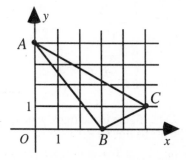

Point A has coordinates $(0, 4)$, point B has coordinates $(3, 0)$, and point C has coordinates $(5, 1)$. Using the distance formula to calculate the distances between points A and B, A and C, and B and C yields

$$\overline{AB} = \sqrt{(0-3)^2 + (4-0)^2} = \sqrt{9+16} = \sqrt{25} = 5$$
$$\overline{AC} = \sqrt{(0-5)^2 + (4-1)^2} = \sqrt{25+9} = \sqrt{34}$$
$$\overline{BC} = \sqrt{(5-3)^2 + (1-0)^2} = \sqrt{4+1} = \sqrt{5}$$

Adding these lengths gives the perimeter of Triangle ABC:

$$\overline{AB} + \overline{AC} + \overline{BC} = 5 + \sqrt{34} + \sqrt{5}$$

The answer is (A).

Problem Set J: Solutions begin on page 568.

1. In the figure to the right, *O* is the center of the circle. What is the area of the circle?

    (A) 2π
    (B) 3π
    (C) 5.5π
    (D) 7π
    (E) 9π

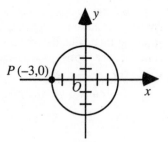

2. In the figure to the right, which one of the following must be true about the value of the *y*-coordinate of point *P* ?

    (A) $y < 6$
    (B) $y > 6$
    (C) $y > 5$
    (D) $y = 6$
    (E) $y < 5$

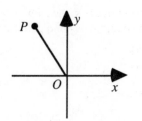

P is a point in the coordinate system and *OP* = 6.

3. In the figure to the right, the equation of the line is $y = px + a$. Which one of the following is the value of *p* ?

    (A) $p = \dfrac{-1}{2}$

    (B) $p = \dfrac{a}{b}$

    (C) $p = \dfrac{-a}{b}$

    (D) $p = \dfrac{b}{a}$

    (E) $p = \dfrac{-b}{a}$

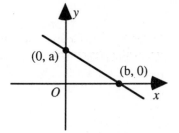

4. In the figure to the right, which one of the following must be true?

    (A) $y < x$
    (B) $y > x$
    (C) $y < 4$
    (D) $y = x$
    (E) $y > 5$

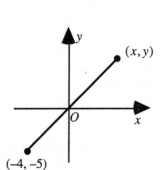

5. In the figure to the right, *a* is the *x*-coordinate of point *P* and *b* is the *y*-coordinate of point *Q*. In which quadrant is the point (*a*,*b*) ?

    (A)   I
    (B)   II
    (C)   III
    (D)   IV
    (E)   cannot be determined from the information given

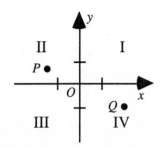

6.   In the figure to the right, if $x = 4$, then $y =$

(A)   1
(B)   2
(C)   3
(D)   4
(E)   5.1

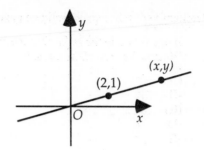

7.   In the figure to the right, which of the following could be the coordinates of a point in the shaded region?

(A)   (1, 2)
(B)   (−2, 3)
(C)   (3, −5)
(D)   (−5, 1)
(E)   (−1, −6)

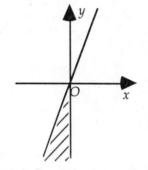

8.   In the figure to the right, which of the following points lies within the circle?

(A)   (3.5, 9.5)
(B)   (−7, 7)
(C)   (−10, 1)
(D)   (0, 11)
(E)   (5.5, 8.5)

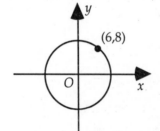

9.   In the figure to the right, the grid consists of unit squares. What is the area of the polygon?

(A)   7
(B)   9
(C)   10
(D)   12
(E)   15

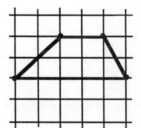

10.   In the figure to the right, which of the following points is three times as far from P as from Q ?

(A)   (0, 3)
(B)   (1, 1)
(C)   (4, 5)
(D)   (2, 3)
(E)   (4, 1)

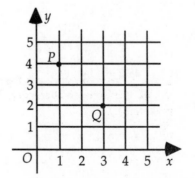

11. In the figure to the right, what is the area of quadrilateral *ABCO* ?

(A)   3
(B)   5
(C)   6.5
(D)   8
(E)   13

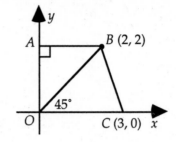

12. In the figure to the right, which quadrants contain points (x,y) such that $xy = -2$?

(A)   I only
(B)   II only
(C)   III and IV only
(D)   II and IV only
(E)   II, III, and IV

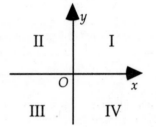

13. If the square in the figure to the right is rotated clockwise about the origin until vertex *V* is on the negative *y*-axis, then the new *y*-coordinate of *V* is

(A) -2
(B) $-2\sqrt{2}$
(C) -4
(D) $-3\sqrt{2}$
(E) -8

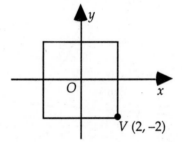

14. In the standard coordinate system, which of the following points is the greatest distance from the origin:

(A) $(-4, -1)$
(B) $(-3, 3)$
(C) $(4, 0)$
(D) $(2, 3)$
(E) $(0, 4)$

15. What is the perimeter of Triangle *ABC* in the figure to the right?

(A) $5 + \sqrt{2} + \sqrt{29}$
(B) $5 + 2\sqrt{2} + \sqrt{29}$
(C) $5 + 4\sqrt{2} + \sqrt{29}$
(D) $3\sqrt{2} + \sqrt{34}$
(E) $4\sqrt{2} + \sqrt{34}$

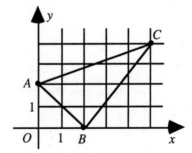

Elimination Strategies

1.   On hard problems, if you are asked to find the least (or greatest) number, then eliminate the least (or greatest) answer-choice.

This rule also applies to easy and medium problems. When people guess on these types of problems, they most often choose either the least or the greatest number. But if the least or the greatest number were the answer, most people would answer the problem correctly, and it therefore would not be a hard problem.

Note: 45% of the time the second smallest (or second largest) number is the answer. For easy and medium problems, this is true 40% of the time.

Example: What is the maximum number of points common to the intersection of a square and a triangle if no two sides coincide?

(A)   4
(B)   5
(C)   6
(D)   8
(E)   9

By the above rule, we eliminate answer-choice (E).

2.   On hard problems, eliminate the answer-choice "not enough information."

When people cannot solve a problem, they most often choose the answer-choice "not enough information." But if this were the answer, then it would not be a "hard" problem.

3.   On hard problems, eliminate answer-choices that <u>merely</u> repeat numbers from the problem.

Example: If the sum of x and 20 is 8 more than the difference of 10 and y, what is the value of $x + y$?

(A)   −2
(B)   8
(C)   9
(D)   28
(E)   not enough information

By the above rule, we eliminate choice (B) since it merely repeats the number 8 from the problem. By Strategy 2, we would also eliminate choice (E). **Caution:** If choice (B) contained more than the number 8, say, $8 + \sqrt{2}$, then it would not be eliminated by the above rule.

4.   On hard problems, eliminate answer-choices that can be derived from elementary operations.

Example: In the figure to the right, what is the
perimeter of parallelogram ABCD?

(A)   12
(B) $10 + 6\sqrt{2}$
(C) $20 + \sqrt{2}$
(D)   24
(E)   not enough information

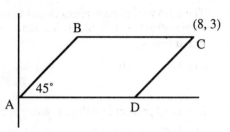

Using the above rule, we eliminate choice (D) since $24 = 8 \cdot 3$. Further, using Strategy 2, eliminate choice
(E). Note, 12 was offered as an answer-choice because some people will interpret the drawing as a
rectangle tilted halfway on its side and therefore expect it to have one-half its original area.

5.   **After you have eliminated as many answer-choices as you can, choose from the more
complicated or more unusual answer-choices remaining.**

Example: Suppose you were offered the following answer-choices:

(A) $4 + \sqrt{3}$
(B) $4 + 2\sqrt{3}$
(C)   8
(D)   10
(E)   12

Then you would choose either (A) or (B).

Problem Set K:

Solutions begin on page 574.

1.   What is the maximum number of 3x3 squares that
can be formed from the squares in the 6x6 checker
board to the right?

(A)   4
(B)   6
(C)   12
(D)   16
(E)   24

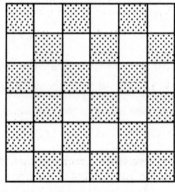

2.   Let P stand for the product of the first 5 positive integers. What is the greatest possible value of m if
$\dfrac{P}{10^m}$ is an integer?

(A)   1
(B)   2
(C)   3
(D)   5
(E)   10

3.   After being marked down 20 percent, a calculator sells for $10. The original selling price was

(A) $20
(B) $12.5
(C) $12
(D) $9
(E) $7

4.   The distance between cities A and B is 120 miles. A car travels from A to B at 60 miles per hour and returns from B to A along the same route at 40 miles per hour. What is the average speed for the round trip?

(A) 48   (B) 50   (C) 52   (D) 56   (E) 58

5.   If **w** is 10 percent less than **x**, and **y** is 30 percent less than **z**, then **wy** is what percent less than **xz**?

(A) 10%   (B) 20%   (C) 37%   (D) 40%   (E) 100%

6.   In the game of chess, the Knight can make any of the moves displayed in the diagram to the right. If a Knight is the only piece on the board, what is the greatest number of spaces from which not all 8 moves are possible?

(A)   8
(B)   24
(C)   38
(D)   48
(E)   56

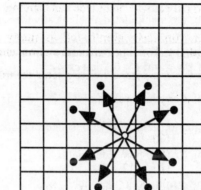

7.   How many different ways can 3 cubes be painted if each cube is painted one color and only the 3 colors red, blue, and green are available? (Order is not considered, for example, green, green, blue is considered the same as green, blue, green.)

(A) 2   (B) 3   (C) 9   (D) 10   (E) 27

8.   What is the greatest prime factor of $\left(2^4\right)^2 - 1$?

(A) 3   (B) 5   (C) 11   (D) 17   (E) 19

9.   Suppose five circles, each 4 inches in diameter, are cut from a rectangular strip of paper 12 inches long. If the least amount of paper is to be wasted, what is the width of the paper strip?

(A)   5
(B) $4 + 2\sqrt{3}$
(C)   8
(D) $4\left(1 + \sqrt{3}\right)$
(E)   not enough information

10.   Let C and K be constants. If $x^2 + Kx + 5$ factors into $(x + 1)(x + C)$, the value of K is

(A) 0   (B) 5   (C) 6   (D) 8   (E) not enough information

Inequalities

Inequalities are manipulated algebraically the same way as equations with one exception:

Multiplying or dividing both sides of an inequality by a negative number reverses the inequality. That is, if $x > y$ and $c < 0$, then $cx < cy$.

Example: For which values of x is $4x + 3 > 6x - 8$?

As with equations, our goal is to isolate x on one side:

Subtracting $6x$ from both sides yields $\qquad\qquad\qquad\qquad\qquad -2x + 3 > -8$

Subtracting 3 from both sides yields $\qquad\qquad\qquad\qquad\qquad -2x > -11$

Dividing both sides by -2 and reversing the inequality yields $\qquad\qquad x < \dfrac{11}{2}$

Positive & Negative Numbers

A number greater than 0 is positive. On the number line, positive numbers are to the right of 0. A number less than 0 is negative. On the number line, negative numbers are to the left of 0. Zero is the only number that is neither positive nor negative; it divides the two sets of numbers. On the number line, numbers increase to the right and decrease to the left.

The expression $x > y$ means that x is greater than y. In other words, x is to the right of y on the number line:

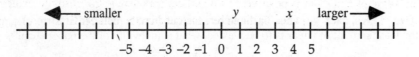

We usually have no trouble determining which of two numbers is larger when both are positive or one is positive and the other negative (e.g., $5 > 2$ and $3.1 > -2$). However, we sometimes hesitate when both numbers are negative (e.g., $-2 > -4.5$). When in doubt, think of the number line: if one number is to the right of the number, then it is larger. As the number line below illustrates, -2 is to the right of -4.5. Hence, -2 is larger than -4.5.

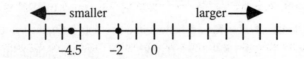

Miscellaneous Properties of Positive and Negative Numbers

1. The product (quotient) of positive numbers is positive.
2. The product (quotient) of a positive number and a negative number is negative.
3. The product (quotient) of an even number of negative numbers is positive.
4. The product (quotient) of an odd number of negative numbers is negative.
5. The sum of negative numbers is negative.
6. A number raised to an even exponent is greater than or equal to zero.

Example: If $xy^2z < 0$, then which one of the following statements must also be true?

    I. $xz < 0$

    II. $z < 0$

    III. $xyz < 0$

    (A) None   (B) I only   (C) III only   (D) I and II   (E) II and III

Since a number raised to an even exponent is greater than or equal to zero, we know that y^2 is positive (it cannot be zero because the product xy^2z would then be zero). Hence, we can divide both sides of the inequality $xy^2z < 0$ by y^2:

$$\frac{xy^2z}{y^2} < \frac{0}{y^2}$$

Simplifying yields $xz < 0$

Therefore, I is true, which eliminates (A), (C), and (E). Now, the following illustrates that $z < 0$ is not necessarily true:

$$-1 \cdot 2^2 \cdot 3 = -12 < 0$$

This eliminates (D). Hence, the answer is (B).

Absolute Value

The absolute value of a number is its distance on the number line from 0. Since distance is a positive number, absolute value of a number is positive. Two vertical bars denote the absolute value of a number: $|x|$. For example, $|3| = 3$ and $|-3| = 3$. This can be illustrated on the number line:

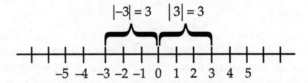

Students rarely struggle with the absolute value of numbers: if the number is negative, simply make it positive; and if it is already positive, leave it as is. For example, since –2.4 is negative, $|-24| = 2.4$ and since 5.01 is positive $|5.01| = 5.01$.

Further, students rarely struggle with the absolute value of positive variables: if the variable is positive, simply drop the absolute value symbol. For example, if $x > 0$, then $|x| = x$.

However, negative variables can cause students much consternation. If x is negative, then $|x| = -x$. This often confuses students because the absolute value is positive but the $-x$ appears to be negative. It is actually positive—it is the negative of a negative number, which is positive. To see this more clearly let $x = -k$, where k is a <u>positive</u> number. Then x is a negative number. So $|x| = -x = -(-k) = k$. Since k is positive so is $-x$. Another way to view this is $|x| = -x = (-1) \cdot x = (-1)(\text{a negative number}) = \text{a positive number}$.

Example: If $x = -|x|$, then which one of the following statements could be true?

    I. $x = 0$

    II. $x < 0$

    III. $x > 0$

    (A) None   (B) I only   (C) III only   (D) I and II   (E) II and III

Statement I could be true because $-|0| = -(+0) = -(0) = 0$. Statement II could be true because the right side of the equation is always negative $[-|x| = -(\text{a positive number}) = \text{a negative number}]$. Now, if one side of an equation is always negative, then the other side must always be negative, otherwise the opposite sides of the equation would not be equal. Since Statement III is the opposite of Statement II, it must be false. But let's show this explicitly: Suppose x were positive. Then $|x| = x$, and the equation $x = -|x|$ becomes $x = -x$. Dividing both sides of this equation by x yields $1 = -1$. This is contradiction. Hence, x cannot be positive. The answer is (D).

Higher Order Inequalities

These inequalities have variables whose exponents are greater than 1. For example, $x^2 + 4 < 2$ and $x^3 - 9 > 0$. The number line is often helpful in solving these types of inequalities.

Example: For which values of x is $x^2 > -6x - 5$?

First, replace the inequality symbol with an equal symbol:	$x^2 = -6x - 5$
Adding $6x$ and 5 to both sides yields	$x^2 + 6x + 5 = 0$
Factoring yields (see General Trinomials in the chapter Factoring)	$(x + 5)(x + 1) = 0$
Setting each factor to 0 yields	$x + 5 = 0$ and $x + 1 = 0$
Or	$x = -5$ and $x = -1$

Now, the only numbers at which the expression can change sign are -5 and -1. So -5 and -1 divide the number line into three intervals. Let's set up a number line and choose test points in each interval:

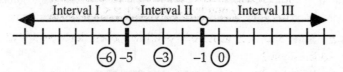

When $x = -6$, $x^2 > -6x - 5$ becomes $36 > 31$. This is true. Hence, all numbers in Interval I satisfy the inequality. That is, $x < -5$. When $x = -3$, $x^2 > -6x - 5$ becomes $9 > 13$. This is false. Hence, no numbers in Interval II satisfy the inequality. When $x = 0$, $x^2 > -6x - 5$ becomes $0 > -5$. This is true. Hence, all numbers in Interval III satisfy the inequality. That is, $x > -1$. The graph of the solution follows:

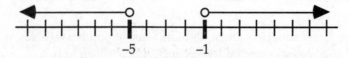

Note, if the original inequality had included the greater-than-or-equal symbol, $\geq$, the solution set would have included both -5 and -1. On the graph, this would have been indicated by filling in the circles above -5 and -1. The open circles indicate that -5 and -1 are not part of the solution.

Summary of steps for solving higher order inequalities:

1. Replace the inequality symbol with an equal symbol.
2. Move all terms to one side of the equation (usually the left side).
3. Factor the equation.
4. Set the factors equal to 0 to find zeros.
5. Choose test points on either side of the zeros.
6. If a test point satisfies the original inequality, then all numbers in that interval satisfy the inequality. Similarly, if a test point does not satisfy the inequality, then no numbers in that interval satisfy the inequality.

Transitive Property

$$\text{If } x < y \text{ and } y < z, \text{ then } x < z.$$

Example: If $\dfrac{1}{Q} > 1$, which of the following must be true?

(A) $1 < Q^2$ (B) $\dfrac{1}{Q^2} > 2$ (C) $1 > Q^2$ (D) $\dfrac{1}{Q^2} < 1$ (E) $Q < Q^2$

Since $\dfrac{1}{Q} > 1$ and $1 > 0$, we know from the transitive property that $\dfrac{1}{Q}$ is positive. Hence, Q is positive.

Therefore, we can multiply both sides of $\dfrac{1}{Q} > 1$ by Q without reversing the inequality:

$$Q \cdot \frac{1}{Q} > 1 \cdot Q$$

Reducing yields

$$1 > Q$$

Multiplying both sides again by Q yields

$$Q > Q^2$$

Using the transitive property to combine the last two inequalities yields

$$1 > Q^2$$

The answer is (C).

Like Inequalities Can Be Added

$$\text{If } x < y \text{ and } w < z, \text{ then } x + w < y + z.$$

Example: If $2 < x < 5$ and $3 < y < 5$, which of the following best describes $x - y$?

(A) $-3 < x - y < 2$
(B) $-3 < x - y < 5$
(C) $0 < x - y < 2$
(D) $3 < x - y < 5$
(E) $2 < x - y < 5$

Multiplying both sides of $3 < y < 5$ by -1 yields $-3 > -y > -5$. Now, we usually write the smaller number on the left side of the inequality. So $-3 > -y > -5$ becomes $-5 < -y < -3$. Add this inequality to the like inequality $2 < x < 5$:

$$2 < x < 5$$
$$(+) \quad -5 < -y < -3$$
$$\overline{\; -3 < x - y < 2}$$

The answer is (A).

Problem Set L: Solutions begin on page 580.

1.   If $1 < x < y$, which of the following must be true?

(A) $-x^2 < -y^2$ (B) $\dfrac{x}{y} < \dfrac{y}{x}$ (C) $\dfrac{y}{x} < \dfrac{x}{y}$ (D) $\dfrac{-x}{y} < \dfrac{-y}{x}$ (E) $x^2 > y^2$

2.   If $-3 < x < -1$ and $3 < y < 7$, which of the following best describes $\dfrac{x-y}{2}$?

(A) $-5 < \dfrac{x-y}{2} < -2$

(B) $-3 < \dfrac{x-y}{2} < -1$

(C) $-2 < \dfrac{x-y}{2} < 0$

(D) $2 < \dfrac{x-y}{2} < 5$

(E) $3 < \dfrac{x-y}{2} < 7$

3.   If x is an integer and $y = -2x - 8$, what is the least value of x for which y is less than 9?

(A) –9   (B) –8   (C) –7   (D) –6   (E) –5

4.   Which one of the following could be the graph of $3 - 6x \leq \dfrac{4x+2}{-2}$?

5.   If line segment AD has midpoint M_1 and line segment M_1D has midpoint M_2, what is the value of $\dfrac{M_1D}{AM_2}$?

(A) $\dfrac{1}{2}$ (B) $\dfrac{2}{3}$ (C) $\dfrac{3}{4}$ (D) $\dfrac{4}{5}$ (E) $\dfrac{5}{6}$

6.   If $x < y < -1$, which of the following must be true?

(A) $\dfrac{x}{y} > xy$ (B) $\dfrac{y}{x} > x + y$ (C) $\dfrac{y}{x} > xy$ (D) $\dfrac{y}{x} < x + y$ (E) $\dfrac{y}{x} > \dfrac{x}{y}$

7.   Which of the following represents all solutions of the inequality $x^2 < 2x$?

(A) $-1 < x < 1$ (B) $0 < x < 2$ (C) $1 < x < 3$ (D) $2 < x < 4$ (E) $4 < x < 6$

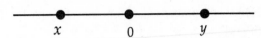

8. Given the positions of numbers x and y on the number line above, which of the following must be true?

 I. $xy > 0$

 II. $\dfrac{x}{y} < 0$

 III. $x - y > 0$

 (A) I only
 (B) II only
 (C) III only
 (D) I and II only
 (E) I, II, and III

9. If , which of the following must be true?

 (A) $x > y$ (B) $y > x$ (C) $x = y$ (D) $x < 0$ (E) $y > 0$

10. If n is an integer, what is the least value of n such that $\dfrac{1}{3^n} < 0.01$?

 (A) 2
 (B) 3
 (C) 4
 (D) 5
 (E) 6

11. If the average of 10, 14, and n is greater than or equal to 8 and less than or equal to 12, what is the least possible value of n ?

 (A) –12   (B) –6   (C) 0   (D) 6   (E) 12

12. If $\begin{array}{c} 3x + y < 4 \\ x > 3 \end{array}$, which of the following must be true?

 (A) $y < -5$ (B) $y < -10$ (C) $x = y$ (D) $x < 3$ (E) $y > 0$

$$2 - 3x \ ? \ 5$$

13. Of the following symbols, which one can be substituted for the question mark in the above expression to make a true statement for all values of x such that $-1 < x \le 2$?

 (A) =   (B) <   (C) $\ge$ (D) >   (E) $\le$

14. Let x, y, z be three different positive integers each less than 20. What is the smallest possible value of expression $\dfrac{x - y}{-z}$?

 (A) –18   (B) –17   (C) –14   (D) –11   (E) –9

15. If $x > 0$ and $|x| = \dfrac{1}{x}$, then $x =$

 (A) –1   (B) 0   (C) 1   (D) 2   (E) 3

16. Four letters—a, b, c, and d—represent one number each from one through four. No two letters represent the same number. It is known that $c > a$ and $a > d$. If $b = 2$, then $a =$

   (A)   1
   (B)   2
   (C)   3
   (D)   4
   (E)   Not enough information to decide.

17. If $r > t$ and $r < 1$ and $rt = 1$, then which one of the following must be true?

   (A) $r > 0$ and $t < -1$
   (B) $r > -1$ and $t < -1$
   (C) $r < -1$ and $t > -1$
   (D) $r < 1$ and $t > 1$
   (E) $r > 1$ and $t < 0$

18. If $x > y > 0$ and $p > q > 0$, then which one of the following expressions must be greater than 1?

   (A) $\dfrac{x + p}{y + q}$

   (B) $\dfrac{x + q}{y + p}$

   (C) $\dfrac{x}{p}$

   (D) $\dfrac{xq}{yp}$

   (E) $\dfrac{yq}{xp}$

19. If $2x + y > m$ and $2y + x < n$, then $x - y$ must be greater than

   (A) $m + n$
   (B) $m - n$
   (C) mn
   (D) $2m + n$
   (E) $n - m$

20. If $p > 2$, then which one of the following inequalities must be false?

   (A) $2p > 7$
   (B) $3p < 7$
   (C) $p < 3$
   (D) $p > 4$
   (E) $3p < 6$

Fractions & Decimals

Fractions

A fraction consists of two parts: a numerator and a denominator.

$$\frac{numerator}{denominator}$$

If the numerator is smaller than the denominator, the fraction is called *proper* and is less than one. For example: $\frac{1}{2}$, $\frac{4}{5}$, and $\frac{3}{\pi}$ are all proper fractions and therefore less than 1.

If the numerator is larger than the denominator, the fraction is called *improper* and is greater than 1. For example: $\frac{3}{2}$, $\frac{5}{4}$, and $\frac{\pi}{3}$ are all improper fractions and therefore greater than 1.

An improper fraction can be converted into a *mixed fraction* by dividing its denominator into its numerator. For example, since 2 divides into 7 three times with a remainder of 1, we get

$$\frac{7}{2} = 3\frac{1}{2}$$

To convert a mixed fraction into an improper fraction, multiply the denominator and the integer and then add the numerator. Then, write the result over the denominator. For example, $5\frac{2}{3} = \frac{3\cdot5+2}{3} = \frac{17}{3}$.

In a negative fraction, the negative symbol can be written on the top, in the middle, or on the bottom; however, when a negative symbol appears on the bottom, it is usually moved to the top or the middle: $\frac{5}{-3} = \frac{-5}{3} = -\frac{5}{3}$. If both terms in the denominator of a fraction are negative, the negative symbol is often factored out and moved to the top or middle of the fraction: $\frac{1}{-x-2} = \frac{1}{-(x+2)} = -\frac{1}{x+2}$ or $\frac{-1}{x+2}$.

• **To compare two fractions, cross-multiply. The larger number will be on the same side as the larger fraction.**

Example: Which of the following fractions is larger?

$$\frac{9}{10} \qquad\qquad\qquad \frac{10}{11}$$

Cross-multiplying gives $9\cdot11$ versus $10\cdot10$, which reduces to 99 versus 100. Now, 100 is greater than 99. Hence, $\frac{10}{11}$ is greater than $\frac{9}{10}$.

- **Always reduce a fraction to its lowest terms.**

Example: If $x \neq -1$, then $\dfrac{2x^2 + 4x + 2}{(x+1)^2} =$

(A) 0   (B) 1   (C) 2   (D) 4   (E) 6

Factor out the 2 in the expression:

$$\frac{2\left(x^2 + 2x + 1\right)}{(x+1)^2}$$

Factor the quadratic expressions:

$$\frac{2(x+1)(x+1)}{(x+1)(x+1)}$$

Finally, canceling the $(x + 1)$'s gives 2. The answer is (C).

- **To solve a fractional equation, multiply both sides by the LCD (lowest common denominator) to clear fractions.**

Example: If $\dfrac{x+3}{x-3} = y$, what is the value of x in terms of y?

(A) $3 - y$ (B) $\dfrac{3}{y}$ (C) $\sqrt{y+12}$ (D) $\dfrac{-3y-3}{1-y}$ (E) $3y^2$

First, multiply both sides of the equation by $x - 3$:

$$(x-3)\frac{x+3}{x-3} = (x-3)y$$

Cancel the $(x - 3)$'s on the left side of the equation: $x + 3 = (x - 3)y$
Distribute the y: $x + 3 = xy - 3y$
Subtract xy and 3 from both sides: $x - xy = -3y - 3$
Factor out the x on the left side of the equation: $x(1 - y) = -3y - 3$

Finally, divide both sides of the equation by $1 - y$: $x = \dfrac{-3y-3}{1-y}$

Hence, the answer is (D).

- **Complex Fractions: When dividing a fraction by a whole number (or vice versa), you must keep track of the main division bar:**

$$\frac{a}{b/c} = a \cdot \frac{c}{b} = \frac{ac}{b}. \text{ But } \frac{a/b}{c} = \frac{a}{b} \cdot \frac{1}{c} = \frac{a}{bc}.$$

Example: $\dfrac{1 - \dfrac{1}{2}}{3} =$

(A) 6   (B) 3   (C) $\dfrac{1}{3}$ (D) $\dfrac{1}{6}$ (E) $\dfrac{1}{8}$

Solution: $\dfrac{1 - \dfrac{1}{2}}{3} = \dfrac{\dfrac{2}{2} - \dfrac{1}{2}}{3} = \dfrac{\dfrac{2-1}{2}}{3} = \dfrac{\dfrac{1}{2}}{3} = \dfrac{1}{2} \cdot \dfrac{1}{3} = \dfrac{1}{6}$. The answer is (D).

Example: If $z \neq 0$ and $yz \neq 1$, then $\dfrac{1}{y - \dfrac{1}{z}} =$

(A) $\dfrac{yz}{zy-1}$ (B) $\dfrac{y-z}{z}$ (C) $\dfrac{yz-z}{z-1}$ (D) $\dfrac{z}{zy-1}$ (E) $\dfrac{y-z}{zy-1}$

Solution: $\dfrac{1}{y - \dfrac{1}{z}} = \dfrac{1}{\dfrac{z}{z}y - \dfrac{1}{z}} = \dfrac{1}{\dfrac{zy-1}{z}} = 1 \cdot \dfrac{z}{zy-1} = \dfrac{z}{zy-1}$. The answer is (D).

- **Multiplying fractions is routine: merely multiply the numerators and multiply the denominators:**
$\dfrac{a}{b} \cdot \dfrac{c}{d} = \dfrac{ac}{bd}$. For example, $\dfrac{1}{2} \cdot \dfrac{3}{4} = \dfrac{1 \cdot 3}{2 \cdot 4} = \dfrac{3}{8}$.

- **Two fractions can be added quickly by cross-multiplying:** $\dfrac{a}{b} \pm \dfrac{c}{d} = \dfrac{ad \pm bc}{bd}$

Example: $\dfrac{1}{2} - \dfrac{3}{4} =$

(A) $-\dfrac{5}{4}$ (B) $-\dfrac{2}{3}$ (C) $-\dfrac{1}{4}$ (D) $\dfrac{1}{2}$ (E) $\dfrac{2}{3}$

Cross multiplying the expression $\dfrac{1}{2} - \dfrac{3}{4}$ yields $\dfrac{1 \cdot 4 - 2 \cdot 3}{2 \cdot 4} = \dfrac{4-6}{8} = \dfrac{-2}{8} = -\dfrac{1}{4}$. Hence, the answer is (C).

Example: Which of the following equals the average of x and $\dfrac{1}{x}$?

(A) $\dfrac{x+2}{x}$ (B) $\dfrac{x^2+1}{2x}$ (C) $\dfrac{x+1}{x^2}$ (D) $\dfrac{2x^2+1}{x}$ (E) $\dfrac{x+1}{x}$

The average of x and $\dfrac{1}{x}$ is $\dfrac{x + \dfrac{1}{x}}{2} = \dfrac{\dfrac{x^2+1}{x}}{2} = \dfrac{x^2+1}{x} \cdot \dfrac{1}{2} = \dfrac{x^2+1}{2x}$. Thus, the answer is (B).

- **To add three or more fractions with different denominators, you need to form a common denominator of all the fractions.**

For example, to add the fractions in the expression $\dfrac{1}{3} + \dfrac{1}{4} + \dfrac{1}{18}$, we have to change the denominator of each fraction into the common denominator 36 (note, 36 is a common denominator because 3, 4, and 18 all divide into it evenly). This is done by multiply the top and bottom of each fraction by an appropriate number (this does not change the value of the expression because any number divided by itself equals 1):

$$\frac{1}{3}\left(\frac{12}{12}\right) + \frac{1}{4}\left(\frac{9}{9}\right) + \frac{1}{18}\left(\frac{2}{2}\right) = \frac{12}{36} + \frac{9}{36} + \frac{2}{36} = \frac{12+9+2}{36} = \frac{23}{36}$$

You may remember from algebra that to find a common denominator of a set of fractions, you prime factor the denominators and then select each factor the greatest number of times it occurs in any of the factorizations. That is too cumbersome, however. A better way is to simply add the largest denominator to itself until all the other denominators divide into it evenly. In the above example, we just add 18 to itself to get the common denominator 36.

- **To find a common denominator of a set of fractions, simply add the largest denominator to itself until all the other denominators divide into it evenly.**

- **Fractions often behave in unusual ways: Squaring a fraction makes it smaller, and taking the square root of a fraction makes it larger.** (**Caution:** This is true only for proper fractions, that is, fractions between 0 and 1.)

Example: $\left(\dfrac{1}{3}\right)^2 = \dfrac{1}{9}$ and $\dfrac{1}{9}$ is less than $\dfrac{1}{3}$. Also $\sqrt{\dfrac{1}{4}} = \dfrac{1}{2}$ and $\dfrac{1}{2}$ is greater than $\dfrac{1}{4}$.

- **You can cancel only over multiplication, not over addition or subtraction.**

For example, the c's in the expression $\dfrac{c+x}{c}$ cannot be canceled. However, the c's in the expression $\dfrac{cx+c}{c}$ can be canceled as follows: $\dfrac{cx+c}{c} = \dfrac{\cancel{c}(x+1)}{\cancel{c}} = x+1$.

Decimals

If a fraction's denominator is a power of 10, it can be written in a special form called a *decimal fraction*. Some common decimals are $\dfrac{1}{10} = .1, \dfrac{2}{100} = .02, \dfrac{3}{1000} = .003$. Notice that the number of decimal places corresponds to the number of zeros in the denominator of the fraction. Also note that the value of the decimal place decreases to the right of the decimal point:

$$\overset{\text{tenths}\quad\text{hundredths}\quad\text{thousandths}\quad\text{ten-thousandths}}{.1 \quad 2 \quad 3 \quad 4}$$

This decimal can be written in expanded form as follows:

$$.1234 = \dfrac{1}{10} + \dfrac{2}{100} + \dfrac{3}{1000} + \dfrac{4}{10000}$$

Sometimes a zero is placed before the decimal point to prevent misreading the decimal as a whole number. The zero has no affect on the value of the decimal. For example, $.2 = 0.2$.

Fractions can be converted to decimals by dividing the denominator into the numerator. For example, to convert $\dfrac{5}{8}$ to a decimal, divide 8 into 5 (note, a decimal point and as many zeros as necessary are added after the 5):

$$
\begin{array}{r}
.625 \\
8\overline{)5.000} \\
\underline{48} \\
20 \\
\underline{16} \\
40 \\
\underline{40} \\
0
\end{array}
$$

The procedures for adding, subtracting, multiplying, and dividing decimals are the same as for whole numbers, except for a few small adjustments.

- **Adding and Subtracting Decimals:** To add or subtract decimals, merely align the decimal points and then add or subtract as you would with whole numbers.

$$
\begin{array}{r}
1.369 \\
+ \quad 9.7 \\
\hline
11.069
\end{array}
\qquad
\begin{array}{r}
12.45 \\
- \quad 6.367 \\
\hline
6.083
\end{array}
$$

- **Multiplying Decimals:** Multiply decimals as you would with whole numbers. The answer will have as many decimal places as the sum of the number of decimal places in the numbers being multiplied.

$$\begin{array}{r} 1.23 \\ \times\ 2.4 \\ \hline 492 \\ 246 \\ \hline 2.952 \end{array}$$

  1.23 — 2 decimal places
  × 2.4 — 1 decimal place
  2.952 — 3 decimal places

- **Dividing Decimals:** Before dividing decimals, move the decimal point of the divisor all the way to the right and move the decimal point of the dividend the same number of spaces to the right (adding zeros if necessary). Then divide as you would with whole numbers.

$$.24\overline{)\,.6} = 24\overline{)60.0}$$

$$\begin{array}{r} 2.5 \\ 24\overline{)60.0} \\ 48 \\ \hline 120 \\ 120 \\ \hline 0 \end{array}$$

Example: $\frac{1}{5}$ of .1 percent equals:

(A) 2   (B) .2   (C) .02   (D) .002   (E) .0002

Recall that percent means to divide by 100. So .1 percent equals $\frac{.1}{100} = .001$. To convert $\frac{1}{5}$ to a decimal, divide 5 into 1:

$$\begin{array}{r} .2 \\ 5\overline{)1.0} \\ 10 \\ \hline 0 \end{array}$$

In percent problems, "of" means multiplication. So multiplying .2 and .001 yields

$$\begin{array}{r} .001 \\ \times\ \ .2 \\ \hline .0002 \end{array}$$

Hence, the answer is (E). Note, you may be surprised to learn that the SAT would consider this to be a hard problem.

Example: The decimal .1 is how many times greater than the decimal $(.001)^3$?

(A) 10   (B) 10^2 (C) 10^5 (D) 10^8 (E) 10^{10}

Converting .001 to a fraction gives $\frac{1}{1000}$. This fraction, in turn, can be written as $\frac{1}{10^3}$, or 10^{-3}. Cubing this expression yields $(.001)^3 = (10^{-3})^3 = 10^{-9}$. Now, dividing the larger number, .1, by the smaller number, $(.001)^3$, yields

$$\frac{.1}{(.001)^3} = \frac{10^{-1}}{10^{-9}} = 10^{-1-(-9)} = 10^{-1+9} = 10^8$$

Hence, .1 is 10^8 times as large as $(.001)^3$. The answer is (D).

Example: Let $x = .99$, $y = \sqrt{.99}$, and $z = (.99)^2$. Then which of the following is true?

      (A) $x < z < y$ (B) $z < y < x$ (C) $z < x < y$ (D) $y < x < z$ (E) $y < z < x$

Converting .99 into a fraction gives $\dfrac{99}{100}$. Since $\dfrac{99}{100}$ is between 0 and 1, squaring it will make it smaller and taking its square root will make it larger. Hence, $(.99)^2 < .99 < \sqrt{.99}$. The answer is (C). Note, this property holds for all proper decimals (decimals between 0 and 1) just as it does for all proper fractions.

Problem Set M:

Solutions begin on page 586.

1. $\dfrac{2}{\dfrac{4}{3}} =$

    (A) $\dfrac{1}{6}$ (B) $\dfrac{3}{8}$ (C) $\dfrac{3}{2}$ (D) $\dfrac{8}{3}$ (E) 6

2.   Which one of the following fractions is greatest?

    (A) $\dfrac{5}{6}$ (B) $\dfrac{4}{5}$ (C) $\dfrac{1}{2}$ (D) $\dfrac{2}{3}$ (E) $\dfrac{3}{4}$

3.   If $x \neq \pm 3$, then $\dfrac{x^2 + 6x + 9}{x + 3} \cdot \dfrac{x^2 - 9}{x - 3} =$

    (A) $\dfrac{x+3}{x-3}$ (B) -1 (C) $(x+3)^2$ (D) $\left(\dfrac{x+3}{x-3}\right)^2$ (E) 1

4. $\dfrac{1}{\dfrac{4}{3} - 1} =$

    (A) $-\dfrac{1}{3}$ (B) $-\dfrac{1}{4}$ (C) $\dfrac{3}{4}$ (D) 3   (E) $\dfrac{9}{2}$

5.   If $0 < x < 1$, which of the following must be true?

    I. $x^2 < x$ II. $x < \dfrac{1}{x^2}$ III. $\sqrt{x} < x$

    (A) I only   (B) II only   (C) III only   (D) I and II only   (E) I, II, and III

6.   In the following pairs of numbers, which are reciprocals of each other?

    I. 1 and 1   II. $\dfrac{1}{11}$ and -11 III. $\sqrt{5}$ and $\dfrac{\sqrt{5}}{5}$

    (A) I only   (B) II only   (C) I and II only   (D) I and III only   (E) II and III only

7. $\dfrac{6^4 - 6^3}{5} =$

    (A) $\dfrac{1}{5}$ (B) 6^3 (C) $\dfrac{6}{5}$ (D) 6^4 (E) $\dfrac{6^3}{5}$

8. $\dfrac{1}{1-\dfrac{1}{1-\dfrac{1}{2}}} =$

    (A) –2   (B) –1   (C) $\dfrac{3}{2}$ (D) 2   (E) 4

9. $\dfrac{1}{10^9} - \dfrac{1}{10^{10}} =$

    (A) $-\dfrac{1}{10}$ (B) $-\dfrac{1}{10^9}$ (C) $-\dfrac{1}{10^{19}}$ (D) $\dfrac{9}{10^{10}}$ (E) $\dfrac{9}{10}$

10. If $x \neq \pm 1$, then $\dfrac{\dfrac{2x^2-2}{x-1}}{2(x+1)} =$

    (A) $x+1$ (B) 1   (C) x^2-1 (D) $x-1$ (E) 2

11. If $\left(x^2-4\right)\left(\dfrac{4}{x}-5\right) = 0$, then $x =$

    (A) –4   (B) –1   (C) $-\dfrac{4}{5}$ (D) $\dfrac{4}{5}$ (E) 4

12. If $m = 3^{n-1} = 3^{3n+1}$, what is the value of $\dfrac{m}{n}$?

    (A) 0   (B) $-\dfrac{1}{20}$ (C) $-\dfrac{1}{10}$ (D) $-\dfrac{1}{9}$ (E) –2

13. For all $p \neq \dfrac{1}{4}$ define p^* by the equation $p^* = \dfrac{\dfrac{p}{2}}{4p-1}$. If $q = 1^*$, then $q^* =$

    (A) $-\dfrac{5}{7}$ (B) $-\dfrac{1}{3}$ (C) $-\dfrac{1}{4}$ (D) $\dfrac{2}{3}$ (E) $\dfrac{3}{4}$

14. If $\dfrac{1}{x} + \dfrac{1}{y} \neq 0$, then which one of the following is equal to the negative reciprocal of $\dfrac{1}{x} + \dfrac{1}{y}$?

    (A) $\dfrac{xy}{x+y}$ (B) $-\dfrac{x+y}{xy}$ (C) $-(x+y)$ (D) $\dfrac{x-y}{xy}$ (E) $\dfrac{-xy}{x+y}$

15. Let x and y be prime numbers such that $x > y$. If $q = x/y$, then q must be

    (A)   An integer greater than one.
    (B)   An integer less than one.
    (C)   A fraction less than one.
    (D)   A fraction greater than one.
    (E)   An even number.

Equations

When simplifying algebraic expressions, we perform operations within parentheses first and then exponents and then multiplication and then division and then addition and lastly subtraction. This can be remembered by the mnemonic:

PEMDAS
Please **E**xcuse **M**y **D**ear **A**unt **S**ally

When solving equations, however, we apply the mnemonic in reverse order: **SADMEP**. This is often expressed as follows: inverse operations in inverse order. The goal in solving an equation is to isolate the variable on one side of the equal sign (usually the left side). This is done by identifying the main operation—addition, multiplication, etc.—and then performing the opposite operation.

Example: Solve the following equation for x: $2x + y = 5$

Solution: The main operation is addition (remember addition now comes before multiplication, SADMEP), so subtracting y from both sides yields

$$2x + y - y = 5 - y$$

Simplifying yields

$$2x = 5 - y$$

The only operation remaining on the left side is multiplication. Undoing the multiplication by dividing both sides by 2 yields

$$\frac{2x}{2} = \frac{5 - y}{2}$$

Canceling the 2 on the left side yields

$$x = \frac{5 - y}{2}$$

Example: Solve the following equation for x: $3x - 4 = 2(x - 5)$

Solution: Here x appears on both sides of the equal sign, so let's move the x on the right side to the left side. But the x is trapped inside the parentheses. To release it, distribute the 2:

$$3x - 4 = 2x - 10$$

Now, subtracting $2x$ from both sides yields[*]

$$x - 4 = -10$$

Finally, adding 4 to both sides yields

$$x = -6$$

We often manipulate equations without thinking about what the equations actually say. The SAT likes to test this oversight. Equations are packed with information. Take for example the simple equation $3x + 2 = 5$. Since 5 is positive, the expression $3x + 2$ must be positive as well. And since 5 is prime, the expression $3x + 2$ must be prime as well. An equation means that the terms on either side of the equal sign are equal in

---

[*] Note, students often mistakenly add $2x$ to both sides of this equation because of the minus symbol between $2x$ and 10. But $2x$ is positive, so we subtract it. This can be seen more clearly by rewriting the right side of the equation as $-10 + 2x$.

every way. Hence, any property one side of an equation has the other side will have as well. Following are some immediate deductions that can be made from simple equations.

Equation	Deduction
$y - x = 1$	$y > x$
$y^2 = x^2$	$y = \pm x$, or $|y| = |x|$. That is, x and y can differ only in sign.
$y^3 = x^3$	$y = x$
$y = x^2$	$y \geq 0$
$\dfrac{y}{x^2} = 1$	$y > 0$
$\dfrac{y}{x^3} = 2$	Both x and y are positive or both x and y are negative.
$x^2 + y^2 = 0$	$y = x = 0$
$3y = 4x$ and $x > 0$	$y > x$ and y is positive.
$3y = 4x$ and $x < 0$	$y < x$ and y is negative.
$y = \sqrt{x + 2}$	$y \geq 0$ and $x \geq -2$
$y = 2x$	y is even
$y = 2x + 1$	y is odd
$yx = 0$	$y = 0$ or $x = 0$, or both

• **In Algebra, you solve an equation for, say, y by isolating y on one side of the equality symbol. On the SAT, however, you are often asked to solve for an entire term, say, $3 - y$ by isolating it on one side.**

Example: If $a + 3a$ is 4 less than $b + 3b$, then $a - b =$

(A) -4 (B) -1 (C) $\dfrac{1}{5}$ (D) $\dfrac{1}{3}$ (E) 2

Translating the sentence into an equation gives $a + 3a = b + 3b - 4$

Combining like terms gives $4a = 4b - 4$

Subtracting $4b$ from both sides gives $4a - 4b = -4$

Finally, dividing by 4 gives $a - b = -1$

Hence, the answer is (B).

• **Sometimes on the SAT, a system of 3 equations will be written as one long "triple" equation. For example, the three equations $x = y$, $y = z$, $x = z$, can be written more compactly as $x = y = z$.**

Example: If $w \neq 0$ and $w = 2x = \sqrt{2}y$, what is the value of $w - x$ in terms of y ?

(A) $2y$ (B) $\dfrac{\sqrt{2}}{2}y$ (C) $\sqrt{2y}$ (D) $\dfrac{4}{\sqrt{2}}y$ (E) y

The equation $w = 2x = \sqrt{2}y$ stands for three equations: $w = 2x$, $2x = \sqrt{2}y$, and $w = \sqrt{2}y$. From the last equation, we get $w = \sqrt{2}y$, and from the second equation we get $x = \dfrac{\sqrt{2}}{2}y$. Hence,

$w - x = \sqrt{2}y - \dfrac{\sqrt{2}}{2}y = \dfrac{2}{2}\sqrt{2}y - \dfrac{\sqrt{2}}{2}y = \dfrac{2\sqrt{2}y - \sqrt{2}y}{2} = \dfrac{\sqrt{2}y}{2}$. Hence, the answer is (B).

- **Often on the SAT, you can solve a system of two equations in two unknowns by merely adding or subtracting the equations—instead of solving for one of the variables and then substituting it into the other equation.**

Example: If p and q are positive, $p^2 + q^2 = 16$, and $p^2 - q^2 = 8$, then $q =$

(A) 2   (B) 4   (C) 8   (D) $2\sqrt{2}$ (E) $2\sqrt{6}$

Subtract the second equation from the first:

$$p^2 + q^2 = 16$$
$$(-)\quad p^2 - q^2 = 8$$
$$2q^2 = 8$$

Dividing both sides of the equation by 2 gives $q^2 = 4$

Finally, taking the square root of both sides gives $q = \pm 2$

Hence, the answer is (A).

METHOD OF SUBSTITUTION (Four-Step Method)

Although on the SAT you can usually solve a system of two equations in two unknowns by merely adding or subtracting the equations, you still need to know a standard method for solving these types of systems.

The four-step method will be illustrated with the following system:

$$2x + y = 10$$
$$5x - 2y = 7$$

1) *Solve one of the equations for one of the variables*:

   Solving the top equation for y yields $y = 10 - 2x$.

2) *Substitute the result from Step 1 into the other equation*:

   Substituting $y = 10 - 2x$ into the bottom equation yields $5x - 2(10 - 2x) = 7$.

3) *Solve the resulting equation*:

$$5x - 2(10 - 2x) = 7$$
$$5x - 20 + 4x = 7$$
$$9x - 20 = 7$$
$$9x = 27$$
$$x = 3$$

4) *Substitute the result from Step 3 into the equation derived in Step 1*:

   Substituting $x = 3$ into $y = 10 - 2x$ yields $y = 10 - 2(3) = 10 - 6 = 4$.

Hence, the solution of the system of equations is the ordered pair (3, 4).

Problem Set N: Solutions begin on page 589.

1. If $a > 0$ and $6a = 5b$, which of the following must be true?

    (A) $a = \dfrac{6}{5}b$ (B) $ab < 0$ (C) $a > b$ (D) $b = \dfrac{5}{6}a$ (E) $b > a$

2. If $p - q + r = 4$ and $p + q + r = 8$, then $p + r =$
    (A) 2 (B) 4 (C) 6 (D) 8 (E) 10

3. Suppose $x = y - 2 = \dfrac{y + 5}{2}$. Then x equals

    (A) $\dfrac{1}{3}$ (B) 1 (C) $\dfrac{7}{6}$ (D) 2 (E) 7

4. Let $p = 3^{q+1}$ and $q = 2r$. Then $\dfrac{p}{3^2} =$

    (A) 3^{2r-1} (B) 3^{2r} (C) 3 (D) r (E) 3^{2r+1}

5. k is a constant in the equation $\dfrac{u - v}{k} = 8$. If $u = 18$ when $v = 2$, then what is the value of u when $v = 4$?

    (A) -3 (B) 0 (C) 10 (D) $\dfrac{23}{2}$ (E) 20

6. If $x = 3y = 4z$, which of the following must equal $6x$?

    I. $18y$ II. $3y + 20z$ III. $\dfrac{4y + 10z}{3}$

    (A) I only (B) II only (C) III only (D) I and II only (E) I and III only

7. Let $P = (x + y)k$. If $P = 10$ and $k = 3$, what is the average of x and y?
    (A) 0 (B) $\dfrac{1}{2}$ (C) $\dfrac{5}{3}$ (D) $\dfrac{10}{3}$ (E) $\dfrac{7}{2}$

8. Let $\dfrac{x}{y} + \dfrac{w}{z} = 2$. Then the value of $\dfrac{y}{x} + \dfrac{z}{w}$ is

    (A) $\dfrac{1}{2}$

    (B) $\dfrac{3}{4}$
    (C) 1
    (D) 5
    (E) It cannot be determined from the information given.

9. If 4 percent of $(p + q)$ is 8 and p is a positive integer, what is the greatest possible value of q?
    (A) 196 (B) 197 (C) 198 (D) 199 (E) 200

10. If $x^5 = 4$ and $x^4 = \dfrac{7}{y}$, then what is the value of x in terms of y?

(A) $\dfrac{7}{4}y$ (B) $\dfrac{4}{7}y$ (C) $\dfrac{1}{7}y$ (D) $7y$ (E) $7 + \dfrac{5}{y}$

11.
$$2x + y = 3$$
$$3y = 9 - 6x$$

How many solutions does the above system of equations have?

(A) None (B) One (C) Two (D) Four (E) An infinite number

12. If $\dfrac{p}{19}$ is 1 less than 3 times $\dfrac{q}{19}$, then p equals which of the following expressions?

(A) $3q + 19$ (B) $3q + 38$ (C) $\dfrac{19}{2}$ (D) $3q - 38$ (E) $3q - 19$

13. If n is a number such that $(-8)^{2n} = 2^{8+2n}$, then $n =$

(A) $\dfrac{1}{2}$ (B) 2 (C) $\dfrac{3}{2}$ (D) 4 (E) 5 .

14. If $m = 3^{n-1}$ and $3^{4n-1} = 27$, what is the value of $\dfrac{m}{n}$?

(A) 0 (B) 1 (C) $\dfrac{7}{3}$ (D) $\dfrac{9}{2}$ (E) 6

15. If $s + S \neq 0$ and $\dfrac{1}{3} = \dfrac{1}{4}\dfrac{s-S}{s+S}$, then what is s in terms of S?

(A) $s = S + 3$ (B) $s = 4S$ (C) $s = \dfrac{S}{12}$ (D) $s = -7S$ (E) $s = 4S - 6$

16. If $3^x = 81$, then $\left(3^{x+3}\right)\left(4^{x+1}\right) =$

(A) $5(7)^5$ (B) $9(7)^5$ (C) $2(12)^4$ (D) $9(12)^5$ (E) $2(12)^7$

17. If $x = y/2$ and $y = z/2$, then $\sqrt{x/z} =$

(A) 4
(B) 2
(C) 1
(D) 1/2
(E) 1/4

18. If $a = b/c$ and $b = a/c$, then $c =$

(A) b/a
(B) a/b
(C) -1
(D) a
(E) $-b$

19. If $x + 3y = 5$ and $3x + y = 7$, then $x + y =$

    (A) 1
    (B) 2
    (C) 3
    (D) 4
    (E) 5

20. If $7x - y = 23$ and $7y - x = 31$, then $x + y =$

    (A) 4
    (B) 6
    (C) 7
    (D) 8
    (E) 9

21. If $x + y = 4a/5$, $y + z = 7a/5$ and $z + x = 9a/5$, then $x + y + z =$

    (A) $7a/15$
    (B) a
    (C) $2a$
    (D) $3a$
    (E) $4a$

Averages

Problems involving averages are very common on the SAT. They can be classified into four major categories as follows.

I. The average of N numbers is their sum divided by N, that is, $average = \dfrac{sum}{N}$.

Example 1: What is the average of x, $2x$, and 6?
(A) $x/2$
(B) $2x$
(C) $\dfrac{x+2}{6}$
(D) $x+2$
(E) $\dfrac{x+2}{3}$

By the definition of an average, we get $\dfrac{x+2x+6}{3} = \dfrac{3x+6}{3} = \dfrac{3(x+2)}{3} = x+2$. Hence, the answer is (D).

II. *Weighted average:* **The average between two sets of numbers is closer to the set with more numbers.**

Example 2: If on a test three people answered 90% of the questions correctly and two people answered 80% correctly, then the average for the group is not 85% but rather $\dfrac{3 \cdot 90 + 2 \cdot 80}{5} = \dfrac{430}{5} = 86$. Here, 90 has a weight of 3—it occurs 3 times. Whereas 80 has a weight of 2—it occurs 2 times. So the average is closer to 90 than to 80 as we have just calculated.

III. Using an average to find a number.

Sometimes you will be asked to find a number by using a given average. An example will illustrate.

Example 3: If the average of five numbers is -10, and the sum of three of the numbers is 16, then what is the average of the other two numbers?

(A) −33
(B) −1
(C) 5
(D) 20
(E) 25

Let the five numbers be a, b, c, d, e. Then their average is $\dfrac{a+b+c+d+e}{5} = -10$. Now three of the numbers have a sum of 16, say, $a + b + c = 16$. So substitute 16 for $a + b + c$ in the average above: $\dfrac{16+d+e}{5} = -10$. Solving this equation for $d + e$ gives $d + e = -66$. Finally, dividing by 2 (to form the average) gives $\dfrac{d+e}{2} = -33$. Hence, the answer is (A).

IV. *Average Speed =* $\dfrac{Total\ Distance}{Total\ Time}$

Although the formula for average speed is simple, few people solve these problems correctly because most fail to find both the <u>total distance</u> and the <u>total time</u>.

Example 4: In traveling from city A to city B, John drove for 1 hour at 50 mph and for 3 hours at 60 mph. What was his average speed for the whole trip?

(A) 50
(B) 53½
(C) 55
(D) 56
(E) 57½

The total distance is $1 \cdot 50 + 3 \cdot 60 = 230$. And the total time is 4 hours. Hence,

$$Average\ Speed = \frac{Total\ Distance}{Total\ Time} = \frac{230}{4} = 57\frac{1}{2}$$

The answer is (E). Note, the answer is not the mere average of 50 and 60. Rather the average is closer to 60 because he traveled longer at 60 mph (3 hrs) than at 50 mph (1 hr).

Problem Set O: Solutions begin on page 593.

1. If the average of p and $4p$ is 10, then $p =$
   (A) 1   (B) 3   (C) 4   (D) 10   (E) 18

2. The average of six consecutive integers in increasing order of size is $9\frac{1}{2}$. What is the average of the last three integers?
   (A) 8   (B) $9\frac{1}{2}$ (C) 10   (D) 11   (E) 19

3. If S denotes the sum and A the average of the consecutive positive integers 1 through n, then which of the following must be true?

   I. $A = \dfrac{S}{n}$

   II. $S = \dfrac{A}{n}$

   III. $A - S = n$

   (A) I only
   (B) II only
   (C) III only
   (D) I and II only
   (E) I, II, and III

4. Cars X and Y leave City A at the same time and travel the same route to City B. Car X takes 30 minutes to complete the trip and car Y takes 20 minutes. Which of the following must be true?
   I. The average miles per hour at which car X traveled was greater than the average miles per hour at which car Y traveled.
   II. The distance between the cities is 30 miles.
   III. The average miles per hour at which car Y traveled was greater than the average miles per hour at which car X traveled.
   (A) I only
   (B) II only
   (C) III only
   (D) I and II only
   (E) I and III only

5. If $p + q = r$, what is the average of p, q, and r?

    (A) $\dfrac{r}{3}$

    (B) $\dfrac{p+q}{3}$

    (C) $\dfrac{2r}{3}$

    (D) $\dfrac{r}{2}$

    (E) $\dfrac{p+q}{2}$

6. Suppose a train travels x miles in y hours and 15 minutes. Its average speed in miles per hour is

    (A) $\dfrac{y+15}{x}$

    (B) $x\left(y-\dfrac{1}{4}\right)$

    (C) $\dfrac{x}{y+\dfrac{1}{4}}$

    (D) $\dfrac{x}{y+15}$

    (E) $\dfrac{y+\dfrac{1}{4}}{x}$

7. The average of five numbers is 6.9. If one of the numbers is deleted, the average of the remaining numbers is 4.4. What is the value of the number deleted?

    (A) 6.8   (B) 7.4   (C) 12.5   (D) 16.9   (E) 17.2

8. The average of four numbers is 20. If one of the numbers is removed, the average of the remaining numbers is 15. What number was removed?

    (A) 10   (B) 15   (C) 30   (D) 35   (E) 45

9. The average of two numbers is $\dfrac{\pi}{2}$, and one of the numbers is x. What is the other number in terms of x?

    (A) $\dfrac{\pi}{2}-x$ (B) $\dfrac{\pi}{2}+x$ (C) $\pi-x$ (D) $\pi+x$ (E) $2\pi+x$

10. A shopper spends \$25 to purchase floppy disks at 50¢ each. The next day, the disks go on sale for 30¢ each and the shopper spends \$45 to purchase more disks. What was the average price per disk purchased?

    (A) 25¢   (B) 30¢   (C) 35¢   (D) 40¢   (E) 45¢

11. The average of 8 numbers is A, and one of the numbers is 14. If 14 is replaced with 28, then what is the new average in terms of A?

    (A) $A+\dfrac{7}{4}$ (B) $A+\dfrac{1}{2}$ (C) $A+2$ (D) $2A+1$ (E) $A+4$

Ratio & Proportion

RATIO

A ratio is simply a fraction. The following notations all express the ratio of x to y: $x:y$, $x \div y$, or $\frac{x}{y}$.

Writing two numbers as a ratio provides a convenient way to compare their sizes. For example, since $\frac{3}{\pi} < 1$, we know that 3 is less than π. A ratio compares two numbers. Just as you cannot compare apples and oranges, so to must the numbers you are comparing have the same units. For example, you cannot form the ratio of 2 feet to 4 yards because the two numbers are expressed in different units—feet vs. yards. It is quite common for the SAT to ask for the ratio of two numbers with different units. Before you form any ratio, make sure the two numbers are expressed in the same units.

Example 1: What is the ratio of 2 feet to 4 yards?

(A) 1:9   (B) 1:8   (C) 1:7   (D) 1:6   (E) 1:5

The ratio cannot be formed until the numbers are expressed in the same units. Let's turn the yards into feet. Since there are 3 feet in a yard, 4 yards = 4×3 feet = 12 feet. Forming the ratio yields

$$\frac{2 \ feet}{12 \ feet} = \frac{1}{6} \ or \ 1:6$$

The answer is (D).

Note, taking the reciprocal of a fraction usually changes its size. For example, $\frac{3}{4} \neq \frac{4}{3}$. So order is important in a ratio: $3:4 \neq 4:3$.

PROPORTION

A proportion is simply an equality between two ratios (fractions). For example, the ratio of x to y is equal to the ratio of 3 to 2 is translated as

$$\frac{x}{y} = \frac{3}{2}$$

or in ratio notation,

$$x:y::3:2$$

Two variables are *directly proportional* if one is a constant multiple of the other:
$$y = kx$$
where k is a constant.

The above equation shows that as x increases (or decreases) so does y. This simple concept has numerous applications in mathematics. For example, in constant velocity problems, distance is directly proportional to time: $d = vt$, where v is a constant. Note, sometimes the word *directly* is suppressed.

Example 2:   If the ratio of y to x is equal to 3 and the sum of y and x is 80, what is the value of y?

(A) –10   (B) –2   (C) 5   (D) 20   (E) 60

Translating *"the ratio of y to x is equal to 3"* into an equation yields

$$\frac{y}{x} = 3$$

Translating *"the sum of y and x is 80"* into an equation yields

$$y + x = 80$$

Solving the first equation for y gives $y = 3x$. Substituting this into the second equation yields

$$3x + x = 80$$
$$4x = 80$$
$$x = 20$$

Hence, $y = 3x = 3 \cdot 20 = 60$. The answer is (E).

In many word problems, as one quantity increases (decreases), another quantity also increases (decreases). This type of problem can be solved by setting up a *direct* proportion.

Example 3:   If Biff can shape 3 surfboards in 50 minutes, how many surfboards can he shape in 5 hours?

(A) 16   (B) 17   (C) 18   (D) 19   (E) 20

As time increases so does the number of shaped surfboards. Hence, we set up a direct proportion. First, convert 5 hours into minutes: *5 hours = 5 × 60 minutes = 300 minutes*. Next, let x be the number of surfboards shaped in 5 hours. Finally, forming the proportion yields

$$\frac{3}{50} = \frac{x}{300}$$

$$\frac{3 \cdot 300}{50} = x$$

$$18 = x$$

The answer is (C).

Example 4:   On a map, 1 inch represents 150 miles. What is the actual distance between two cities if they are $3\frac{1}{2}$ inches apart on the map?

(A) 225   (B) 300   (C) 450   (D) 525   (E) 600

As the distance on the map increases so does the actual distance. Hence, we set up a direct proportion. Let x be the actual distance between the cities. Forming the proportion yields

$$\frac{1\,in}{150\,mi} = \frac{3\frac{1}{2}\,in}{x\,mi}$$

$$x = 3\frac{1}{2} \times 150$$

$$x = 525$$

The answer is (D).

Note, you need not worry about how you form the direct proportion so long as the order is the same on both sides of the equal sign. The proportion in Example 4 could have been written as $\dfrac{1\,in}{3\frac{1}{2}\,in} = \dfrac{150\,mi}{x\,mi}$. In this case, the order is inches to inches and miles to miles. However, the following is not a direct proportion because the order is not the same on both sides of the equal sign: $\dfrac{1\,in}{150\,mi} = \dfrac{x\,mi}{3\frac{1}{2}\,in}$. In this case, the order is inches to miles on the left side of the equal sign but miles to inches on the right side.

If one quantity increases (or decreases) while another quantity decreases (or increases), the quantities are said to be *inversely* proportional. The statement "*y* is inversely proportional to *x*" is written as

$$y = \frac{k}{x}$$

where *k* is a constant.

Multiplying both sides of $y = \frac{k}{x}$ by *x* yields

$$yx = k$$

Hence, in an inverse proportion, the product of the two quantities is constant. Therefore, instead of setting ratios equal, we set products equal.

In many word problems, as one quantity increases (decreases), another quantity decreases (increases). This type of problem can be solved by setting up a product of terms.

Example 5: If 7 workers can assemble a car in 8 hours, how long would it take 12 workers to assemble the same car?

(A) 3hrs (B) $3\frac{1}{2}$ hrs (C) $4\frac{2}{3}$ hrs (D) 5hrs (E) $6\frac{1}{3}$ hrs

As the number of workers increases, the amount time required to assemble the car decreases. Hence, we set the products of the terms equal. Let *x* be the time it takes the 12 workers to assemble the car. Forming the equation yields

$$7 \cdot 8 = 12 \cdot x$$
$$\frac{56}{12} = x$$
$$4\frac{2}{3} = x$$

The answer is (C).

To summarize: if one quantity increases (decreases) as another quantity also increases (decreases), set ratios equal. If one quantity increases (decreases) as another quantity decreases (increases), set products equal.

The concept of proportion can be generalized to three or more ratios. *A*, *B*, and *C* are in the ratio 3:4:5 means $\frac{A}{B} = \frac{3}{4}$, $\frac{A}{C} = \frac{3}{5}$, and $\frac{B}{C} = \frac{4}{5}$.

Example 6: In the figure to the right, the angles *A*, *B*, *C* of the triangle are in the ratio 5:12:13. What is the measure of angle *A*?

(A) 15
(B) 27
(C) 30
(D) 34
(E) 40

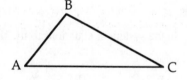

Since the angle sum of a triangle is 180°, *A* + *B* + *C* = 180. Forming two of the ratios yields

$$\frac{A}{B} = \frac{5}{12} \qquad \frac{A}{C} = \frac{5}{13}$$

Solving the first equation for *B* yields $\qquad B = \frac{12}{5}A$

Solving the second equation for *C* yields $\qquad C = \frac{13}{5}A$

Hence, $180 = A + B + C = A + \frac{12}{5}A + \frac{13}{5}A = 6A$. Therefore, $180 = 6A$, or $A = 30$. The answer is choice (C).

Problem Set P: Solutions begin on page 596.

1. What is the ratio of 2 ft. 3 in. to 2 yds?

    (A) $\dfrac{1}{4}$ (B) $\dfrac{1}{3}$ (C) $\dfrac{3}{8}$ (D) $\dfrac{1}{2}$ (E) $\dfrac{3}{4}$

2. The ratio of two numbers is 10 and their difference is 18. What is the value of the smaller number?

    (A) 2   (B) 5   (C) 10   (D) 21   (E) 27

3. If the degree measures of two angles of an isosceles triangle are in the ratio 1:3, what is the degree measure of the largest angle if it is not a base angle?

    (A) 26°   (B) 36°   (C) 51°   (D) 92°   (E) 108°

4. A jet uses 80 gallons of fuel to fly 320 miles. At this rate, how many gallons of fuel are needed for a 700 mile flight?

    (A) 150   (B) 155   (C) 160   (D) 170   (E) 175

5. Two boys can mow a lawn in 2 hours and 30 minutes If they are joined by three other boys, how many hours will it take to mow the lawn?

    (A) 1 hr.   (B) $1\tfrac{1}{4}$ hrs.   (C) $1\tfrac{1}{2}$ hrs.   (D) $1\tfrac{3}{4}$ hrs.   (E) 2 hrs.

6. A recipe requires $\dfrac{1}{2}$ lb. of shortening and 14 oz. of flour. If the chef accidentally pours in 21 oz. of flour, how many ounces of shortening should be added?

    (A) 9   (B) 10   (C) 11   (D) 12   (E) 13

7. If w widgets cost d dollars, then at this rate how many dollars will 2000 widgets cost?

    (A) $\dfrac{wd}{2000}$ (B) $\dfrac{2000w}{d}$ (C) $\dfrac{2000d}{w}$ (D) $\dfrac{d}{2000w}$ (E) $\dfrac{2000}{wd}$

8. In the system of equations to the right, $z \neq 0$. What is ratio of x to z?

    $$x + 2y - z = 1$$
    $$3x - 2y - 8z = -1$$

    (A) $-\dfrac{9}{4}$ (B) $-\dfrac{1}{3}$ (C) $\dfrac{1}{3}$ (D) $\dfrac{4}{9}$ (E) $\dfrac{9}{4}$

9. If a sprinter takes 30 steps in 9 seconds, how many steps does he take in 54 seconds?

    (A) 130   (B) 170   (C) 173   (D) 180   (E) 200

10. If $5x = 6y$, then the ratio of x to y is

    (A) 5:11   (B) 5:6   (C) 1:1   (D) 6:5   (E) 11:6

Exponents & Roots

EXPONENTS

Exponents afford a convenient way of expressing long products of the same number. The expression b^n is called a power and it stands for $b \times b \times b \times \cdots \times b$, where there are n factors of b. b is called the base, and n is called the exponent. By definition, $b^0 = 1$.

There are six rules that govern the behavior of exponents:

Rule 1: $x^a \cdot x^b = x^{a+b}$ Example, $2^3 \cdot 2^2 = 2^{3+2} = 2^5 = 32$. Caution, $x^a + x^b \neq x^{a+b}$

Rule 2: $\left(x^a\right)^b = x^{ab}$ Example, $\left(2^3\right)^2 = 2^{3\cdot2} = 2^6 = 64$

Rule 3: $(xy)^a = x^a \cdot y^a$ Example, $(2y)^3 = 2^3 \cdot y^3 = 8y^3$

Rule 4: $\left(\dfrac{x}{y}\right)^a = \dfrac{x^a}{y^a}$ Example, $\left(\dfrac{x}{3}\right)^2 = \dfrac{x^2}{3^2} = \dfrac{x^2}{9}$

Rule 5: $\dfrac{x^a}{x^b} = x^{a-b}$, if $a > b$.   Example, $\dfrac{2^6}{2^3} = 2^{6-3} = 2^3 = 8$

       $\dfrac{x^a}{x^b} = \dfrac{1}{x^{b-a}}$, if $b > a$.   Example, $\dfrac{2^3}{2^6} = \dfrac{1}{2^{6-3}} = \dfrac{1}{2^3} = \dfrac{1}{8}$

Rule 6: $x^{-a} = \dfrac{1}{x^a}$ Example, $z^{-3} = \dfrac{1}{z^3}$ Caution, a negative exponent does not make the number negative; it merely indicates that the base should be reciprocated. For example, $3^{-2} \neq -\dfrac{1}{3^2}$ or $-\dfrac{1}{9}$.

Problems involving these six rules are common on the SAT, and they are often listed as hard problems. However, the process of solving these problems is quite mechanical: simply apply the six rules until they can no longer be applied.

Example 1: If $x \neq 0$, $\dfrac{x\left(x^5\right)^2}{x^4} =$

     (A) x^5 (B) x^6 (C) x^7 (D) x^8 (E) x^9

First, apply the rule $\left(x^a\right)^b = x^{ab}$ to the expression $\dfrac{x\left(x^5\right)^2}{x^4}$:

$$\frac{x \cdot x^{5\cdot2}}{x^4} = \frac{x \cdot x^{10}}{x^4}$$

Next, apply the rule $x^a \cdot x^b = x^{a+b}$:

$$\frac{x \cdot x^{10}}{x^4} = \frac{x^{11}}{x^4}$$

Finally, apply the rule $\dfrac{x^a}{x^b} = x^{a-b}$:

$$\frac{x^{11}}{x^4} = x^{11-4} = x^7$$

The answer is (C).

Note: Typically, there are many ways of solving these types of problems. For this example, we could have begun with Rule 5, $\dfrac{x^a}{x^b} = \dfrac{1}{x^{b-a}}$:

$$\frac{x\left(x^5\right)^2}{x^4} = \frac{\left(x^5\right)^2}{x^{4-1}} = \frac{\left(x^5\right)^2}{x^3}$$

Then apply Rule 2, $\left(x^a\right)^b = x^{ab}$:

$$\frac{\left(x^5\right)^2}{x^3} = \frac{x^{10}}{x^3}$$

Finally, apply the other version of Rule 5, $\dfrac{x^a}{x^b} = x^{a-b}$:

$$\frac{x^{10}}{x^3} = x^7$$

Example 2: $\dfrac{3\cdot 3\cdot 3\cdot 3}{9\cdot 9\cdot 9\cdot 9} =$

(A) $\left(\dfrac{1}{3}\right)^4$ (B) $\left(\dfrac{1}{3}\right)^3$ (C) $\dfrac{1}{3}$ (D) $\dfrac{4}{9}$ (E) $\dfrac{4}{3}$

Canceling the common factor 3 yields $\dfrac{1\cdot 1\cdot 1\cdot 1}{3\cdot 3\cdot 3\cdot 3}$, or $\dfrac{1}{3}\cdot\dfrac{1}{3}\cdot\dfrac{1}{3}\cdot\dfrac{1}{3}$. Now, by the definition of a power, $\dfrac{1}{3}\cdot\dfrac{1}{3}\cdot\dfrac{1}{3}\cdot\dfrac{1}{3} = \left(\dfrac{1}{3}\right)^4$ Hence, the answer is (A).

Example 3: $\dfrac{6^4}{3^2} =$

(A) 2^4 (B) $2^3\cdot 3$ (C) 6^2 (D) $2^4\cdot 3^2$ (E) $2^2\cdot 3^4$

First, factor the top of the fraction:

$$\frac{(2\cdot 3)^4}{3^2}$$

Next, apply the rule $(xy)^a = x^a\cdot y^a$:

$$\frac{2^4\cdot 3^4}{3^2}$$

Finally, apply the rule $\dfrac{x^a}{x^b} = x^{a-b}$:

$$2^4\cdot 3^2$$

Hence, the answer is (D).

ROOTS

The symbol $\sqrt[n]{b}$ is read the *n*th root of *b*, where *n* is called the index, *b* is called the base, and $\sqrt{}$ is called the radical. $\sqrt[n]{b}$ denotes that number which raised to the *n*th power yields *b*. In other words, *a* is the *n*th root of *b* if $a^n = b$. For example, $\sqrt{9} = 3^*$ because $3^2 = 9$, and $\sqrt[3]{-8} = -2$ because $(-2)^3 = -8$. Even roots occur in pairs: both a positive root and a negative root. For example, $\sqrt[4]{16} = 2$ since $2^4 = 16$, and $\sqrt[4]{16} = -2$ since $(-2)^4 = 16$. Odd roots occur alone and have the same sign as the base: $\sqrt[3]{-27} = -3$ since $(-3)^3 = -27$. If given an even root, you are to assume it is the positive root. However, if you introduce even roots by solving an equation, then you <u>must</u> consider both the positive and negative roots:

$$x^2 = 9$$
$$\sqrt{x^2} = \pm\sqrt{9}$$
$$x = \pm 3$$

Square roots and cube roots can be simplified by removing perfect squares and perfect cubes, respectively. For example,

$$\sqrt{8} = \sqrt{4 \cdot 2} = \sqrt{4}\sqrt{2} = 2\sqrt{2}$$
$$\sqrt[3]{54} = \sqrt[3]{27 \cdot 2} = \sqrt[3]{27}\sqrt[3]{2} = 3\sqrt[3]{2}$$

Radicals are often written with fractional exponents. The expression $\sqrt[n]{b}$ can be written as $b^{1/n}$. This can be generalized as follows:

$$b^{m/n} = \left(\sqrt[n]{b}\right)^m = \sqrt[n]{b^m}$$

Usually, the form $\left(\sqrt[n]{b}\right)^m$ is better when calculating because the part under the radical is smaller in this case. For example, $27^{2/3} = \left(\sqrt[3]{27}\right)^2 = 3^2 = 9$. Using the form $\sqrt[n]{b^m}$ would be much harder in this case: $27^{2/3} = \sqrt[3]{27^2} = \sqrt[3]{729} = 9$. Most students know the value of $\sqrt[3]{27}$, but few know the value of $\sqrt[3]{729}$.

If *n* is even, then

$$\sqrt[n]{x^n} = |x|$$

For example, $\sqrt[4]{(-2)^4} = |-2| = 2$. With odd roots, the absolute value symbol is not needed. For example, $\sqrt[3]{(-2)^3} = \sqrt[3]{-8} = -2$.

To solve radical equations, just apply the rules of exponents to undo the radicals. For example, to solve the radical equation $x^{2/3} = 4$, we cube both sides to eliminate the cube root:

$$\left(x^{2/3}\right)^3 = 4^3$$
$$x^2 = 64$$
$$\sqrt{x^2} = \sqrt{64}$$
$$|x| = 8$$
$$x = \pm 8$$

---

* With square roots, the index is not written, $\sqrt[2]{9} = \sqrt{9}$.

Even roots of negative numbers do not appear on the SAT. For example, you will not see expressions of the form $\sqrt{-4}$; expressions of this type are called complex numbers.

The following rules are useful for manipulating roots:

$$\sqrt[n]{xy} = \sqrt[n]{x}\sqrt[n]{y} \qquad \text{For example, } \sqrt{3x} = \sqrt{3}\sqrt{x}.$$

$$\sqrt[n]{\frac{x}{y}} = \frac{\sqrt[n]{x}}{\sqrt[n]{y}} \qquad \text{For example, } \sqrt[3]{\frac{x}{8}} = \frac{\sqrt[3]{x}}{\sqrt[3]{8}} = \frac{\sqrt[3]{x}}{2}.$$

Caution: $\sqrt[n]{x+y} \neq \sqrt[n]{x} + \sqrt[n]{y}$. For example, $\sqrt{x+5} \neq \sqrt{x} + \sqrt{5}$. Also, $\sqrt{x^2 + y^2} \neq x + y$. This common mistake occurs because it is similar to the following valid property: $\sqrt{(x+y)^2} = x + y$ (If $x + y$ can be negative, then it must be written with the absolute value symbol: $|x + y|$). Note, in the valid formula, it's the whole term, $x + y$, that is squared, not the individual x and y.

To add two roots, both the index and the base must be the same. For example, $\sqrt[3]{2} + \sqrt[4]{2}$ cannot be added because the indices are different, nor can $\sqrt{2} + \sqrt{3}$ be added because the bases are different. However, $\sqrt[3]{2} + \sqrt[3]{2} = 2\sqrt[3]{2}$. In this case, the roots can be added because both the indices and bases are the same. Sometimes radicals with different bases can actually be added once they have been simplified to look alike. For example, $\sqrt{28} + \sqrt{7} = \sqrt{4 \cdot 7} + \sqrt{7} = \sqrt{4}\sqrt{7} + \sqrt{7} = 2\sqrt{7} + \sqrt{7} = 3\sqrt{7}$.

You need to know the approximations of the following roots: $\sqrt{2} \approx 1.4 \qquad \sqrt{3} \approx 1.7 \qquad \sqrt{5} \approx 2.2$

Example 4:   Given the system $\begin{aligned} x^2 &= 4 \\ y^3 &= -8 \end{aligned}$, which of the following is NOT necessarily true?

(A) $y < 0$ (B) $x < 5$ (C) y is an integer   (D) $x > y$ (E) $\dfrac{x}{y}$ is an integer

$y^3 = -8$ yields one cube root, $y = -2$. However, $x^2 = 4$ yields two square roots, $x = \pm 2$. Now, if $x = 2$, then $x > y$; but if $x = -2$, then $x = y$. Hence, choice (D) is not necessarily true. The answer is (D).

Example 5:   If $x < 0$ and y is 5 more than the square of x, which one of the following expresses x in terms of y?

(A) $x = \sqrt{y-5}$ (B) $x = -\sqrt{y-5}$ (C) $x = \sqrt{y+5}$ (D) $x = \sqrt{y^2-5}$ (E) $x = -\sqrt{y^2-5}$

Translating the expression *"y is 5 more than the square of x"* into an equation yields:

$$y = x^2 + 5$$

$$y - 5 = x^2$$

$$\pm\sqrt{y-5} = x$$

Since we are given that $x < 0$, we take the negative root, $-\sqrt{y-5} = x$. The answer is (B).

RATIONALIZING

A fraction is not considered simplified until all the radicals have been removed from the denominator. If a denominator contains a single term with a square root, it can be rationalized by multiplying both the numerator and denominator by that square root. If the denominator contains square roots separated by a plus or minus sign, then multiply both the numerator and denominator by the conjugate, which is formed by merely changing the sign between the roots.

Example :   Rationalize the fraction $\dfrac{2}{3\sqrt{5}}$.

Multiply top and bottom of the fraction by $\sqrt{5}$:

$$\dfrac{2}{3\sqrt{5}}\cdot\dfrac{\sqrt{5}}{\sqrt{5}}=\dfrac{2\sqrt{5}}{3\cdot\sqrt{25}}=\dfrac{2\sqrt{5}}{3\cdot 5}=\dfrac{2\sqrt{5}}{15}$$

Example :   Rationalize the fraction $\dfrac{2}{3-\sqrt{5}}$.

Multiply top and bottom of the fraction by the conjugate $3+\sqrt{5}$:

$$\dfrac{2}{3-\sqrt{5}}\cdot\dfrac{3+\sqrt{5}}{3+\sqrt{5}}=\dfrac{2\left(3+\sqrt{5}\right)}{3^2+3\sqrt{5}-3\sqrt{5}-\left(\sqrt{5}\right)^2}=\dfrac{2\left(3+\sqrt{5}\right)}{9-5}=\dfrac{2\left(3+\sqrt{5}\right)}{4}=\dfrac{3+\sqrt{5}}{2}$$

Problem Set Q: Solutions begin on page 598.

1.   If $x \neq 0$, $\left(\dfrac{2y^3}{x^2}\right)^4 \cdot x^{10} =$

(A) $16y^{12}x^2$ (B) $8y^7x^2$ (C) $16\dfrac{y^{12}}{x^8}$ (D) $8\dfrac{y^{12}}{x^8}$ (E) $\dfrac{y^{12}}{16x^8}$

2. $\sqrt{(31-6)(16+9)} =$

(A) 5   (B) 10   (C) 25   (D) 50   (E) 625

3.   What is the largest integer n such that 2^n is a factor of 20^8?

(A) 1   (B) 2   (C) 4   (D) 8   (E) 16

4. $\dfrac{55^5}{5^{55}} =$

(A) $\dfrac{11}{5^{50}}$ (B) $\dfrac{11}{5^{55}}$ (C) $\dfrac{11^5}{5^{50}}$ (D) $\dfrac{11^5}{5^5}$ (E) $\dfrac{11^5}{5}$

5.   If $x = \dfrac{1}{9}$, then $\sqrt{x} - x^2 =$

(A) 0   (B) $\dfrac{1}{9}$ (C) $\dfrac{26}{81}$ (D) $\dfrac{1}{3}$ (E) 1

6. $\left(9^x\right)^3 =$

    (A) 3^{3x} (B) 3^{2+3x} (C) 3^{6x} (D) $729x^3$ (E) 9^{x^3}

7. If $x = 4$, then $-2^{2\sqrt{x}} + 2 =$

    (A) -14 (B) -8 (C) -2 (D) 0 (E) 18

8. $\sqrt{\dfrac{25 + 10x + x^2}{2}} =$

    (A) $\dfrac{\sqrt{2}(5-x)}{2}$ (B) $\dfrac{\sqrt{5+x}}{\sqrt{2}}$ (C) $\dfrac{\sqrt{2}(5+x)}{2}$ (D) $\dfrac{5+x}{2}$ (E) $\dfrac{5-x}{2}$

9. $\dfrac{2 + \sqrt{5}}{2 - \sqrt{5}} =$

    (A) $-9 - 4\sqrt{5}$ (B) $-1 - \dfrac{4}{9}\sqrt{5}$ (C) $1 + \dfrac{4}{9}\sqrt{5}$ (D) $9 + 4\sqrt{5}$ (E) 20

10. $2^{12} + 2^{12} + 2^{12} + 2^{12} =$

    (A) 4^{12} (B) 2^{14} (C) 2^{16} (D) 4^{16} (E) 2^{48}

11. $\left(\dfrac{\left(x^2 y\right)^3 z}{xyz}\right)^3 =$

    (A) $x^8 y^5$ (B) xy^6 (C) $x^{15} y^6 z$ (D) $x^3 y^6$ (E) $x^{15} y^6$

12. If $2^{2x} = 16^{x+2}$, what is the value of x ?

    (A) -4 (B) -2 (C) 0 (D) 2 (E) 4

13. If $(x-y)^{\frac{1}{3}} = (x+y)^{-\frac{1}{3}}$, then which one of the following must be true?

    (A) $x = 1$ (B) $y = 1$ (C) $x^2 - y^2 = 1$ (D) $x + y^2 = 1$ (E) $x^2 - 2xy + y^2 = 1$

Factoring

To factor an algebraic expression is to rewrite it as a product of two or more expressions, called factors. In general, any expression on the SAT that can be factored should be factored, and any expression that can be unfactored (multiplied out) should be unfactored.

DISTRIBUTIVE RULE

The most basic type of factoring involves the distributive rule:

$$ax + ay = a(x + y)$$

When this rule is applied from left to right, it is called factoring. When the rule is applied from right to left, it is called distributing.

For example, $3h + 3k = 3(h + k)$, and $5xy + 45x = 5xy + 9 \cdot 5x = 5x(y + 9)$. The distributive rule can be generalized to any number of terms. For three terms, it looks like $ax + ay + az = a(x + y + z)$. For example, $2x + 4y + 8 = 2x + 2 \cdot 2y + 2 \cdot 4 = 2(x + 2y + 4)$. For another example, $x^2 y^2 + xy^3 + y^5 = y^2 \left(x^2 + xy + y^3 \right)$.

Example 1: If $x - y = 9$, then $\left(x - \dfrac{y}{3} \right) - \left(y - \dfrac{x}{3} \right) =$

(A) -4 (B) -3 (C) 0   (D) 12   (E) 27

$$\left(x - \frac{y}{3} \right) - \left(y - \frac{x}{3} \right) =$$

$x - \dfrac{y}{3} - y + \dfrac{x}{3} =$ by distributing the negative sign

$\dfrac{4}{3}x - \dfrac{4}{3}y =$ by combining the fractions

$\dfrac{4}{3}(x - y) =$ by factoring out the common factor $\dfrac{4}{3}$

$\dfrac{4}{3}(9) =$ since $x - y = 9$

12

The answer is (D).

Example 2: $\dfrac{2^{20} - 2^{19}}{2^{11}} =$

(A) $2^9 - 2^{19}$ (B) $\dfrac{1}{2^{11}}$ (C) 2^8 (D) 2^{10} (E) 2^{28}

$$\frac{2^{20} - 2^{19}}{2^{11}} = \frac{2^{19+1} - 2^{19}}{2^{11}} =$$

$$\frac{2^{19} \cdot 2^1 - 2^{19}}{2^{11}} = \qquad \text{by the rule } x^a \cdot x^b = x^{a+b}$$

$$\frac{2^{19}(2 - 1)}{2^{11}} = \qquad \text{by the distributive property } ax + ay = a(x + y)$$

$$\frac{2^{19}}{2^{11}} =$$

$$2^8 \qquad \text{by the rule } \frac{x^a}{x^b} = x^{a-b}$$

The answer is (C).

DIFFERENCE OF SQUARES

One of the most important formulas on the SAT is the difference of squares:

$$\boxed{x^2 - y^2 = (x + y)(x - y)}$$

Caution: a sum of squares, $x^2 + y^2$, does not factor.

Example 3: If $x \neq -2$, then $\dfrac{8x^2 - 32}{4x + 8} =$

(A) $2(x - 2)$ (B) $2(x - 4)$ (C) $8(x + 2)$ (D) $x - 2$ (E) $x + 4$

In most algebraic expressions involving multiplication or division, you won't actually multiply or divide, rather you will factor and cancel, as in this problem.

$$\frac{8x^2 - 32}{4x + 8} =$$

$$\frac{8(x^2 - 4)}{4(x + 2)} = \qquad \text{by the distributive property } ax + ay = a(x + y)$$

$$\frac{8(x + 2)(x - 2)}{4(x + 2)} = \qquad \text{by the difference of squares } x^2 - y^2 = (x + y)(x - y)$$

$$2(x - 2) \qquad \text{by canceling common factors}$$

The answer is (A).

PERFECT SQUARE TRINOMIALS

Like the difference of squares formula, perfect square trinomial formulas are very common on the SAT.

$$x^2 + 2xy + y^2 = (x+y)^2$$
$$x^2 - 2xy + y^2 = (x-y)^2$$

For example, $x^2 + 6x + 9 = x^2 + 2(3x) + 3^2 = (x+3)^2$. Note, in a perfect square trinomial, the middle term is twice the product of the square roots of the outer terms.

Example 4: If $r^2 - 2rs + s^2 = 4$, then $(r-s)^6 =$

      (A) −4   (B) 4   (C) 8   (D) 16   (E) 64

$$r^2 - 2rs + s^2 = 4$$

$$(r-s)^2 = 4 \qquad \text{by the formula } x^2 - 2xy + y^2 = (x-y)^2$$

$$\left[(r-s)^2\right]^3 = 4^3 \qquad \text{by cubing both sides of the equation}$$

$$(r-s)^6 = 64 \qquad \text{by the rule } \left(x^a\right)^b = x^{ab}$$

The answer is (E).

GENERAL TRINOMIALS

$$x^2 + (a+b)x + ab = (x+a)(x+b)$$

The expression $x^2 + (a+b)x + ab$ tells us that we need two numbers whose product is the last term and whose sum is the coefficient of the middle term. Consider the trinomial $x^2 + 5x + 6$. Now, two factors of 6 are 1 and 6, but $1 + 6 \neq 5$. However, 2 and 3 are also factors of 6, and $2 + 3 = 5$. Hence, $x^2 + 5x + 6 = (x+2)(x+3)$.

Example 5: Which of the following could be a solution of the equation $x^2 - 7x - 18 = 0$?

      (A) −1   (B) 0   (C) 2   (D) 7   (E) 9

Now, both 2 and −9 are factors of 18, and $2 + (-9) = -7$. Hence, $x^2 - 7x - 18 = (x+2)(x-9) = 0$. Setting each factor equal to zero yields $x + 2 = 0$ and $x - 9 = 0$. Solving these equations yields $x = -2$ and 9. The answer is (E).

COMPLETE FACTORING

When factoring an expression, first check for a common factor, then check for a difference of squares, then for a perfect square trinomial, and then for a general trinomial.

Example 6: Factor the expression $2x^3 - 2x^2 - 12x$ completely.

Solution: First check for a common factor: $2x$ is common to each term. Factoring $2x$ out of each term yields $2x\left(x^2 - x - 6\right)$. Next, there is no difference of squares, and $x^2 - x - 6$ is not a perfect square trinomial since x does not equal twice the product of the square roots of x^2 and 6. Now, −3 and 2 are factors of −6 whose sum is −1. Hence, $2x\left(x^2 - x - 6\right)$ factors into $2x(x-3)(x+2)$.

Problem Set R: Solutions begin on page 601.

1.   If $3y + 5 = 7x$, then $21y - 49x =$

   (A) –40   (B) –35   (C) –10   (D) 0   (E) 15

2.   If $x - y = p$, then $2x^2 - 4xy + 2y^2 =$

   (A) p (B) $2p$ (C) $4p$ (D) p^2 (E) $2p^2$

3.   If $p \neq 0$ and $p = \sqrt{2pq - q^2}$, then in terms of q, $p =$

   (A) q (B) q^2 (C) $2q$ (D) $-2q$ (E) $\dfrac{q}{4}$

4.   If $\dfrac{x^2 + 2x - 10}{5} = 1$, then x could equal

   (A) –5   (B) –3   (C) 0   (D) 10   (E) 15

5.   What is the absolute value of twice the difference of the roots of the equation $5y^2 - 20y + 15 = 0$?

   (A) 0   (B) 1   (C) 2   (D) 3   (E) 4

6.   If $x \neq -2$, then $\dfrac{7x^2 + 28x + 28}{(x+2)^2} =$

   (A) 7   (B) 8   (C) 9   (D) 10   (E) 11

7. $\dfrac{7^9 + 7^8}{8} =$

   (A) $\dfrac{1}{8}$ (B) $\dfrac{7}{8}$ (C) $\dfrac{7^7}{8}$ (D) 7^8 (E) 7^9

8.   If $x + y = 10$ and $x - y = 5$, then $x^2 - y^2 =$

   (A) 50   (B) 60   (C) 75   (D) 80   (E) 100

9. $x(x - y) - z(x - y) =$

   (A) $x - y$ (B) $x - z$ (C) $(x - y)(x - z)$ (D) $(x - y)(x + z)$ (E) $(x - y)(z - x)$

10.   If $(x - y)^2 = x^2 + y^2$, then which one of the following statements must also be true?

   I. $x = 0$
   II. $y = 0$
   III. $xy = 0$

   (A) None   (B) I only   (C) II only   (D) III only   (E) II and III only

11. If x and y are prime numbers such that $x > y > 2$, then $x^2 - y^2$ must be divisible by which one of the following numbers?

   (A) 3
   (B) 4
   (C) 5
   (D) 9
   (E) 12

12. If $\dfrac{x+y}{x-y} = \dfrac{1}{2}$, then $\dfrac{xy+x^2}{xy-x^2} =$

   (A) −4.2
   (B) −1/2
   (C) 1.1
   (D) 3
   (E) 5.3

13. If $x + y = 2\sqrt{xy}$, then which one of the following must be true?

   (A) $x < y$
   (B) $x = 2$
   (C) $x = y$
   (D) $x > y$
   (E) $x = 4$

Algebraic Expressions

A mathematical expression that contains a variable is called an algebraic expression. Some examples of algebraic expressions are x^2, $3x - 2y$, $2z(y^3 - \frac{1}{z^2})$. Two algebraic expressions are called like terms if both the variable parts and the exponents are identical. That is, the only parts of the expressions that can differ are the coefficients. For example, $5y^3$ and $\frac{3}{2}y^3$ are like terms, as are $x + y^2$ and $-7(x + y^2)$. However, x^3 and y^3 are not like terms, nor are $x - y$ and $2 - y$.

ADDING & SUBTRACTING ALGEBRAIC EXPRESSIONS

Only like terms may be added or subtracted. To add or subtract like terms, merely add or subtract their coefficients:

$$x^2 + 3x^2 = (1 + 3)x^2 = 4x^2$$

$$2\sqrt{x} - 5\sqrt{x} = (2 - 5)\sqrt{x} = -3\sqrt{x}$$

$$.5\left(x + \frac{1}{y}\right)^2 + .2\left(x + \frac{1}{y}\right)^2 = (.5 + .2)\left(x + \frac{1}{y}\right)^2 = .7\left(x + \frac{1}{y}\right)^2$$

$$\left(3x^3 + 7x^2 + 2x + 4\right) + \left(2x^2 - 2x - 6\right) = 3x^3 + (7 + 2)x^2 + (2 - 2)x + (4 - 6) = 3x^3 + 9x^2 - 2$$

You may add or multiply algebraic expressions in any order. This is called the commutative property:

$$x + y = y + x$$

$$xy = yx$$

For example, $-2x + 5x = 5x + (-2x) = (5 - 2)x = -3x$ and $(x - y)(-3) = (-3)(x - y) = (-3)x - (-3)y = -3x + 3y$.

Caution: the commutative property does not apply to division or subtraction: $2 = 6 \div 3 \neq 3 \div 6 = \frac{1}{2}$ and $-1 = 2 - 3 \neq 3 - 2 = 1$.

When adding or multiplying algebraic expressions, you may regroup the terms. This is called the associative property:

$$x + (y + z) = (x + y) + z$$

$$x(yz) = (xy)z$$

Notice in these formulas that the variables have not been moved, only the way they are grouped has changed: on the left side of the formulas the last two variables are grouped together, and on the right side of the formulas the first two variables are grouped together.

For example, $(x - 2x) + 5x = (x + [-2x]) + 5x = x + (-2x + 5x) = x + 3x = 4x$

and

$24x = 2x(12x) = 2x(3x4x) = (2x3x)4x = 6x4x = 24x.$

The associative property doesn't apply to division or subtraction: $4 = 8 \div 2 = 8 \div (4 \div 2) \neq (8 \div 4) \div 2 = 2 \div 2 = 1$

and

$-6 = -3 - 3 = (-1 - 2) - 3 \neq -1 - (2 - 3) = -1 - (-1) = -1 + 1 = 0.$

Notice in the first example that we changed the subtraction into negative addition: $(x - 2x) = (x + [-2x])$. This allowed us to apply the associative property over addition.

PARENTHESES

When simplifying expressions with nested parentheses, work from the inner most parentheses out:

$$5x + (y - (2x - 3x)) = 5x + (y - (-x)) = 5x + (y + x) = 6x + y$$

Sometimes when an expression involves several pairs of parentheses, one or more pairs are written as brackets. This makes the expression easier to read:

$$2x(x - [y + 2(x - y)]) =$$
$$2x(x - [y + 2x - 2y]) =$$
$$2x(x - [2x - y]) =$$
$$2x(x - 2x + y) =$$
$$2x(-x + y) =$$
$$-2x^2 + 2xy$$

ORDER OF OPERATIONS: (PEMDAS)

When simplifying algebraic expressions, perform operations within parentheses first and then exponents and then multiplication and then division and then addition and lastly subtraction. This can be remembered by the mnemonic:

PEMDAS
Please Excuse My Dear Aunt Sally

This mnemonic isn't quite precise enough. Multiplication and division are actually tied in order of operation, as is the pair addition and subtraction. When multiplication and division, or addition and subtraction, appear at the same level in an expression, perform the operations from left to right. For example, $6 \div 2 \times 4 = (6 \div 2) \times 4 = 3 \times 4 = 12$. To emphasize this left-to-right order, we can use parentheses in the mnemonic: **PE(MD)(AS)**.

Example 1: $2 - \left(5 - 3^3[4 \div 2 + 1]\right) =$

       (A) –21   (B) 32   (C) 45   (D) 60   (E) 78

$2 - \left(5 - 3^3[4 \div 2 + 1]\right) =$

$\quad 2 - \left(5 - 3^3[2 + 1]\right) =$ By performing the division within the innermost parentheses

$\quad\quad 2 - \left(5 - 3^3[3]\right) =$ By performing the addition within the innermost parentheses

$\quad\quad 2 - (5 - 27[3]) =$ By performing the exponentiation

$\quad\quad\quad 2 - (5 - 81) =$ By performing the multiplication within the parentheses

$\quad\quad\quad 2 - (-76) =$ By performing the subtraction within the parentheses

$\quad\quad\quad\quad 2 + 76 =$ By multiplying the two negatives

$\quad\quad\quad\quad\quad 78$

The answer is (E).

FOIL MULTIPLICATION

You may recall from algebra that when multiplying two expressions you use the FOIL method: First, Outer, Inner, Last:

$$(x + y)(x + y) = xx + xy + xy + yy$$

Simplifying the right side yields $(x+y)(x+y) = x^2 + 2xy + y^2$. For the product $(x-y)(x-y)$ we get $(x-y)(x-y) = x^2 - 2xy + y^2$. These types of products occur often, so it is worthwhile to memorize the formulas. Nevertheless, you should still learn the FOIL method of multiplying because the formulas do not apply in all cases.

Examples (FOIL):

$$(2-y)(x-y^2) = 2x - 2y^2 - xy + yy^2 = 2x - 2y^2 - xy + y^3$$

$$\left(\frac{1}{x} - y\right)\left(x - \frac{1}{y}\right) = \frac{1}{x}x - \frac{1}{x}\frac{1}{y} - xy + y\frac{1}{y} = 1 - \frac{1}{xy} - xy + 1 = 2 - \frac{1}{xy} - xy$$

$$\left(\frac{1}{2} - y\right)^2 = \left(\frac{1}{2} - y\right)\left(\frac{1}{2} - y\right) = \left(\frac{1}{2}\right)^2 - 2\left(\frac{1}{2}\right)y + y^2 = \frac{1}{4} - y + y^2$$

DIVISION OF ALGEBRAIC EXPRESSIONS

When dividing algebraic expressions, the following formula is useful:

$$\frac{x+y}{z} = \frac{x}{z} + \frac{y}{z}$$

This formula generalizes to any number of terms.

Examples:

$$\frac{x^2 + y}{x} = \frac{x^2}{x} + \frac{y}{x} = x^{2-1} + \frac{y}{x} = x + \frac{y}{x}$$

$$\frac{x^2 + 2y - x^3}{x^2} = \frac{x^2}{x^2} + \frac{2y}{x^2} - \frac{x^3}{x^2} = x^{2-2} + \frac{2y}{x^2} - x^{3-2} = x^0 + \frac{2y}{x^2} - x = 1 + \frac{2y}{x^2} - x$$

When there is more than a single variable in the denomination, we usually factor the expression and then cancel, instead of using the above formula.

Example 2: $\dfrac{x^2 - 2x + 1}{x - 1} =$

(A) $x+1$ (B) $-x-1$ (C) $-x+1$ (D) $x-1$ (E) $x-2$

$\dfrac{x^2 - 2x + 1}{x-1} = \dfrac{(x-1)(x-1)}{x-1} = x - 1$. The answer is (D).

Problem Set S: Solutions begin on page 604.

1. If $\left(x^2 + 2\right)\left(x - x^3\right) =$

    (A) $x^4 - x^2 + 2$ (B) $-x^5 - x^3 + 2x$ (C) $x^5 - 2x$ (D) $3x^3 + 2x$ (E) $x^5 + x^3 + 2x$

2. $-2\left(3 - x\left[\dfrac{5 + y - 2}{x}\right] - 7 + 2 \cdot 3^2\right) =$

    (A) $2y - 11$ (B) $2y + 1$ (C) $x - 2$ (D) $x + 22$ (E) $2y - 22$

3. For all real numbers a and b, where $a \cdot b \neq 0$, let $a \lozenge b = ab - 1$, which of the following must be true?

    I. $a \lozenge b = b \lozenge a$
    II. $\dfrac{a \lozenge a}{a} = 1 \lozenge 1$
    III. $(a \lozenge b) \lozenge c = a \lozenge (b \lozenge c)$

    (A) I only   (B) II only   (C) III only   (D) I and II only   (E) I and III only

4. $\left(x + \dfrac{1}{2}\right)^2 - (2x - 4)^2 =$

    (A) $-3x^2 - 15x + \dfrac{65}{4}$ (B) $3x^2 + 16x$ (C) $-3x^2 + 17x - \dfrac{63}{4}$ (D) $5x^2 + \dfrac{65}{4}$ (E) $3x^2$

5. If $x = 2$ and $y = -3$, then $y^2 - \left(x - \left[y + \dfrac{1}{2}\right]\right) - 2 \cdot 3 =$

    (A) $-\dfrac{39}{2}$ (B) $-\dfrac{3}{2}$ (C) 0 (D) 31 (E) 43

6. $4(xy)^3 + \left(x^3 - y^3\right)^2 =$

    (A) $x^3 - y^3$ (B) $\left(x^2 + y^2\right)^3$ (C) $\left(x^3 + y^3\right)^3$ (D) $\left(x^3 - y^3\right)^2$ (E) $\left(x^3 + y^3\right)^2$

7. If $\dfrac{a}{b} = -\dfrac{2}{3}$, then $\dfrac{b - a}{a} =$

    (A) $-\dfrac{5}{2}$ (B) $-\dfrac{5}{3}$ (C) $-\dfrac{1}{3}$ (D) 0 (E) 7

8. The operation $*$ is defined for all non-zero x and y by the equation $x * y = \dfrac{x}{y}$. Then the expression $(x - 2)^2 * x$ is equal to

    (A) $x - 4 + \dfrac{4}{x}$ (B) $4 + \dfrac{4}{x}$ (C) $\dfrac{4}{x}$ (D) $1 + \dfrac{4}{x}$ (E) $1 - 4x + \dfrac{4}{x}$

9. $\left(2 + \sqrt{7}\right)\left(4 - \sqrt{7}\right)(-2x) =$

    (A) $78x - 4x\sqrt{7}$ (B) $\sqrt{7}x$ (C) $-2x - 4x\sqrt{7}$ (D) $-2x$ (E) $4x\sqrt{7}$

10. If the operation $*$ is defined for all non-zero x and y by the equation $x * y = (xy)^2$, then $(x * y) * z =$

    (A) $x^2 y^2 z^2$ (B) $x^4 y^4 z^2$ (C) $x^2 y^4 z^2$ (D) $x^4 y^2 z^2$ (E) $x^4 y^4 z^4$

11. If $p = z + 1/z$ and $q = z - 1/z$, where z is a real number not equal to zero, then $(p + q)(p - q) =$

    (A) 2
    (B) 4.
    (C) z^2
    (D) $\dfrac{1}{z^2}$
    (E) $z^2 - \dfrac{1}{z^2}$

12. If $x^2 + y^2 = xy$, then $(x + y)^4 =$

    (A) xy
    (B) $x^2 y^2$
    (C) $9x^2 y^2$
    (D) $\left(x^2 + y^2\right)^2$
    (E) $x^4 + y^4$

13. $(2 + x)(2 + y) - (2 + x) - (2 + y) =$

    (A) $2y$
    (B) xy
    (C) $x + y$
    (D) $x - y$
    (E) $x + y + xy$

14. If $x^2 + y^2 = 2ab$ and $2xy = a^2 + b^2$, with $a, b, x, y > 0$, then $x + y =$

    (A) ab
    (B) $a - b$
    (C) $a + b$
    (D) $\sqrt{a^2 + b^2}$
    (E) $\sqrt{a^2 - b^2}$

Percents

Problems involving percent are common on the SAT. The word *percent* means "divided by one hundred." When you see the word "percent," or the symbol %, remember it means $\frac{1}{100}$. For example,

$$25 \text{ percent}$$
$$\downarrow \quad \downarrow$$
$$25 \times \frac{1}{100} = \frac{1}{4}$$

To convert a decimal into a percent, move the decimal point two places to the right. For example,

$$0.25 = 25\%$$
$$0.023 = 2.3\%$$
$$1.3 = 130\%$$

Conversely, to convert a percent into a decimal, move the decimal point two places to the left. For example,

$$47\% = .47$$
$$3.4\% = .034$$
$$175\% = 1.75$$

To convert a fraction into a percent, first change it into a decimal (by dividing the denominator [bottom] into the numerator [top]) and then move the decimal point two places to the right. For example,

$$\frac{7}{8} = 0.875 = 87.5\%$$

Conversely, to convert a percent into a fraction, first change it into a decimal and then change the decimal into a fraction. For example,

$$80\% = .80 = \frac{80}{100} = \frac{4}{5}$$

Following are the most common fractional equivalents of percents:

$$33\frac{1}{3}\% = \frac{1}{3} \qquad\qquad 20\% = \frac{1}{5}$$

$$66\frac{1}{3}\% = \frac{2}{3} \qquad\qquad 40\% = \frac{2}{5}$$

$$25\% = \frac{1}{4} \qquad\qquad 60\% = \frac{3}{5}$$

$$50\% = \frac{1}{2} \qquad\qquad 80\% = \frac{4}{5}$$

Percent problems often require you to translate a sentence into a mathematical equation.

Example 1:   What percent of 25 is 5?

(A) 10%   (B) 20%   (C) 30%   (D) 35%   (E) 40%

Translate the sentence into a mathematical equation as follows:

$$\begin{array}{cccccc} \text{What} & \text{percent} & \text{of} & 25 & \text{is} & 5 \\ \downarrow & \downarrow & \downarrow & \downarrow & \downarrow & \downarrow \\ x & \dfrac{1}{100} & \cdot & 25 & = & 5 \end{array}$$

$$\frac{25}{100}x = 5$$

$$\frac{1}{4}x = 5$$

$$x = 20$$

The answer is (B).

Example 2:   2 is 10% of what number

(A) 10   (B) 12   (C) 20   (D) 24   (E) 32

Translate the sentence into a mathematical equation as follows:

$$\begin{array}{cccccc} 2 & \text{is} & 10 & \% & \text{of} & \underline{\text{what number}} \\ \downarrow & \downarrow & \downarrow & \downarrow & \downarrow & \downarrow \\ 2 & = & 10 & \dfrac{1}{100} & \cdot & x \end{array}$$

$$2 = \frac{10}{100}x$$

$$2 = \frac{1}{10}x$$

$$20 = x$$

The answer is (C).

Example 3:   What percent of a is $3a$?

(A) 100%   (B) 150%   (C) 200%   (D) 300%   (E) 350%

Translate the sentence into a mathematical equation as follows:

$$\begin{array}{cccccc} \text{What} & \text{percent} & \text{of} & a & \text{is} & 3a \\ \downarrow & \downarrow & \downarrow & \downarrow & \downarrow & \downarrow \\ x & \dfrac{1}{100} & \cdot & a & = & 3a \end{array}$$

$$\frac{x}{100} \cdot a = 3a$$

$$\frac{x}{100} = 3 \quad \text{(by canceling the } a\text{'s)}$$

$$x = 300$$

The answer is (D).

Example 4:   If there are 15 boys and 25 girls in a class, what percent of the class is boys?

(A)   10%
(B)   15%
(C)   18%
(D)   25%
(E)   37.5%

The total number of students in the class is $15 + 25 = 40$. Now, translate the main part of the sentence into a mathematical equation:

what	percent	of	the class	is	boys
↓	↓	↓	↓	↓	↓
x	$\dfrac{1}{100}$	$\cdot$	40	$=$	15

$$\frac{40}{100}x = 15$$

$$\frac{2}{5}x = 15$$

$$2x = 75$$

$$x = 37.5$$

The answer is (E).

Often you will need to find the percent of increase (or decrease). To find it, calculate the increase (or decrease) and divide it by the original amount:

Percent of change: $\dfrac{Amount\ of\ change}{Original\ amount} \times 100\%$

Example 5:   The population of a town was 12,000 in 1980 and 16,000 in 1990. What was the percent increase in the population of the town during this period?

(A) $33\dfrac{1}{3}\%$
(B)   50%
(C)   75%
(D)   80%
(E)   120%

The population increased from 12,000 to 16,000. Hence, the change in population was 4,000. Now, translate the main part of the sentence into a mathematical equation:

Percent of change:

$$\frac{Amount\ of\ change}{Original\ amount} \times 100\% =$$

$$\frac{4000}{12000} \times 100\% =$$

$$\frac{1}{3} \times 100\% = \quad \text{(by canceling 4000)}$$

$$33\frac{1}{3}\%$$

The answer is (A).

Problem Set T: Solutions begin on page 607.

1. John spent $25, which is 15 percent of his monthly wage. What is his monthly wage?

   (A) $80   (B) 166\frac{2}{3}$ (C) $225   (D) $312.5   (E) $375

2. If a = 4b, what percent of 2a is 2b?
   (A) 10%   (B) 20%   (C) 25%   (D) 26%   (E) 40%

3. If $p = 5q > 0$, then 40 percent of $3p$ equals
   (A) $6q$ (B) $5.52q$ (C) $13.3q$ (D) $9q$ (E) $20.1q$

4. A jar contains 24 blue balls and 40 red balls. Which one of the following is 50% of the blue balls?
   (A) 10   (B) 11   (C) 12   (D) 13   (E) 14

5. In a company with 180 employees, 108 of the employees are female. What percent of the employees are male?

   (A) 5%   (B) 25%   (C) 35%   (D) 40%   (E) 60%

6. John bought a shirt, a pair of pants, and a pair of shoes, which cost $10, $20, and $30, respectively. What percent of the total expense was spent for the pants?

   (A) 16$\frac{2}{3}$%   (B) 20%   (C) 30%   (D) 33$\frac{1}{3}$%   (E) 60%

7. Last year Jenny was 5 feet tall, and this year she is 5 feet 6 inches. What is the percent increase of her height?

   (A) 5%   (B) 10%   (C) 15%   (D) 20%   (E) 40%

8. Last month the price of a particular pen was $1.20. This month the price of the same pen is $1.50. What is the percent increase in the price of the pen?

   (A) 5%   (B) 10%   (C) 25%   (D) 30%   (E) 33$\frac{1}{3}$%

9. Stella paid $1,500 for a computer after receiving a 20 percent discount. What was the price of the computer before the discount?

   (A) $300   (B) $1,500   (C) $1,875   (D) $2,000   (E) $3,000

10. A town has a population growth rate of 10% per year. The population in 1990 was 2000. What was the population in 1992?

    (A) 1600   (B) 2200   (C) 2400   (D) 2420   (E) 4000

11. In a class of 200 students, forty percent are girls. Twenty-five percent of the boys and 10 percent of the girls signed up for a tour to Washington DC. What percent of the class signed up for the tour?

    (A) 19%   (B) 23%   (C) 25%   (D) 27%   (E) 35%

12. If 15% of a number is 4.5, then 45% of the same number is
    (A) 1.5   (B) 3.5   (C) 13.5   (D) 15   (E) 45

Graphs

Questions involving graphs are more common on the new SAT. Rarely do these questions involve any significant calculating. Usually, the solution is merely a matter of interpreting the graph.

Questions 1-4 refer to the following graphs.

SALES AND EARNINGS OF CONSOLIDATED CONGLOMERATE

Sales
(in millions of dollars)

Earnings
(in millions of dollars)

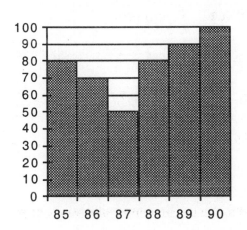

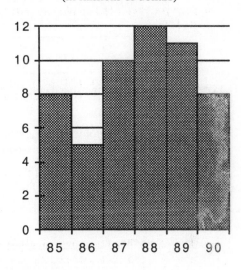

Note: Figure drawn to scale.

1.   During which year was the company's earnings 10 percent of its sales?

    (A) 85   (B) 86   (C) 87   (D) 88   (E) 90

Reading from the graph, we see that in 1985 the company's earnings were $8 million and its sales were $80 million. This gives

$$\frac{8}{10} = \frac{1}{10} = \frac{10}{100} = 10\%$$

The answer is (A).

2.   During the years 1986 through 1988, what were the average earnings per year?

    (A) 6 million   (B) 7.5 million   (C) 9 million   (D) 10 million   (E) 27 million

The graph yields the following information:

Year	Earnings
1986	$5 million
1987	$10 million
1988	$12 million

Forming the average yields $\dfrac{5+10+12}{3} = \dfrac{27}{3} = 9$. The answer is (C).

3.   In which year did sales increase by the greatest percentage over the previous year?

(A) 86   (B) 87   (C) 88   (D) 89   (E) 90

To find the percentage increase (or decrease), divide the numerical change by the original amount. This yields

Year	Percentage increase
86	$\dfrac{70-80}{80} = \dfrac{-10}{80} = \dfrac{-1}{8} = -12.5\%$
87	$\dfrac{50-70}{70} = \dfrac{-20}{70} = \dfrac{-2}{7} \approx -29\%$
88	$\dfrac{80-50}{50} = \dfrac{30}{50} = \dfrac{3}{5} = 60\%$
89	$\dfrac{90-80}{80} = \dfrac{10}{80} = \dfrac{1}{8} = 12.5\%$
90	$\dfrac{100-90}{90} = \dfrac{10}{90} = \dfrac{1}{9} \approx 11\%$

The largest number in the right-hand column, 60%, corresponds to the year 1988. The answer is (C).

4.   If Consolidated Conglomerate's earnings are less than or equal to 10 percent of sales during a year, then the stockholders must take a dividend cut at the end of the year. In how many years did the stockholders of Consolidated Conglomerate suffer a dividend cut?

(A) None   (B) One   (C) Two   (D) Three   (E) Four

Calculating 10 percent of the sales for each year yields

Year	10% of Sales (millions)	Earnings (millions)
85	$.10 \times 80 = 8$	8
86	$.10 \times 70 = 7$	5
87	$.10 \times 50 = 5$	10
88	$.10 \times 80 = 8$	12
89	$.10 \times 90 = 9$	11
90	$.10 \times 100 = 10$	8

Comparing the right columns shows that earnings were 10 percent or less of sales in 1985, 1986, and 1990. The answer is (D).

Problem Set U: Solutions begin on page 611.

Questions 1–5 refer to the following graphs.

Profit And Revenue Distribution For Zippy Printing, 1990–1993, Copying And Printing.

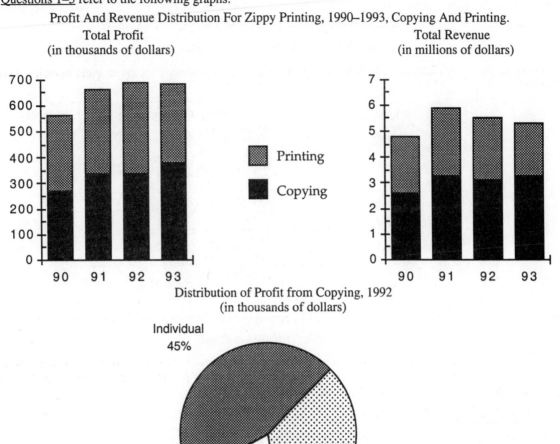

Total Profit
(in thousands of dollars)

Total Revenue
(in millions of dollars)

Distribution of Profit from Copying, 1992
(in thousands of dollars)

1.   In 1993, the total profit was approximately how much greater than the total profit in 1990?

    (A) 50 thousand   (B) 75 thousand   (C) 120 thousand   (D) 200 thousand   (E) 350 thousand

2.   In 1990, the profit from copying was approximately what percent of the revenue from copying?

    (A) 2%   (B) 10%   (C) 20%   (D) 35%   (E) 50%

3.   In 1992, the profit from copying for corporate customers was approximately how much greater than the profit from copying for government customers?

    (A) 50 thousand   (B) 80 thousand   (C) 105 thousand   (D) 190 thousand   (E) 260 thousand

4.   During the two years in which total profit was most nearly equal, the combined revenue from printing was closest to

    (A) 1 million   (B) 2 million   (C) 4.5 million   (D) 6 million   (E) 6.5 million

5.   The amount of profit made from government copy sales in 1992 was

    (A) 70 thousand   (B) 100 thousand   (C) 150 thousand   (D) 200 thousand   (E) 350 thousand

Questions 6–10 refer to the following graphs.

DISTRIBUTION OF CRIMINAL ACTIVITY BY CATEGORY OF CRIME FOR COUNTRY X IN 1990
AND PROJECTED FOR 2000.

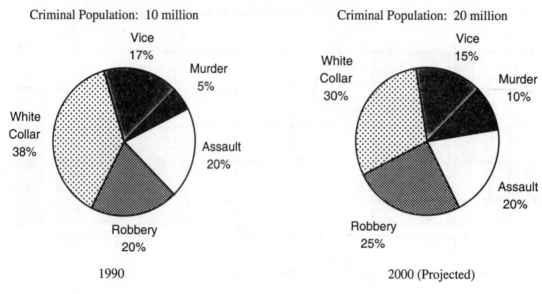

6.   What is the projected number of white-collar criminals in 2000?

   (A)   1 million
   (B)   3.8 million
   (C)   6 million
   (D)   8 million
   (E)   10 million

7.   The ratio of the number of robbers in 1990 to the number of projected robbers in 2000 is

   (A) $\frac{2}{5}$ (B) $\frac{3}{5}$ (C) 1   (D) $\frac{3}{2}$ (E) $\frac{5}{2}$

8.   From 1990 to 2000, there is a projected decrease in the number of criminals for which of the following categories?

   I.   Vice
   II.   Assault
   III.   White Collar

   (A) None   (B) I only   (C) II only   (D) II and III only   (E) I, II, and III

9.   What is the approximate projected percent increase between 1990 and 2000 in the number of criminals involved in vice?

   (A) 25%   (B) 40%   (C) 60%   (D) 75%   (E) 85%

10.   The projected number of Robbers in 2000 will exceed the number of white-collar criminals in 1990 by
   (A) 1.2 million   (B) 2.3 million   (C) 3.4 million   (D) 5.8 million   (E) 7.2 million

Questions 11–15 refer to the following graph.

SALES BY CATEGORY FOR GRAMMERCY PRESS, 1980–1989
(in thousands of books)

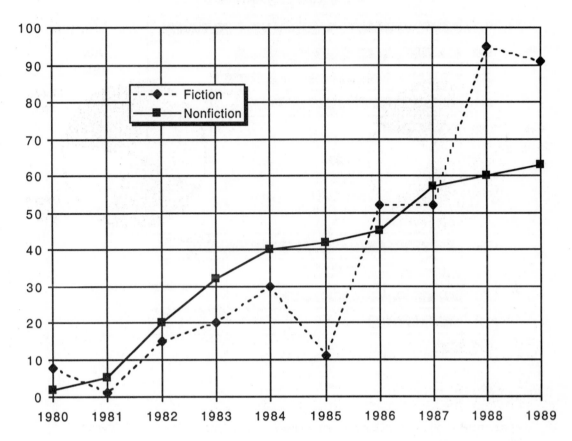

11. In how many years did the sales of nonfiction titles exceed the sales of fiction titles ?

    (A) 2   (B) 3   (C) 4   (D) 5   (E) 6

12. Which of the following best approximates the amount by which the increase in sales of fiction titles from 1985 to 1986 exceeded the increase in sales of fiction titles from 1983 to 1984?

    (A)   31.5   thousand
    (B)   40   thousand
    (C)   49.3   thousand
    (D)   50.9   thousand
    (E)   68   thousand

13. Which of the following periods showed a continual increase in the sales of fiction titles?

    (A) 1980–1982   (B) 1982–1984   (C) 1984–1986   (D) 1986–1988   (E) 1987–1989

14. What was the approximate average number of sales of fiction titles from 1984 to 1988?

    (A) 15 thousand   (B) 30 thousand   (C) 40 thousand   (D) 48 thousand   (E) 60 thousand

15. By approximately what percent did the sale of nonfiction titles increase from 1984 to 1987?

    (A) 42%   (B) 50%   (C) 70%   (D) 90%   (E) 110%

Questions 16–20 refer to the following graph.

AUTOMOBILE ACCIDENTS IN COUNTRY X: 1990 TO 1994
(in ten thousands)

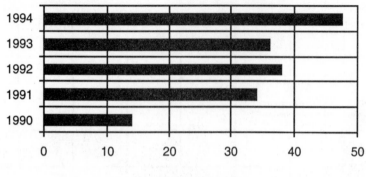

CARS IN COUNTRY X
(in millions)

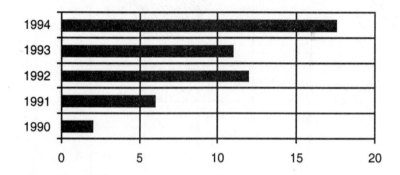

16. Approximately how many millions of cars were in Country X in 1994?

(A) 1.0   (B) 4.7   (C) 9.0   (D) 15.5   (E) 17.5

17. The amount by which the number of cars in 1990 exceeded the number of accidents in 1991 was approximately

(A) 0.3 million   (B) 0.7 million   (C) 1.0 million   (D) 1.7 million   (E) 2.5 million

18. The number of accidents in 1993 was approximately what percentage of the number of cars?

(A) 1%   (B) 1.5%   (C) 3%   (D) 5%   (E) 10%

19. In which of the following years will the number of accidents exceed 500 thousand?

(A)   1994
(B)   1995
(C)   1998
(D)   2000
(E)   It cannot be determined from the information given.

20. If no car in 1993 was involved in more than four accidents, what is the minimum number of cars that could have been in accidents in 1993?

(A) 50 thousand   (B) 60 thousand   (C) 70 thousand   (D) 80 thousand   (E) 90 thousand

Questions 21–25 refer to the following graphs.

DISTRIBUTION OF IMPORTS AND EXPORTS FOR COUNTRY X IN 1994.

Imports
200 million items

Exports
100 million items

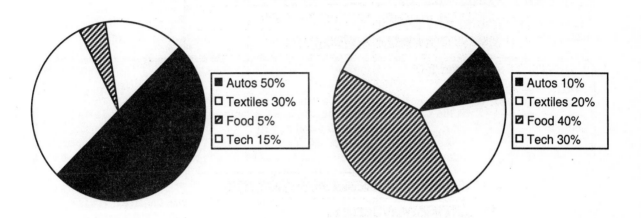

21. How many autos did Country X export in 1994?

(A) 10 million
(B) 15 million
(C) 16 million
(D) 20 million
(E) 30 million

22. In how many categories did the total number of items (import and export) exceed 75 million?

(A) 1   (B) 2   (C) 3   (D) 4   (E) none

23. The ratio of the number of technology items imported in 1994 to the number of textile items exported in 1994 is

(A) $\frac{1}{3}$ (B) $\frac{3}{5}$ (C) 1   (D) $\frac{6}{5}$ (E) $\frac{3}{2}$

24. If in 1995 the number of autos exported was 16 million, then the percent increase from 1994 in the number of autos exported is

(A) 40%   (B) 47%   (C) 50%   (D) 60%   (E) 65%

25. In 1994, if twice as many autos imported to Country X broke down as autos exported from Country X and 20 percent of the exported autos broke down, what percent of the imported autos broke down?

(A) 1%   (B) 1.5%   (C) 2%   (D) 4%   (E) 5.5%

Word Problems

Before we begin solving word problems, we need to be very comfortable with translating words into mathematical symbols. Following is a partial list of words and their mathematical equivalents.

Concept	Symbol	Words	Example	Translation
equality	=	is	2 plus 2 is 4	$2 + 2 = 4$
		equals	x minus 5 equals 2	$x - 5 = 2$
		is the same as	multiplying x by 2 is the same as dividing x by 7	$2x = x/7$
addition	+	sum	the sum of y and π is 20	$y + \pi = 20$
		plus	x plus y equals 5	$x + y = 5$
		add	how many marbles must John add to collection P so that he has 13 marbles	$x + P = 13$
		increase	a number is increased by 10%	$x + 10\%x$
		more	the perimeter of the square is 3 more than the area	$P = 3 + A$
subtraction	−	minus	x minus y	$x - y$
		difference	the difference of x and y is 8	$|x - y| = 8$
		subtracted	x subtracted from y	$y - x$ *
		less than	the circumference is 5 less than the area	$C = A - 5$
multiplication	$\times$ *or* $\bullet$	times	the acceleration is 5 times the velocity	$a = 5v$
		product	the product of two consecutive integers	$x(x + 1)$
		of	x is 125% of y	$x = 125\%y$
division	÷	quotient	the quotient of x and y is 9	$x \div y = 9$
		divided	if x is divided by y, the result is 4	$x \div y = 4$

Although exact steps for solving word problems cannot be given, the following guidelines will help:

(1) First, choose a variable to stand for the least unknown quantity, and then try to write the other unknown quantities in terms of that variable.

For example, suppose we are given that Sue's age is 5 years less than twice Jane's and the sum of their ages is 16. Then Jane's age would be the least unknown, and we let $x = Jane's\ age$. Expressing Sue's age in terms of x gives *Sue's age* $= 2x - 5$.

(2) Second, write an equation that involves the expressions in Step 1. Most (though not all) word problems pivot on the fact that two quantities in the problem are equal. Deciding which two quantities should be set equal is usually the hardest part in solving a word problem since it can require considerable ingenuity to discover which expressions are equal.

For the example above, we would get $(2x - 5) + x = 16$.

(3) Third, solve the equation in Step 2 and interpret the result.

For the example above, we would get by adding the x's: $3x - 5 = 16$

Then adding 5 to both sides gives $3x = 21$

Finally, dividing by 3 gives $x = 7$

Hence, Jane is 7 years old and Sue is $2x - 5 = 2 \cdot 7 - 5 = 9$ years old.

---

* Notice that with "minus" and "difference" the terms are subtracted in the same order as they are written, from left to right (x minus $y \longrightarrow x - y$). However, with "subtracted" and "less than," the order of subtraction is reversed (x subtracted from $y \longrightarrow y - x$). Many students translate "subtracted from" in the wrong order.

MOTION PROBLEMS

Virtually, all motion problems involve the formula *Distance* = *Rate* × *Time*, or

$$D = R \times T$$

Overtake: In this type of problem, one person catches up with or overtakes another person. The key to these problems is that at the moment one person overtakes the other they have traveled the same distance.

Example : Scott starts jogging from point X to point Y. A half-hour later his friend Garrett who jogs 1 mile per hour slower than twice Scott's rate starts from the same point and follows the same path. If Garrett overtakes Scott in 2 hours, how many miles will Garrett have covered?

(A) $2\dfrac{1}{5}$ (B) $3\dfrac{1}{3}$ (C) 4 (D) 6 (E) $6\dfrac{2}{3}$

Following Guideline 1, we let r = *Scott's rate*. Then $2r - 1$ = *Garrett's rate*. Turning to Guideline 2, we look for two quantities that are equal to each other. When Garrett overtakes Scott, they will have traveled the same distance. Now, from the formula $D = R \times T$, Scott's distance is $D = r \times 2\dfrac{1}{2}$

and Garrett's distance is $D = (2r - 1)2 = 4r - 2$

Setting these expressions equal to each other gives $4r - 2 = r \times 2\dfrac{1}{2}$

Solving this equation for r gives $r = \dfrac{4}{3}$

Hence, Garrett will have traveled $D = 4r - 2 = 4\left(\dfrac{4}{3}\right) - 2 = 3\dfrac{1}{3}$ miles. The answer is (B).

Opposite Directions: In this type of problem, two people start at the same point and travel in opposite directions. The key to these problems is that the total distance traveled is the sum of the individual distances traveled.

Example: Two people start jogging at the same point and time but in opposite directions. If the rate of one jogger is 2 mph faster than the other and after 3 hours they are 30 miles apart, what is the rate of the faster jogger?

(A) 3 (B) 4 (C) 5 (D) 6 (E) 7

Let r be the rate of the slower jogger. Then the rate of the faster jogger is $r + 2$. Since they are jogging for 3 hours, the distance traveled by the slower jogger is $D = rt = 3r$, and the distance traveled by the faster jogger is $3(r + 2)$. Since they are 30 miles apart, adding the distances traveled gives

$$3r + 3(r + 2) = 30$$
$$3r + 3r + 6 = 30$$
$$6r + 6 = 30$$
$$6r = 24$$
$$r = 4$$

Hence, the rate of the faster jogger is $r + 2 = 4 + 2 = 6$. The answer is (D).

Round Trip: The key to these problems is that the distance going is the same as the distance returning.

Example: A cyclist travels 20 miles at a speed of 15 miles per hour. If he returns along the same path and the entire trip takes 2 hours, at what speed did he return?

(A) 15 mph   (B) 20 mph   (C) 22 mph   (D) 30 mph   (E) 34 mph

Solving the formula $D = R \times T$ for T yields $T = \dfrac{D}{R}$. For the first half of the trip, this yields $T = \dfrac{20}{15} = \dfrac{4}{3}$ hours. Since the entire trip takes 2 hours, the return trip takes $2 - \dfrac{4}{3}$ hours, or $\dfrac{2}{3}$ hours. Now, the return trip is also 20 miles, so solving the formula $D = R \times T$ for R yields $R = \dfrac{D}{T} = \dfrac{20}{2/3} = 20 \cdot \dfrac{3}{2} = 30$. The answer is (D).

Compass Headings: In this type of problem, typically two people are traveling in perpendicular directions. The key to these problems is often the Pythagorean Theorem.

Example: At 1 PM, Ship A leaves port heading due west at x miles per hour. Two hours later, Ship B is 100 miles due south of the same port and heading due north at y miles per hour. At 5 PM, how far apart are the ships?

(A) $\sqrt{(4x)^2 + (100 + 2y)^2}$

(B) $x + y$

(C) $\sqrt{x^2 + y^2}$

(D) $\sqrt{(4x)^2 + (2y)^2}$

(E) $\sqrt{(4x)^2 + (100 - 2y)^2}$

Since Ship A is traveling at x miles per hour, its distance traveled at 5 PM is $D = rt = 4x$. The distance traveled by Ship B is $D = rt = 2y$. This can be represented by the following diagram:

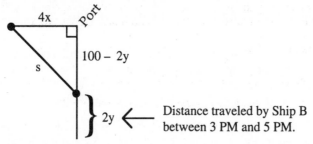

Applying the Pythagorean Theorem yields $s^2 = (4x)^2 + (100 - 2y)^2$. Taking the square root of this equation gives $s = \sqrt{(4x)^2 + (100 - 2y)^2}$. The answer is (E).

Circular Motion: In this type of problem, the key is often the arc length formula $S = R\theta$, where S is the arc length (or distance traveled), R is the radius of the circle, and θ is the angle.

Example: The figure to the right shows the path of a car moving around a circular racetrack. How many miles does the car travel in going from point A to point B ?

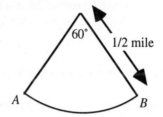

(A) $\dfrac{\pi}{6}$ (B) $\dfrac{\pi}{3}$ (C) π (D) 30   (E) 60

When calculating distance, degree measure must be converted to radian measure. To convert degree measure to radian measure, multiply by the conversion factor $\dfrac{\pi}{180}$. Multiplying 60° by $\dfrac{\pi}{180}$ yields $60 \cdot \dfrac{\pi}{180} = \dfrac{\pi}{3}$. Now, the length of arc traveled by the car in moving from point A to point B is S. Plugging this information into the formula $S = R\theta$ yields $S = \dfrac{1}{2} \cdot \dfrac{\pi}{3} = \dfrac{\pi}{6}$. The answer is (A).

Example : If a wheel is spinning at 1200 revolutions per minute, how many revolutions will it make in t seconds?

   (A) $2t$ (B) $10t$ (C) $20t$ (D) $48t$ (E) $72t$

Since the question asks for the number of revolutions in t seconds, we need to find the number of revolutions per second and multiply that number by t. Since the wheel is spinning at 1200 revolutions per minute and there are 60 seconds in a minute, we get $\dfrac{1200\ revolutions}{60\ seconds} = 20\ rev/sec$. Hence, in t seconds, the wheel will make $20t$ revolutions. The answer is (C).

WORK PROBLEMS

The formula for work problems is $Work = Rate \times Time$, or $W = R \times T$. The amount of work done is usually 1 unit. Hence, the formula becomes $1 = R \times T$. Solving this for R gives $R = \dfrac{1}{T}$.

Example : If Johnny can mow the lawn in 30 minutes and with the help of his brother, Bobby, they can mow the lawn 20 minutes, how long would it take Bobby working alone to mow the lawn?

   (A) $\dfrac{1}{2}$ hour   (B) $\dfrac{3}{4}$ hour   (C) 1 hour   (D) $\dfrac{3}{2}$ hours   (E) 2 hours

Let $r = 1/t$ be Bobby's rate. Now, the rate at which they work together is merely the sum of their rates:

$$Total\ Rate = Johnny's\ Rate + Bobby's\ Rate$$

$$\frac{1}{20} = \frac{1}{30} + \frac{1}{t}$$

$$\frac{1}{20} - \frac{1}{30} = \frac{1}{t}$$

$$\frac{30 - 20}{30 \cdot 20} = \frac{1}{t}$$

$$\frac{1}{60} = \frac{1}{t}$$

$$t = 60$$

Hence, working alone, Bobby can do the job in 1 hour. The answer is (C).

Example: A tank is being drained at a constant rate. If it takes 3 hours to drain $\frac{6}{7}$ of its capacity, how much longer will it take to drain the tank completely?

(A) $\frac{1}{2}$ hour   (B) $\frac{3}{4}$ hour   (C) 1 hour   (D) $\frac{3}{2}$ hours   (E) 2 hours

Since $\frac{6}{7}$ of the tank's capacity was drained in 3 hours, the formula $W = R \times T$ becomes $\frac{6}{7} = R \times 3$. Solving for R gives $R = \frac{2}{7}$. Now, since $\frac{6}{7}$ of the work has been completed, $\frac{1}{7}$ of the work remains. Plugging this information into the formula $W = R \times T$ gives $\frac{1}{7} = \frac{2}{7} \times T$. Solving for T gives $T = \frac{1}{2}$. The answer is (A).

MIXTURE PROBLEMS

The key to these problems is that the combined total of the concentrations in the two parts must be the same as the whole mixture.

Example :   How many ounces of a solution that is 30 percent salt must be added to a 50-ounce solution that is 10 percent salt so that the resulting solution is 20 percent salt?

(A) 20   (B) 30   (C) 40   (D) 50   (E) 60

Let x be the ounces of the 30 percent solution. Then $30\%x$ is the amount of salt in that solution. The final solution will be $50 + x$ ounces, and its concentration of salt will be $20\%(50 + x)$. The original amount of salt in the solution is $10\% \cdot 50$. Now, the concentration of salt in the original solution plus the concentration of salt in the added solution must equal the concentration of salt in the resulting solution:

$$10\% \cdot 50 + 30\%x = 20\%(50 + x)$$

Multiply this equation by 100 to clear the percent symbol and then solving for x yields $x = 50$. The answer is (D).

COIN PROBLEMS

The key to these problems is to keep the quantity of coins distinct from the value of the coins. An example will illustrate.

Example :   Laura has 20 coins consisting of quarters and dimes. If she has a total of $3.05, how many dimes does she have?

(A) 3   (B) 7   (C) 10   (D) 13   (E) 16

Let D stand for the number of dimes, and let Q stand for the number of quarters. Since the total number of coins in 20, we get $D + Q = 20$, or $Q = 20 - D$. Now, each dime is worth 10¢, so the value of the dimes is $10D$. Similarly, the value of the quarters is $25Q = 25(20 - D)$. Summarizing this information in a table yields

	Dimes	Quarters	Total
Number	D	$20 - D$	20
Value	$10D$	$25(20 - D)$	305

Notice that the total value entry in the table was converted from $3.05 to 305¢. Adding up the value of the dimes and the quarters yields the following equation:

$$10D + 25(20 - D) = 305$$
$$10D + 500 - 25D = 305$$
$$-15D = -195$$
$$D = 13$$

Hence, there are 13 dimes, and the answer is (D).

AGE PROBLEMS

Typically, in these problems, we start by letting x be a person's current age and then the person's age a years ago will be $x - a$ and the person's age a years in future will be $x + a$. An example will illustrate.

Example : John is 20 years older than Steve. In 10 years, Steve's age will be half that of John's. What is Steve's age?

(A) 2   (B) 8   (C) 10   (D) 20   (E) 25

Steve's age is the most unknown quantity. So we let x = Steve's age and then $x + 20$ is John's age. Ten years from now, Steve and John's ages will be $x + 10$ and $x + 30$, respectively. Summarizing this information in a table yields

	Age now	**Age in 10 years**
Steve	x	$x + 10$
John	$x + 20$	$x + 30$

Since "in 10 years, Steve's age will be half that of John's," we get

$$\frac{1}{2}(x + 30) = x + 10$$
$$x + 30 = 2(x + 10)$$
$$x + 30 = 2x + 20$$
$$x = 10$$

Hence, Steve is 10 years old, and the answer is (C).

INTEREST PROBLEMS

These problems are based on the formula

$$\text{INTEREST} = \text{AMOUNT} \times \text{TIME} \times \text{RATE}$$

Often, the key to these problems is that the interest earned from one account plus the interest earned from another account equals the total interest earned:

Total Interest = (Interest from first account) + (Interest from second account)

An example will illustrate.

Example : A total of $1200 is deposited in two savings accounts for one year, part at 5% and the remainder at 7%. If $72 was earned in interest, how much was deposited at 5%?

(A) 410   (B) 520   (C) 600   (D) 650   (E) 760

Let x be the amount deposited at 5%. Then $1200 - x$ is the amount deposited at 7%. The interest on these investments is $.05x$ and $.07(1200 - x)$. Since the total interest is $72, we get

$$.05x + .07(1200 - x) = 72$$
$$.05x + 84 - .07x = 72$$
$$-.02x + 84 = 72$$
$$-.02x = -12$$
$$x = 600$$

The answer is (C).

Problem Set V: Solutions begin on page 619.

1. Seven years ago, Scott was 3 times as old as Kathy was at that time. If Scott is now 5 years older than Kathy, how old is Scott?

    (A) 12 ½   (B) 13   (C) 13 ½   (D) 14   (E) 14 ½

Duals

2. A dress was initially listed at a price that would have given the store a profit of 20 percent of the wholesale cost. After reducing the asking price by 10 percent, the dress sold for a net profit of 10 dollars. What was the wholesale cost of the dress?

    (A) 200   (B) 125   (C) 100   (D) 20   (E) 10

3. A dress was initially listed at a price that would have given the store a profit of 20 percent of the wholesale cost. The dress sold for 50 dollars. What was the wholesale cost of the dress?

    (A) 100   (B) 90   (C) 75   (D) 60   (E) Not enough information to decide

Duals

4. The capacity of glass X is 80 percent of the capacity of glass Y. Further, glass X contains 6 ounces of punch and is half-full, while glass Y is full. Glass Y contains how many more ounces of punch than glass X?

    (A) 1   (B) 3   (C) 6   (D) 9   (E) Not enough information to decide

5. The capacity of glass X is 80 percent of the capacity of glass Y. Further, Glass X is 70 percent full, and glass Y is 30 percent full. Glass X contains how many more ounces of punch than glass Y?

    (A) 1   (B) 3   (C) 6   (D) 8   (E) Not enough information to decide

6. Car X traveled from city A to city B in 30 minutes. The first half of the distance was covered at 50 miles per hour, and the second half of the distance was covered at 60 miles per hour. What was the average speed of car X?

    (A) $\dfrac{200}{11}$ (B) $\dfrac{400}{11}$ (C) $\dfrac{500}{11}$ (D) $\dfrac{600}{11}$ (E) $\dfrac{700}{11}$

7. Steve bought some apples at a cost of \$.60 each and some oranges at a cost of \$.50 each. If he paid a total of \$4.10 for a total of 8 apples and oranges, how many apples did Steve buy?

    (A) 1   (B) 2   (C) 3   (D) 5   (E) 6

8. Cyclist M leaves point P at 12 noon and travels in a straight path at a constant velocity of 20 miles per hour. Cyclist N leaves point P at 2 PM, travels the same path at a constant velocity, and overtakes M at 4 PM. What was the average speed of N?

    (A) 15   (B) 24   (C) 30   (D) 35   (E) 40

9. A pair of pants and matching shirt cost \$52.50. The pants cost two and a half times as much as the shirt. What is the cost of the shirt alone?

    (A) 10   (B) 15   (C) 20   (D) 27   (E) 30

10. Jennifer and Alice are 4 miles apart. If Jennifer starts walking toward Alice at 3 miles per hour and at the same time Alice starts walking toward Jennifer at 2 miles per hour, how much time will pass before they meet?

    (A) 20 minutes   (B) 28 minutes   (C) 43 minutes   (D) 48 minutes   (E) 60 minutes

11. If Robert can assemble a model car in 30 minutes and Craig can assemble the same model car in 20 minutes, how long would it take them, working together, to assemble the model car?

    (A) 12 minutes   (B) 13 minutes   (C) 14 minutes   (D) 15 minutes   (E) 16 minutes

12. How many ounces of nuts costing 80 cents a pound must be mixed with nuts costing 60 cents a pound to make a 10-ounce mixture costing 70 cents a pound?

    (A) 3   (B) 4   (C) 5   (D) 7   (E) 8

13. Tom is 10 years older than Carrie. However, 5 years ago Tom was twice as old as Carrie. How old is Carrie?

    (A) 5   (B) 10   (C) 12   (D) 15   (E) 25

14. Two cars start at the same point and travel in opposite directions. If one car travels at 45 miles per hour and the other at 60 miles per hour, how much time will pass before they are 210 miles apart?

    (A) .5 hours   (B) 1 hour   (C) 1.5 hours   (D) 2 hours   (E) 2.5 hours

15. If the value of x quarters is equal to the value of $x + 32$ nickels, $x =$

    (A) 8   (B) 11   (C) 14   (D) 17   (E) 20

16. Steve has $5.25 in nickels and dimes. If he has 15 more dimes than nickels, how many nickels does he have?

    (A) 20   (B) 25   (C) 27   (D) 30   (E) 33

17. Cathy has equal numbers of nickels and quarters worth a total of $7.50. How many coins does she have?

    (A) 20   (B) 25   (C) 50   (D) 62   (E) 70

18. Richard leaves to visit his friend who lives 200 miles down Interstate 10. One hour later his friend Steve leaves to visit Richard via Interstate 10. If Richard drives at 60 mph and Steve drives at 40 mph, how many miles will Steve have driven when they cross paths?

    (A) 56   (B) 58   (C) 60   (D) 65   (E) 80

19. At 1 PM, Ship A leaves port traveling 15 mph. Three hours later, Ship B leaves the same port in the same direction traveling 25 mph. At what time does Ship B pass Ship A?

    (A) 8:30 PM   (B) 8:35 PM   (C) 9 PM   (D) 9:15 PM   (E) 9:30 PM

20. In x hours and y minutes a car traveled z miles. What is the car's speed in miles per hour?

    (A) $\dfrac{z}{60 + y}$ (B) $\dfrac{60z}{60x + y}$ (C) $\dfrac{60}{60 + y}$ (D) $\dfrac{z}{x + y}$ (E) $\dfrac{60 + y}{60z}$

21.   A 30% discount reduces the price of a commodity by $90. If the discount is reduced to 20%, then the price of the commodity will be

   (A) $180   (B) $210   (C) $240   (D) $270   (E) $300

22.   In a class of 40 students, the number of students who passed the math exam is equal to half the number of students who passed the science exam. Each student in the class passed at least one of the two exams. If 5 students passed both exams, then the number of students who passed the math exam is

   (A) 5   (B) 10   (C) 15   (D) 20   (E) 25

23.   A train of length l, traveling at a constant velocity, passes a pole in t seconds. If the same train traveling at the same velocity passes a platform in $3t$ seconds, then the length of the platform is

   (A) $0.5l$ (B) l (C) $1.5l$ (D) $2l$ (E) $3l$

24.   If two workers can assemble a car in 8 hours and a third worker can assemble the same car in 12 hours, then how long would it take the three workers together to assemble the car?

   (A) $\dfrac{5}{12}$ hrs

   (B) $2\dfrac{2}{5}$ hrs

   (C) $2\dfrac{4}{5}$ hrs

   (D) $3\dfrac{1}{2}$ hrs

   (E) $4\dfrac{4}{5}$ hrs

25.   The age of B is half the sum of the ages of A and C. If B is 2 years younger than A and C is 32 years old, then the age of B must be

   (A)   28
   (B)   30
   (C)   32
   (D)   34
   (E)   36

26.   The ages of three people are such that the age of one person is twice the age of the second person and three times the age of the third person. If the sum of the ages of the three people is 33, then the age of the youngest person is

   (A)   3
   (B)   6
   (C)   9
   (D)   11
   (E)   18

Sequences & Series

SEQUENCES

A sequence is an ordered list of numbers. The following is a sequence of odd numbers:

$$1, 3, 5, 7, \ldots$$

A term of a sequence is identified by its position in the sequence. In the above sequence, 1 is the first term, 3 is the second term, etc. The ellipsis symbol (. . .) indicates that the sequence continues forever.

Example 1: In sequence S, the 3rd term is 4, the 2nd term is three times the 1st, and the 3rd term is four times the 2nd. What is the 1st term in sequence S?

(A) 0   (B) $\dfrac{1}{3}$ (C) 1   (D) $\dfrac{3}{2}$ (E) 4

We know *"the 3rd term of S is 4,"* and that *"the 3rd term is four times the 2nd."* This is equivalent to saying the 2nd term is $\dfrac{1}{4}$ the 3rd term: $\dfrac{1}{4} \cdot 4 = 1$. Further, we know *"the 2nd term is three times the 1st."* This is equivalent to saying the 1st term is $\dfrac{1}{3}$ the 2nd term: $\dfrac{1}{3} \cdot 1 = \dfrac{1}{3}$. Hence, the first term of the sequence is fully determined:

$$\frac{1}{3}, 1, 4$$

The answer is (B).

Example 2: Except for the first two numbers, every number in the sequence $-1, 3, -3, \ldots$ is the product of the two immediately preceding numbers. How many numbers of this sequence are odd?

(A) one   (B) two   (C) three   (D) four   (E) more than four

Since *"every number in the sequence $-1, 3, -3, \ldots$ is the product of the two immediately preceding numbers,"* the forth term of the sequence is $-9 = 3(-3)$. The first 6 terms of this sequence are

$$-1, 3, -3, -9, 27, -243, \ldots$$

At least six numbers in this sequence are odd: $-1, 3, -3, -9, 27, -243$. The answer is (E).

Arithmetic Progressions

An arithmetic progression is a sequence in which the difference between any two consecutive terms is the same. This is the same as saying: each term exceeds the previous term by a fixed amount. For example, $0, 6, 12, 18, \ldots$ is an arithmetic progression in which the common difference is 6. The sequence $8, 4, 0, -4, \ldots$ is arithmetic with a common difference of -4.

Example 3:   The seventh number in a sequence of numbers is 31 and each number after the first number in the sequence is 4 less than the number immediately preceding it. What is the fourth number in the sequence?

(A) 15   (B) 19   (C) 35   (D) 43   (E) 51

Since each number *"in the sequence is 4 less than the number immediately preceding it,"* the sixth term is $31 + 4 = 35$; the fifth number in the sequence is $35 + 4 = 39$; and the fourth number in the sequence is $39 + 4 = 43$. The answer is (D). Following is the sequence written out:

$$55, 51, 47, 43, 39, 35, 31, 27, 23, 19, 15, 11, \ldots$$

Advanced concepts: (Sequence Formulas)

Students with strong backgrounds in mathematics may prefer to solve sequence problems by using formulas. Note, none of the formulas in this section are necessary to answer questions about sequences on the SAT.

Since each term of an arithmetic progression *"exceeds the previous term by a fixed amount,"* we get the following:

first term	$a + 0d$	where a is the first term and d is the common difference
second term	$a + 1d$	
third term	$a + 2d$	
fourth term	$a + 3d$	
	$\ldots$	
nth term	$a + (n - 1)d$	This formula generates the nth term

The sum of the first n terms of an arithmetic sequence is

$$\frac{n}{2}\big[2a + (n-1)d\big]$$

Geometric Progressions

A geometric progression is a sequence in which the ratio of any two consecutive terms is the same. Thus, each term is generated by multiplying the preceding term by a fixed number. For example, $-3, 6, -12, 24, \ldots$ is a geometric progression in which the common ratio is -2. The sequence $32, 16, 8, 4, \ldots$ is geometric with common ratio $1/2$.

Example 4:   What is the sixth term of the sequence $90, -30, 10, -\dfrac{10}{3}, \ldots$?

(A) $\dfrac{1}{3}$ (B) 0 (C) $-\dfrac{10}{27}$ (D) -3 (E) $-\dfrac{100}{3}$

Since the common ratio between any two consecutive terms is $-\dfrac{1}{3}$, the fifth term is $\dfrac{10}{9} = \left(-\dfrac{1}{3}\right) \cdot \left(-\dfrac{10}{3}\right)$.

Hence, the sixth number in the sequence is $-\dfrac{10}{27} = \left(-\dfrac{1}{3}\right) \cdot \left(\dfrac{10}{9}\right)$. The answer is (C).

Advanced concepts: (Sequence Formulas)

Note, none of the formulas in this section are necessary to answer questions about sequences on the SAT.

Since each term of a geometric progression *"is generated by multiplying the preceding term by a fixed number,"* we get the following:

first term $\quad\quad a$

second term $\quad\quad ar^1 \quad\quad\quad$ where r is the common ratio

third term $\quad\quad ar^2$

fourth term $\quad\quad ar^3$

$\quad\quad\quad\quad\quad \ldots$

nth term $\quad\quad a_n = ar^{n-1} \quad\quad$ This formula generates the nth term

The sum of the first n terms of an geometric sequence is

$$\frac{a\left(1 - r^n\right)}{1 - r}$$

SERIES

A series is simply the sum of the terms of a sequence. The following is a series of even numbers formed from the sequence 2, 4, 6, 8, . . . :

$$2 + 4 + 6 + 8 + \cdots$$

A term of a series is identified by its position in the series. In the above series, 2 is the first term, 4 is the second term, etc. The ellipsis symbol (. . .) indicates that the series continues forever.

Example 5: The sum of the squares of the first n positive integers $1^2 + 2^2 + 3^2 + \ldots + n^2$ is $\frac{n(n+1)(2n+1)}{6}$. What is the sum of the squares of the first 9 positive integers?

(A) 90 $\quad\quad$ (B) 125 $\quad\quad$ (C) 200 $\quad\quad$ (D) 285 $\quad\quad$ (E) 682

We are given a formula for the sum of the squares of the first n positive integers. Plugging $n = 9$ into this formula yields

$$\frac{n(n+1)(2n+1)}{6} = \frac{9(9+1)(2 \cdot 9 + 1)}{6} = \frac{9(10)(19)}{6} = 285$$

The answer is (D).

Example 6: For all integers $x > 1$, $\langle x \rangle = 2x + (2x - 1) + (2x - 2) + \ldots + 2 + 1$. What is the value of $\langle 3 \rangle \cdot \langle 2 \rangle$?

(A) 60 $\quad\quad$ (B) 116 $\quad\quad$ (C) 210 $\quad\quad$ (D) 263 $\quad\quad$ (E) 478

$$\langle 3 \rangle = 2(3) + (2 \cdot 3 - 1) + (2 \cdot 3 - 2) + (2 \cdot 3 - 3) + (2 \cdot 3 - 4) + (2 \cdot 3 - 5) = 6 + 5 + 4 + 3 + 2 + 1 = 21$$

$$\langle 2 \rangle = 2(2) + (2 \cdot 2 - 1) + (2 \cdot 2 - 2) + (2 \cdot 2 - 3) = 4 + 3 + 2 + 1 = 10$$

Hence, $\langle 3 \rangle \cdot \langle 2 \rangle = 21 \cdot 10 = 210$, and the answer is (C).

Problem Set W: Solutions begin on page 625.

1. By dividing 21 into 1, the fraction $\dfrac{1}{21}$ can be written as a repeating decimal: 0.476190476190 . . . where the block of digits 476190 repeats. What is the 54th digit following the decimal point?

    (A) 0   (B) 4   (C) 6   (D) 7   (E) 9

2. The positive integers *P, Q, R, S,* and *T* increase in order of size such that the value of each successive integer is one more than the preceding integer and the value of *T* is 6. What is the value of *R*?

    (A) 0   (B) 1   (C) 2   (D) 3   (E) 4

3. Let *u* represent the sum of the integers from 1 through 20, and let *v* represent the sum of the integers from 21 through 40. What is the value of $v - u$?

    (A) 21   (B) 39   (C) 200   (D) 320   (E) 400

4. In the pattern of dots to the right, each row after the first row has two more dots than the row immediately above it. Row 6 contains how many dots?

    (A) 6   (B) 8   (C) 10   (D) 11   (E) 12

5. In sequence S, all odd numbered terms are equal and all even numbered terms are equal. The first term in the sequence is $\sqrt{2}$ and the second term is –2. What is approximately the sum of two consecutive terms of the sequence?

    (A) –2   (B) –0.6   (C) 0   (D) 2   (E) 0.8

6. The sum of the first *n* even, positive integers is $2 + 4 + 6 + \cdots + 2n$ is $n(n + 1)$. What is the sum of the first 20 even, positive integers?

    (A) 120   (B) 188   (C) 362   (D) 406   (E) 420

7. In the array of numbers to the right, each number above the bottom row is equal to three times the number immediately below it. What is value of $x + y$?

27	x	81	–108
9	–18	27	–36
3	–6	y	–12
1	–2	3	–4

    (A) –45   (B) –15   (C) –2   (D) 20   (E) 77

8. The first term of a sequence is 2. All subsequent terms are found by adding 3 to the immediately preceding term and then multiplying the sum by 2. Which of the following describes the terms of the sequence?

    (A) Each term is odd   (B) Each term is even   (C) The terms are: even, odd, even, odd, etc.
    (D) The terms are: even, odd, odd, odd, etc.   (E) The terms are: even, odd, odd, even, odd, odd, etc.

9. Except for the first two numbers, every number in the sequence –1, 3, 2, . . . is the sum of the two immediately preceding numbers. How many numbers of this sequence are even?

    (A) none   (B) one   (C) two   (D) three   (E) more than three

10. In the sequence w, x, y, 30, adding any one of the first three terms to the term immediately following it yields $\dfrac{w}{2}$. What is the value of *w* ?

    (A) –60   (B) –30   (C) 0   (D) 5   (E) 25

Counting

Counting may have been one of humankind's first thought processes; nevertheless, counting can be deceptively hard. In part, because we often forget some of the principles of counting, but also because counting can be inherently difficult.

> **When counting elements that are in overlapping sets, the total number will equal the number in one group plus the number in the other group minus the number common to both groups. Venn diagrams are very helpful with these problems.**

Example 1: If in a certain school 20 students are taking math and 10 are taking history and 7 are taking both, how many students are taking either math or history?

    (A) 20   (B) 22   (C) 23   (D) 25   (E) 29

Solution:

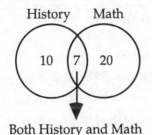

Both History and Math

By the principle stated above, we add 10 and 20 and then subtract 7 from the result. Thus, there are (10 + 20) – 7 = 23 students. The answer is (C).

> **The number of integers between two integers <u>inclusive</u> is one more than their difference.**

Example 2: How many integers are there between 49 and 101, inclusive?

    (A) 50   (B) 51   (C) 52   (D) 53   (E) 54

By the principle stated above, the number of integers between 49 and 101 inclusive is (101 – 49) + 1 = 53. The answer is (D). To see this more clearly, choose smaller numbers, say, 9 and 11. The difference between 9 and 11 is 2. But there are three numbers between them inclusive—9, 10, and 11—one more than their difference.

> *Fundamental Principle of Counting*: **If an event occurs m times, and each of the m events is followed by a second event which occurs k times, then the first event follows the second event $m \cdot k$ times.**

The following diagram illustrates the fundamental principle of counting for an event that occurs 3 times with each occurrence being followed by a second event that occurs 2 times for a total of $3 \cdot 2 = 6$ events:

Event One: 3 times

Total number of events:
$m \cdot k = 3 \cdot 2 = 6$

Event Two: 2 times for each
occurrence of Event One

Example 3:   A drum contains 3 to 5 jars each of which contains 30 to 40 marbles. If 10 percent of the marbles are flawed, what is the greatest possible number of flawed marbles in the drum?

(A) 51   (B) 40   (C) 30   (D) 20   (E) 12

There is at most 5 jars each of which contains at most 40 marbles; so by the fundamental counting principle, there is at most $5 \cdot 40 = 200$ marbles in the drum. Since 10 percent of the marbles are flawed, there is at most $20 = 10\% \cdot 200$ flawed marbles. The answer is (D).

MISCELLANEOUS COUNTING PROBLEMS

Example 4:   In a legislative body of 200 people, the number of Democrats is 50 less than 4 times the number of Republicans. If one fifth of the legislators are neither Republican nor Democrat, how many of the legislators are Republicans?

(A) 42   (B) 50   (C) 71   (D) 95   (E) 124

Let D be the number of Democrats and let R be the number of Republicans. "One fifth of the legislators are neither Republican nor Democrat," so there are $\frac{1}{5} \cdot 200 = 40$ legislators who are neither Republican nor Democrat. Hence, there are $200 - 40 = 160$ Democrats and Republicans, or $D + R = 160$. Translating the clause "the number of Democrats is 50 less than 4 times the number of Republicans" into an equation yields $D = 4R - 50$. Plugging this into the equation $D + R = 160$ yields

$$4R - 50 + R = 160$$
$$5R - 50 = 160$$
$$5R = 210$$
$$R = 42$$

The answer is (A).

Example 5:   Speed bumps are being placed at 20 foot intervals along a road 1015 feet long. If the first speed bump is placed at one end of the road, how many speed bumps are needed?

(A) 49   (B) 50   (C) 51   (D) 52   (E) 53

Since the road is 1015 feet long and the speed bumps are 20 feet apart, there are $\frac{1015}{20} = 50.75$, or 50 full sections in the road. If we ignore the first speed bump and associate the speed bump at the end of each section with that section, then there are 50 speed bumps (one for each of the fifty full sections). Counting the first speed bump gives a total of 51 speed bumps. The answer is (C).

SETS

A *set* is a collection of objects, and the objects are called *elements* of the set. You may be asked to form the *union* of two sets, which contains all the objects from either set. You may also be asked to form the *intersection* of two sets, which contains only the objects that are in both sets. For example, if Set A = {1, 2, 5} and Set B = {5, 10, 21}, then the union of sets A and B would be {1, 2, 5, 10, 21} and the intersection would be {5}.

Problem Set X: Solutions begin on page 627.

1.   The number of integers between 29 and 69, inclusive is

   (A) 39   (B) 40   (C) 41   (D) 42   (E) 43

2.   A school has a total enrollment of 150 students.   There are 63 students taking French, 48 taking chemistry, and 21 taking both.   How many students are taking <u>neither</u> French nor chemistry?

   (A) 60   (B) 65   (C) 71   (D) 75   (E) 97

3.   The number of minutes in $1\frac{1}{3}$ hours is

   (A) 60   (B) 65   (C) 71   (D) 80   (E) 97

4.   A web press prints 5 pages every 2 seconds.   At this rate, how many pages will the press print in 7 minutes?

   (A) 350   (B) 540   (C) 700   (D) 950   (E) 1050

5.   A school has a total enrollment of 90 students.   There are 30 students taking physics, 25 taking English, and 13 taking both.   What percentage of the students are taking either physics or English?

   (A) 30%   (B) 36%   (C) 47%   (D) 51%   (E) 58%

6.   Callers 49 through 91 to a radio show won a prize.   How many callers won a prize?

   (A) 42   (B) 43   (C) 44   (D) 45   (E) 46

7.   A rancher is constructing a fence by stringing wire between posts 20 feet apart.   If the fence is 400 feet long, how many posts must the rancher use?

   (A) 18   (B) 19   (C) 20   (D) 21   (E) 22

8.   The number of marbles in x jars , each containing 15 marbles, plus the number of marbles in $3x$ jars , each containing 20 marbles is

   (A) $65x$ (B) $70x$ (C) $75x$ (D) $80x$ (E) $85x$

9.   The number of integers from 2 to 10^3 , inclusive is

   (A) 997   (B) 998   (C) 999   (D) 1000   (E) 1001

10.   In a small town, 16 people own Fords and 11 people own Toyotas.   If exactly 15 people own only one of the two types of cars, how many people own both types of cars.

   (A) 2   (B) 6   (C) 7   (D) 12   (E) 14

Probability & Statistics

PROBABILITY

We know what probability means, but what is its formal definition? Let's use our intuition to define it. If there is no chance that an event will occur, then its probability of occurring should be 0. On the other extreme, if an event is certain to occur, then its probability of occurring should be 100%, or 1. Hence, our *probability* should be a number between 0 and 1, inclusive. But what kind of number? Suppose your favorite actor has a 1 in 3 chance of winning the Oscar for best actor. This can be measured by forming the fraction 1/3. Hence, a *probability* is a fraction where the top is the number of ways an event can occur and the bottom is the total number of possible events:

$$P = \frac{Number\ of\ ways\ an\ event\ can\ occur}{Number\ of\ total\ possible\ events}$$

Example: *Flipping a coin*

What's the probability of getting heads when flipping a coin?

There is only one way to get heads in a coin toss. Hence, the top of the probability fraction is 1. There are two possible results: heads or tails. Forming the probability fraction gives 1/2.

Example: *Tossing a die*

What's the probability of getting a 3 when tossing a die?

A die (a cube) has six faces, numbered 1 through 6. There is only one way to get a 3. Hence, the top of the fraction is 1. There are 6 possible results: 1, 2, 3, 4, 5, and 6. Forming the probability fraction gives 1/6.

Example: *Drawing a card from a deck*

What's the probability of getting a king when drawing a card from a deck of cards?

A deck of cards has four kings, so there are 4 ways to get a king. Hence, the top of the fraction is 4. There are 52 total cards in a deck. Forming the probability fraction gives 4/52, which reduces to 1/13. Hence, there is 1 chance in 13 of getting a king.

Example: *Drawing marbles from a bowl*

What's the probability of drawing a blue marble from a bowl containing 4 red marbles, 5 blue marbles, and 5 green marbles?

There are five ways of drawing a blue marble. Hence, the top of the fraction is 5. There are 14 (= 4 + 5 + 5) possible results. Forming the probability fraction gives 5/14.

Example: *Drawing marbles from a bowl (second drawing)*

What's the probability of drawing a red marble from the same bowl, given that the first marble drawn was blue and was not placed back in the bowl?

There are four ways of drawing a red marble. Hence, the top of the fraction is 4. Since the blue marble from the first drawing was not replaced, there are only 4 blue marbles remaining. Hence, there are 13 (= 4 + 4 + 5) possible results. Forming the probability fraction gives 4/13.

Consecutive Probabilities

What's the probability of getting heads twice in a row when flipping a coin twice? Previously we calculated the probability for the first flip to be 1/2. Since the second flip is not affected by the first (these are called *mutually exclusive* events), its probability is also 1/2. Forming the product yields the probability of two heads in a row: $\frac{1}{2} \times \frac{1}{2} = \frac{1}{4}$.

490

What's the probability of drawing a blue marble and then a red marble from a bowl containing 4 red marbles, 5 blue marbles, and 5 green marbles? (Assume that the marbles are not replaced after being selected.) As calculated before, there is a 5/14 likelihood of selecting a blue marble first and a 4/13 likelihood of selecting a red marble second. Forming the product yields the probability of a blue marble immediately followed by a red marble: $\frac{5}{14} \times \frac{4}{13} = \frac{20}{182} = \frac{10}{91}$.

These two examples can be generalized into the following rule for calculating consecutive probabilities:

To calculate consecutive probabilities, multiply the individual probabilities.

This rule applies to two, three, or any number of consecutive probabilities.

Either-Or Probabilities

What's the probability of getting either heads or tails when flipping a coin once? Since the only possible outcomes are heads or tails, we expect the probability to be 100%, or 1: $\frac{1}{2} + \frac{1}{2} = 1$. Note that the events heads and tails are mutually exclusive. That is, if heads occurs, then tails cannot (and vice versa).

What's the probability of drawing a red marble or a green marble from a bowl containing 4 red marbles, 5 blue marbles, and 5 green marbles? There are 4 red marbles out of 14 total marbles. So the probability of selecting a red marble is 4/14 = 2/7. Similarly, the probability of selecting a green marble is 5/14. So the probability of selecting a red or green marble is $\frac{2}{7} + \frac{5}{14} = \frac{9}{14}$. Note again that the events are mutually exclusive. For instance, if a red marble is selected, then neither a blue marble nor a green marble is selected.

These two examples can be generalized into the following rule for calculating *either-or* probabilities:

To calculate *either-or* probabilities, add the individual probabilities (only if the events are mutually exclusive).

The probabilities in the two immediately preceding examples can be calculated more naturally by adding up the events that occur and then dividing by the total number of possible events. For the coin example, we get 2 events (heads or tails) divided by the total number of possible events, 2 (heads and tails): 2/2 = 1. For the marble example, we get 9 (= 4 + 5) ways the event can occur divided by 14 (= 4 + 5 + 5) possible events: 9/14.

If it's more natural to calculate the *either-or* probabilities above by adding up the events that occur and then dividing by the total number of possible events, why did we introduce a second way of calculating the probabilities? Because in some cases, you may have to add the individual probabilities. For example, you may be given the individual probabilities of two mutually exclusive events and be asked for the probability that either could occur. You now know to merely add their individual probabilities.

Geometric Probability

In this type of problem, you will be given two figures, with one inside the other. You'll then be asked what is the probability that a randomly selected point will be in the smaller figure. These problems are solved with the same principle we have been using: $Probability = \dfrac{desired\ outcome}{possible\ outcomes}$.

Example: In the figure to the right, the smaller square has sides of length 2 and the larger square has sides of length 4. If a point is chosen at random from the large square, what is the probability that it will be from the small square?

Applying the probability principle, we get $Probability = \dfrac{area\ of\ the\ small\ square}{area\ of\ the\ large\ square} = \dfrac{2^2}{4^2} = \dfrac{4}{16} = \dfrac{1}{4}$.

STATISTICS

Statistics is the study of the patterns and relationships of numbers and data. There are four main concepts that may appear on the test:

Median

When a set of numbers is arranged in order of size, the *median* is the middle number. For example, the median of the set {8, 9, 10, 11, 12} is 10 because it is the middle number. In this case, the median is also the mean (average). But this is usually not the case. For example, the median of the set {8, 9, 10, 11, 17} is 10 because it is the middle number, but the mean is $11 = \dfrac{8+9+10+11+17}{5}$. If a set contains an even number of elements, then the median is the average of the two middle elements. For example, the median of the set {1, 5, 8, 20} is $6.5\left(=\dfrac{5+8}{2}\right)$.

Example: What is the median of $0, -2, 256, 18, \sqrt{2}$?

Arranging the numbers from smallest to largest (we could also arrange the numbers from the largest to smallest; the answer would be the same), we get $-2, 0, \sqrt{2}, 18, 256$. The median is the middle number, $\sqrt{2}$.

Mode

The *mode* is the number or numbers that appear most frequently in a set. Note that this definition allows a set of numbers to have more than one mode.

Example: What is the mode of $3, -4, 3, 7, 9, 7.5$?

The number 3 is the mode because it is the only number that is listed more than once.

Example: What is the mode of $2, \pi, 2, -9, \pi, 5$?

Both 2 and π are modes because each occurs twice, which is the greatest number of occurrences for any number in the list.

Range

The *range* is the distance between the smallest and largest numbers in a set. To calculate the range, merely subtract the smallest number from the largest number.

Example: What is the range of $2, 8, 1, -6, \pi, 1/2$?

The largest number in this set is 8, and the smallest number is –6. Hence, the range is $8 - (-6) = 8 + 6 = 14$.

Standard Deviation

On the test, you are not expected to know the definition of standard deviation. However, you may be presented with the definition of standard deviation and then be asked a question based on the definition. To make sure we cover all possible bases, we'll briefly discuss this concept.

Standard deviation measures how far the numbers in a set vary from the set's mean. If the numbers are scattered far from the set's mean, then the standard deviation is large. If the numbers are bunched up near the set's mean, then the standard deviation is small.

Example: Which of the following sets has the larger standard deviation?

$$A = \{1, 2, 3, 4, 5\}$$
$$B = \{1, 4, 15, 21, 27\}$$

All the numbers in Set A are within 2 units of the mean, 3. All the numbers in Set B are greater than 5 units from the mean, 15. Hence, the standard deviation of Set B is greater.

Problem Set Y: Solutions begin on page 629.

1. The median is larger than the average for which one of the following sets of integers?

    (A) {8, 9, 10, 11, 12}
    (B) {8, 9, 10, 11, 13}
    (C) {8, 10, 10, 10, 12}
    (D) {10, 10, 10, 10, 10}
    (E) {7, 9, 10, 11, 12}

2. A hat contains 15 marbles, and each marble is numbered with one and only one of the numbers 1, 2, 3. From a group of 15 people, each person selects exactly 1 marble from the hat.

Numbered Marble	Number of People Who Selected The Marble
1	4
2	5
3	6

    What is the probability that a person selected at random picked a marble numbered 2 or greater?

    (A) 5/15   (B) 9/15   (C) 10/15   (D) 11/15   (E) 1

3. Sarah cannot completely remember her four-digit ATM pin number. She does remember the first two digits, and she knows that each of the last two digits is greater than 5. The ATM will allow her three tries before it blocks further access. If she randomly guesses the last two digits, what is the probability that she will get access to her account?

    (A) 1/2   (B) 1/4   (C) 3/16   (D) 3/18   (E) 1/32

4. If $x < y < z$, $z = ky$, $x = 0$, and the average of the numbers x, y, and z is 3 times the median, what is the value of k?

    (A) –2   (B) 3   (C) 5.5   (D) 6   (E) 8

5. Three positive numbers x, y, and z have the following relationships $y = x + 2$ and $z = y + 2$. When the median of x, y, and z is subtracted from the product of the smallest number and the median, the result is 0. What is the value of the largest number?

    (A) –2   (B) π (C) 5   (D) 8   (E) 21/2

6. A jar contains only three types of objects: red, blue, and silver paper clips. The probability of selecting a red paper clip is 1/4, and the probability of selecting a blue paper clip is 1/6. What is the probability of selecting a silver paper clip?

    (A) 5/12   (B) 1/2   (C) 7/12   (D) 3/4   (E) 11/12

7. A bowl contains one marble labeled 0, one marble labeled 1, one marble labeled 2, and one marble labeled 3. The bowl contains no other objects. If two marbles are drawn randomly without replacement, what is the probability that they will add up to 3?

    (A) 1/12   (B) 1/8   (C) 1/6   (D) 1/4   (E) 1/3

8. A housing subdivision contains only two types of homes: ranch-style homes and townhomes. There are twice as many townhomes as ranch-style homes. There are 3 times as many townhomes with pools than without pools. What is the probability that a home selected at random from the subdivision will be a townhome with a pool?

    (A) 1/6   (B) 1/5   (C) 1/4   (D) 1/3   (E) 1/2

9. The figure to the right shows a small equilateral triangle inscribed in the large equilateral triangle. If a point is chosen at random from the large triangle, what is the probability that it will be from the small triangle?

    (A) 1/8   (B) 1/5   (C) 1/4   (D) 1/3   (E) 1/2

Miscellaneous Problems

Example 1:   The language Q has the following properties:

(1)   ABC is the base word.

(2)   If C immediately follows B, then C can be moved to the front of the code word to generate another word.

Which one of the following is a code word in language Q?

(A) CAB   (B) BCA   (C) AAA   (D) ABA   (E) CCC

From (1), ABC is a code word.

From (2), the C in the code word ABC can be moved to the front of the word: CAB.

Hence, CAB is a code word and the answer is (A).

Example 2:   Bowl S contains only marbles. If $\dfrac{1}{4}$ of the marbles were removed, the bowl would be filled to $\dfrac{1}{2}$ of its capacity. If 100 marbles were added, the bowl would be full. How many marbles are in bowl S?

(A) 100   (B) 200   (C) 250   (D) 300   (E) 400

Let n be the number of marbles in the bowl, and let c be the capacity of the bowl. Then translating *"if $\dfrac{1}{4}$ of the marbles were removed, the bowl would be filled to $\dfrac{1}{2}$ of its capacity"* into an equation yields

$$n - \frac{1}{4}n = \frac{1}{2}c, \text{ or } \frac{3}{2}n = c.$$

Next, translating *"if 100 marbles were added, the bowl would be full"* into an equation yields

$$100 + n = c$$

Hence, we have the system:

$$\frac{3}{2}n = c$$

$$100 + n = c$$

Combining the two above equations yields

$$\frac{3}{2}n = 100 + n$$

$$3n = 200 + 2n$$

$$n = 200$$

The answer is (B).

Method II (Plugging in):

Suppose there are 100 marbles in the bowl—choice (A). Removing 1/4 of them would leave 75 marbles in the bowl. Since this is 1/2 the capacity of the bowl, the capacity of the bowl is 150. But if we add 100 marbles to the original 100, we get 200 marbles, not 150. This eliminates (A).

Next, suppose there are 200 marbles in the bowl—choice (B). Removing 1/4 of them would leave 150 marbles in the bowl. Since this is 1/2 the capacity of the bowl, the capacity of the bowl is 300. Now, if we add 100 marbles to the original 200, we get 300 marbles—the capacity of the bowl. The answer is (B).

Problem Set Z: Solutions begin on page 630.

1. A certain brand of computer can be bought with or without a hard drive. The computer with the hard drive costs 2,900 dollars. The computer without the hard drive costs 1,950 dollars more than the hard drive alone. What is the cost of the hard drive?

    (A) 400   (B) 450   (C) 475   (D) 500   (E) 525

2. At Peabody Tech, 72 students are enrolled in History, and 40 students are enrolled in both History and Math. How many students are enrolled in Math, but not History?

    (A) 30   (B) 31   (C) 32   (D) 33   (E) not enough information to decide

3. Half of the people who take the SAT score above 1000 and half of the people score below 1000. What is the average (arithmetic mean) score on the SAT?

    (A) 999   (B) 1000   (C) 1001   (D) 1002   (E) not enough information to decide

4. The buyer of a particular car must choose 2 of 3 optional colors and 3 of 4 optional luxury features. In how many different ways can the buyer select the colors and luxury features?

    (A) 3   (B) 6   (C) 9   (D) 12   (E) 20

5. A bowl contains 500 marbles. There are x red marbles and y blue marbles in the bowl. Which one of the following expresses the number marbles in the bowl that are neither red nor blue?

    (A) $500 + x - y$
    (B) $500 - x + y$
    (C) $500 - x - y$
    (D) $500 + x + y$
    (E) $500 - x - y/2$

6. What is 0.12345 rounded to the nearest thousandth?

    (A) 0.12   (B) 0.123   (C) 0.1235   (D) 0.1234   (E) 0.12346

$$\frac{v+w}{x/yz}$$

7. To halve the value of the expression above by doubling exactly one of the variables, one must double which one of the following variables?

    (A) v (B) w (C) x (D) y (E) z

8. The picture above represents 4,250 apples. How many apples does each apple stand for?

    (A) 400   (B) 450   (C) 500   (D) 625   (E) 710

Grid-ins

The only difference between grid-in questions and multiple-choice questions is in the way you mark the answer. Instead of choosing from five given answer-choices, grid-in questions require you to write your *numerical* answer in a grid.

Because the grid can accommodate only numerical answers, many of the questions will be on arithmetic. There will still be algebra questions, but variables will not appear in the answers.

Like the rest of the test, there is no partial credit given for showing your work on grid-ins. Unlike, the rest of the test, there is no guessing penalty on the grid-in section. However, unless you have a good idea of what the answer is, the chances of guessing the answer are virtually nil. So don't waste time guessing on these questions.

Often you will be able to write your answer in more than one form. For example, you can grid-in either 1/2 or .5:

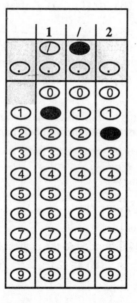

You don't need to put a zero before the .5, though it is still correct if you do. In the above example .5 was placed on the right side of the grid. It could also have been placed on the left side or in the center:

You must convert all mixed fractions to improper fractions or decimals before gridding them in. The computer scoring the test will read $2\frac{1}{2}$ as $\frac{21}{2}$. You must convert it to $\frac{5}{2}$ or 2.5 before gridding it in.

Incorrect and correct ways of gridding in $2\frac{1}{2}$

Wrong!

Correct

Correct

Below are the directions for grid-in questions; the wording has been changed slightly from the SAT to make it clearer. Be sure you know them cold before taking the test. You should never have to look at the instructions during the test.

Directions for Grid-in Questions

In the following questions (16-25), you are to record your answer by filling in the ovals in the grid, as shown in the examples below:

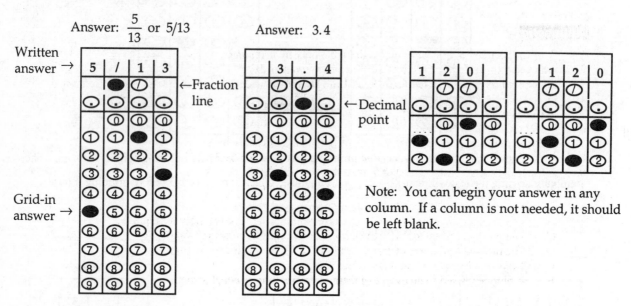

- Mark at most one oval in any column.

- Credit is given to a response only if the oval is filled in correctly.

- To avoid mistakes, it may be helpful to write your answer in the boxes at the top of the columns.

- If a problem has more than one answer, grid only one of the answers.

- Negative answers do not appear.

- **A mixed number** such as $3\frac{1}{2}$ must be converted into an improper fraction (7/2) or a decimal (3.5) before being gridded. (The answer grid will be interpreted as $\frac{31}{2}$, not $3\frac{1}{2}$.)

- <u>Decimal Accuracy:</u> For decimal answers, **enter the most accurate value the grid will allow.** For example, an answer such as $0.3333...$ should be entered as .333. **The less accurate values .33 and .3 are unacceptable.**

Acceptable ways to grid $\frac{1}{3}$ = .3333...

Summary of Math Properties

Arithmetic

1.   A *prime number* is an integer that is divisible only by itself and 1.
2.   An even number is divisible by 2, and can be written as $2x$.
3.   An odd number is not divisible by 2, and can be written as $2x + 1$.
4.   Division by zero is undefined.
5.   Perfect squares: 1, 4, 9, 16, 25, 36, 49, 64, 81 . . .
6.   Perfect cubes: 1, 8, 27, 64, 125 . . .
7.   If the last digit of a integer is 0, 2, 4, 6, or 8, then it is divisible by 2.
8.   An integer is divisible by 3 if the sum of its digits is divisible by 3.
9.   If the last digit of a integer is 0 or 5, then it is divisible by 5.
10. Miscellaneous Properties of Positive and Negative Numbers:

   A.   The product (quotient) of positive numbers is positive.
   B.   The product (quotient) of a positive number and a negative number is negative.
   C.   The product (quotient) of an even number of negative numbers is positive.
   D.   The product (quotient) of an odd number of negative numbers is negative.
   E.   The sum of negative numbers is negative.
   F.   A number raised to an even exponent is greater than or equal to zero.

$$even \times even = even$$
$$odd \times odd = odd$$
$$even \times odd = even$$

$$even + even = even$$
$$odd + odd = even$$
$$even + odd = odd$$

11. Consecutive integers are written as $x, x + 1, x + 2,\ldots$
12. Consecutive even or odd integers are written as $x, x + 2, x + 4,\ldots$
13. The integer zero is neither positive nor negative, but it is even: $0 = 2 \cdot 0$.
14. Commutative property: $x + y = y + x$. Example: $5 + 4 = 4 + 5$.
15. Associative property: $(x + y) + z = x + (y + z)$. Example: $(1 + 2) + 3 = 1 + (2 + 3)$.
16. Order of operations: Parentheses, Exponents, Multiplication, Division, Addition, Subtraction.
17. $-\dfrac{x}{y} = \dfrac{-x}{y} = \dfrac{x}{-y}$. Example: $-\dfrac{2}{3} = \dfrac{-2}{3} = \dfrac{2}{-3}$

18.
$$33\frac{1}{3}\% = \frac{1}{3} \qquad 20\% = \frac{1}{5}$$
$$66\frac{2}{3}\% = \frac{2}{3} \qquad 40\% = \frac{2}{5}$$
$$25\% = \frac{1}{4} \qquad 60\% = \frac{3}{5}$$
$$50\% = \frac{1}{2} \qquad 80\% = \frac{4}{5}$$

19.

$$\frac{1}{100} = .01 \qquad \frac{1}{10} = .1 \qquad \frac{2}{5} = .4$$

$$\frac{1}{50} = .02 \qquad \frac{1}{5} = .2 \qquad \frac{1}{2} = .5$$

$$\frac{1}{25} = .04 \qquad \frac{1}{4} = .25 \qquad \frac{2}{3} = .666...$$

$$\frac{1}{20} = .05 \qquad \frac{1}{3} = .333... \qquad \frac{3}{4} = .75$$

20. Common measurements:
    1 foot = 12 inches
    1 yard = 3 feet
    1 quart = 2 pints
    1 gallon = 4 quarts
    1 pound = 16 ounces

21. Important approximations: $\sqrt{2} \approx 1.4 \qquad \sqrt{3} \approx 1.7 \qquad \pi \approx 3.14$

22. *"The remainder is r when p is divided by q"* means $p = qz + r$; the integer z is called the quotient.
    For instance, *"The remainder is 1 when 7 is divided by 3"* means $7 = 3 \cdot 2 + 1$.

23. $Probability = \dfrac{number\ of\ outcomes}{total\ number\ of\ possible\ outcomes}$

Algebra

24. Multiplying or dividing both sides of an inequality by a negative number reverses the inequality. That is, if $x > y$ and $c < 0$, then $cx < cy$.

25. Transitive Property: If $x < y$ and $y < z$, then $x < z$.

26. Like Inequalities Can Be Added: If $x < y$ and $w < z$, then $x + w < y + z$.

27. Rules for exponents:

$$x^a \cdot x^b = x^{a+b} \quad \text{Caution, } x^a + x^b \neq x^{a+b}$$

$$\left(x^a\right)^b = x^{ab}$$

$$(xy)^a = x^a \cdot y^a$$

$$\left(\frac{x}{y}\right)^a = \frac{x^a}{y^a}$$

$$\frac{x^a}{x^b} = x^{a-b}, \text{ if } a > b. \qquad \frac{x^a}{x^b} = \frac{1}{x^{b-a}}, \text{ if } b > a.$$

$$x^0 = 1$$

28. There are only two rules for roots that you need to know for the SAT:

$$\sqrt[n]{xy} = \sqrt[n]{x}\sqrt[n]{y} \qquad \text{For example, } \sqrt{3x} = \sqrt{3}\sqrt{x}.$$

$$\sqrt[n]{\frac{x}{y}} = \frac{\sqrt[n]{x}}{\sqrt[n]{y}} \qquad \text{For example, } \sqrt[3]{\frac{x}{8}} = \frac{\sqrt[3]{x}}{\sqrt[3]{8}} = \frac{\sqrt[3]{x}}{2}.$$

$$\text{Caution: } \sqrt[n]{x+y} \neq \sqrt[n]{x} + \sqrt[n]{y}.$$

29. Factoring formulas:

$$x(y+z) = xy + xz$$
$$x^2 - y^2 = (x+y)(x-y)$$
$$(x-y)^2 = x^2 - 2xy + y^2$$
$$(x+y)^2 = x^2 + 2xy + y^2$$
$$-(x-y) = y - x$$

30. Adding, multiplying, and dividing fractions:

$$\frac{x}{y} + \frac{z}{y} = \frac{x+z}{y} \quad \text{and} \quad \frac{x}{y} - \frac{z}{y} = \frac{x-z}{y}$$

Example: $\dfrac{2}{4} + \dfrac{3}{4} = \dfrac{2+3}{4} = \dfrac{5}{4}$.

$$\frac{w}{x} \cdot \frac{y}{z} = \frac{wy}{xz}$$

Example: $\dfrac{1}{2} \cdot \dfrac{3}{4} = \dfrac{1 \cdot 3}{2 \cdot 4} = \dfrac{3}{8}$.

$$\frac{w}{x} \div \frac{y}{z} = \frac{w}{x} \cdot \frac{z}{y}$$

Example: $\dfrac{1}{2} \div \dfrac{3}{4} = \dfrac{1}{2} \cdot \dfrac{4}{3} = \dfrac{4}{6} = \dfrac{2}{3}$.

31. $x\% = \dfrac{x}{100}$

32. Quadratic Formula: $x = \dfrac{-b \pm \sqrt{b^2 - 4ac}}{2a}$ are the solutions of the equation $ax^2 + bx + c = 0$.

Geometry

33. There are four major types of angle measures:

An **acute angle** has measure less than 90°:

A **right angle** has measure 90°:

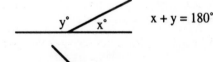

90°

An **obtuse angle** has measure greater than 90°:

A **straight angle** has measure 180°:

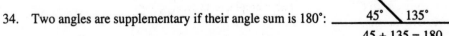

$y°$ $x°$ $x + y = 180°$

34. Two angles are supplementary if their angle sum is 180°: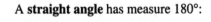

45° 135°

45 + 135 = 180

35. Two angles are complementary if their angle sum is 90°:

60°

30°

30 + 60 = 90

36. Perpendicular lines meet at right angles:

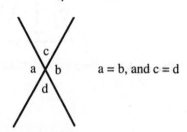

$l_1 \perp l_2$

37. When two straight lines meet at a point, they form four angles. The angles opposite each other are called vertical angles, and they are congruent (equal). In the figure to the right, $a = b$, and $c = d$.

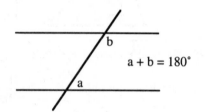

$a = b$, and $c = d$

38. When parallel lines are cut by a transversal, three important angle relationships exist:

Alternate interior angles are equal.

Corresponding angles are equal.

Interior angles on the same side of the transversal are supplementary.

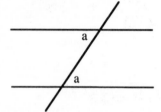

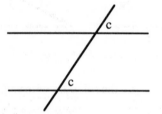

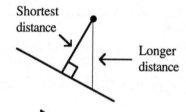

$a + b = 180°$

39. The shortest distance from a point not on a line to the line is along a perpendicular line.

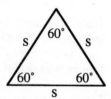

Shortest distance

Longer distance

40. A triangle containing a right angle is called a *right triangle*. The right angle is denoted by a small square:

41. A triangle with two equal sides is called isosceles. The angles opposite the equal sides are called the base angles:

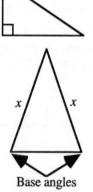

x x

Base angles

42. In an equilateral triangle all three sides are equal, and each angle is 60°:

60°

s s

60°   60°

s

43. The altitude to the base of an isosceles or equilateral triangle bisects the base and bisects the vertex angle:

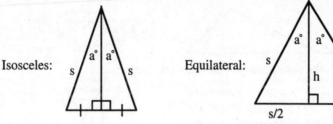

Isosceles: Equilateral: $h = \dfrac{s\sqrt{3}}{2}$

44. The angle sum of a triangle is 180°:

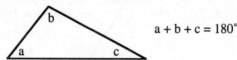

$$a + b + c = 180°$$

45. The area of a triangle is $\dfrac{1}{2}bh$, where b is the base and h is the height.

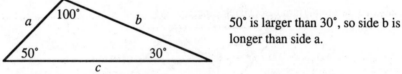

$$A = \dfrac{1}{2}bh$$

46. In a triangle, the longer side is opposite the larger angle, and vice versa:

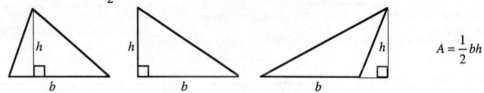

50° is larger than 30°, so side b is longer than side a.

47. Pythagorean Theorem (right triangles only): The square of the hypotenuse is equal to the sum of the squares of the legs.

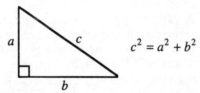

$$c^2 = a^2 + b^2$$

48. A Pythagorean triple: the numbers 3, 4, and 5 can always represent the sides of a right triangle and they appear very often: $5^2 = 3^2 + 4^2$.

49. Two triangles are similar (same shape and usually different size) if their corresponding angles are equal. If two triangles are similar, their corresponding sides are proportional:

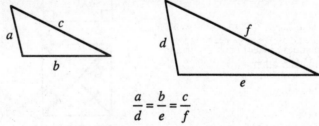

$$\dfrac{a}{d} = \dfrac{b}{e} = \dfrac{c}{f}$$

50. If two angles of a triangle are congruent to two angles of another triangle, the triangles are similar.

In the figure to the right, the large and small triangles are similar because both contain a right angle and they share $\angle A$.

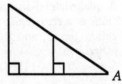

51. Two triangles are congruent (identical) if they have the same size and shape.

52. In a triangle, an exterior angle is equal to the sum of its remote interior angles and is therefore greater than either of them:

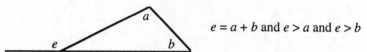

$e = a + b$ and $e > a$ and $e > b$

53. In a 30°–60°–90° triangle, the sides have the following relationships:

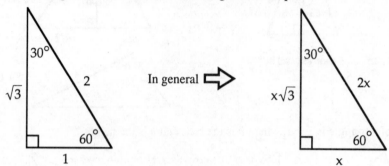

In general ⇒

54. Opposite sides of a parallelogram are both parallel and congruent:

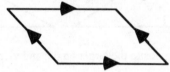

55. The diagonals of a parallelogram bisect each other:

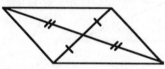

56. A parallelogram with four right angles is a *rectangle*. If w is the width and l is the length of a rectangle, then its area is $A = lw$ and its perimeter is $P = 2w + 2l$:

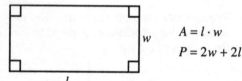

$A = l \cdot w$

$P = 2w + 2l$

57. If the opposite sides of a rectangle are equal, it is a square and its area is $A = s^2$ and its perimeter is $P = 4s$, where s is the length of a side:

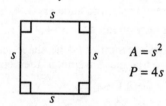

$A = s^2$

$P = 4s$

58. The diagonals of a square bisect each other and are perpendicular to each other:

59. A quadrilateral with only one pair of parallel sides is a *trapezoid*. The parallel sides are called *bases*, and the non-parallel sides are called *legs*:

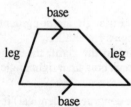

60. The area of a trapezoid is the average of the bases times the height:

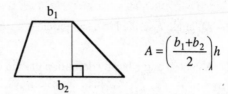

$$A = \left(\frac{b_1 + b_2}{2}\right)h$$

61. The volume of a rectangular solid (a box) is the product of the length, width, and height. The surface area is the sum of the area of the six faces:

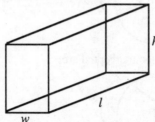

$$V = l \cdot w \cdot h$$
$$S = 2wl + 2hl + 2wh$$

62. If the length, width, and height of a rectangular solid (a box) are the same, it is a cube. Its volume is the cube of one of its sides, and its surface area is the sum of the areas of the six faces:

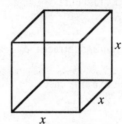

$$V = x^3$$
$$S = 6x^2$$

63. The volume of a cylinder is $V = \pi r^2 h$, and the lateral surface (excluding the top and bottom) is $S = 2\pi rh$, where r is the radius and h is the height:

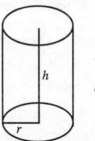

$$V = \pi r^2 h$$
$$S = 2\pi rh + 2\pi r^2$$

64. A line segment form the circle to its center is a *radius*.
A line segment with both end points on a circle is a *chord*.
A chord passing though the center of a circle is a *diameter*.
A diameter can be viewed as two radii, and hence a diameter's length is twice that of a radius.
A line passing through two points on a circle is a *secant*.
A piece of the circumference is an *arc*.
The area bounded by the circumference and an angle with vertex at the center of the circle is a *sector*.

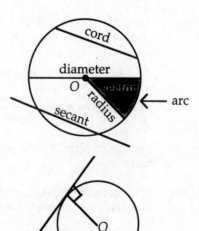

65. A tangent line to a circle intersects the circle at only one point. The radius of the circle is perpendicular to the tangent line at the point of tangency:

66. An angle inscribed in a semicircle is a right angle:

67. A central angle has by definition the same measure as its intercepted arc.

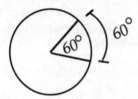

68. An inscribed angle has one-half the measure of its intercepted arc.

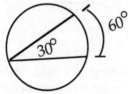

69. The area of a circle is πr^2, where r is the radius.

70. The circumference of a circle is $2\pi r$.

71. To find the area of the shaded region of a figure, subtract the area of the unshaded region from the area of the entire figure.

72. When drawing geometric figures, don't forget extreme cases.

Miscellaneous

73. To compare two fractions, cross-multiply. The larger product will be on the same side as the larger fraction.

74. Taking the square root of a fraction between 0 and 1 makes it larger.

Caution: This is not true for fractions greater than 1. For example, $\sqrt{\dfrac{9}{4}} = \dfrac{3}{2}$. But $\dfrac{3}{2} < \dfrac{9}{4}$.

75. Squaring a fraction between 0 and 1 makes it smaller.

76. $ax^2 \neq (ax)^2$. In fact, $a^2 x^2 = (ax)^2$.

77. $\dfrac{1/a}{b} \neq \dfrac{1}{a/b}$. In fact, $\dfrac{1/a}{b} = \dfrac{1}{ab}$ and $\dfrac{1}{a/b} = \dfrac{b}{a}$.

78. $-(a + b) \neq -a + b$. In fact, $-(a + b) = -a - b$.

79. $percentage\ increase = \dfrac{increase}{original\ amount}$

80. Systems of simultaneous equations can most often be solved by merely adding or subtracting the equations.

81. When counting elements that are in overlapping sets, the total number will equal the number in one group plus the number in the other group minus the number common to both groups.

82. The number of integers between two integers <u>inclusive</u> is one more than their difference.

83. Elimination strategies:
   A.   On hard problems, if you are asked to find the least (or greatest) number, then eliminate the least (or greatest) answer-choice.
   B.   On hard problems, eliminate the answer-choice "not enough information."
   C.   On hard problems, eliminate answer-choices that <u>merely</u> repeat numbers from the problem.
   D.   On hard problems, eliminate answer-choices that can be derived from elementary operations.
   E.   After you have eliminated as many answer-choices as you can, choose from the more complicated or more unusual answer-choices remaining.

84. To solve a fractional equation, multiply both sides by the LCD (lowest common denominator) to clear fractions.

85. You can cancel only over multiplication, not over addition or subtraction. For example, the c's in the expression $\dfrac{c+x}{c}$ cannot be canceled.

86. The average of N numbers is their sum divided by N, that is, $average = \dfrac{sum}{N}$.

87. *Weighted average:* The average between two sets of numbers is closer to the set with more numbers.

88. $Average\ Speed = \dfrac{Total\ Distance}{Total\ Time}$

89. Distance = Rate × Time

90. $Work = Rate \times Time$, or $W = R \times T$. The amount of work done is usually 1 unit. Hence, the formula becomes $1 = R \times T$. Solving this for R gives $R = \dfrac{1}{T}$.

91. $Interest = Amount \times Time \times Rate$

Diagnostic/Review Math Test

This diagnostic test appears at the end of the math section because it is probably best for you to use it as a review test. Unless your math skills are very strong, you should thoroughly study every math chapter. Afterwards, you can use this diagnostic/review test to determine which math chapters you need to work on more. If you do not have much time to study, this test can also be used to concentrate your studies on your weakest areas.

1. If $3x + 9 = 15$, then $x + 2 =$

   (A) 2
   (B) 3
   (C) 4
   (D) 5
   (E) 6

2. If $a = 3b$, $b^2 = 2c$, $9c = d$, then $\dfrac{a^2}{d} =$

   (A) 1/2
   (B) 2
   (C) 10/3
   (D) 5
   (E) 6

$$a + b + c/2 = 60$$
$$-a - b + c/2 = -10$$

3. In the system of equations above, what is the value of b ?

   (A) 8
   (B) 20
   (C) 35
   (D) 50
   (E) Not enough information to decide.

4. $3 - (2^3 - 2[3 - 16 \div 2]) =$

   (A) −15
   (B) −5
   (C) 1
   (D) 2
   (E) 30

5. $(x - 2)(x + 4) - (x - 3)(x - 1) = 0$

   (A) −5
   (B) −1
   (C) 0
   (D) 1/2
   (E) 11/6

6. $-2^4 - \left(x^2 - 1\right)^2 =$

   (A) $-x^4 + 2x^2 + 15$
   (B) $-x^4 - 2x^2 + 17$
   (C) $-x^4 + 2x^2 - 17$
   (D) $-x^4 + 2x^2 - 15$
   (E) $-x^4 + 2x^2 + 17$

7. The smallest prime number greater than 48 is

   (A) 49
   (B) 50
   (C) 51
   (D) 52
   (E) 53

8. If a, b, and c are consecutive integers and $a < b < c$, which of the following must be true?

   (A) b^2 is a prime number
   (B) $\dfrac{a + c}{2} = b$
   (C) $a + b$ is even
   (D) $\dfrac{ab}{3}$ is an integer
   (E) $c - a = b$

9. $\sqrt{(42 - 6)(20 + 16)} =$

   (A) 2
   (B) 20
   (C) 28
   (D) 30
   (E) 36

10. $\left(4^x\right)^2 =$

   (A) 2^{4x}
   (B) 4^{x+2}
   (C) 2^{2x+2}
   (D) 4^{x^2}
   (E) 2^{2x^2}

11. If $8^{13} = 2^z$, then $z =$

   (A) 10
   (B) 13
   (C) 19
   (D) 26
   (E) 39

12. 1/2 of 0.2 percent equals

   (A) 1
   (B) 0.1
   (C) 0.01
   (D) 0.001
   (E) 0.0001

13. $\dfrac{4}{\frac{1}{3} + 1} =$

   (A) 1
   (B) 1/2
   (C) 2
   (D) 3
   (E) 4

14. If $x + y = k$, then $3x^2 + 6xy + 3y^2 =$

(A) k
(B) $3k$
(C) $6k$
(D) k^2
(E) $3k^2$

15. $8x^2 - 18 =$

(A) $8(x^2 - 2)$
(B) $2(2x + 3)(2x - 3)$
(C) $2(4x + 3)(4x - 3)$
(D) $2(2x + 9)(2x - 9)$
(E) $2(4x + 3)(x - 3)$

16. For which values of x is the following inequality true: $x^2 < 2x$.

(A) $x < 0$
(B) $0 < x < 2$
(C) $-2 < x < 2$
(D) $x < 2$
(E) $x > 2$

17. If x is an integer and $y = -3x + 7$, what is the least value of x for which y is less than 1?

(A) 1
(B) 2
(C) 3
(D) 4
(E) 5

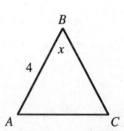

Note, figure not drawn to scale

18. In the figure above, triangle ABC is isosceles with base AC. If $x = 60°$, then $AC =$

(A) 2
(B) 3
(C) 4
(D) $\dfrac{14}{3}$
(E) $\sqrt{30}$

19. A unit square is circumscribed about a circle. If the circumference of the circle is $q\pi$, what is the value of q?

(A) 1
(B) 2
(C) π
(D) 2π
(E) 5π

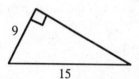

20. What is the area of the triangle above?

(A) 20
(B) 24
(C) 30
(D) 54
(E) 64

21. If the average of $2x$ and $4x$ is 12, then $x =$

(A) 1
(B) 2
(C) 3
(D) 4
(E) 24

22. The average of x, y, and z is 8 and the average of y and z is 4. What is the value of x?

(A) 4
(B) 9
(C) 16
(D) 20
(E) 24

23. If the ratio of two numbers is 6 and their sum is 21, what is the value of the larger number?

(A) 1
(B) 5
(C) 12
(D) 17
(E) 18

24. What percent of $3x$ is $6y$ if $x = 4y$?

(A) 50%
(B) 40%
(C) 30%
(D) 20%
(E) 18%

25. If $y = 3x$, then the value of 10% of y is

 (A) .003x
 (B) .3x
 (C) 3x
 (D) 30x
 (E) 300x

26. How many ounces of water must be added to a 30-ounce solution that is 40 percent alcohol to dilute the solution to 25 percent alcohol?

 (A) 9
 (B) 10
 (C) 15
 (D) 16
 (E) 18

27. What is the value 201st term of a sequence if the first term of the sequence is 2 and each successive term is 4 more the term immediately preceding it?

 (A) 798
 (B) 800
 (C) 802
 (D) 804
 (E) 806

28. A particular carmaker sells four models of cars, and each model comes with 5 options. How many different types of cars does the carmaker sell?

 (A) 15
 (B) 16
 (C) 17
 (D) 18
 (E) 20

29. Define a @ b to be $a^3 - 1$. What is the value of x @ 1 ?

 (A) 0
 (B) a^3
 (C) $x^3 - 1$
 (D) $x^3 + 1$
 (E) 2

30. Define the symbol * by the following equation: $x* = 1 - x$, for all non-negative x. If $((1-x)*)* = (1-x)*$, then $x =$

 (A) 1/2
 (B) 3/4
 (C) 1
 (D) 2
 (E) 3

1. Dividing both sides of the equation by 3 yields

$$x + 3 = 5$$

Subtracting 1 from both sides of this equation (because we are looking for $x + 2$) yields

$$x + 2 = 4$$

The answer is (C).

2.

$$\frac{a^2}{d} =$$

$$\frac{(3b)^2}{9c} = \quad \text{since } a = 3b \text{ and } 9c = d$$

$$\frac{9b^2}{9c} =$$

$$\frac{b^2}{c} =$$

$$\frac{2c}{c} = \quad \text{since } b^2 = 2c$$

$$2$$

The answer is (B).

3. Merely adding the two equations yields

$$c = 50$$

Next, multiplying the bottom equation by -1 and then adding the equations yields

$$\begin{array}{r} a + b + c/2 = 60 \\ (+) \quad \underline{a + b - c/2 = 10} \\ 2a + 2b = 70 \end{array}$$

Dividing this equation by 2 yields

$$a + b = 35$$

This equation does not allow us to determine the value of b. For example, if $a = 0$, then $b = 35$. Now suppose, is $a = -15$, then $b = 50$. This is a double case and therefore the answer is (E), not enough information to decide.

4.

$3 - (2^3 - 2[3 - 16 \div 2]) =$ Within the innermost parentheses, division is performed before subtraction:

$$3 - (2^3 - 2[3 - 8]) =$$
$$3 - (2^3 - 2[-5]) =$$
$$3 - (8 - 2[-5]) =$$
$$3 - (8 + 10) =$$
$$3 - 18 =$$
$$-15$$

The answer is (A).

5. Multiplying (using foil multiplication) both terms in the expression yields

$$x^2 + 4x - 2x - 8 - (x^2 - x - 3x + 3) = 0$$

(Notice that parentheses are used in the second expansion but not in the first. Parentheses must be used in the second expansion because the negative sign must be distributed to *every* term within the parentheses.)

Combining like terms yields

$$x^2 + 2x - 8 - (x^2 - 4x + 3) = 0$$

Distributing the negative sign to every term within the parentheses yields

$$x^2 + 2x - 8 - x^2 + 4x - 3 = 0$$

(Note, although distributing the negative sign over the parentheses is an elementary operation, many, if not most, students will apply the negative sign to only the first term:

$$-x^2 - 4x + 3$$

The writers of the test are aware of this common mistake and structure the test so that there are many opportunities to make this mistake.)

Grouping like terms together yields

$$(x^2 - x^2) + (2x + 4x) + (-8 - 3) = 0$$

Combining the like terms yields

$$6x - 11 = 0$$
$$6x = 11$$
$$x = 11/6$$

The answer is (E).

6.

$$-2^4 - (x^2 - 1)^2 =$$
$$-16 - [(x^2)^2 - 2x^2 + 1] =$$
$$-16 - [x^4 - 2x^2 + 1] =$$
$$-16 - x^4 + 2x^2 - 1 =$$
$$-x^4 + 2x^2 - 17$$

The answer is (C).

Notice that $-2^4 = -16$, not 16. This is one of the most common mistakes on the test. To see why $-2^4 = -16$ more clearly, rewrite -2^4 as follows:

$$-2^4 = (-1)2^4$$

In this form, it is clearer that the exponent, 4, applies only to the number 2, not to the number -1. So $-2^4 = (-1)2^4 = (-1)16 = -16$.

To make the answer positive 16, the -2 could be placed in parentheses:

$$(-2)^4 = [(-1)2]^4 = (-1)^4 \, 2^4 = (+1)16 = 16$$

7. Since the question asks for the *smallest* prime greater then 48, we start with the smallest answer-choice. Now, 49 is not prime since $49 = 7 \cdot 7$. Next, 50 is not prime since $50 = 5 \cdot 10$. Next, 51 is not prime since $51 = 3 \cdot 17$. Next, 52 is not prime since $52 = 2 \cdot 26$. Finally, 53 *is* prime since it is divisible by only itself and 1. The answer is (E).

Note, an integer is prime if it greater than 1 and divisible by only itself and 1. The number 2 is the smallest prime (and the only even prime) because the only integers that divide into it evenly are 1 and 2. The number 3 is the next larger prime. The number 4 is not prime because $4 = 2 \cdot 2$. Following is a partial list of the prime numbers. You should memorize it.

$$2, 3, 5, 7, 11, 13, 17, 19, 23, 29, 31, \ldots$$

8. Recall that an integer is prime if it is divisible by only itself and 1. In other words, an integer is prime if it cannot be written as a product of two other integers, other than itself and 1. Now, $b^2 = bb$. Since b^2 can be written as a product of b and b, it is not prime. Statement (A) is false.

Turning to Choice (B), since a, b, and c are consecutive integers, in that order, b is one unit larger than a: $b = a + 1$, and c is one unit larger than b: $c = b + 1 = (a + 1) + 1 = a + 2$. Now, plugging this information into the expression $\dfrac{a+c}{2}$ yields

$$\frac{a+c}{2} =$$
$$\frac{a+(a+2)}{2} =$$
$$\frac{2a+2}{2} =$$
$$\frac{2a}{2} + \frac{2}{2} =$$
$$a + 1 =$$
$$b$$

The answer is (B).

Regarding the other answer-choices, Choice (C) is true in some cases and false in others. To show that it can be false, let's plug in some numbers satisfying the given conditions. How about $a = 1$ and $b = 2$. In this case, $a + b = 1 + 2 = 3$, which is odd, not even. This eliminates Choice (C). Notice that to show a statement is false, we need only find one exception. However, to show a statement is true by plugging in numbers, you usually have to plug in more than one set of numbers because the statement may be true for one set of numbers but not for another set. We'll discuss in detail later the conditions under which you can say that a statement is true by plugging in numbers.

Choice (D) is not necessarily true. For instance, let $a = 1$ and $b = 2$. Then $\dfrac{ab}{3} = \dfrac{1 \cdot 2}{3} = \dfrac{2}{3}$, which is not an integer. This eliminates Choice (D).

Finally, $c - a = b$ is not necessarily true. For instance, let $a = 2$, $b = 3$, and $c = 4$. Then $c - a = 4 - 2 = 2 \neq 3$. This eliminates Choice (E).

9.
$$\sqrt{(42-6)(20+16)} =$$
$$\sqrt{(36)(36)} =$$
$$\sqrt{36}\sqrt{36} = \qquad \text{from the rule } \sqrt{xy} = \sqrt{x}\sqrt{y}$$
$$6 \cdot 6 =$$
$$36$$

The answer is (E).

10.
$$\left(4^x\right)^2 =$$
$$4^{2x} = \qquad \text{by the rule } \left(x^a\right)^b = x^{ab}$$
$$\left(2^2\right)^{2x} = \qquad \text{by replacing 4 with } 2^2$$
$$(2)^{4x} \qquad \text{by the rule } \left(x^a\right)^b = x^{ab}$$

The answer is (A). Note, this is considered to be a hard problem.

As to the other answer-choices, Choice (B) wrongly adds the exponents x and 2. The exponents are added when the same bases are multiplied:

$$a^x a^y = a^{x+y}$$

For example: $2^3 2^2 = 2^{3+2} = 2^5 = 32$. Be careful not to multiply unlike bases. For example, do not add exponents in the following expression: $2^3 4^2$. The exponents cannot be added here because the bases, 2 and 4, are not the same.

Choice (C), first changes 4 into 2^2, and then correctly multiplies 2 and x: $\left(2^2\right)^x = 2^{2x}$. However, it then errs in adding $2x$ and 2: $\left(2^{2x}\right)^2 \neq 2^{2x+2}$.

Choice (D) wrongly squares the x. When a power is raised to another power, the powers are multiplied:

$$\left(x^a\right)^b = x^{ab}$$

So $\left(4^x\right)^2 = 4^{2x}$.

Choice (E) makes the same mistake as in Choice (D).

11. The number 8 can be written as 2^3. Plugging this into the equation $8^{13} = 2^z$ yields

$$\left(2^3\right)^{13} = 2^z$$

Applying the rule $\left(x^a\right)^b = x^{ab}$ yields

$$2^{39} = 2^z$$

Since the bases are the same, the exponents must be the same. Hence, $z = 39$, and the answer is (E).

12. Recall that percent means to divide by 100. So .2 percent equals .2/100 = .002. (Recall that the decimal point is moved to the left one space for each zero in the denominator.) Now, as a decimal 1/2 = .5.

In percent problems, "of" means multiplication. So multiplying .5 and .002 yields

$$\begin{array}{r} .002 \\ \times\quad .5 \\ \hline .001 \end{array}$$

Hence, the answer is (D).

13.

$$\frac{4}{\dfrac{1}{3}+1} =$$

$$\frac{4}{\dfrac{1}{3}+\dfrac{3}{3}} = \qquad \text{by creating a common denominator of 3}$$

$$\frac{4}{\dfrac{1+3}{3}} =$$

$$\frac{4}{\dfrac{4}{3}} =$$

$$4 \cdot \frac{3}{4} = \qquad \text{Recall: "to divide" means to invert and multiply}$$

$$3 \qquad\qquad \text{by canceling the 4's}$$

Hence, the answer is (D).

14. $3x^2 + 6xy + 3y^2 =$
    $3(x^2 + 2xy + y^2) = \qquad$ by factoring out the common factor 3
    $3(x + y)^2 = \qquad\qquad$ by the perfect square trinomial formula $x^2 + 2xy + y^2 = (x+y)^2$
    $3k^2$

Hence, the answer is (E).

15. $8x^2 - 18 =$

    $2(4x^2 - 9) =$ by the distributive property $ax + ay = a(x + y)$

    $2(2^2x^2 - 3^2) =$

    $2([2x]^2 - 3^2) =$

    $2(2x + 3)(2x - 3)$ by the difference of squares formula $x^2 - y^2 = (x + y)(x - y)$

The answer is (B).

It is common for students to wrongly apply the difference of squares formula to a perfect square:

$$(x - y)^2 \neq (x + y)(x - y)$$

The correct formulas follow. Notice that the first formula is the square of a difference, and the second formula is the difference of two squares.

Perfect square trinomial: $(x - y)^2 = x^2 - 2xy + y^2$

Difference of squares: $x^2 - y^2 = (x + y)(x - y)$

It is also common for students to wrongly distribute the 2 in a perfect square:

$$(x - y)^2 \neq x^2 - y^2$$

Note, there is no factoring formula for a sum of squares: $x^2 + y^2$. It cannot be factored.

16. First, replace the inequality symbol with an equal symbol: $x^2 = 2x$

Subtracting $2x$ from both sides yields $x^2 - 2x = 0$

Factoring by the distributive rule yields $x(x - 2) = 0$

Setting each factor to 0 yields $x = 0$ and $x - 2 = 0$

Or $x = 0$ and $x = 2$

Now, the only numbers at which the expression can change sign are 0 and 2. So 0 and 2 divide the number line into three intervals. Let's set up a number line and choose test points in each interval:

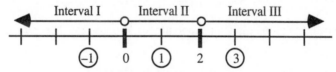

When $x = -1$, $x^2 < 2x$ becomes $1 < -2$. This is false. Hence, no numbers in Interval I satisfy the inequality. When $x = 1$, $x^2 < 2x$ becomes $1 < 2$. This is true. Hence, all numbers in Interval II satisfy the inequality. That is, $0 < x < 2$. When $x = 3$, $x^2 < 2x$ becomes $9 < 6$. This is false. Hence, no numbers in Interval III satisfy the inequality. The answer is (B). The graph of the solution follows:

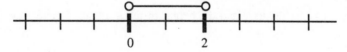

17. Since y is to be less than 1 and $y = -3x + 7$, we get

         $-3x + 7 < 1$

         $-3x < -6$ by subtracting 7 from both sides of the inequality

         $x > 2$ by dividing both sides of the inequality by -3

(Note that the inequality changes direction when we divide both sides by a negative number. This is also the case if you multiply both sides of an inequality by a negative number.)

Since x is an integer and is to be as small as possible, $x = 3$. The answer is (C).

18. Since the triangle is isosceles, with base AC, the base angles are congruent (equal). That is, $A = C$. Since the angle sum of a triangle is 180, we get

$$A + C + x = 180$$

Replacing C with A and x with 60 gives

$$A + A + 60 = 180$$
$$A + A + 60 = 180$$
$$2A + 60 = 180$$
$$2A = 120$$
$$A = 60$$

Hence, the triangle is equilateral (all three sides are congruent). Since we are given that side AB has length 4, side AC also has length 4. The answer is (C).

19. Since the unit square is circumscribed about the circle, the diameter of the circle is 1 and the radius of the circle is r = d/2 = 1/2. This is illustrated in the following figure:

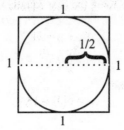

Now, the circumference of a circle is given by the formula $2\pi r$. For this circle the formula becomes $2\pi r = 2\pi(1/2) = \pi$. We are told that the circumference of the circle is $q\pi$. Setting these two expressions equal yields

$$\pi = q\pi$$

Dividing both sides of this equation by π yields

$$1 = q$$

The answer is (A).

20. Let x be the unknown side of the triangle. Applying the Pythagorean Theorem yields

$$9^2 + x^2 = 15^2$$
$$81 + x^2 = 225 \qquad \text{by squaring the terms}$$
$$x^2 = 144 \qquad \text{by subtracting 81 from both sides of the equation}$$
$$x = \pm\sqrt{144} \qquad \text{by taking the square root of both sides of the equation}$$
$$x = 12 \qquad \text{since we are looking for a length, we take the positive root}$$

In a right triangle, the legs are the base and the height of the triangle. Hence, $A = \dfrac{1}{2}bh = \dfrac{1}{2} \cdot 9 \cdot 12 = 54$. The answer is (D).

21. Since the average of $2x$ and $4x$ is 12, we get

$$\frac{2x + 4x}{2} = 12$$
$$\frac{6x}{2} = 12$$
$$3x = 12$$
$$x = 4$$

The answer is (D).

22. Recall that the average of N numbers is their sum divided by N. That is, average = sum/N. Since the average of x, y, and z is 8 and the average of y and z is 4, this formula yields

$$\frac{x+y+z}{3} = 8$$

$$\frac{y+z}{2} = 4$$

Solving the bottom equation for $y + z$ yields $y + z = 8$. Plugging this into the top equation gives

$$\frac{x+8}{3} = 8$$

$$x + 8 = 24$$

$$x = 16$$

The answer is (C).

23. Let the two numbers be x and y. Now, a ratio is simply a fraction. Forming the fraction yields $x/y = 6$, and forming the sum yields $x + y = 21$. Solving the first equation for x yields $x = 6y$. Plugging this into the second equation yields

$$6y + y = 21$$
$$7y = 21$$
$$y = 3$$

Plugging this into the equation $x = 6y$ yields

$$x = 6(3) = 18$$

The answer is (E).

24. Let $z\%$ represent the unknown percent. Now, when solving percent problems, "of" means times. Translating the statement "What percent of $3x$ is $6y$" into an equation yields

$$z\%(3x) = 6y$$

Substituting $x = 4y$ into this equation yields

$$z\%(3 \cdot 4y) = 6y$$

$$z\%(12y) = 6y$$

$$z\% = \frac{6y}{12y}$$

$$z\% = 1/2 = .50 = 50\%$$

The answer is (A).

25. The percent symbol, %, means to divide by 100. So $10\% = 10/100 = .10$. Hence, the expression 10% of y trunlsates into $.10y$. Since $y = 3x$, this becomes $.10y = .10(3x) = .30x$. The answer is (B).

26. Let x be the amount of water added. Since there is no alcohol in the water, the percent of alcohol in the water is $0\%x$. The amount of alcohol in the original solution is $40\%(30)$, and the amount of alcohol in the final solution will be $25\%(30 + x)$. Now, the concentration of alcohol in the original solution plus the concentration of alcohol in the added solution (water) must equal the concentration of alcohol in the resulting solution:

$$40\%(30) + 0\%x = 25\%(30 + x)$$

Multiplying this equation by 100 to clear the percent symbol yields

$$40(30) + 0 = 25(30 + x)$$
$$1200 = 750 + 25x$$
$$450 = 25x$$
$$18 = x$$

The answer is (E).

27. Except for the first term, each term of the sequence is found by adding 4 to the term immediately preceding it. In other words, we are simply adding 4 to the sequence 200 times. This yields

$$4 \cdot 200 = 800$$

Adding the 2 in the first term gives $800 + 2 = 802$. The answer is (C).

We can also solve this problem formally. The first term of the sequence is 2, and since each successive term is 4 more than the term immediately preceding it, the second term is $2 + 4$, and the third term is $(2 + 4) + 4$, and the fourth term is $[(2 + 4) + 4] + 4$, etc. Regrouping yields (note that we rewrite the first term as $2 + 4(0)$. You'll see why in a moment.)

$$2 + 4(0), 2 + 4(1), 2 + 4(2), 2 + 4(3), \ldots$$

Notice that the number within each pair of parentheses is 1 less than the numerical order of the term. For instance, the *first* term has a 0 within the parentheses, the *second* term has a 1 within the parentheses, etc. Hence, the nth term of the sequence is

$$2 + 4(n - 1)$$

Using this formula, the 201st term is $2 + 4(201 - 1) = 2 + 4(200) = 2 + 800 = 802$.

28. For the first model, there are 5 options. So there are 5 different types of cars in this model. For the second model, there are the same number of different types of cars. Likewise, for the other two types of models. Hence, there are $5 + 5 + 5 + 5 = 20$ different types of cars. The answer is (E).

This problem illustrates the *Fundamental Principle of Counting*:

> If an event occurs *m* times, and each of the *m* events is followed by a second event which occurs *k* times, then the first event follows the second event $m \cdot k$ times.

29. This is considered to be a hard problem. However, it is actually quite easy. By the definition given, the function @ merely cubes the term on the left and then subtracts 1 from it (the value of the term on the right is irrelevant). The term on the left is x. Hence, $x @ 1 = x^3 - 1$, and the answer is (C).

30.

$$((1 - x)*)* = (1 - x)*$$
$$(1 - (1 - x))* = (1 - x)*$$
$$(1 - 1 + x)* = (1 - x)*$$
$$(x)* = (1 - x)*$$
$$1 - x = 1 - (1 - x)$$
$$1 - x = 1 - 1 + x$$
$$1 - x = x$$
$$1 = 2x$$
$$\frac{1}{2} = x$$

The answer is (A).

Study Plan

Use the list below to review the appropriate chapters for any questions you missed.

Solutions To Problems

Problem Set A:

1. Choose $n = 1$. Then $\dfrac{n}{2} = \dfrac{1}{2}$, which is not even—eliminate (A). Next, $4n + 3 = 4 \cdot 1 + 3 = 7$, which is not even—eliminate (B). Next, $2n = 2 \cdot 1 = 2$, which is even and may therefore be the answer. Next, both (D) and (E) equal 1, which is not even. Hence, the answer is (C).

2. Choose $x = 4$ and $y = 9$. Then $x^2 = 4^2 = 16$, which is a perfect square. (Note, we cannot eliminate x^2 because it may not be a perfect square for another choice of x.) Next, $xy = 4 \cdot 9 = 36$, which is a perfect square. Next, $4x = 4 \cdot 4 = 16$, which is a perfect square. Next, $x + y = 4 + 9 = 13$, which is <u>not</u> a perfect square. Hence, the answer is (D).

3. Choose $x = 1$ and $y = 2$. Then $3x + \dfrac{y}{2} = 3 \cdot 1 + \dfrac{2}{2} = 4$, which is even. The answer is (A). Note: We don't need to check the other answer-choices because the problem asked for the expression that *could be* even. Thus, the first answer-choice that turns out even is the answer.

4. Choose $k = \dfrac{1}{4}$. Then $\dfrac{3}{2}k = \dfrac{3}{2} \cdot \dfrac{1}{4} = \dfrac{3}{8} > \dfrac{1}{4}$; eliminate (A). Next, $\dfrac{1}{k} = \dfrac{1}{1/4} = 4 > \dfrac{1}{4}$; eliminate (B). Next, $|k| = \left|\dfrac{1}{4}\right| = \dfrac{1}{4}$; eliminate (C). Next, $\sqrt{k} = \sqrt{\dfrac{1}{4}} = \dfrac{1}{2} > \dfrac{1}{4}$; eliminate (D). Thus, by process of elimination, the answer is (E).

5. Without substitution, this is a hard problem. With substitution, it's quite easy. Suppose you begin reading on page 1 and stop on page 2. Then you will have read 2 pages. Now, merely substitute $h = 1$ and $k = 2$ into the answer-choices to see which one(s) equal 2. Only $k - h + 1 = 2 - 1 + 1 = 2$ does. (Verify this.) The answer is (E).

6. Suppose $m = 2$, an even integer. Then $4m + 1 = 9$, which is odd. Hence, the next even integer greater than 9 is 10. And the next even integer after 10 is 12. Now, $10 + 12 = 22$. So look for an answer-choice which equals 22 when $m = 2$.
    Begin with choice (A). Since $m = 2$, $8m + 2 = 18$—eliminate (A). Next, $8m + 4 = 20$—eliminate (B). Next, $8m + 6 = 22$. Hence, the answer is (C).

7. Suppose $x^2 = 4$. Then $x = 2$ or $x = -2$. In either case, x is even. Hence, Statement I need not be true, which eliminates (A) and (D). Further, $x^3 = 8$ or $x^3 = -8$. In either case, x^3 is even. Hence, Statement III need not be true, which eliminates (C) and (E). Therefore, by process of elimination, the answer is (B).

8. Suppose $x = 8$. Then x is divisible by 8 and is not divisible by 3. Now, $\dfrac{x}{2} = 4$, $\dfrac{x}{4} = 2$, $\dfrac{x}{8} = 1$, and $x = 8$, which are all integers—eliminate (A), (B), (D), and (E). Hence, by process of elimination, the answer is (C).

9. Let $p = 1$ and $q = 2$. Then $pq = 2$ and $p(q + 2) = 4$. This scenario has one integer, 3, greater than pq and less than $p(q + 2)$. Now, we plug $p = 1$ and $q = 2$ into the answer-choices until we find one that has the value 1. Look at choice (D): $2p - 1 = (2)(1) - 1 = 1$. Thus, the answer is (D).

10. If $x = 3$ and $y = 2$, then $x - y = 3 - 2 = 1$. This eliminates (A). If $x = 5$ and $y = 3$, then $x - y = 5 - 3 = 2$. This eliminates (B). If $x = 17$ and $y = 3$, then $x - y = 17 - 3 = 14$. This eliminates (D). If $x = 23$ and $y = 3$, then $x - y = 23 - 3 = 20$. This eliminates (E). Hence, by process of elimination, the answer is (C).
    Method II (without substitution): Suppose $x - y = 13$. Now, let x and y be distinct prime numbers, both greater than 2. Then both x and y are odd numbers since the only even prime is 2. Hence, $x = 2k + 1$, and $y = 2h + 1$, for some positive integers k and h. And $x - y = (2k + 1) - (2h + 1) = 2k - 2h = 2(k - h)$. Hence, $x - y$ is even. This contradicts the assumption that $x - y = 13$, an odd number. Hence, x and y cannot both

be greater than 2. Next, suppose $y = 2$, then $x - y = 13$ becomes $x - 2 = 13$. Solving yields $x = 15$. But 15 is not prime. Hence, there does not exist prime numbers x and y such that $x - y = 13$. The answer is (C).

11. Suppose $x = 1$, an integer. Then $2(x + 1) = 2(1 + 1) = 4$. The next two integers greater than 4 are 5 and 6, and their product is 30. Now, check which of the answer-choices equal 30 when $x = 1$. Begin with (A): $4x^2 + 14x + 12 = 4(1)^2 + 14 \cdot 1 + 12 = 30$. No other answer-choice equals 30 when $x = 1$. Hence, the answer is (A).

12. The number 3 itself is divisible by 3 but not by 2. With this value for x, Choice (A) becomes $\frac{3+1}{2} = \frac{4}{2} = 2$, eliminate; Choice (C) becomes $\frac{3^2}{3} = \frac{9}{3} = 3$, eliminate; Choice (D) becomes $\frac{3^3}{3} = \frac{27}{3} = 9$, eliminate. Next, if $x = 21$, then Choice (B) becomes $\frac{21}{7} = 3$, eliminate. Hence, by process of elimination, the answer is (E).

13. If $x = y = 2$, then $y^{x-1} = 2^{2-1} = 2^1 = 2$, which is even. But $y - 1 = 2 - 1 = 1$ is odd, and $x/2 = 2/2 = 1$ is also odd. This eliminates choices (B), (C), (D), and (E). The answer is (A).

14.   We could solve the equation, but it is much faster to just plug in the answer-choices. Begin with 0:

$$x^4 - 2x^2 = 0^4 - 2 \cdot 0^2 = 0 - 0 = 0$$

Hence, eliminate (A). Next, plug in 1:

$$x^4 - 2x^2 = 1^4 - 2 \cdot 1^2 = 1 - 2 = -1$$

Hence, the answer is (B).

15. If $x = 0$, then $\frac{3 - 4x}{5}$ becomes $\frac{3}{5}$ and the answer-choices become

(A) $\frac{5}{4}$

(B) $\frac{10}{3}$

(C) $-\frac{10}{3}$

(D) $\frac{3}{5}$

(E) $-\frac{3}{10}$

Multiplying Choice (C) by $\frac{3}{5}$, gives $\left(\frac{3}{5}\right)\left(-\frac{10}{3}\right) = -2$. The answer is (C).

Problem Set B:

1. The ten's digit must be twice the unit's digit. This eliminates (A), (C), and (E). Now reversing the digits in choice (B) yields 12. But $21 - 12 \neq 27$. This eliminates (B). Hence, by process of elimination, the answer is (D). $(63 - 36 = 27.)$

2. Here we need only plug in answer-choices until we find the one that yields a result of 1. Start with 1, the easiest number to calculate with. $\dfrac{1+1}{1^2} = 2 \neq 1$. Eliminate (C). Next, choosing $N = 2$, we get

$\dfrac{2+2}{2^2} = \dfrac{4}{4} = 1$. Hence, the answer is (D).

3. Suppose there were 8 people on the bus—choice (C). Then after the first stop, there would be 4 people left on the bus. After the second stop, there would be 2 people left on the bus. After the third stop, there would be only one person left on the bus. Hence, on the third stop the next to last person would have exited the bus. The answer is (C).

4. In choice (D), $3 + 9 = 12$ and $3 = \dfrac{1}{3} \cdot 9$. Hence, the answer is (D).

5. We could solve the equation, but it is much faster to just plug in the answer-choices. Begin with 1: $\dfrac{1^6 - 5(1)^3 - 16}{8} = \dfrac{1 - 5 - 16}{8} = \dfrac{-20}{8}$. Hence, eliminate (A). Next, plug in 2: $\dfrac{2^6 - 5(2)^3 - 16}{8} =$ $\dfrac{64 - 5(8) - 16}{8} = \dfrac{64 - 40 - 16}{8} = \dfrac{8}{8} = 1$. Hence, the answer is (B).

6. Begin with 0: $x^4 - 2x^2 = 0^4 - 2 \cdot 0^2 = 0 - 0 = 0$. Hence, eliminate (A). Next, plug in 1: $x^4 - 2x^2 = 1^4 - 2 \cdot 1^2 = 1 - 2 = -1$. Hence, the answer is (B).

Problem Set C:

1. Substituting $p = 3$ into the equation $p^* = \dfrac{p+5}{p-2}$ gives $3^* = \dfrac{3+5}{3-2} = \dfrac{8}{1} = 8$. The answer is (E).

2. SAT answer-choices are usually listed in ascending order of size—occasionally they are listed in descending order. Hence, start with choice (C). If it is less than 2, then turn to choice (D). If it is greater than 2, then turn to choice (B).

Now, $\boxed{6} = \dfrac{6^2}{2} = \dfrac{36}{2} = 18$, which is greater than 2. So we next check choice (B). Now,

$\boxed{4} = \dfrac{4^2}{2} = \dfrac{16}{2} = 8$, which is greater than 2. Therefore, by process of elimination, the answer is (A). Let's

verify this: $\boxed{2} = \dfrac{2^2}{2} = \dfrac{4}{2} = 2$.

3. $2 \# 3 = -\sqrt{(2+3)^2} = -\sqrt{5^2} = -\sqrt{25} = -5$. The answer is (B).

4. The area of a circle is πr^2 (where r is the radius), or $\pi \left(\dfrac{d}{2}\right)^2$ (where d is the diameter). This formula

yields $\boxed{4} \cdot \boxed{6} = \pi \left(\dfrac{4}{2}\right)^2 \cdot \pi \left(\dfrac{6}{2}\right)^2 = \pi 4 \cdot \pi 9 = 36\pi^2$. Now, $\pi \cdot \boxed{12} = \pi \cdot \pi \left(\dfrac{12}{2}\right)^2 = \pi^2 6^2 = 36\pi^2$.

Hence, the answer is (D).

5. $\xleftrightarrow{0,1,a} = (0-1)a = -a$, and $\xleftrightarrow{1,a,0} = (1-a)0 = 0$. Setting these results equal to each other yields $-a = 0$. Multiplying by -1 yields $a = 0$. Hence, the answer is (C).

6. $\boxed{2} = 2^2 - 2 = 2$, and $\boxed{x} = x^2 - 2$. Substituting these values into the equation $\boxed{2} - \boxed{x} = x^2$ yields

$$2 - \left(x^2 - 2\right) = x^2$$
$$2 - x^2 + 2 = x^2$$
$$4 - x^2 = x^2$$
$$4 = 2x^2$$
$$2 = x^2$$
$$\sqrt{2} = x$$

The answer is (A).

7.   Statement I is false. For instance, $1 \Diamond 2 = 1 \cdot 2 - \dfrac{1}{2} = \dfrac{3}{2}$, but $2 \Diamond 1 = 2 \cdot 1 - \dfrac{2}{1} = 0$. This eliminates (A), (D), and (E). Statement II is true: $a \Diamond a = aa - \dfrac{a}{a} = a^2 - 1 = (a+1)(a-1)$. This eliminates (C). Hence, by process of elimination, the answer is (B). Note: The expression $a \cdot b \neq 0$ insures that neither a nor b equals 0: if $a \cdot b = 0$, then either $a = 0$ or $b = 0$, or both.

8. $(x * y) * z = \left(\dfrac{x}{y}\right) * z = \dfrac{\left(\dfrac{x}{y}\right)}{z} = \dfrac{x}{y} \cdot \dfrac{1}{z} = \dfrac{x}{yz}$. Hence, the answer is (E).

9.   From the equation $x \Theta y = -y$, we get

$$x\sqrt{y} - y - 2x = -y$$
$$x\sqrt{y} - 2x = 0$$
$$x\left(\sqrt{y} - 2\right) = 0$$

Now, if $x = 0$, then $x\left(\sqrt{y} - 2\right) = 0$ will be true regardless the value of y since the product of zero and any number is zero. The answer is (A).

10. $\left(64^*\right)^* = \left(\dfrac{\sqrt{64}}{2}\right)^* = \left(\dfrac{8}{2}\right)^* = 4^* = \dfrac{\sqrt{4}}{2} = \dfrac{2}{2} = 1$. The answer is (A).

11. $\boxed{x+2} - \boxed{x-2} = \left([x+2]+2\right)[x+2] - \left([x-2]+2\right)[x-2]$

$$= (x+4)[x+2] - x[x-2]$$
$$= x^2 + 6x + 8 - \left(x^2 - 2x\right)$$
$$= x^2 + 6x + 8 - x^2 + 2x$$
$$= 8x + 8$$
$$= 8(x + 1)$$

The answer is (E).

12. Following is the set of all integers greater than –2.1:

$$\{-2, -1, 0, 1, 2, \ldots\}$$

The least integer in this set is –2. The answer is (C).

13. $(2 \lozenge 8) - (3 \lozenge 3) = \sqrt{2 \cdot 8} - \sqrt{3 \cdot 3} = \sqrt{16} - \sqrt{9} = 4 - 3 = 1$. The answer is (B).

14. Statement I is true:

$$a \phi 1 =$$
$$1 \phi a = \qquad \text{[Since } a \phi b = b \phi a\text{]}$$
$$1 \qquad \text{[Since } 1 \phi a = 1\text{]}$$

This eliminates (B) and (C). Statement III is true:

$$\frac{1 \phi a}{b \phi 1} =$$
$$\frac{1 \phi a}{1 \phi b} = \qquad \text{[Since } a \phi b = b \phi a\text{]}$$
$$\frac{1}{1} = \qquad \text{[Since } 1 \phi a = 1\text{]}$$
$$1$$

This eliminates (A) and (D). Hence, by process of elimination, the answer is (E).

15. From $1 \ominus 1 = 1$, we know that $\ominus$ must denote multiplication or division; and from $0 \ominus 0 = 0$, we know that $\ominus$ must denote multiplication, addition, or subtraction. The only operation common to these two groups is multiplication. Hence, the value of $\pi \ominus \sqrt{2}$ can be uniquely determined:

$$\pi \ominus \sqrt{2} = \pi \cdot \sqrt{2}$$

The answer is (C).

16. Since $4 < 12$, we use the bottom half of the definition of #:

$$4 \, \# \, 12 = 4 + \frac{12}{4} = 4 + 3 = 7$$

The answer is (B).

17. Statement I is possible: $\left(-\frac{4}{5}\right) \# \left(-\frac{4}{5}\right) = -\frac{4}{5} + \frac{(-4/5)}{4} = -\frac{4}{5} - \frac{1}{5} = -\frac{5}{5} = -1$. Statement II is not possible: since $x > y$, the top part of the definition of # applies. But a square cannot be negative (i.e., cannot equal –1). Statement III is possible: $-1 < 0$. So by the bottom half of the definition, $-1 \, \# \, 0 = -1 + \frac{0}{4} = -1$. The answer is (D).

18. $(a + b^*)^* = (a + [2 - b])^* = (a + 2 - b)^* = 2 - (a + 2 - b) = 2 - a - 2 + b = -a + b = b - a$. The answer is (A).

19.
$$(2 - x)^* = (x - 2)^*$$
$$2 - (2 - x) = 2 - (x - 2)$$
$$2 - 2 + x = 2 - x + 2$$
$$x = 4 - x$$
$$2x = 4$$
$$x = 2$$

The answer is (C).

Problem Set D:

1. Let's change the fractional notation to radical notation: $g(x) = \sqrt[4]{2x - 3} + 1$. Since we have an even root, the expression under the radical must be greater than or equal to zero. Hence, $2x - 3 \geq 0$. Adding 3 to both sides of this inequality yields $2x \geq 3$. Dividing both sides by 2 yields $x \geq 3/2$. The answer is (C).

2. We need to plug the x table values into each given function to find the one that returns the function values in the bottom row of the table. Let's start with $x = 0$ since zero is the easiest number to calculate with. According to the table $f(0) = 3$. This eliminates Choice (A) since $f(0) = -2(0)^2 = -2(0) = 0$; and it eliminates Choice (D) since $f(0) = -2(0)^2 - 3 = -2 \cdot 0 - 3 = 0 - 3 = -3$. Now, choose $x = 1$. The next easiest number to calculate with. According to the table $f(1) = 1$. This eliminates Choice (B) since $f(1) = 1^2 + 3 = 1 + 3 = 4$; and it eliminates Choice (C) since $f(1) = -(1)^2 + 3 = -1 + 3 = 2$. Hence, by process of elimination, the answer is (E).

3. The graph has a height of 2 for every value of x between 2 and 3; it also has a height of 2 at about $x = -2$. The only number offered in this interval is 2.5. This is illustrated by the dot and the thick line in the following graph:

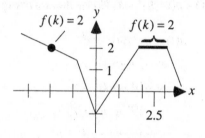

The answer is (D).

4. Evaluating the function $h(x) = \sqrt{x} + 2$ at v yields $h(v) = \sqrt{v} + 2$. Plugging this into the equation $3h(v) = 18$ yields

$$3\left(\sqrt{v} + 2\right) = 18$$
$$\sqrt{v} + 2 = 6 \qquad \text{by dividing both sides by 3}$$
$$\sqrt{v} = 4 \qquad \text{by subtracting 2 from both sides}$$
$$\left(\sqrt{v}\right)^2 = 4^2 \qquad \text{by squaring both sides}$$
$$v = 16 \qquad \text{since } \left(\sqrt{v}\right)^2 = v$$

Plugging $v = 16$ into $h\left(\dfrac{v}{4}\right)$ yields

$$h\left(\frac{v}{4}\right) = h\left(\frac{16}{4}\right) = h(4) = \sqrt{4} + 2 = 2 + 2 = 4$$

The answer is (E).

5. Since the graph is symmetric about the x-axis, its base graph is $x = y^2$. Since the graph opens to the left, we know that exterior of the base function is multiplied by negative one: $-y^2$. Since the graph is shifted one unit to the left, we know that one is added to the interior of the function: $x = -(y + 1)^2$. The answer is (A).

6. We are asked to find the value of x for which revenue is \$110. In mathematical terms, we need to solve the equation $r(x) = 110$. Since $r(x) = 50\sqrt{x} - 40$, we get

$$50\sqrt{x} - 40 = 110$$
$$50\sqrt{x} = 150$$
$$\sqrt{x} = 3$$
$$\left(\sqrt{x}\right)^2 = 3^2$$
$$|x| = 9$$
$$x = 9 \quad \text{or} \quad x = -9$$

Since $x = -9$ has no physical interpretation for this problem, we know that $x = 9$. The answer is (E).

7. **Method I:**

Recall that when a quadratic function is written in the form $y = a(x-h)^2 + k$, its vertex (in this case, the maximum height of the projectile) occurs at the point (h, k). So let's rewrite the function $h(t) = p - 10(q-t)^2$ in the form $h(t) = a(t-h)^2 + k$. Notice that we changed y to $h(t)$ and x to t.

$$
\begin{aligned}
h(t) &= p - 10(q-t)^2 \\
&= -10(q-t)^2 + p \\
&= -10(q-t)^2 + p \\
&= -10(-[-q+t])^2 + p \\
&= -10(-[t-q])^2 + p \\
&= -10([-1]^2[t-q])^2 + p \\
&= -10([+1][t-q])^2 + p \\
&= -10(t-q)^2 + p
\end{aligned}
$$

In this form, we can see that the vertex (maximum) occurs at the point (q, p). We are given that the maximum height of 100 occurs when t is 3. Hence, $q = 3$ and $p = 100$. Plugging this into our function yields

$$h(t) = -10(t-q)^2 + p = -10(t-3)^2 + 100$$

We are asked to find the height of the projectile when $t = 4$. Evaluating our function at 4 yields

$$
\begin{aligned}
h(4) &= -10(4-3)^2 + 100 \\
&= -10(1)^2 + 100 \\
&= -10 \cdot 1 + 100 \\
&= -10 + 100 \\
&= 90
\end{aligned}
$$

The answer is (E).

Method II:

In this method, we are going to solve a system of two equations in two unknowns in order to determine the values of p and q in the function $h(t) = p - 10(q-t)^2$. At time $t = 0$, the projectile had a height of 10 feet. In other words, $h(0) = 10$. At time $t = 3$, the projectile had a height of 100 feet. In other words, $h(3) = 100$. Plugging this information into the function $h(t) = p - 10(q-t)^2$ yields

$$h(0) = 10 \quad \Rightarrow \quad 10 = p - 10(q-0)^2$$
$$h(3) = 100 \quad \Rightarrow \quad 100 = p - 10(q-3)^2$$

Now, we solve this system of equations by subtracting the bottom equation from the top equation:

$$10 = p - 10q^2$$
$$(-) \quad 100 = p - 10(q-3)^2$$
$$\overline{-90 = -10q^2 + 10(q-3)^2}$$

Solving this equation for q yields

$$-90 = -10q^2 + 10(q-3)^2$$
$$-90 = -10q^2 + 10(q^2 - 6q + 9)$$
$$-90 = -10q^2 + 10q^2 - 60q + 90$$
$$-90 = -60q + 90$$
$$-180 = -60q$$
$$3 = q$$

Plugging $q = 3$ into the equation $10 = p - 10q^2$ yields

$$10 = p - 10 \cdot 3^2$$
$$10 = p - 10 \cdot 9$$
$$10 = p - 90$$
$$100 = p$$

Hence, the function $h(t) = p - 10(q-t)^2$ becomes $h(t) = 100 - 10(3-t)^2$. We are asked to find the height of the projectile when $t = 4$. Evaluating this function at 4 yields

$$h(4) = 100 - 10(3-4)^2$$
$$= 100 - 10(-1)^2$$
$$= 100 - 10 \cdot 1$$
$$= 100 - 10$$
$$= 90$$

The answer is (E).

8. Let s denote the length of a side of square *ABCD*. Since the area of the square is 16, we get $s^2 = 16$. Taking the square root of both sides of this equation yields $s = 4$. Hence, line segment *AB* has length 4. Since the parabola is symmetric about the y-axis, Point *B* is 2 units from the y-axis (as is Point *A*). That is, the x-coordinate of Point *B* is 2. Since line segment *BC* has length 4, the coordinates of Point *B* are (2, 4). Since the square and the parabola intersect at Point *B*, the point (2, 4) must satisfy the equation $y = a - x^2$:

$$4 = a - 2^2$$
$$4 = a - 4$$
$$8 = a$$

The answer is (D).

Problem Set E:

1. From the formula $a^2 x^2 = (ax)^2$, we see that $(2x)^2 = 2^2 \cdot x^2 = 4x^2$. Now, since $x \neq 0$, $4x^2$ is clearly larger than $2x^2$. Hence, the answer is (B).

2. Begin by comparing $\dfrac{15}{16}$ to each of the other answer-choices. Cross-multiplying $\dfrac{15}{16}$ and $\dfrac{7}{9}$ gives 135 vs. 112. Now, 135 is greater than 112, so $\dfrac{15}{16}$ is greater than $\dfrac{7}{9}$. Using this procedure to compare $\dfrac{15}{16}$ to each of the remaining answer-choices shows that $\dfrac{15}{16}$ is the greatest fraction listed. The answer is (A).

3. $1 + \dfrac{1}{1 - \dfrac{1}{2}} = 1 + \dfrac{1}{\frac{1}{2}} = 1 + 2 = 3$. The answer is (A).

4. "The ratio of $\dfrac{1}{5}$ to $\dfrac{1}{4}$ is equal to the ratio of $\dfrac{1}{4}$ to x" means $\dfrac{\frac{1}{5}}{\frac{1}{4}} = \dfrac{\frac{1}{4}}{x}$, or $\dfrac{1}{5} \cdot \dfrac{4}{1} = \dfrac{1}{4} \cdot \dfrac{1}{x}$. This in turn reduces to $\dfrac{4}{5} = \dfrac{1}{4x}$. Cross-multiplying yields $16x = 5$, or $x = \dfrac{5}{16}$. The answer is (A).

5. Squaring a fraction between 0 and 1 makes it smaller, and taking the square root of it makes it larger. Hence, Choice (A) is smaller than Choice (B). Choices (C), (D), (E) are all greater than one since 8/7 > 1. The answer is (A).

6. $x\#(-y) = -(-y)^4 = -y^4$. Note: The exponent applies only to the negative inside the parentheses. The answer is (C).

7. $\dfrac{1}{1 - (.2)^2} = \dfrac{1}{1 - .04} = \dfrac{1}{.96} = \dfrac{1}{\frac{96}{100}} = 1 \cdot \dfrac{100}{96} = \dfrac{100}{96} = \dfrac{25}{24}$. The answer is (A).

8. Since x is a fraction between 0 and 1, $\sqrt{x}$ is greater than either x^3 or x^4. It's also greater than $\dfrac{1}{\pi}x$ since $\dfrac{1}{\pi}x$ is less than x. To tell which is greater between $\sqrt{x}$ and $\dfrac{1}{\sqrt{x}}$, let $x = \dfrac{1}{4}$ and plug it into each expression: $\sqrt{x} = \sqrt{\dfrac{1}{4}} = \dfrac{1}{2}$ and $\dfrac{1}{\sqrt{x}} = \dfrac{1}{\sqrt{\frac{1}{4}}} = \dfrac{1}{\frac{1}{2}} = 2$. Hence, $\dfrac{1}{\sqrt{x}}$ is greater than $\sqrt{x}$. The answer is (A).

9. Squaring a fraction between 0 and 1 makes it smaller, and taking the square root of it makes it larger. Therefore, Statement I is true since the top part of the fraction is larger than the bottom. This eliminates (B). Next, Statement II is false. Squaring a fraction makes it smaller only if the fraction is between 0 and 1. This eliminates (C) and (E). Finally, Statement III is false. Since $\dfrac{5}{6} < \sqrt{\dfrac{5}{6}}$, we get

$$\dfrac{\frac{5}{6}}{\sqrt{\frac{5}{6}}} < 1$$

Although taking the square root of this expression will make it larger, it will still be less than 1. The answer is (A).

10. Statement I is not necessarily true. For example, if $x = 2$ and $y = 1$, then $\dfrac{x+2}{y+2} = \dfrac{2+2}{1+2} = \dfrac{4}{3} \ne 2 =$

$\dfrac{2}{1} = \dfrac{x}{y}$. This is also a counterexample to Statement II. Hence, we can eliminate (A), (B), (D), and (E).

Thus, by process of elimination, the answer is (C).

However, it is instructive to prove that Statement III is true. From the expression $x > y > 0$, we get

$$x + 2 > y + 2$$

Since $y + 2 > 0$, dividing both sides of the above expression by $y + 2$ will not reverse the inequality:

$$\frac{x+2}{y+2} > 1$$

Hence, Statement III is necessarily true.

Problem Set F:

1.   The statement *"the remainder is 1 when m is divided by 2"* translates into

$$m = 2u + 1$$

The statement *"the remainder is 3 when n is divided by 4"* translates into

$$n = 4v + 3$$

Forming the sum of m and n gives

$$m + n = 2u + 1 + 4v + 3 = 2u + 4v + 4 = 2(u + 2v + 2)$$

Since we have written $m + n$ as a multiple of 2, it is even. The answer is (C).

Method II (Substitution)
Let $m = 3$ and $n = 7$. Then

$$3 = 2 \cdot 1 + 1$$

and

$$7 = 4 \cdot 1 + 3$$

Now, both 3 and 7 are odd, which eliminates (A) and (B). Further, $3 \cdot 7 = 21$ is odd, which eliminates (D).

Finally, $\dfrac{3}{7}$ is not an integer, which eliminates (E). Hence, by process of elimination, the answer is (C).

2.   Since x and y are prime and greater than 2, xy is the product of two odd numbers and is therefore odd. Hence, 2 cannot be a divisor of xy. The answer is (A).

3.   Since 2 divides evenly into x, we get $x = 2z$. Hence, $5x = 5(2z) = 10z$. In other words, $5x$ is divisible by 10. A similar analysis shows that $5y$ is also divisible by 10. Since 10 is the greatest number listed, the answer is (E).

4.   Let a, $a + 2$, $a + 4$ stand for the consecutive even integers a, b, and c, in that order. Forming the average of a, b, and c yields

$$\frac{a+b+c}{3} = \frac{a+a+2+a+4}{3} = \frac{3a+6}{3} = a+2$$

Setting this less than $\dfrac{1}{3}a$ gives $a + 2 < \dfrac{1}{3}a$

Multiplying by 3 yields $3a + 6 < a$

Subtracting 6 and a from both sides yields $2a < -6$

Dividing by 2 yields $a < -3$

Hence, a is negative, and the best answer is (E).

5. If $x = 1$ and $y = 3$, then

$$y \neq 5x$$

and

$$\frac{x+5}{y} = \frac{1+5}{3} = \frac{6}{3} = 2,$$

which is prime and not odd. Hence, Statements I and III are not necessarily true. Next, let $x = 3$ and $y = 4$. Then y is not prime and

$$\frac{x+5}{y} = \frac{3+5}{4} = \frac{8}{4} = 2,$$

which is prime. Hence, Statement II is not necessarily true. The answer is (A).

6. Since x is both a cube and between 2 and 200, we are looking at the integers:

$$2^3, \ 3^3, \ 4^3, \ 5^3$$

which reduce to

$$8, 27, 64, 125$$

There is only one perfect square, $64 = 8^2$, in this set. The answer is (C).

7. Since the sum of the digits is 4, x must be 13, 22, 31, or 40. Further, since the difference of the digits is 4, x must be 40, 51, 15, 62, 26, 73, 37, 84, 48, 95, or 59. We see that 40 and only 40 is common to the two sets of choices for x. Hence, x must be 40. The answer is (C).

8. First, let's briefly review the concept of division. "Seven divided by 3 leaves a remainder of 1" means that $7 = 3 \cdot 2 + 1$. By analogy, "x divided by y leaves a remainder of 1" means that $x = y \cdot q + 1$, where q is an integer.

Hence, *"p divided by 9 leaves a remainder of 1"* translates into $p = 9 \cdot q + 1$. If $q = 1$, then $p = 10$ which is even. But if $q = 2$, then $p = 19$ which is odd. Hence, neither Statement I nor Statement II need be true. This eliminates (A), (B), (D), and (E). Hence, the answer is (C).

Let's verify that Statement III is true. $p = 9 \cdot q + 1 = 3(3q) + 1 = 3z + 1$, where $z = 3q$.

9. Statement I is true: From *"If p is divided by 2, the remainder is 1,"* $p = 2u + 1$; and from *"if q is divided by 6, the remainder is 1,"* $q = 6v + 1$. Hence, $pq + 1 =$

$$(2u+1)(6v+1) + 1 =$$

$$12uv + 2u + 6v + 1 + 1 =$$

$$12uv + 2u + 6v + 2 =$$

$$2(6uv + u + 3v + 1)$$

Since we have written $pq + 1$ as a multiple of 2, it is even.

Method II

Since p and q each leave a remainder of 1 when divided by an even number, both are odd. Now, the product of two odd numbers is another odd number. Hence, pq is odd, and therefore $pq + 1$ is even.

Now, since $pq + 1$ is even, pq is odd. Hence, $\frac{pq}{2}$ is not an integer, and Statement II is not necessarily true. Next, Statement III is not necessarily true. For example, if $p = 3$ and $q = 7$, then $pq = 21$, which is not a multiple of 12. The answer is (A).

10. Since the question asks for the *smallest* prime greater than 53, we start with the smallest answer-choice. 54 is not prime since 54 = 2(27). 55 is not prime since 55 = 5(11). 57 is not prime since 57 = 3(19). Now, 59 *is* prime. Hence, the answer is (D).

11. $27^5 = \left(3^3\right)^5 = 3^{15}$. Hence, $x = 15$ and the answer is (D).

12. Since x and y are consecutive integers, one of them must be even. Hence, the product xy is even and Statement I is true. As to Statement II, suppose z is odd, then x must be odd as well. Now, the difference of two odd numbers is an even number. Next, suppose z is even, then x must be even as well. Now, the difference of two even numbers is again an even number. Hence, Statement II is true. As to Statement III, let $x = 1$, then $z = 3$ and $x^z = 1^3 = 1$, which is odd. Thus, Statement III is not necessarily true. The answer is (D).

13. Working from the innermost parentheses out, we get

$$-x - 2 = -\left|-(6-2)\right|$$
$$-x - 2 = -\left|-4\right|$$
$$-x - 2 = -(+4)$$
$$-x - 2 = -4$$
$$-x = -2$$
$$x = 2$$

The answer is (D).

14. We are told that the sum of the prime numbers x and y is odd. For a sum of two numbers to be odd, one number must be odd and another even. There is only one even prime number—2; all others are odd. Hence, either x or y must be 2. Thus, the product of x and y is a multiple of 2 and therefore is divisible by 2. The answer is (A).

15. Solution: $\dfrac{x+y}{x-y} = 3$. Multiplying both sides of this equation by $(x-y)$ yields

$$x + y = 3(x - y)$$
$$x + y = 3x - 3y$$
$$-2x = -4y$$
$$x = 2y$$

Since we have expressed x as 2 times an integer, it is even. The answer is (D).

16. Let the original number be represented by xy. (Note: here xy does not denote multiplication, but merely the position of the digits: x first, then y.). Reversing the digits of xy gives yx. We are told that $yx > xy$. This implies that $y > x$. (For example, 73 > 69 because 7 > 6.) If $x = 9$, then the condition $y > x$ cannot be satisfied. Hence, x cannot equal 9. The answer is (E).

Method II:
Let the original number be represented by xy. In expanded form, xy can be written as $10x + y$. For example, 53 = 5(10) + 3. Similarly, $yx = 10y + x$. Since $yx > xy$, we get $10y + x > 10x + y$. Subtracting x and y from both sides of this equation yields $9y > 9x$. Dividing this equation by 9 yields $y > x$. Now, if $x = 9$, then the inequality $y > x$ cannot be satisfied. The answer is (E).

17. Cross multiplying the equation $a/b = b/c$ yields

$$ac = b^2$$

Dividing by a yields $\quad\quad\quad\quad\quad c = b^2/a$

We are given that a is a perfect square. Hence, $a = k^2$, for some number k. Replacing a in the bottom equation with k^2, we get $c = b^2/k^2 = (b/k)^2$. Since we have written c as the square of a number, it is a perfect square. The answer is (C).

18. Observe that n and $(n + 1)$ are consecutive integers. Hence, one of the numbers is even. Therefore, the 2 in the denominator divides evenly into either n or $(n + 1)$, eliminating 2 from the denominator. Thus, S can be reduced to a product of two integers. Remember, a prime number cannot be written as the product of two integers (other than itself and 1). Hence, S is not a prime number, and the answer is (D).

19. The set of numbers greater than 5 and divisible by 5 is {10, 15, 20, 25, 30, 35, . . .}. Since n is odd, the possible values for n are 15, 25, 35, ... Any number in this list, when divided by 10, leaves a remainder of 5. The answer is (C).

20. A number divisible by all three numbers 2, 3, and 4 is also divisible by 12. Hence, each number can be written as a multiple of 12. Let the first number be represented as $12a$ and the second number as $12b$. Assuming $a > b$, the difference between the two numbers is $12a - 12b = 12(a - b)$. Observe that this number is also a multiple of 12. Hence, the answer must also be divisible by 12. Since 72 is the only answer-choice divisible by 12, the answer is (B).

21. We are told that the remainder is 7 when the number is divided by 12. Hence, we can represent the number as $12x + 7$. Now, 7 can be written as $6 + 1$. Plugging this into the expression yields

$$
\begin{array}{ll}
12x + (6 + 1) = & \\
(12x + 6) + 1 = & \text{by regrouping} \\
6(2x + 1) + 1 & \text{by factoring 6 out of the first two terms}
\end{array}
$$

This shows that the remainder is 1 when the expression $12x + 7$ is divided by 6. The answer is (A).

Method II (Substitution):
Choose the number 19, which gives a remainder of 7 when divided by 12. Now, divide 19 by 6:

$$\frac{19}{6} =$$

$$3\frac{1}{6}$$

This shows that 6 divides into 19 with a remainder of 1. The answer is (A).

22. Let's take a two-digit number whose digits add up to 9, say, 72. Adding 10 to this number gives 82. The sum of the digits of this number is 10. Now, let's choose another two-digit number whose digits add up to 9, say, 90. Then $x + 10 = 90 + 10 = 100$. The sum of the digits of this number is 1. Hence, the sum of the numbers is either 1 or 10. The answer is (E).

23. Observe that all the digits of the dividend 39693 are divisible by 3. So 3 will divide the dividend into such a number that each of its digits will be 1/3 the corresponding digit in the dividend (i.e., 39693). For example, the third digit in the dividend is 6, and hence the third digit in the quotient will be 2, which is 1/3 of 6. Applying the same process to all digits gives the quotient 13231. The answer is (B).

24. In the ordered set of integers from 1 through 999, every third integer is a multiple of 3. Hence, the number of integers in this set of 999 integers that are multiples of 3 is 999/3 = 333. The answer is (B).

25. . Suppose $n = 1$. Then $n^3 = 1^3 = 1$, which is odd. Now, we plug this value for n into each of the answer-choices to see which ones are even. Thus, $2n^2 + 1$ becomes $2(1)^2 + 1 = 3$, which is not even. So eliminate (A). Next, $n^4 = 1^4 = 1$ is not even—eliminate (B). Next, $n^2 + 1 = 1^2 + 1 = 2$ is even, so the answer is possibly (C). Next, $n(n + 2) = 1(1 + 2) = 3$ is not even—eliminate (D). Finally, $n = 1$, which is not even—eliminate (E). Hence, by the process of elimination, the answer is (C).

26. If the product of the two numbers is odd, then each number in the product must be odd. Recall that the sum of two odd numbers is an even number. The answer is (B).

27. Suppose the odd number n is added to itself an odd number of times, say m times. The result would be mn, which is the product of two odd numbers. Recall that the product of two odd numbers is odd. The answer is (A).

28. Let the three consecutive integers be x, $x + 1$, and $x + 2$. The sum of these integers is $3x + 3$. According to the question, this sum is odd. Hence $3x + 3$ is odd. Recall that if the sum of two integers is odd, then one of the integers is odd and the other one is even. Since 3 in the expression $3x + 3$ is odd, $3x$ must be even. Now, recall that the product of two numbers is odd only when one of the numbers is odd and the other is even. So x must be even. If x is an even number, then $x + 2$ is also even. Thus, the first and the last integers must both be even. The answer is (D).

29. We are given that l, m, and n are three positive integers such that $l < m < n$. This implies that l, m, and n are each greater than zero and not equal to each other. Since n is less than 4, the numbers l, m, and n must have the values 1, 2, and 3, respectively. Hence, the answer is (C).

30. Dividing both sides of the equation $p = 4q$ by 4, we get $q = p/4$. We are also given that $p < 8$. Dividing both sides of this inequality by 4 yields, $p/4 < 8/4$. Simplifying it, we get $p/4 < 2$. But $q = p/4$. Hence, $q < 2$. The only non-zero positive integer less than 2 is 1. Hence, $q = 1$. The answer is (A).

31. Answer-choice (C) consists of the product of two consecutive integers. Now, of any two consecutive integers, one of the integers must be even. Hence, their product must be even. The answer is (C).

32. Since $pq/2$ is prime, it is an integer. Hence, either p or q must be even; otherwise, the 2 would not cancel and $pq/2$ would be a fraction. The only even prime number is 2. Hence, either p or q, but not both, must be 2. The other one is an odd prime number. Now, the sum of an even number and an odd number is an odd number. The answer is (A).

33. Let the three consecutive positive integers be n, $n + 1$, and $n + 2$. The sum of these three positive integers is

$$n + (n + 1) + (n + 2) =$$
$$3n + 3 =$$
$$3(n + 1)$$

Since we have written the sum as a multiple of 3, it is divisible by 3. The answer is (B).

Problem Set G:

1. In the figure to the right, what is the value of y ?

    (A) $\sqrt{23}$
    (B) $\sqrt{27}$
    (C) $\sqrt{29}$
    (D) $\sqrt{33}$
    (E) $\sqrt{35}$

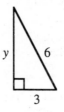

Since we have a right triangle, the Pythagorean Theorem yields $\quad\quad y^2 + 3^2 = 6^2$

Simplifying yields $\quad\quad y^2 + 9 = 36$

Subtracting 9 from both sides yields $\quad\quad y^2 = 27$

Taking the square root of both sides yields $\quad\quad y = \sqrt{27}$

The answer is (B).

2. In the figure to the right, circle P has diameter 2 and circle Q has diameter 1. What is the area of the shaded region?

    (A) $\dfrac{3}{4}\pi$
    (B) 3π
    (C) $\dfrac{7}{2}\pi$
    (D) 5π
    (E) 6π

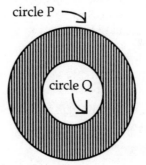

Since the diameter of circle P is 2, its radius is 1. So the area of circle P is $\pi(1)^2 = \pi$. Since the diameter of circle Q is 1, its radius is $\dfrac{1}{2}$. So the area of circle Q is $\pi\left(\dfrac{1}{2}\right)^2 = \dfrac{1}{4}\pi$. The area of the shaded region is the difference between the area of circle P and the area of circle Q: $\pi - \dfrac{1}{4}\pi = \dfrac{3}{4}\pi$. The answer is (A).

3. In the figure to the right, QRST is a square. If the shaded region is bounded by arcs of circles with centers at Q, R, S, and T, then the area of the shaded region is

    (A) 9
    (B) 36
    (C) $36 - 9\pi$
    (D) $36 - \pi$
    (E) $9 - 3\pi$

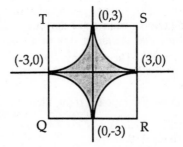

Each arc forms a quarter of a circle. Taken together the four arcs constitute one whole circle. From the drawing, we see that the radii of the arcs are each length 3, so the area of the four arcs together is $\pi(3)^2 = 9\pi$. Since the square has sides of length 6, its area is 36. Hence, the area of the shaded region is $36 - 9\pi$. The answer is (C).

4.   In the figure to the right, QRST is a square. If the area of each circle is 2π, then the area of square QRST is

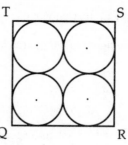

   (A) $\sqrt{2}$
   (B)   4
   (C) $\sqrt{2}\pi$
   (D) $4\sqrt{2}$
   (E)   32

Setting the area of a circle equal to 2π gives $\pi r^2 = 2\pi$

Dividing both sides of this equation by π gives $r^2 = 2$

Taking the square root of both sides gives $r = \sqrt{2}$

Hence, the diameter of each circle is $d = 2r = 2\sqrt{2}$

Adding the diameters to the diagram gives

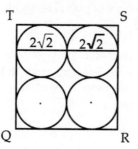

Clearly, in this diagram, the sides of the square are length $2\sqrt{2} + 2\sqrt{2} = 4\sqrt{2}$. Hence, the area of the square is $4\sqrt{2} \cdot 4\sqrt{2} = 16 \cdot 2 = 32$. The answer is (E).

5.   In the figure to the right, if O is the center of the circle, then $y =$

   (A)   75
   (B)   76
   (C)   77
   (D)   78
   (E)   79

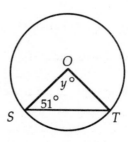

OS and *OT* are equal since they are radii of the circle. Hence, ΔSOT is isosceles. Therefore, $S = T = 51°$. Recalling that the angle sum of a triangle is 180°, we get $S + T + y = 51° + 51° + y = 180°$. Solving for y gives $y = 78°$. The answer is (D).

6.   In the figure to the right, the value of $a + b$ is

   (A)   118
   (B)   119
   (C)   120
   (D)   121
   (E)   122

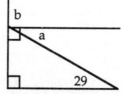

Since the two horizontal lines are parallel (Why?), angle a and the angle with measure 29 are alternate interior angles and therefore are equal. Further, from the drawing, angle b is 90°. Hence, $a + b = 29 + 90 = 119$. The answer is (B).

7. If $l_1 \| l_2$ in the figure to the right, what is the value of x?

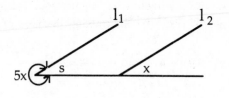

    (A)   30
    (B)   45
    (C)   60
    (D)   72
    (E)   90

Since $l_1 \| l_2$, s and x are corresponding angles and therefore are congruent.

Now, about any point there are 360°. Hence,	$5x + s = 360$
Substituting x for s in this equation gives	$5x + x = 360$
Combining like terms gives	$6x = 360$
Dividing by 6 gives	$x = 60$

The answer is (C).

8. In the figure to the right, O is the center of the circle. Which one of the following must be true?

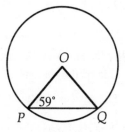

    (A)   PQ > OQ
    (B)   OP ≥ OQ
    (C)   PQ = OQ
    (D)   OQ < OP
    (E)   PQ ≤ OP

$\triangle OPQ$ is isosceles. (Why?). Hence, $P = Q = 59°$. Now, the angle sum of a triangle is 180. So

$$O + P + Q = 180.$$

Substituting $P = Q = 59°$ into this equation gives	$O + 59 + 59 = 180.$
Solving for O gives	$O = 62.$

Now, since O is the largest angle in $\triangle OPQ$, the side opposite it, PQ, is the longest side of the triangle. The answer is (A).

9. In the figure to the right, x is both the radius of the larger circle and the diameter of the smaller circle. The area of the shaded region is

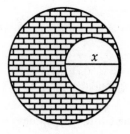

    (A) $\dfrac{3}{4}\pi x^2$

    (B) $\dfrac{\pi}{3}$

    (C) $\dfrac{4}{3}\pi x^2$

    (D) $\dfrac{3}{5}\pi x^2$

    (E) πx^2

Since x is the radius of the larger circle, the area of the larger circle is πx^2. Since x is the diameter of the smaller circle, the radius of the smaller circle is $\dfrac{x}{2}$. Therefore, the area of the smaller circle is

$\pi\left(\dfrac{x}{2}\right)^2 = \pi\dfrac{x^2}{4}$. Subtracting the area of the smaller circle from the area of the larger circle gives

$\pi x^2 - \pi\dfrac{x^2}{4} = \dfrac{4}{4}\pi x^2 - \pi\dfrac{x^2}{4} = \dfrac{4\pi x^2 - \pi x^2}{4} = \dfrac{3\pi x^2}{4}$. The answer is (A).

10. In the figure to the right, the circle with center O is inscribed in the square PQRS. The combined area of the shaded regions is

   (A) $36 - 9\pi$
   (B) $36 - \dfrac{9}{2}\pi$
   (C) $\dfrac{36 - 9\pi}{2}$
   (D) $18 - 9\pi$
   (E) $9 - \dfrac{9}{4}\pi$

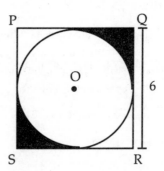

The area of square PQRS is $6^2 = 36$. Now, the radius of the circle is 3. (Why?) So the area of the circle is $\pi(3)^2 = 9\pi$. Subtracting the area of the circle from the area of the square yields $36 - 9\pi$. This is the combined area of the regions outside the circle and inside the square. Dividing this quantity by 2 gives $\dfrac{36 - 9\pi}{2}$. The answer is (C).

11. In the figure to the right, the length of QS is

   (A) $\sqrt{51}$
   (B) $\sqrt{61}$
   (C) $\sqrt{69}$
   (D) $\sqrt{77}$
   (E) $\sqrt{89}$

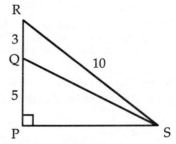

The length of *PR* is $PR = 3 + 5 = 8$. Applying the Pythagorean Theorem to triangle *PRS* yields

$$8^2 + (PS)^2 = 10^2$$

Squaring yields

$$64 + (PS)^2 = 100$$

Subtracting 64 from both sides yields

$$(PS)^2 = 36$$

Taking the square root of both sides yields

$$PS = \sqrt{36} = 6$$

Now, applying the Pythagorean Theorem to triangle *PQS* yields

$$(QS)^2 = 5^2 + 6^2$$

Squaring and adding yields

$$(QS)^2 = 61$$

Taking the square root of both sides yields

$$QS = \sqrt{61}$$

The answer is (B).

12. In the figure to the right, which one of the following must be true about y ?

    (A) $y > 37$
    (B) $y < 35$
    (C) $y > 40$
    (D) $y > 42$
    (E) $y > 45$

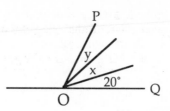

$\angle\, POQ = 70°$ and $x > 15$

Since $\angle\, POQ = 70°$, we get $x + y + 20 = 70$. Solving this equation for y yields $y = 50 - x$. Now, we are given that $x > 15$. Hence, the expression $50 - x$ must be less than 35:

$$x > 15$$
$$-x < -15$$
$$50 - x < 50 - 15$$
$$50 - x < 35$$

The answer is (B).

13. In the figure to the right, if $l \| k$, then what is the value of y ?

    (A)   20
    (B)   45
    (C)   55
    (D)   75
    (E)   110

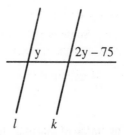

Since lines l and k are parallel, we know that the corresponding angles are equal. Hence, $y = 2y - 75$. Solving this equation for y gives $y = 75$. The answer is (D).

14. In the figure to the right, both triangles are right triangles. The area of the shaded region is

    (A)   1/2
    (B)   2/3
    (C)   7/8
    (D)   3/2
    (E)   5/2

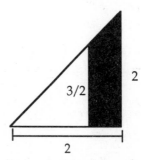

Since the height and base of the larger triangle are the same, the slope of the hypotenuse is 45°. Hence, the base of the smaller triangle is the same as its height, $\dfrac{3}{2}$. Thus, the area of the shaded region = (area of the larger triangle) – (area of the smaller triangle) = $\left(\dfrac{1}{2} \cdot 2 \cdot 2 \right) - \left(\dfrac{1}{2} \cdot \dfrac{3}{2} \cdot \dfrac{3}{2} \right) = 2 - \dfrac{9}{8} = \dfrac{7}{8}$. The answer is (C).

15. In the figure to the right, the radius of the larger circle is twice that of the smaller circle. If the circles are concentric, what is the ratio of the shaded region's area to the area of the smaller circle?

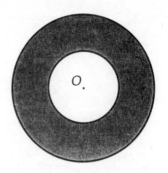

(A) 10:1
(B) 9:1
(C) 3:1
(D) 2:1
(E) 1:1

Suppose the radius of the larger circle is 2 and the radius of the smaller circle is 1. Then the area of the larger circle is $\pi r^2 = \pi(2)^2 = 4\pi$, and the area of the smaller circle is $\pi r^2 = \pi(1)^2 = \pi$. Hence, the area of the shaded region is $4\pi - \pi = 3\pi$. Now, $\dfrac{area\ of\ shaded\ region}{area\ of\ smaller\ circle} = \dfrac{3\pi}{\pi} = \dfrac{3}{1}$. The answer is (C).

16. In the figure to the right, ΔPST is an isosceles right triangle, and $PS = 2$. What is the area of the shaded region URST?

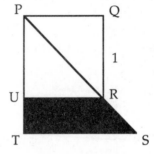

(A) 4
(B) 2
(C) 5/4
(D) 5/6
(E) 1/2

Let x stand for the distances TP and TS. Applying the Pythagorean Theorem to the right triangle PST gives

$$TP^2 + TS^2 = PS^2$$

Substituting x for TP and TS and substituting 2 for PS gives

$$x^2 + x^2 = 2^2$$

Squaring and combining like terms gives

$$2x^2 = 4$$

Dividing by 2 gives

$$x^2 = 2$$

Finally, taking the square root gives

$$x = \sqrt{2}$$

Adding this information to the diagram gives

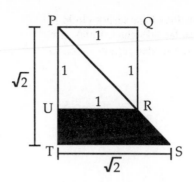

Now, the area of the shaded region equals *(area of triangle PST) – (area of triangle PRU)* = $\left(\dfrac{1}{2}\cdot\sqrt{2}\cdot\sqrt{2}\right)-\left(\dfrac{1}{2}\cdot1\cdot1\right)=\left(\dfrac{1}{2}\cdot2\right)-\left(\dfrac{1}{2}\right)=1-\dfrac{1}{2}=\dfrac{1}{2}$. The answer is (E).

17. In the figure to the right, the area of $\triangle PQR$ is 40. What is the area of $\triangle QRS$?

    (A) 10
    (B) 15
    (C) 20
    (D) 25
    (E) 45

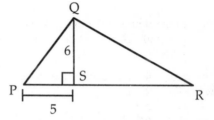

The area of triangle PQS is $\dfrac{1}{2}\cdot5\cdot6=15$. Now, (the area of $\triangle QRS$) = (the area of $\triangle PQR$) – (the area of $\triangle PQS$) = 40 – 15 = 25. The answer is (D).

18. In the figure to the right, PQRS is a square and M and N are midpoints of their respective sides. What is the area of quadrilateral PMRN?

    (A) 8
    (B) 10
    (C) 12
    (D) 14
    (E) 16

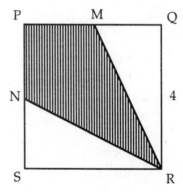

Since M is the midpoint of side PQ, the length of MQ is 2. Hence, the area of triangle MQR is $\dfrac{1}{2}\cdot2\cdot4=4$.

A similar analysis shows that the area of triangle NSR is 4. Thus, the unshaded area of the figure is 4 + 4 = 8. Subtracting this from the area of the square gives 16 – 8 = 8. The answer is (A).

19. In the figure to the right, O is the center of the circle. If the area of the circle is 9π, then the perimeter of the sector *PRQO* is

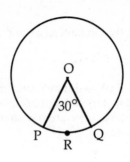

(A) $\dfrac{\pi}{2} - 6$

(B) $\dfrac{\pi}{2} + 6$

(C) $\dfrac{3}{4}\pi + 6$

(D) $\dfrac{\pi}{2} + 18$

(E) $\dfrac{3}{4}\pi + 18$

Since the area of the circle is 9π, we get

$$\pi r^2 = 9\pi$$
$$r^2 = 9$$
$$r = 3$$

Now, the circumference of the circle is

$$C = 2\pi r = 2\pi 3 = 6\pi$$

Since the central angle is 30°, the length of arc PRQ is

$$\frac{30}{360}C = \frac{1}{12} \cdot 6\pi = \frac{1}{2}\pi$$

Hence, the perimeter of the sector is

$$\frac{1}{2}\pi + 3 + 3 = \frac{1}{2}\pi + 6$$

The answer is (B).

20. Let A denote the area of a circular region. Which of the following denotes the circumference of that circular region?

(A) $\sqrt{\dfrac{A}{\pi}}$

(B) $2\dfrac{A}{\sqrt{\pi}}$

(C) $2\pi\sqrt{A}$

(D) $2\sqrt{\dfrac{A}{\pi}}$

(E) $2\pi\sqrt{\dfrac{A}{\pi}}$

Since A denotes the area of the circular region, we get

$$A = \pi r^2$$
$$\frac{A}{\pi} = r^2$$
$$\sqrt{\frac{A}{\pi}} = r$$

Hence, the circumference is $C = 2\pi r = 2\pi\sqrt{\dfrac{A}{\pi}}$

The answer is (E).

21. Ship X and ship Y are 5 miles apart and are on a collision course. Ship X is sailing directly north, and ship Y is sailing directly east. If the point of impact is 1 mile closer to the current position of ship X than to the current position of ship Y, how many miles away from the point of impact is ship Y at this time?

  (A) 1
  (B) 2
  (C) 3
  (D) 4
  (E) 5

Let d be the distance ship Y is from the point of collision. Then the distance ship X is from the point of collision is d – 1. The following diagram depicts the situation:

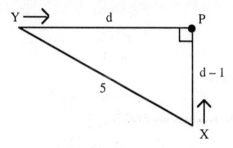

Applying the Pythagorean Theorem to the diagram yields

$$d^2 + (d-1)^2 = 5^2$$

$$d^2 + d^2 - 2d + 1 = 25$$

$$2d^2 - 2d - 24 = 0$$

$$d^2 - d - 12 = 0$$

$$(d-4)(d+3) = 0$$

$$d = 4 \quad \text{or} \quad d = -3$$

Since *d* denotes distance, we reject $d = -3$. Hence, $d = 4$ and the answer is (D).

22. The figure to the right represents a square with sides of length 4 surmounted by a circle with center *O*. What is the outer perimeter of the figure?

  (A) $\dfrac{5}{6}\pi + 12$

  (B) $\pi + 12$

  (C) $\dfrac{49}{9}\pi + 12$

  (D) $\dfrac{20}{3}\pi + 12$

  (E) $9\pi + 12$

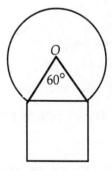

Since two sides of the triangle are radii of the circle, they are equal. Hence, the triangle is isosceles, and the base angles are equal:

Since the angle sum of a triangle is 180, we get

$$x + x + 60 = 180$$

$$2x = 120$$

$$x = 60$$

Hence, the triangle is equilateral. Therefore, the radius of the circle is 4, and the circumference is $C = 2\pi r = 2\pi 4 = 8\pi$. Now, the portion of the perimeter formed by the circle has length $\dfrac{360 - 60}{360} \cdot C = \dfrac{5}{6} \cdot 8\pi = \dfrac{20}{3}\pi$. Adding the three sides of the square to this expression gives $\dfrac{20}{3}\pi + 12$. The answer is (D).

23. In $\triangle ABC$ to the right, $AB = AC$ and $x = 30$. What is the value of y?
    (A)   30
    (B)   40
    (C)   50
    (D)   65
    (E)   75

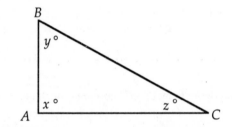

Note, figure not drawn to scale.

Since $AB = AC$, $\triangle ABC$ is isosceles. Hence, its base angles are equal: $y = z$. Since the angle sum of a triangle is 180°, we get $x + y + z = 180$. Replacing z with y and x with 30 in this equation and then simplifying yields

$$30 + y + y = 180$$
$$30 + 2y = 180$$
$$2y = 150$$
$$y = 75$$

The answer is (E).

24. In the figure to the right, $c^2 = 6^2 + 8^2$. What is the area of the triangle?

    (A)   12
    (B)   18
    (C)   24
    (D)   30
    (E)   36

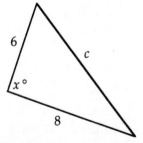

Recall that a triangle is a right triangle if and only if the square of the longest side is equal to the sum of the squares of the shorter sides (Pythagorean Theorem). Hence, $c^2 = 6^2 + 8^2$ implies that the triangle is a right triangle. So the area of the triangle is $\dfrac{1}{2} \cdot 6 \cdot 8 = 24$. The answer is (C).

25. If the total surface area of cube S is 22, what is the volume of S?

(A) $\dfrac{1}{3}\sqrt{\dfrac{11}{3}}$

(B) $\dfrac{\sqrt{11}}{3}$

(C) $\dfrac{11}{3}$

(D) $\dfrac{11}{3}\sqrt{\dfrac{11}{3}}$

(E) $\dfrac{121}{9}$

Since the total surface area of the cube is 22 and each of the cube's six faces has the same area, the area of each face is $\dfrac{22}{6}$, or $\dfrac{11}{3}$. Now, each face of the cube is a square with area $\dfrac{11}{3}$, so the length of a side of the cube is $\sqrt{\dfrac{11}{3}}$. Hence, the volume of the cube is $\sqrt{\dfrac{11}{3}}\cdot\sqrt{\dfrac{11}{3}}\cdot\sqrt{\dfrac{11}{3}}=\dfrac{11}{3}\cdot\sqrt{\dfrac{11}{3}}$. The answer is (D).

26. In the figure to the right, what is the area of the triangle?

(A) 5
(B) 9
(C) 10
(D) 15
(E) It cannot be determined from the information given

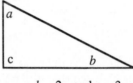

$a = x$, $b = 2x$, and $c = 3x$.

From the information given, we can determine the measures of the angles:

$$a + b + c = x + 2x + 3x = 6x = 180$$

Dividing the last equation by 6 gives

$$x = 30$$

Hence, $a = 30$, $b = 60$, and $c = 90$. However, different size triangles can have these angle measures, as the diagram below illustrates:

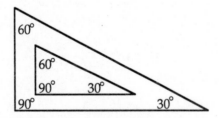

Hence, the information given is not sufficient to determine the area of the triangle. The answer is (E).

27. In the figure to the right, $\triangle ABC$ is inscribed in the circle and AB is a diameter of the circle. What is the radius of the circle?

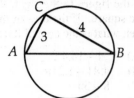

   (A)   3/2
   (B)   2
   (C)   5/2
   (D)   5
   (E)   6

Recall from geometry that a triangle inscribed in a semicircle is a right triangle. Hence, we can use the Pythagorean Theorem to calculate the length of AB:

$$AC^2 + BC^2 = AB^2$$

or

$$3^2 + 4^2 = AB^2$$

or

$$25 = AB^2$$

or

$$5 = AB$$

Hence, the radius of the circle is $\dfrac{diameter}{2} = \dfrac{5}{2}$. The answer is (C).

28. In the figure to the right, the circle is inscribed in the square. If the area of the square is 16 square feet, what is the area of the shaded region?

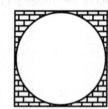

   (A) $16 - 16\pi$
   (B) $16 - 4.4\pi$
   (C) $16 - 4\pi$
   (D) 2π
   (E) 4π

Since the area of the square is 16, the length of a side is

$$\sqrt{16} = 4$$

Since the circle is inscribed in the square, a diameter of the circle has the same length as a side of the square. Hence, the radius of the circle is

$$\frac{diameter}{2} = \frac{4}{2} = 2$$

Therefore, the area of the circle is

$$\pi \cdot 2^2 = 4\pi$$

and the area of the shaded region is

$$16 - 4\pi$$

The answer is (C).

29. In the figure to the right, the circle is inscribed in the square. If the area of the circle is 1.21π square feet, what is the area of the shaded region?

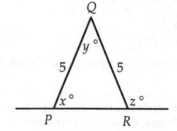

(A) $14 - 14.4\pi$
(B) $4.84 - 1.21\pi$
(C) $8 - 3\pi$
(D) 1.21π
(E) $\dfrac{11}{2}\pi$

Since the area of the circle is 1.21π, we get

$$\pi r^2 = 1.21\pi$$

Dividing by π yields

$$r^2 = 1.21$$

Taking the square root of both sides gives

$$r = 1.1$$

So the diameter of the circle is

$$d = 2r = 2(1.1) = 2.2$$

Hence, a side of the square has length 2.2, and the area of the square is

$$(2.2)^2 = 4.84$$

Therefore, the area of the shaded region is

$$4.84 - 1.21\pi$$

The answer is (B).

30. In $\triangle PQR$ to the right, $x = 60$. What is the value of y?

(A) 60
(B) 55
(C) 50
(D) 45
(E) 40

Since $\triangle PQR$ is isosceles, its base angles are equal:

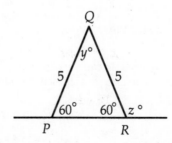

Remembering that the angle sum of a triangle is $180°$, we see y is also $60°$. The answer is (A).

31. In $\triangle PQR$ to the right, $y + z = 150$. What is the
     value of y?

     (A)   60
     (B)   55
     (C)   50
     (D)   45
     (E)   40

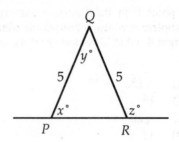

Again since the base angles of an isosceles triangle are equal, the diagram becomes

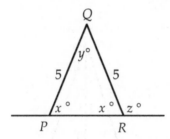

Since x and z form a straight angle, $x + z = 180$. Hence, we have the system:

$$x + z = 180$$
$$y + z = 150$$

Subtracting these equations yields $x - y = 30$. Since there are two variables and only one equation, we need another equation in order to determine y. However, since the angle sum of a triangle is $180°$, $x + x + y = 180$, or $2x + y = 180$. This yields the system:

$$x - y = 30$$
$$2x + y = 180$$

Adding the equations gives $3x = 210$. Hence, $x = 70$. Plugging this value for x back into either equation gives $y = 40$. The answer is (E).

32. In the figure to the right, what is the area of the
     triangle?

     (A)   5
     (B)   9
     (C)   10
     (D)   15
     (E)   It cannot be determined from the information
           given

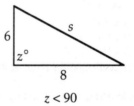

Since we do not know the value of z, the triangle can vary in size. Each of the triangles illustrated below satisfies the given information, yet one has an area greater than the other:

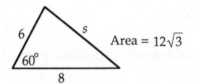

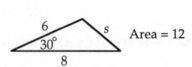

The answer is (E).

33. If point P in the figure to the right makes one complete revolution around the triangle which has height 4, what is the length of the path traveled by P?

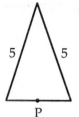

(A) $\sqrt{150}$
(B)   14
(C) $\sqrt{200}$
(D)   15
(E)   16

Add the height to the diagram:

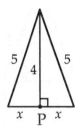

Applying the Pythagorean Theorem to either of the right triangles formed above yields

$$x^2 + 4^2 = 5^2$$

Solving for x yields

$$x = 3$$

Hence, the base of the triangle is $2x = 2(3) = 6$, and therefore the perimeter is $5 + 5 + 6 = 16$. The answer is (E).

34. The opposite sides of quadrilateral Q are parallel and one of the four angles of Q is 90 degrees. If θ is an angle of quadrilateral Q, which one of the following must be true?

(A) $\theta = 80°$
(B) $\theta = 88°$
(C) $\theta = 90°$
(D) $\theta = 91°$
(E)   It cannot be determined from the information given

Note, a quadrilateral is a closed figure formed by four straight lines. Now, the given information generates the following diagram:

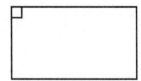

Here, our goal is to show that the other three angles are also 90 degrees. It will help to extend the sides as follows:

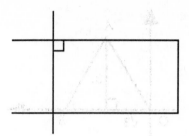

Since corresponding angles are congruent, we get

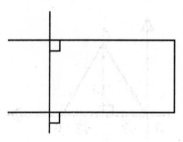

Or

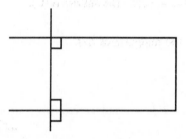

Continuing in this manner will show that the other two angles are also 90 degrees. Hence, θ is 90°. The answer is (C).

35.   In the figure to the right, the coordinates of A are $(\sqrt{3}, 3)$. If $\triangle ABO$ is equilateral, what is the area of $\triangle ABO$?

(A) $\dfrac{1}{2}\sqrt{3}$

(B) $\dfrac{3}{2}\sqrt{3}$

(C) $3\sqrt{3}$

(D) $6\sqrt{3}$

(E) $9\sqrt{3}$

Since the coordinates of A are $(\sqrt{3}, 3)$, the diagram becomes

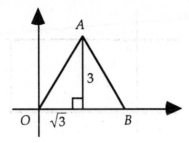

Further, since $\triangle ABO$ is equilateral, the diagram becomes

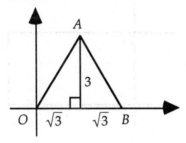

Hence, the area is $\dfrac{1}{2} \cdot b \cdot h = \dfrac{1}{2} \cdot 2\sqrt{3} \cdot 3 = 3\sqrt{3}$. The answer is (C).

36. In the figure to the right, E is the midpoint of AD.
What is the length of EB?

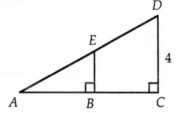

(A) 1
(B) 2
(C) 11/5
(D) 5/2
(E) 3

Recall from geometry that if two angles of one triangle are equal to two angles of another triangle then the triangles are similar. Hence, $\triangle ACD$ is similar to $\triangle ABE$ since they share angle A and both are right triangles.

Since E is the midpoint of AD, the diagram becomes

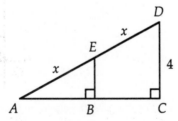

Since $\triangle ABE$ and $\triangle ACD$ are similar, their corresponding sides are proportional:

$$\frac{EB}{EA} = \frac{DC}{DA}$$

or

$$\frac{EB}{x} = \frac{4}{2x}$$

Solving for EB yields

$$EB = 2$$

The answer is (B).

37.   If the sides x of the rectangle to the right are
      increased by 3 units, the resulting figure is a square
      with area 20. What was the original area?

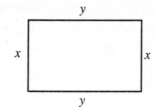

(A) $20 - 3\sqrt{20}$
(B) $20 - 2\sqrt{20}$
(C) $20 - \sqrt{20}$
(D) $20 - \sqrt{2}$
(E)   19

The area of the original rectangle is $A = xy$. So the goal in this problem is to find the values of x and y.

Lengthening side x of the original figure by 3 units yields

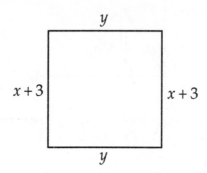

The area of this figure is $y(x + 3) = 20$. Since the resulting figure is a square, $y = x + 3$. Hence, we have the system:

$$y(x + 3) = 20$$
$$y = x + 3$$

Solving this system gives $x = \sqrt{20} - 3$ and $y = \sqrt{20}$. Hence, the area is $A = xy = \left(\sqrt{20} - 3\right)\left(\sqrt{20}\right) =$

$20 - 3\sqrt{20}$. The answer is (A).

38.   In the figure to the right, h denotes the height and b
      the base of the triangle. If $2b + h = 6$, what is the
      area of the triangle?

(A)   1
(B)   2
(C)   3
(D)   4
(E)   Not enough information

The area of a triangle is $\dfrac{1}{2} base \times height$. For the given triangle, this becomes

$$Area = \frac{1}{2}b \times h$$

Solving the equation $2b + h = 6$ for h gives $h = 6 - 2b$. Plugging this into the area formula gives

$$Area = \frac{1}{2}b(6 - 2b)$$

Since the value of b is not given, we cannot determine the area. Hence, there is not enough information, and the answer is (E).

39. In the figure to the right, h denotes the height and b the base of the triangle. If $(bh)^2 = 16$, what is the area of the triangle?

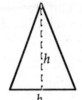

(A) 1
(B) 2
(C) 3
(D) 4
(E) Not enough information

Taking the square root of both sides of the equation $(bh)^2 = 16$ gives

$$bh = 4$$

Plugging this into the area formula gives

$$Area = \frac{1}{2} \cdot b \cdot h = \frac{1}{2} \cdot 4 = 2$$

Hence, the answer is (B).

40. If the ratio of an edge of cube S and the greatest distance between two points on the cube is $1:\sqrt{3}$, then the volume of cube S must be

(A) greater than 8
(B) less than 8
(C) equal to 8
(D) greater than or equal to 8
(E) Not enough information

There is not enough information to decide since different size cubes can have the ratio $1:\sqrt{3}$:

Ratio: $\dfrac{2}{2\sqrt{3}} = \dfrac{1}{\sqrt{3}}$

Ratio: $\dfrac{1}{\sqrt{3}}$

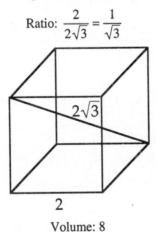

Volume: 8

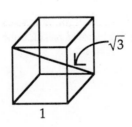

Volume: 1

The answer is (E).

41. If the length of a diagonal across a face of cube S is 2, then the volume of cube S must be

(A) greater than 8
(B) less than 8
(C) equal to 8
(D) greater than or equal to 8
(E) Not enough information to decide

A diagram illustrating the situation is shown below:

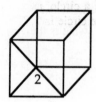

Looking at the face in isolation gives

Applying the Pythagorean Theorem to this diagram gives

$$x^2 + x^2 = 2^2$$

$$2x^2 = 4$$

$$x^2 = 2$$

$$x = \sqrt{2}$$

Hence, the volume of the cube is $V = x^3 = \left(\sqrt{2}\right)^3 < 8$. The answer is (B).

42. In the parallelogram to the right, $\angle BAD + \angle BCD = 140$. What is the measure of $\angle ABC$?

(A) 100
(B) 110
(C) 120
(D) 125
(E) 142

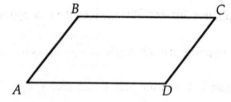

Since opposite angles of a parallelogram are equal, $\angle ABC = \angle ADC$. Further, since there are $360°$ in a parallelogram,

$$\angle ABC + \angle ADC + \angle BAD + \angle BCD = 360$$

$$\angle ABC + \angle ADC + 140 = 360$$

$$\angle ABC + \angle ABC = 220$$

$$2\angle ABC = 220$$

$$\angle ABC = 110$$

The answer is (B).

43. An equilateral triangle is inscribed in a circle, as shown to the right. If the radius of the circle is 2, what is the area of the triangle?

(A) $\dfrac{\sqrt{2}}{2}$

(B) $\sqrt{2}$

(C) $\sqrt{3}$

(D) $3\sqrt{3}$

(E) $10\sqrt{3}$

Adding radii to the diagram yields

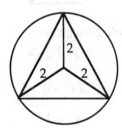

Now, viewing the bottom triangle in isolation yields

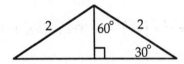

Recall, in a 30°–60°–90° triangle, the side opposite the 30° angle is $\dfrac{1}{2}$ the length of the hypotenuse, and the

side opposite the 60° angle is $\dfrac{\sqrt{3}}{2}$ times the length of the hypotenuse. Hence, the altitude of the above

triangle is 1, and the base is $\sqrt{3}+\sqrt{3}=2\sqrt{3}$. Thus, the area of the triangle is $A=\dfrac{1}{2}\cdot 2\sqrt{3}\cdot 1=\sqrt{3}$. By

symmetry, the area of the inscribed triangle is $3A=3\sqrt{3}$. The answer is (D).

44. The triangle to the right has side DC of the square as its base. If $DM = 5$ and M is the midpoint of side AB, what is the area of the shaded region?

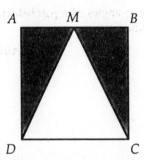

(A) $\dfrac{5}{2}$

(B) $\sqrt{10}$

(C) $\sqrt{15}$

(D) 4

(E) 10

Adding the given information to the diagram gives

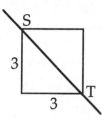

Applying the Pythagorean Theorem yields

$$x^2 + (2x)^2 = 5^2$$

$$x^2 + 4x^2 = 5^2$$

$$5x^2 = 5^2$$

$$x^2 = 5$$

$$x = \sqrt{5}$$

Hence, the area of the square is $2x \cdot 2x = 2\sqrt{5} \cdot 2\sqrt{5} = 20$. Since the height of the unshaded triangle is the same as the length of a side of the square, the area of the triangle is

$$A = \frac{1}{2}\left(2\sqrt{5}\right)\left(2\sqrt{5}\right) = 10$$

Subtracting this from the area of the square gives

$$20 - 10 = 10$$

The answer is (E).

45. A square with sides of length 3 is intersected by a line at S and T. What is the maximum possible distance between S and T?

(A) $\sqrt{6}$ (B) $2\sqrt{3}$ (C) $3\sqrt{2}$ (D) $2\sqrt{5}$ (E) 9

The maximum possible distance between S and T will occur when the line intersects the square at opposite vertices:

Hence, the maximum distance is the length of the diagonal of the square. Applying the Pythagorean Theorem yields

$$ST^2 = 3^2 + 3^2$$

$$ST^2 = 18$$

$$ST = \sqrt{18} = 3\sqrt{2}$$

The answer is (C).

46. In the triangle to the right, what is the value of
     $\dfrac{x+y+z}{15}$?

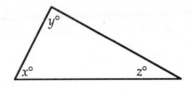

(A)   9
(B)   10
(C)   11
(D)   12
(E)   13

Since the angle sum of a triangle is 180°, $x + y + z = 180$. Plugging this into the expression $\dfrac{x+y+z}{15}$ yields

$$\frac{x+y+z}{15} = \frac{180}{15} = 12$$

The answer is (D)

47. If a square has an area of a^2 and a right-angled isosceles triangle also has area is a^2, then which one of the following must be true?

(A)   The perimeter of the square is greater than the perimeter of the triangle.
(B)   The perimeter of the square is less than the perimeter of the triangle.
(C)   The perimeter of the square is equal to the perimeter of the triangle.
(D)   The perimeter of the square is greater than or equal to the perimeter of the triangle.
(E)   It cannot be determined which perimeter is greater from the information given

Remember that the area of a square is equal to the length of its side squared. Since the area of the square is a^2, the side of the square is a. Hence, the perimeter of the square is $P = a + a + a + a = 4a$.

Now, let b represent the length of the equal sides of the right-angled isosceles triangle, and let c represent the length of the hypotenuse:

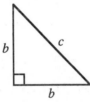

Since the hypotenuse of a right triangle is opposite the right angle, the sides labeled b are the base and height of the triangle. The area of the triangle is $\dfrac{1}{2}$ base $\times$ height $= \dfrac{1}{2}bb = \dfrac{1}{2}b^2$. We are given that the area of the triangle is a^2. Hence, $\dfrac{1}{2}b^2 = a^2$. Solving this equation for b yields $b = \sqrt{2}a$. To calculate the hypotenuse, c, of the triangle we apply the Pythagorean Theorem:

$$c^2 = b^2 + b^2$$
$$c^2 = 2b^2$$
$$c = \sqrt{2b^2}$$
$$c = \sqrt{2}b$$
$$c = \sqrt{2}\sqrt{2}a \qquad (\text{since } b = \sqrt{2}a)$$
$$c = 2a$$

The perimeter of the triangle is $P = b + b + c = 2b + c = 2\sqrt{2}a + 2a = a(2\sqrt{2} + 2)$. Recall that $\sqrt{2} \approx 1.4$. Hence, $a(2\sqrt{2} + 2) \approx a(2.8 + 2) = 4.48a > 4a$. Hence, the perimeter of the triangle is greater than the perimeter of the square, and the answer is (B).

48. The perimeter of a square is equal to the perimeter of a rectangle whose length and width are 6*m* and 4*m*, respectively. The side of the square is

(A) 3*m*
(B) 4*m*
(C) 5*m*
(D) 6*m*
(E) 7*m*

The length of the rectangle is 6*m* and the width of the rectangle is 4*m*. From the standard formula for the perimeter of a rectangle, we get

$$P = 2L + 2W = 2(6m) + 2(4m) = 20m$$

Now, the formula for the perimeter of a square is 4*x*, where *x* represents the length of a side of the square. Since we are given that the perimeter of the square is equal to that of the rectangle, we write

$$4x = 20m$$

$$x = \frac{20m}{4} = 5m$$

The answer is (C).

49. If the circumference of a circle is 4*m*, then the ratio of circumference of the circle to the diameter of the circle is

(A) π
(B) 4
(C) 2π
(D) 4π
(E) 16

The formula for the circumference of a circle with diameter *d* is $C = 2\pi r = \pi(2r) = \pi d$ (since the diameter is twice the radius, $d = 2r$). Hence, the ratio of the circumference of the circle to its diameter is

$$\frac{C}{d} =$$

$$\frac{\pi d}{d} =$$

$$\pi$$

The answer is (A).

Note: The fact that the circumference of the circle is 4*m* was not used in solving the problem. Thus, the answer is independent of the size of the circle. In other words, the ratio of the circumference of a circle to its diameter is always π.

50. In Triangle *ABC*, $\angle A$ is 10 degrees greater than $\angle B$, and $\angle B$ is 10 degrees greater than $\angle C$. The value of angle B is

(A) 30   (B) 40   (C) 50   (D) 60   (E) 70

We are given that $\angle A$ is 10 degrees greater than $\angle B$. Expressing this as an equation gives

$$\angle A = \angle B + 10$$

We are also given that $\angle B$ is 10 degrees greater than $\angle C$. Expressing this as an equation gives

$$\angle B = \angle C + 10$$

In a triangle, the sum of the three angles is 180 degrees. Expressing this as an equation gives

$$\angle A + \angle B + \angle C = 180$$

Solving these three equations for $\angle B$, we get $\angle B = 60$ degrees. The answer is (D).

51.   Two squares each with sides of length *s* are joined to form a rectangle. The area of the rectangle is

(A) s^2
(B) $2s^2$
(C) $4s^2$
(D) $8s^2$
(E) $16s^2$

The area of a square with side *s* is s^2. On joining two such squares, the resulting area will be twice the area of either square: $2s^2$. The answer is (B).

52.   A person travels 16 miles due north and then 12 miles due east. How far is the person from his initial location?

(A)   4 miles
(B)   8 miles
(C)   14 miles
(D)   20 miles
(E)   28 miles

Solution:

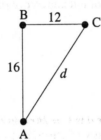

A: Initial position
B: Second position
C: Final position

The path taken by the person can be represented diagrammatically as shown. Let *d* be the distance between his initial location and his final location. Since a person traveling due north has to turn 90 degrees to travel due east, the Angle ABC is a right angle. Hence, we can apply the Pythagorean Theorem to the triangle, which yields

$$d^2 = 12^2 + 16^2$$
$$d^2 = 400$$
$$d = \sqrt{400}$$
$$d = 20$$

The answer is (D).

53.   The area of Triangle *PQR* is 6. If *PR* = 4, then the length of the hypotenuse *QR* is

(A)   1
(B)   2
(C)   3
(D)   4
(E)   5

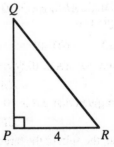

Triangle *PQR* is a right triangle with the base *PR* equal to 4 and height *PQ*. The area of Triangle *PQR* is $\frac{1}{2}bh = 6$. Substituting the known quantities into this formula yields $\frac{1}{2}(4)(PQ) = 6$. Solving this equation for *PQ* yields *PQ* = 3. Applying the Pythagorean Theorem to the triangle yields

$$(PQ)^2 + (PR)^2 = (QR)^2$$
$$3^2 + 4^2 = (QR)^2 \qquad \text{by substitution}$$
$$25 = (QR)^2$$
$$5 = QR \qquad \text{by taking the square root of both sides}$$

The answer is (E).

54. In the figure, the equation of line AB is $y = -\dfrac{5}{3}x + 10$.

The area of the shaded portion is

(A) 12
(B) 30
(C) 100/3
(D) 60
(E) 100

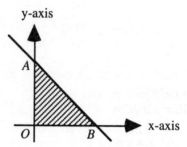

To find the y-intercept of a line, we set $x = 0$: $y = -\dfrac{5}{3}(0) + 10 = 10$. Hence, the height of the triangle is 10.

To find the x-intercept of a line, we set $y = 0$: $-\dfrac{5}{3}x + 10 = 0$. Solving this equation for x yields $x = 6$. Hence, the base of the triangle is 6. Therefore, the area of shaded portion (which is a triangle) is $\dfrac{1}{2} \cdot 6 \cdot 10 = 30$. The answer is (B).

55. In the figure to the right, which one of the following must be true about the angle θ?

(A) $\theta = 60°$
(B) $\theta < 60°$
(C) $\theta > 60°$
(D) $\theta > 70°$
(E) It cannot be determined from the information given

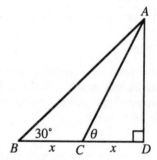

In the figure, $CD = x$ and AC is the hypotenuse of the right triangle ADC. Recall that in a right triangle the hypotenuse is the longest side. Hence, $AC > x$. Now, consider triangle ABC. Observe that $\angle B$ is opposite side AC and $\angle BAC$ is opposite side BC. Since, $BC = x$ and $AC > x$, we can write that $AC > BC$. Recall that in a triangle, the angle opposite the greater side is the greater angle. Hence, $\angle B > \angle BAC$. Since $\angle B = 30°$, $\angle BAC$ must be less than 30°. From the exterior angle theorem, $\theta = \angle B + \angle BAC = 30 + \angle BAC$. We have already derived that $\angle BAC < 30°$. Adding 30 to both sides of this inequality yields $30 + \angle BAC < 60$. Replacing $30 + \angle BAC$ with θ, we get $\theta < 60$. The answer is (B).

56. In the figure, if $x = 54°$ and $y = 72°$, then $z =$

(A) 54°
(B) 56°
(C) 72°
(D) 76°
(E) 98°

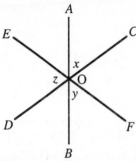

O is the point of intersection of the three lines in the figure.

From the figure, observe that $\angle AOC$ and $\angle BOD$ are vertical angles between the lines AB and CD. Hence, $\angle AOC = \angle BOD = x$. Since a straight angle has 180°, we get the following equation:

$\angle EOD + \angle BOD + \angle BOF = 180$
$z + x + y = 180$ since $\angle EOD = z$, $\angle BOD = x$, $\angle BOF = y$
$z + 54 + 72 = 180$ since $x = 54°$ and $y = 72°$
$z = 180 - 54 - 72 = 54$

The answer is (A)

57. If one of the sides of the rectangle shown in the figure has a length of 3, then the area of the rectangle is

(A) 9
(B) 13.5
(C) 18
(D) 27
(E) 54

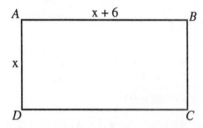

We are given that one of the sides of the rectangle has length 3. This implies that either x or $x + 6$ equals 3. If $x + 6$ equals 3, then x must be -3, which is impossible since a length cannot be negative. Hence, $x = 3$ and $x + 6 = 3 + 6 = 9$. The area of the rectangle, being the product of two adjacent sides of the rectangle, is $x(x + 6) = 3(9) = 27$. The answer is (D).

58. The value of $x + y + z =$

(A) 120°
(B) 160°
(C) 180°
(D) 270°
(E) 360°

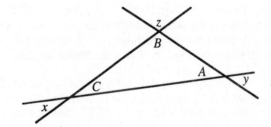

Since angles A, B, and C are the interior angles of the triangle, their angle sum is 180°. Hence, $A + B + C = 180$. Since A and y are vertical angles, they are equal. This is also true for angles B and z and angles C and x. Substituting these values into the equation yields $y + z + x = 180$. The answer is (C).

59. In the figure, what is the area of Triangle *ABC* ?

(A) 25
(B) 50
(C) $100/\sqrt{2}$
(D) 100
(E) $100\sqrt{2}$

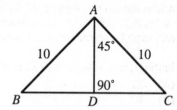

In a triangle, the sum of the interior angles is 180 degrees. Applying this to Triangle *ADC* yields

$$\angle DAC + \angle C + \angle CDA = 180$$
$$45 + \angle C + 90 = 180 \qquad \text{since } \angle DAC = 45° \text{ and } \angle CDA = 90°$$
$$\angle C = 180 - 90 - 45 = 45$$

In Triangle *ABC*, *AB = AC*. Recall that angles opposite equal sides of a triangle are equal. Hence, $\angle B = \angle C$. We have already derived that $\angle C = 45°$. Hence, $\angle B = \angle C = 45°$. Again, the sum of the interior angles of a triangle is 180 degrees. Applying this to Triangle *ABC* yields

$$\angle A + \angle B + \angle C = 180$$
$$\angle A + 45 + 45 = 180$$
$$\angle A = 90$$

This implies that Triangle *ABC* is a right triangle with right angle at *A*. Hence, the area of the triangle is

$$\frac{1}{2}\left(\text{the product of the sides containing the right angle}\right) =$$

$$\frac{1}{2}AB \cdot AC =$$

$$\frac{1}{2}10 \cdot 10 =$$

$$50$$

The answer is (B).

60. In the triangle to the right, $y/x = 3$. Which one of the following must be true?

(A) $4x > z$
(B) $4x < z$
(C) $4x \leq z$
(D) $4x = z$
(E) It cannot be determined from the information given

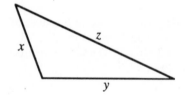

In a triangle, the sum of any two sides is greater than the third side. Hence, $x + y > z$. We are given $y/x = 3$. Multiplying both sides of this equation by *x* yields $y = 3x$. Substituting this into the inequality $x + y > z$, we get $x + 3x > z$, or $4x > z$. Hence, the answer is (A).

61. In the figure to the right, which one of the following statements about the circumference *C* of the circle and the perimeter *P* of Square *PQRS* must be true?

(A) $C > P$
(B) $C < P$
(C) $C \leq P$
(D) $C = P$
(E) It cannot be determined from the information given

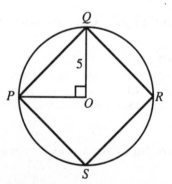

O is the center of the circle, and the radius of the circle is 5.

The shortest distance between two points is along the line joining them. So, the lengths of the arcs *PQ*, *QR*, *RS*, and *SP* are greater than the lengths of the sides *PQ*, *QR*, *RS*, and *SP*, respectively. The circumference of the circle is the sum of lengths of the arcs *PQ*, *QR*, *RS*, and *SP*, and the perimeter of the square is the sum of the sides *PQ*, *QR*, *RS*, and *SP*. Since each arc is greater than the corresponding side, the circumference of the circle must be greater than the perimeter of the square. Hence, the answer is (A).

62. In the figure, what is the value of *x*?

    (A) 20°
    (B) 30°
    (C) 40°
    (D) 50°
    (E) 60°

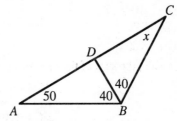

In the figure, ∠*B* is the sum of ∠*ABD* and ∠*DBC*. So, ∠*B* = ∠*ABD* + ∠*DBC* = 40 + 40 = 80. Now, recall that the sum of the angles in a triangle is 180°. Hence,

$$\angle A + \angle B + \angle C = 180$$
$$50 + 80 + x = 180 \qquad \text{since } \angle A = 50 \text{ and } \angle B = 80$$
$$130 + x = 180$$
$$x = 50$$

The answer is (D).

63. The area of the Triangle *ABC* shown in the figure is 30. The area of Triangle *ADC* is

    (A) 5
    (B) 10
    (C) 15
    (D) 20
    (E) 25

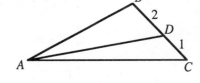

Let's add an altitude to Triangle *ABC* by extending side *BC* as shown in the figure below.

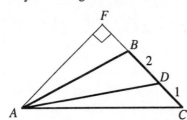

The formula for the area of a triangle is *A* = (1/2)(base)(height). Hence, the area of Triangle *ABC* = (1/2)(*BC*)(*AF*) = (1/2)(2 + 1)(*AF*) = (3/2)(*AF*) = 30 (the area of Triangle *ABC* is given to be 30). Solving this equation for *AF* yields *AF* = 20. Now, the area of Triangle *ADC* = (1/2)(*DC*)(*AF*) = (1/2)(1)(20) = 10. The answer is (B).

64. In the figure, what is the value of *y* ?

    (A) 7.5
    (B) 15
    (C) 30
    (D) 40
    (E) 45

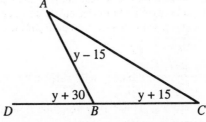

Observe that ∠*DBA* is an exterior angle of Triangle *ABC*. Applying the exterior angle theorem yields

$$\angle DBA = \angle A + \angle C$$
$$y + 30 = (y - 15) + (y + 15)$$
$$y + 30 = 2y \qquad \text{by adding like terms}$$
$$30 = y \qquad \text{by subtracting } y \text{ from both sides}$$

The answer is (C).

65. A circle is depicted in the rectangular coordinate system as shown. The value of x is

   (A) 4
   (B) 6
   (C) 8
   (D) 10
   (E) 12

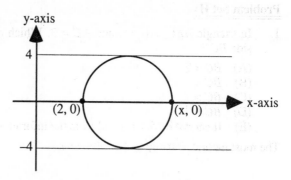

The figure shows that the circle is located between the lines $y = 4$ and $y = -4$ and that the circle is symmetric to x-axis. From this, we make two observations: 1) The center of the circle is on the x-axis. 2) The diameter of the circle is 8. Since the center of the circle is on the x-axis, the points $(2, 0)$ and $(x, 0)$ must be diametrically opposite points of the circle. That is, they are end points of a diameter of the circle. Hence, the distance between the two points, $x - 2$, must equal the length of the diameter. Hence, $x - 2 = 8$. Adding 2 to both sides of this equation, we get $x = 10$. The answer is (D).

66. In the figure, the ratio of x to y is 2. What is the value of y?

   (A) 108
   (B) 90
   (C) 68
   (D) 45
   (E) 36

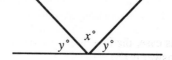

Since the ratio of x to y is 2, we get $x/y = 2$. Solving this equation for x yields $x = 2y$. Since the sum of the angles made by a line is 180°, $y + x + y = 180$. Substituting $2y$ for x in this equation yields

$$y + 2y + y = 180$$
$$4y = 180$$
$$y = 45$$

The answer is (D).

67. In the figure, the equation of line AB is $y = x + 2$. The difference of the x- and y-coordinates of any point on the line is equal to:

   (A) −4
   (B) −2
   (C) 0
   (D) 2
   (E) 4

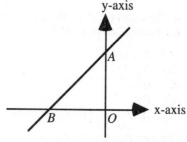

Since the coordinates x and y are on the line, we know that $y = x + 2$. Hence, the difference of x and y is

$$x - y = x - (x + 2) = -2$$

The answer is (B).

Problem Set H:

1. In triangle *ABC*, *AB* = 5 and *AC* = 3. Which one of the following is the measure of the length of side *BC* ?

    (A) *BC* < 7
    (B) *BC* = 7
    (C) *BC* > 7
    (D) *BC* ≤ 7
    (E) It cannot be determined from the information given

The most natural drawing is the following:

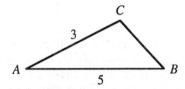

In this case, the length of side *BC* is less than 7. However, there is another drawing possible, as follows:

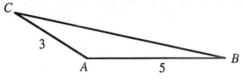

In this case, the length of side *BC* is greater than 7. Hence, there is not enough information to decide, and the answer is (E).

2. In the figure to the right, what is the area of △*ABC* ?

    (A) 6
    (B) 7
    (C) 8
    (D) 9
    (E) It cannot be determined from the information given

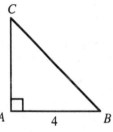

Although the drawing looks to be an isosceles triangle, that cannot be assumed. We are not given the length of side AC: it could be 4 units long or 100 units long, we don't know. Hence, the answer is (E).

3. In the figure to the right, which one of the following is the measure of angle θ ?

    (A) θ < 45°
    (B) θ > 45°
    (C) θ = 45°
    (D) θ ≤ 45°
    (E) It cannot be determined from the information given

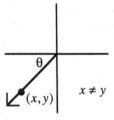

There are two possible drawings:

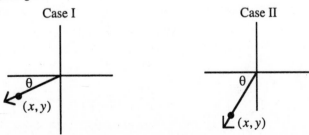

In Case I, θ < 45°. Whereas, in Case II, θ > 45°. This is a double case, and the answer therefore is (E).

4.   In isosceles triangle ABC, $CA = CB = 4$. Which one of the following is the area of triangle ABC ?

(A) 7
(B) 8
(C) 9
(D) 10
(E) It cannot be determined from the information given

There are many possible drawings for the triangle, two of which are listed below:

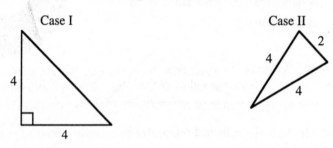

In Case I, the area is 8. In Case II, the area is $\sqrt{15}$ This is a double case and therefore the answer is (E).

Problem Set I:

1. In the figure to the right, the radius of the larger circle is twice that of the smaller circle. If the circles are concentric, what is the ratio of the shaded region's area to the area of the smaller circle?

    (A) 10:1
    (B) 9:1
    (C) 3:1
    (D) 2:1
    (E) 1:1

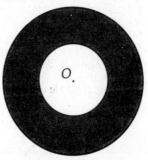

The area of the shaded region appears to be about three times the area of the smaller circle, so the answer should be (C). Let's verify this. Suppose the radius of the larger circle is 2 and the radius of the smaller circle is 1. Then the area of the larger circle is $\pi r^2 = \pi(2)^2 = 4\pi$, and the area of the smaller circle is $\pi r^2 = \pi(1)^2 = \pi$. Hence, the area of the shaded region is $4\pi - \pi = 3\pi$. Now, $\dfrac{area\ of\ shaded\ region}{area\ of\ smaller\ circle} = \dfrac{3\pi}{\pi} = \dfrac{3}{1}$. The answer is (C).

2. In the figure to the right, ΔPST is an isosceles right triangle, and $PS = 2$. What is the area of the shaded region URST?

    (A) 4
    (B) 2
    (C) 5/4
    (D) 5/6
    (E) 1/2

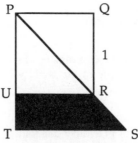

The area of the square is $1^2 = 1$. Now, the area of the shaded region appears to be about half that of the square. Hence, the area of the shaded region is about 1/2. The answer is (E).

3. In the figure to the right, the area of ΔPQR is 40. What is the area of ΔQRS?

    (A) 10
    (B) 15
    (C) 20
    (D) 25
    (E) 45

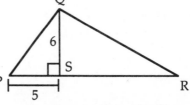

Clearly from the drawing, the area of ΔQRS is greater than half the area of ΔPQR. This eliminates (A), (B), and (C). Now, the area of ΔQRS cannot be greater than the area of ΔPQR. This eliminates (E). The answer is (D).

4. In the figure to the right, PQRS is a square and M and N are midpoints of their respective sides. What is the area of quadrilateral PMRN?

    (A) 8
    (B) 10
    (C) 12
    (D) 14
    (E) 16

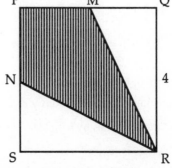

Since the square has sides of length 4, its area is 16. Now, the area of the shaded region appears to be half that of the square. Hence, its area is 8. The answer is (A).

Problem Set J:

1.   In the figure to the right, O is the center of the circle.
      What is the area of the circle?

      (A) 2π
      (B) 3π
      (C) 5.5π
      (D) 7π
      (E) 9π

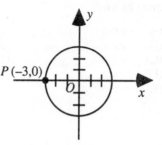

Since the circle is centered at the origin and passes through the point $(-3,0)$, the radius of the circle is 3.
Hence, the area is $A = \pi r^2 = \pi 3^2 = 9\pi$. The answer is (E).

2.   In the figure to the right, which one of the following
      must be true about the value of the y-coordinate of
      point P ?

      (A) $y < 6$
      (B) $y > 6$
      (C) $y > 5$
      (D) $y = 6$
      (E) $y < 5$

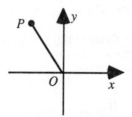

P is a point in the coordinate
system and $OP = 6$.

Whatever the coordinates of P are, the line OP is the hypotenuse of a right triangle with sides being the
absolute value of the x and y coordinates. Hence, OP is greater than the y-coordinate of point P. The
answer is (A).
      This problem brings up the issue of how much you can assume when viewing a diagram. We are told
that P is a point in the coordinate system and that it appears in the second quadrant. Could P be on one of
the axes or in another quadrant? No. Although P could be anywhere in Quadrant II (not necessarily where
it is displayed), P could not be on the y-axis because the "position of points, angles, regions, etc. can be
assumed to be in the order shown." If P were on the y-axis, then it would not be to the left of the y-axis, as
it is in the diagram. That is, the order would be different.

3.   In the figure to the right, the equation of the line is
      $y = px + a$. Which one of the following is the value of
      p ?

      (A) $p = \dfrac{-1}{2}$

      (B) $p = \dfrac{a}{b}$

      (C) $p = \dfrac{-a}{b}$

      (D) $p = \dfrac{b}{a}$

      (E) $p = \dfrac{-b}{a}$

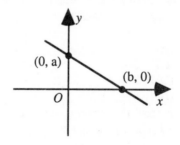

Since $(b, 0)$ is the x-intercept of the line, it must satisfy the equation: $0 = pb + a$

Subtracting a from both sides yields $-a = pb$

Dividing both sides by b yields $\dfrac{-a}{b} = p$

The answer is (C).

4. In the figure to the right, which one of the following must be true?

    (A) $y < x$
    (B) $y > x$
    (C) $y < 4$
    (D) $y = x$
    (E) $y > 5$

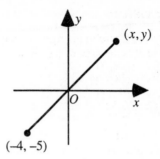

Since the line passes through (–4, –5) and (0, 0), its slope is $m = \dfrac{rise}{run} = \dfrac{-5-0}{-4-0} = \dfrac{5}{4}$. Notice that the rise, 5, is larger than the run, 4. Hence, the y-coordinate will always be larger in absolute value than the x-coordinate. The answer is (B).

5. In the figure to the right, a is the x-coordinate of point P and b is the y-coordinate of point Q. In which quadrant is the point (a,b)?

    (A) I
    (B) II
    (C) III
    (D) IV
    (E) cannot be determined from the information given

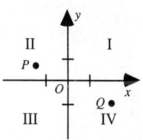

Since P is in Quadrant II, its x-coordinate is negative. That is, a is negative. Since Q is in Quadrant IV, its y-coordinate is negative. That is, b is negative. Hence, (a,b) is in Quadrant III. The answer is (C).

6. In the figure to the right, if $x = 4$, then $y =$

    (A) 1
    (B) 2
    (C) 3
    (D) 4
    (E) 5.1

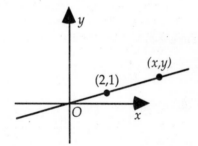

Let's write the equation of the line, using the slope-intercept form, $y = mx + b$. Since the line passes through the origin, $b = 0$. This reduces the equation to $y = mx$. Calculating the slope between (2,1) and (0,0) yields $m = \dfrac{1-0}{2-0} = \dfrac{1}{2}$. Plugging this into the equation yields $y = \dfrac{1}{2}x$. Since $x = 4$, we get

$y = \dfrac{1}{2} \cdot 4 = 2$. The answer is (B).

7. In the figure to the right, which of the following could be the coordinates of a point in the shaded region?

    (A) (1, 2)
    (B) (–2, 3)
    (C) (3, –5)
    (D) (–5, 1)
    (E) (–1, –6)

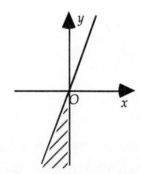

The shaded region is entirely within the third quadrant. Now, both coordinates of any point in Quadrant III are negative. The only point listed with both coordinates negative is (–1,–6). The answer is (E).

8.   In the figure to the right, which of the following points lies within the circle?

    (A)   (3.5, 9.5)
    (B)   (–7, 7)
    (C)   (–10, 1)
    (D)   (0, 11)
    (E)   (5.5, 8.5)

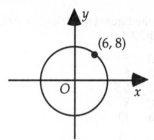

For a point to be within a circle, its distance from the center of the circle must be less than the radius of the circle. The distance from (6, 8) to (0, 0) is the radius of the circle: $R = \sqrt{(6-0)^2 + (8-0)^2} = \sqrt{36+64} = \sqrt{100} = 10$. Now, let's calculate the distance between (–7, 7) and (0, 0) $R = \sqrt{(-7-0)^2 + (7-0)^2} = \sqrt{49+49} = \sqrt{98} < 10$. The answer is (B).

9.   In the figure to the right, the grid consists of unit squares. What is the area of the polygon?

    (A)   7
    (B)   9
    (C)   10
    (D)   12
    (E)   15

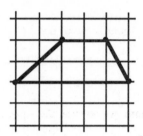

Dividing the polygon into triangles and squares yields

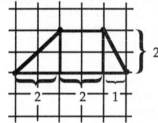

The triangle furthest to the left has area $A = \frac{1}{2}bh = \frac{1}{2} \cdot 2 \cdot 2 = 2$. The square has area $A = s^2 = 2^2 = 4$. The triangle furthest to the right has area $A = \frac{1}{2} \cdot 1 \cdot 2 = 1$. The sum of the areas of these three figures is $2 + 4 + 1 = 7$. The answer is (A).

10.   In the figure to the right, which of the following points is three times as far from P as from Q ?

    (A)   (0, 3)
    (B)   (1, 1)
    (C)   (4, 5)
    (D)   (2, 3)
    (E)   (4, 1)

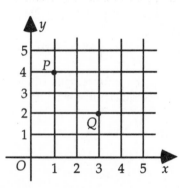

From the distance formula, the distance between (4,1) and Q is $\sqrt{2}$, and the distance between (4,1) and P is $\sqrt{(4-1)^2 + (1-4)^2} = \sqrt{3^2 + (-3)^2} = \sqrt{2 \cdot 3^2} = 3\sqrt{2}$. The answer is (E).

11. In the figure to the right, what is the area of quadrilateral
     ABCO ?

     (A) 3
     (B) 5
     (C) 6.5
     (D) 8
     (E) 13

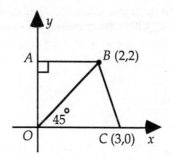

Dropping a vertical line from point *B* perpendicular to the *x*-axis will form a square and a triangle:

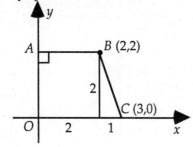

From the figure, we see that the square has area $s^2 = 2^2 = 4$, and the triangle has area $\frac{1}{2}bh = \frac{1}{2} \cdot 1 \cdot 2 = 1$.

Hence, the area of the quadrilateral is $4 + 1 = 5$. The answer is (B). Note, with this particular solution, we did not need to use the properties of the diagonal line in the original diagram.

12. In the figure to the right, which quadrants contain points
     (x, y) such that $xy = -2$?

     (A) I only
     (B) II only
     (C) III and IV only
     (D) II and IV only
     (E) II, III, and IV

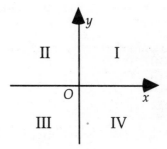

If the product of two numbers is negative, the numbers must have opposite signs. Now, only the coordinates of points in quadrants II and IV have opposite signs. The diagram below illustrates the sign pattern of points for all four quadrants. The answer is (D).

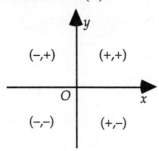

13.   If the square in the figure to the right is rotated clockwise about the origin until vertex *V* is on the negative *y*-axis, then the new *y*-coordinate of *V* is

(A)   –2
(B) $-2\sqrt{2}$
(C)   –4
(D) $-3\sqrt{2}$
(E)   –8

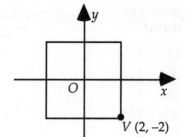

Calculating the distance between *V* and the origin yields $\sqrt{(2-0)^2 + (-2-0)^2} = \sqrt{4+4} = \sqrt{8} = 2\sqrt{2}$. Since the square is rotated about the origin, the distance between the origin and *V* is fix. Hence, the new *y*-coordinate of *V* is $-2\sqrt{2}$. The diagram below illustrates the position of *V* after the rotation. The answer is (B).

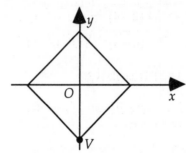

14.   In the standard coordinate system, which of the following points is the greatest distance from the origin:

(A)   (–4,–1)
(B)   (–3,3)
(C)   (4,0)
(D)   (2,3)
(E)   (0,4)

Using the distance formula to calculate the distance of each point from the origin yields

$$d = \sqrt{(-4)^2 + (-1)^2} = \sqrt{17}$$
$$d = \sqrt{(-3)^2 + (3)^2} = \sqrt{18}$$
$$d = \sqrt{(4)^2 + (0)^2} = \sqrt{16}$$
$$d = \sqrt{(2)^2 + (3)^2} = \sqrt{13}$$
$$d = \sqrt{(0)^2 + (4)^2} = \sqrt{16}$$

The answer is (B).

15. What is the perimeter of Triangle *ABC* in the figure to the right?

(A) $5 + \sqrt{2} + \sqrt{29}$

(B) $5 + 2\sqrt{2} + \sqrt{29}$

(C) $5 + 4\sqrt{2} + \sqrt{29}$

(D) $3\sqrt{2} + \sqrt{34}$

(E) $4\sqrt{2} + \sqrt{34}$

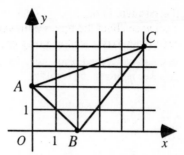

Point *A* has coordinates (0, 2), point *B* has coordinates (2, 0), and point *C* has coordinates (5, 4). Using the distance formula to calculate the distances between points *A* and *B*, *A* and *C*, and *B* and *C* yields

$$\overline{AB} = \sqrt{(0-2)^2 + (2-0)^2} = \sqrt{4+4} = \sqrt{8} = 2\sqrt{2}$$

$$\overline{AC} = \sqrt{(0-5)^2 + (2-4)^2} = \sqrt{25+4} = \sqrt{29}$$

$$\overline{BC} = \sqrt{(2-5)^2 + (0-4)^2} = \sqrt{9+16} = 5$$

Adding these lengths gives the perimeter of Triangle *ABC*:

$$\overline{AB} + \overline{AC} + \overline{BC} = 2\sqrt{2} + \sqrt{29} + 5$$

The answer is (B).

Problem Set K:

1. What is the maximum number of 3x3 squares
    that can be formed from the squares in the 6x6
    checker board to the right?

    (A)   4
    (B)   6
    (C)   12
    (D)   16
    (E)   24

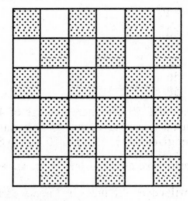

Clearly, there are more than four 3x3 squares in the checker board—eliminate (A). Next, eliminate (B)
since it merely repeats a number from the problem. Further, eliminate (E) since it is the greatest. This
leaves choices (C) and (D). If you count carefully, you will find sixteen 3x3 squares in the checker board.
The answer is (D).

2. Let P stand for the product of the first 5 positive integers. What is the greatest possible value of m if
    $\dfrac{P}{10^m}$ is an integer?

    (A)   1
    (B)   2
    (C)   3
    (D)   5
    (E)   10

Since we are to find the greatest value of m, we eliminate (E)—the greatest. Also, eliminate 5 because it is
repeated from the problem. Now, since we are looking for the largest number, start with the greatest
number remaining and work toward the smallest number. The first number that works will be the answer.
To this end, let $m = 3$. Then $\dfrac{P}{10^m} = \dfrac{1 \cdot 2 \cdot 3 \cdot 4 \cdot 5}{10^3} = \dfrac{120}{1000} = \dfrac{3}{25}$. This is not an integer, so eliminate (C).
Next, let $m = 2$. Then $\dfrac{P}{10^m} = \dfrac{1 \cdot 2 \cdot 3 \cdot 4 \cdot 5}{10^2} = \dfrac{120}{100} = \dfrac{6}{5}$. This still is not an integer, so eliminate (B). Hence,
by process of elimination, the answer is (A).

3. After being marked down 20 percent, a calculator sells for $10. The original selling price was

    (A) $20
    (B) $12.5
    (C) $12
    (D) $9
    (E) $7

Twenty dollars is too large. The discount was only 20 percent—eliminate (A). Both (D) and (E) are
impossible since they are less than the selling price—eliminate. 12 is the eye-catcher: 20% of 10 is 2 and
$10 + 2 = 12$. This is too easy for a hard problem—eliminate. Thus, by process of elimination, the answer is
(B).

4.   The distance between cities A and B is 120 miles. A car travels from A to B at 60 miles per hour and returns from B to A along the same route at 40 miles per hour. What is the average speed for the round trip?

   (A)   48
   (B)   50
   (C)   52
   (D)   56
   (E)   58

We can eliminate 50 (the mere average of 40 and 60) since that would be too elementary. Now, the average must be closer to 40 than to 60 because the car travels for a longer time at 40 mph. But 48 is the only number given that is closer to 40 than to 60. The answer is (A).

It's instructive to also calculate the answer. $Average\ Speed = \dfrac{Total\ Distance}{Total\ Time}$. Now, a car traveling at 40 mph will cover 120 miles in 3 hours. And a car traveling at 60 mph will cover the same 120 miles in 2 hours. So the total traveling time is 5 hours. Hence, for the round trip, the average speed is $\dfrac{120+120}{5} = 48$.

5.   If **w** is 10 percent less than **x,** and **y** is 30 percent less than **z,** then **wy** is what percent less than **xz**?

   (A)   10%
   (B)   20%
   (C)   37%
   (D)   40%
   (E)   100%

We eliminate (A) since it repeats the number 10 from the problem. We can also eliminate choices (B), (D), and (E) since they are derivable from elementary operations:

$$20 = 30 - 10$$
$$40 = 30 + 10$$
$$100 = 10 \cdot 10$$

This leaves choice (C) as the answer.

   Let's also solve this problem directly. The clause

   w is 10 percent less than x

translates into

$$w = x - .10x$$

Simplifying yields

   1) $w = .9x$

Next, the clause

   y is 30 percent less than **z**

translates into

$$y = z - .30z$$

Simplifying yields

   2) $y = .7z$

Multiplying 1) and 2) gives

$$wy = (.9x)(.7z) = .63xz = xz - .37xz$$

Hence, **wy** is 37 percent less than **xz**. The answer is (C).

6. In the game of chess, the Knight can make any of the moves displayed in the diagram to the right. If a Knight is the only piece on the board, what is the greatest number of spaces from which not all 8 moves are possible?

    (A)   8
    (B)   24
    (C)   38
    (D)   48
    (E)   56

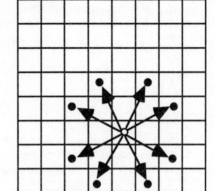

Since we are looking for the <u>greatest</u> number of spaces from which not all 8 moves are possible, we can eliminate the greatest number, 56. Now, clearly not all 8 moves are possible from the outer squares, and there are 28 outer squares—not 32. Also, not all 8 moves are possible from the next to outer squares, and there are 20 of them—not 24. All 8 moves are possible from the remaining squares. Hence, the answer is 28 + 20 = 48. The answer is (D). Notice that 56, (32 + 24), is given as an answer-choice to catch those who don't add carefully.

7. How many different ways can 3 cubes be painted if each cube is painted one color and only the 3 colors red, blue, and green are available? (Order is not considered, for example, green, green, blue is considered the same as green, blue, green.)

    (A)   2
    (B)   3
    (C)   9
    (D)   10
    (E)   27

Clearly, there are more than 3 color combinations possible. This eliminates (A) and (B). We can also eliminate (C) and (E) because they are both multiples of 3, and that would be too ordinary, too easy, to be the answer. Hence, by process of elimination, the answer is (D).

Let's also solve this problem directly. The following list displays all 27 $(= 3 \cdot 3 \cdot 3)$ color combinations possible (without restriction):

RRR	BBB	GGG
RRB	BBR	GGR
RRG	BBG	GGB
RBR	BRB	GRG
RBB	BRR	GRR
RBG	BRG	GRB
RGR	BGB	GBG
RGB	BGR	GBR
RGG	BGG	GBB

If order is not considered, then there are 10 distinct color combinations in this list. You should count them.

8. What is the greatest prime factor of $\left(2^4\right)^2 - 1$?

   (A)   3
   (B)   5
   (C)   11
   (D)   17
   (E)   19

$\left(2^4\right)^2 - 1 = (16)^2 - 1 = 256 - 1 = 255$. Since the question asks for the <u>greatest</u> prime factor, we eliminate 19, the greatest number. Now, we start with the next largest number and work our way up the list; the first number that divides into 255 evenly will be the answer. Dividing 17 into 255 gives

$$17\overline{)255} = 15$$

Hence, 17 is the largest prime factor of $\left(2^4\right)^2 - 1$. The answer is (D).

9. Suppose five circles, each 4 inches in diameter, are cut from a rectangular strip of paper 12 inches long. If the least amount of paper is to be wasted, what is the width of the paper strip?

   (A)   5
   (B) $4 + 2\sqrt{3}$
   (C)   8
   (D) $4\left(1 + \sqrt{3}\right)$
   (E)   not enough information

Since this is a hard problem, we can eliminate (E), "not enough information." And because it is too easily derived, we can eliminate (C), $(8 = 4 + 4)$. Further, we can eliminate (A), 5, because answer-choices (B) and (D) form a more complicated set. At this stage we cannot apply any more elimination rules; so if we could not solve the problem, we would guess either (B) or (D).

Let's solve the problem directly. The drawing below shows the position of the circles so that the paper width is a minimum.

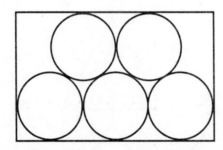

Now, take three of the circles in isolation, and connect the centers of these circles to form a triangle:

Since the triangle connects the centers of circles of diameter 4, the triangle is equilateral with sides of length 4.

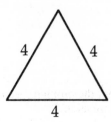

Drawing an altitude gives

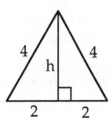

Applying the Pythagorean Theorem to either right triangle gives	$h^2 + 2^2 = 4^2$
Squaring yields	$h^2 + 4 = 16$
Subtracting 4 from both sides of this equation yields	$h^2 = 12$
Taking the square root of both sides yields	$h = \sqrt{12} = \sqrt{4 \cdot 3}$
Removing the perfect square 4 from the radical yields	$h = 2\sqrt{3}$

Summarizing gives

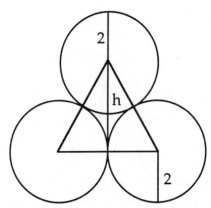

Adding to the height, $h = 2\sqrt{3}$, the distance above the triangle and the distance below the triangle to the edges of the paper strip gives

$$width = (2 + 2) + 2\sqrt{3} = 4 + 2\sqrt{3}$$

The answer is (B).

10. Let C and K be constants. If $x^2 + Kx + 5$ factors into $(x + 1)(x + C)$, the value of K is

  (A)   0
  (B)   5
  (C)   6
  (D)   8
  (E)   not enough information

Since the number 5 is merely repeated from the problem, we eliminate (B). Further, since this is a hard problem, we eliminate (E), "not enough information."

Now, since 5 is prime, its only factors are 1 and 5. So the constant C in the expression $(x + 1)(x + C)$ must be 5:

$$(x + 1)(x + 5)$$

Multiplying out this expression yields

$$(x+1)(x+5) = x^2 + 5x + x + 5$$

Combining like terms yields

$$(x+1)(x+5) = x^2 + 6x + 5$$

Hence, $K = 6$, and the answer is (C).

Problem Set L:

1.   If $1 < x < y$, which one of the following must be true?

(A) $-x^2 < -y^2$ (B) $\dfrac{x}{y} < \dfrac{y}{x}$ (C) $\dfrac{y}{x} < \dfrac{x}{y}$ (D) $\dfrac{-x}{y} < \dfrac{-y}{x}$ (E) $x^2 > y^2$

From $1 < x < y$, we know that both x and y are positive. So dividing both sides of $x < y$ by x yields $1 < \dfrac{y}{x}$; and dividing both sides of $x < y$ by y yields $\dfrac{x}{y} < 1$. Hence, $\dfrac{x}{y} < 1 < \dfrac{y}{x}$. By the transitive property of inequalities, $\dfrac{x}{y} < \dfrac{y}{x}$. The answer is (B).

2.   If $-3 < x < -1$ and $3 < y < 7$, which of the following best describes $\dfrac{x - y}{2}$?

(A) $-5 < \dfrac{x - y}{2} < -2$

(B) $-3 < \dfrac{x - y}{2} < -1$

(C) $-2 < \dfrac{x - y}{2} < 0$

(D) $2 < \dfrac{x - y}{2} < 5$

(E) $3 < \dfrac{x - y}{2} < 7$

Multiplying both sides of $3 < y < 7$ by -1 yields $-3 > -y > -7$. Now, we usually write the smaller number on the left side of an inequality. So $-3 > -y > -7$ becomes $-7 < -y < -3$. Add this inequality to the like inequality $-3 < x < -1$:

$$
\begin{array}{r}
-3 < x < -1 \\
(+) \quad \underline{-7 < -y < -3} \\
-10 < x - y < -4
\end{array}
$$

Dividing $-10 < x - y < -4$ by 2 yields $\dfrac{-10}{2} < \dfrac{x - y}{2} < \dfrac{-4}{2}$, or $-5 < \dfrac{x - y}{2} < -2$. The answer is (A).

3.   If x is an integer and $y = -2x - 8$, what is the least value of x for which y is less than 9?

(A) -9 (B) -8 (C) -7 (D) -6 (E) -5

Since y is less than 9 and $y = -2x - 8$, we get $-2x - 8 < 9$
Adding 8 to both sides of this inequality yields $-2x < 17$

Dividing by -2 and reversing the inequality yields $x > -\dfrac{17}{2} = -8.5$

Since x is an integer and is to be as small as possible, $x = -8$
The answer is (B).

4. Which one of the following could be the graph of $3 - 6x \le \dfrac{4x + 2}{-2}$?

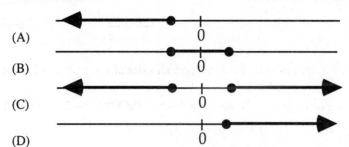

(A)

(B)

(C)

(D)

(E)

Multiplying both sides of the inequality by –2 yields	$-2(3 - 6x) \ge 4x + 2$
Distributing the –2 yields	$-6 + 12x \ge 4x + 2$
Subtracting $4x$ and adding 6 to both sides yields	$8x \ge 8$
Dividing both sides of the inequality by 8 yields	$x \ge 1$

The answer is (D).

5. If line segment AD has midpoint M_1 and line segment M_1D has midpoint M_2, what is the value of $\dfrac{M_1D}{AM_2}$?

(A) $\dfrac{1}{2}$ (B) $\dfrac{2}{3}$ (C) $\dfrac{3}{4}$ (D) $\dfrac{4}{5}$ (E) $\dfrac{5}{6}$

Let 4 be the length of line segment AD. Since M_1 is the midpoint of AD, this yields

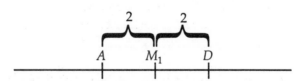

Now, since M_2 is the midpoint of M_1D, this yields

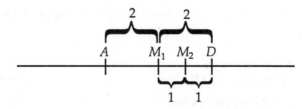

From the diagram, we see that $M_1D = 2$ and $AM_2 = 3$. Hence, $\dfrac{M_1D}{AM_2} = \dfrac{2}{3}$. The answer is (B).

6. If $x < y < -1$, which of the following must be true?

    (A) $\dfrac{x}{y} > xy$ (B) $\dfrac{y}{x} > x + y$ (C) $\dfrac{y}{x} > xy$ (D) $\dfrac{y}{x} < x + y$ (E) $\dfrac{y}{x} > \dfrac{x}{y}$

Since the sum of negative numbers is negative, $x + y$ is negative. Since the quotient of an even number of negative numbers is positive, $\dfrac{y}{x}$ is positive. Hence, $\dfrac{y}{x} > x + y$. The answer is (B).

7. Which of the following represents all solutions of the inequality $x^2 < 2x$?

    (A) $-1 < x < 1$ (B) $0 < x < 2$ (C) $1 < x < 3$ (D) $2 < x < 4$ (E) $4 < x < 6$

Forming an equation from $x^2 < 2x$ yields $x^2 = 2x$
Subtracting $2x$ from both sides yields $x^2 - 2x = 0$
Factoring yields $x(x - 2) = 0$
Setting each factor to zero yields $x = 0$ and $x - 2 = 0$
Solving yields $x = 0$ and $x = 2$
Setting up a number line and choosing test points (the circled numbers on the number line below) yields

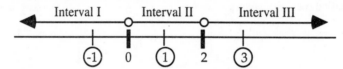

Now, if $x = -1$, the inequality $x^2 < 2x$ becomes $(-1)^2 < 2(-1)$, or $1 < -2$. This is false. Hence, Interval I is not a solution. If $x = 1$, the inequality $x^2 < 2x$ becomes $1^2 < 2(1)$, or $1 < 2$. This is true. Hence, Interval II is a solution. If $x = 3$, the inequality $x^2 < 2x$ becomes $3^2 < 2(3)$, or $9 < 6$. This is false. Hence, Interval III is not a solution. Thus, only Interval II is a solution:

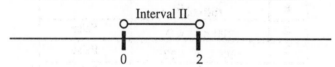

The answer is (B).

8. Given the positions of numbers x and y on the number line above, which of the following must be true?

    I. $xy > 0$

    II. $\dfrac{x}{y} < 0$

    III. $x - y > 0$

    (A) I only
    (B) II only
    (C) III only
    (D) I and II only
    (E) I, II, and III

Since x is to the left of zero on the number line, it's negative. Since y is to the right of zero, it's positive. Now, the product or quotient of a positive number and a negative number is negative. Hence, Statement I is false and Statement II is true. Regarding Statement III, since x is to the left of y on the number line, $x < y$. Subtracting y from both sides of this inequality yields $x - y < 0$. Hence, Statement III is false. Therefore, the answer is (B).

9.   If $\begin{array}{l} x^4 y < 0 \\ xy^4 > 0 \end{array}$, which of the following must be true?

(A) $x > y$ (B) $y > x$ (C) $x = y$ (D) $x < 0$ (E) $y > 0$

Since x is raised to an even exponent, it is greater than or equal to zero. Further, since $x^4 y \neq 0$, we know that neither x nor y is zero (otherwise $x^4 y = 0$). Hence, we may divide $x^4 y < 0$ by x^4 without reversing the inequality:

$$\frac{x^4 y}{x^4} < \frac{0}{x^4}$$

Simplifying yields $y < 0$

A similar analysis of the inequality $xy^4 > 0$ shows that $x > 0$. Hence, $x > y$. The answer is (A).

10.   If n is an integer, what is the least value of n such that $\dfrac{1}{3^n} < 0.01$?

(A)   2
(B)   3
(C)   4
(D)   5
(E)   6

Replacing 0.01 with its fractional equivalent, $\dfrac{1}{100}$, yields $\dfrac{1}{3^n} < \dfrac{1}{100}$

Multiplying both sides by 3^n and 100 and then simplifying yields $100 < 3^n$

Beginning with $n = 2$, we plug in larger and larger values of n until we reach one that makes $100 < 3^n$ true. The table below summarizes the results:

n	$100 < 3^n$	
2	$100 < 3^2 = 9$	False
3	$100 < 3^3 = 27$	False
4	$100 < 3^4 = 81$	False
5	$100 < 3^5 = 243$	True

Since 5 is the first integer to work, the answer is (D).

11.   If the average of 10, 14, and n is greater than or equal to 8 and less than or equal to 12, what is the least possible value of n ?

(A)   –12
(B)   –6
(C)   0
(D)   6
(E)   12

Translating the clause "the average of 10, 14, and n is greater than or equal to 8 and less than or equal to 12" into an inequality yields

$$8 \leq \frac{10 + 14 + n}{3} \leq 12$$

Adding 10 and 14 yields $8 \leq \dfrac{24 + n}{3} \leq 12$

Multiplying <u>each</u> term by 3 yields $24 \leq 24 + n \leq 36$

Subtracting 24 from each term yields $0 \leq n \leq 12$

Hence, the least possible value of n is 0. The answer is (C).

12. If $\begin{array}{c} 3x + y < 4 \\ x > 3 \end{array}$, which of the following must be true?

    (A) $y < -5$ (B) $y < -10$ (C) $x = y$ (D) $x < 3$ (E) $y > 0$

Subtracting $3x$ from both sides of $3x + y < 4$ yields $y < 4 - 3x$. Now, multiplying both sides of $x > 3$ by -3 yields $-3x < -9$. Adding 4 to both sides yields $4 - 3x < -5$. Now, using the transitive property to combine $y < 4 - 3x$ and $4 - 3x < -5$ yields $y < 4 - 3x < -5$. Hence, $y < -5$. The answer is (A).

$$2 - 3x \; ? \; 5$$

13. Of the following symbols, which one can be substituted for the question mark in the above expression to make a true statement for all values of x such that $-1 < x \le 2$?

    (A) $=$ (B) $<$ (C) $\ge$ (D) $>$ (E) $\le$

Multiply each term of the inequality $-1 < x \le 2$ by -3 (this is done because the original expression involves $-3x$):

$$3 > -3x \ge -6$$

Add 2 to each term of this inequality (this is done because the original expression adds 2 and $-3x$):

$$5 > 2 - 3x \ge -4$$

Rewrite the inequality in standard form (with the smaller number on the left and the larger number on the right):

$$-4 \le 2 - 3x < 5$$

The answer is (B).

14. Let x, y, z be three different positive integers each less than 20. What is the smallest possible value of expression $\dfrac{x - y}{-z}$ is

    (A) -18 (B) -17 (C) -14 (D) -11 (E) -9

First, bring the negative symbol in the expression $\dfrac{x - y}{-z}$ to the top:

$$\frac{-(x - y)}{z}$$

Then distribute the negative symbol:

$$\frac{y - x}{z}$$

To make this expression as small as possible, we need to make both the $y - x$ and z as small as possible. To make $y - x$ as small as possible, let $y = 1$ and $x = 19$. Then $y - x = 1 - 19 = -18$. With these choices for y and x, the smallest remaining value for z is 2. This gives

$$\frac{y - x}{z} = \frac{1 - 19}{2} = \frac{-18}{2} = -9$$

In this case, we made the numerator as small as possible. Now, let's make the denominator as small as possible. To that end, chose $z = 1$ and $y = 2$ and $x = 19$. This gives

$$\frac{y - x}{z} = \frac{2 - 19}{1} = \frac{-17}{1} = -17$$

The answer is (B).

15. If $x > 0$ and $|x| = \dfrac{1}{x}$, then $x =$

    (A) –1   (B) 0   (C) 1   (D) 2   (E) 3

Since $x > 0$, $|x| = x$. And the equation $|x| = \dfrac{1}{x}$ becomes $x = \dfrac{1}{x}$. Multiplying both sides of this equation by x yields $x^2 = 1$. Taking the square root of both sides gives $x = \pm 1$. Since we are given that $x > 0$, x must equal 1. The answer is (C).

16. Four letters—a, b, c, and d—represent one number each from one through four. No two letters represent the same number. It is known that $c > a$ and $a > d$. If b = 2, then $a =$

    (A)   1
    (B)   2
    (C)   3
    (D)   4
    (E)   Not enough information to decide.

Combining the inequalities $c > a$ and $a > d$ gives $c > a > d$. Since $b = 2$, a, c, and d must represent the remaining numbers 1, 3, and 4—not necessarily in that order. In order to satisfy the condition $c > a > d$, c must be 4, a must be 3, and d must be 1. The answer is (C).

17. If $r > t$ and $r < 1$ and $rt = 1$, then which one of the following must be true?

    (A) $r > 0$ and $t < -1$
    (B) $r > -1$ and $t < -1$
    (C) $r < -1$ and $t > -1$
    (D) $r < 1$ and $t > 1$
    (E) $r > 1$ and $t < 0$

Note that the product of r and t is 1. The product of two numbers is positive only if both numbers are positive or both numbers are negative. Since $rt = 1$ and $r > t$, there are two possibilities:

$$\text{Case I (both negative): } -1 < r < 0 \text{ and } t < -1$$
$$\text{Case II (both positive): } 0 < t < 1 \text{ and } r > 1$$

The second case violates the condition $r < 1$. Hence, Case I is true, and the answer is (B).

18. If $x > y > 0$ and $p > q > 0$, then which one of the following expressions must be greater than 1?

    (A) $\dfrac{x+p}{y+q}$

    (B) $\dfrac{x+q}{y+p}$

    (C) $\dfrac{x}{p}$

    (D) $\dfrac{xq}{yp}$

    (E) $\dfrac{yq}{xp}$

Adding the given inequalities $x > y > 0$ and $p > q > 0$ yields

$$x + p > y + q > 0$$

Since $y + q$ is positive, dividing the inequality by $y + q$ will not reverse the inequality:

$$\frac{x+p}{y+q} > \frac{y+q}{y+q}$$

$$\frac{x+p}{y+q} > 1$$

Hence, the answer is (A).

19. If $2x + y > m$ and $2y + x < n$, then $x - y$ must be greater than

    (A) $m + n$
    (B) $m - n$
    (C) mn
    (D) $2m + n$
    (E) $n - m$

Aligning the system of inequalities vertically yields

$$2x + y > m$$
$$2y + x < n$$

Multiplying both sides of the bottom inequality by -1 and flipping the direction of the inequality yields

$$-2y - x > -n$$

Adding this inequality to the top inequality yields

$$(2x + y) + (-2y - x) > m - n$$
$$(2x - x) + (-2y + y) > m - n$$
$$x - y > m - n$$

The answer is (B).

20. If $p > 2$, then which one of the following inequalities must be false?

    (A) $2p > 7$
    (B) $3p < 7$
    (C) $p < 3$
    (D) $p > 4$
    (E) $3p < 6$

We are given that $p > 2$. Multiplying both sides of this inequality by 3 yields $3p > 6$. The answer is (E).

Problem Set M:

1. $\dfrac{\frac{2}{4}}{3} = 2 \cdot \dfrac{3}{4} = \dfrac{6}{4} = \dfrac{3}{2}$. The answer is (C).

2. Begin with $\dfrac{5}{6}$ and $\dfrac{4}{5}$. Cross-multiplying gives 25 versus 24. Hence, $\dfrac{5}{6} > \dfrac{4}{5}$. Continuing in this manner will show that $\dfrac{5}{6}$ is the greatest fraction listed. The answer is (A).

3. First, factor the expression $\dfrac{x^2 + 6x + 9}{x + 3} \cdot \dfrac{x^2 - 9}{x - 3}$:

$$\dfrac{(x+3)(x+3)}{x+3} \cdot \dfrac{(x+3)(x-3)}{x-3}$$

Next, cancel the $x + 3$ and the $x - 3$:

$$(x+3) \cdot (x+3)$$

or

$$(x+3)^2$$

The answer is (C).

4. $\dfrac{1}{\dfrac{4}{3}-1}=\dfrac{1}{\dfrac{4}{3}-\dfrac{3}{3}}=\dfrac{1}{\dfrac{1}{3}}=3$. The answer is (D).

5. Since squaring a fraction between 0 and 1 makes it smaller, we know Statement I is true. This eliminates both (B) and (C). Also, since taking the square root of a fraction between 0 and 1 makes it larger, we know Statement III is false. This eliminates (E). To analyze Statement II, we'll use substitution. Since $0 < x < 1$, we need only check one fraction, say, $x=\dfrac{1}{2}$. Then $\dfrac{1}{x^2}=\dfrac{1}{\left(\dfrac{1}{2}\right)^2}=\dfrac{1}{\left(\dfrac{1}{4}\right)}=1\cdot\dfrac{4}{1}=4$. Now,

$\dfrac{1}{2} < 4$. Hence, Statement II is true, and the answer is (D).

6. Let's take the first number in each pair, form its reciprocal, and then try to reduce it to the second number. Now, $1 \Rightarrow \dfrac{1}{1}=1$. Hence, the pair 1 and 1 are reciprocals of each other. Next,

$\dfrac{1}{11} \Rightarrow \dfrac{1}{\dfrac{1}{11}}=1\cdot\dfrac{11}{1}=11\neq -11$. Hence, the pair $\dfrac{1}{11}$ and -11 are not reciprocals of each other. Finally,

$\sqrt{5} \Rightarrow \dfrac{1}{\sqrt{5}}=\dfrac{1}{\sqrt{5}}\cdot\dfrac{\sqrt{5}}{\sqrt{5}}=\dfrac{\sqrt{5}}{5}$. Hence, the pair $\sqrt{5}$ and $\dfrac{\sqrt{5}}{5}$ are reciprocals of each other. The answer is (D).

7. $\dfrac{6^4-6^3}{5}=\dfrac{6^3(6-1)}{5}=\dfrac{6^3\cdot 5}{5}=6^3$. The answer is (B).

8. $\dfrac{1}{1-\dfrac{1}{1-\dfrac{1}{2}}}=\dfrac{1}{1-\dfrac{1}{\dfrac{2}{2}-\dfrac{1}{2}}}=\dfrac{1}{1-\dfrac{1}{\dfrac{1}{2}}}=\dfrac{1}{1-2}=\dfrac{1}{-1}=-1$. The answer is (B).

9. $\dfrac{1}{10^9}-\dfrac{1}{10^{10}}=\dfrac{1}{10^9}-\dfrac{1}{10^9}\cdot\dfrac{1}{10}=\dfrac{1}{10^9}\left(1-\dfrac{1}{10}\right)=\dfrac{1}{10^9}\left(\dfrac{9}{10}\right)=\dfrac{9}{10^{10}}$. The answer is (D).

10. $\dfrac{\dfrac{2x^2-2}{x-1}}{2(x+1)}=\dfrac{2x^2-2}{x-1}\cdot\dfrac{1}{2(x+1)}=\dfrac{2(x^2-1)}{x-1}\cdot\dfrac{1}{2(x+1)}=\dfrac{2(x+1)(x-1)}{x-1}\cdot\dfrac{1}{2(x+1)}=\dfrac{2}{2}\cdot\dfrac{x+1}{x+1}\cdot\dfrac{x-1}{x-1}=1$.
The answer is (B).

11. From the equation $\left(x^2-4\right)\left(\dfrac{4}{x}-5\right)=0$, we get $x^2-4=0$ or $\dfrac{4}{x}-5=0$. Consider the equation $x^2-4=0$ first. Factoring gives

$$(x+2)(x-2)=0$$

Setting each factor to zero gives

$$x+2=0 \ \text{ or } \ x-2=0$$

Hence, $x = 2$ or $x = -2$. But neither number is offered as an answer-choice. So we turn to the equation $\frac{4}{x} - 5 = 0$. Adding 5 to both sides yields

$$\frac{4}{x} = 5$$

Multiplying both sides by x gives

$$4 = 5x$$

Dividing both sides by 5 gives

$$\frac{4}{5} = x$$

The answer is (D).

12.
$$3^{n-1} = 3^{3n+1}$$
$$n - 1 = 3n + 1$$
$$-2n = 2$$
$$n = -1$$

Since $n = -1$, $m = 3^{n-1} = 3^{-1-1} = 3^{-2} = \frac{1}{3^2} = \frac{1}{9}$. Hence, $\frac{m}{n} = \frac{\frac{1}{9}}{-1} = -\frac{1}{9}$, and the answer is (D).

13. $q = 1* = \dfrac{\frac{1}{2}}{4 \cdot 1 - 1} = \dfrac{\frac{1}{2}}{3} = \dfrac{1}{2} \cdot \dfrac{1}{3} = \dfrac{1}{6}$. Hence, $q* = \dfrac{\frac{1}{6}}{4 \cdot \frac{1}{6} - 1} = \dfrac{\frac{1}{6} \cdot \frac{1}{2}}{\frac{2}{3} - 1} = \dfrac{\frac{1}{12}}{-\frac{1}{3}} = \dfrac{1}{12}\left(-\dfrac{3}{1}\right) = -\dfrac{3}{12} = -\dfrac{1}{4}$

The answer is (C).

14. Forming the negative reciprocal of $\dfrac{1}{x} + \dfrac{1}{y}$ yields

$$\dfrac{-1}{\dfrac{1}{x} + \dfrac{1}{y}}$$

Adding the fractions in the denominator yields

$$\dfrac{-1}{\dfrac{y + x}{xy}}$$

Reciprocating the denominator yields

$$-1 \cdot \dfrac{xy}{x + y}$$

Or

$$\dfrac{-xy}{x + y}$$

The answer is (E).

15. Since x and y are prime numbers and $x > y$, we know that $x > y > 0$. Dividing this inequality by y yields $x/y > y/y > 0/y$. Reducing yields $x/y > 1$. Since x and y are prime numbers, they will not have any common factors that could reduce x/y to an integer. Therefore, x/y is an irreducible fraction greater than one. The answer is (D).

Problem Set N:

1. Dividing both sides of the equation $6a = 5b$ by 6 gives $a = \dfrac{5}{6}b$. Thus, a is a fraction of b. But b is greater than zero and therefore b is greater than a. (Note, had we been given that a was less than zero, then a would have been greater than b.) The answer is (E).

2. Adding the two equations $\begin{array}{l} p - q + r = 4 \\ p + q + r = 8 \end{array}$ gives $2p + 2r = 12$

    Then dividing by 2 gives $p + r = 6$

    Hence, the answer is (C).

3. Clearing fractions in the equation $y - 2 = \dfrac{y + 5}{2}$ gives $2(y - 2) = y + 5$

    Distributing the 2 gives $2y - 4 = y + 5$
    Subtracting y and adding 4 to both sides gives $y = 9$
    Now, replacing y with 9 in the equation $x = y - 2$ gives $x = y - 2 = 9 - 2 = 7$
    Hence, the answer is (E).

4. Replacing p with 3^{q+1} in the expression $\dfrac{p}{3^2}$ gives $\dfrac{p}{3^2} = \dfrac{3^{q+1}}{3^2} = 3^{q+1-2} = 3^{q-1}$

    Now, replacing q with $2r$ in the expression 3^{q-1} gives $3^{q-1} = 3^{2r-1}$
    Hence, the answer is (A).

5. Substituting $u = 18$ and $v = 2$ into the equation $\dfrac{u - v}{k} = 8$ gives $\dfrac{18 - 2}{k} = 8$

    Subtracting gives $\dfrac{16}{k} = 8$

    Multiplying both sides of this equation by k gives $16 = 8k$

    Dividing by 8 gives $2 = k$

    With this value for k, the original equation becomes $\dfrac{u - v}{2} = 8$

    Now, we are asked to find u when $v = 4$.

    Replacing v with 4 in the equation $\dfrac{u - v}{2} = 8$ gives $\dfrac{u - 4}{2} = 8$

    Multiplying by 2 gives $u - 4 = 16$

    Adding 4 gives $u = 20$

    Hence, the answer is (E).

6. The equation $x = 3y = 4z$ contains three equations:

    $$x = 3y$$
    $$3y = 4z$$
    $$x = 4z$$

    Multiplying both sides of the equation $x = 3y$ by 6 gives $6x = 18y$. Hence, Statement I is true. This eliminates (B) and (C). Next, $3y + 20z = 3y + 5(4z)$. Substituting x for $3y$ and for $4z$ in this equation gives $3y + 20z = 3y + 5(4z) = x + 5x = 6x$. Hence, Statement II is true. This eliminates (A) and (E). Hence, by process of elimination, the answer is (D).

7.   Plugging $P = 10$ and $k = 3$ into the equation $P = (x + y)k$ gives $10 = (x + y)3$. Dividing by 3 gives $x + y = \dfrac{10}{3}$. Finally, to form the average, divide both sides of this equation by 2: $\dfrac{x + y}{2} = \dfrac{10}{6} = \dfrac{5}{3}$. Hence, the answer is (C).

8.   There are many different values for w, x, y, and z such that $\dfrac{x}{y} + \dfrac{w}{z} = 2$. Two particular cases are listed below:

If $x = y = w = z = 1$, then $\dfrac{x}{y} + \dfrac{w}{z} = \dfrac{1}{1} + \dfrac{1}{1} = 1 + 1 = 2$ and $\dfrac{y}{x} + \dfrac{z}{w} = \dfrac{1}{1} + \dfrac{1}{1} = 1 + 1 = 2$.

If $x = 3$, $y = 2$, $w = 1$, and $z = 2$, then $\dfrac{x}{y} + \dfrac{w}{z} = \dfrac{3}{2} + \dfrac{1}{2} = \dfrac{3+1}{2} = \dfrac{4}{2} = 2$ and $\dfrac{y}{x} + \dfrac{z}{w} = \dfrac{2}{3} + \dfrac{2}{1} = \dfrac{2}{3} + \dfrac{2}{1} \cdot \dfrac{3}{3} = \dfrac{2}{3} + \dfrac{6}{3} = \dfrac{2+6}{3} = \dfrac{8}{3}$.

This is a double case. Hence, the answer is (E).

9.   Translating the clause "4 percent of $(p + q)$ is 8" into a mathematical expression yields

$$.04(p + q) = 8$$

Dividing both sides of this equation by .04 yields

$$p + q = \dfrac{8}{.04} = 200$$

Subtracting p from both sides yields

$$q = 200 - p$$

This expression will be greatest when p is as small as possible. This is when $p = 1$:

$$q = 200 - 1 = 199$$

The answer is (D).

10.   The expression $x^5 = 4$ can be rewritten as

$$x \cdot x^4 = 4$$

Replacing x^4 in this expression with $\dfrac{7}{y}$ yields

$$x \cdot \dfrac{7}{y} = 4$$

Multiplying both sides of this equation by y gives

$$x \cdot 7 = 4 \cdot y$$

Dividing both sides of this equation by 7 yields

$$x = \dfrac{4}{7} \cdot y$$

Hence, the answer is (B).

11.   Start with the bottom equation $3y = 9 - 6x$:

Dividing by 3 yields $y = 3 - 2x$

Adding $2x$ yields $2x + y = 3$

Notice that this is the top equation in the system. Hence, the system is only one equation in two different forms. Thus, there are an infinite number of solutions. For example, the pair $x = 2$, $y = -1$ is a solution as is the pair $x = 0$, $y = 3$. The answer is (E).

12. The clause " $\dfrac{p}{19}$ *is 1 less than 3 times* $\dfrac{q}{19}$ " translates into:

$$\frac{p}{19} = 3 \cdot \frac{q}{19} - 1$$

Multiplying both sides of this equation by 19 gives

$$p = 3 \cdot q - 19$$

The answer is (E).

13. Since the right side of the equation is positive, the left side must also be positive. Thus, $(-8)^{2n}$ is equal to

$$8^{2n}$$

This in turn can be written as

$$\left(2^3\right)^{2n}$$

Multiplying the exponents gives

$$2^{6n}$$

Plugging this into the original equation gives

$$2^{6n} = 2^{8+2n}$$

Now, since the bases are the same, the exponents must be equal:

$$6n = 8 + 2n$$

Solving this equation gives

$$n = 2$$

The answer is (B).

14.
$$3^{4n-1} = 27$$
$$3^{4n-1} = 3^3$$
$$4n - 1 = 3$$
$$4n = 4$$
$$n = 1$$

Since $n = 1$, $m = 3^{n-1} = 3^{1-1} = 3^0 = 1$. Hence, $\dfrac{m}{n} = \dfrac{1}{1} = 1$, and the answer is (B).

15. First, clear fractions by multiplying both sides by $12(s + S)$: $4(s + S) = 3(s - S)$

Next, distribute the 3 and 4: $4s + 4S = 3s - 3S$

Finally, subtract $3s$ and $4S$ from both sides: $s = -7S$

The answer is (D).

16. $3^x = 81 = 3^4$. Hence, $x = 4$. Replacing x with 4 in the expression $\left(3^{x+3}\right)\left(4^{x+1}\right)$ yields

$$\left(3^{4+3}\right)\left(4^{4+1}\right) =$$

$$3^7 \cdot 4^5 =$$

$$3^2 \cdot 3^5 \cdot 4^5 =$$

$$3^2(3 \cdot 4)^5 =$$

$$9(12)^5$$

The answer is (D).

17. We are given the equations: $x = y/2$
$y = z/2$

Solving the bottom equation for z yields $z = 2y$. Replacing x and z in the expression $\sqrt{x/z}$ with $y/2$ and $2y$, respectively, yields

$$\sqrt{x/z} = \sqrt{\frac{y/2}{2y}} = \sqrt{\frac{y}{2} \cdot \frac{1}{2y}} = \sqrt{\frac{1}{4}} = \frac{1}{2}$$

The answer is (D).

18. We are given $a = b/c$
$b = a/c$

Replacing b in the top equation with a/c (since $b = a/c$ according to the bottom equation) yields

$$a = \frac{a/c}{c}$$

$$a = \frac{a}{c} \cdot \frac{1}{c}$$

$$a = \frac{a}{c^2}$$

$$1 = \frac{1}{c^2} \qquad \text{(by canceling } a \text{ from both sides)}$$

$$c^2 = 1$$

$$c = \pm\sqrt{1} = \pm 1$$

Since one of the two possible answers is –1, the answer is (C).

19. Forming a system from the two given equations yields

$$x + 3y = 5$$
$$3x + y = 7$$

Adding the two equations yields

$$4x + 4y = 12$$

$$4(x + y) = 12 \qquad \text{by factoring out 4}$$

$$x + y = 12/4 = 3 \qquad \text{by dividing by 4}$$

The answer is (C).

20. Aligning the system of equations vertically yields

$$7x - y = 23$$
$$7y - x = 31$$

Adding the system of equations yields

$$(7x - y) + (7y - x) = 23 + 31$$
$$(7x - x) + (7y - y) = 54 \qquad \text{by collecting like terms}$$
$$6x + 6y = 54 \qquad \text{by adding like terms}$$
$$6(x + y) = 54 \qquad \text{by factoring out 6}$$
$$x + y = 9 \qquad \text{by dividing both sides by 6}$$

The answer is (E).

21. Writing the system of given equations vertically yields

$$x + y = 4a/5$$
$$y + z = 7a/5$$
$$z + x = 9a/5$$

Adding the three equations yields

$$(x + y) + (y + z) + (z + x) = 4a/5 + 7a/5 + 9a/5$$
$$2x + 2y + 2z = 20a/5 \qquad \text{by adding like terms}$$
$$2(x + y + z) = 4a$$
$$x + y + z = 2a \qquad \text{by dividing both sides by 2}$$

The answer is (C).

Problem Set O:

1. Since the average of p and $4p$ is 10, we get
$$\frac{p + 4p}{2} = 10$$

Combining the p's gives
$$\frac{5p}{2} = 10$$

Multiplying by 2 yields
$$5p = 20$$
Finally, dividing by 5 gives
$$p = 4$$
The answer is (C).

2. We have six consecutive integers whose average is $9\frac{1}{2}$, so we have the first three integers less than $9\frac{1}{2}$ and the first three integers greater than $9\frac{1}{2}$. That is, we are dealing with the numbers 7, 8, 9, 10, 11, 12. Clearly, the average of the last three numbers in this list is 11. Hence, the answer is (D).

3. The average of the consecutive positive integers 1 through n is $A = \dfrac{1 + 2 + \ldots + n}{n}$. Now, we are given that S denotes the sum of the consecutive positive integers 1 through n, that is, $S = 1 + 2 + \cdots + n$.. Plugging this into the formula for the average gives $A = \dfrac{S}{n}$. Hence, Statement I is true, which eliminates (B) and (C). Next, solving the equation $A = \dfrac{S}{n}$ for S yields $S = A \cdot n$. Thus, Statement II is false, which eliminates (D) and (E). Therefore, the answer is (A).

4.   The average speed at which car X traveled is $\dfrac{Total\ Distance}{30}$.

The average speed at which car Y traveled is $\dfrac{Total\ Distance}{20}$.

The two fractions have the same numerators, and the denominator for car Y is smaller. Hence, the average miles per hour at which car Y traveled is greater than the average miles per hour at which car X traveled. Thus, Statement I is false and Statement III is true. As to Statement II, we do not have enough information to calculate the distance between the cities. Hence, Statement II need not be true. The answer is (C).

5.   The average of p, q, and r is $\dfrac{p+q+r}{3}$. Replacing $p+q$ with r gives $\dfrac{r+r}{3} = \dfrac{2r}{3}$. The answer is (C).

6.   Often on the SAT you will be given numbers in different units. When this occurs, you must convert the numbers into the same units. (This is obnoxious but it does occur on the SAT, so be alert to it.) In this problem, we must convert 15 minutes into hours: $15 \cdot \dfrac{1}{60} = \dfrac{1}{4}\ hr$. Hence, the average speed is $\dfrac{Total\ Distance}{Total\ Time} = \dfrac{x}{y+\dfrac{1}{4}}$. The answer is (C).

7.   Forming the average of the five numbers gives

$$\frac{v+w+x+y+z}{5} = 6.9$$

Let the deleted number be z. Then forming the average of the remaining four numbers gives

$$\frac{v+w+x+y}{4} = 4.4$$

Multiplying both sides of this equation by 4 gives

$$v+w+x+y = 17.6$$

Plugging this value into the original average gives

$$\frac{17.6+z}{5} = 6.9$$

Solving this equation for z gives

$$z = 16.9$$

The answer is (D).

8.   Let the four numbers be a, b, c, and d. Since their average is 20, we get

$$\frac{a+b+c+d}{4} = 20$$

Let d be the number that is removed. Since the average of the remaining numbers is 15, we get

$$\frac{a+b+c}{3} = 15$$

Solving for $a+b+c$ yields

$$a+b+c = 45$$

Substituting this into the first equation yields

$$\frac{45+d}{4} = 20$$

Multiplying both sides of this equation by 4 yields

$$45 + d = 80$$

Subtracting 45 from both sides of this equation yields

$$d = 35$$

The answer is (D).

9. Let the other number be y. Since the average of the two numbers is $\dfrac{\pi}{2}$, we get

$$\frac{x+y}{2} = \frac{\pi}{2}$$

Multiplying both sides of this equation by 2 yields

$$x + y = \pi$$

Subtracting x from both sides of this equation yields

$$y = \pi - x$$

The answer is (C).

10. This is a weighted-average problem because more disks were purchased on the second day. Let x be the number of disks purchased on the first day. Then $.50x = 25$. Solving for x yields $x = 50$. Let y be the number of disks purchased on the second day. Then $.30y = 45$. Solving for y yields $y = 150$. Forming the weighted average, we get

$$Average\ Cost = \frac{Total\ Cost}{Total\ Number} = \frac{25+45}{50+150} = \frac{70}{200} = .35$$

The answer is (C).

11. Let the seven unknown numbers be represented by $x_1, x_2, \cdots, x_7$. Forming the average of the eight numbers yields

$$\frac{x_1 + x_2 + \cdots + x_7 + 14}{8} = A$$

Replacing 14 with 28 ($= 14 + 14$), and forming the average yields

$$\frac{x_1 + x_2 + \cdots + x_7 + (14+14)}{8}$$

Breaking up the fraction into the sum of two fractions yields

$$\frac{x_1 + x_2 + \cdots + x_7 + 14}{8} + \frac{14}{8}$$

Since $\dfrac{x_1 + x_2 + \cdots + x_7 + 14}{8} = A$, this becomes

$$A + \frac{14}{8}$$

Reducing the fraction yields

$$A + \frac{7}{4}$$

The answer is (A).

Problem Set P:

1.   First change all the units to inches: 2 ft. 3 in. = 27 in., and 2 yds. = 72 in. Forming the ratio yields

$$\frac{2\ ft.\ 3\ in.}{2\ yds.} = \frac{27\ in.}{72\ in.} = \frac{3}{8}$$

The answer is (C).

2.   Let x and y denote the numbers. Then $\frac{x}{y} = 10$ and $x - y = 18$. Solving the first equation for x and plugging it into the second equation yields

$$10y - y = 18$$

$$9y = 18$$

$$y = 2$$

Plugging this into the equation $x - y = 18$ yields $x = 20$. Hence, y is the smaller number. The answer is (A).

3.   Let x and y denote the angles: Then $\frac{x}{y} = \frac{1}{3}$ and since the angle sum of a triangle is $180°$, $x + x + y = 180$. Solving the first equation for y and plugging it into the second equation yields

$$2x + 3x = 180$$

$$5x = 180$$

$$x = 36$$

Plugging this into the equation $\frac{x}{y} = \frac{1}{3}$ yields $y = 108$. The answer is (E).

4.   This is a direct proportion: as the distance increases, the gallons of fuel consumed also increases. Setting ratios equal yields

$$\frac{80\ gal.}{320\ mi.} = \frac{x\ gal.}{700\ mi.}$$

$$\frac{700 \cdot 80}{320} = x$$

$$175 = x$$

The answer is (E).

5.   This is an inverse proportion: as the number of boys increases the time required to complete the job decreases. Setting products equal yields

$$2 \times 2.5 = 5 \times t$$

$$1 = t$$

The answer is (A).

6. This is a direct proportion: as the amount of flour increases so must the amount of shortening. First change $\frac{1}{2}$ lb. into 8 oz., Setting ratios equal yields

$$\frac{8}{14} = \frac{x}{21}$$

$$\frac{21 \cdot 8}{14} = x$$

$$12 = x$$

The answer is (D).

7. Most students struggle with this type of problem, and the SAT considers them to be difficult. However, if you can identify whether a problem is a direct proportion or an inverse proportion, then it is not so challenging. In this problem, as the number of widgets increases so does the absolute cost. This is a direct proportion, and therefore we set ratios equal:

$$\frac{w}{d} = \frac{2000}{x}$$

Cross multiplying yields

$$w \cdot x = 2000 \cdot d$$

Dividing by w yields

$$x = \frac{2000d}{w}$$

The answer is (C).

8. This is considered to be a hard problem. Begin by adding the two equations:

$$x + 2y - z = 1$$
$$\underline{3x - 2y - 8z = -1}$$
$$4x - 9z = 0$$
$$4x = 9z$$
$$\frac{x}{z} = \frac{9}{4}$$

The answer is (E).

9. This is a direct proportion: as the time increases so does the number of steps that the sprinter takes. Setting ratios equal yields

$$\frac{30}{9} = \frac{x}{54}$$

$$\frac{30 \cdot 54}{9} = x$$

$$180 = x$$

The answer is (D).

10. Dividing the equation $5x = 6y$ by $5y$ yields

$$\frac{x}{y} = \frac{6}{5} \quad \text{ratio of } x \text{ to } y$$

or in ratio notation

$$x : y = 6 : 5$$

The answer is (D).

Problem Set Q:

1.

$$\left(\frac{2y^3}{x^2}\right)^4 \cdot x^{10} = \frac{\left(2y^3\right)^4}{\left(x^2\right)^4} \cdot x^{10} = \qquad \text{by the rule } \left(\frac{x}{y}\right)^a = \frac{x^a}{y^a}$$

$$\frac{2^4 \cdot \left(y^3\right)^4}{\left(x^2\right)^4} \cdot x^{10} = \qquad \text{by the rule } (xy)^a = x^a \cdot y^a$$

$$\frac{2^4 \cdot y^{12}}{x^8} \cdot x^{10} = \qquad \text{by the rule } \left(x^a\right)^b = x^{ab}$$

$$2^4 \cdot y^{12} \cdot x^2 = \qquad \text{by the rule } \frac{x^a}{x^b} = x^{a-b}$$

$$16 \cdot y^{12} \cdot x^2$$

The answer is (A).

2.

$$\sqrt{(31-6)(16+9)} =$$
$$\sqrt{25 \cdot 25} =$$
$$\sqrt{25}\sqrt{25} =$$
$$5 \cdot 5 =$$
$$25$$

The answer is (C).

3.   Begin by completely factoring 20:

$$20^8 = (2 \cdot 2 \cdot 5)^8 =$$
$$2^8 \cdot 2^8 \cdot 5^8 = \qquad \text{by Rule 3, } (xy)^a = x^a \cdot y^a *$$
$$2^{16} \cdot 5^8 \qquad \text{by Rule 1, } x^a \cdot x^b = x^{a+b}$$

The expression 2^{16} represents all the factors of 20^8 of the form 2^n. Hence, 16 is the largest such number, and the answer is (E).

4.   Begin by factoring 55 in the top of the fraction:

$$\frac{55^5}{5^{55}} = \frac{(5 \cdot 11)^5}{5^{55}} =$$
$$\frac{5^5 \cdot 11^5}{5^{55}} = \qquad \text{by Rule 3, } (xy)^a = x^a \cdot y^a$$
$$\frac{11^5}{5^{50}} \qquad \text{by Rule 5, } \frac{x^a}{x^b} = \frac{1}{x^{b-a}}$$

The answer is (C).

---

* Note, Rule 3 can be extended to any number of terms by repeatedly applying the rule. For example,

$$(xyz)^a = ([xy]z)^a = [xy]^a \cdot z^a = x^a y^a z^a.$$

5. $\sqrt{x} - x^2 = \sqrt{\dfrac{1}{9}} - \left(\dfrac{1}{9}\right)^2 = \dfrac{1}{3} - \dfrac{1}{81} = \dfrac{27}{27} \cdot \dfrac{1}{3} - \dfrac{1}{81} = \dfrac{27-1}{81} = \dfrac{26}{81}$. The answer is (C).

6.

$$\left(9^x\right)^3 = 9^{3x} = \qquad \text{by the rule } \left(x^a\right)^b = x^{ab}$$

$$\left(3^2\right)^{3x} = \qquad \text{since } 9 = 3^2$$

$$3^{6x} \qquad \text{again by the rule } \left(x^a\right)^b = x^{ab}$$

The answer is (C). Note, this is considered to be a hard problem.

7. Plugging $x = 4$ into the expression $-2^{2\sqrt{x}} + 2$ yields

$$-2^{2\sqrt{4}} + 2 = -2^{2\cdot2} + 2 = -2^4 + 2 = -16 + 2 = -14$$

The answer is (A).

8.

$$\sqrt{\dfrac{25 + 10x + x^2}{2}} = \sqrt{\dfrac{(5+x)^2}{2}} = \qquad \text{since } 25 + 10x + x^2 \text{ factors into } (5+x)^2$$

$$\dfrac{\sqrt{(5+x)^2}}{\sqrt{2}} = \qquad \text{by the rule } \sqrt[n]{\dfrac{x}{y}} = \dfrac{\sqrt[n]{x}}{\sqrt[n]{y}}$$

$$\dfrac{5+x}{\sqrt{2}} = \qquad \text{since } \sqrt{x^2} = x$$

$$\dfrac{5+x}{\sqrt{2}} \cdot \dfrac{\sqrt{2}}{\sqrt{2}} = \qquad \text{rationalizing the denominator}$$

$$\dfrac{\sqrt{2}(5+x)}{2}$$

Hence, the answer is (C).

9. $\dfrac{2+\sqrt{5}}{2-\sqrt{5}} = \dfrac{2+\sqrt{5}}{2-\sqrt{5}} \cdot \dfrac{2+\sqrt{5}}{2+\sqrt{5}} = \dfrac{4+4\sqrt{5}+5}{4-5} = \dfrac{9+4\sqrt{5}}{-1} = -9-4\sqrt{5}$. Hence, the answer is (A).

10. $2^{12} + 2^{12} + 2^{12} + 2^{12} = 4 \cdot 2^{12} = 2^2 \cdot 2^{12} = 2^{2+12} = 2^{14}$. The answer is (B).

11. $\left(\dfrac{\left(x^2 y\right)^3 z}{xyz}\right)^3 = \left(\dfrac{\left(x^2 y\right)^3}{xy}\right)^3 = \left(\dfrac{\left(x^2\right)^3 y^3}{xy}\right)^3 = \left(\dfrac{x^6 y^3}{xy}\right)^3 = \left(x^5 y^2\right)^3 = \left(x^5\right)^3 \left(y^2\right)^3 = x^{15} y^6$

Hence, the answer is (E).

12. Our goal here is to write both sides of the equation in terms of the base 2 and then equate the exponents. To that end, write 16 as 2^4:

$$2^{2x} = \left(2^4\right)^{x+2}$$
$$2^{2x} = 2^{4(x+2)}$$

Since we have written both sides of the equation in terms of the base 2, we now equate the exponents:

$$2x = 4(x + 2)$$
$$2x = 4x + 8$$
$$-2x = 8$$
$$x = -4$$

The answer is (A).

13. First, let's reciprocate the expression $(x + y)^{-\frac{1}{3}}$ to eliminate the negative exponent:

$$(x - y)^{\frac{1}{3}} = \frac{1}{(x + y)^{\frac{1}{3}}}$$

Cubing both sides of this equation to eliminate the cube roots yields

$$x - y = \frac{1}{x + y}$$

Multiplying both sides of this equation by $x + y$ yields

$$(x - y)(x + y) = 1$$

Multiplying out the left side of this equation yields

$$x^2 - xy + xy + y^2 = 1$$

Reducing yields

$$x^2 + y^2 = 1$$

The answer is (C).

Problem Set R:

1.   First, interchanging 5 and $7x$ in the expression $3y + 5 = 7x$ yields $3y - 7x = -5$. Next, factoring $21y - 49x$ yields

$$21y - 49x =$$
$$7 \cdot 3y - 7 \cdot 7x =$$
$$7(3y - 7x) =$$
$$7(-5) = \qquad \text{since } 3y - 7x = -5$$
$$-35$$

The answer is (B).

2.

$$2x^2 - 4xy + 2y^2 =$$

$$2\left(x^2 - 2xy + y^2\right) = \qquad \text{by factoring out the common factor 2}$$

$$2(x - y)^2 = \qquad \text{by the formula } x^2 - 2xy + y^2 = (x - y)^2$$

$$2p^2 \qquad \text{since } x - y = p$$

The answer is (E).

3.

$$p = \sqrt{2pq - q^2}$$
$$p^2 = 2pq - q^2 \qquad \text{by squaring both sides}$$
$$p^2 - 2pq + q^2 = 0 \qquad \text{by subtracting } 2pq \text{ and adding } q^2 \text{ to both sides}$$
$$(p - q)^2 = 0 \qquad \text{by the formula } x^2 - 2xy + y^2 = (x - y)^2$$
$$p - q = 0 \qquad \text{by taking the square root of both sides}$$
$$p = q \qquad \text{by adding } q \text{ to both sides}$$

The answer is (A).

4.

$$\frac{x^2 + 2x - 10}{5} = 1$$
$$x^2 + 2x - 10 = 5 \qquad \text{by multiplying both sides by 5}$$
$$x^2 + 2x - 15 = 0 \qquad \text{by subtracting 5 from both sides}$$
$$(x + 5)(x - 3) = 0 \qquad \text{since } 5 \cdot 3 = 15 \text{ and } 5 - 3 = 2$$
$$x + 5 = 0 \text{ and } x - 3 = 0 \qquad \text{by setting each factor equal to zero}$$
$$x = -5 \text{ and } x = 3$$

The answer is (A).

5.

Begin by factoring out the common factor in the equation $5y^2 - 20y + 15 = 0$:

$$5\left(y^2 - 4y + 3\right) = 0$$

Dividing both sides of this equation by 5 yields $y^2 - 4y + 3 = 0$
Since $3 + 1 = 4$, the trinomial factors into $(y - 3)(y - 1) = 0$
Setting each factor equal to zero yields $y - 3 = 0$ and $y - 1 = 0$

Solving these equations yields $y = 3$ and $y = 1$. Now, the difference of 3 and 1 is 2 and twice 2 is 4. Further, the difference of 1 and 3 is -2 and twice -2 is -4. Now, the absolute value of both 4 and -4 is 4. The answer is (E).

6.

$$\frac{7x^2 + 28x + 28}{(x+2)^2} =$$

$$\frac{7\left(x^2 + 4x + 4\right)}{(x+2)^2} = \qquad \text{by factoring out 7}$$

$$\frac{7(x+2)^2}{(x+2)^2} = \qquad \text{by the formula } x^2 + 2xy + y^2 = (x+y)^2$$

$$7 \qquad \text{by canceling the common factor } (x+2)^2$$

The answer is (A).

7.

$$\frac{7^9 + 7^8}{8} =$$

$$\frac{7^8 \cdot 7 + 7^8}{8} = \qquad \text{since } 7^9 = 7^8 \cdot 7$$

$$\frac{7^8(7+1)}{8} = \qquad \text{by factoring out the common factor } 7^8$$

$$\frac{7^8(8)}{8} =$$

$$7^8$$

Hence, the answer is (D). Note, this is considered to be a very hard problem.

8.

$$x^2 - y^2 =$$

$$(x+y)(x-y) = \qquad \text{since } x^2 - y^2 \text{ is a difference of squares}$$

$$(10)(5) = \qquad \text{since } x+y = 10 \text{ and } x-y = 5$$

$$50$$

The answer is (A). This problem can also be solved by adding the two equations. However, that approach will lead to long, messy fractions. Writers of the SAT put questions like this one on the SAT to see whether you will discover the short cut. The premise being that those students who do not see the short cut will take longer to solve the problem and therefore will have less time to finish the test.

9.   Noticing that $x - y$ is a common factor, we factor it out:

$$x(x-y) - z(x-y) = (x-y)(x-z)$$

The answer is (C).

Method II

Sometimes a complicated expression can be simplified by making a substitution. In the expression $x(x-y) - z(x-y)$ replace $x - y$ with w:

$$xw - zw$$

Now, the structure appears much simpler. Factoring out the common factor w yields

$$w(x-z)$$

Finally, re-substitute $x - y$ for w:

$$(x-y)(x-z)$$

10.

$$(x-y)^2 = x^2 + y^2$$

$$x^2 - 2xy + y^2 = x^2 + y^2 \quad \text{by the formula } x^2 - 2xy + y^2 = (x-y)^2$$

$$-2xy = 0 \qquad \text{by subtracting } x^2 \text{ and } y^2 \text{ from both sides of the equation}$$

$$xy = 0 \quad \text{by dividing both sides of the equation by } -2$$

Hence, Statement III is true, which eliminates choices (A), (B), and (C). However, Statement II is false. For example, if $y = 5$ and $x = 0$, then $xy = 0 \cdot 5 = 0$. A similar analysis shows that Statement I is false. The answer is (D).

11. The Difference of Squares formula yields $x^2 - y^2 = (x + y)(x - y)$. Now, both x and y must be odd because 2 is the only even prime and $x > y > 2$. Remember that the sum (or difference) of two odd numbers is even. Hence, $(x + y)(x - y)$ is the product of two even numbers and therefore is divisible by 4. To show this explicitly, let $x + y = 2p$ and let $x - y = 2q$. Then $(x + y)(x - y) = 2p \cdot 2q = 4pq$. Since we have written $(x + y)(x - y)$ as a multiple of 4, it is divisible by 4. The answer is (B).

Method II (substitution):

Let $x = 5$ and $y = 3$, then $x > y > 2$ and $x^2 - y^2 = 5^2 - 3^2 = 25 - 9 = 16$. Since 4 is the only number listed that divides evenly into 16, the answer is (B).

12. Solution:

$$\frac{xy + x^2}{xy - x^2} =$$

$$\frac{x(y + x)}{x(y - x)} = \qquad \text{by factoring out } x \text{ from both the top and bottom expressions}$$

$$\frac{y + x}{y - x} = \qquad \text{by canceling the common factor } x$$

$$\frac{x + y}{-(x - y)} = \qquad \text{by factoring out the negative sign in the bottom and then rearranging}$$

$$-\frac{x + y}{x - y} = \qquad \text{by recalling that a negative fraction can be written three ways: } \frac{a}{-b} = -\frac{a}{b} = \frac{-a}{b}$$

$$-\frac{1}{2} \qquad \text{by replacing } \frac{x + y}{x - y} \text{ with } \frac{1}{2}$$

The answer is (B).

13. The only information we have to work with is the equation $x + y = 2\sqrt{xy}$. Since radicals are awkward to work with, let's square both sides of this equation to eliminate the radical:

$$(x+y)^2 = \left(2\sqrt{xy}\right)^2$$

Applying the Perfect Square Trinomial Formula to the left side and simplifying the right side yields

$$x^2 + 2xy + y^2 = 4xy$$

Subtracting $4xy$ from both sides yields

$$x^2 - 2xy + y^2 = 0$$

Using the Perfect Square Trinomial Formula again yields

$$(x-y)^2 = 0$$

Taking the square root of both sides yields

$$\sqrt{(x-y)^2} = \pm\sqrt{0}$$

Simplifying yields

$$x - y = 0$$

Finally, adding y to both sides yields

$$x = y$$

The answer is (C).

Problem Set S:

1.
$\left(x^2+2\right)\left(x-x^3\right) = x^2x - x^2x^3 + 2x - 2x^3 = x^3 - x^5 + 2x - 2x^3 = -x^5 - x^3 + 2x$. Thus, the answer is (B).

2.

$$-2\left(3 - x\left[\frac{5+y-2}{x}\right] - 7 + 2\cdot3^2\right) =$$
$$-2\left(3 - x\left[\frac{3+y}{x}\right] - 7 + 2\cdot3^2\right) =$$
$$-2\left(3 - [3+y] - 7 + 2\cdot3^2\right) =$$
$$-2\left(3 - 3 - y - 7 + 2\cdot3^2\right) =$$
$$-2(3 - 3 - y - 7 + 2\cdot9) =$$
$$-2(3 - 3 - y - 7 + 18) =$$
$$-2(-y + 11) =$$
$$2y - 22$$

The answer is (E).

3.
$a\lozenge b = ab - 1 = ba - 1 = b\lozenge a$. Thus, I is true, which eliminates (B) and (C).

$\dfrac{a\lozenge a}{a} = \dfrac{aa-1}{a} \neq 1\cdot1 - 1 = 1 - 1 = 0 = 1\lozenge1$. Thus, II is false, which eliminates (D).

$(a\lozenge b)\lozenge c = (ab-1)\lozenge c = (ab-1)c - 1 = abc - c - 1 \neq a\lozenge(bc-1) = a(bc-1) - 1 = abc - a - 1 = a\lozenge(b\lozenge c)$. Thus, III is false, which eliminates (E). Hence, the answer is (A).

4.

$$\left(x+\frac{1}{2}\right)^2 - (2x-4)^2 =$$

$$x^2 + 2x\frac{1}{2} + \left(\frac{1}{2}\right)^2 - \left[(2x)^2 - 2(2x)4 + 4^2\right] =$$

$$x^2 + x + \frac{1}{4} - 4x^2 + 16x - 16 =$$

$$-3x^2 + 17x - \frac{63}{4}$$

Hence, the answer is (C).

5.

$$y^2 - \left(x - \left[y + \frac{1}{2}\right]\right) - 2\cdot3 =$$

$$(-3)^2 - \left(2 - \left[-3 + \frac{1}{2}\right]\right) - 2\cdot3 =$$

$$(-3)^2 - \left(2 - \left[-\frac{5}{2}\right]\right) - 2\cdot3 =$$

$$(-3)^2 - \left(2 + \frac{5}{2}\right) - 2\cdot3 =$$

$$(-3)^2 - \frac{9}{2} - 2\cdot3 =$$

$$9 - \frac{9}{2} - 2\cdot3 =$$

$$9 - \frac{9}{2} - 6 =$$

$$3 - \frac{9}{2} =$$

$$-\frac{3}{2}$$

The answer is (B).

6.

$$4(xy)^3 + \left(x^3 - y^3\right)^2 =$$

$$4x^3y^3 + \left(x^3\right)^2 - 2x^3y^3 + \left(y^3\right)^2 =$$

$$\left(x^3\right)^2 + 2x^3y^3 + \left(y^3\right)^2 =$$

$$\left(x^3 + y^3\right)^2$$

The answer is (E).

7.

$$\frac{b-a}{a} = \frac{b}{a} - \frac{a}{a} = \frac{b}{a} - 1 = \frac{-3}{2} - 1 = \frac{-3}{2} - \frac{2}{2} = \frac{-3-2}{2} = \frac{-5}{2}.$$ The answer is (A).

8. $(x-2)^2 * x = \dfrac{(x-2)^2}{x} = \dfrac{x^2 - 4x + 4}{x} = \dfrac{x^2}{x} - \dfrac{4x}{x} + \dfrac{4}{x} = x - 4 + \dfrac{4}{x}$. The answer is (A).

9.
$$(2+\sqrt{7})(4-\sqrt{7})(-2x) =$$
$$(2\cdot 4 - 2\sqrt{7} + 4\sqrt{7} - \sqrt{7}\sqrt{7})(-2x) =$$
$$(8 + 2\sqrt{7} - 7)(-2x) =$$
$$(1 + 2\sqrt{7})(-2x) =$$
$$1(-2x) + 2\sqrt{7}(-2x) =$$
$$-2x - 4x\sqrt{7}$$

The answer is (C).

10. $(x*y)*z = (xy)^2 * z = \left((xy)^2 z\right)^2 = \left((xy)^2\right)^2 z^2 = (xy)^4 z^2 = x^4 y^4 z^2$. The answer is (B).

11. Since we are given that $p = z + 1/z$ and $q = z - 1/z$,
$$p + q = (z + 1/z) + (z - 1/z) = z + 1/z + z - 1/z = 2z.$$
$$p - q = (z + 1/z) - (z - 1/z) = z + 1/z - z + 1/z = 2/z.$$
Therefore, $(p + q)(p - q) = (2z)(2/z) = 4$. The answer is (B).

12. Adding $2xy$ to both sides of the equation $x^2 + y^2 = xy$ yields

$$x^2 + y^2 + 2xy = 3xy$$
$$(x+y)^2 = 3xy \qquad \text{from the formula } (x+y)^2 = x^2 + 2xy + y^2$$

Squaring both sides of this equation yields

$$(x+y)^4 = (3xy)^2 = 9x^2 y^2$$

The answer is (C).

13.
Solution:
$$(2+x)(2+y) - (2+x) - (2+y) =$$
$$4 + 2y + 2x + xy - 2 - x - 2 - y =$$
$$x + y + xy$$

The answer is (E).

14. Writing the system of equations vertically yields

$$x^2 + y^2 = 2ab$$
$$2xy = a^2 + b^2$$

Adding the equations yields

$$x^2 + 2xy + y^2 = a^2 + 2ab + b^2$$

Applying the Perfect Square Trinomial formula to both the sides of the equation yields

$$(x+y)^2 = (a+b)^2$$
$$x + y = a + b \qquad \text{by taking the square root of both sides and noting all numbers are positive}$$

The answer is (C).

Problem Set T:

1. Consider the first sentence: John spent \$25, which is 15 percent of his monthly wage. Now, translate the main part of the sentence into a mathematical equation as follows:

25	is	15	%	of	his monthly wage
↓	↓	↓	↓	↓	↓

$$25 \quad = \quad 15 \quad \frac{1}{100} \quad \cdot \quad\quad x$$

$$25 = \frac{15}{100}x$$

$$2500 = 15x$$

$$x = \frac{2500}{15} = \frac{500}{3} = 166\frac{2}{3}$$

The answer is (B).

2. Translate the main part of the sentence into a mathematical equation as follows:

What	percent	of	2a	is	2b
↓	↓	↓	↓	↓	↓

$$x \quad \frac{1}{100} \quad \cdot \quad 2a \quad = \quad 2b$$

$$\frac{x}{100} \cdot 2a = 2b$$

$$\frac{x}{100} \cdot 2(4b) = 2b \qquad \text{(substituting } a = 4b\text{)}$$

$$\frac{x}{100} \cdot 8 = 2 \qquad \text{(canceling } b \text{ from both sides)}$$

$$\frac{8x}{100} = 2$$

$$8x = 200$$

$$x = 25$$

The answer is (C).

Remark: You can substitute $b = a/4$ instead of $a = 4b$. Whichever letter you substitute, you will get the same answer. However, depending on the question, one substitution may be easier than another.

3. Since more than one letter is used in this question, we need to substitute one of the letters for the other to minimize the number of unknown quantities (letters).

40	percent	of	3p
↓	↓	↓	↓

$$40 \quad \frac{1}{100} \quad \times \quad 3p$$

$$= \frac{40}{100} \times 3p$$

$$= \frac{40}{100} \times 3(5q) \qquad \text{(substituting } p \ = \ 5q\text{)}$$

$$= \frac{600q}{100}$$

$$= 6q$$

The answer is (A).

4.

50	%	of	the blue balls
↓	↓	↓	↓
50	$\dfrac{1}{100}$	×	24

$$= \frac{50 \times 24}{100}$$

$$= \frac{1200}{100}$$

$$= 12$$

The answer is (C).

5. Since female employees are 108 out of 180, there are $180 - 108 = 72$ male employees. Now, translate the main part of the sentence into a mathematical equation as follows:

What	percent	of	the employees	are	male
↓	↓	↓	↓	↓	↓
x	$\dfrac{1}{100}$	·	180	=	72

$$\frac{180}{100}x = 72$$

$$\frac{100}{180} \times \frac{180}{100}x = \frac{100}{180} \times 72$$

$$x = 40$$

The answer is (D).

6. The total expense is the sum of expenses for the shirt, pants, and shoes, which is $\$10 + \$20 + \$30 = \$60$. Now, translate the main part of the sentence into a mathematical equation:

What	percent	of	the total expense	was spent for	the pants
↓	↓	↓	↓	↓	↓
x	$\dfrac{1}{100}$	·	60	=	20

$$\frac{60}{100}x = 20$$

$60x = 2000$ (by multiplying both sides of the equation by 100)

$x = \dfrac{2000}{60}$ (by dividing both sides of the equation by 60)

$x = \dfrac{100}{3} = 33\dfrac{1}{3}$

The answer is (D).

7. First, express all the numbers in the same units (inches):

The original height is $5\ feet = 5\ feet \times \dfrac{12\ inches}{1\ feet} = 60\ inches$

The change in height is $(5\ feet\ 6\ inches) - (5\ feet) = 6\ inches$.
Now, use the formula for percent of change.

Percent of change: $\dfrac{Amount\ of\ change}{Original\ amount} \times 100\% =$

$\dfrac{6}{60} \times 100\% =$

$\dfrac{1}{10} \times 100\% =$ (by canceling 6)

10%

The answer is (B).

8. The change in price is $\$1.50 - \$1.20 = \$.30$. Now, use the formula for percent of change.

$\dfrac{Amount\ of\ change}{Original\ amount} \times 100\% =$

$\dfrac{.30}{1.20} \times 100\% =$

$\dfrac{1}{4} \times 100\% =$

25%

The answer is (C).

9. Let x be the price before the discount. Since Stella received a 20 percent discount, she paid 80 percent of the original price. Thus, 80 percent of the original price is $\$1,500$. Now, translate this sentence into a mathematical equation:

80	percent	of	<u>the original price</u>	is	$1,500
↓	↓	↓	↓	↓	↓
80	$\dfrac{1}{100}$	$\cdot$	x	$=$	1500

$\dfrac{80}{100}x = 1500$

$\dfrac{100}{80}\dfrac{80}{100}x = \dfrac{100}{80}1500$ (by multiplying both sides by the reciprocal of $\dfrac{80}{100}$)

$x = 1875$

The answer is (C).

10. Since the population increased at a rate of 10% per year, the population of any year is the population of the previous year + 10% of that same year. Hence, the population in 1991 is the population of 1990 + 10% of the population of 1990:

$$2000 + 10\% \text{ of } 2000 =$$
$$2000 + 200 =$$
$$2200$$

Similarly, the population in 1992 is the population of 1991 + 10% of the population of 1991:

$$2200 + 10\% \text{ of } 2200 =$$
$$2200 + 220 =$$
$$2420$$

Hence, the answer is (D).

11. Let g be the number of girls, and b the number of boys. Calculate the number of girls in the class:

Girls	are	40	percent	of	the class
↓	↓	↓	↓	↓	↓
g	=	40	$\dfrac{1}{100}$	×	200

$$g = \frac{40}{100} \times 200 = 80$$

The number of boys equals the total number of students minus the number of girls:

$$b = 200 - 80 = 120$$

Next, calculate the number of boys and girls who signed up for the tour:

25 percent of boys ($\dfrac{25}{100} \times 120 = 30$) and 10 percent of girls ($\dfrac{10}{100} \times 80 = 8$) signed up for the tour. Thus, $30 + 8 = 38$ students signed up. Now, translate the main part of the question with a little modification into a mathematical equation:

What	percent	of	the class	is	the students who signed up for the tour
↓	↓	↓	↓	↓	↓
x	$\dfrac{1}{100}$	·	200	=	38

$$\frac{200}{100}x = 38$$

$$x = 19$$

The answer is (A).

12. Let x be the number of which the percentage is being calculated. Then 15% of the number x is $.15x$. We are told this is equal to 4.5. Hence,

$$.15x = 4.5$$

Solving this equation by dividing both sides by .15 yields

$$x = \frac{4.5}{.15} = 30$$

Now, 45% of 30 is

$$.45(30)$$

Multiplying out this expression gives 13.5. The answer is (C).

Problem Set U:

Questions 1–5 refer to the following graphs.

Profit And Revenue Distribution For Zippy Printing, 1990–1993, Copying And Printing.

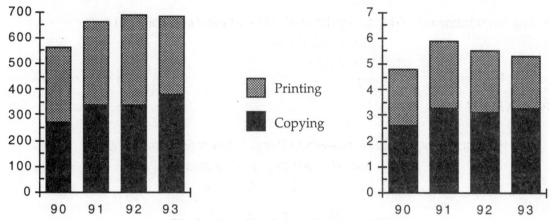

Total Profit
(in thousands of dollars)

Total Revenue
(in millions of dollars)

Distribution of Profit from Copying, 1992
(in thousands of dollars)

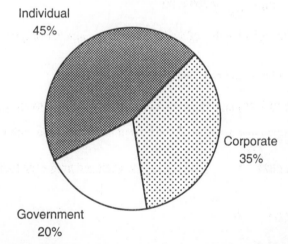

1.   In 1993, the total profit was approximately how much greater than the total profit in 1990?

(A) 50 thousand   (B) 75 thousand   (C) 120 thousand   (D) 200 thousand   (E) 350 thousand

Remember, rarely does a graph question involve significant computation. For this question, we need merely to read the bar graph. The Total Profit graph shows that in 1993 approximately 680 thousand was earned, and in 1990 approximately 560 thousand was earned. Subtracting these numbers yields 680 − 560 = 120. The answer is (C).

2.   In 1990, the profit from copying was approximately what percent of the revenue from copying?

(A) 2%   (B) 10%   (C) 20%   (D) 35%   (E) 50%

The Total Revenue graph indicates that in 1990 the revenue from copying was about \$2,600,000. The Total Profit graph shows the profit from copying in that same year was about \$270,000. The profit margin is

$$\frac{\text{Profit}}{\text{Revenue}} = \frac{270,000}{2,600,000} \approx 10\%$$

The answer is (B).

3.   In 1992, the profit from copying for corporate customers was approximately how much greater than the profit from copying for government customers?

   (A) 50 thousand   (B) 80 thousand   (C) 105 thousand   (D) 190 thousand   (E) 260 thousand

From the chart, the profit in 1992 was approximately $700,000 of which 35% x $700,000 = $245,000 was from corporate customers and 20% x $700,000 = $140,000 was from government customers. Subtracting these amounts yields $245,000 – $140,000 = $105,000. The answer is (C).

4.   During the two years in which total profit was most nearly equal, the combined revenue from printing was closest to

   (A) 1 million   (B) 2 million   (C) 4.5 million   (D) 6 million   (E) 6.5 million

The Total Profit graph shows that 1992 and 1993 are clearly the two years in which total profit was most nearly equal. Turning to the Total Revenue graph, we see that in 1992 the revenue from printing sales was approximately 2.5 million, and that in 1993 the revenue from printing sales was approximately 2 million. This gives a total of 4.5 million in total printing sales revenue for the period. The answer is (C).

5.   The amount of profit made from government copy sales in 1992 was

   (A) 70 thousand   (B) 100 thousand   (C) 150 thousand   (D) 200 thousand   (E) 350 thousand

The Total Profit graph shows that Zippy Printing earned about $340,000 from copying in 1992. The Pie Chart indicates that 20% of this was earned from government sales. Multiplying these numbers gives $340,000 \times 20\% \approx \$70,000$. The answer is (A).

Questions 6–10 refer to the following graphs.

DISTRIBUTION OF CRIMINAL ACTIVITY BY CATEGORY OF CRIME FOR COUNTRY X IN 1990 AND PROJECTED FOR 2000.

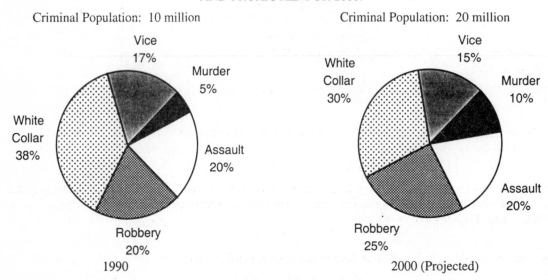

6.   What is the projected number of white-collar criminals in 2000?

   (A)   1 million
   (B)   3.8 million
   (C)   6 million
   (D)   8 million
   (E)   10 million

From the projected-crime graph, we see that the criminal population will be 20 million and of these 30 percent are projected to be involved in white-collar crime. Hence, the number of white-collar criminals is $(30\%)(20\ million) = (.30)(20\ million) = 6\ million$. The answer is (C).

7. The ratio of the number of robbers in 1990 to the number of projected robbers in 2000 is

(A) $\dfrac{2}{5}$ (B) $\dfrac{3}{5}$ (C) 1   (D) $\dfrac{3}{2}$ (E) $\dfrac{5}{2}$

In 1990, there were 10 million criminals and 20% were robbers. Thus, the number of robbers in 1990 was

$$(20\%)(10 \text{ million}) = (.20)(10 \text{ million}) = 2 \text{ million}$$

In 2000, there are projected to be 20 million criminals of which 25% are projected to be robbers. Thus, the number of robbers in 2000 is projected to be

$$(25\%)(20 \text{ million}) = (.25)(20 \text{ million}) = 5 \text{ million}$$

Forming the ratio of the above numbers yields

$$\frac{number\ of\ robbers\ in\ 1990}{number\ of\ robbers\ in\ 2000} = \frac{2}{5}$$

The answer is (A).

8. From 1990 to 2000, there is a projected decrease in the number of criminals for which of the following categories?

  I. Vice
  II. Assault
  III. White Collar

(A) None   (B) I only   (C) II only   (D) II and III only   (E) I, II, and III

The following table lists the number of criminals by category for 1990 and 2000 and the projected increase or decrease:

Category	Number in 1990 (millions)	Number in 2000 (millions)	Projected increase (millions)	Projected decrease (millions)
Vice	1.7	3	1.3	None
Assault	2	4	2	None
White Collar	3.8	6	2.2	None

As the table displays, there is a projected increase (not decrease) in all three categories. Hence, the answer is (A).

9. What is the approximate projected percent increase between 1990 and 2000 in the number of criminals involved in vice?

(A) 25%   (B) 40%   (C) 60%   (D) 75%   (E) 85%

Remember, to calculate the percentage increase, find the absolute increase and divide it by the original number. Now, in 1990, the number of criminals in vice was 1.7 million, and in 2000 it is projected to be 3 million. The absolute increase is thus:

$$3 - 1.7 = 1.3$$

Hence the projected percent increase in the number of criminals in vice is

$$\frac{absolute\ increase}{original\ number} = \frac{1.3}{1.7} \approx 75\%.$$

The answer is (D).

10. The projected number of Robbers in 2000 will exceed the number of white-collar criminals in 1990 by

(A) 1.2 million   (B) 2.3 million   (C) 3.4 million   (D) 5.8 million   (E) 7.2 million

In 1990, the number of white-collar criminals was (38%)(10 million) = 3.8 million. From the projected-crime graph, we see that the criminal population in the year 2000 will be 20 million and of these (25%)(20 million) = 5 million will be robbers. Hence, the projected number of Robbers in 2000 will exceed the number of white-collar criminals in 1990 by 5 – 3.8 = 1.2 million. The answer is (A).

Questions 11–15 refer to the following graph.

SALES BY CATEGORY FOR GRAMMERCY PRESS, 1980–1989
(in thousands of books)

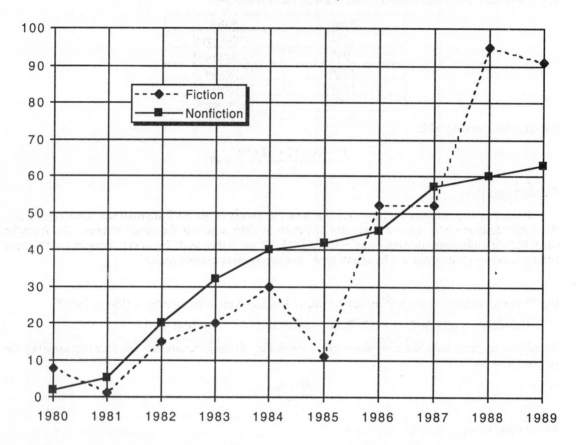

11.   In how many years did the sales of nonfiction titles exceed the sales of fiction titles ?

(A) 2   (B) 3   (C) 4   (D) 5   (E) 6

The graph shows that nonfiction sales exceeded fiction sales in '81, '82, '83, '84, '85, and '87. The answer is (E).

12. Which of the following best approximates the amount by which the increase in sales of fiction titles from 1985 to 1986 exceeded the increase in sales of fiction titles from 1983 to 1984?

(A)   31.5   thousand
(B)   40   thousand
(C)   49.3   thousand
(D)   50.9   thousand
(E)   68   thousand

The graph shows that the increase in sales of fiction titles from 1985 to 1986 was approximately 40 thousand and the increase in sales of fiction titles from 1983 to 1984 was approximately 10 thousand. Hence, the difference is 40 – 10 = 30. Choice (A) is the only answer-choice close to 30 thousand.

13.   Which of the following periods showed a continual increase in the sales of fiction titles?

(A) 1980–1982   (B) 1982–1984   (C) 1984–1986   (D) 1986–1988   (E) 1987–1989

According to the chart, sales of fiction increased from 15,000 to 20,000 to 30,000 between 1982 and 1984. The answer is (B).

14. What was the approximate average number of sales of fiction titles from 1984 to 1988?

   (A) 15 thousand   (B) 30 thousand   (C) 40 thousand   (D) 48 thousand   (E) 60 thousand

The following chart summarizes the sales for the years 1984 to 1988:

Year	Sales
1984	30 thousand
1985	11 thousand
1986	52 thousand
1987	52 thousand
1988	95 thousand

Forming the average yields:

$$\frac{30 + 11 + 52 + 52 + 95}{5} = 48$$

The answer is (D).

   Note, it is important to develop a feel for how the writers of the SAT approximate when calculating. We used 52 thousand to calculate the sales of fiction in 1986, which is the actual number. But from the chart, it is difficult to whether the actual number is 51, 52, or 53 thousand. However, using any of the these numbers, the average would still be nearer to 40 than to any other answer-choice.

15. By approximately what percent did the sale of nonfiction titles increase from 1984 to 1987?

   (A) 42%   (B) 50%   (C) 70%   (D) 90%   (E) 110%

Recall that the percentage increase (decrease) is formed by dividing the absolute increase (decrease) by the original amount:

$$\frac{57 - 40}{40} = 42$$

The answer is (A).

Questions 16–20 refer to the following graph.

AUTOMOBILE ACCIDENTS IN COUNTRY X: 1990 TO 1994
(in ten thousands)

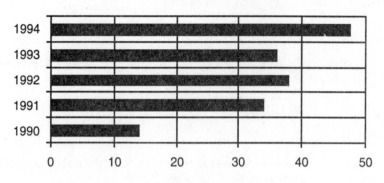

CARS IN COUNTRY X
(in millions)

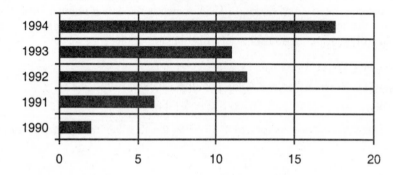

16.   Approximately how many millions of cars were in Country X in 1994?

   (A) 1.0   (B) 4.7   (C) 9.0   (D) 15.5   (E) 17.5

In the bottom chart, the bar for 1994 ends half way between 15 and 20. Thus, there were about 17.5 million cars in 1994. The answer is (E).

17.   The amount by which the number of cars in 1990 exceeded the number of accidents in 1991 was approximately

   (A) 0.3 million   (B) 0.7 million   (C) 1.0 million   (D) 1.7 million   (E) 2.5 million

From the bottom chart, there were 2 million cars in 1990; and from the top chart, there were 340 thousand accidents in 1991. Forming the difference yields

$$2,000,000 - 340,000 = 1,660,000$$

Rounding 1.66 million off yields 1.7 million. The answer is (D).

18.   The number of accidents in 1993 was approximately what percentage of the number of cars?

   (A) 1%   (B) 1.5%   (C) 3%   (D) 5%   (E) 10%

From the charts, the number of accidents in 1993 was 360,000 and the number of cars was 11,000,000. Forming the percentage yields

$$\frac{360,000}{11,000,000} \approx 3\%$$

The answer is (C).

19. In which of the following years will the number of accidents exceed 500 thousand?

   (A) 1994
   (B) 1995
   (C) 1998
   (D) 2000
   (E) It cannot be determined from the information given.

From the graphs, there is no way to predict what will happen in the future. The number of accidents could continually decrease after 1994. The answer is (E).

20. If no car in 1993 was involved in more than four accidents, what is the minimum number of cars that could have been in accidents in 1993?

   (A) 50 thousand   (B) 60 thousand   (C) 70 thousand   (D) 80 thousand   (E) 90 thousand

The number of cars involved in accidents will be minimized when each car has exactly 4 accidents. Now, from the top chart, there were 360,000 accidents in 1993. Dividing 360,000 by 4 yields

$$\frac{360,000}{4} = 90,000$$

The answer is (E).

Questions 21–25 refer to the following graphs.

DISTRIBUTION OF IMPORTS AND EXPORTS FOR COUNTRY X IN 1994.

Imports
200 million items

Exports
100 million items

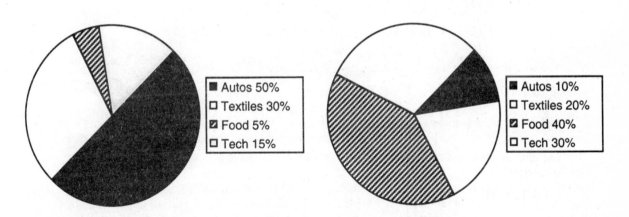

21. How many autos did Country X export in 1994?

   (A) 10 million
   (B) 15 million
   (C) 16 million
   (D) 20 million
   (E) 30 million

The graph shows that 100 million items were exported in 1994 and 10% were autos. Hence, 10 million autos were exported. The answer is (A).

22. In how many categories did the total number of items (import and export) exceed 75 million?

   (A) 1   (B) 2   (C) 3   (D) 4   (E) none

The chart shows that only autos and textiles exceeded 75 million total items. The answer is (B).

23. The ratio of the number of technology items imported in 1994 to the number of textile items exported in 1994 is

(A) $\dfrac{1}{3}$ (B) $\dfrac{3}{5}$ (C) 1   (D) $\dfrac{6}{5}$ (E) $\dfrac{3}{2}$

In 1994, there were 200 million items imported of which 15% were technology items. Thus, the number of technology items imported was

$$(15\%)(200 \text{ million}) = (.15)(200 \text{ million}) = 30 \text{ million}$$

In 1994, there were 100 million items exported of which 20% were textile items. Thus, the number of textile items exported was

$$(20\%)(100 \text{ million}) = (.20)(100 \text{ million}) = 20 \text{ million}$$

Forming the ratio of the above numbers yields

$$\frac{number\ of\ technology\ items\ imported}{number\ of\ textile\ items\ exp\,orted} = \frac{30}{20} = \frac{3}{2}$$

The answer is (E).

24. If in 1995 the number of autos exported was 16 million, then the percent increase from 1994 in the number of autos exported is

(A) 40%   (B) 47%   (C) 50%   (D) 60%   (E) 65%

Remember, to calculate the percentage increase, find the absolute increase and divide it by the original number. Now, in 1994, the number of autos exported was 10 million (100x10%), and in 1995 it was 16 million. The absolute increase is thus:

$$16 - 10 = 6$$

Hence the percent increase in the number of autos exported is

$$\frac{absolute\ increase}{original\ number} = \frac{6}{10} = 60\%$$

The answer is (D).

25. In 1994, if twice as many autos imported to Country X broke down as autos exported from Country X and 20 percent of the exported autos broke down, what percent of the imported autos broke down?

(A) 1%   (B) 1.5%   (C) 2%   (D) 4%   (E) 5.5%

If 20% of the exports broke down, then 2 million autos broke down (20%x10). Since "twice as many autos imported to Country X broke down as autos exported from Country X," 4 million imported autos broke down. Further, Country X imported 100 million autos (50%x200). Forming the percentage yields $\dfrac{4}{100} = 0.04 = 4\%$. The answer is (D).

Problem Set V:

1. Let S be Scott's age and K be Kathy's age. Then translating the sentence·*"If Scott is now 5 years older than Kathy, how old is Scott"* into an equation yields

$$S = K + 5$$

Now, Scott's age 7 years ago can be represented as $S = -7$, and Kathy's age can be represented as $K = -7$. Then translating the sentence *"Seven years ago, Scott was 3 times as old as Kathy was at that time"* into an equation yields $S - 7 = 3(K - 7)$.

Combining this equation with $S = K + 5$ yields the system:

$$S - 7 = 3(K - 7)$$
$$S = K + 5$$

Solving this system gives $S = 14 \frac{1}{2}$. The answer is (E).

2. Since the store would have made a profit of 20 percent on the wholesale cost, the original price P of the dress was 120 percent of the cost: $P = 1.2C$. Now, translating *"After reducing the asking price by 10 percent, the dress sold for a net profit of 10 dollars"* into an equation yields:
$$P - .1P = C + 10$$

Simplifying gives $$.9P = C + 10$$

Solving for P yields $$P = \frac{C + 10}{.9}$$

Plugging this expression for P into $P = 1.2C$ gives

$$\frac{C + 10}{.9} = 1.2C$$

Solving this equation for C yields $C = 125$. The answer is (B).

3. There is not sufficient information since the selling price is not related to any other information. Note, the phrase "initially listed" implies that there was more than one asking price. If it wasn't for that phrase, the information would be sufficient. The answer is (E).

4. Since *"the capacity of glass X is 80 percent of the capacity of glass Y,"* we get

$$X = .8Y$$

Since *"glass X contains 6 ounces of punch and is half-full,"* the capacity of glass X is 12 ounces. Plugging this into the equation yields

$$12 = .8Y$$

$$\frac{12}{.8} = Y$$

$$15 = Y$$

Hence, glass Y contains $15 - 6 = 9$ more ounces of punch than glass X. The answer is (D).

5.   Now, there is not sufficient information to solve the problem since it does not provide any absolute numbers. The following diagram shows two situations: one in which Glass X contains 5.2 more ounces of punch than glass Y, and one in which Glass X contains 2.6 more ounces than glass Y.

Scenario I (Glass X contains 5.2 more ounces than glass Y.)

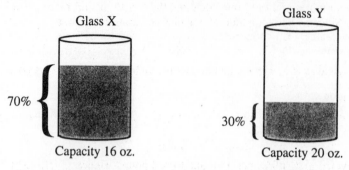

Scenario II (Glass X contains 2.6 more ounces than glass Y.)

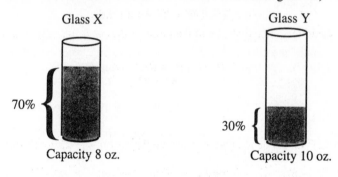

The answer is (E).

6.   Recall that $Average\ Speed = \dfrac{Total\ Distance}{Total\ Time}$. Now, the setup to the question gives the total time for the trip—30 minutes. Hence, to answer the question, we need to find the distance of the trip.

Let t equal the time for the first half of the trip. Then since the whole trip took 30 minutes (or $\frac{1}{2}$ hour), the second half of the trip took $\frac{1}{2} - t$ hours. Now, from the formula $Distance = Rate \times Time$, we get for the first half of the trip:

$$\frac{d}{2} = 50 \cdot t$$

And for the second half of the trip, we get

$$\frac{d}{2} = 60\left(\frac{1}{2} - t\right)$$

Solving this system yields

$$d = \frac{300}{11}$$

Hence, the $Average\ Speed = \dfrac{Total\ Distance}{Total\ Time} = \dfrac{300/11}{1/2} = \dfrac{600}{11}$. The answer is (D).

7.   Let x denote the number of apples bought, and let y denote the number of oranges bought. Then, translating the sentence *"Steve bought some apples at a cost of $.60 each and some oranges at a cost of $.50 each"* into an equation yields

$$.60x + .50y = 4.10$$

Since there are two variables and only one equation, the key to this problem is finding a second equation that relates x and y. Since he bought a total of 8 apples and oranges, we get

$$x + y = 8$$

Solving this system yields $x = 1$. Hence, he bought one apple, and the answer is (A).

8.   Recall the formula *Distance = Rate × Time*, or $D = R \cdot T$. From the second sentence, we get for Cyclist N:

$$D = R \cdot 2$$

Now, Cyclist M traveled at 20 miles per hour and took 4 hours. Hence, Cyclist M traveled a total distance of

$$D = R \cdot T = 20 \cdot 4 = 80 \text{ miles}$$

Since the cyclists covered the same distance at the moment they met, we can plug this value for D into the equation $D = R \cdot 2$:

$$80 = R \cdot 2$$
$$40 = R$$

The answer is (E).

9.   Let p denote the cost of the pants, and let s denote the cost of the shirt. Then from the question setup, $p + s = 52.50$.

Translating *"The pants cost two and a half times as much as the shirt"* into an equation gives $p = 2.5s$. Plugging this into the above equation gives

$$2.5s + s = 52.50$$

$$3.5s = 52.50$$

$$s = 15$$

The answer is (B).

10. Let the distance Jennifer walks be x. Then since they are 4 miles apart, Alice will walk $4 - x$ miles. The key to this problem is that when they meet each person will have walked for an equal amount of time.

Solving the equation $D = R \times T$ for T yields $T = \dfrac{D}{R}$. Hence,

$$\frac{x}{3} = \frac{4 - x}{2}$$
$$2x = 3(4 - x)$$
$$2x = 12 - 3x$$
$$5x = 12$$
$$x = \frac{12}{5}$$

Therefore, the time that Jennifer walks is $T = \dfrac{D}{R} = \dfrac{12/5}{3} = \dfrac{12}{5} \times \dfrac{1}{3} = \dfrac{4}{5}$ of an hour. Converting this into minutes gives $\dfrac{4}{5} \times 60 = 48$ minutes. The answer is (D).

11. ILet t be the time it takes the boys, working together, to assemble the model car. Then their combined rate is $\dfrac{1}{t}$, and their individual rates are $\dfrac{1}{30}$ and $\dfrac{1}{20}$. Now, their combined rate is merely the sum of their individual rates:

$$\frac{1}{t} = \frac{1}{30} + \frac{1}{20}$$

Solving this equation for t yields $t = 12$. The answer is (A).

12. Let x be the amount of nuts at 80 cents a pound. Then $10 - x$ is the amount of nuts at 60 cents a pound. The cost of the 80-cent nuts is $80x$, the cost of the 60-cent nuts is $60(10 - x)$, and the cost of the mixture is $70(10)$ cents. Since the cost of the mixture is the sum of the costs of the 70- and 80-cent nuts, we get

$$80x + 60(10 - x) = 70(10)$$

Solving this equation for x yields $x = 5$. The answer is (C).

13. Let C be Carrie's age. Then Tom's age is $C + 10$. Now, 5 years ago, Carrie's age was $C - 5$ and Tom's age was $(C + 10) - 5 = C + 5$. Since at that time, Tom was twice as old as Carrie, we get $5 + C = 2(C - 5)$. Solving this equation for C yields $C = 15$. The answer is (D).

14. Since the cars start at the same time, the time each has traveled is the same. Let t be the time when the cars are 210 miles apart. The equation $D = R \times T$, yields

$$210 = 45 \cdot t + 60 \cdot t$$
$$210 = 105 \cdot t$$
$$2 = t$$

The answer is (D).

15. The value of the x quarters is $25x$, and the value of the $x + 32$ nickels is $5(x + 32)$. Since these two quantities are equal, we get

$$25x = 5(x + 32)$$
$$25x = 5x + 160$$
$$20x = 160$$
$$x = 8$$

The answer is (A).

16. Let N stand for the number of nickels. Then the number of dimes is $N + 15$. The value of the nickels is $5N$, and the value of the dimes is $10(N + 15)$. Since the total value of the nickels and dimes is 525¢, we get

$$5N + 10(N + 15) = 525$$
$$15N + 150 = 525$$
$$15N = 375$$
$$N = 25$$

Hence, there are 25 nickels, and the answer is (B).

17. Let x stand for both the number of nickels and the number of quarters. Then the value of the nickels is $5x$ and the value of the quarters is $25x$. Since the total value of the coins is \$7.50, we get

$$5x + 25x = 750$$
$$30x = 750$$
$$x = 25$$

Hence, she has $x + x = 25 + 25 = 50$ coins. The answer is (C).

18. Let t be time that Steve has been driving. Then $t + 1$ is time that Richard has been driving. Now, the distance traveled by Steve is $D = rt = 40t$, and Richard's distance is $60(t + 1)$. At the moment they cross paths, they will have traveled a combined distance of 200 miles. Hence,

$$40t + 60(t + 1) = 200$$
$$40t + 60t + 60 = 200$$
$$100t + 60 = 200$$
$$100t = 140$$
$$t = 1.4$$

Therefore, Steve will have traveled $D = rt = 40(1.4) = 56$ miles. The answer is (A).

19. Let t be time that Ship B has been traveling. Then $t + 3$ is time that Ship A has been traveling. The distance traveled by Ship B is $D = rt = 25t$, and Ship A's distance is $15(t + 3)$. At the moment Ship B passes Ship A, they will have traveled the same distance. Hence,

$$25t = 15(t + 3)$$
$$25t = 15t + 45$$
$$10t = 45$$
$$t = 4.5$$

Since Ship B left port at 4 PM and overtook Ship A in 4.5 hours, it passed Ship A at 8:30 PM. The answer is (A).

20. Since the time is given in mixed units, we need to change the minutes into hours. Since there are 60 minutes in an hour, y minutes is equivalent to $\dfrac{y}{60}$ hours. Hence, the car's travel time, "x hours and y minutes," is $x + \dfrac{y}{60}$ hours. Plugging this along with the distance traveled, z, into the formula $d = rt$ yields

$$z = r\left(x + \frac{y}{60}\right)$$
$$z = r\left(\frac{60}{60}x + \frac{y}{60}\right)$$
$$z = r\left(\frac{60x + y}{60}\right)$$
$$\frac{60z}{60x + y} = r$$

The answer is (B).

21. Let the original price of the commodity be x. The reduction in price due to the 30% discount is $0.3x$. It is given that the 30% discount reduced the price of the commodity by $90. Expressing this as an equation yields

$$0.3x = 90$$

Solving for x yields

$$x = 300$$

Hence, the original price of the commodity was $300. The value of a 20% discount on $300 is

$$.20(300) = 60$$

Hence, the new selling price of the commodity is

$$\$300 - \$60 = \$240$$

The answer is (C).

22. Let x represent the number of students in the class who passed the math exam. Since it is given that the number of students who passed the math exam is half the number of students who passed the science exam, the number of students in the class who passed the science exam is $2x$. It is given that 5 students passed both exams. Hence, the number of students who passed only the math exam is $(x - 5)$, and the number of students who passed only the science exam is $(2x - 5)$. Since it is given that each student in the class passed at least one of the two exams, the number of students who failed both exams is 0.

We can divide the class into four groups:

1) Group of students who passed only the math exam: $(x - 5)$
2) Group of students who passed only the science exam: $(2x - 5)$
3) Group of students who passed both exams: 5
4) Group of students who failed both exams: 0

The sum of the number of students from each of these four categories is equal to the number of students in the class—40. Expressing this as an equation yields

$$(x - 5) + (2x - 5) + 5 + 0 = 40$$
$$3x - 5 = 40$$
$$3x = 45$$
$$x = 15$$

Thus, the number of students who passed the math exam is 15. The answer is (C).

23. The distance traveled by the train while passing the pole is l (which is the length of the train). The train takes t seconds to pass the pole. Recall the formula velocity = distance/time. Applying this formula, we get

$$\text{velocity} = \frac{l}{t}$$

While passing the platform, the train travels a distance of $l + x$, where x is the length of the platform. The train takes $3t$ seconds at the velocity of l/t to cross the platform. Recalling the formula distance = velocity $\times$ time and substituting the values for the respective variables, we get

$$l + x = \frac{l}{t} \times 3t \qquad \text{by substitution}$$
$$l + x = 3l \qquad \text{by canceling } t$$
$$x = 2l \qquad \text{by subtracting } l \text{ from both sides}$$

Hence, the length of the platform is $2l$. The answer is (D).

24. The fraction of work done in 1 hour by the first two people working together is 1/8. The fraction of work done in 1 hour by the third person is 1/12. When the three people work together, the total amount of work done in 1 hour is 1/8 + 1/12 = 5/24. The time taken by the people working together to complete the job is

$$\frac{1}{\text{fraction of work done per unit time}} =$$

$$\frac{1}{5/24} =$$

$$\frac{24}{5} =$$

$$4\frac{4}{5}$$

The answer is (E).

25. Let a represent the age of A and let c represent the age of C. If b represents the age of B, then according to the question $b = \frac{a+c}{2}$. We are told that B is 2 years younger than A. This generates the equation $a = b + 2$. We know that the age of C is 32. Substituting these values into the equation $b = \frac{a+c}{2}$ yields $b = \frac{(b+2)+32}{2}$. Solving this equation for b yields $b = 34$. The answer is (D).

26. Let a represent the age of the oldest person, b the age of the age of second person, and c the age of youngest person. The age of first person is twice the age of the second person and three times the age of the third person. This can be expressed as $a = 2b$ and $a = 3c$. Solving these equations for b and c yields $b = a/2$ and $c = a/3$. The sum of the ages of the three people is $a + b + c = 33$. Substituting for b and c in this equation, we get

$$a + a/2 + a/3 = 33$$
$$6a + 3a + 2a = 198 \quad \text{by multiplying both sides by 6}$$
$$11a = 198$$
$$a = 198/11 = 18 \quad \text{by dividing both sides by 11}$$

Since $c = a/3$, we get

$$c = a/3 = 18/3 = 6$$

The answer is (B).

Problem Set W:

1. The sixth digit following the decimal point is the number zero: 0.476190476190 . . . Since the digits repeat in blocks of six numbers, 0 will appear in the space for all multiples of six. Since 54 is a multiple of six, the 54th digit following the decimal point is 0. The answer is (A).

2. We know that T is 6; and therefore from the fact that *"each successive integer is one more than the preceding integer"* we see that S is 5. Continuing in this manner yields the following unique sequence:

P	Q	R	S	T
2	3	4	5	6

Hence, the value of R is 4. The answer is (E).

3.   Forming the series for u and v yields

$$u = 1 + 2 + \cdots + 19 + 20$$

$$v = 21 + 22 + \cdots + 39 + 40$$

Subtracting the series for u from the series for v yields

$$v - u = \underbrace{20 + 20 + \cdots + 20 + 20}_{20 \text{ times}} = 20 \cdot 20 = 400$$

The answer is (E).

4.   Extending the dots to six rows yields

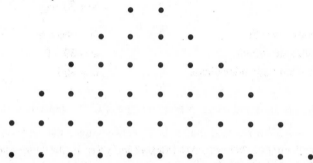

Row 6 has twelve dots. Hence, the answer is (E).

5.   Since the *"the first term in the sequence is $\sqrt{2}$"* and *"all odd numbered terms are equal,"* all odd numbered terms equal $\sqrt{2}$. Since the *"the second term is –2"* and *"all even numbered terms are equal,"* all even numbered terms equal –2. Hence, the sum of any two consecutive terms of the sequence is $\sqrt{2} + (-2) \approx -0.6$ (remember, $\sqrt{2} \approx 1.4$). The answer is (B).

6.   We are given a formula for the sum of the first n even, positive integers. Plugging $n = 20$ into this formula yields

$$n(n + 1) = 20(20 + 1) = 20(21) = 420$$

The answer is (E).

7.   Since *"each number above the bottom row is equal to three times the number immediately below it,"* $x = 3(-18) = -54$ and $y = 3(3) = 9$. Hence, $x + y = -54 + 9 = -45$. The answer is (A).

8.   The first term is even, and all subsequent terms are found by multiplying a number by 2. Hence, all terms of the sequence are even. The answer is (B). Following is the sequence:

$$2, 10, 26, 58, \ldots$$

9.   Since *"every number in the sequence –1, 3, 2, . . . is the sum of the two immediately preceding numbers,"* the forth term of the sequence is $5 = 3 + 2$. The first 12 terms of this sequence are

$$-1, 3, 2, 5, 7, 12, 19, 31, 50, 81, 131, 212, \ldots$$

At least four numbers in this sequence are even: 2, 12, 50, and 212. The answer is (E).

10. Since *"adding any one of the first three terms to the term immediately following it yields $\frac{w}{2}$,"* we get

$$w + x = \frac{w}{2}$$

$$x + y = \frac{w}{2}$$

$$y + 30 = \frac{w}{2}$$

Subtracting the last equation from the second equation yields $x - 30 = 0$. That is $x = 30$. Plugging $x = 30$ into the first equation yields

$$w + 30 = \frac{w}{2}$$

Multiplying both sides by 2 yields $\qquad\qquad\qquad\qquad 2w + 60 = w$

Subtracting w from both sides yields $\qquad\qquad\qquad w + 60 = 0$

Finally, subtracting 60 from both sides yields $\qquad\qquad w = -60$

The answer is (A).

Problem Set X:

1. Since the number of integers between two integers inclusive is one more than their difference, we get $69 - 29 + 1 = 41$ integers. The answer is (C).

2. First display the information in a Venn diagram:

French   Chemistry

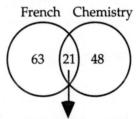

Both French and Chemistry

Adding the number of students taking French and the number of students taking chemistry and then subtracting the number of students taking both yields $(63 + 48) - 21 = 90$. This is the number of students enrolled in *either* French or chemistry or both. Since the total school enrollment is 150, there are $150 - 90 = 60$ students enrolled in *neither* French nor chemistry. The answer is (A).

3. There are 60 minutes in an hour. Hence, there are $1\frac{1}{3} \cdot 60 = 80$ minutes in $1\frac{1}{3}$ hours. The answer is (D).

4. Since there are 60 seconds in a minute and the press prints 5 pages every 2 seconds, the press prints $5 \cdot 30 = 150$ pages in one minute. Hence, in 7 minutes, the press will print $7 \cdot 150 = 1050$ pages. The answer is (E).

5.   First display the information in a Venn diagram:

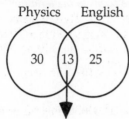

Both Physics and English

Adding the number of students taking physics and the number of students taking English and then subtracting the number of students taking both yields $(30 + 25) = -13 = 42$. This is the number of students enrolled in *either* physics or English or both. The total school enrollment is 90, so forming the ratio yields

$$\frac{physics\ or\ math\ enrollment}{total\ enrollment} = \frac{42}{90} \approx .47 = 47\%$$

The answer is (C).

6.   Since the number of integers between two integers inclusive is one more than their difference, $(91 - 49) + 1 = 43$ callers won a prize. The answer is (B).

7.   Since the fence is 400 feet long and the posts are 20 feet apart, there are $\frac{400}{20} = 20$ sections in the fence. Now, if we ignore the first post and associate the post at the end of each section with that section, then there are 20 posts (one for each of the twenty sections). Counting the first post gives a total of 21 posts. The answer is (D).

8.   The x jars have $15x$ marbles, and the $3x$ jars have $20 \cdot 3x = 60x$ marbles. Hence, there is a total of $15x + 60x = 75x$ marbles. The answer is (C).

9.   Since the number of integers between two integers inclusive is one more than their difference, we have $\left(10^3 - 2\right) + 1 = (1000 - 2) + 1 = 999$ integers. The answer is (C).

10. This is a hard problem. Let x be the number of people who own both types of cars. Then the number of people who own only Fords is $16 - x$, and the number of people who own only Toyotas is $11 - x$. Adding these two expressions gives the number of people who own only one of the two types of cars, which we are told is 15:

$$(16 - x) + (11 - x) = 15$$

Add like terms: $27 - 2x = 15$

Subtract 27 from both sides of the equation: $-2x = -12$

Finally, divide both sides of the equation by –2: $x = 6$

The answer is (B).

Problem Set Y:

1. The median in all five answer-choices is 10. By symmetry, the average in answer-choices (A), (C), and (D) is 10 as well. The average in choice (B) is larger than 10 because 13 is further away from 10 than 8 is. Similarly, the average in choice (E) is smaller than 10 because 7 is further away from 10 than 12 is. The exact average is $\dfrac{7+9+10+11+12}{5} = \dfrac{49}{5} < 10$. The answer is (E).

2. There are 11 (= 5 + 6) people who selected a number 2 or number 3 marble, and there are 15 total people. Hence, the probability of selecting a number 2 or number 3 marble is 11/15, and the answer is (D).

3. Randomly guessing either of the last two digits does not affect the choice of the other, which means that these events are mutually exclusive and we are dealing with consecutive probabilities. Since each of the last two digits is greater than 5, Sarah has four digits to choose from: 6, 7, 8, 9. Her chance of guessing correctly on the first choice is 1/4, and on the second choice also 1/4. Her chance of guessing correctly on both choices is

$$\frac{1}{4} \cdot \frac{1}{4} = \frac{1}{16}$$

Since she gets three tries, the total probability is $\dfrac{1}{16} + \dfrac{1}{16} + \dfrac{1}{16} = \dfrac{3}{16}$. The answer is (C).

4. Since y is the middle number, it is the median. Forming the average of x, y, and z and setting it equal to 3 times the median yields

$$\frac{x+y+z}{3} = 3y$$

Replacing x with 0 and z with ky yields

$$\frac{0+y+ky}{3} = 3y$$

Multiplying both sides of this equation by 3 yields $y + ky = 9y$

Subtracting $9y$ from both sides yields $-8y + ky = 0$

Factoring out y yields $y(-8 + k) = 0$

Since $y \ne 0$ (why?), $-8 + k = 0$. Hence, $k = 8$ and the answer is (E).

5. Plugging $y = x + 2$ into the equation $z = y + 2$ gives $z = (x + 2) + 2 = x + 4$. Hence, in terms of x, the three numbers x, y, and z are

$$x, x + 2, x + 4$$

Clearly, x is the smallest number. Further, since $x + 2$ is smaller than $x + 4$, $x + 2$ is the median. Subtracting the median from the product of the smallest number and the median and setting the result equal to 0 yields

$$x(x + 2) - (x + 2) = 0$$

Factoring out the common factor $x + 2$ yields

$$(x + 2)(x - 1) = 0$$

Setting each factor equal to 0 yields

$$x + 2 = 0 \text{ or } x - 1 = 0$$

Hence, $x = -2$ or $x = 1$. Since the three numbers are positive, x must be 1. Hence, the largest number is $x + 4 = 1 + 4 = 5$. The answer is (C).

6. First, let's calculate the probability of selecting a red or a blue paper clip. This is an either-or probability and is therefore the sum of the individual probabilities:

$$1/4 + 1/6 = 5/12$$

Now, since there are only three types of objects, the sum of their probabilities must be 1 (Remember that the sum of the probabilities of all possible outcomes is always 1):

$$P(r) + P(b) + P(s) = 1,$$

where r stands for red, b stands for blue, and s stands for silver.

Replacing $P(r) + P(b)$ with 5/12 yields $5/12 + P(s) = 1$

Subtracting 5/12 from both sides of this equation yields $P(s) = 1 - 5/12$

Performing the subtraction yields $P(s) = 7/12$

The answer is (C).

7.   The following list shows all 12 ways of selecting the two marbles:

(0, 1)	(1, 0)	(2, 0)	**(3, 0)**
(0, 2)	**(1, 2)**	**(2, 1)**	(3, 1)
(0, 3)	(1, 3)	(2, 3)	(3, 2)

The four pairs in bold are the only ones whose sum is 3. Hence, the probability that two randomly drawn marbles will have a sum of 3 is

$$4/12 = 1/3$$

The answer is (E).

8.   Since there are twice as many townhomes as ranch-style homes, the probability of selecting a townhome is 2/3.[*] Now, "there are 3 times as many townhomes with pools than without pools." So the probability that a townhome will have a pool is 3/4. Hence, the probability of selecting a townhome with a pool is

$$\frac{2}{3} \cdot \frac{3}{4} = \frac{1}{2}$$

The answer is (E).

9.   In the figure, it appears that the small inscribed triangle divides the large triangle into four congruent triangles. Hence, the probability that a point chosen at random from the large triangle will also be from the small triangle is 1/4. (As an exercise, prove that small inscribed triangle divides the large triangle into four congruent triangles.) The answer is (C).

Problem Set Z:

1.   Let C be the cost of the computer without the hard drive, and let H be the cost of the hard drive. Then translating *"The computer with the hard drive costs 2,900 dollars"* into an equation yields

$$C + H = 2,900$$

Next, translating *"The computer without the hard drive costs 1,950 dollars more than the hard drive alone"* into an equation yields

$$C = H + 1,950$$

Combining these equations, we get the system:

$$C + H = 2,900$$
$$C = H + 1,950$$

Solving this system for H, yields $H = 475$. The answer is (C).

---

[*] Caution: Were you tempted to choose 1/2 for the probability because there are "twice" as many townhomes? One-half (= 50%) would be the probability if there were an equal number of townhomes and ranch-style homes. Remember the probability of selecting a townhome is not the ratio of townhomes to ranch-style homes, but the ratio of townhomes to the total number of homes. To see this more clearly, suppose there are 3 homes in the subdivision. Then 2 would be townhomes and 1 would be a ranch-style home. So the ratio of townhomes to total homes would be 2/3.

2.   The given information does tell us the number of History students who are <u>not</u> taking Math—32; however, the statements do not tell us the number of students enrolled in Math. The following Venn diagrams show two scenarios that satisfy the given information. Yet in the first case, less than 32 students are enrolled in Math; and in the second case, more than 32 students enrolled in Math:

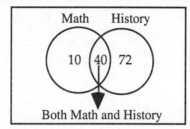   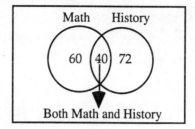

The answer is (E).

3.   Many students mistakenly think that the given information implies the average is 1000. Suppose just 2 people take the test and one scores 1200 (above 1000) and the other scores 900 (below 1000). Clearly, the average score for the two test-takers is not 1000. The answer is (E).

4.   Let A, B, C stand for the three colors, and let W, X, Y, Z stand for the four luxury features. There are three ways of selecting the colors:

| A | B | | A | C | | B | C |

There are four ways of selecting the luxury features:

| W | X | Y | | W | Y | Z | | W | X | Z | | X | Y | Z |

Hence, there are $3 \times 4 = 12$ ways of selecting all the features. The answer is (D).

5.   There are $x + y$ red and blue marbles in the bowl. Subtracting this from the total of 500 marbles yields the number of marbles that are neither red nor blue:

$$500 - (x + y) = 500 - x - y$$

Hence, the answer is (C).

6.   The convention used for rounding numbers is *"if the following digit is less than five, then the preceding digit is not changed. But if the following digit is greater than or equal to five, then the preceding digit is increased by one."*

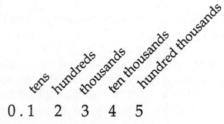

Since 3 is in the thousands position and the following digit, 4, is less than 5, the digit 3 is not changed. Hence, rounded to the nearest thousandth 0.12345, is 0.123. The answer is (B).

7.   Doubling the x in the expression yields $\dfrac{v+w}{2x/yz} = \dfrac{1}{2}\left(\dfrac{v+w}{x/yz}\right)$. Since we have written the expression as 1/2 times the original expression, doubling the x halved the original expression. The answer is (C).

8.   There are 8.5 apples in the picture. Dividing the total number of apples by 8.5 yields $\dfrac{4,250}{8.5} = 500$. The answer is (C).

Software

<u>INSTALLATION DIRECTIONS FOR SAT PREPCOURSE SOFTWARE</u>

Windows:
1. Insert the disk into the CD-ROM drive.
2. From the Start menu, select Run and then select Browse.
3. Select your CD-ROM drive from the Browse menu.
4. Select the file sat.exe
5. Click Open and then click OK.

Macintosh:
1. Insert the disk into the CD-ROM drive.
2. If necessary, double click the disk icon.
3. Double click the icon: sat.sea
4. Select a folder into which you would like to place the file.
5. Click Save.

<u>SOFTWARE ORIENTATION</u>

If you are familiar with computers and software, you are unlikely to need to read this orientation: We put considerable thought into making the software as simple and intuitive as possible.

A. Main Menu

You start a test by clicking either the Mentor Mode or Test Mode button of the test you want to take. In Mentor Mode, you can immediately see a solution to each problem and you will not be timed. Select this mode for studying. In Test Mode, you will not see solutions of the problems and you will be timed. Select this mode for practice at taking timed SATs.

1. **Select Section Screen**

   When you click Mentor Mode, the Select Section Screen appears. On this screen, click the section of the test you want to study. If you have chosen Test Mode instead of Mentor Mode, this screen will not appear and you will be taken directly to the first section of the test.

2. **Section/Direction Screen**

   After clicking the section you want to study, the program takes you to the first page of the section—the Directions page. To see the first question, click Next.

3. **Selecting an Answer**

   You select an answer by clicking its letter (or typing its letter). This highlights the letter, and, if you are in Mentor Mode, presents a feedback box that explains why your selection is correct or incorrect. You can change your answers as often as you like. Some solutions to the questions are too long to display all at once in the feedback box. In these cases, use the scroll bar to scroll through the solution. When there is more text to be viewed, the scroll bar will be highlighted.

B. Navigation

There are three ways to reach other questions.

1. **Questions Near By**

   If the question is near by, merely click Next (or Back) the appropriate number of times.

2. **Questions Moderately Far Away**

   If the question is farther away, press the Right Arrow Key on the keyboard the appropriate number of times (this is available only on extended keyboards). If you are on Question 3 and want to go to Question 7, then press the Right Arrow Key four times

3. **Questions Far Away**

   If the question is far away, click the Status Button, which takes you to the Status Display. From there, you can go to any question by merely clicking the question. If you are on Question 3 and want to go to Question 26, click the Status Button and then click Question 26.

C. The Navigation Strip

The Navigation Strip is present at the bottom of the screen when questions are present.

1. **Status Button**

   Clicking the Status Button takes you to the Status Display which lists the questions you have answered correctly or incorrectly (in Test Mode, it states only whether the questions have been answered). The Status Display is also a convenient and fast way to reach far away questions. If you are on Question 21 and want to go to Question 2, then click the Status Button and then click Question 2.

2. **Time Button**

   The Time Button displays the time you have been working on a section and the time you have remaining.

3. **Stop Button**

   The Stop Button gives you access to your current score (and from there access to the Score Conversion Chart). It also allows you to navigate to other sections of the test or to return to the Main Menu.

   A. **Return to the Section Button**

   The Return to the Section Button takes you back to the question you were working on.

   B. **Switch Sections (Go to Next Section)**

   The Switch Sections Button takes you to the Switch Sections Screen from which you can choose another section of the test.

   In Test Mode, the Switch Sections Button is labeled Go to Next Section, and it takes you directly to the next section. If you want to skip that section, just click the Stop Button and then click the Go to Next Section Button. By doing this, you will be unable to return to the skipped section. Although this is inconvenient, it is how the paper and pencil test is administered.

   C. **Return to Main Menu Button**

   The Return to Main Menu Button takes you back to the Main Menu. When you select this option, the Are You Sure dialog box will appear reminding you that your current score and status will be erased. (Note, changing sections within a test does not erase your score or status.)

   D. **Show Score Button**

   The Show Score Button takes you to the Score Display which shows your current score for the entire test and for each section.

Additional Educational Titles from Nova Press

Master The LSAT offers the prelaw student a complete and rigorous analysis of the LSAT. In addition, it contains actual LSAT questions, including a complete and official LSAT test.

The LSAT is the most intellectually demanding entrance exam. To prepare for it, students need an equally challenging book. MASTER THE LSAT fills that need.

$29.95   Pages 560

Law School Basics presents a thorough overview of law school, legal reasoning, and legal writing. It was written for those who are considering law school and for those who are about to start law school.

Law School Basics was written with one overriding goal: to enlighten you about everything the author wishes he had known before starting law school.

$14.95   Pages 224

The LSAT is a logic test. Although this makes the test hard, it also makes the test predictable—it is based on fundamental principles of logic. LSAT Prep Course Software analyzes and codifies these basic principles: the contrapositive, the if-then, etc.

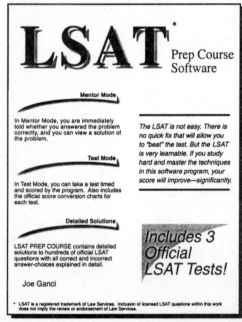

You no longer need to worry that the problems you are studying are like those on the LSAT. Now, you can study official LSATs. Order and download from the Web: www.novapress.net

$29.95   Windows and Macintosh

Every year students pay $600+ to test prep companies to prepare for the GMAT. Now you can get the same preparation in a book. GMAT PREP COURSE provides the equivalent of a two month, 50 hour course.

Mentor Exercises: These exercises provide hints, insight, and partial solutions to ease your transition from seeing problems solved to solving them on your own.

$29.95   Pages 624

GRE PREP COURSE presents a thorough analysis of the GRE and introduces numerous analytic techniques that will help you immensely, not only on the GRE but in graduate school as well.

Detailed Solutions: We have found that students are frustrated and angered by books in which they cannot get the author's "drift," so all solutions are written in step-by-step detail.

$29.95   Pages 624

The MCAT Physics Book presents a thorough analysis of MCAT physics and introduces numerous analytic techniques that will help you immensely, not only on the MCAT but in medical school as well.

Detailed Solutions: We have found that students are frustrated and angered by books in which they cannot get the author's "drift," so all solutions are written in step-by-step detail.

$29.95   Pages 444

The MCAT Biology Book presents a thorough analysis of MCAT biology and introduces numerous analytic techniques that will help you immensely, not only on the MCAT but in medical school as well.

Detailed Solutions: We have found that students are frustrated and angered by books in which they cannot get the author's "drift," so all solutions are written in step-by-step detail.

$29.95   Pages 416

The MCAT Chemistry Book presents a thorough analysis of MCAT chemistry and introduces numerous analytic techniques that will help you immensely, not only on the MCAT but in medical school as well.

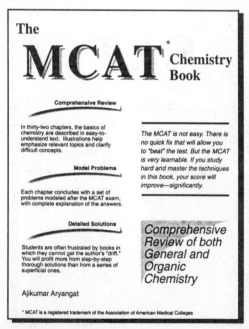

Detailed Solutions: We have found that students are frustrated and angered by books in which they cannot get the author's "drift," so all solutions are written in step-by-step detail.

$29.95   Pages 492

ORDER FORM

Product	Quantity	Price
GRE Prep Course		$29.95
GMAT Prep Course		$29.95
Master The LSAT		$29.95
The MCAT Physics Book		$29.95
The MCAT Biology Book		$29.95
The MCAT Chemistry Book		$29.95
SAT Prep Course		$29.95
Law School Basics		$14.95
Vocabulary 4000		$9.95

Name:	
Address:	
City: State: Zip:	
Phone: ( )	

Books are shipped Priority Mail. For delivery, allow 2 to 4 days from the day we receive the order. The shipping charge for any size order is $4. There is no tax.

Make check payable and mail to:
NOVA PRESS
11659 Mayfield Ave., Suite 1
Los Angeles, CA 90049

Credit card information

☐ Visa   ☐ MasterCard   ☐ Discovery   ☐ American Express
Name (as printed on card):
Credit card number:
Expiration date:

To Order by Phone, Call
1-800-949-6175

To Order from Our Website, Go to
www.novapress.net

Overnight delivery is available

Printed in Canada